THE GALLANT SEVENTY-EIGHTH
Colonel William Sirwell and The Pennsylvania Seventy-Eighth
Stones River to Pickett's Mill
Second Edition

THE GALLANT SEVENTY-EIGHTH
Colonel William Sirwell and The Pennsylvania Seventy-Eighth
Stones River to Pickett's Mill

Second Edition

Ronald S. Gancas

Published by
Mark V Enterprises
Plum Boro, Pennsylvania
1997

the
Gallant Seventy-Eighth

TO
MY FATHER

STANLEY LOUIS GANCAS

ROBYN, ELIZABETH, JONATHAN

MARISA, CAMRYN

AND

MY FAMILY

THE GALLANT SEVENTY-EIGHTH
Colonel William Sirwell and The Pennsylvania Seventy-Eighth
Stones River to Pickett's Mill
Second Edition

by Ron Gancas

I have always had a fervent appreciation of American history and the people that have affected the course of that history. By the time I reached the age of reason, I was well aware that somewhere back in time my great-great grandfather, Colonel William Sirwell, had been a "hero" in the Civil War. Anna Sirwell Beuth, my grandmother, dramatically told and retold stories of her famous grandfather. I relished the stories and believed every word as the gospel truth.

My mother and father fostered my consuming interest in politics, American History and the Civil War when I was a young boy. They took me to the homes of Washington, Lee and Jefferson. I walked the halls of Custis Lee's mansion at Arlington and imagined the heroes of my youth who walked those same halls hundreds of years before. On many vacations we visited the houses of Congress, the White House, or Williamsburg. I will never be able to watch a political convention without thinking of the ones I watched with my mother. I would lay on the living room floor watching the snowy screened Dumont television while she stood at her ironing board. Between sweeps of her iron she would point out the famous and not so famous politicians and statesmen of the day. Her explanations of speeches and what she thought were the results of the back room machinations always held my attention.

As time passed, my father's interest in the Civil War and that of his older brother, Joe, caused me to study this era more closely. Through the many years of enjoyable reading and research, I became aware that little information existed on my great, great grandfather. After closer study of the battles that Sirwell's Pennsylvania Seventy-Eighth participated in and deeper research into the life of William Sirwell, it also became apparent that many of my grandmother's stories were "family legends." There was always a ring of truth to the legends, but never the factual background. Unfortunately, at the time of a historical water mark of the Civil War local newspapers, as late as 1990, reprinted these legends and because of incorrect assumptions, added to them. Therefore, I decided to put together as true a history as possible of Colonel William Sirwell and his Pennsylvania Seventy-Eighth Volunteer Infantry Regiment.

THE GALLANT SEVENTY-EIGHTH is the story of William Sirwell, regimental commander of the Pennsylvania Seventy-Eighth, and the men from Western Pennsylvania who followed him. It is the story of the Army of the Cumberland and primarily the New Year's Eve 1862, battle of Stones River fought near Murfreesboro, Tennessee. To complete the story of this courageous regiment, the book also follows the history of the unit from their victory at Stones River to their last battle at Pickett's Mill, Georgia. It is the story of valiant young adversaries from Tennessee. It is a story of friends and neighbors who became brothers.

With little thought or regard to the cost in human suffering, the advent of war is an exhilarating time. In 1861, it was no different. The debates over states rights, slavery, or an agrarian versus an industrial society were irrelevant. The young boys from

Armstrong County and Western Pennsylvania, happily left their homes to join the great adventure of the American Civil War.

ACKNOWLEDGMENTS

Research on any subject cannot be completed without the help of innumerable people. One of the greatest joys in doing research for me was meeting people who shared my interest in the Civil War and the Pennsylvania Seventy-Eighth. I would like to thank the many people who have helped me over the years. Their kindnesses made my work and research much more enjoyable.

The original Company I "Company Orders," book became a focal point of my story. This record along with the personal letters of Lt. George Washington Black, of Company I, Pennsylvania Seventy-Eighth Regiment, were given to me by his grand daughter, Miss Elizabeth Buzzard, of Apollo, Pennsylvania. I am most appreciative of her generosity.

Bill May, "Private Christian Hinchberger", of Butler, Pennsylvania, who re-enacts the war years of his great-grandfather Christian Hinchberger, a member of the Seventy-Eighth, supplied information, research and pictures for this book. His help was invaluable James Coulson of Lower Burrell graciously gave me the letters of his great grandfather, Sergeant Major Samuel Dumm. Margaret Stivenson Krecota of Ford City, Pennsylvania kindly supplied old newspaper articles. Eric McCandless of Zelienople kindly shared information he had gathered on members of the regiment and regimental reunions. Ronn Palm of Kittanning, supplied photographs and updated material for the second addition through regimental reunion reports and regimental enlistment records. Rick Sauers of the Allegheny County Soldiers and Sailors Memorial in Pittsburgh was a great help. Much of the material supplied by these people became linchpins for my story.

Carol F. Kaplan of the Nashville, Tennessee Ben West Library was most kind to a distant telephone voice. Ms. Kaplan is the great-great granddaughter of Mitchell Cobb of the Confederate First Tennessee, a unit that fought Sirwell's Seventy-Eighth. Her efforts in researching the histories of the First Tennessee and the Rock City Guards was inestimable.

Fran Shell of the Tennessee State Library and Archives in Nashville was instrumental in adding to the information on the Tennessee Sixteenth, Twenty-Sixth, and Twenty-Seventh regiments. Her efforts further enhanced my historical and personal knowledge.

Carol Hall of New Kensington, Pennsylvania, painstakingly corrected this book for grammatical and structural errors committed by a man who did not pay attention in her Senior High English class when he was a boy. Unfortunately, last minute changes and additions have not been corrected; for that I take responsibility.

Without the help of the personnel of the United States National Park services, I would not have been able to learn about the unique aspects of the battlefield at Stones River. Janice Martin of the Stones River National Battlefield was an immense help in searching records of members of the regiment buried in Murfreesboro and Nashville. Charles Spearman of Lookout Mountain was of great assistance in my research of the actual battlefield.

Through my uncle, Joe Gancas, I made the acquaintance of Dr. M. Jay Luvaas of the Army War College in Carlisle, Pennsylvania. I sincerely wish to thank Jay for his tireless efforts over these past eighteen years in teaching me more about the Civil War. Studying the battles with Jay, General Hal Nelson and the "Battlefield Trampers" has been most enjoyable.

Jack Blair of Apollo kept my efforts constantly in the forefront of business transacted by the Sons of Union Veterans of the Civil War, John T. Crawford Camp in Kittanning, Pennsylvania. Jack was also extremely helpful in proofing the original manuscript and correcting omissions in regard to regimental personnel. Bill McMaster Sr. of Kittanning was also very helpful in getting information for the history of the Seventy-Eighth.

I wish to remember H.R. "Hap" Fleming of Kittanning. His knowledge of the history of Armstrong County and the Pennsylvania Seventy-Eighth helped bring this work to a more vivid story form.

My sincere appreciation goes to my uncle, Simon William Beuth, for sharing his pictures, memorabilia, knowledge, and understanding of the history of the Seventy-Eighth.

It is with a great deal of fondness that I mention the support given to me by my family. Without their help, encouragement, and enthusiasm, this book could not have been completed. My wife, Marjorie, along with my children, Robert and Caroline urged me to write this story and assisted building the story line. My son Rod meticulously corrected numerous "points of order." My sister, Carolyn Gancas Haser, added her talents to this effort by advising me on the reproduction maps and printing procedures for this book.

Lastly, and most importantly, I cannot forget the one person who above all had faith in my abilities and gave me the confidence to finish this book, my mother, Dorothy Beuth Gancas, great grand daughter of Colonel William Sirwell.

R.G.   September 1997

Picture of Colonel William Graham Sirwell   Cover
          Courtesy of Simon Beuth, Lakeland, Florida
PREFACE   pg. V
ACKNOWLEDGMENTS   pg. VI
MAPS AND PHOTOS   pg. VIII
Picture of Colonel William Graham Sirwell   pg. X
          Courtesy of Ronn Palm, Kittanning, PA
RALLY ROUND THE FLAG!   pg. 1
TO ARMS, TO ARMS!   pg. 4
"THE KID HAS GONE TO THE COLORS"   pg. 9
          Picture of Colonel William Sirwell   pg. 12
          Picture of Father Richard Christy   pg. 17
THE BONNIE BLUE FLAG   pg. 18
CAMP FIRES IN KENTUCKY   pg. 20
DON CARLOS THE FIRST   pg. 29
          Picture of General James Negley   pg. 31
          Lieutenant G.W. Black Letter   pg. 34
"TRAMP! TRAMP! TRAMP"   pg. 36
THE CITY BIDES THE FOE   pg. 42
SEEING THE ELEPHANT   pg. 45
          Battle of Lavergne, map.   pg. 46
OLD ROSEY TAKES COMMAND   pg. 52
          Picture of William Rosecrans   pg. 53
ONWARD CHRISTIAN SOLDIERS   pg. 60
          Chain of Command at Stones River   pg. 62
"WE MOVE TOMORROW, GENTLEMEN"   pg. 68
          Movement to Murfreesboro, map   pg. 75
          Picture of General George Thomas*   pg. 79
"THE BALL OPENED"   pg. 80
          Sirwell's Regimental Formation   pg. 81
          Position of Seventy-Eighth, 30 December   pg. 83
SHOUT! SHOUT! THE BATTLE CRY OF FREEDOM   pg. 86
          Battlefield Positions December 31   pg. 87
          Seventy-Eighth position December 30   pg. 90
          Picture of Major Augustus B. Bonnaffon   pg. 91
INTO LINE, MEN! INTO LINE!   pg. 92
          Seventy-Eighth position 9:00 A.M. on 31st   pg. 93
          Bragg's force attacking Seventy-Eighth   pg. 95
CUT YOUR WAY OUT!   pg. 98
          Attack upon the Seventh-Eighth   pg. 100
HELL'S HALF ACRE   pg. 107
"THIS ARMY DOES NOT RETREAT"   pg. 109
NEW YEAR'S DAY, 1863   pg. 111
          Picture of Colonel John Franklin Miller   pg. 113

FIRST TO CROSS   pg. 114
        Battlefield positions on January 2   pg. 115
        Bragg's force attacked by Seventy-Eighth   pg. 117
        Picture of Jimmy Thorne   pg. 121
ASHES, ASHES! WE ALL FALL DOWN!   pg. 125
TENTING TONIGHT   pg. 137
"WE ARE COMING, FATHER ABRA'AM"   pg. 150
        Map of Tullahoma Campaign   pg. 151
"WEEPING SAD AND LONELY"   pg. 156
        Map of Davis Crossroads   pg. 158
        Chain of Command, Chickamauga   pg. 160
        Map of Snodgrass Hill   pg. 163
        Picture William Sirwell and Staff   pg. 173
ON TO ATLANTA   pg. 175
        Map of Atlanta Campaign   pg. 176
        Chain of Command, Atlanta Campaign   pg. 178
        Picture Archibald Blakeley   pg. 180
I AM IN THE FRONT RANKS YET!   pg. 181
        Map of Battlefield at Pumpkin Vine Creek   pg. 183
        Picture Franklin Mechling   pg. 185
GOIN' HOME   pg. 186
BLOOD OF THE DYING SUN   pg. 190
        Picture of William Sirwell   pg. 194
O CAPTAIN! MY CAPTAIN   pg. 196
FOOTNOTES   pg. 199
BIBLIOGRAPHY   pg. 211
INDEX   pg. 216
Regimental Roster Codes   pg. 235
Regimental Roster   pg. 237
Regimental Roster, Second Regiment   pg. 368
* The History of the Seventy-Eighth Pennsylvania Volunteer Infantry

Picture of Colonel William Graham Sirwell
Courtesy of Ronn Palm, Kittanning, PA

THE GALLANT SEVENTY-EIGHTH
Colonel William Sirwell and The Pennsylvania Seventy-Eighth
Stones River to Pickett's Mill

RALLY ROUND THE FLAG!

In the cold pre-dawn hours the fog drifted along the course of the Stones River. It meandered between the lines of the eighty-thousand Confederate and Union troops gathered for battle just outside Murfreesboro, Tennessee. Union regimental commander, Colonel William Sirwell, rode slowly from his regiment to brigade headquarters for last minute orders. In the freezing rain and darkness of December 31, 1862, his troops and many other fatigued troops began to stir from a night of little sleep.

Sleep, warmth and decent food were now only memories. Whatever rest that could be had was on the icy, rocky ground with no blankets or tents. For most, an out stretched arm, a limestone rock or cold rifle served as a pillow. The men were hungry and anxious. The hundreds of miles that separated them from their homes and Murfreesboro had brought to Pennsylvania's Seventy-Eighth Infantry Regiment the hardships associated with campaigning and camp life.

Fifteen months in the field had also taught these boys the realities of death. Many of their comrades had already died from typhoid, dysentery and flu. There had been a lesser number of friends that had been killed in small battles and skirmishes during their campaigns with the Army of the Cumberland, but on that New Year's Eve the Pennsylvanians faced what would be the greatest battle of their lives.

Within two days, Colonel Sirwell and his regiment, of mostly farm boys, would lead a charge a few miles from their current post across Stones River that would affect the outcome of the battle and the subsequent history of the Civil War. Through their courage and example the Pennsylvania Seventy-Eighth would turn a potential defeat into victory. They would be hailed by newspapers within the Union as "The Gallant Seventy-Eighth." Many of the boys from Armstrong County and Western Pennsylvania who answered the call to arms would lose their lives along this river near a town very similar to their home.

Murfreesboro was a small, active agrarian community at the outbreak of the Civil War. The county seat of Rutherford County, Tennessee, lay in the central part of state about thirty miles southeast of Nashville. Situated just east of Stones River, Murfreesboro was simply home to the people of the area, but the fact that the railroad from Nashville to Chattanooga passed through the town gave it significant military importance to both sides of the American conflict.

The Federal command saw the sleepy town as another point necessary to move its armies deeper into Southern territory and eventually split the Confederacy. Conversely, the Confederates viewed it as a necessary rail stop to continue receiving the advantages of Tennessee's resources and food stuff. It was also the point where Braxton Bragg and his Confederate Army of the Tennessee must destroy the Union army or lose their hold on the entire state. By December of 1862, Braxton Bragg had garrisoned his gray army in the town and William Starke Rosecrans made the decision to attack him.

Many of the boys in Bragg's army who had answered the call to their new flag of the Confederacy were from the surrounding counties of central Tennessee. It was the

Christmas holiday season and, to many of the boys in gray friends, families and festivities made it a happy time. Irrespective of the festivities there must have been the thought in the back of most of the Southrons minds that they must stem the blue tide that was moving south to Atlanta.

The soldiers of the Seventy-Eighth Pennsylvania and their comrades in the Army of the Cumberland were far from those they loved. For them it was a somber second Christmas away from home. They suspected all too well what lay ahead in Murfreesboro as they followed General William Rosecrans to the tumultuous battle at Stones River.

William Rosecrans' subsequent victory in central Tennessee has been appraised by some historians as a tactical draw. However, that is poppycock. If the outcome of this battle at Murfreesboro had been less than the reported hollow victory, the defeat would have been a dramatic setback for the Union cause. During this period, British and French recognition of the Confederacy was still a distinct possibility. Ambrose Burnside's Army of the Potomac had suffered a catastrophic defeat at the hands of Robert E. Lee in Fredericksburg, Virginia. General William Sherman was defeated at Chickasaw Bluffs, while affecting General Ulysses Grant's plan to capture Vicksburg, Mississippi. More over, at almost the same time, Federal troops also under Grant's area of responsibility were defeated at Holly Springs, in northern Mississippi. If there had been an additional Union loss at Stones River, it would have been devastating to President Lincoln's purposes in December of 1862.

Naturally, Abraham Lincoln's main goal was to pursue the war to a victorious end. However, in September, after General McClellan's dubious victory at the battle of Antietam, President Lincoln made it known that he planned to release his Emancipation Proclamation on January 1, 1863. The official unveiling of this historic document to impel the United States into removing slavery from their society would definitely have been marred by a calamitous loss at Stones River.

The battle of Stones River, fought in what was referred to as the western theater, has never received the recognition or in-depth study as compared to the other major battles of the war, even though it stands as the eighth largest fight in terms of battle losses. Only two current day defined works deal solely with Stones River: James Lee McDonough's *Stones River-Bloody Winter in Tennessee* published in 1980 and Peter Cozzens' recent *No Better Place to Die* published in 1990. The remainder of the works on the battle of Stones River were published in the late nineteenth century. Alexander Stevenson authored *The Battle of Stones River* in 1884. Four histories dealing with the Army of the Cumberland as their focal point touch on the battle of Stones River. Ken Burn's recent Civil War video study virtually ignored this horrendous struggle on the road to Atlanta.

Why then does the notoriety afforded to the "linchpin" battle at Stones River pale in contrast to other major battles? Numerous books have been written in great detail regarding the machinations of the Army of the Potomac. In comparison, there are decidedly fewer relating to the battles of the Western theater. A number of factors contributed to the greater fame of the Army of the Potomac. Primarily, it operated near the nation's capital. With the operations of an army so near to the center of power, a greater number of reporters followed its exploits. Maybe more importantly most newspapers spent a greater percentage of their money in the East. In addition to the written word, the burgeoning science of photography also followed Mr. Lincoln's army in the East. Matthew Brady the most prolific photographer of the war, spent a greater part of his time practicing his new art with the Army of the Potomac.

What could have detracted from this epic battle? Rosecrans himself may have affected the publicity of his army, because of his recalcitrant character. William Rosecrans had the ability to inspire his troops. He had the intelligence to plan well for battle. Long after the battle at Stones River, he had the record of a winner. However, he also had the ability to provoke those in power above him. Samuel Eliot Morison calls Rosecrans a "second-rater who had most of McClellan's faults without his ability." [1]

This statement is somewhat harsh to say the least. It can be said that like McClellan, Rosecrans was a planner, he did nag his superiors for supplies, and he did move slowly to battle. But unlike McClellan, he was not an egomaniac, he harbored no higher political aspirations, he did not relinquish real estate he had fought so hard to acquire, and more importantly his army *did advance.*

Regardless of history's claim of an indecisive victory, Stones River is still one of the great battles of the Civil War, and it deserves a better station in history. General Rosecrans persevered at Stones River through personal courage and inspiration. In the face of virtual annihilation, Rosecrans and his officers displayed leadership, and the character of his foot soldiers helped carry the day. After the severe punishment by the Confederates on the first day's battle, the tenacity of the volunteer Union soldier drove the Rebels from the battlefield and gained victory. William Sirwell's Pennsylvania Seventy-Eighth was in the vanguard of regiments that routed the Confederates on the second day of fighting and brought that victory home.

Throughout the history of these United States, thousands upon thousands of young men just as William Sirwell and his regiment, "the volunteer soldiers," have always been the backbone of the American fighting forces. Although they have been led to their deaths by self-serving politicians and inept generals, America's volunteers have always fought willingly for their beliefs. Historians, many times, have portrayed generals in the light of grand chess masters pondering tactics and moves on a strategic board, when in reality they are more like irrational children playing games of checkers or hide and seek. Although not quite children, William Sirwell and his vaunted 78th Regiment were typical of the soldiers both North and South, that engaged each other in the battle at Stones River. Despite the short-comings of William Rosecrans and Braxton Bragg during the battle, Colonel Sirwell and his Pennsylvanians, their oft adversaries, Hume Feild, John Lillard and their Tennesseans, and most of the volunteer soldiers courageously struggled and died. They had a belief in themselves; they had a belief in a cause. From the lowest private to many officers, most were citizen-soldiers fighting for their way of life. They were willing participants in a conflict that would determine the destiny of this great experiment in democracy.

TO ARMS, TO ARMS!

After decades of acrimonious political debate, it had come. A civil war that had been threatened for years was now a reality. The batteries of cannon that had ruptured the walls of Fort Sumter also divided the nation. They ignited a fire storm that would eradicate a way of life and completely change the course of American history. By April of 1861, seven southern states had officially seceded from the Union to form the Confederate States of America. Jefferson Davis' call for volunteers in early March and Abraham Lincoln's appeal for soldiers in mid April precipitated a flood of eager young men to both flags. In thousands of towns and villages across the United States wealthy or prominent citizens formed companies of young men to go off and fight for the rights of their friends and neighbors. As in the past Kittanning answered the call of their country.

Kittanning, Pennsylvania, was an enterprising, small community in 1861. Like Murfreesboro it was the hub to the agricultural society that surrounded it and the county seat of Armstrong County. The town, situated in the tree-lined valley along the Allegheny River that flows the thirty or so miles southwest to Pittsburgh, could trace its roots to a time before the Revolutionary War. And down through the history of Pennsylvania the men of Armstrong County had patriotically answered war's dreaded alarm whenever they were called upon to defend their way of life. In the coming War of the Rebellion, it would be no different.

William Sirwell, a leading citizen of Kittanning, was a jeweler by trade; however, he had spent most of his life as a soldier. Sirwell was not wealthy. He was only prominent to the extent that he touched the lives of others in his community through his jewelry business, his brick business, the church, and his military activities. He had been a member of the Pennsylvania Militia for over twenty years and was the founder of two surviving local militia units, the Kittanning Yeagers and the Brady Alpines. During the Mexican War, William Sirwell had offered his services and that of his unit, the Washington Blues, to the government. However, the state never accepted his offer since their quota of soldiers had been filled. The advent of the Civil War once again gave Sirwell the opportunity to serve his country.

With the election of Abraham Lincoln, by April 1, 1861, it was the prevailing opinion throughout the country, and also in Armstrong County, that there would be a war, and soon. With that thought in mind, William Sirwell tendered the services of his company, a combination of the two militia units, to Governor Curtin. He quickly received notice from the Adjutant General of Pennsylvania that the offer of his company had been received and "had been placed on file."

At the firing of the first Confederate gun at Fort Sumter, South Carolina, on April 12, 1861, Captain Bill Sirwell received orders to form his company and proceed to Harrisburg, Pennsylvania. The Armstrong County History states, "When this order was received the day was very pleasant and the town was quiet as though it were Sunday. Within an hour the whole town of Kittanning was up in arms." The peace and tranquillity of the Allegheny Valley had quickly become awash in a sea of jubilation and preparation for war. In less than six days after President Lincoln issued his call for seventy-five thousand men to put down the rebellion, a company of one hundred and fourteen men from Armstrong County was raised by Captain Sirwell.

Little directly written by William Sirwell regarding his personal opinions about the causes of the war or why he fought exists today. However, there are a few sources that could be indicative of beliefs. Sirwell had an extensive library covering subjects ranging from history to science and the humanities. One of his books has managed to survive, *The African Slave Trade and the Political History of Slavery in the United States*. The book, published in 1859, deals with the history of slavery from ancient Greece to the Dred Scott decision. Although not an out and out condemnation of slavery, its Preface states: "Each human being retains inherently the right to his own person, and can neither sell himself, nor be legally bound by any act of aggression on his natural liberty. Slavery therefore can never be a legal relation. Slavery is also inconsistent with the moral nature of man." Sirwell's signature and notes on various pages still exist. This book and its premise, along with the fact that William Sirwell's father, Richard, had "two free colored" living with him at the time of the 1830 census would cause one to suppose that Sirwell believed in the abolition of slavery. However, this ideal was in no way proposed by Sirwell within his contribution to the county history.

The Northern abolitionists and many Southerners saw the Civil War as a struggle over slavery and its future. Charles Dana was the managing editor of Horace Greelcy's powerful *New York Tribune* before the war. He rallied Northerners by referring to Southerners as "slavebreeders and slavetraders." An Alabama newspaper undoubtedly galvanized its readers when it reported the asinine premise that the North would free the slaves and force amalgamation on the Southern whites.

William Sirwell made no such outlandish or inflammatory comments. Sirwell was instrumental in writing the Civil War section for the county history that was published in 1883. *The History of Armstrong County, Pennsylvania* by Robert Walter Smith has an "exhaustive chapter" on Armstrong County in the War of the Rebellion. Irrespective of slavery or states' rights, the premise put forward in the history concludes that the Western Pennsylvania soldiers, "Marched off to aid the government in repossessing the forts, arsenals, and other national property which had been violently seized by the insurgents, and in re-establishing law, order, and the dominion of the legitimate government."

Born in 1820, just outside Pittsburgh, Pennsylvania, William Graham Sirwell was raised until age seven at the United States arsenal in Lawrenceville. His father, Richard Sirwell, a native of Warwick, England, came to the Pittsburgh area with his wife, Elizabeth Graham Sirwell, in early 1820. He enlisted in the United States Army for a term that ran from June 1821, to June 1827, at the Allegheny Arsenal. The arsenal dealt in the repair and manufacturer of military weapons and equipment. Richard Sirwell spent his six years in the service as a private engaged in the skilled, delicate work of repairing fire arms. He carried the title of "artificer" during his time in the military.

William Sirwell was raised in an atmosphere of brass bands, military balls, and -- to a young boy -- dashing uniforms. It was only natural that the soldierly flare passed from father to son. Young William Sirwell joined the state militia in 1839. Very early in his career he commanded the City Blues of Pittsburgh. Evidently William Sirwell was totally affected by his father who had also been a watchmaker in England. Prior to his enlistment in the militia, William Sirwell contracted an apprenticeship with a Pittsburgh watch maker. He finished his apprenticeship and eventually worked with his father at Sirwell's Watch Making Shop in Pittsburgh's old Diamond Market.

In 1845, Sirwell and Elizabeth McCandless Sirwell, his wife of almost five years, moved to Kittanning. William Sirwell was now well over six feet tall. Because of his height, he was lean at two hundred pounds and had a long face that sported a walrus mustache that covered a large toothy smile. For the next ten years he operated his various businesses. "[In 1851, Sirwell]...erected the first dry-house and made the first pressed brick in [the] county." But his businesses always took second place when the military was involved. For years he was the brigade inspector for all of the Armstrong County militia units. He personally formed and commanded various military companies distinctively named the German or Kittanning Yeagers and the Washington Blues. In 1854, he volunteered to move to Iowa where he trained state militia in Davenport. During his absence from Armstrong County, Andrew Jack of Manor Township, commanded the 30-plus man militia contingent now named the Sirwell Blues.

In 1855, upon his return to Pennsylvania, Sirwell organized a company of African-American troops in Pittsburgh. Named the Hannibal Guards this company is supposedly "the first colored unit" to be formed in the United States Army. Reportedly, with the advent of the Civil War many of these young black men left Pittsburgh to join Massachusetts' famed Fifty-Fourth "Colored" regiment. For Sirwell these years of military education and command experiences made him the ideal choice to lead a company of young soldiers.

On April 18th, 1861, under a clear sky, the Brady Alpines formed at the Diamond in Kittanning. The company was most impressive as they marched to the Allegheny Valley Railroad depot. Two young enlisted musicians, bursting with pride, marched with Captain Sirwell. Danny Golden was twelve years old and Teddy Barrett was all of fourteen. It is so easy to imagine the bands playing and the flags waving. The jubilation and thrills of war with its unknown adventures caused a virtual state of euphoria among the green troops. The company of soldiers made an imposing sight. They were young, most of them six feet in height or more, and made a handsome sight. Their height at one time was a prerequisite of membership in the Alpines.

Captain Sirwell's wife, Elizabeth, carrying baby Emma watched proudly as her husband led his company to the train depot. Sirwell's son, William, and daughters Lucinda, Sarah, Mary, and Elizabeth excitedly waved to their father and their eighteen year-old cousin, George McCandless who marched in the enlisted ranks. It was a time that families could be proud. It was also a time when young men of the county could show off their new found patriotism. One can almost see the gaily dressed, young girls calling out the name of their favored warrior as they marched through the town. In the bright, spring sunshine the boys of Armstrong County marched off to defeat the enemies of their nation. It is difficult to determine the motives for their enlistment. They may have joined to serve God, to serve country, or to abolish slavery, but their reasons did not matter. For $11 a month, it was going to be a grand adventure. The company rode the train south through Pittsburgh and then due east to Harrisburg, Pennsylvania, the state capitol.

Within forty eight hours of their departure from Kittanning, the Brady Alpines gathered with men from throughout the state at Camp Curtin near Harrisburg. Bill Sirwell's company was officially mustered into the three month service on April 22, 1861, and designated as Company B, 9th Regiment, Pennsylvania Volunteer Infantry under the command of Colonel Henry C. Longnecker of Allentown, Pennsylvania.   The Brady Alpines had reported in with their company of one hundred and fourteen men.

Unknowingly, the original company that Sirwell had tendered to the state back on April 1st, had contained seventy-eight men and that is all the government would now pay and supply. Sirwell was forced to reduce the size of his company by thirty-six men. Eighteen men willingly joined other companies and regiments.   Sirwell made arrangements to get three men attached to the quartermaster's department. Fifteen men from Armstrong County refused to leave the company and offered to serve for nothing. It was decided that they could stay. During their three months of service, Sirwell divided his pay with those men. Obviously a very generous man, Sirwell was also shrewd. The men that he had attached to the quartermaster's department made sure that there were ample uniforms, supplies, and rations for "all" the men of Company B, even those fifteen men not on the muster rolls. [1]

From early May until early June of 1861, the Ninth Regiment including Sirwell's Company spent their time in purely boring duty. They rode a series of trains from Harrisburg through Pennsylvania and into Delaware. Intelligence had been received indicating that there were instruction camps set up for the explicit purpose of training men sympathetic to the Confederacy. The Ninth was encamped at Hare's Corners, between Wilmington and New Castle, Delaware to strengthen the state's loyalists. Their specific charge was to prevent the movement southward of any citizens supportive of the Confederate cause.

On June 6th, Company B and the Pennsylvania Ninth were attached to the army of Major General Robert Patterson. General Patterson of Pennsylvania, was born in County Tyrone, Ireland in 1792. He was over 69 years-old at the war's start. In all likelihood, he received his command because of his friendship with the commander of Federal forces, General Winfield Scott. General Patterson did not appear to be a competent officer. He had served with some minor distinction in the war of 1812, and in the Mexican war. He is quoted as saying during that earlier war: "The President can make generals, but he cannot make soldiers." [2]   Coincidentally, by the outbreak of the Civil War, General Patterson had lived up to his declaration. Neither Lincoln or Scott would be able to make him into a soldier. Like his friend Scott, he was simply too old, but unlike General Scott, he was also too slow and too timid to handle an active field command.

Under Patterson's command, the Pennsylvania Ninth was moved back to Chambersburg, Pennsylvania, and then to Williamsport, Maryland, and Martinsburg, Virginia in search of a real army of Rebels. [3]

At Harper's Ferry, Virginia, Patterson's army was opposed by crusty Major General Joseph E. Johnston. Johnston, at age 54, had been a ranking officer in the "old" army where he had risen to brigadier after a distinguished career. Despite his personal conflicts on and off the battlefield, he was an able military commander. In anticipation of a battle at Bull Run, General Irvin McDowell hoped that General Patterson would simply engage Johnston's troops and prohibit them from joining General Pierre G.T. Beauregard on the plains of Manassas. [4]

Patterson held a council of war on July 9th, and at that meeting it became, although plausible, the absurd consensus of opinion that Patterson's army should not fear Johnston's movement to Bull Run, but should fear the movement of Rebel troops from Manassas to Winchester. There was genuine concern on Patterson's part that twelve thousand men would be moved to Johnston. This larger force would then be able to defeat Patterson, immediately return to Manassas, and rejoin Beauregard. Patterson's assessment was to move his army to join McDowell's and leave Winchester to the Confederates. [5] General Scott would not even consider that option.

The main battle at Bull Run began on 21 July 1861. On the 18th, Patterson had wired from Charlestown in western Virginia to General Winfield Scott in Washington with a basic question regarding Johnston's force: "Shall I attack?" Scott replied: "I have certainly been expecting you to beat the enemy."

Regrettably for McDowell, Johnston's advance had left Winchester on the same day that Patterson's wire left Charlestown. Johnston had joined Beauregard's army. His men would be instrumental in defeating the Federals. While the battle of First Bull Run raged to the south, the ninety-day enlistment of many companies in Patterson's army, including William Sirwell's, expired.

After three months of riding trains in search of an elusive enemy, drilling, marching, and tolerating inept leadership, Armstrong County's finest were heading home. Captain Sirwell and his men once more boarded trains and headed for the Allegheny River valley. The Brady Alpines were honorably discharged in Pittsburgh on August 14th, 1861. Little if any time passed before William Sirwell formed a new regiment. The Armstrong County history states that the men from Company B virtually became the essence of all military organizations that left Armstrong County during the war.

For his failure to hold Johnston in position, Patterson would never again have an active role in the war. His lack of initiative in engaging the enemy in battle caused him the loss of his or any future command. He tried to explain his passive battle plan by saying he had not received orders to attack. He was mustered out of the army on July 27, 1861. [6]

"THE KID HAS GONE TO THE COLORS"

The main source for the events, character, and movements of the Pennsylvania Seventy-Eighth regiment came from: *The War of the Rebellion: A Compilation of the Official Records of the Union and Confederate Armies*, its regimental history, the letters, dairies and service records of a number of its members, and the company order book of the Seventy-Eighth's Company I. However, in an attempt to give this work the view of the regular soldier, many other regimental histories, diaries, autobiographies and biographies were used in assessing the perception of those people from a bygone era.

A majority of Civil War regimental histories were written with the political and financial support of their home state. Therefore, there were political pressures placed upon the regimental historians to record a chronicle acceptable to the state. Most of these works were also written in the faded light of years past and often in the spirit of reconciliation with the enemy. It is also evident that in order to present the image of the consecrated, untainted warrior, many works were expurgated to further mask the actual character of the "boys."

A most important fact to be remembered is that J. Thompson Gibson the editor, who headed the committee that wrote the regimental history of the 78th, was by 1905, a member of the clergy and thusly a sympathetic chronologer. The letters and diaries of the soldiers were more honest in their opinions and only diverged from the facts when not wanting to worry a loved one far from the war's front. For the most part, these memoirs more often than not kept closer to the truth.

Most of the autobiographies and biographies of this era were self serving and written to conform to a popularly held idea. Naturally, much of the information written by generals such as Ulysses Grant, William Sherman and Phil Sheridan was recorded in the hope that it would become the popular opinion. Notwithstanding, whether it be these personal recollections, newspapers, or the Official Record, most writings were guarded or slanted. As with all events reality lies somewhere betwixt the facts, the opinions and perceptions of each writer.

The History of the Seventy-Eighth Pennsylvania Volunteer Infantry, begins with its origins in Kittanning, Armstrong County, Pennsylvania. Reverend Gibson begins with, "By order of the Secretary of War, Camp Orr, on the Northeastern bank of the Allegheny River, about two miles above Kittanning, was authorized as a rendezvous for the organization of troops and the encampment of new recruits." Camp Orr was erected on the land of the Armstrong County Fair Grounds originally the site of an old Delaware Indian town that had been previously used as a military training camp once before in 1774, during the Revolutionary War.

Throughout the country small groups of men and boys formed up to make up squads, companies and regiments. Reverend DeWitt Hervey of Slate Lick, Pennsylvania was typical of many company commanders in respect to how he forged his company. He created the nucleus for his company within his Union Baptist Church. Other men from the area filled the necessary one-hundred man quota. On the day noted to leave for Camp Orr, Reverend Hervey had his men – in full uniform – meet at his church. After a short service, the men filed out of the church, fell into ranks and marched off to Kittanning.

The first company of the 78th reported in on August 14th, 1861. It was designated as Company B and was comprised of men from Kittanning. The companies that composed the regiment were identical to their brother regiments of the North and their opposition regiments from the Confederacy. Throughout the country companies and regiments were formed in a specific town or county. The boys all went off to war with acquaintances, friends, and relatives. The Seventy-Eighth Infantry Regiment was formed in counties from the south western section of Pennsylvania: Armstrong, Butler, Allegheny, Indiana, Westmoreland, and Clarion. The regimental roster also listed members from Chester, York, Mifflin, Berks, Lancaster, Cambria and Crawford counties and the city of Philadelphia. All ten companies were in Camp Orr by mid-September of 1861.

The ideal compliment for a Civil War Union regiment was a roster of one thousand men; ten companies of one hundred men each. Although many of the counties in Pennsylvania are represented as the origin of the soldiers, over six companies were recruited in Armstrong County. If a company was shy the necessary aggregate of troops to make up a "proper" company, the newly promoted regimental commander, Colonel William Sirwell, simply shifted men around to make equal company strengths. Of the 980 men listed on the original roster, 641 men claimed Armstrong County as their home.

Although numerous professions were listed for the members of the regiment, the regiment consisted of mostly farmers. There were lumbermen, coopers and mechanics in all companies. Teachers, lawyers, and doctors made up a small percentage of the regiment. A few of the boys listed themselves as students. Private Absalom Lloyd of Company K was the only mortician and Sergeant Bill Huff of Company F recorded himself as a "Gentleman." [1]

When one considers the short time frame of the return of Company B and the emergence of the fifteen-hundred man regiment, it would seem like an impossible task for Sirwell to accomplish. However, Sirwell obviously felt that the three-month soldiers would not end the rebellion of the South. Contrary to the popular opinion that the war would end before most men would be afforded the honor of reaching the battlefield, Sirwell seemed to sense something different.

When Company B left Kittanning in April, Sirwell left behind twenty-six men of the Kittanning Yeagers and the Brady Alpines to recruit and organize companies for a future regiment. Sirwell, the ever resourceful militia captain, had hand picked older men to remain behind and canvas the county for new recruits. The advanced age of Sirwell's "recruiters" would have made it difficult for them to survive the arduous campaigning ahead. Bill Sirwell realized they were more valuable in another capacity. Perhaps they could not campaign with the young, but these "elder statesmen" were popular, out-going fellows. Their personal qualities and the patriotic zeal that existed within the country would keep the county's young boys available for new regiments, not to mention some very handsome bonuses or bounties offered to new recruits; Butler County paid each three-year recruit $100. Sirwell's personal recruiters would, through their charm and persuasive demeanor, enlist more than fifteen hundred men in Armstrong County during the three months that Company B was with General Patterson. This number was more than what was needed for a regiment of one thousand. Therefore, the remaining four to five-hundred men were enough to eventually begin another Armstrong County regiment, the Pennsylvania 103rd. [2]

The new-fashioned regiment would spend three months training before entering the war. The time spent at Camp Orr involved the customary squad, company, and regimental drills. However, training a group of farmers, lumbermen, teachers, and varying clerks and professionals to work in concert must have been a difficult task at best. Although Colonel Sirwell was of a firm military bearing, he and his captains attempted to keep the new doses of military rules and regulations to a minimum. In these still early days of the war, many breeches of military conduct and order by the young friends and neighbors were dismissed with a temperate reprimand. [3]

During the three years of the regiment's enlistment discipline would never be very stiff. William Sirwell was a soft spoken man. To him these young men serving their country were his boys. Although Sirwell demanded a proper military bearing, he rarely invoked punishment stronger than a reprimand or extra duty for what he considered small infractions of the Army regulations. The troops in his regiment became very fond of this man more than twice their age in most cases. In return this gentle man truly came to love his boys. He could come to the point of threatening a fellow officer with a "sound thrashing" for moving his men to a poorer camping position.

General James Negley, Sirwell's direct superior for most of the war, would incur Sirwell's wrath and a number of threats of resignation when "Old Bill" thought his boys were being treated unfairly. Negley, not one to back down, would have Sirwell "arrested" a number of times when he felt the members of the Seventy-Eighth had committed "crimes" with Sirwell's knowledge or acceptance. Bill Sirwell saw no great harm in young boys taking leave when there was no great battle to be fought and supplementing their life by living off of the land. Although Sirwell did not condone Absence Without Official Leave or stealing, neither did he condone harsh punishment for his troops.

On October 12th, 1861, Sirwell's regiment was officially mustered into the service of the United States in a ceremony at Camp Orr, Kittanning, Pennsylvania. A noisy, excited crowd watched as Captain A.B. Hays, a mustering and recruiting officer from Pittsburgh, performed the swearing in ceremony.

The time for organization had passed; it was time to join their brothers and enter the war. Two days later, in the bright, clear autumn sun, the Regiment marched out of Camp Orr, its home for the last three months. The soldiers marching through Kittanning presented a dashing, military appearance to the excited throng of spectators as they moved down Jefferson Street to the depot and boarded the open rail cars of the Allegheny Valley Railroad for the train ride to Pittsburgh.

Major Augustus Bonnaffon and the company commanders over saw the boarding of the troops. The crowds cheered and the bands played as the train smoked, belched, and churned its way out of the town. It traveled down through the tree-lined river valley toward Pennsylvania's teeming gateway to the West. It is doubtful that few if any of the anxious young men appreciated the spectacular crimson, red, deep purple or gold of the oaks, maples and sycamores that revealed their autumn splendor as they had for a thousand years before. A number of these young men would never see a Pennsylvania autumn again. They would fall prey to camp disease and death on some distant battlefield.

Colonel Sirwell was not with his regiment. He had preceded them to Pittsburgh by a few days and had checked into the St. Charles Hotel along with his friends, Lieutenant Sam Lee and Dr. William McCullough. His second-in-command, Lieutenant Colonel

Colonel William Graham Sirwell
Courtesy of Ronn Palm, Kittanning, Pennsylvania

David Barclay was also registered at the hotel. The planning needed for the movement of his regiment took precedence over a farewell ceremony. There were last minute meetings with General Negley and his staff. There were logistical details to attend to in preparation for the brigade's embarkation to the theater of war. [4]

Forty year-old Captain Charles Gillespie, commander of Freeport's Company F, was not with the regiment either. On the 13th he had married his sweetheart, Sue Brunker, at the Sugar Creek Roman Catholic Church in Armstrong County. He hurried to Pittsburgh after a short honeymoon.

The advent of the "War of the Rebellion," brought continued growth and increased prominence to Pittsburgh, Pennsylvania. Already a burgeoning center for production and manufacturing, the city attracted droves of people in search of new wealth in the flourishing war time economy. In 1861, Pittsburgh and Allegheny City, the sister city across the Allegheny River, had rapidly grown to a combined population of about 78,000, while Allegheny County that surrounded the cities had a population of over 178,000. The war would again make the population grow to greater heights.

At the outbreak of the Civil War, Pittsburgh was already noted for its steel and iron production. It boasted twenty-six rolling mills and was also noted for the extensive construction of machinery, locomotives, and steamboats. The title prophecy of Samuel Young's 1845 crime thriller "The Smoky City" had become a reality, and the war would increase the output of steel and iron in the form of cannon. The skies of Pittsburgh were filled with smoke during the day and fire storms billowing from the blast furnaces at night. The United States arsenal at Lawrenceville, where Sirwell was born, was now heavily engaged in the manufacture of munitions.

Pittsburgh's rail lines and its three rivers made it an ideal location for shipping manufactured goods. Freight moved to all points in the country through the city's rail hub. Steamboats plying their trade on the nation's rivers lined the shores of the Monongahela and Allegheny River banks. Black smoke and soot poured from their stacks as they waited to transfer their cargo. The streets were filled with wagons, buggies, and people going about their business. Hotels and restaurants, filled with soldiers and businessmen, fed and housed hundreds in rooms overflowing with cigar smoke and noise. Even Mrs. Black's house of ill repute on Third Street was doing a booming business.

This then was the frantic hustle and bustle that the boys of the Seventy-Eighth were greeted with upon their arrival to the city in mid-October of 1861. The immensity, activity, and excitement of the big city must have been virtually overwhelming. [5]

In addition to the shipment of manufactured goods and draw material, Pittsburgh's railroads and the city's three rivers also made it an ideal staging area for many regiments leaving for the different theaters of the war. Pittsburgh was the jump off point for the Seventy-Eighth. The regiment arrived to a glorious welcome for its short stay in the city. They were encamped at the old fair grounds, now Camp Wilkens, on Penn Avenue and Twenty-Sixth, just below Lawrenceville.

The day after their arrival the regiment was formed into a brigade under Brigadier General James Negley with the obligatory ceremonies, presentations, and speeches. Along with Sirwell's regiment, there were also the Pennsylvania Seventy-Seventh, which had been formed in Chambersburg, Pennsylvania, and was commanded by Frederick Stambaugh, and the Seventy-Ninth, recruited in Lancaster County, Pennsylvania, and commanded by Henry Hambright.   Charles F. Muehler's Light Artillery Battery, recruited in Erie, Pennsylvania, rounded out the membership in the brigade.

At a ceremony at Camp Wilkens, the brigade received a special flag sent to General Negley's Brigade by a Mr. Collins, reportedly a friend of Sirwell's, from London. Obviously, while England's political leaders would take a long time deciding whether to recognize the Southern Confederacy, Mr. Collins chose sides very early in the war. The brigade proudly paraded their new flag and arms. Negley had already received rifles and ammunition for his men, and new guns and horses for his battery were on their way. [6]

James Scott Negley, the 78th's new brigade commander was a stout man of medium height, both affable and courteous. Of Swiss decent, Negley was a native of the East Liberty section of Pittsburgh. He attended the Western University of Pennsylvania, the present day University of Pittsburgh. His interest and education gave him an excellent background in horticulture. During the coming campaigns through the South, Negley would be seen reining in his horse, dismounting and taking particular interest in a flower. Although Negley never had the military education offered to a West Point graduate, he did serve a number of years in the state militia. Negley had left college and served during the Mexican War as a private in the First Pennsylvania Infantry. He had fought with General Winfield Scott at Cerro Gordo. In the years between the Mexican War and the Civil War, Negley had risen to the rank of brigadier general of the Pennsylvania state militia. He was thirty-five years old, when he was commissioned a brigadier general of volunteers in April of 1861, and given command of the Pennsylvania militia in Pittsburgh. Like William Sirwell, Negley served with the inept General Patterson in Virginia during the early months of the war.

Negley had been on the committee to welcome President Lincoln to Pittsburgh as the president-elect passed through the city on February 14th, 1861. He headed up a contingent of soldiers from the Pennsylvania Dragoons, the Washington Infantry, and the Jackson Blues that acted as Lincoln's honor guard and security screen. Negley could not persuade his old Mexican War unit, the Duquesne Grays, to join the honor guard. They refused to favor a back-woods, rail-splitting, abolitionist, Republican. [7]

Throughout the few days that the brigade formed in Pittsburgh, there were various activities to enjoy and disappointments for a few of the troops. In addition to Mrs. Black and her eight "ladies of the night", Uncle Tom's Cabin was playing at the Pittsburgh Theater, and Prime Oysters were available at Mr. Young's on Fifth Street. Colonel Hambright had to appear before Judge Wilson McCandless of the U.S. District Court with one of his enlistees on a writ of habeas corpus. Private Aaron Sutman of the Seventy-Ninth had lied about his age to enlist. His irate father came to Pittsburgh; he brought charges against Hambright and the regiment. Young Sutman was discharged and sent home with his father. [8]

At this stage of the war, petty politics often occurred within the development of army units from the army level down through corps, divisions and brigades and even to the company level. Negley had appointed the twenty-eight year old, Pittsburgher James Lowrie as his Assistant Adjutant General. Lowrie, who was the son of Pennsylvania Chief Justice W.H. Lowrie, although gaining his position through friendship and politics, would prove to be a loyal and competent officer. However, General Negley had difficulty appointing each and every political hack searching for an important position in his brigade. Although never being specific, the *Pittsburgh Gazette* alluded to Negley's oft political problems. These problems usually occurred when various individuals viewed the Civil War as an opportunity to advance their careers, their personal fortunes or both. William Sirwell had a formidable problem within his own regiment.

Evidently, at this eleventh hour of the embarkation of the brigade for the theater of operations, a disagreement arose between Sirwell and his second-in-command. Reportedly, while traveling home from Virginia, Sirwell stopped for a night at the Monongahela House in Pittsburgh where he made the acquaintance of David Barclay, a lawyer from Butler, Pennsylvania. According to Barclay, "Some weeks ago I met Col. Sirwell...who informed me that his friends were pressing him to undertake the formation of a regiment in Armstrong and the adjoining counties. He had so far refused, yet if I would agree to give him my aid he would make the attempt. I consented to do so...I rode through the sunshine and rain, day and night, for weeks [helping to form the regiment]."

Barclay's story seems somewhat far fetched. Sirwell's regiment had been in Camp Orr for almost eight weeks and it already had fourteen hundred to fifteen hundred recruits when he supposedly met Barclay. It would follow that Barclay did not have much to do with the actual recruitment or formation of the regiment.

Because of Barclay's prosperous law practice, Sirwell supposedly agreed to permit him to continue part-time operation of his office. But now as the regiment prepared to leave, Sirwell informed Barclay he needed more than a part time second-in-command. He would not tolerate Barclay commuting back and forth from the war zone to Butler. Barclay, maybe rightly so, perceived that Sirwell went back on his word. He surmised, that because of his efforts he deserved special considerations. He took his case to General Negley. James Negley would not over rule Sirwell; he referred Barclay back to his command. A good politician with problems of his own knew better than to come between one of his regimental commanders and a political "hot potato."

Returning to his regiment, Barclay restated his case once again, but Colonel Sirwell could not be swayed from his original decision. An angry Barclay resigned his commission on October 16th. He forwarded a copy of his resignation and letter stating his position to be printed in the *Pittsburgh Gazette*. No information has ever surfaced regarding any exchange between Sirwell or Barclay; however, the regiment sailed away with a new second-in-command, Lieutenant Colonel Archibald Blakeley, who had mustered into the regiment on September 17th.

Archibald Blakeley, a thirty-three year-old lawyer from Butler, Pennsylvania, came to the Seventy-Eighth with outstanding credentials. A native of Butler County, Blakeley had been a delegate to the first state Republican Convention in 1855. He served as the Butler county district attorney in 1853. Colonel Sirwell had known Blakeley's older brother William who was currently serving as the district attorney for Armstrong County. [9]

Although command personnel and officers could be petty, the enlisted men could be equally antagonistic. These western Pennsylvanians, no matter what their profession were cut from the same cloth. They were friends and neighbors of the same ilk. They not only shared political ideas, but also thought alike as to religion. That commonality of opinions brought about an unusually delicate problem. This regiment, comprised mostly of Protestants, had appointed a Roman Catholic priest, as its chaplain.

It should be remembered that during this time there was a great deal of anti-Catholic sentiment in the country as a whole. Resentment of Catholics had existed for many years. The "Know Nothings", a secret society, exerted a great deal of political influence from 1852 to 1860. The American Party, or Know Nothings, were recognized to be anti-Catholic, anti-immigrant, and anti-liquor. Pittsburgh had a strong following of Know Nothings. In the years before the war there was a great deal of resentment for the "paddies," but despite the pronounced religious bigotry, most of the people of the local Catholic parishes were staunch Unionists and willing to fight. However, the philosophical differences of the church leaders ultimately affected the thinking of the flock; both Catholic and Protestant, and the younger men from the farm lands of Western Pennsylvania were no different from their city cousins. They obviously admired and respected Sirwell, but they were not pleased with his selection of Father Christy. A segment of the regiment did not want a papist as their spiritual leader.

Although the political power of the Know Nothings dissipated, because of differences within their party after the elections of 1854, the anti-Catholic sentiment was still alive. Because of these broad based bigotries, the appointment of a Roman Catholic chaplain in the 78th was not only controversial within the regiment, but obviously caused interest outside the regiment. With no editorial comment, the *Pittsburgh Gazette* reported on October 17, 1861, that Colonel Sirwell's regiment had appointed Father Richard Christy of the Butler County Catholic Church as its chaplain. The tiny article noted that one company commander and two other men within the ranks were Protestant clergymen. Statement of this fact would suggest that the "voice of the people" questioned the appointment of a Catholic priest when a number of ministers were available. If the truth be known, not one person enlisting with the Seventy-Eighth stated his profession was that of an ordained minister.

It is unknown if any ordained minister was willing to take the position of chaplain. Evidently, the Reverend Captain DeWitt Hervey of Company K, the Baptist minister, was only interested in remaining with his boys from Slate Lick as a company commander. The thirty-one year-old minister had left his pulpit, his wife Kate and their four children for glory. In point of fact, Reverend Hervey did not list any profession in the *Original Roster and Descriptive List of the 78TH Pennsylvania Volunteer Infantry*. Clearly, he did not want the "ignoble" position of regimental chaplain. At the same time, a meeting of the deacons of the First Presbyterian Church in Kittanning produced no volunteer for the position of regimental chaplain. On the 19th, after the brigade had left Pittsburgh the newspaper reported again, "We are now authorized to state that Father Christy's appointment was not confirmed. Someone else will be picked."

The *Gazette* was incorrect in its report. Bill Sirwell, with whom the ultimate responsibility of the appointment had to be placed, was not inclined to change his decision. Richard Christy, the former pastor of St. John's Roman Catholic Church in Clearfield Township of Butler County, would stay with the regiment. Evidently the newspaper did not know or neglected to mention that Sirwell was also a Catholic. Sirwell was one of the original members of St. Mary's Roman Catholic Church in Kittanning in 1852. The first mass held in Kittanning in 1847, was observed in Sirwell's home, and this practice continued on a frequent basis until a church could be built. [10]

Despite the serious objections to Father Christy by certain numbers of the regiment, time would show him to be an admired and respected member of the regiment and the Society of the Army of the Cumberland.

Father Richard Christy
Courtesy of Bill May, Butler, Pennsylvania

THE BONNIE BLUE FLAG

While Negley's Brigade was being sworn in and prepared for the movement south, similar scenes played themselves out in the Confederate states. Brothers Mitchell and Thomas Cobb, and their friends from central Tennessee, like many of their Northern counterparts, rushed to the flag of Dixie with the outbreak of the war. During the latter part of April 1861, while William Sirwell was forming up his Brady Alpines in Harrisburg, Pennsylvania, three companies of Tennessee "Volunteers" formed the Rock City Guards in Nashville. These three companies would become companies A, B, and C of the proud, Rebel First Tennessee. The other companies of the First Tennessee would be formed in the counties surrounding the towns of Nashville, Franklin, Murfreesboro, Columbia and Pulaski. Many months away the First Tennessee would meet the Pennsylvania Seventy-Eighth in deadly combat.

In early May, after the usual flag presentations and ceremonies in Nashville, Sam Watkins with the Company of Maury Grays left home as Company H, First Tennessee Regiment, for two months training at Camp Cheatham. The camp was north of Nashville about six miles from Springfield. Negley's brigade would enter Kentucky with new rifles. Regrettably, the Tennessee boys would not have the same luxury. They would leave Camp Cheatham with a mishmash of repaired or rebuilt old muskets. But that would not stop the Rebels from fighting the good fight.

In July, to the accompanying brass bands, picnics and the requisite, vivacious, young girls, the First Tennessee set out for the "first and last" battle at Manassas Junction. A young girl, that history records only as "Mary," left a vivid description of Colonel George Maney and his First Tennessee heading off to war. Mary recorded that the streets of Nashville were virtually impassable because of the huge crowd waiting to see the parade of young warriors march out of the city. The First Tennessee Regiment marched to the beat of the drum and playing fifes; a brass band played "Mocking Bird." The colors leading the regiment on parade were a gift of the graduating class of the Nashville Female Academy. Mary's youthful soul could only see invincible heroes march through the streets of the city, "What fine, manly fellows they were. Their guns, as bright as silver, shone in the July sun with unsurpassed splendor. Their upturned, sunburned faces, their eyes beaming with unspeakable enthusiasm and joy..."

The young warriors enjoyed the attention lavished on them. They also enjoyed the excitement and entertainment during their progress through the cities of Nashville, Knoxville and Chattanooga. There were numberless celebrations in each town. A collection of young fellows, enlisted and officers alike, became so drunk in Nashville that they had to be left behind when the regiment embarked for the battle front.

The First Tennessee like the Pennsylvania Ninth did not participate in the battle along Bull Run creek. Unlike their northern counterpart with the absurd and timid leadership of General Patterson, the Tennessee boys were simply late for the battle in Virginia. While the Pennsylvania Seventy-Eighth would spend its time before Stones River in rail guard and small battles, the First Tennessee would find itself in the horrifying carnage at the battle of Shiloh fought at Pittsburg Landing along the Tennessee River. However, the Rock City Guard like the Pennsylvania 78th, would also sit out this major battle. They would perform guard duty in Knoxville. [1]

Mitchell and Tom Cobb did not accompany the First Tennessee to Virginia either. As members of the Rock City Volunteers, they would enter the Confederate service in the latter part of 1861, with Major James M. Hawkins' Battalion. Major Hawkins and his Nashville battalion were assigned to provost guard duty in Nashville itself until its evacuation on February 18th, 1862.

In May of 1862, at Corinth, Mississippi, Hawkins' battalion would be forced to reorganize. In the reorganization Major Hawkins joined General Cheatham's staff. Third Lieutenant now Captain Joseph Fulcher would become the company commander. The troops would merge their three companies into Company L, First Tennessee. Purportedly, the companies were joined together because too many old men filled the original ranks. For the most part, this war would be fought by men young enough to face the hard campaigning ahead. The new organization saw all of these old soldiers fade away. Colonel Maney, a Nashville lawyer and Mexican War veteran, was promoted to Brigadier for gallantry at Shiloh. He succeeded to brigade command and Captain Hume Feild assumed command of the First Tennessee.

Colonel Kit Williams raised a regiment of Southrons in western Tennessee designated the Twenty-Seventh Tennessee. The original regiment of approximately one thousand strong would be worn down from camp diseases. Their wounded and dead at the bloody battle of Shiloh would further deplete their ranks. Shortly before the battle of Murfreesboro they would be combined with the First Tennessee.

The Twenty-Sixth Tennessee was formed with men from the eastern Tennessee region. Soldiers from the counties around Knoxville and Chattanooga would follow Colonel John Lillard of Meigs County through the fighting and capture at Fort Donelson. Reorganized in September of 1862, they would be assigned to General Gideon Pillow's Brigade at Stones River. [2]

Irrespective of the roads traveled; these soldiers would one day meet in the deadly struggle at Murfreesboro, Tennessee. Unknowingly, Bill Sirwell's Pennsylvanians would meet Sam Watkins, Mitchell Cobb and their friends from Tennessee as they were pushed back from the Wilkinson Pike on New Year's Eve 1862. On January 2nd the Seventy-Eighth would attack Colonel John Lillard's Twenty-Sixth Tennessee and capture their regimental colors. The Pennsylvanians would be instrumental in driving General John Breckenridge's brigades back from McFadden's Ford; thus breaking Braxton Bragg's hold middle in Tennessee.

CAMP FIRES IN KENTUCKY

Many of the men who headed off to war with James Negley had never been away from home. A number had been in state militia units, a lesser number had been in the three-month service, and fewer still had ever been in active combat. Few if any regimental or company commanders had military experience. Besides Sirwell, within the 78th, the only military experience among the officers was shared with one staff officer and two company commanders. Major Augustus Bonnaffon, Captain William Jack, Company H, and Captain James Hilberry, Company B were all in the three-month service. Captain Hilberry had been with Sirwell's Company B, Ninth Regiment. Captain William Cummins of Company A had led a militia group in Indiana County, but had no active experience. [1]

To the foot soldiers their experience or lack of it was of no concern. It was an exhilarating time. Most shared the patriotic fervor that gripped every section of the country. They gladly went off to war to be with friends and family. They went with their family's advice and blessings. In a letter to her brother Albert of the Seventy-Eighth, Lida Simkins echoed the opinion of many family members across the land. "I want you my dear boy as you have offered your services to your country to do your best in all cases and never under any circumstances turn your back to your enemy unless by orders of those in command. It will be more to your personal honor as well as to the honor of your country to give up your gun than to run as did our troops at Bull's Run." [2]

War may have been the patriotic thing to do, but it was also an opportunity to get away from the drudgery and boredom of the farmer's life. And there were probably many who enlisted lest they be branded as cowards. No matter what the reason, they were now being paid the princely sum of $13 a month, and there was that ever present opportunity of an absolutely rollicking adventure. Whatever the boys lacked in experience they made up with enthusiasm.

The adventure, excitement, and adulation at Pittsburgh were heady stuff for these untested warriors. On the late Wednesday afternoon of October 16th, the regiments in Negley's brigade were presented with their regimental national ensign at a festive ceremony at Camp Wilkens. That night, the one time Know Nothing, Governor Andrew Curtin with his personal military retinue arrived at the Monongahela House for the following day's ceremonies. The Monongahela House at Smithfield, First Avenue and Water was reportedly the finest of Pittsburgh's seventeen hotels. The grand hotel had housed President-elect Lincoln, when he passed through Pittsburgh in February.

Thursday, October 17th, was a most exciting day for Negley's new brigade. On that autumn afternoon, the brigade marched out of Camp Wilkens at 2 o'clock. Fully uniformed with broad smiles, the men stepped off in a springing gait. The parade of regiments proceeded down Penn Avenue to the Monongahela House. General Negley, his staff, Colonel Stambaugh and Colonel Hambright all rode horses. Colonel Sirwell chose to walk with his boys. Close by his side was the little over four and one-half foot tall, 13 year-old veteran musician, Danny Golden. At the Monongahela House, Governor Curtin, his party, and the Lancaster Brass Band led the brigade out of Pittsburgh to Allegheny City. They crossed the new Suspension Bridge at Sixth Street. The relatively new architectural creation was built by John and Washington Roebling who would go on to build the famous Brooklyn Bridge. The parade marched up Federal Street and formed on the West Commons.

Governor Curtin spoke for a short period, but because of the noisy, excited crowd it was difficult to hear the Governor. Even the press was unable to record the text of the speech. Nonetheless, they did hear the Governor inform the three thousand excited soldiers of their destination. Many of the officers and men of the brigade feared that they would be sent to the humdrum theaters of war in either western Virginia or Missouri, but the announcement that they would be heading for Kentucky brought loud and long cheers. Governor Curtin then presented each regimental commander with a state flag. The azure blue field with the state coat of arms surrounded with thirty-four stars represented the total Union, not one divided by rebellion. After three resounding huzzahs for Curtin and Negley, the brigade moved back to Camp Wilkens. The cloudy skies had not dampened their enthusiasm. [3] Colonel Sirwell returned to Camp Wilkens with 961 combatants.

The original roster had already lost a few of its enlistees. Lt. Colonel Barclay had resigned and a few men never reported in or went AWOL. Those that are listed as deserted, obviously did not share the enthusiasm of their brothers. Corporal George Edmonson of Company I deserted. Privates Brown, Butler, Gap, Alfred Schrecengost and Bill Wheeler of Company G never mustered or went AWOL. [4] Alfred Schrecengost eventually served in the Second Battalion of the Pennsylvania Militia from 1862 until the war's end.

On October 18th, Negley's Brigade was marched to the wharf on the Monongahela River and boarded steam boats for the trip to Kentucky. Thousands of men, women, and children lined the river bank to give the men a rousing send off. The excitement and confusion must have been overwhelming. The Seventy-Eighth was boarded on Captain Thomas Poe's steamboat Clara Poe and the Moderator, while the remainder of the men, horses, and cannon were boarded on the four other steam boats. Adam Johnston, a private in the Pennsylvania 79th regiment, wrote in his diary that the loading of the soldiers and their gear was chaotic to say the least. The Lancaster Brass Band once again was playing for the troops from the upper decks of the Sir William Wallace. An artillery horse became frightened and fell from the gangplank of Captain McCarthy's boat the J.W. Hailman. Later it had to be destroyed. But the rush of soldiers to see the horse flailing in the water caused the weight of the Hugh Campbell's Wallace to shift to the larboard side. The excessive weight of men and baggage caused the front part of the Wallace's hurricane deck to collapse, and many of the soldiers and musicians fell to the lower deck. Colonel Hambright's adjutant, Charles Frailey, Private Dan Landis, and Dan Clemens, a member of the band, were all seriously hurt. Frailey's injuries were such that he was forced to resign his commission at the end of the month. [5] All in all, thirty men from Hambright's command were injured.

At 6:00 P.M., ropes were released, steam whistles sounded, anchors weighed, and the Clara Poe, the Moderator, the Argonaut, the Silver Wave, the J.W. Hailman, and the Sir William Wallace sailed quickly from the Monongahela River onto the Ohio River. The huge river boats spewed smoke, soot, and sparkling ash into the night sky. They floated down the pathway to Kentucky and into the rapidly cooling night. Naturally, through Sirwell's politicing, his regiment enjoyed breathing cleaner air being in the first two boats. Many of the boys stood at the railings and watched the lights of Pittsburgh rapidly disappeared into the fog, smoke, and darkness. The fog became so thick after passing Neville Island, just a few miles from Pittsburgh, that Commander of the Fleet, W.J. Kountz decided to pull into shore until the dense fog dissipated enough to steer. Notably, this was a disappointment for the eager servicemen. [6]

A great deal of the personal information on the men of the Pennsylvania Seventy-Eighth was gleaned from the *Original Roster and Descriptive List of the 78th Pennsylvania Volunteer Infantry*, the original history of the regiment, Bates' *History of Pennsylvania Volunteers* and numerous letters and diaries. It is difficult in some cases to pin point exact information. Many names were spelled phonetically which in turn may show one soldier having as many as six spellings for his name in differing official records. Some lied about their age to be older and some lied to be younger. Coloring was suspect to description: "sallow" vs. pale complexion, dark eyes vs. dark blue or dark brown, while "sandy hair" or "light hair" could be blond or light brown.

The average height of the regiment was 5'7". Most regimental companies stated the height of a soldier to be "5' 9";" however, Company H that listed a great number of students had a scribe who became very exacting and creative. He listed measurements in eighth, quarter or thirds of inches. Some fellows added a few halves to make them taller; presumably none reduced their stature. Solomon Holben of Company B and Solomon Altman of Company C were the tallest at 6'4". Holben would die of typhoid in hospital at Louisville on March 21, 1862, and Altman would be given a medical discharge. All in all, the roster at the end of the book is correct...for the most part!

The group of men and boys in Sirwell's regiment that went off to war averaged about twenty-one years in age. While the ages of most of the men ranged from 18 to 45 there were those younger and those much older. At least twenty-five of the regiment were 13 to 17 years old, the youngest being Dennis "Danny" Golden at twelve. Dennis Golden would serve the longest term of any man on the roster of the Seventy-Eighth. He tramped off with Sirwell's Company in April of 1861, and mustered out in the second regimental organization in September of 1865. John Croyle, who enlisted at 16, would be listed as "missing in action" at Stones River. He never returned and was presumed dead. Henry Weaver, who enlisted at 14 by stating he was sixteen, was the youngest member of the regiment to be killed in battle. George H. Smith of Company H, would die in February of 1862, at Bells Farm in Kentucky. Joseph Lowry, who enlisted at 16, would be promoted to Regimental Staff Commissary Sergeant at approximately age 19. The remaining twenty would be honorably discharged at the end of their terms in November of 1864.

It was somewhat prevalent for young boys to lie about their age in order to follow their family members or friends to war. The French born, Christian Hinchberger of Butler County's Company H enlisted at age seventeen with his father's permission, but many young recruits were forced to lie about their age to enlisting officers. Bill May of Butler, Pennsylvania in his one-man Civil War drama, tells an interesting story of American ingenuity. When under-aged boys faced questioning recruiters, they honestly stated that they were over eighteen; well...that is after placing a piece of paper with the number "18" written on it in their shoe.

In researching the members of the regiment in the *Original Roster and Descriptive List of the 78th Pennsylvania Volunteer Infantry*, Private Sam Steele of Company K listed as being eighteen years old is the most glaring example of falsification. Cross references in newspaper articles and U.S. Census records indicate that Sam was only fourteen. Born in Freeport, Pennsylvania, on April 1, 1847, the son of Isaac and Mary Steele of Slate Lick easily deceived any who would question his age, six months after his fourteenth birthday; he was well built and five feet, eight inches tall. Obviously, Sam went off to war with his father's blessing, since his father, unlike Private Aaron Sutman's of the Pennsylvania Seventy-Ninth, did not come after him.

Not all families sent their sons off to war alone. The Seventy-Eighth was a list of fathers and sons, brothers, uncles, nephews, cousins and at least one grandfather. Mathais Bartlebaugh of Company D marched off with his two grandsons in the company; Sam Bartlebaugh and Jeremiah Cook. Fifty-four year-old Sam Shaffer, Sr. laid ill for over two months before being discharged in September of 1862; his nineteen year-old son, Sam Jr., served out his enlistment. The regimental history list only John W. Geary in Company K. However, research reveals that John W. at 35 marched off with his 15 year-old son John W. Geary, Jr. Both members of Company K would return home. Only Harrison Daniels would come home; brother David would die of wounds received at Stones River. David McQuiston would die of chronic diarrhea in Nashville during February, 1864. David, Jr. would serve until November of 1864. John and Elizabeth Latshaw of Clarion County would lose both sons Ebenezer and Reuben. All 4 members of the McLaughlin family of Co. D would die of disease. Twins John and Sam Hutchison would die within 18 months; Sam of disease and John of wounds at Stones River. All ten members of the Schick families would survive the war. Among the father-son teams in the regiment, a number of fathers died of disease. Campaigning was a young man's adventure.

Many of the "boys" were in their thirties or forties, but roughly ten men of the regiment were "senior citizens." They were all 50 years-old or older, with the eldest honor going to Private Alexander Lowry of Co. G, at 60. Only 2 of 10 finished their term of enlistment. Charles Allen, Co. B, served almost 4 years and mustered out in June of 1865 at age 60. Bill Davis, Co. I, mustered out in November of 1864. A 56 year-old Davis would be honored for his heroism at the battle of Stones River. Alex Lowry was discharged, on a surgeon's certificate, in October of 1862, at age 61. Tom Wilson of, the 58 year-old teamster from Company G, would die within five months. The cold nights, the hard ground, and limited food quickly took their tool on an old man.

Virtually all of the men were born in Western Pennsylvania. At least twenty-five men had been born in either England, Wales, Ireland, France or Germany. [7]

The convey of boats steamed down the Ohio River for three days to their jump-off point at Louisville. When the river boats steamed passed Wheeling, Virginia, people gathered along the river banks and the bridge that crossed the river. They cheered the troops as the boats drifted by. Soldiers from Fort Duty fired a cannon salute and the two bands from the steamers responded with a few merry tunes. The boats continued to follow the flow of the river which for a good part of its course acts as the north-south border for Ohio and Kentucky. When the Ohio River cut between the sister cities of Cincinnati, Ohio, and Covington, Kentucky, it turned to a south westerly direction. Crowds stood along the river banks and shouted their loudest cheers.

As the boats steamed closer to enemy territory, rumors ran wild. The Rebels attacking the flotilla was the most prominent. A group of men with a piece of artillery caused a great deal of anxiety, when they appeared along the Kentucky river bank with a cannon. The puffs of smoke and the boom of the cannon sent a few men scurrying for their weapons, but the cannon fire was not an attack. Thankfully, Sergeant Gibson reported the gun only fired a salute. [8]

On Sunday evening the steam flotilla passed Six-mile Island and formed a line for docking at Louisville's wharf. "...thousands of people, mostly women and children," noted the decidedly Rebel *Louisville Daily Courier*, cheered the arrival of Negley's Brigade. In spite of the warm welcome, the excited troops were kept on board the steamboats until Tuesday morning.

On Monday evening, General Negley, his staff, Colonel Stambaugh, Colonel Hambright and Colonel Sirwell attended dinner with General William Sherman, their commander, at Louisville's famed Galt House. Captain Silas Miller, host of the hotel set out "a sumptuous entertainment."

Many of loyal Kentucky citizens of Louisville gave the troops a hearty welcome as they paraded in review for General Sherman on Tuesday morning. Marching four abreast out First Street and through the town to Camp Oakland the column of soldiers, artillery and horses stretched for over a mile. As the feted warriors passed the staunch Unionist, flag-draped mansion of Mrs. Marshall Halbert on Broadway, they thrilled at the beautiful young ladies of Louisville waving from the garden.

The brigade camped near the Oakland race track, christened Camp Sherman, for only a short time. On October 23rd, at 12:00 A.M., they boarded the rail cars of the Louisville and Nashville Railroad and headed south through the stacked limestone hills of northern Kentucky. The weary soldiers reached McCook Station at midnight the next day and pitched their tents in the nearby woods for some much needed sleep. The next morning they moved into their newly christened home, Camp Nevin. This camp, the first of many for the regiment, was fifty two miles south of Louisville on the north side of Nolin Creek. [9]

The arrival of Sirwell's soldiers into Kentucky came at a time when the state was split into two armed, opposing political camps. The folks in Kentucky like many border states were in an unusual political position. The state itself was considered a slave state, with many of its goods sold to the cotton-growing states and its neighbors to the north. Additionally many of its social and family ties were with the both the Northern and Southern people. The diverse opinions of the Kentuckians had originally led to an absurd policy of "armed neutrality" adopted by local politicians. General Robert Anderson, the defeated commander of Fort Sumter, had tried to maintain the status quo by housing his command in Cincinnati since May. By September 4, 1861, both sides had forces in Kentucky. General Leonidas Polk had moved Southern troops into the state on the rumor of Federal troops entering Kentucky. On the other hand, General Anderson made a counter advance into the state, reportedly in answer to Polk's movement. The incursion of opposing armies into Kentucky ended all hopes of neutrality.

The *Daily Journal*, which supported the Union, was printed in Louisville while the *Louisville Daily Courier*, which supported the Confederacy, was printed in Bowling Green, Kentucky. It was this diverse atmosphere that left the Union troops wondering about the loyalties of each and every native they encountered. Regardless of the sentiments of the Rebel citizens, there were no great battles to be fought. The regiment's time in Kentucky would consist of small skirmishes, camp life, illness, and boredom. [10]

When one holds the image of parades, bands playing, and the added spectacle of "Old Glory" and regimental standards snapping in the autumn breezes as they led newly uniformed soldiers off to war, it becomes quite amusing to read the first order recorded in Company I, Order Book, Pennsylvania 78th Regiment. It would seem that the recently anointed saviors of the Union were taking advantage of their invader status. They were stealing too many chickens.

Headquarters 78th Pennsylvania Volunteer Infantry.
Camp Nevin, Kentucky.
General Order No. 1

There having been a great deal of stealing done last night and the blame attached to this regiment, Notice is given that the captains of companies are held responsible for payment.
There has been a bill [of] Six dollars and fifty cents <$6.50> already settled by the Colonel of this regiment.

> *By Order of Colonel William Sirwell*
> *Commanding*
> *J. W. Powell, Adjutant* [11]

Unburdened by the constraints of home and family, the boys were getting a little wild. Most assuredly many boys were homesick, but many more were having a holiday. It is evident that the grand adventure and its accompanying freedom led to excesses that disturbed the command. Sirwell in one of his first orders stated that "Profane Swearing & obscene language are positively prohibited." Without the authority of their parents, without responsibilities of a home and employment, and without the obligations of wives and children to many this was a escapade to be enjoyed. The bane of all soldiers throughout history is the "waiting." Waiting for assignments, waiting to eat and drill afford the troops in the field a good deal of free time. There was time to lay around, time to read, write letters, "shoot the bull," and "horse around," play games, gamble, drink and use tobacco. The history of the Seventy-Eighth notes that the boys often amused themselves by making cigars of cured tobacco from the local barns. It does not state how the tobacco was acquired. [12]

Sirwell, with his abiding interest in everything, initially made the best of his time in Kentucky. Along with his staff and Father Christy, he took trips to see Kentucky's famed Manmouth Caves and a cabin "on Nolin's Creek near Hodgenville," or what was left of it, reported to be the birth place of Abraham Lincoln. And as did thousands of soldiers that went off to war, he sat for a picture in Louisville. Sitting for the piece of history, Sirwell wore his full dress uniform with all accouterments. But these first days of new found joys quickly passed and reality soon set in.

New, green troops joining up with a large army needed organization. Considering the time away at war, battles were infrequent. Campaigning in the field was mostly camp life. General Order Number 3, issued by Colonel Sirwell five days after arriving in Kentucky, dealt with the daily routine and schedule that would burden the men for the duration of their service. The following order is from the Company I order book. The refinement of musical commands did not appear in Sirwell's orders until a year later. However, the commands are added here for reference. Most regiments both Yankee and Rebel would follow this schedule or something similar to it for the course of the war.

The mundane schedule followed by the volunteer soldiers quickly put an end to visions of heroic deeds in a deadly battle. Bill Sirwell's troops would come to realize that boredom and endless, repetitive tasks would be their fate for the duration of their service. Reveille, policing the compound, breakfast, guard mounting, and drills became the annoyance of the troops. Naturally, the boys passed a good deal of time complaining about drills.

Headquarters 78th Pennsylvania Volunteer Infantry
Camp Nevin, Kentucky.
General Order No. 3, October 26th, 1861.

The following camp duties will be strictly attended to hereafter at the time herein designated.

6:00 A.M. Reveille. Signal: Field Music
Roll call by sergeants to be superintended by a commissioned officer. Immediately after roll call commanders of companies will see that their company quarters are cleaned and put in order.
7:00 A.M. Breakfast Call. Signal: Bugle
8:30 A.M. Regimental Guard Mounting Troop. Signal: Field Music
The detail of each regiment will be marched under the direction of the senior officer of the detail to the parade [ground] in front of the General Headquarters for Brigade Guard Mounting.
8:30 A.M. Company Inspection Signal: Bugle
9:00 A.M. Surgeons Call.
First Sergeants to conduct the sick to the hospital and hand the Surgeon a list of the sick of the company. He will then make out and present his morning report to the Adjutant.
9:00 A.M. Squad Drills. Signal: Field Music
To continue for two hours.
11:00 A.M. Morning Reports.
Morning Report of the Regiments will be returned to the office of the Assistant Adjutant General by Adjutants of Regiments.
12:00 M. Dinner Call. Signal: Bugle
Roll Call superintended by a commissioned officer.
1:00 P.M. Assembly. Signal: Field Music
Company drill for 2 hours in which all commissioned officers in uniform must take part.
4:00 P.M. Battalion drill. Signal: Field Music
For one hour or Brigade drill when ordered by the General Commanding.
5:00 P.M. Dress Parade/Retreat. Signal: Field Music

6:00 P.M. Supper. Signal: Bugle
8:00 P.M. Tattoo. Signal: Bugle
Roll Call superintended by a commissioned officer.
9:00 P.M. Taps. Signal: Drum. [13]

At this stage of the war, a commanding officer had very little time to mold his command into a "well-oiled machine." The best that any commander could hope for was a unit that fired well and moved with enough precision during a battle to be utilized effectively. To accomplish this task a strong organization had to be built. Woefully, many of the sergeants and corporals of the regiment did not measure up to even the volunteer-infantryman standards of the time. Most of the non commissioned officers were named to their positions because of their engaging character and personality. "Good fellows" did not necessarily make good leaders. In every company of the regiment a good percentage of the non commissioned officers were reduced to the rank of private. Colonel Sirwell selected the best leaders available from the personnel available...often six to eight sergeants and six to eight corporals per company. These men would command the respect of their peers and educate the soldiers in the ways of warfare.

In most cases the education of a volunteer soldier was simply teaching him to obey orders. It was a process of teaching organization. There was little if any actual education in simulated battle conditions. For the most part, early in the Civil War regiments learned to fight in actual battles. Therefore, company and regimental drills became most important. The drills may have seemed excessive to the new soldier, but at this phase of their service the movements of most units were blundering and awkward. William Sirwell had the advantage of years of military experience. He made sure that his troops would be well trained. He was keenly aware that the best regiments were those that were well versed in the manual of arms, and basic drill movements. [14] Unfortunately, all drill officers did not think accordingly.

The regimental commanders were left to their own designs in drilling their green troops. Supposedly, the order for drill read, "[the regiment with its command was to be] under arms at three o'clock in the morning, and perform such evolutions as regimental Commanders may direct." Silas Canfield wrote in his *History of the Twenty-First Regiment, Ohio Volunteer Infantry* that Colonel Granville Moody had his 74th Ohio on the drill field in the early morning darkness. "[They were] put through a course of battalion drill each morning, to the great annoyance and disgust of the men." On the other hand, all that was required of the Ohio 21st was, to fall in with arms; they were then dismissed to quarters, and enjoyed some refreshing sleep. [15]

Firing a weapon was of equal importance to troop movements. However, according to the Company I order book target practice was superficial. Although most of the men in the Seventy-Eighth grew up with a knowledge of "hunting" fire arms, the army-issued weapon was in all likelihood quite different from the rifles used at home. Many of the boys in Negley's brigade did not appreciate the unique, individual characteristics of their new weapons. They would exchange "better fitting parts" with their friends. General Negley had to admonish his troops not to swap parts of guns. Exchanging parts could endanger the action of their rifle and render them inoperable.

After the manual of arms, and how to care for a rifle, firing of weapons had to be taught. There was a need of education in loading and firing the army rifle at target practice; it too was lacking. The following order states that only two bullets would be issued to each man for target practice. It does not nearly seem worth the effort.

Brigade Headquarters
Camp Nevin, Kentucky.
October 27th, 1861

Target Practice

General Order No 13
There will be detailed daily (provided other military duties and the weather permits) between the hours of 9 and 11 O'clock A.M., three companies from each regiment [with a] commissioned officer [in charge] for Target Practice. Each man to fire two shots at a target 100 yards distant governed by the following rules:
1. Take a position as to aim with ease
2. Keep the body free from constraint
3. Do not incline the sight right or left
4. Aim with the sight down
5. Aim at the height of a man's breast
6. Guard against recoil or derangement of the aim in pressing the trigger
7. When firing with the sight down under 200 yards target fixed
8. The officer in charge of each company to make a written statement of the
*   experimental firing and the names of the men making the best shots each.*

By Order of Brigadier General James Negley
James A. Lowrie, Assistant Adjutant General
To: Colonel William Sirwell, Commanding 78th Regiment [16]

In this the early days of the war, it is evident that training was very basic. Eventually the army commanders would learn that firing breast high in the excitement of battle saw the projectiles go overhead. The order would soon change to "Fire at their shins." As the war progressed, training of all types, mock battles, situation training and target practice would increase.

DON CARLOS THE FIRST

The Army of the Cumberland, initially christened The Army of the Ohio, had seen a rapid succession of commanders during its brief existence. General Robert Anderson had been the first Federal commander in the Kentucky theater of operations. Although General Anderson never actively campaigned with the army during his short tenure, the men he selected as subordinates would command the army for the course of the war. William Sherman, Don Carlos Buell, and George Thomas were all assigned to Anderson's western command.

There was some difficulty in having Thomas assigned to Anderson's command. Because of Thomas' Southern heritage, President Lincoln was reluctant to place him in an important position. But at the behest of Anderson and a number of important political and military advisers, President Lincoln promoted Thomas to Brigadier and assigned him to the western command. Thomas' loyalty and military skills would bring victories and fame to the Army of the Cumberland. George Thomas, like Negley and Sirwell, had also been with General Patterson in Virginia during the early stages of the war.

General Anderson resigned his command due to poor health on October 7, 1861. When Negley's Pennsylvanians arrived in Kentucky, General William Sherman, who had succeeded Anderson, was the army commander. On November 9th, Sherman, at his own request, resigned and was relieved of command. General Don Carlos Buell assumed command of the Army of the Ohio. Buell's Department of the Ohio covered Ohio, Indiana, Michigan, Tennessee, and the part of Kentucky east of the Cumberland River.

General Buell brought a much different style to the Army of the Ohio. A West Point graduate, he was a career military man. He rose from a lieutenant colonelcy in the adjutant general's department in May 1861, to brigadier general of volunteers. His arrival saw an increase in drills, better camp conditions, and more discipline. He demanded stern punishment for straggling, pillaging, and disobedience of orders. Buell had a violent temper and at times he was harsh and severe. [1] A manner such as this did not sit well with the citizen-soldier.

Buell's harsh treatment of the troops came from the fact that he had very little confidence in the volunteer soldier. As a professional soldier, he held volunteers in contempt. Ulysses Grant stated that Buell "...could not distinguish sufficiently between the volunteer 'enlisted for the war' and the soldier who serves in time of peace. One system embraced men who risked life for a principle...The other includes, as a rule, only men who could not do as well in any other occupation." This attitude of Buell's became evident to the men and they returned their feelings in kind. There was a lack of mutual respect between the army and their commander. [2] It is difficult to determine the image that Buell, who had a difficult time developing his own personal relationships, wished to project for his men, but the fact that he trimmed his hair and beard to resemble portraits of Don Carlos I of Spain, says something peculiar about the ego of the man. [3]

At this stage of the war, according to the regimental history, the army appears to have been well cared for. They had "an adequate supply of comfortable clothing...and each company had, at this time, as much baggage as afterwards sufficed for a whole regiment." The fact of excess baggage may have been true, but was it material that the regiment needed for a better life in the field. It would appear from other writers that this comment was far from reality. Reverend J. Thompson Gibson, a Sergeant in Company A, assuredly had his remembrances dimmed over the forty years since the war ended. [4]

Bates' History states, "owing to the unhealthy location of the camps, Nevin and Negley, and the excessive wet weather, the mortality rate in Negley's brigade was very great." It is possible that there was an enormous amount of "baggage" with the regiment, but warm blankets and tents were not among the wagons.[5] Private Abram Kipp of Company F also painted a dismal picture in letters to his mother. From Camp Nevin, Kentucky on November 8, 1861, Private Abram Kipp wrote, "I like my grub first rate. We get crackers and fat pork. We lay on the ground yet. We ain't got our blankets yet and only one shirt and one pair of drawers and one pair of pants."

The regiment did not receive proper tents or blankets until about November 25th, and many of those were donated by Allegheny County, Pennsylvania. By the 27th, Private Kipp reported in his letters home, "It rained all last night. It is very sickly here now. There are...183 sick in the regiment." Kipp's statement rang true. Poor camping conditions quickly affected the men. During the first nine weeks of the campaign in Kentucky, twenty-one men died from varying diseases. [6]

During the course of the war sickness was the constant companion of the men in the field. Diarrhea was the most common ailment of the soldiers in the field. General Negley had been returned to a Louisville hospital around this time and Sirwell himself became quite ill. He had a difficult time recovering. As was common practice in armies on both sides, when it was feasible, a soldier's wife would visit him in camp. Naturally, an illness would bring wives, mothers or sisters to care for the sick. Elizabeth Sirwell came to Kentucky and cared for her husband until he was healthy. Nine year-old Bill Sirwell Jr. had traveled with his mother. When the time came to leave, he begged his father to remain with the regiment. Young Bill could not see the hardship and illness; he saw only the uniforms and excitement. Much to his dismay, Colonel Sirwell sent him packing.

Corporal Ira Gillaspie of the 11th Michigan, also part of the Army of the Ohio, made entries into his diary that would substantiate Private Kipp's comments in the letters to his mother. "Dec. the 12th - A couple of our men come down with small pox but our surgeons would not own up that it was that...Such a coughing you never heard in our camp for we had to sleep right on the wet muddy ground and not being used to camp life we caught a tremendous cold which settled in our lungs and in the end sent many a poor fellow to his grave... Dec. 16 - We drilled for the first time on knapsack drill. We made so much noise coughing that one could not hear the commands...Some of the boys come down with small pox...the measles and [lung disorders]..." Gillaspie made a number of entries in his diary regarding friends or acquaintances becoming ill and being taken off to the pest house. [7]

It is well documented in many histories of the Civil War that a higher percentage of men died from illness than from battle wounds, and that much of the food, clothing and equipment was of poor quality. Disease was to become more of threat to the soldiers fighting the Civil War than the guns of their respective enemies. Sickness hit soldiers hardest in their first year of service. The Army of the Cumberland housed men from the mid-west and the mid-Atlantic states. Many of these farm boys had never been exposed to the mild, but highly contagious childhood diseases such as measles, mumps, and tonsillitis. Diseases like smallpox, and infectious lung maladies were devastating. Poorly prepared food, lack of proper clothing and cover against the cold along with poor sanitary

Major General James Scott Negley

conditions created the ideal environment for viruses of many types. Those viruses and bacteria caused the three greatest causes of death to the Civil War soldier: diarrhea or dysentery, typhoid, and pneumonia. Ladies of the evening at Lexington, Louisville, and Nashville, in addition to camp followers, were doubtlessly responsible for the number of cases of venereal disease. [8]

Clearly one of the Federal generals did not like reports of illness or substandard equipment in the Kentucky theater of operations. Whitelaw Reid of the *Cincinnati Gazette* was banished from Camp Nevin by General Alexander McCook, when some remarks in one of his letters referred to defective cartridges furnished to the army and the high percentage of sickness in the Indiana regiments. [9]

No matter what the condition of the soldiers there were training assignments and military duties for the soldiers to perform, and sentry duty was one of them. Sentry duty was rarely executed to conform with army regulations. Fatigue, fear and loneliness affected most of the pickets. The boys walking sentry couldn't care less about regulations. In General Order #26 issued by General Negley the brigade commander of the 78th, it is apparent that leaving a post, sitting down for a rest or sleeping was commonplace.

Brigade Headquarters
Camp Nevin, Kentucky. November 12th, 1861.

Duties of Sentries while on Duty
General Order No 26
*   The commanding General regrets the necessity of calling the attention of the officers of the Guard to the very unmilitary practice of beating the drum for relief, allowing fires to burn on the picket line, permitting the Sentinels to set down or stand at post taking no notice when they carry their guns in an improper manner nor when they fire off their musket while on duty. This neglect and want of vigilance has been increased until several of the Sentinels have gone to sleep on their posts others have left their posts without being relieved. In the future the Guards who may violate the articles of war shall be court martialed and made liable to suffer the penalty prescribed.*
*   By Order of Brigadier General James Negley*
*   James A. Lowrie, Assistant Adjutant General* [10]

In the regimental history, sentry duty was addressed in humorous vein, but the stories are indicative of the fear of many of these young boys. In the pitch blackness of the Kentucky skies, skittish boy-soldiers overreacted to every sound and movement. "During our first night on picket in the dense woods, soon after midnight, a cry rang out, 'Halt! halt!! halt!!!' It was loud, louder, loudest, and the last halt was preceded by an expression not found in Hardee's Tactics, and was followed by a loud report [of a rifle]. Hardly a night passed that a horse, a cow or a mule did not pay the penalty with his life for approaching too near the picket line." Fear was a usual companion during the late night watch, but the desire to sleep could be overwhelming. The thin line of sentries that surrounded an army or regiment placed young men in a lonely situation.

In a letter to his wife Ruth, and his daughters, Sarah and Annabelle, in Apollo, Pennsylvania, Lt. George Washington Black of Company I, like the common soldier, felt he was in danger because of the proximity of the Rebel army and the secessionist politics of the people in the area. He also relates a story of how picket duty brought the regiment one of its first casualties.

78th Regiment Company I
Colonel Sirwell, Captain R. D. Elwood,   Camp Nevin, November 15/61
   My Dear Wife I want to let you Know that I have been Sick for a week or So, but I have Got better again. I caught Cold when I was out on Picket duty. Our camp is under Strict discipline.
   We are Still Encamped at Camp Nevin, 56 Miles from Louisville, on the Louisville and Nashville Rail Road. General Buckner the Rebel General Still Occupies Bowling Green 40 Miles from us. Part of his force is at Green River 20 Miles from us. The Main force [at] Nashville is from 60 to a 100 Thousand Rebels. Our whole force is not More than 40 or 50 thousand.
   This is a very nice country. It is very frosty. I think the People are nearly all Secessionists
   I think we will have an engagement before Long. I expect this Battle will take place within ten days. I think our Men will do their duty. We Soon will be called to face the Enemy of our Country. If we Shall be called to face death with all the horrors of war ... if god is on our Side we trust in Success. We know that our cause is just.
   I Notice an accident in our Regiment in Captain Hosey's company [James N. Hosey, Captain, Company "E"]. When on Picket duty the two Pickets where Showing the other that he Must Come to arms Port. [The] gun Slipped out [of] his hands and went off and Shot the other through the thigh and Shattered the bone. The next Morning [they] Cut his Leg off and the Man died the Same day. By now Thorne who died in peace is with god.
   Private Samuel Thorn, Company E, was killed on picket duty November 13, 1861, by his picket companion. His young partner had to be placed under guard for fear that he would kill himself. Many years later, Lieutenant Colonel Blakeley remembered the mournful gathering at the newly dug grave of Samuel Thorn, the first casualty of gun fire. For some unknown reason, General Negley did not want Thorn's funeral to take on any importance. He ordered Sirwell to have only four men at the ceremony. Sirwell threatened to resign his commission or transfer to another brigade if this order stood. In the end, only a small squad and Sirwell's staff assembled for Thorn's interment at a nearby church yard. Sirwell did not resign, but a few of the boys from the regiment threatened to shoot Negley in battle if they had the opportunity. [11]
   It is noteworthy that the letterhead of Lt. Black's letter of this date had a picture of William Rosecrans. Rosey would become their commander a year later.
   By November 27th, the 78th was in their new camp. Camp Negley was situated on the south side of Nolin Creek only about two miles from their old Camp Nevin.
   During the summer of 1862, Buell's 89,000-man army, along with James Negley's brigade, was reorganized. Negley's Brigade was attached to General Alexander McDowell McCook's Division. The Seventy-Seventh Regiment was transferred to General Thomas Wood's Brigade. The Seventy-Ninth Regiment was transferred to John Starkweather's Brigade around July or August of 1862. By August of 1862, Colonel Sirwell's Seventy-Eighth regiment, which served "Unattached" for a short time, would be

BRIG. GEN'L ROSECRANS,
COMMANDING U. S. FORCES IN WESTERN VIRGINIA.

Published and for sale by Mumford & Co., 38 and 40 Fourth St., Cin

78th Regiment Company
Col Sirwell
Capt R. D. Elwood,

Camp Nevin Nov 15/61
My Dear wife I want to
let you know that
I have been sick for
a week or so but I have
Got better again I could
not tell when I was out on
Picket duty Our Camp is under
Strick disiplene we are still
Encamped at Camp Nevin
56 Miles from Louisville on the
Louisville and Nashville Rail Road
Genural Bucker the Rebel Genaral
Still Occupys Bollingreen 40 Miles
from us Part of his force is at
Geen River 30 Miles from us
the Main force is up to Nashville
is now no a 100 Thousand

Lieutenant George Black's Letter
Courtesy of Miss Elizabeth Buzzard

reassigned to Negley and be the only original part of the old Pennsylvania Brigade still in the chain of Negley's new command. [12]

In mid December, the army moved to new camp grounds at Munfordville, Kentucky, a little town on the north bank of the Green River. They left a number of comrades behind. Corporal Ben Truxall, Privates John Hastings, Bob Stark, George Adam, and John Devlin all succumbed to illness at Camp Negley. Private George Roth from Company H died on December 12th, the day the regiment moved out. Fears of the unknown enemy were beginning to show in the men and the rumor spread that Private Roth died from poisoned food or drink accepted from a local woman. That was pure conjecture and was never proven. Records of deaths in the regiment indicate Roth died of a fever.

The brigade arrived at their new home, Camp Wood, and the men were preparing to bed down. The sound of musketry and the roar of artillery came from across the river. The long roll of the drum summoned the men to arms. For most men in the regiment it was the first time that this drum roll had been heard. It called them to battle. When they realized the meaning of this signal there was no fear, only intense excitement. "We were exhilarated rather than alarmed, not so much because we were courageous, as because we did not know the danger," writes J.T. Gibson. Before they could get to the battle it was over. Gibson notes that it was a useless attack on the pickets and inexcusable murder of Union troops. Assuredly, Reverend Gibson still did not realize many years after the war was over, that attacks and killings were part of warfare and "murder" was perceived differently by him and the enemy. [13]

Of the number of holidays that dot the calendar, none makes the pain of separation more forsaken than Christmas. Visions of decorated homes with warm fires burning, the aroma of a roasted goose or turkey, and desserts made from recipes passed down by generations of mothers must have filled the windows of the lonely soldier's mind. The holiday and its wishes of peace aside, it was business as usual. The hardships of the Army of the Ohio continued. The loneliness and depression of a family holiday made these hardships virtually unbearable. Hard crackers or "Mrs. Lincoln's Pies," a small piece of pork fat, and water was the first Christmas feast away from home for the Seventy-Eighth. Most of the men were down with fever and measles. Camp Wood, Kentucky was a lonely place.

"TRAMP! TRAMP! TRAMP"

The war's first great battle took place in Western Tennessee at a place called Pittsburg Landing in early April, 1862. January had seen little movement of either the Yankee or Rebel armies in the East or the West. In the early days of the new year President Lincoln pressed his generals, McClellan, Halleck, and Buell to put their respective armies into action, but to no avail. In March the Union forces began to converge at a point along the Tennessee River for an all out attack on Confederate Albert Sidney Johnston's army at Corinth, Mississippi. To the surprise of many, General Johnston's early morning attack against Grant's bivouacked army on April 6, almost brought defeat to the Union forces, but the Union prevailed. The tumultuous battle near Shiloh Church saw combined casualties of over 23,000 soldiers; a staggering figure that surpassed the total casualties of the nation's three previous wars: the Revolutionary War, the War of 1812, and the Mexican War. General Grant's victory had cost him over 13,000 Union troops. Fresh Union soldiers and Buell's Army of the Cumberland came to Grant's aid and assisted in driving back the Confederate threat.

When General Buell did move his army to support General Grant at Shiloh, the Seventy-Eighth was left behind, along with Negley's troops, to guard communication lines. Colonel Sirwell's troops would spend the better part of 1862, in such trite duty. Mundane and weary tramping through Kentucky, Tennessee, and Alabama would be their fate. Guarding railroad supply lines was their sole objective. The men, naturally, blamed Negley, who they claimed was "drunk half of his time," for their supposed plight and took to calling themselves the "Pennsylvania Volunteer Rail Road Guards."

In early February, the men of the 78th experienced a unique Civil War tradition. While in Camp Wood, a dozen "splendid looking, but poorly armed and equipped" Confederate soldiers warily approached the picket line of Company F under a flag of truce. Bob Boreland of Butler County's Company H, recognized one of the Rebs whom he had worked with in Lexington, Kentucky before the war. Major Bonnaffon met with their leader and Colonel Sirwell approved the visit. The Rebels, most dressed in civilian clothes, riding stolen U.S. horses and wearing U.S. belts and cartridge boxes belonged to Morgan's Cavalry. They asked the Yankees to mail some letters for them. Since they were totally surrounded and not able to send mail home, they looked to their foes for help. Brother enemies readily agreed to see that the letters got through. For the boys of the Seventy-Eighth, it was easy to imagine the appreciation of news to and from their own mothers, wives, and sweethearts so far away. The Rebs stayed all afternoon and amicably "shot the breeze" with their Union hosts. [1]

It is quite evident that early in the war the tradition of meeting during times of inactivity became commonplace. Time would not change any of that. There are numerous reports all through the war, irrespective of the theater of operations, regarding enemy troops meeting during a lull in battles to trade for newspapers, coffee or tobacco, or to have mail sent through the lines. Generous acts between enemies was the gentlemanly thing to do. It seems unusual, when one considers the death and carnage that resulted from even the smallest of conflicts. In light of the uncommon bonds of friendship, this was still a war, and harassment of the enemy was obligatory. But some contemptible acts were found to be more despicable than others. Those small acts made the war more personal.

In early February, the Seventy-Eighth marched from their camp on the Green River to the Barren River at Bowling Green, Kentucky. There was a shortage of water during the campaign and the only supply existed in ponds. These ponds were found all over southwestern Kentucky. They consisted of a rounded hole in the surface rock in the shape of a bowl. The source of the water in these ponds came from melted snow and rain. Although stagnant, the water filled the needs of the local and poorer white and black families and their live stock for most of the year. A large army on the move depended on this same water source. When the Confederates retreated from their Green River line, they caused problems for the Yankees following them by tampering with this water. Within the regimental history it is recorded, "They drove old mules and worn out horses into these ponds and shot them. Dead cats and dogs were also found in them." Despite this vile act, the Seventy-Eighth overcame this problem by carrying water in their wagons. [2]

A myriad of hardships continually plagued the men in the western armies. It is difficult to imagine the continual lack of food, lack of proper cover, and the mundane train guard duties. But the soldiers in the Army of the Cumberland faced these problems every day of their tenure. Lieutenant Black made no judgment of his plight; he simply stated facts to his wife. "We left Munfordville, on the 13th of February. We were marched the whole of the day...at night we lay on the ground with no tents...it snowed three inches during the night...we have little to eat...I enjoyed a bit of corn [stolen] by the boys." [3]

By the time February 1862, rolled around, over thirty men of the regiment had died. The pestilence and disease took their toll. Many of the boys suffered from the "trots." It was a common occurrence to see tent mates clearing out their tent and burning everything that could carry body lice. The filth and cold of this austere life caused many of the viruses for which the farmer-soldier had no immunity. William Hays noted in a letter to his sister, "We have had no snow here yet but what it loses in snowing it makes up in raining." Each day there were increasing numbers of ailing soldiers lined up at the physician's tent, and the deaths continued. Eighteen year-old, Private Richard Tittle's embalmed body was sent home to be buried on the hill overlooking Kittanning. But the army moved on.

Despite the hardships, disease and deaths the army and the Seventy-Eighth moved south, the Federal armies began to take total possession of the first fallen Confederate state capitol. With the fall of Fort Donelson, Albert Sidney Johnston realized that Nashville, Tennessee was no longer defensible. General Johnston's army retreated southward through the city leaving it virtually uncontested to the Union forces. Nathan Bedford Forrest "closed the door and turned out the lights" on the Rock City. On February 25, 1862, the Federal army moved into Nashville, Tennessee. Miss A.B.M. recorded in her diary, "It was a silent surrender with no exclamations of triumph or display of pageant. The Union flag was raised on the capitol building..." The Confederate army had evacuated the city. The only butternut soldiers in the town were those too ill to be moved. Old men, women and children stayed their posts with no resistance offered.

The Union army settled into a city now torn by war, but thankfully, it had not been ravaged by battle; it had only changed protectors. The citizens of Nashville had plundered many of the Confederate warehouses, as Johnston's army had retreated through the streets. General Forrest's troops, the unofficial rear guard for the Rebels, had taken charge of the city. Forrest stopped the looting and sent a good deal of supplies and provisions southeast after the army. Forrest was angered at the Confederate high command. He concluded that "millions of dollars" of [Southern] stores could have been saved if only more men had been left to send supplies southward. Nonetheless, much of the populace had profited from the pilfering of government stores. The Yankee occupation might not be that bad. They had not burned the city and they paid in gold for work done. The Seventy-Eighth did not have to contend themselves with the people of Nashville; they were placed on train guard duty. [4]

The people of Nashville may have not put up an open fight against Buell's soldiers, but now in their daily routine there was the constant threat of enemy sympathizers who would harass these young Federals. The regiment was on train guard duty at the end of March. They were strung out forty-five miles along the Tennessee and Dayton Railroad. Rebel soldiers were not the threat, but citizens of the area were. The Confederate sympathizers continually set fire to the railroad along the path guarded by the Federals. [5]

Many of Buell's men were guarding rail lines and the pro-Southern citizens also harassed them. Colonel John Beatty of the 3rd Ohio was moving his regiment to Huntsville, Alabama during May, when his train was ambushed near the town of Paint Rock. Colonel Beatty became quite angry when several of his troops were wounded. From his memoirs it would appear that Beatty was a sensitive, sympathetic warrior, but apparently, out of utter frustration, he had to stop these attacks. He entered in his diary. "I had the train stopped and taking a file of soldiers, returned to the village. The telegraph line had been cut, and the wire was lying in the street. Calling the citizens together, I said to them that this bushwhacking must cease. Hereafter every time the telegraph wire was cut we would burn a house; every time a train was fired upon we would hang a man; and we would continue to do this until every house was burned and every man was hanged between Decatur and Bridgeport. I then set fire to the town, took three citizens with me, and proceeded to Huntsville." Beatty's actions were no less drastic or less violent than those of Colonel John Turchin's reprisal for an attack on his men. The Russian-born officer turned the town of Athens, Alabama over to his soldiers with the comment, "I shut mine eyes for one hour." Some of the boys from the Nineteenth Illinois beat the proprietor of a hotel being used as the Confederate command post. As they beat the man to within an inch of his life they shouted, "The 19th Illinois is back! Turchin is here!" Calm was restored after a barrel of whiskey soothed the angry Yankees. Nonetheless, the avenging troopers robbed the local citizens of jewelry and other valuables, raped a number of slave girls, and all totaled were accused of taking more than $50,000 worth of goods. [6] Colonel Sirwell's order was not as dramatic, but it was to the point. If the citizens of Franklin, Tennessee "molested" troops, trains or tracks, they were to be shot down. One bold, would-be warrior confronted Bill Sirwell on a city street with a drawn pistol. Colonel Sirwell drew his menacing Colt and took careful aim at his assailant. When the man turned and ran, Sirwell fired a harmless shot over his head. [7]

As provost guards in Edgefield, the volunteers from Pennsylvania had a good opportunity to observe citizens in that town. Some of the women of the city sought to show their contempt for the Union soldier in many ways. However, J.T. Gibson writes, either in kindness or through naïveté, that the soldiers were inclined to believe that this was not a good representation of Southern womanhood. There is no recorded action by Sirwell, Negley or of a higher command that the Southern women should be treated as "ladies of the night" as General Ben Butler had so ordered in New Orleans.

In Nashville, there was open hostility towards the Union troops. On the shutter of a house used as a Union hospital were found the words, "...God Bless the Southern cause! curse the Northern, and all that fight for it!" Despite the secessionists encountered by the army, there were many Union sympathizers in Tennessee. In fact, the populace was almost split in half by their opposing sympathies. Gibson recorded the intensity of convictions held by the parishioners at the Second Presbyterian Church of Nashville. One of the prominent elders related that at prayer services, half of the members stand when praying for the Union and the other half stand when praying for the Confederacy. They all stood when the prayers are offered to the Lord to do what is best.

In March, the regiment was relieved of provost guard duty at Edgefield and moved to Camp "Andy Johnson" two miles south of Nashville. Within days the regiment was marched south to Franklin and Columbia. As of the 25th of March, part of the regiment was in Camp "Bill Sirwell," on Carter's Creek not far from Columbia and the remainder was at Franklin. Morning "sick call" lists had grown during this month from a winter without vegetables. Many on sick call were jaundiced.

Essentially the regiment spent the summer guarding Buell's lines of communication and his base of supply on the railroads running south through Franklin, Columbia, and Pulaski. [8]

Constant movement of the regiment ultimately affected their training. From Camp Bill Sirwell, the Colonel chided his staff and company officers for their laxity in holding required drills. "If troops are not improving they are losing what they already know." He ordered two hours of drill every day except Sunday. Colonel Sirwell was also distressed with the lack of cleanliness in his camp. He demanded a change in personal and house-keeping habits; however, he did not add the threat of punishment for continued offenses. Some personal cleanliness did not have to be addressed by the Colonel Commanding. On a number of occasions the men would once again burn their clothing and even their blankets to rid their immediate quarters of body lice. [9]

During May the regiment tramped the roads from Franklin, Tennessee, to Rogersville, Alabama. There was no permanent camp. The nomadic life wore the men down. When the regiment encamped at Pulaski, Tennessee, many of the men were a lot thinner, without shoes, and in need of clothing.

On August 10th, Colonel Sirwell celebrated his forty-second birthday. The same day, he once again faced the sad duty of reporting the death of one of his troopers. Private David Kenniston of Company F was accidentally killed by a train at Pulaski. The Brookville, Pennsylvania *Jefferson County Republican* reported "Captain" Thomas Hamilton Reynolds, the regiment's sutler, was also killed around this time. Traveling by buggy from Franklin to Columbia, Tennessee, he was attacked and robbed by supposed Rebel sympathizers about eight miles south of Franklin. Reynolds was struck numerous times and killed instantly. The body was "so riddled with bullets that it could not be embalmed." The body was sent back to Kittanning for burial by his brother who had been waiting for him in Columbia. At the end of August the regiment returned to the main body of the army at Nashville.[10]

After seven months in the field, some men in the regiment still had not warmed to their Roman Catholic chaplain. Private Kipp notes: "We had preaching last Sabbath and there were only 24 men out at the church. The priest preached and most of the boys don't like his profession." Private Kipp is one of the few whose letters continuously bring up the negative side of Richard Christy's religion. In a number of other letters home, Lieutenant Black, Sam Dumm and Will Lowery felt that Father Christy was an all right fellow. But Father Christy or not, "there was no lack of preachin'."

The Federal forces in Nashville settled in and along with other concerns they did not avoid religious training. By special order of Colonel John Miller the Second Presbyterian Church of Nashville was "appropriated" for use as a Post Chapel. During the next several months Captain DeWitt Hervey of the Pennsylvania 78th, Colonel Granville Moody of the 74th Ohio and the Reverend John Dillon, Chaplain of the 18th Ohio preached there. Moody and J.H. Lozier, Chaplain of the 37th Indiana would also preach at the Chattanooga Railroad Depot in Nashville. [11]

To these boys with pronounced religious bigotries and with a stated goal of "saving the Union," a decision unique to their way of life now confronted them. The question of slavery and slaves was no longer theoretical. It presented itself in a real form. In June of 1862, Charles W. Bennett of Company G, Ninth Michigan Infantry writes in his historical sketches. "Quite a number of Negro slaves had come into camp and were helping as cooks, teamsters, etc. One day two slave owners came to Colonel Parkhurst and demanded a Negro slave be turned over to them. Parkhurst told them it was a matter he had no control over, but he would order the Negro out of camp and then they could do what they pleased."

The slave catchers had a little problem with the Negro slave. He exited the front of the camp, but ran around the side and re-entered the back gate. Dodging in and around tents, and in and out of the camp, the elusive slave became a center of attention. A large crowd gathered, many of them jeering the slave catchers. Colonel Parkhurst decided to keep the slave in camp. He ordered the slave catchers out of camp and after that refused to help anyone looking for runaway slaves.

Brigadier General Quincy A. Gilmore, a Division commander in the Army of Kentucky posted in Georgetown, Kentucky, viewed the problem of "contrabands" much differently. Although he professed repugnance at the thought of returning slaves to former masters, he also felt the growing number of non-combatants -or "hangers-on of any kind or class"- in the camps was demoralizing to the troops in the field. Additionally, Gilmore was aware that many of "the officers and men of [his] division [were] enticing the colored people [to enter his lines]. On October, 22, 1862, he issued General Order No. 9 which, in part stated that guards and pickets should refuse admission to the division camps those people known as "contrabands." Within days of his order he was assailed by Northern newspapers.

On December 2, 1862, General Gilmore defended his position in a letter to M.R. Keith of Cleveland, Ohio. In part it reads. "I have never returned a slave to any claimant, loyal or disloyal, and never will. I will not even turn them out of my line if I know or suspect their owners or their agents are in waiting to seize them." Gilmore alludes to the fact that too many of the soldiers were not only using Blacks to work in their camps, but were also taking Black women as mistresses. He felt that if this were not restricted "... every soldier, restrained only by individual caprice or lust, would have with him a negro man or negro woman, and this colossal and debauching abuse would find its only practical limit in satiety." Gilmore expressed his belief that he wished for the slaves to be free; however, that was not his charge in Kentucky. Irrespective of any commanders feelings the Blacks remained in camps to some degree. [12]

If Negroes were working in the camps of the Ninth Michigan and Gilmore's Division, they were in other camps of regiments throughout Buell's army. There are instances when J.T. Gibson notes Negroes working in the camps of the Seventy-Eighth, but he virtually avoids the subject. Many of those who corresponded with family and friends rarely spoke of the Negroes; however, it was not unusual to find references to "niggers" in all letters. Irrespective of the reasons for this war, the boys used blacks as laborers and the blacks were willing to take some abuse, at this point, for the freedom they now had. In reality, many of these former slaves were runaways and were happy to work in the Union camps. The soldiers themselves may have protected these slaves, but the extra hands performing unpleasant tasks had to be part of their motivation.

Within the Seventy-Eighth, there were instances when a young black would get cuffed for not working at his best or for stealing. However, there are few recorded instances of this behavior. The cooks in the Seventy-Eighth made use of a young black man by the name of Dudley. After a day of heavy chores, Dudley would sit around the camp fire and impose himself on the men to teach him to read and write. He professed a desire to become a preacher. Dudley learned quickly, but he did not enter the clergy. He did become the first and one of the most prominent black dentists in Nashville. Born in 1850, Dudley took the name of the white lawyer from Columbia, Tennessee, who became his mentor. Frank "Dudley" Dunnington married in 1870, but had no children. He practiced dentistry from 1882 until his death in 1913.

Private James Wilson Reed was a Tennessee-born slave. He enlisted in Company K of the 78th shortly after the fall of Nashville. James Wilson - his real name - served until November of 1864. With his enlistment fulfilled he returned North with the Pennsylvanians. Jim Wilson was a cook at the Franklin Hotel in Franklin, Venango County. He married, raised a family and died in Franklin, PA in 1917.

Albeit, there was no real stated policy regarding slaves or slave catchers. In the army at this point in the war, many regimental commanders undoubtedly made their own policies and the Black learned to exist in their new found freedom. There is no record, to date, of any policies regarding Blacks that were adopted by Colonel Sirwell.

On September 2nd, the regiment encamped five miles south of Nashville, at "Camp Lucinda." Named for Lucinda Sirwell the eldest daughter of Colonel Sirwell, the new camp brought back together all parts of the regiment. While Sergeant Gibson recorded the mundane marching and guard duty experienced by the 78th, Colonel Sirwell was having a quarrel with General Negley. For the third time under Negley's command William Sirwell threatened to resign his command or have his regiment transferred. And as usual the argument was over what Sirwell felt was poor treatment of his boys. Nonetheless, two months back pay for his companies and new sky blue pants for the regiment mollified Colonel Sirwell, for the time being. Thomas Blakeley's gift of a half box of cigars also made the Colonel happy. [13]

"THE CITY BIDES THE FOE"

By the summer of 1862, the deployment of armies in exacting battle lines in the theaters of operation, both east and west, were not really clear cut. There was no definite line of demarcation signaling friendly or enemy territory. Throughout the duration of the war spies and "scouts" operated within the opposition territory. Unlike the Southern armies that never really penetrated the North for any length of time, the Union armies operated in "enemy" territory, for most of the war. But unlike the supply lines of the Army of the Potomac, the Union supply lines in Kentucky and Tennessee were constantly in danger. In addition to this ever present threat, the position of attacking Confederate troops on their own soil led to an advantage that the North was never able to remove, a loyal, local population. The citizens of these occupied areas were an adjunct to army spies and of great value to Southern armies.

The Army of the Cumberland, during the campaigns through Kentucky, Tennessee, Georgia, and Alabama, was under the constant menace of being harassed by the local population or being attacked by Confederate cavalry. Wily cavalry raiders under the command of Nathan Bedford Forrest or John Hunt Morgan usually struck the Union supply line at some vulnerable point. They destroyed or seized millions of dollars worth of supplies, rifles, and wagons over the years.

During early 1862, the Union troops under Don Carlos Buell garrisoned Louisville, Bowling Green, Nashville and Murfreesboro. They campaigned throughout the four-state area of Kentucky, Tennessee, Alabama and Georgia. However, constant harassment and stinging attacks from Confederate cavalry left Buell's Union forces virtually powerless and quite confused.

In June, forces under James Negley, minus the 78th, had actually moved over sixty miles southeast of Nashville and had attacked Chattanooga. The 6000 man force under Negley shelled Chattanooga, but was ordered back in light of Confederate threats throughout Tennessee and Kentucky.

Other than Stonewall Jackson's Shenandoah Valley campaigns and Jeb Stuart's dashing cavalry raids during General McClellan's Peninsular Campaign, there are few instances where the Army of the Potomac had to contend with raids all around them. The Army of the Cumberland had to be wary of their rear supply lines being cut during most of the war. In July, Rebel Colonel John Hunt Morgan attacked and captured Union forces at Tompkinsville, Kentucky. In the same raid he attacked Cynthiana, a small hamlet south of Cincinnati. The proximity of the threatening, Confederate, horse soldiers to a Northern city spread anguish and terror throughout the Ohio River valley.

On July 13th, at the same time as Morgan was reeking havoc in Kentucky, the pugnacious Nathan Forrest rode through Tennessee and captured the Union garrison at Murfreesboro. He and his cavalry swept into the town at 4:30 A.M., and swiftly convinced the divided parts of the Union garrison to surrender. With a force that was equal in size to the Federal force, he bluffed that his was much greater in numbers. The threat to "have ever man put to the sword" without their unconditional surrender brought an end to the fighting. Brigadier General Thomas T. Crittenden, first cousin to Major General Thomas L. Crittenden, had commanded the garrison for a little over twenty-four hours. He and his staff were among the prizes of victory. By night fall of the same day, Forrest had released prisoners held by the Federals, gathered needed stores in fifty wagons with full horse teams, set bridges afire, tore up rail track, and ridden out of town. A few weeks later, Forrest attacked close to Nashville itself, burned three railroad bridges, and captured 97 Union soldiers.

In mid-August Colonel Morgan attacked Gallatin, Tennessee. At the crucial point between the rail heads of Nashville, Tennessee and Bowling Green, Kentucky, the dashing Morgan destroyed the depot, burned some trestles, and caused the collapse of an 800-foot railroad tunnel.

On September 5th, General Buell arrived at an abandoned Murfreesboro, only to learn that the Confederates were north of him once again. General Kirby Smith had captured Lexington and General Polk was at Sparta, Tennessee moving north. General Smith had placed General McCown in charge of the mundane task of protecting Chattanooga while he headed for glory in the Bluegrass state. Buell swiftly moved back to Nashville and prepared to move to the defense of Louisville, Bragg's new target. It appeared that the Federal armies were never going to secure a foothold on the total area of occupation.

In early Autumn, Braxton Bragg moved his army into a position to interpose between Buell at Nashville and capture Louisville to the north. General Buell had taken the main body of his army northward to confront General Bragg. The two armies began a race to determine which one would occupy this strategic point. Despite the importance of Louisville, Buell left Thomas, Negley, and Palmer at Nashville because he felt holding this city was equally important. Governor Andrew Johnson also demanded that a force be left to protect his capital. This was probably the overriding reason. Originally, Thomas had been placed in command of Nashville. When Buell learned that Bragg was receiving additional troops, he ordered Thomas to force march his division into action and placed James Negley in charge of the remaining garrison at Nashville.

Negley was left to his own designs in holding the Tennessee state capital. From the 8th of September until the 8th of November, Negley's approximate 12,000 man-force was virtually surrounded and existed under a state of siege at Nashville. The two Union brigades were, for the most part, essentially cut off from news of the outside world. They were literally ignorant of the condition or successes of General Buell's army to the north in Kentucky.

As commander of the Union garrison, Negley became responsible for his own defense and supplies. Confederate troops hovered around the city, frequently attacking. However, guard details and sentinel stations protected the army from these surprise attacks. Negley directed his chief engineer, Captain James Morton, to complete a set of forts named Negley, Casino, Confiscation, and Andrew Johnson. The forts and entrenched lines were essentially completed by October 17. Fort Negley would become one of the largest forts built to surround the city. On many Sundays, thousands of people would gather within the walls of this fort to watch the dress parades of regiments.

The construction of such large proportion took a great deal of manpower. Since all communication had been cut off from Louisville, it was impossible to receive government monies. It would follow that the army was not able to pay the citizen-laborers. Negley put out a list of prominent Southern sympathizers with a predetermined assessment next to their name. All of the money was receipted and turned over to Morton to pay the workers. When there were not enough soldiers or workers to help Captain Morton, Negley ordered the impressment of all able-bodied male Negroes to work on the projects.

Many of the slaveholders tried to hide their "property," but Negley's troops found them and put them to work.

The *Nashville Union* reported tongue in cheek on the number of people forced into labor gangs building the fortifications. In Frank Parrish's barber shop a black man proposed a riddle.

"Jim, what's the difference between General Lincoln and General Negley?"

"Go away, fool nigger, dey's had no difference ever I heard of," was the reply.

"Oh yes, dey has; General Lincoln started the irrepressible conflict, and General Negley started the pressible conflict."

The black man was not able to enjoy the laughter of his play on words. The press-gang hauled him off to a work crew.

Negley worked diligently to affect a more organized defense system in all areas. He established better picket lines and also strengthened his rifle pits with heavy abatis [trees felled toward the direction of an attacking enemy, many times with pointed ends]. Many houses, reportedly, were barricaded and "provided with loopholes for musketry." He reorganized the regiments and fractured brigades that were left behind. He also formed a regiment from the able-bodied convalescents to provide guard duty. [1]

The besieged Federals became their own commissary department. Food became scarce. Butter rose to $1.00 per pound, potatoes to a dollar a peck and a head of cabbage brought fifty cents. Many farmers were afraid that if they ventured into town to sell their goods the Federals might impress their wagons, but those willing to take the chance and move food and goods were making a great deal of money. Foraging expeditions with escorts were sent out every few days from ten to fifteen miles from the city.

Concerned for the safety of his troops, Negley was forced to take some harsh actions. He had a number of outspoken Southern patriots arrested and even threatened to hang a few, although he never did. For the protection of army personnel, he ordered that all weapons of private citizens be turned over to military authorities. To bolster his "request," Negley placed a $25.00 reward on information leading to the confiscation of arms or ammunition.

Skirmishes and battles around Nashville were serious and frequent. They resulted in casualties, but were not grand or news worthy. Since there were no spectacular battles to report, one reporter felt that his news articles needed some "pumping up." The *Louisville Journal* reported that a sharp skirmish took place on the Franklin Pike, south of Nashville, between General Negley's troops and the enemy. A reporter from the *Cincinnati Commercial* found out that the story was much different than reported. The foragers in brigade strength had fired on a frightened Negro and his mule. The sun seen reflecting off the menacing Confederate bayonets was in reality reflecting off the axe carried by the black man.

Buell's army eventually maneuvered Bragg away from Louisville. It can be better put that Bragg gave up the chase. Nonetheless by the 29th, the Union forces were in possession of Louisville. [2]

SEEING THE ELEPHANT

Marauders around Nashville were a constant threat. For the most part, General Negley was able to protect the city against the stinging attacks of these raiders with his system of entrenched forts. A build up of approximately twenty-five hundred Confederates under General S.R. Anderson about fifteen miles southeast of Nashville near Lavergne was not a force powerful enough to defeat Negley or retake the city, but could eventually prove to be a problem especially if they were permitted to reinforce their position from Murfreesboro. From his headquarters on High Street, Negley determined that in this instance his best defense must be an aggressive offense. Negley would attack.

His order of October 6th, reprinted in the *Nashville Union*, fortunately after the battle, on October 8th, laid out the plan for General Palmer to attack the Confederate forces under General Anderson at Lavergne. Negley correctly assumed that "... by deploying left and right to surround the enemy, and give play to your artillery... the enemy's forces being poorly organized, armed and drilled [could] ... easily be startled into a sudden panic." Negley's only fear was that Rebel troops from Murfreesboro, Green Hill or Nolensville could reinforce Anderson.

General Negley ordered the huge, flaxen-haired General John Palmer to move with his command, and instructed Colonel John Miller to cooperate in the attack on the Confederate forces at Lavergne. Palmer in command of the 21st Illinois, the 1st Kentucky Battery, Houghtaling's Illinois Battery and two squadrons of cavalry, the 1st Middle Tennessee and the 7th Pennsylvania led the Union force. Miller commanded a brigade made up from parts of four regiments: the 14th Michigan, the 21st Ohio, the 18th Ohio and the 78th Pennsylvania.

Sirwell's Regiment was now part of Colonel John Miller's Brigade. Miller, a native of South Bend, Indiana, had been the regimental commander of the 29th Indiana. Colonel Miller and his Hoosiers, formed in Laporte, Indiana, had been in the service since August of 1861. But Miller had only remained with his regiment a short time. He was promoted to brigade command under Negley shortly after arriving in Nashville. Major Bonnaffon of the 78th was promoted to his staff.

Up until now, the boys from Pennsylvania had seen no real fighting. There had been no great battles. There had only been the remote possibility of death. And in the vernacular of the day the men had not experienced the maddening effect of "a landscape turned red" from an intense battle or the more comical euphemism of "seeing the elephant." The deeper movement into the enemy's region would test the élan of these young men, and everyone sensed it.

Negley's attacking force moved out of Nashville promptly at nine o'clock Monday night, the 6th of October. Palmer's eight hundred man-force took the direct route to Lavergne via the Nashville-Murfreesboro Pike. Miller's brigade numbering about eighteen hundred men marched south on a circuitous path toward the enemy hoping to flank them or attack them from the rear. After moving south on the road to Triune, Miller's Brigade traveled about five miles on the Nolensville Road and then on to Lavergne.

With the Twenty-First Ohio in the lead, Sirwell's boys marched smartly out of Nashville. As time and the miles passed the pace was not as brisk, but Colonel Sirwell

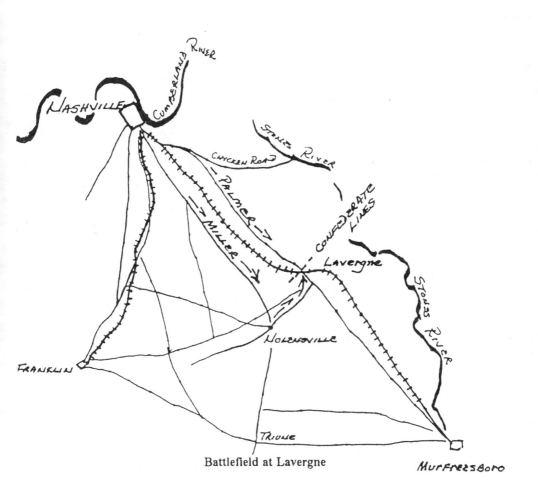

Battlefield at Lavergne

kept them in an acceptable formation. Despite the pace the intermittent "larking" persisted until the wee hours of the morning when they were almost to Lavergne. Small group discussions, jokes and abrupt laughter pierced the night along their path. Silent tramping brought about the apprehensions of first battle.

Palmer arrived at Lavergne at half-past three on Tuesday morning and attacked the Confederates shortly before daybreak. The 32nd Alabama, Biffle's Tennesseans, Major Douglas' Battalion and Colonel John T. Morgan's Alabama Cavalry were taken completely by surprise, but initially made a strong stand. Miller's arrival and attack at shortly after daybreak, and after the battle began, threw the Confederates into confusion.

The Thirty-Second Alabama made a powerful demonstration to flank Palmer on his right, but Miller, moving through a cornfield, "surprised both friend and foe" when he threw his brigade in front of the Confederate line on the right of the Murfreesboro road. Colonel Miller's force quickly routed the Rebels. In the excitement the 78th was attacked by the Alabama cavalry and cut off from the main force; they were virtually surrounded. Sirwell ordered his regiment to close ranks and attack the heaviest part of the Alabama line. As the attack movement became evident, Sirwell reversed his force and attacked the weakest point of the Confederate line. The 32nd Alabama broke and began to retreat. Colonel Sirwell rapidly flanked the Alabama troops when they attempted to flee. His enveloping movement completely blocked the withdrawal of the enemy. Meanwhile, Charles Houghtaling's battery played upon the rebels with telling effect.

The Rebel cavalry dashed against the ranks of the 78th in an attempt to break the Union line, but was met by a succession of volleys of musketry that drove them back. Sirwell's force and the 7th Pennsylvania Cavalry charged the Alabama 32nd once again and they quickly threw down their arms. Their cavalry also capitulated. The Rebel cavalry displayed a white flag indicating total surrender. Unfortunately, the artillery did not see the flag and kept firing. The Confederate cavalry then broke and fled in great confusion into the woods. [1]

The "ragged...and very dirty," Alabama boys surrendered quickly because they did not seem to have their heart in the battle. The Rebels were "green" recruits and "they were sick of the war." They had a generally poor opinion of their Tennessee brothers. At least one member of Mobile's, Thirty-Second Alabama, left an unusual perspective of the campaigns in Tennessee. J. Morgan Smith wrote, "I hate the state [Tennessee], the institutions and the people and really feel as if I am fighting for the Yankee side..." [2]

In the engagement at Lavergne, the Yankees had captured: the one and only Rebel cannon, four hundred small arms, a regimental stand of colors, fifty-six loads of flour, several hundred-weight of bacon, forty beef cattle, and a large number of horses. The beef cattle would alleviate some of the hunger in Nashville. The Yankees also cornered three hundred rebel prisoners of which the 78th accounted for the capture of 100 enlisted and 2 officers belonging to the Alabama 32nd, one of the officers being a very sick Lieutenant Colonel James Murray. James Murray would later die in a Chattanooga military hospital. Sirwell's boys also captured a stand of 100 arms. Buck Simkins personally "captured Lieutenant Colonel Sanford's saber belt." In the quick-hitting battle Corporal George Langdon, Company D, 78th Regiment, was mortally wounded. He was the first man in the regiment killed in a pitched battle. Major Augustus Bonnaffon was captured; however, he was exchanged a few days later. The whole Federal force lost four men and had seven wounded. The Confederates had thirty men killed and eighty more wounded.

Nathan Forrest was in Murfreesboro when he heard of the attack. He immediately set about taking a force to Lavergne to battle the Yankees. His fears of a Yankee victory were proved out when during his dash to Lavergne he encountered, "streams of fugitives riding to the rear, many of them without arms, others riding horses without saddles, still others clad only in the garments in which they had been sleeping." The wide-eyed Confederates were running for their lives. Major Sparks of the Texas Rangers was with Forrest when they encountered the fleeing Alabama warriors. He related that, "...they were the worst skeered set of fellers I ever saw...they said they wanted [to go home] to Jackson county, Alabama."

Despite the urging and threats of General Forrest the boys from Jackson County would not return to the fight. Why should they fight; their officers had reportedly ran before them. The men claimed that General Anderson who had left before the battle to get reinforcements at Murfreesboro, was never seen by them again. Forrest cussed out the Rebel boys and pushed his battalion northward to within six miles of Nashville in the hopes of engaging the enemy, but they had already entered the city.

Early on Tuesday morning Negley had become anxious about his attack force and personally led a contingent of reinforcements from the 22nd Illinois, the 10th and 11th Michigan and a battery, but his concern was unwarranted. The relief detachment was met by the returning, victorious forces. Around 10:30 A.M. within a mile of the Nashville Insane Asylum, General Negley met a smiling Colonel Stokes cantering ahead of his Tennessee Cavalry. The tired, dusty colonel hollered, "General, we've got 'em." Crowds of people waving flags and handkerchiefs turned out on Nashville's Church, High and Cedar Streets to welcome the returning "army" and their catch of "woe-begone" prisoners.

In this early stage of the war, prisoners like Major Bonnaffon were still paroled and exchanged. The day after the battle a detachment from the Seventy-Eighth escorted part of the prisoners through the Union lines to Lavergne. The Confederates had been paroled. The capture and parole of prisoners was a sham, and the boys knew it. A number of men from Negley's command and a few from the Seventy-Eighth had been captured while on picket or guard duty. Corporal Bill Boyd of Company H was captured in November by Confederate guerrillas dressed in Federal uniforms, but escaped. When Michael Davis, Company K, from Butler was captured, he was back in his tent within a few days. As soon as any parolee was sent back, Negley returned them to duty. He had little respect for the parole oath.

In their baptism of fire the Seventy-Eighth had performed admirably. Colonel Sirwell was complimented by General Negley and Andrew Johnson, then military governor of Tennessee. Sirwell made sure that the boys were keenly aware that he was proud of their accomplishment. The regiment had experienced soldiering and battle. They had performed well. They could at last say they had "seen the elephant." [3]

The Federals continued to keep Nashville secure and drove off any skirmishers. The outside threats were controlled, but the siege conditions, the mundane daily routine, the marching, and counter marching began to affect the soldiers. Discipline was breaking down in, probably, more than a few squads. Some of the troops were virtually out of hand. Laxity persisted within the ranks and thievery grew. Brigadier General Negley published his General Order #8 in the Nashville Union on the first of October which dealt with the number of complaints at his headquarters relating to unlawful and unordered searches of private property. Colonel Miller addressed the conduct of the soldiers in mid-October.

Headquarters 7th Brigade
Nashville, Tennessee, October 13th, 1862.
General Order No 10

Hereafter until further orders this entire command including all officers of whatever rank and all men fit for duty will appear under arms at Four A.M. promptly Each day and remain under arms until after inspection at five o'clock A.M.

Regimental Commanders will cause the Articles of War to be read at the head of each Company on the first and third Saturday of each month.

Certain soldiers at this post have become so base and degraded as to commit the heinous crime of house breaking and robbing and have brought dishonor upon the name of the American soldier by stealing the apparel and jewels of helpless women the toys and clothing of little children. Some have even gone so far in their course of crime as to rob filthy Negro Slaves of their vile and tattered garments. If there be a soldier of the 7th Brigade who has been guilty of such offense let him be branded as a coward and a traitor to the cause in which we are engaged, worthy of the scorn and contempt of all brave and honest men.

If anyone found hereafter engaged in the commission of like crime, it is ordered that Any officer or soldier who may be present shall immediately arrest him or them and bring them to the proper authority for punishment, and if resistance in such case be made against that arrest sufficient force shall be used to accomplish it even at the expense of the life of the offenders. Any officer or soldier who may be present at the perpetration of such offense and shall fail or neglect to do all in his power to cause the arrest of the guilty parties will be deemed guilty as principal in the crime and suffer accordingly.

The Colonel Commanding desires to express confidence in the bravery of the men under his command and his high appreciation of their good conduct [and] enviable character. No brave man will ever become a thief. It is believed therefor that there can be but a few in the 7th Brigade who would be so vicious as to commit such offenses. Good soldiers will unite in bringing such to punishment that the good name of all may be preserved.

> *By Order of Colonel John F. Miller*
> *Commanding 7th Brigade*
>> *By Order of Colonel William Sirwell*
>> *Commanding Pennsylvania 78th*
>> *Lieutenant Henry M. Cist [74th Ohio]*
>> *Acting Assistant Adjutant General* [4]

J.T. Gibson added a few comments to the regimental history around this time almost as if an answer to Colonel Miller's order. "The average soldier believed that the Government they served should provide him the food, shelter, and comforts of army life, and demand such confiscation as might be necessary to furnish these comforts, but did not regard legal confiscation as theft. We cannot speak for the whole Army, but we can say for the 78th Regiment that nine out of every ten would have considered it as disgraceful to steal anything in the Army as they would have considered it to steal anything at home. In sport, in order to vary the monotony of life, they might take fruit or corn, just as a party of raccoon hunters from Western Pennsylvania, would take corn from a neighboring corn field to furnish the camp fire feast, but good soldiers were always willing to pay full price for anything that might have been taken in any such spirit of merriment." From Reverend Gibson's view the boys didn't steal, they were just having fun. However, despite Gibson's claim, it is doubtful that little if anything was taken for sport. And if Colonel Sirwell and his company commanders were paying bills for stolen chickens, it is inconceivable that any of the boys offered to willingly pay for their plunder. [5]

Corporal Ira Gillaspie of the Eleventh Michigan Infantry, a most interesting diarist, essentially put forth the same rationale as Sergeant Gibson. The Eleventh Michigan was not in Miller's brigade, but was in Negley's division. Gillaspie reports in his diary an unadulterated picture of some of the troops in the Kentucky-Tennessee theater of operations since, for the most part, he makes little attempt to gloss over the shortcomings of his fellow soldiers or himself.

In early September, Gillaspie makes a humorous addition to his diary. "Some of our boys went out and pressed some fowls into the service of the 11th Mich. Reg. They was good companions at supper but I tell you hunger and half rations will cause a soldier to do many things he would not do was he at home in a land of freedom and plenty."

The crimes of the boys in blue were petty for the most part, but General Negley did not find them amusing. Colonel Sirwell was arrested, charged and court martialed when men from the 19th Illinois in his foraging detail confiscated and killed several hogs and turkeys. Bill Sirwell was confined and gave up a month's pay. Major Bonnaffon commanded the regiment during his forced absence. Will Lowry wrote his parents adding a picture of Sirwell: "Colonel Bill Sirwell, one of the best colonels in the field...[was] not the man to look on and see his men suffer for anything." [6]

Drinking was another fault of the Civil War soldier. No matter the rank or army a good deal of drinking took place. Assistant Surgeon, Will Knox, fell to the hard pavement in Louisville while in a drunken stupor. Milton Welsh of Company H stabbed Hugh Morgan of the same company while drunk. He fractured his skull and died. Colonel Sirwell's nephew, Private George McCandless, also of Company H, fractured a Freeport man's head with a club when in a drunken rage. He was arrested, but broke out of jail. No record exists as to the fate of McCandless; however, being the Colonel's nephew undoubtedly helped. Lieutenant Joe Mechling was not so fortunate. He was forced to resign after being found drunk and absent from his post. Abram Kipp blamed the meanness of some officers on too much liquor.

Most of the so called crimes of the soldier listed by Colonel Miller in his October order were petty in nature. Being caught at any crime could have a stiff penalty, but usually the boys would laugh or scoff at these punishments. Extra duty was usually the cost of transgressions in the 78th. At the same time, although there was resolute acceptance of severe punishment for certain crimes committed by their fellow soldiers, it was never tolerated by Sirwell. Certain officers were chastised by Colonel Sirwell for "bucking and gagging" soldiers for some offenses. It was then made clear to all officers that no man in the Seventy-Eighth would be punished in that fashion. Any officer using harsh punishment risked being cashiered. [7]

On October 20, 1862, the Seventy-Eighth attacked a camp of Confederate cavalry and guerrillas at Neeley's Bend, Tennessee. The regimental history lists the size of the enemy force at 1500, but it was substantially less. The Confederates were driven across the Cumberland River at Hermitage Ford. The enemy formed a line of battle on the opposite bank of the river and opened fire. Private Daniel Zerby, of Company F was killed and several men of the advance party were wounded. When the main body of the regiment arrived and returned fire the Rebs retreated. The Union troops did not follow. [8]

Although Miller's whole force was sent out after the enemy, the Seventy-Eighth was accorded special mention in Negley's report.

Head-Quarters U.S. Forces
Nashville, Tennessee, October 20, 1862.

Yesterday General Forrest commenced crossing a considerable force of cavalry over the Cumberland [River]. The advance, about one thousand strong, encamped on the Gallatin pike seven miles from Nashville. I immediately sent a force under Colonel Miller, who attacked the enemy at daylight, speedily routing and driving them back over the river. In their consternation they lost one of their cannon overboard from a flat boat and strewed the pathway of their flight with arms (all new) and knapsacks. They had few killed or wounded.
A number of prisoners were taken, including a colonel. The Pennsylvania 78th behaved handsomely. The result was very satisfactory, - especially as it is the third time we have completely routed the enemy's forces near Nashville.

James S. Negley Brigadier General
Commanding
To: Colonel James B. Fry, Adjutant General and Chief of Staff

In mid November, a contingent of new recruits from Armstrong County arrived in Nashville. Among the recruits Privates Samuel Dumm, Lemuel Rea, Hamilton Smith, Sam Minteer, Wilson Boney, Daniel Colbert, James Gillam, William Ritchey along with Washington and John Doty all reported into the regiment after the siege was lifted. They had all received a $29 bounty for enlisting. But in reality the bounty had not enticed them into the service of their country. They had traveled by trains from Harrisburg to Indianapolis and Louisville. They had marched through the cold, and rains, and snow of Kentucky and Tennessee to join their comrades and fight for the Union. [9]

OLD ROSEY TAKES COMMAND

On October 23rd, 1862, President Lincoln relieved Major General Don Carlos Buell of command of the Army of the Ohio. He replaced Buell with Major General William Starke Rosecrans. Rosecrans' new command officially created the new Department of the Cumberland with the men in the field designated the Fourteenth Army Corps; the Army of the Cumberland as history would come to remember the Army of the Ohio. Braxton Bragg did not need spies to learn of his new adversary. Kentucky and Tennessee newspapers trumpeted the news.

In his *History of the Army of the Cumberland*, Henry Cist makes no mention, other than factual, of Buell's replacement. However, he definitely tries to show Buell in a positive light. As for Henry Halleck, the General-in-Chief and Lincoln's military adviser, he had no respect. "The military affairs of the nation at this time were unfortunately in [the] charge of General Halleck, [in Washington]. Halleck, invested by the Administration with supreme powers, designed a campaign into East Tennessee, on paper in Washington, and ordered Buell to execute it." Buell ultimately refused to comply with Halleck's directive and that cost him his job. Cist makes his point that planning in Washington, over five hundred miles away, without knowledge of the immediate situation leads to a poor blueprint. [1]

Cist, who eventually served on Rosecrans' and Thomas' staffs may have been correct in his assumptions regarding Halleck, but a much more deeply rooted problem caused Buell's downfall. He did not receive the support of his soldiers. His contempt for the citizen-soldier and his strict disciplinary measures never did endear him to a recalcitrant, volunteer army. It is quite evident that Buell never realized that he needed their support to carry out his plans.

Buell not only lost the support of his troops; he earned the antipathy of some powerful politicians. His overbearing attitude brought him into direct conflict with the equally proud Republican war time governor of Indiana, Oliver P. Morton and the military governor of Tennessee, future president, Andrew Johnson. Both men had a great deal of power in Washington and they brought that power to bear on a man they each despised for their own personal reasons. Johnson, in particular, had the most to lose with a poor Union showing. He held an ineffectual governor's chair without Federal victories in Tennessee. Buell did not supply the victories; hence Governor Johnson did not have any real power. Nonetheless, Buell could have survived the brickbats and charges of these two men had it not been for the indecisive blood bath at the battle of Perryville in October and the sluggish pursuit of Bragg's army.

On October 8th, Braxton Bragg ordered an attack on General Buell's Union forces near Perryville, Kentucky. Once again the Seventy-Eighth was not with the main army. They were still with Negley in Nashville. Unknown to Bragg, he had assaulted a much superior force. Surprisingly, the Confederates bloodied their adversaries, but not without excessive losses themselves. A combination of the First, Sixth, Ninth and Twenty-Seventh Tennessee, and Forty-First Georgia made up Colonel Maney's Brigade. Maney lost almost half of the men taken into battle. Colonel Maney's horse had been wounded in the opening salvos and Colonel Hume Feild of the First Tennessee took command of the

Major General William Starke Rosecrans

charging force. Holding a position on the extreme right of the battlefield, they drove the Union forces before them and captured four twelve-pound Napoleons.

The Confederate force performed heroically. Nonetheless, Bragg upon learning the real strength of the enemy that he faced, retired from the field and abandoned his strategy to move north and join General Kirby Smith.

An open rift between Bragg and some of his generals surfaced after the battle. John Breckenridge, Bishop Polk, Pat Cleburne, and William Hardee criticized Bragg for his actions at Perryville. They were not critical of the fact that Bragg attacked a superior force. They were, however, critical of the fact that he did not follow through when the tide of battle was in his favor. His retreat from Kentucky may have been abhorrent to privates and generals alike, but Bragg did not lose his command. However, the bickering and accusations would haunt the Army of the Tennessee in the subsequent battles at Stones River, Tullahoma, Chickamauga, and Chattanooga.

The battle at Perryville ended any real Confederate presence in Kentucky. Don Carlos Buell failed to follow up on Bragg's retreat. Buell did not have to contend with the criticism of his generals as Bragg did; however, he had a greater problem, his President had lost faith in him. In the end, Lincoln could not tolerate Buell's lack of initiative or his inability to take direction. He was fired and replaced by Rosecrans. [2]

William Rosecrans had earned his new position by his performance over the sixteen months since the war began. Although a West Point graduate, Rosecrans was not in the army at the outbreak of the war. However, eleven days after the bombardment of Fort Sumter, he became a major on General George McClellan's staff. Returning to his home state of Ohio he performed various duties for Governor Dennison. The state legislature created the position of chief of engineers specifically for Rosecrans. Within two months of returning to the service, he won the field service he desired as colonel of the 23rd Ohio Volunteer Infantry. The 23rd Ohio was undoubtedly the most unusual regiment of the war. Two future Presidents, Rutherford B. Hayes and William McKinley, marched in its ranks.

Physically Rosecrans was an imposing man. The burly, six-foot tall Rosecrans was 42 years old, the same age as Sirwell. When Rosecrans reported in to Nashville he was approximately one month shy of his forty-third birthday. He had blond hair, sported a close-cropped beard to cover burn scars from an explosion, and he had a large, "intensified Roman nose."

Rosecrans was gifted, lovable, irritable, and peculiar. He was a convert to Roman Catholicism. He loved to discuss religion along with literature and history in his late night "bull sessions" with the men. The matter of creeds and faiths appears to have been discussed in good spirit, with nobody yielding much or becoming provoked. He was also an excellent student of geology, mineralogy, and military history. For the most part, William Rosecrans, the one-time Assistant Professor of Philosophy and Engineering at West Point, enjoyed any stimulating conversation or debate.

Rosecrans and Sirwell shared great many similarities, and some significant differences. William Sirwell, a Catholic from birth, married Elizabeth McCandless in 1840. Sirwell's wife shared the same strong faith as Rosecrans; she had also converted to Catholicism. Rosecrans had his chaplain, Father Trecy, and Sirwell had Father Christy. Like Rosecrans, Sirwell was interested in a variety of subjects. In an interview with Nellie Bly shortly before his death, Sirwell indicated he was quite interested in geology and mineralogy. His jeweler's profession and curiosity led to an extensive collection of minerals and precious stones. He had a piece of the scaffolding that John Brown was hung from, a piece of Plymouth Rock, and numerous books on philosophy, science, and history.

Both Sirwell and Rosecrans were of a Prussian-Germanic background. Sirwell's family changed their name and migrated to the United States through England. Rosecrans' family migrated to Ohio through Holland, New York and Pennsylvania. Sirwell loved German music and collected German sheet music. He had a 150 year-old German, family prayer book.

William Sirwell had a true, lasting affection for his men. Rosecrans also displayed a great affection for the "boys." Some officers were disturbed with Rosecrans habit of chatting with the common soldiers in a jocular manner during inspections. He always spoke pleasantly to the enlisted, saving severe rebukes for his officers. The men came to like Rosecrans quickly and dubbed him "Old Rosey."

Sirwell would dress for photos or inspections in full military attire, but his everyday uniform was his old captain's uniform with colonel straps added. Rosecrans was impeccable in dress ... most of the time. One officer said, "He looked more like a third-rate wagon master than a great general." However, he exacted neatness, military posture, and close attentiveness to a proper military bearing from his aides. He insisted that his staff ride handsome mounts. His own horses were magnificent and spirited. "Boney," was a handsome bay, and his favorite "Robey," was a slim-angled gray. He also required that his "sandy fellows," his name for his young aides, also lack experience. Rosey's line of thinking was if they were inexperienced they would not be predisposed to inflexible thought or action.

Unlike Sirwell, a man of few words, Rosecrans was excitable and loquacious. His speech, ordinarily rapid, became hurried to the point of stammering when he was excited. Some said that he was even emotionally unstable, but from anger, never from fear. During an emotional outburst he used rough language, but like his more than moderate drinking he made definite distinctions. While sometimes profane, he never blasphemed. While he could consume quantities of whiskey, he was no drunkard. [3]

Sirwell was known to enjoy a good stiff drink as did the General-in-command. Although controlled and restrained in manner, Sirwell could be provoked to near physical violence if he thought his boys were being poorly treated. Like many men of the time, both Sirwell and Old Rosey enjoyed a good cigar. Bill Sirwell or Bill Rosecrans could be seen most times with a short, dark cigar clenched between their teeth.

General Rosecrans reported to Cincinnati on October 25th to take control of his army, now second in size only to the Army of the Potomac. Upon assumption of the command of Buell's army, he quickly realized that he had a manpower and supply problem. He did not have the needed supplies to mount an extended offensive and his army was seriously depleted and demoralized. Of the 100,000 men carried on the rolls over one-third were absent. He found 26,482 were absent with authority and another 6,484 were absent without authority. [4]

Alfred Reed, of Company H, was one of those absent without leave. He had placed Sirwell in a particularly bad situation. Reed wanted to return to Butler and try to get an officer's position in another regiment. Negley had ordered Sirwell not to give out any furloughs at this time. Sirwell permitted Reed to return to Butler with a promise to return within 10 days. When Reed did not return, and Negley learned of Sirwell's duplicity, he threatened to court martial Sirwell for his actions. With a sharp rebuke, before charges could be brought against Bill Sirwell, Negley had Sirwell released from "house arrest." Colonel Sirwell would be needed for the coming battle.

Rosecrans and his staff arrived in Nashville on November 10, 1862, and took up headquarters near Negley's on High Street. He and his staff went to work the next day. The Union troops came to respect and admire their new commander almost immediately. Along with his easy way of speaking to the enlisted he had a way of making the men feel special. Although many ranking officers ignored the salutes of the "lowly" soldiers, Rosey made a distinct effort to return the salutes of the enlisted personnel. Private Kipp wrote his mother: "I have every confidence in our general, Rosecrans. He inspected our division the other day and told us that our regiment marched better to the front than any regiment he ever saw." A number of regimental histories from the Army of the Cumberland have remarks of the same ilk. However, Rosey's flattering comments were not all fluff. Negley was widely noted as a good drillmaster. When Rosecrans and his staff reviewed and rated the Army of the Cumberland, they listed Negley's division among the "very best" in appearance and discipline.

Obviously, Old Rosey, knew the value of flattery, but that seemed to be reserved only for his soldiers; his officers and interfering politicians faced a different man. He possessed many of the qualities of a genius; he was intelligent, energetic, and animated. But he could also be intolerant, indiscreet and impulsive. General Thomas L. Crittenden thought Rosecrans was "of the first order of military mind...both brave and generous." He also concluded that his excitability led to gallantry under fire and his major flaw was issuing too many orders during a battle. [5]

On November 13th, six days after McCook's army arrived, James Negley's garrison drove away the last of John Hunt Morgan's small, but menacing cavalry command. Nashville was now free and Rosecrans set up permanent headquarters. To his credit, Rosecrans was a tireless laborer and upon assuming command immediately began to rebuild his army.

Before arriving in Nashville, Rosecrans had requested that Secretary of War Stanton give him the authority to muster officers out of the service for "flagrant misdemeanors and crimes - such as pillaging, drunkenness and misbehavior in the presence of the enemy or on guard duty." Rosecrans wanted to cashier these officers without the time consuming, cumbersome court martial system. Immediately upon assuming command in Nashville he began relieving officers unfit for command. Although no reason was given in the History of the Seventy-Eighth, within two weeks two company commanders and four company officers resigned. Lt. Samuel Crosby of Company I was discharged, probably in response to Rosecrans effort to rid his army of incompetent officers.

There was one resignation that did not sit well with the enlisted men in Company K, that of Captain DeWitt Hervey. Reverend Hervey had actually put in his resignation in June. Sirwell had not accepted it, but he did put First Lieutenant Joe Mechling of Company H in command of the company. The boys felt Hervey had made some promises many months before from his Baptist pulpit in Slate Lick; now he was going back on his word. He had not been the best company commander and a few fellows wrote home stating so. Reverend Hervey threatened to court martial anyone he found spreading detrimental rumors -- relating to him -- through their letters. The young minister did not want any "bad press" leaking back to his flock. Before Hervey left his command he attempted to have the men sign a letter attesting to his good character. Many were reluctant to do so. In mid November, Joe Mechling would be found drunk and away from his post. He was court martialed and cashiered at the end of the month.

When Rosecrans assumed command of the army, most of the soldiers were disheartened by Buell's dictates. There had been a universal feeling that perks and punishments were meted out on an unequal basis. Many of Buell's rules and regulations were arbitrary or harsh. Punishments for infractions of those rules were not always fairly given out. To the joy of the troops, discipline became fair and universal. Officers were placed on the same footing as the enlisted men in many instances. In order to keep a good accounting of his strength numbers, General Rosecrans demanded that all officers and enlisted men be required to present written passes when outside their camps. [6]

Shortly after Rosecrans entered the city, Sirwell was addressing the same subject of passes. In his orders of November 16th, 1862, Sirwell made it clear that like the enlisted men, commissioned officers would not be permitted to leave their quarters without a pass from his adjutant, Lieutenant Henry Torbett.

Rosecrans struggled to recast his army. His desire was to make it more effective and disciplined. A number of roll calls were affected during the day. Those failing to respond were given extra duty. At sick call the regimental surgeon separated the malingerers from the legitimately sick soldiers. Additional drill, guard duty and dress parade filled the day. Regimental inspections were held every Sunday morning at 10 A.M. and the articles of war were read to the men. Rosey was taking charge. All of these actions had the effect Rosecrans desired, morale improved. Sensing the change, the men rapidly developed respect for their new commander. [7]

Despite Rosey's entrance into the city and Negley's success in driving the Rebels from the city gates, the small stinging skirmishes did not stop. During the siege of Nashville and subsequent to Rosecrans' arrival, skirmishing between the Union pickets and enemy scouting parties had been constant. A system of pickets and block houses were devised by Lt. Colonel Alexander Von Schrader of the 74th Ohio. These guard houses kept the city virtually safe from attack. Von Schrader, a trained Prussian Army officer and a former street car conductor from Cincinnati, was noted for his military capabilities and for paying personal attention to detail, as the following order demonstrates. He personally attended to certain details so the system worked as flawlessly as possible. [8] Without a doubt, Rosey appreciated Colonel Von Schrader's military bearing and follow through.

Headquarters 78th Pennsylvania Volunteer Infantry.
Nashville, Tennessee, October 31st, 1862.
To: Captain R. D. Elwood
   You are hereby detailed to act as Division officer of the Picket to report to Lieutenant Colonel Von Schrader [74th Ohio] on the corner of Broad and Spruce Streets this Evening at 7 o'clock.
      By Order of Colonel William Sirwell, Commanding [9]

The Tennessee state capital was now the headquarters for General Rosecrans' army and the center of its supply base. The Yankee occupation filled the streets and dirty hotels of Nashville with Union personnel and businessmen. William Rosecrans was the supreme military, police and legal power in Nashville. He was not only responsible for the army's problems, but also for the community's problems. The butternut-citizens of the city came to Union headquarters with many dubious requests. The ladies of the city were particularly troublesome. In a short period of time, hundreds of women applied to the Union command for passes to leave the city.

Captain William Wiles, Provost Marshal General dealt with the many appeals. The young Wiles had been on Rosey's staff before and had showed unique abilities and loyalty. He now carefully screened the petitions of Nashville's citizens, since he was well aware that many of the needs of the Confederate army were smuggled out of the city by the female inhabitants. Underneath the large hoop skirts of the women, Union female detectives found quinine, morphine, clothing, needles, thread, gray material, shoes, and even cavalry boots. When the passes became sparse because of this blatant smuggling, the sorrowful ladies of the South applied to the virtually inaccessible Commanding General. Their pleas to visit families and especially sick members of their family went unanswered. General Rosecrans, reportedly told a gaggle of Nashville women, "I have a sick uncle. When my Uncle Sam recovers from his severe indisposition, I may consider the propriety of granting passes to Rebel women." [10]

While the men in the Army of the Cumberland fought skirmishes with General Bragg's Confederates and Rosey prepared his army to move, Ambrose Burnside's army was defeated by General Robert E. Lee on December 13th, in the fierce battle at Fredericksburg, Virginia. Approximately 13,000 Federals were wounded or uselessly slaughtered, while the Confederates sustained fifty-one hundred losses. [11]

A number of relatives of men from Armstrong County suffered at Fredericksburg or in other battles of the Army of the Potomac. As previously stated, many of the men in the 78th had relatives within the regiment. They also had friends and relatives in other regiments fighting in different theaters of the war. Nineteen year-old Sam Stahl II transferred to the Fourth U.S. Cavalry while twenty-one year-old Cousin Sam Stahl I stayed with the Seventy-Eighth. Sam I would muster out with the regiment; Sam II would die in Andersonville Prison. Archibald and Thomas Blakeley kept in close touch with their brother William Blakeley who now served as a lieutenant colonel in the Pennsylvania Fourteenth Cavalry. Their brother Harvey served in the Seventy-Seventh Pennsylvania; he would die from wounds received in the Atlanta Campaign. Sirwell's young nephew, George McCandless, who lived with him in Kittanning, had marched off with the Brady Alpines and now served in Company H of the regiment.

Samuel McCandless, unlike his brother-in-law, Sirwell, or his nephew, George, did not join the Seventy-Eighth. He joined the Pennsylvania Eighth Reserve Infantry. It was probably after the siege of Nashville that Sirwell learned of the wounds received by Sam McCandless in battle. Sergeant McCandless, his wife's brother and a close friend, who also lived with Sirwell from 1850, was wounded both at South Mountain and Antietam in September of 1862. Promoted to a First Lieutenant in Company A of the Eighth Reserve, McCandless was wounded fighting in Major General George Gordon Meade's division. He was wounded once again at the ferocious battle of Fredericksburg in Magilton's Second Brigade attack on Jackson's Corps in the early morning of December 13, 1862.

Alfred Reed, who, with Sirwell's permission, had gone AWOL to get his officers straps died of wounds received at Fredericksburg. First Lieutenant Reed was mortally wounded assaulting Marye's Heights with the Pennsylvania 134th, part of General Hooker's Center Grand Division. [12] In the Eastern theater, Lee, Jackson, and Longstreet would make Christmas 1862, a sad time in many Northern homes.

While the Federal army struggled for life in the eastern theater the Union suffered another set back in their attempt to capture Vicksburg on December 20th. General Earl Van Dorn's Southerners attacked the Federal supply depot at Holly Springs, approximately 50 miles south of Memphis on the Mississippi Central Railroad. The depot held the stores for the staging area of the Union forces advancing on Vicksburg. Even though Colonel R.C. Murphy of the 8th Wisconsin had been warned by Grant on the 19th of December to be on alert for a Confederate attack, he took no real defensive action. When the Rebels attacked, he immediately surrendered.

The Confederates raiders gained a total victory. They captured valuable bales of cotton and much needed flour. Whatever they could not carry away they burned and destroyed. Two locomotives along with forty to fifty cars and the arsenal were destroyed. Murphy was supposed to have one thousand men in his command; however, the *Richmond Dispatch* claimed the capture of eighteen hundred men and one hundred and fifty officers.

The Rebels claimed to have taken or destroyed $4,000,000 worth of supplies and material. Bruce Catton lists a more realistic figure of $1,500,000. Horace Greeley called Murphy an imbecile and a traitor. Grant relieved Murphy of duty.

It is both interesting and amusing to note the ridiculous, distorted manner in which the *Richmond Dispatch* reported the surprise attack. "The scene was wild, exciting and tumultuous. Yankees running; tents burning; torches flaming; Confederates shouting; guns popping; sabers clanking; Abolitionists begging for mercy; Rebels shouting exultantly; women en dishabille [en deshabille literally meaning in a state of undress] clapping their hands, frantic with joy. The ladies rushed out from the houses, wild with joy, crying out, 'There's some at the Fair Grounds; chase them! Kill them for God's sake!'" It is difficult to appreciate where this reporter was during the attack; especially when one tries to consider what type of woman would run from her home naked to shout for anything. It is hard to imagine a well-bred southern woman doing such a thing. [13]

ONWARD CHRISTIAN SOLDIERS

For soldiers in the field campaigning is a grueling chore at best. Adequate shelter, good meals, and warm clothing were not routine, even within the Northern army. Campaigning in the Tennessee winter was particularly burdensome for the armies moving into battle. A compendium of comments gleaned from the reports of the Official Record, the regimental histories, and the soldiers personal diaries both North and South, indicate that cold, rain, sleet, and mud were constant companions of the armies from the beginning of the campaign until well after the battle at Murfreesboro. Springtime may be a better time to fight and die, but Rosecrans had decided to assault his enemy now.

On December 22nd, James Negley's thirty-sixth birthday, General Rosecrans affected the plan for his advance against Bragg. His primary responsibility before moving was to protect his base at Nashville. In order to achieve the best possible defense of these areas of operation certain divisions, many unhappily, were selected to stay behind while the remainder of his army was deployed for the move. Rumor spread throughout the 78th that Negley's "Volunteer Rail Road Guard" would remain with Miller's Brigade in Nashville.

General Thomas was responsible for the protection of the Nashville base, the supply lines from Louisville to Murfreesboro. Of the five divisions that comprised Thomas' Center Wing of Rosecrans' army, only two would go into battle. General Joseph Reynolds' Division and two brigades of General Speed Fry's Division were given the responsibility of guarding the Louisville and Nashville Railroad. General Robert Mitchell's Division was assigned to the Nashville garrison duty. This left Thomas with James Negley's and Lovell Rousseau's Divisions to follow him into the active campaign.

Colonel Moses B. Walker's Brigade of Fry's Division was to join Thomas, but was instead relegated to guard rail lines from Nashville to Murfreesboro. Not reaching the battlefield until the 31st, Walker's Brigade was used to halt the flow of fugitives scurrying back to safety in Nashville. Walker's unit was never engaged in any heavy combat.

The other corps commanders would have three divisions each for the battle, minus some regiments also relegated to guard duty. McCook commanded the Right Wing with Johnson's, Davis' and Sheridan's divisions, while Crittenden commanded the Left Wing with its three divisions of Wood, Palmer and Van Cleve. [1]

Rosecrans' Wing commanders were men of individual character. George Thomas, was a competent field commander and a fighter. He would prove to be Rosey's most dependable corps commander. Alexander McCook and Thomas Crittenden had questionable military credentials. General McCook's courage was never an issue, but many questioned his ability to handle large numbers of men. Crittenden like McCook had limited corps command experience.

Despite the fact that Major General Thomas became Rosey's most trusted and closest advisor, initially their old friendship was strained. At the outbreak of the war, Thomas, a native Virginian, chose to remain with the Union. This fact would haunt him for the duration of the war, and in fact, for the rest of his life. During the war, there was always a reluctance on the part of Northern politicians to completely trust him. Thomas knew of these feelings, but remained loyal to the Union. He was a proud and honorable man. He had been offered the command of the Army of the Ohio, when Buell was still in power, but in deference to Buell's coming battle at Perryville he respectfully declined. However, with the removal of Buell, Thomas was distressed that William Rosecrans, his junior, was given command of the army.

General Thomas appealed directly to General Halleck regarding what he felt was a gross discourtesy and in his honest, open fashion confronted Rosecrans with his feelings. He also requested a transfer out of the Army of the Cumberland. He thought of asking for a transfer to the Texas theater. Abraham Lincoln solved the problem by back-dating Rosecrans promotion making him Thomas' senior.

Rosecrans was headed for what he knew to be an important and difficult campaign; he needed the robust George Thomas. Rosecrans had known Thomas since he was a cadet at West Point. At that time he called him, "General Washington" because he felt that Thomas displayed many of the traits of President George Washington. Following the days at the Military Academy, Rosecrans recommended Thomas for the position as Chief of Artillery at the Academy and also for the position at the Virginia Military Institute.

Realizing that there was a problem in his command, Rosecrans respectfully confronted Thomas and expressed his need of this competent soldier, valued advisor, and old friend. In their meeting Rosecrans laid all of his cards on the table. "You well know my friendship for you...whatever you want, you can have. I will divide the army...and give you the largest of the three divisions, or you may be second in command." Thomas acquiesced to Rosecrans request and remained with the army under the condition that he would command the Center Wing of the army. He did not want to be relegated to the empty second in command position. Rosecrans quickly agreed.

George Thomas was not a rash individual. He was deliberate and calculating in his actions, and it is a testament to his consideration for his soldiers that they in turn affectionately called him "Pap." In lighter moments the boys facetiously referred to their commander as "Old Slow Trot." The nickname came from Thomas' deliberate riding style. When his cavalry escort moved out too quickly, the large, over-weight Thomas would call out, "Slow Trot!"

Major General Alexander McDowell McCook, a member of the famed "fighting McCook family" of Ohio, had been a tactics instructor at West Point. Like his nine brothers serving in the Union army, he was a courageous warrior. He had won promotions for gallantry at both Bull Run and Shiloh. His brother Daniel was also a member of the Army of the Cumberland. Despite his courage, Alexander McCook was widely regarded as incompetent; he was relatively unpopular. Although good-natured and jovial, he was a profane man who came across in a manner that many considered undignified. Northern abolitionists thought that he was Southern and Democrat in his sympathies.

Major General Thomas Leonidas Crittenden was commissioned a brigadier general in 1861. His position was a clear indication of the power of his family in Kentucky and that states' importance to the Union. Promoted to Major General for his actions at Shiloh, Crittenden had risen to rank because he was also a member of the powerful Crittenden family of Kentucky. His father, John Jordan Crittenden, was a United States Senator from Kentucky. As with many families in the border states, the Crittenden family experienced the "brother against brother" scenario. John's other son, George, rose to the rank of Major General in the army of the Confederacy. George Crittenden was censured and resigned for his defeat at Logan's Cross Roads, Kentucky in October of 1862.

CHAIN OF COMMAND
THE PENNSYLVANIA SEVENTY-EIGHTH [4]
Troops Engaged

ARMY OF THE CUMBERLAND
Fourteenth Army Corps

COMMAND
Major General William Rosecrans

ROSECRANS' CENTER WING
Major General George Thomas

THOMAS' SECOND DIVISION
Brigadier General James Scott Negley

NEGLEY'S SECOND BRIGADE
Colonel Timothy R. Stanley
18th Ohio, Lieutenant Colonel Josiah Given
19th Illinois Colonel Joseph R. Scott
11th Michigan, Colonel William L. Stoughton
69th Ohio Colonel William B. Cassily

ARTILLERY
1st Ohio, Battery M, Captain Fredrick Schultz

NEGLEY'S THIRD BRIGADE
Colonel John F. Miller
21st Ohio, Lieutenant Colonel James M. Neibling
37th Indiana Colonel James S. Hull
74th Ohio, Colonel Granville Moody
78th Pennsylvania, Colonel William G. Sirwell

ARTILLERY
1st Kentucky, Battery B, Lieutenant Alban A. Ellsworth
1st Ohio, Battery G, Lieutenant Alexander Marshall

Self-serving and also irreverent, Thomas Crittenden had only minimal military experience as an aide to General Zachary Taylor during the war with Mexico.

Rosecrans selected all of his subordinates for their abilities and qualities. General David Stanley, chief of cavalry, was a good organizer for the horse soldiers that had been neglected under Buell. He was extremely loyal. Colonel Julius Garesché, the near-sighted, Cuban born, Frenchman was Rosecrans' chief of staff. Garesché was an old, very close friend of the General's. He had been instrumental in Rosey's conversion to Catholicism. He was equally intelligent and refined. Stanley and Garesché were selected for Rosecrans' staff for their competence, and not for their Roman Catholic religion as it was rumored. A youthful Captain James St. Clair Morton was Rosey's choice for chief engineering officer. Morton was permitted to develop an independent command, drawing volunteers from any regiment of infantry. Morton enlisted approximately seventeen hundred troops which he organized into three battalions. This brigade of "combat engineers" was the resourceful idea of General Rosecrans. They were to build field fortifications, corduroy roads, and build or repair bridges. [2]

All of Rosecrans' corps commanders and division commanders had years of military experience. Except for John Palmer of Crittenden's Corps, they had either been at West Point or in the Mexican War. Two of the three corps commanders and four of the eight division commanders had been trained at the Military Academy. McCook, Thomas, David Stanley, Garesché, and Morton were all products of West Point, as were Johnson, Sheridan, Wood and Van Cleve. Crittenden, Thomas, Davis, Negley and Rousseau had participated in the war with Mexico. All of these men had served the Union virtually since the beginning of the Civil War. [3]

Indiana General Jefferson C. Davis, who served with Robert Anderson at Fort Sumter, was the most unusual officer in Rosecrans' command. In September of 1862, Davis had killed his defenseless, commander, General William "Bull" Nelson, at the Galt House in Louisville. Although charged with the crime, he was never tried. Indiana governor Oliver Morton put pressure on authorities to have Davis freed. Now this dastardly murderer served under Rosecrans. [4]

As part of General Thomas' Center Wing, James Negley commanded three brigades. The brigade commanded by General James Spears, did not arrive on the battlefield until the 3rd of January, and was only then permanently attached to Negley. The remaining two brigades were commanded by two men who were both Republican lawyers, and political appointees. Although neither man had any prior military experience at the outbreak of the war, both were steadfast and dependable men: Colonel Timothy Stanley of Ohio and Colonel John Miller of Indiana. Colonel Sirwell's regiment served with John Miller. [5]

The ten company commanders in the Seventy-Eighth were from varying backgrounds; their military experience was representative of most company commanders. For the most part they had little or no military experience before the Civil War. But, all in all, they would prove to be competent, loyal officers. Captain Jack, Company H, had been in the three month service. Captain Cummins, Company A, was a merchant from Indiana County, Pennsylvania. Captain Brinker, a businessman from Clarion County headed Company C. Captain Forbes of Company D, was a lumberman also from Indiana County. Captain Hosey of Company E, was a graduate of Allegheny College in Meadville, Pennsylvania, and a teacher. Captain Gillespie was a physician from Freeport,

Pennsylvania, and commanded Company F. Captain Jordan led Company G, after recruiting it. Captain Elwood, a canal packet captain, commanded Company I.

Two company commanders resigned before the battle. Captain Hilberry, Company B, who had been in Sirwell's three month company, resigned on Christmas Day, and was replaced with Martin McCanna. Captain Hervey, the commander of Company K, was granted his requested resignation on November 17th. Command of the company was given to the forty year-old Lieutenant Matthew Halstead of North Buffalo Township. The boys in Company K were not pleased with Halstead's promotion over other lieutenants. Questioning his military leadership by referring to him as "the Off Wheel Ox or that Damned Hog Drover" would soon be replaced with their admiration of his unfailing courage. [6]

Shortly after Rosecrans appointment as commander of the Army of the Cumberland, the highly political General Halleck began to pressure him. Henry Cist applied his poison pen to the character of Henry Halleck. "General Halleck's brilliant paper campaign into East Tennessee again was produced and aired with a show of the most profound wisdom, based on the extreme of ignorance of the situation and surroundings." Halleck immediately urged Rosecrans to move his army and attack Bragg. There were even suggestions to Rosecrans' removal if he took no action. [7]

Halleck notified Rosecrans that Lincoln was most anxious to have the Army of the Cumberland move against Braxton Bragg. Halleck warned him: "If you remain one more week in Nashville I cannot prevent your removal." Rosecrans would not be threatened. He replied: "I will not move for popular effect. To threats of removal or the like I must be permitted to say that I am insensible." [8]

Rosey took his time regrouping, resupplying and organizing his army. When he went into battle, he wanted his boys to be prepared. He also needed a sufficient amount of supplies to sustain his troops in the event rail service was interrupted between Nashville and Murfreesboro. [9] This decision would prove to be wise in light of the Rebel cavalry harassment to his supply lines when he marched his army to meet Bragg.

It was becoming more apparent to Jefferson Davis that if the Confederacy could not stem the tide of Federal advances in the West the dream of an independent nation would die. With that thought in mind he decided to visit his western armies and evaluate them. So in early December, President Davis, his aide, Robert E. Lee's son, Custis, and his new Western commander, General Joe Johnston, personally visited his army at Murfreesboro. Johnston was the overall commander of Bragg's army in Tennessee, and of Pemberton's in Vicksburg, Mississippi.

Unfortunately, after a review of the Army of the Tennessee, the assumption that Rosecrans would not move against the Southern army during the winter months led to a decision that yielded nine thousand men from Bragg to Pemberton. In spite of Bragg's objections, Davis could not be dissuaded from transferring Major General Carter Stevenson's Division. Many distinguished military historians have stated that this dreadful decision had a far reaching effect on the outcome of the ensuing battle. It may be true that Stevenson's Division could have swayed the outcome of the battle in Bragg's favor. However, in playing the "what if game" it could be supposed that if Rosecrans had the over fourteen thousand Union troops on detached service in Clarksville, Gallatin, Bowling Green, and Nashville he could have not only routed Bragg, but totally crushed his army. [10]

General Bragg's objections to weakening his forces might have been stronger, but he was relatively as confident as his commanders-in-chief that Rosecrans would not move against him. Despite this belief, he would hedge his bet; he deployed Wheeler's cavalry to keep him continuously informed of Federal positions and actions. As he told President Jefferson Davis, he planned to attack Rosecrans at Nashville in the spring.

With a good many Tennessee boys in his command, Bragg gave little thought to intelligence. The Rutherford Rifles, Company I of the First Tennessee, were formed in the county surrounding Murfreesboro. Rosecrans, on the other hand, had only a minimal working knowledge of the local geography. To overcome this distinct disadvantage, Colonel William Truesdail, Chief of Army Police, gathered about himself an effective group of "scouts" and spies, in order that Rosecrans would have the best intelligence possible. General Sheridan of McCook's corps had come to trust and employ an east Tennessee "drummer," one James Card and two of his brothers. As a native of the state, Card was knowledgeable about the area; his days of peddling books in middle, east Tennessee and Georgia only enhanced that knowledge. Card and his brothers infiltrated and spied on the Rebel army, then reported back to General Sheridan. Card's reports were so precise that Rosecrans used them to check the information of his own scouts and spies. [11]

With many channels of information, General Rosecrans was also well aware of the disposition of Braxton Bragg's soldiers. His spies and soldiers kept him informed. Bishop Polk, headquartered at Murfreesboro, had strong outposts at Stewart's Creek and Lavergne. General McCown was on the right flank at Readyville. Hardee's corps, the army's left flank, was on the turnpike to Shelbyville and on Nolensville pike between Triune and Eaglesville, with and advanced guard at Nolensville and Knob's Gap. [12]

Intelligence sources may have been good, but they could not overcome the fact that the countryside that Rosey's soldiers had to move through was fraught with rough terrain and an insidious adversary. These well-placed Confederates would definitely slow the army's movement. The short thirty miles between Nashville and Murfreesboro was now a more dangerous path. Along with Bragg's soldiers, his new, young commander of cavalry, Major General Joseph Wheeler, would harass the Union army during its initial movement toward Murfreesboro and threaten its supply line during the battle of Stones River itself.

Joseph Wheeler, who would one day command Federal troops again in the Spanish-American War, left behind the true picture of a cavalier dandy equal to that of Jeb Stuart. The twenty-six year-old Wheeler had the physical stature of a thin boy. His appearance and fame may not have come down through history equal to Stuart's, but his exuberance cannot be over shadowed. His reported way of announcing a raid to his staff paints a picture of a dashing, confident, young warrior, "The War Child rides tonight." [13]

Scouts and spies were one form of an intelligence gathering system, but old fashioned lookouts could be just as effective. The 24th of December was a clear, bright day, and the 78th Regiment spent the day reconnoitering. The signal corps of the Army was not thoroughly organized and sentinels were stationed on the tops of the hills in the neighborhood to keep a lookout for the enemy. A squad from Sirwell's Regiment spent the day overlooking all the roads leading in the direction of Murfreesboro. There were several sharp skirmishes during the day, and the Keystone state troops could hear the distant boom of the cannon and see the smoke of other skirmishes. [14]

Rosecrans had worked diligently to prepare his army for the coming campaign. His reluctance to move in early December was due to the fact that he had only accumulated five days of supplies, but by Christmas Day he had built up enough supplies to last his army until approximately February 1st. He planned his movements and assault, evaluated the positions of his adversary, and now issued orders to advance at dawn on Christmas Day. Possibly in light of the holiday the order was withdrawn in lieu of one for an advance on the 26th. Reason for the delay was known only to Rosey, but his strong religious beliefs may have had something to do with his decision. William Shanks of the *New York Herald* suspected an important move, but could not get a confirmation from Rosecrans. He incorrectly assumed that the army might be retreating, and would abandon Nashville. He subsequently learned from George Thomas' Inspector General that the wagons were being moved back into Nashville to make way for the army's advance. Naturally he immediately informed the *Herald*. [15]

In the almost fifteen months of guard duty, small skirmishes, and camp diseases the regiment could only muster five hundred and fifty-five effectives for the coming battle. This number was reported by Colonel Sirwell, but it is approximate. The record keeping within the regiment was adequate. However, conflicting spelling of names, the listing of one man in two different companies, and discrepancies of the exact number of men placed in hospitals in Nashville make all totals suspect.

The Seventy-Eighth had left Pittsburgh in October of 1861, with approximately 980 men on their roster. By December of 1862, 177 men had officially listed as no longer belonging to the regiment. Five of those men were killed. Seventy-nine men had died from various causes: "camp fever," typhoid, dysentery, diphtheria, and consumption. Fifty-six men had been discharged on a surgeon's certificate, and three discharged for other reasons. Six officers and one surgeon had resigned, and one officer had been discharged. There had been five desertions. Three men transferred to the Veteran Reserve. Seventeen men had transferred to the 4th U.S. Cavalry, and were placed in Company A, in a squad commanded by Armstrong County native, Sergeant John Watson from Sarver, Pennsylvania. Alf Reed had transferred to the Pennsylvania 134th. Another three hundred and fifty-eight men were not with the regiment for various reasons.

The troops not listed with the regiment were either ill or on assignment. Lieutenant Colonel Blakeley had gone on furlough because of illness in late November. A goodly number of men, like Private Elias Rettinger of Company B, were in Nashville hospitals. They would spend the time during the battle in hospital at Nashville or Hospital #1 in Louisville. Unlike their brothers in the field, although ill, they would enjoy the home cooked meals of turkey with all the "fixins" while in the hospital. Prior to the battle of Stones River a number of men from the regiment like Georgie McCandless volunteered for the Pioneer Brigade, or were assigned to artillery units, and headquarter aide positions. [16]

There had been one hundred and ten replacements that had joined the regiment. Six men had joined Company A, in November of 1862, for a $29.00 bounty. James Carnahan, one of the "bounty soldiers" would lose his life at the battle of Stones River. Colonel Sirwell personally enlisted three Southern-born young men at Nashville in early December. James Thorne, at age twelve, would go down in history. The young

Tennessean would become famous after the picture of him riding a captured Rebel cannon appeared in *Frank Leslie's Magazine*. Pulaski neighbors James A. Champion and John L. Tanner former co-workers in Samuel Nicholson's cotton factory were initial members of Company G, Tenth Tennessee Union Volunteers Infantry. Sam Nicholson was a native of Massachusetts and a Pulaski magistrate. This could indicate that he was pro-Union or neutral. In all likelihood he may have influenced Champion and Tanner to join the Union cause. Nonetheless, the seventeen year-old Champion joined the Seventy-Eighth and would go on to serve out his three-year term. He would be wounded during the battle at Murfreesboro, his birth place.

John L. Tanner, of Company I, Pennsylvania 78th, also listed in various Union records as John L. Tarmer would fight at Stones River and according to the regimental *Descriptive List* would reportedly die of pneumonia in his home town during January of 1863. There is even a grave listing of John Tanner at the National Cemetery in Nashville. But a grave listing means virtually nothing.

Interestingly, a Private John L. Tanner of the Confederate Sixteenth Tennessee deserted the Southern army and gave himself up to Colonel Geza Mihalotzy's Twenty-Fourth Illinois posted in Chattanooga on January 20, 1864. Since John L. Tanner is shown to be buried at Nashville, it could follow that he did die at home. However there are five cases where men never listed in any regimental records are listed as members of the 78th buried at Nashville: Mark Brown, L.P. Henry, Valentine Ryers, F. Wissa and John Sheilds. George Fox shows interment at Nashville and Andersonville. Jacob J. Angless is noted to be buried at Nashville. He died years later in Clarion County, Pennsylvania. [17]

It is a distinct possibility that there were two John L. Tanners; however, a search of the service records show a very suspicious pattern. A John L. Tanner did join the Confederate Sixteenth Tennessee on May 15, 1861; subsequently he was discharged at Corinth, Mississippi, on May 28, 1862. One John L. Tanner enlisted in the Union Tenth Tennessee and is recorded as being present from September 1862, until he "deserted" on November 22, 1862. Private John L. Tanner was enlisted by Sirwell on December 17, 1862. After his brief month with the Pennsylvania 78th, John L. Tanner again shows up in the records of the Confederate Sixteenth Tennessee from January 1863, until his "desertion" in 1864. It may be possible that John L. Tanner, Tennessean, was fickle and could not decide on his allegiance, or he was one of those many Southrons spying for the Confederate cause. [18]

"WE MOVE TOMORROW, GENTLEMEN"

December 25, 1862, Christmas Day, was celebrated in many American homes, both North and South. However, it was a holiday celebrated that year with an ever present sadness. During that time of warmth and peace, memories flooded back of those lost in the war. Around the battlefield at Fredericksburg and in the hospitals that dotted the roads to both Washington and Richmond young men were dying of their wounds. Burial parties and undertakers committed more young Americans to the Virginia soil. Soon the boys in Rosecrans' army would be fighting and dying, too.

This was the second Christmas in the field for Bill Sirwell's regiment, and the 78th had changed. Seasoned veterans now spent a quite Christmas day in Camp Hamilton, six miles south of Nashville. These soldiers had been tested under fire at Lavergne. They had experienced sickness and death. They had suffered, at times, from a lack of adequate or proper food, shelter, and clothing. They had lived under siege at Nashville and had seen the hatred of the Rebel sympathizers. Now they were headed for one of the large battles of the war. William Rosecrans announced to his officers and staff, "We move tomorrow, gentlemen."

By December 1862, after nine full months of Yankee occupation, Nashville had changed. It was one of the biggest Union bases in the West. Soldiers outnumbered citizens by more than two-to-one. Soldiers took up residence in houses that had been abandoned. Hotels and schools were turned into hospitals. The Rock City was an exciting home for boys from distant farm communities. The hustle and bustle of Nashville equaled and surpassed that of Pittsburgh. There was also excitement and entertainment to be found. There were dances, plays and other shows. Business boomed and prices soared. Butter was 80¢ a pound. Apples and potatoes sold for 75¢ per peck. A coat costing $10 in Kittanning went for $40 in Nashville. Sugar was scarce at any price and prostitutes were plentiful.

So many prostitutes plied their trade in Nashville that an Ohio soldier declared the army's very existence was threatened. Appalled by numerous "ladies of the night," the Federal authorities finally took a provost guard, rounded up fifteen hundred of the women, and moved them by rail, under guard all the way to Louisville, with clear orders not to return. Nothing is recorded pertaining to Louisville's acceptance of Nashville's exports. [1]

Unlike his fellow Ohioian, Ira Gillaspie did not see the threat from female companionship. He had no problem with the ladies in Nashville. They were his favorite pastime. While in camp near Nashville he wrote, "In the evening, I stole out of camp and went to see some of my friends in town I having the countersign. I found the ladies...very agreeable...At 3 AM I bid good by to my female friends and came back to camp again." [2]

Many of the soldiers availed themselves of the prostitutes on Nashville's "Smokey Row" and after the white prostitutes were moved out of town they began visiting the black ones. A number of the boys in the Seventy-Eighth visited prostitutes and a few even came to enjoy the company of black prostitutes. Negroes were becoming more a part of their daily lives.

Samuel Dumm wrote to his sister to tell her that he now saw more Negroes in one day than he previously saw in a year. Droves of young black "Pie Boys" descended on the camps selling "pies, Ginger Bread and sweet milk or eggs and chickens." Negro women would enter the camps to sell cakes and apples. Negroes passed by their encampment all during the day, "some driving carriages, and all dressed up like gentlemen in better clothes than we can afford at home to wear to church. And the 'Dinahs' dress up in their best, tripping through the street like so many New York belles," Sam related to his sister. Nonetheless, the soldiers heading for battle would miss their adopted home in Nashville.

Unfortunately, all of the problems that accompany any army of occupation were present. There was a constant danger from Southern sympathizers. Soldiers learned not to walk the streets alone at night. Thievery was rampant. Union supplies and medicines were continuously being smuggled out of Nashville to the Rebel army. And there were many cases where a Union sympathizer or soldier could make a quick dollar by aiding the Southern cause.

The regimental history says little about the Christmas season or Christmas day 1862, but it would seem that there was entertainment and merriment to be had. Gambling was a favorite pastime of most soldiers both Yankee and Rebel. The Pennsylvanians were no different. Although the soldiers in the Army of the Cumberland were paid their thirteen dollars a month, many times they would not receive pay for three to four months. J.T. Gibson states that many of the men sent as much as two-thirds of their pay home, but that there were also those who enjoyed "cards and chuckaluck" and those that spent their money at the sutlers on unnecessary things that "did them no good."

Thirty miles away, Christmas in Murfreesboro was celebrated with that warm feeling held by all Americans on a great holiday. There was the naive belief on the part of the Confederates that Rosecrans, because of the winter weather and the constant cavalry harassment under which his army existed, could not move out of Nashville until spring. Essentially, Bragg and his troops had no desire to see the Yankees move. Army life wasn't too bad. Middle Tennessee supplied the Confederacy with valuable items such as food, forage, leather, cloth, and other essentials. For Bragg's soldiers there was plenty to eat, plenty to wear. There was a mild out-break of smallpox in some of Cheatham's regiments, but that was quickly contained. For the most part the camps were healthy. In his memoirs, General Arthur Middleton Manigault stated that the men were able to recover from their fatigue and losses. "Blankets, clothing and shoes were issued to the men, their spirits were excellent, everybody was cheerful, the ordinary duties of the soldier were performed with spirit..."

Festivities and celebrations were in abundance in the Southern camps. There was a gala wedding performed on December 14th, during the holiday season. General "Bishop" Polk joined in marriage the dashing, thirty-seven year old, Rebel, cavalry General John Hunt Morgan to Murfreesboro's nubile, seventeen year-old, spit-fire, Yankee-hater, Miss Mattie Ready. On Christmas Day in the spirit of Southern aristocracy the Confederate officers paid social calls in and around Murfreesboro. They also got up horse races, while the troops played games. Gambling was flagrant. An Alabama soldier wrote about the excessive amount of gambling in the Confederate camps and the fact that "...some Loose all that they have got." The headquarters officers had planned an elaborate ball for the 26th. The festive dance at the courthouse would be the last for many; a ball of a different type was already in the operational stage. In a few days the courthouse would be filled with the moans of dying men instead of music. [3]

The cheerful, Rebel spirit was turned to anger at various times. Naturally, the General Commanding was the crux of the problem. General Bragg aggravated his soldiers by executing four boys for desertion the day after Christmas. Three were shot while one was hung. Many of the officers and men of Breckenridge's command had been particularly disconcerted with the execution of Asa Lewis of the Sixth Kentucky the day after Christmas. Private Lewis left to go home after his one year enlistment. In spite of the change in required service time, Lewis felt he was bound only by his original agreement. He wanted to return home to help his recently widowed mother and younger siblings. The general commanding did not see things as Private Lewis did. Lewis was charged with desertion and sentenced to death. General Breckenridge was outraged when Bragg refused his personal request to commute the young man's sentence. [4]

Bragg's harsh actions and the threat of an enemy attack did not stop the troops who wanted to celebrate. Ignorance of enemy plans was bliss; death, a constant companion, was soon forgotten. So, the Rebels engaged in merrymaking. Along with games and dances, the Confederate army that now happily occupied Murfreesboro also found their own entertainment for the holiday season. Alcohol consumption and drunkenness were commonplace. Sam Watkins of the First Tennessee described it this way: "It was Christmas. John Barleycorn was general-in-chief. Our generals, and colonels, and captains, had kissed *John* a little too often." [5] The officers of the Confederate Twentieth Tennessee Infantry had purchased a barrel of whiskey for the men, that they might spend a merry Christmas. The result was not too merry. One soldier of the regiment reported: "We had many a drunken fight and knock-down before the day closed." [6] Not to be outdone, Bill Rogers of the Thirteenth Tennessee recorded in his diary that the captains, lieutenants and privates also got drunk. In line with the Christmas holiday, eggnog was very "fashionable." [7]

The boys of the Twentieth Tennessee may have engaged in a "knock down, drag out" fight, but Bragg and much of his senior command, although not physical, were engaged in their own squabbles. Bragg was still at odds with his corps commanders and some of his division commanders over his retreat from Perryville. On Christmas Day, the high command of the Confederate army in Murfreesboro was still torn by dissension. President Davis and General Johnston may have left thinking that they had patched up the problems in Bragg's command, but they had not.

The first of Bragg's corps commanders was Lieutenant General Leonidas Polk. The sanctimonious "Bishop" Polk, an Episcopalian bishop, held Bragg up to scorn. He visited President Davis in Richmond and after placing singular blame for the failure of the Kentucky campaign squarely on Bragg's shoulders suggested that Bragg be replaced by Joe Johnston. Jefferson Davis would not even think of complying with Polk's suggestion.

General Polk led a corps containing two strong division commanders, the Nashville native, tobacco-chewing, profane, hard drinking and hard fighting Major General Benjamin Franklin Cheatham, and Major General Jones Withers one of the few close friends and loyal subordinates of Braxton Bragg.

Lieutenant General William Hardee commanded Bragg's second corps. Hardee, a West Pointer, was a professional soldier. He was lauded in both North and South as a leading military scholar for his pre war two-volume Rifle and Light Infantry Tactics endorsed by the War Department in 1855. A handsome, affable fellow with a reputation as a devoted ladies' man, Hardee also suggested the removal of Bragg.

General Hardee had three division commanders. The hard-fighting Patrick Ronayne Cleburne had little problem with Bragg and made little or no attempt to undermine him. John McCown of Kirby Smith's old corps was at present attached to Hardee's corps. He did not relish the idea of serving with Bragg. Major General John Breckenridge, James Buchannan's Vice President, who held Bragg in open disdain, led the first division. [8]

Braxton Bragg himself was an enigma. A West Point graduate in 1837, General Bragg had become over the last two years of command a contradictory picture of competence and failure. He was loved by some and hated by others. Only forty-five years old at the battle of Stones River, the cantankerous, ill-tempered General Bragg had been, by then, in poor health during most of his adult life. One officer in his army wrote that he should have been in bed most of the time instead of in the saddle. Bragg suffered from rheumatism, gastrointestinal disorders, and boils. Nervousness, migraine headaches, and other ailments, possibly psychosomatic, reportedly, increased with his responsibilities. Despite his personal problems, Bragg the martinet could be affable. He would join his staff around the camp-fire and regale them with stories about his adventures in the Mexican War serving under General Zachary Taylor, and tales of his old friends and acquaintances: Bill Sherman, Don Carlos Buell, and George Thomas.

At Stones River, similar to the battle at Perryville, Braxton Bragg would initially gain the upper hand, but indecision and ineptness would cause him to withdraw. Professor James Lee McDonough states that his greatest strength lay in organization and logistics, not tactics. His career path during the Civil War proved this out. [9] After taking command of Beauregard's unruly army in June of 1862, Bragg built an effective, organized, and disciplined fighting force. Both admired and liked by Jefferson Davis, but far from the mistaken impression of a strong friendship, Bragg continued in command with the President's apparent confidence. [10]

In mid-December, as the Confederate army settled into Murfreesboro, Bragg made various organizational changes that affected the First Tennessee. The losses of men from battle and from disease made it necessary to combine units. The First Tennessee was combined with the Twenty-Seventh Tennessee. General Maney remained in brigade command. Colonel Hume Feild commanded the combined regiment.

On Christmas day, Braxton Bragg was still assured by his spies that the Union army had gone into winter quarters. It was virtually a time of peace. As the Confederates prepared for their dance and the troops celebrated, General Rosecrans prepared to move. William Sirwell merely noted in his report of the battle: "I received orders [this] evening, to have my Command in line for marching at 6 o'clock A.M. on the morning of the 26th instant." [11] The enemy that had eluded the soldiers under Sirwell's command for so many months was now present. Ten leagues from Nashville, Bragg's army was waiting. A number of the Union troops wrote "last" letters home to loved ones. It was apparent that the coming battle would not be a hit and run skirmish.

In the wee hours of the morning on December 26th, reveille sounded through the pre-dawn mist, an hour before first light. Within the company streets of the Seventy-Eighth at Camp Hamilton, tents were quickly "struck," and at daybreak the army moved out on the macadamized roads that weaved through the rolling Tennessee hills shrouded by heavy clouds. [12] Negley's division, in the advance of Thomas' command, moved out promptly to Brentwood on the Franklin Pike, and from there advanced on the Wilson Road to Owen's store where the troops were to be encamped for the night. Since General Negley did not have a good working knowledge of the area he enlisted the aid of one of the local men as a guide. The normally benevolent Negley warned his reluctant pathfinder that he faced possible death if he led the division astray.

General Thomas' Corps, in the center position of the line of march, was deployed so that at Nolensville it could aid Crittenden to the left or McCook to the right if they were attacked. [13]

The Seventy-Eighth was in General Thomas' Center Corps, but initially did not accompany Negley's other regiments. The Regiment and their comrades had encountered the picket lines and skirmishers of the Confederates shortly after leaving Nashville. Brisk skirmishing was kept up during the day. Colonel Sirwell noted in his after-action report: "My Regiment was on picket duty [and] by some mistake I was not relieved until the troops of the Divisions had taken up the line of march. [This] threw me as rear guard of a large train of one hundred and fifty wagons."

The Seventy-Eighth took up the line of march about 9:00 A.M. and trudged down the Franklin Pike to a given point, where it left the road abruptly and moved onto Wilson's Road. The unit was headed towards Nolensville, for the purpose of striking out to Murfreesboro. The country road they traveled was a "hilly," rough road cut through dense cedars in many places. The virtual dirt path was rendered almost impassable by the heavy rain. It had rained almost incessantly during the day, and the roads were very muddy. The heavy wagons plowed equal distant furrows in the mud. Furrows that would never be planted, but would only point the direction to battle. It took all of the strength of horses, mules, and men to push, pull and drag the wagons. A few wagons turned over and there were times that they became stuck after only "three and four rods." The singing that had occurred in the early stages of the march quickly had died away. After a tedious and toilsome march the 78th encamped about five miles west of Nolensville in the woods. Many of the boys hacked boughs from the cedar trees and used them as beds. [14]

Sirwell was correct in his assumption of not being relieved. Negley simply gave no orders to Sirwell. However, in his after-action report Sirwell showed his practice at the art of politics. He did not state that he was not given orders. He used the word "mistake" which could protect Negley. Nevertheless, at the sound of Davis' embattled guns, Negley changed his plans. He pushed forward with his troops to Nolensville to help Davis, as was the designed support plan of Thomas' Corps. It is apparent that to the contrary the 78th was not left behind. Negley simply neglected to send orders to Colonel Sirwell. He needed someone to protect his trains and obviously he trusted his regimental commander to act properly. [15] On the evening of the 27th, General Negley reported to the command, that he now ordered Colonel Sirwell to bring up the wagons. This adds to the premise that Negley was in complete control of his division. He also knew how to cover his ass. [16]

At a time when the Union forces moved forward to defeat the "enemies of freedom" the *Louisville Daily Journal* reported that members of the Union-biased Tennessee state government including Andrew Johnson signed a "memorial" to be presented to President Lincoln. The document requested that the President not make the Emancipation Proclamation applicable to the state of Tennessee. Near Paris, Kentucky a collection of slaves was prepared for their eventual sale in late January. Those slaves, the object of this wretched war, would bring a price of $166 to $800 each.

While his "wings" advanced on Braxton Bragg, Rosey finished up last minute details. About 11:30 A.M., he rode out of Nashville with his staff. "Captain" William Bickham, a volunteer aide-de-camp and also a reporter for the *Cincinnati Commercial*, rode with the Commanding General's cadre. It was time to catch up with the army. At approximately 3:00 o'clock, Bickham noted the gun fire to their right, but was assured that it was only skirmishers. Bickham stated that as the thunder of hostile guns grew louder, every rider sat up a little straighter. The group followed Crittenden's army for most of the day. The First/Twenty-Seventh Tennessee on picket duty near Lavergne knowingly assessed the sound of the approaching Union army. Southeast of Nashville, the distant roll of cannon fire reverberating through the rolling Tennessee hills signaled the Confederates that Rosecrans was on the move.

General Rosecrans' cadre followed Crittenden's Corps for most of the day. At the same hour as the Southrons became aware of the Union advance the Commanding General was ready to camp, but he wanted to meet with McCook. The riding party wound through the hills and dales through which the army passed, but had little luck reaching McCook's headquarters. Around eight o'clock it became evident to Bickham that the group was lost. An old woman who could not give them directions because she claimed to never have been more than three miles from her home probably put a greater scare into the reporter when she announced that Reb cavalry had been in the area. One of the General's staff found a guide and after another hour's ride they reached McCook's camp.

After the meeting with General McCook, Rosey was ready to return to his camp. Bickham noted that Rosecrans mounted his horse at approximately ten o'clock, with McCook's pledge that, "I will whip my friend Hardee tomorrow." The night was dark and wet. The riding party got lost three times again and never arrived at Rosecrans' camp until three A.M. They almost wandered into a Confederate picket line at one point. Everyone was "ravenously hungry and utterly exhausted" after fifteen hours in the saddle. [17]

Most reports and regimental histories note the immediate skirmishes that took place as the three wings of Rosecrans' army departed Nashville. Bragg had many of his troops in a "fire and fall back" position from Nashville to Murfreesboro. But a good deal of the harassment taken by the Federals was dealt out by Bragg's cavalry.

Although he had made meticulous preparations for the battle, Rosecrans could not overcome Bragg's advantage in cavalry. In addition to Wheeler's horsemen directly under his command, Bragg could count on Morgan and Forrest, who operated independently of the Army of the Tennessee, to cause their share of consternation within Rosecrans' military district. Morgan and Forrest with several hundred men in each command raided throughout the area occupied by the Yankee soldiers and constantly threatened Yankee held towns or positions. The "War Child" and his cavalier companions burned bridges, attacked trains, and tore up rail lines. Their small, biting attacks on the advancing Union army caused wounds, deaths, and supply losses.

General Wheeler's cavalry soon reaffirmed the news of the Union army movement to Bragg. It is safe to say that, although Bragg did not anticipate Rosey's movement, his placement of troops and cavalry were done to protect his army against such a surprise. Needless to say, advance of the army brought a halt to the plans for the dance. Bragg quickly set into motions his plan to meet the enemy. [18]

The Union army moved to battle, but there was still a few in their ranks who wished to prolong the merriment of the Christmas season, once they encamped for the day. Ira Gillaspie notes, "We got to Nolensville just [after] dark. It rained hard and long during the night. Some of the 19th Illinois Regiment pressed a couple of barrels of whiskey. They had a jolly time of it, I wager, judging from the sound of them." [19]

The continuous rain and the poor conditions of the road slowed the army. For many days to follow, cold rains, wind, mud, and fog would hamper the movement of both armies and make the men miserable. On December 27, Colonel Sirwell was only able to move his command six miles. Moving through Nolensville, a cluster of about 20 log houses and two frame homes, they camped approximately one mile east of the town next to the road leading to Stewartsboro. [20]

The three wings of Rosecrans' army plodded forward. McCook, who had seventy-five men killed on the first day, lost some of his cavalry to friendly fire. The fog, in the early morning of the 27th, caused some of his infantry to fire on his cavalry. As his skirmishers pushed forward to Triune, they found the Confederates had burned the bridge at Wilson's Creek, and pulled back. Crittenden's Corps fought their way through Lavergne and camped with the army at Stewartsboro on the 28th. [21]

While the Union army advanced, Bragg, his officers, and local citizens prepared for the battle. As Bill Sirwell was struggling through the mud on the road to Nolensville, the Confederates were cutting roads through the cedars, and preparing river crossings in the fields around Murfreesboro. A number of high ranking Confederate officers rode through the fields checking the lay of the terrain. General Arthur Manigault left a dramatic description of the anxious families that resided in the area of Stones River. "Interspersed amongst [the military wagons] here and there or perhaps toiling along, with some interval between them, would appear the larger and more cumbrous machine of some unfortunate farmer, his household goods piled to an immense height, far beyond what one would suppose to be the capacity of the vehicle, women and children occupying every available position, apparently at great risk to their necks. Horses, cows, sheep, hogs, and pigs, formed an attendant drove, in [the] charge of the lads or Negroes belonging to the family, the proprietor himself assisting in some way or superintending everything, leaving behind his once happy home...and seeking shelter and protection in the rear of our lines..." James Haynie left the doleful picture of an abandoned small log house that he supposed was owned by a young couple. The one room cottage still held the belongings of Haynie's romantic newly married couple. "...there were the beginnings of a garden, some cribs and pens, a few chickens. and a pig...Inside the cabin, the bed was nicely made up..." [22] In all probability, within days, this picturesque setting and most of the homes in the area would be ransacked and destroyed.

The foul weather and cold affected the soldiers both blue and gray. Amandus Silsby of the 24th Wisconsin, Sill's Brigade marched the roads with McCook's Corp. "During the

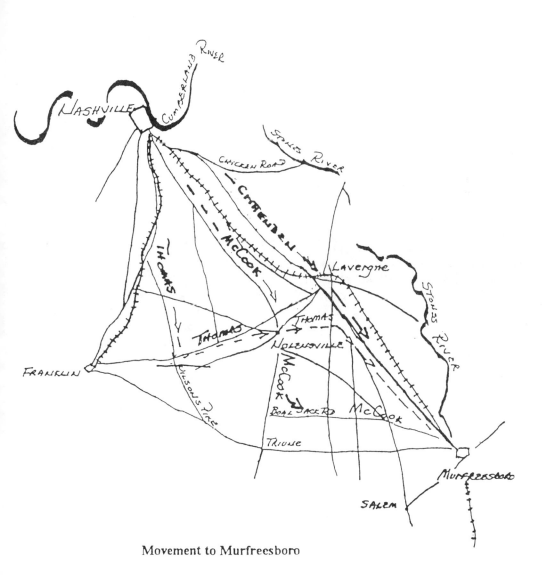

Movement to Murfreesboro

march...to Murfreesboro, it was nothing but a continual rain day and night, so that we were wet through. The roads were full of mud and slush, so the four days before the fight my feet were wet soaking all the time. (Monday night) all that was left of my shoes gave way, so I had to walk barefooted." Silsby's graphic account of his march leaves quite a different picture of the Union soldier. The impression of the perfectly clad "Billy Yank" versus the picture of his poorly uniformed adversary has persisted down through history. However, the image of the boys in blue marching shoeless through cold, rain, and mud equals those of the tattered, barefooted "Johnny Reb."

Johnny Green of the Ninth Kentucky, Hanson's Brigade, suffered with his comrades in Southern gray. "The weather is a cold drizzle (but) we are not permitted to have fires for General Bragg does not wish the enemy to be able to locate our line. Beef & corn meal issued to us uncooked...Colonel Hunt ordered a detail sent back to the wagons from each company to cook the rations & bring them to us." [23]

No matter what the conditions are for an army on the move, there are always a few men under arms who are able to overcome adversity. Diarist James Marshall recorded that he found a comfortable place to sleep. Although most of the army had no cover for their rest, Mr. Marshall was able to find a place, at least out of the direct rain. He spent the night sleeping in an ambulance with Colonel Miller's adjutant, Major Augustus Bonnaffon of the Pennsylvania Seventy-Eighth. [24]

On the morning of December 28th, Sirwell's men once again took up the line of march with more favorable weather and better roads. In and around Murfreesboro, the day was raw and cold. The roads were slippery and icicles hung from the trees. General Polk and some of his officers once again rode out the Nashville/Murfreesboro Pike to reconnoiter the area. Regiments traversed the fields getting into position for the fight. At the same time as Polk was surveying the terrain around Stones River, General Willich of McCook's Corps, and units of General Stanley's cavalry reported back to Rosecrans that the retreating Rebels had left the Shelbyville Road, and headed for Murfreesboro. Bragg was concentrating his forces. [25]

During the Federal progress on Murfreesboro, General Wheeler's cavalry continually attacked the Union convey. In a daring race begun on the night of the 29th, Wheeler after being reinforced by Colonel James Carter's First Tennessee Cavalry, completely circled the Union army. In effective attacks at Jefferson, Lavergne, Rock Springs, and Nolensville, the "War Child's" Cavalry killed and wounded many Yankees. They captured hundreds of prisoners, large wagon trains, stores, and arms. Hundreds of thousands of dollars of stores, wagons, and arms were also destroyed. The actions by Wheeler's cavalry would have been enough to drive McClellan, Hooker or Pope from the field or at least would have halted offensive operations. Rosey did not hesitate; he pushed forward.

In spite of the superiority of the Confederate cavalry, David Stanley's cavalry unit performed admirably. Colonel Minty with Crittenden's Corps, Colonel Zahm with McCook's, and General Stanley, personally leading the reserves at the head of McCook's Wing, did an effective job in protecting trains, rails, and wagons. They routed the enemy and drove them back from their lines. David Stanley's horsemen remained in the saddle for the duration of the campaign. Although, not equal to Wheeler and his horse soldiers, General Stanley's troopers had a positive effect on the outcome of the fray. [26]

The Seventy-Eighth was still in charge of protecting Negley's wagons. Although not directly attacked, they safely guarded their freight. They spent the day moving to Stewartsboro. Because of Rosecrans' standing policy for the Sabbath, there had been little movement by any of the other divisions, but Sirwell and his companies would have little rest. They were forced to ride along slowly with the wagons until they joined up with the main body of Negley's Division.

That evening, after the wagon train finally reached Miller's camp, the regiment received orders from Lieutenant Henry Cist, Colonel John Miller's acting adjutant, to bivouac for the night. Sirwell's regiment had been three days on the march until they rejoined their command. Although there had been cavalry activity, light skirmishing, and the sound of heavy cannonading flowing through the countryside from where General McCook was engaging the enemy at Triune, the men remained steady and turned over all the wagons. Unfortunately, before the men of the division could claim any of their baggage or belongings, the order was passed to "reduce baggage." [27]

After morning mass, while his army rested, General Rosecrans and his staff rode down the Murfreesboro Pike to the north bank of Stewart's Creek, and reconnoitered the enemy positions. After considering various options for the advance, Rosecrans returned to his headquarters at Lavergne. While Rosey had been attending mass, General Bragg met with Generals Polk and Hardee to discuss the developing situation and subsequent plans. There were no church bells to bring the townspeople of Murfreesboro to services. Their fear grew as the Union army gathered. [28]

The countryside around Murfreesboro was somewhat hilly and jagged, with thickets of cedar, intersected by small streams, with rocky, bluff banks. The roads were rough and muddy from the days of rain and excessive usage. It was only through the utmost of efforts that the teams pulling wagons and guns could be gotten through. When the army marched again, Bill Sirwell frequently dismounted, pulled off his coat, and rolled up his sleeves and assisted the teamsters in pulling their charges through. [29] Regardless of the time or place in the history of warfare, it has always been impressive to the common soldier to see an officer and especially a colonel willing to pitch in to get the job done. The sight of Sirwell struggling in mud with the "boys" placed an indelible mark on his record as a leader by small acts such as this.

The Seventy-Eighth took up the line of march again on Monday morning the 29th. Upon leaving Stewartsboro, Crittenden's troops were assigned to the Murfreesboro Pike, so Negley's soldiers were moved onto a very rough by-road that paralleled the Pike. About three miles down this country road a sharp skirmish ensued between the Federal forces and those of the enemy. The skirmish over, the troops moved once again. The fields, roads and forests were filled with the sounds of an army on the move. The rumble of cannon and wagon wheels, the clanking of rifles and tin eating utensils, the voices, the tramp of the foot soldier filled the countryside with the cacophony of a bizarre orchestra. The regiment pressed on; the fighting was continuous between the enemy's pickets and the regiment's advance. The 78th proceeded on for considerable distance until they struck the Murfreesboro Pike near a bridge that crosses Overall Creek. All divisions, brigades and regiments were marching in line with their relative conformity to their eventual battle line. During a rest break Colonel Sirwell's troops traded speculation and rumors with the troops of Colonel Nicholas Anderson's, 6th Ohio Regiment of Crittenden's Corps.

There was some confusion between the commanding General and General Crittenden. An assumption was made that the Rebels would abandon Murfreesboro at the arrival of the advance units of the Union army. General Rosecrans had actually ordered that one of Crittenden's divisions occupy the town upon its arrival.   After skirmishing with Confederate forces on the approaches to the town, Generals Wood and Palmer went to see Crittenden. They both expressed the folly in committing their divisions against Bragg's entire force, especially with Van Cleve and Negley still struggling to bring up their divisions. Crittenden would not over rule Rosecrans' order, but did delay its execution. Upon reaching the intended battlefield Rosecrans withdrew the order. He would bring up all forces before engaging the enemy.

The 78th "saddled up and moved out" until within approximately two and one-half miles from Murfreesboro. The regiment camped for the night near a dense cedar grove on the right of the Murfreesboro Pike. Colonel Sirwell's regiment camped with Miller's Brigade near Lt. Marshall's battery of the First Ohio Artillery. In spite of the rain and cold the regiment prepared hot coffee, cooked some fatty bacon, and chewed on hardtack. When they stacked arms, many did so by sticking the bayoneted rifle into the ground to keep their loads dry. All of Rosey's soldiers lay down to sleep on the wet ground, most without fires, under a drenching rain. [30]

A number of men from the 78th had been placed or volunteered for duty in other utility units or positions. Various troops were placed in artillery units or teamster positions. Major Augustus Bonnaffon was serving as topographical engineer on Colonel Miller's staff, Lieutenant Alfred Ayres of Company H was serving as Miller's aide-de-camp, and Private Saegers was serving with Ellsworth's Battery.   Colonel Sirwell's nephew, George McCandless, volunteered for the Pioneer Brigade. [31]

During that day, unbeknown to Rosecrans' troops in the field, the Northern armies had another set back in the Mississippi campaign to capture Vicksburg. The Federal forces commanded by General William Sherman clashed with the Confederates at Chickasaw Bayou, north of Vicksburg. Sherman's Right Wing of the Army of the Tennessee made a concerted effort to break through the defenses at Chickasaw Bluff.   But the well entrenched and fortified Rebels on the precipitous bluff threw back the Yanks attempting to displace them. Sherman's 30,000 men who had wallowed through mud, swamps and abysmal mire from Johnston's Landing were defeated. [32]

Abraham Lincoln faced troublesome times as the year drew to a close. Along with military losses, he faced the dissolution of his cabinet with the resignations of Secretary of War, William Seward and Treasury Secretary, Salmon Chase. On the 30th of December, the vaunted ironclad, USS Monitor, would sink in a storm off Cape Hatteras, losing a combined sixteen seamen and officers. It was widely rumored that England and France would withdraw their unconditional support of the Union and recognize the Confederate states of America. The anti-war, Democratic *Kittanning Mentor* stated that, "The news in Europe of the Federal defeat at Fredericksburg was viewed as very unfavorable to the Union. They predict a dissolution of the Cabinet and government, and a repudiation of the war debt by the people."

Several of the boys in the Seventy-Eighth were surreptitiously sent copies of The *Mentor*, since it was believed by some that the Republican dominated postal system prevented its delivery. The newspaper arrived stuffed in shoes, clothes and the lining for food boxes. In spite of the fact that copies of the hometown anti-war newspaper did reach the regiment, the boys stayed their course. [33]

In the waning days of 1862, Rosecrans' army became the sole standard bearer for the Federal cause. Irrespective of the outcome of the impending battle at Murfreesboro, Lincoln would issue his Emancipation Proclamation. It would sit better if the battle news was incontestable.

Major General George "Pap" Thomas

"THE BALL OPENED"

The Tennessee countryside leading from Nashville to Murfreesboro is rolling and rough. The roads in 1862, were poor and the battlefield selected was no better. The area was relatively flat with few imposing hills for artillery or observation. The terrain had rolling, low hills and shallow swales. The land was broken by numerous and sometimes large limestone outcroppings which in some areas gave prominence to the land. It was heavily wooded with red cedars and pines, Black Cherry, American Elm, Orange Osage, Kentucky Coffeetree, oaks, and maples. The coming of winter had caused the fruit of the Orange Osage and Coffeetree to fall from their branches. Mistletoe covered many of the leafless trees.

In some fields cotton still clung to their opened bolls on brown, shriveled plants. There were some open fields harvested of their corn. The most prominent feature of the area was the river running south to north through the intended battlefield. Stones River was more or less easy to wade across, but in many places its banks were steep and lined with trees. To Rosecrans' advantage, the terrain did not lend itself well to the effective use of the somewhat superior Rebel cavalry. The dense cedars afforded some protection for both sides. [1]

The full winter season had set into the Nashville Basin. December 30th saw a smattering of weather that had plagued the armies from the 26th of December, and would continue until January 4th as the Confederates retreated out the Wartrace and Shelbyville roads in a cold, winter rain. On this next to last day of the year, several diarists reported heavy showers, bitter cold, and ice on the river. During the ten dismal days of the campaign, it rained and or sleeted on seven days. It snowed on December 31st. The sun fought through the mist and fog on one day, January 1st, otherwise the sky was filled with low hanging, dark clouds. In a number of areas the water pooled and froze in the shallow, limestone lined swales.

In the vernacular of the day, Colonel Sirwell announced, in his after-action report, "The ball opened this morning [December 30th]." Miller's brigade, as it marched into the assigned battle line, closed in on Crittenden's Left Wing. They advanced and took a position to the right of General Palmer's Second Division and proceeded through the cedars. Negley's division had lined up its right with Sheridan's division. Sheridan's men had skirmished continuously during their march down the six mile long Wilkinson Pike from Stewart's Creek. The Pioneer Brigade had busied themselves cutting roads through the thick stands of cedars in order that Negley could easily move cannon, ammunition wagons, and ambulances. The Federal batteries commenced shelling the enemy as soon as they were in position. The Rebels did not respond immediately, but in their turn opened a corresponding deadly fire on the Yankees. The fight of the day would principally be with artillery and small skirmishes.

In the chilly morning mist Colonel Miller ordered skirmishers from the Seventy-Eighth Pennsylvania, the Nineteenth Illinois and the Thirty-Seventh Indiana southward across the Wilkinson Pike. At 8:30 A.M., Sirwell deployed his skirmishers as ordered; Martin McCanna's Company B, and William Jack's Company H, the selected companies moved to their positions. First Lieutenant McCanna, although new to his command, had the Colonel's confidence. As noted, Captain James Hilberry, commander of Company B, had resigned on Christmas day, and it was only on the 26th, that Lieutenant McCanna

Right Flank

Company A
Captain Cummins
⇐
Company F
Acting Lieutenant Weaver
⇐
Company D
Captain Forbes
⇐
Company I
Captain Elwood
⇐
Company C
Captain Brinker
⇐

Regimental   Regimental Colors
Front   Sergeant Hamm
                              ⇐
Company H
Captain Jack
⇐
Company K
Lieutenant Halstead
⇐
Company E
Captain Hosey
⇐
Company G
Lieutenant Maize
⇐
Company B
Captain McCanna
⇐

Left Flank

Colonel Sirwell's Order for the Regimental Battle Formation at Stones River [2]

had been placed in command of the company. Despite the change in commander Sirwell still showed his confidence in the boys from Kittanning by selecting them along with Captain Jack's company to deploy as primary skirmishers. The youthful Captain William Cummins leading Company A and Company F were deployed as a reserve skirmish line. Captain Charles Gillespie had been replaced by Acting Lieutenant Absolom Weaver as commander of Company F. Gillespie like Blakeley before him had been selected for court martial duty in Nashville. Colonel Hull of the 37th Indiana had deployed companies D and E of his regiment as his skirmishers.

The Union skirmishers drove the Confederates southward across the Wilkinson Pike. Moving at the double-quick the Yankees soon adopted a style of Indian fighting. As they pursued the Rebels they frequently took advantage of the trees; stopping in safety they fired at the retreating foe. The thrill of the chase quickly ended when a large Confederate force near the Giles Harding house and the brick kiln near it opened a blazing volley into the Union ranks. The Hoosier skirmishers, leading the assault, took a fierce pounding. When the boys from Indiana began to falter, the 78th moved forward, passed them, and engaged the Rebels near the brick kiln east of the Harding home.

The regiment's skirmishers exchanged deadly rounds with the enemy and drove them back. With a lull in the fighting, Sirwell was ordered to withdraw to make room for Colonel George Roberts' Illinois command of Sheridan's Division. Phil Sheridan's Third Division had fought their way into place. The 78th was ordered to lie in that position for some time and was eventually ordered to advance and remain on picket near the edge of dense woods. At noon, they were relieved by the Twenty-First Ohio. The efforts of Sheridan's and Negley's brigades drove back the Confederates and brought about the occupation of the home, gin-house, and other out buildings belonging to Mr. Harding. General Negley wrote in his after action report that the 78th and the 19th Illinois admirably drove back the Confederates skirmishers. [3]

In the annals of warfare, many officers were noted to be drunkards, incompetent or both, and they did not fight. The most unusual and equally amusing incident related at the battle of Stones River concerned two Confederate officers that could not determine who the enemy was. Lieutenant W.N. Mercer Otey of General Polk's staff leaves a humorous picture of two overly pugnacious Rebel officers. "(Early Tuesday) morning General Polk...sent his aide-de-camp,...(Lt.) William B. Richmond, [to order] (a) regiment of infantry to pull down a rail fence which was an obstruction to the movement of troops. ...Richmond rode to the officer in command, Colonel (S.S.) Stanton, of the...(84th) Tennessee...and transmitted the order.

Some words passed that led to blows, and though the bullets were flying thick and fast, here was seen the ludicrous spectacle of two [Confederate] officers engaged in a personal fight on the battlefield. Stanton had got Richmond's thumb in his mouth, while Richmond was gnawing away at Stanton's ear. ..." [4]

While the two Confederates attempted to settle their dispute, the sporadic skirmishing and cannon duels increased along the front between the Yankees and Rebels. The army commanders were feeling their way into a major battle.

Although many reports in the Official Record indicate there was little or no fights for many brigades on the 30th, the fighting for Miller's command was somewhat heated. Private James Myers of the 78th's Company H was killed in the early skirmishing action

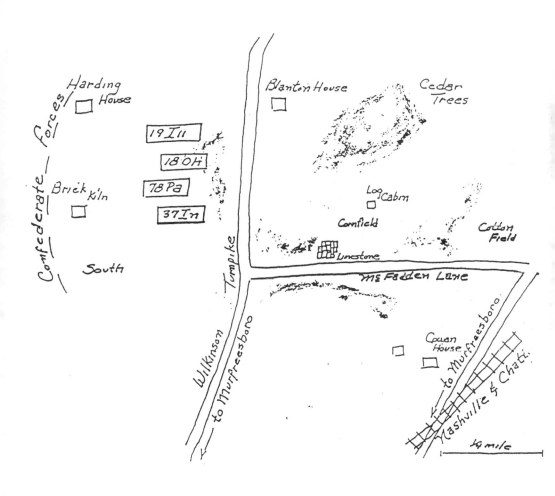

December 30, 1862

near the Harding house. Reverend Gibson noted years later that he was the first man to be killed in the battle, but more than likely he had the wretched distinction of being the first from the Seventy- Eighth killed in the "great" battle. Colonel Miller lost about 20 killed and wounded during the day.

By the mid-afternoon the earlier flush of battle had worn off; the reality of combat had set in. J.T. Gibson related an event in the regimental history which could be indicative of the universal feelings of the men after they saw the effects of battle. "In the afternoon we overheard one of General Thomas' staff talking to General Negley about the possibility of capturing some rifle pits about a thousand yards in our front, where we supposed there were masked batteries. General Negley replied, 'We can take them if you say so.' A captain remarked in an undertone, 'He might add, 'But we would rather not.'" The men were ready to fight, but attacking those distant rifle pits made no real sense.

By evening the clouds of the bleak, dreary day were swept away and the stars peeped out for a short time. Rosecrans' and Bragg's armies lay along a four mile front. From the banks of the Stones River to the north the lines extended southwesterly to the Franklin Turnpike, awaiting the coming fury.[5] In the clear, dark, biting cold Negley's Division ended the day to the left of Sheridan's division with their right flank resting on the east-west Wilkinson pike at the junction of McFadden's Lane. They were perpendicular to the pike and fronted south eastward while stretching approximately one-half mile in a convex line to the rough road leading north to McFadden's Ford.

There is no mention of McFadden's Lane within any of the after action reports on the battle of Stones River. However, it appears on all of the maps made at the time. General Manigault drew the road on his map. In Captain Bickham's book he refers to the road that today is named Van Cleve's Lane as a "trace." For ease of understanding the positions and movements of the troops it is referred to in this book as McFadden's Lane; the name historically attached to the trace by the National Park Service brochure of Stones River. [6]

Timothy Stanley's brigade of Negley's Division anchored the far right of the division on the Wilkinson Pike. His brigade ensconced in a cedar thicket butted against Robert's brigade of Sheridan's division. John Miller's brigade anchored the far left of the division at a point on McFadden's Lane, approximately one-half mile from the Nashville Turnpike and the railroad. [7]

At the approach of Rosecrans' army, Bragg had wasted no time in setting a well-defined line of battle. Bragg's army was split into two corps. Lieutenant General Leonidas Polk commanded one and Lieutenant General William Hardee the other. Hardee's Corps as the left wing and Polk's Corps as the center were ordered to the west side of the river. Major General John Breckenridge's Division anchored the right flank. It remained posted on the east side of Stones River to afford protection to the town.

The armies rested fitfully after the day's stinging fire fights, but Rosecrans was not resting. He began to shift his overall alignment once again. He had placed his corps from right to left: McCook, Thomas and Crittenden. His grand design was to have Crittenden attack Breckenridge, Bragg's right. Thomas would move forward against "Bishop" Polk concurrently with Crittenden and McCook to hold his ground against Hardee and serve as anchor to the right wheel.

By first capturing the high ground east of Stones River near McFadden's Ford at Rosecrans' left, Wood's batteries would be able to enfilade the Rebels in front of Negley and Palmer. Negley's right flank, that section held by Timothy Stanley's brigade, would be the pivot of the entire wheel movement. By crushing Bragg's right flank with Crittenden's assault, Rosecrans intended to sweep through Murfreesboro. In doing so, he would cut off any route of escape and destroy the Confederate army.

Rosecrans had the plan and the troop positions, but he wanted to weigh the odds more in his favor. He devised a plan to draw Bragg's attention away from Crittenden's all important left flank attack to McCook on the right flank. At 6:00 P.M. Rosecrans ordered McCook to deceptively extend his right flank with additional large camp fires to make it appear that more troops were massed there. Fires were built extending nearly a mile from the actual right of McCook's line. The bogus campsites would definitely get Bragg's attention, but they also affected the strength of Rosecrans' troops. Despite the numbers of men in his Right Wing, the men needed to build and keep these fires going now thinned McCook's lines all the more. [8]

When McCook lit off his fires, Bragg took the bait. Unfortunately, for the Union army Bragg "over reacted" to the ploy. He conceived an offense of his own that was strikingly similar to Rosecrans'. Bragg's pre-dawn execution of that plan would lead to the eventual rout of the boys in blue on the next day.

Although Bragg would not be able to effectively utilize his cavalry superiority in the battle, he had a slight advantage over Rosecrans in this terrain. The number of roads originating in Murfreesboro made it easier for him to move his soldiers. He had already moved J.P. McCown's Division to his left. Now in support of that flank he moved Cleburne's Division and the remainder of Hardee Corps to oppose McCook. Both commanding generals now had identical strategies. Bragg planned to drive McCook back against the Union center and then by crushing the Federal line capture the Nashville turnpike and railroad. By cutting off Rosecrans' escape route he could destroy the Union army. [9]

At 9:00 P.M., Rosecrans met with his corps commanders at his headquarters in order to issue final instructions. In the cedars near the Murfreesboro Pike the three commanders learned the details of the battle plan. McCook would secure the right of the line and hold the Confederate force at his front. This was the key to the whole plan; McCook's ability to refuse the right for at least three hours. Thomas would engage the enemy center. Crittenden would push the attack from his left position and sweep the Rebel right from the field, move through Murfreesboro, and cut off any route of escape for the Rebels. Everyone left the meeting with confidence in the plan. [10]

Just before tattoo, a number of regimental bands began a battle of their own. Private Sam Seay, Company C, Rock City Guards, of the First Tennessee recorded "an incident [that]...history seldom records." The opposing forces competed with their national songs. "Dixie, Yankee Doodle, Hail Columbia, and The Bonnie Blue Flag" filled the cold night air. Eventually, one band began to play "Home Sweet Home," the competing bands took up the national favorite until all of the musicians played in concert. The gut wrenching feeling of those melancholy words, "There's no place like home," brought visions of home and family to the men of both armies. The strains of final song floated into the dark night leaving each man with his private thoughts. The men of the 78th lay quietly along Stones River with their comrades and enemies. The silence was an omen of the coming storm. [11]

SHOUT! SHOUT! THE BATTLE CRY OF FREEDOM

If there was any sleep to be had that night, it was a fitful sleep. The Yankees did not know exactly what was afoot over in the Rebel line, but they were sure that something was amiss. During the late night and pre-dawn hours of December 31st, the sounds of troop movements in the Confederate camps were noted by a number of soldiers in McCook's corps. The truth of the matter was that General Bragg, in response to McCook's supposed lines, was briskly shifting men to his left flank. To mask their actions the Rebels had laid straw and hay over the stony parts of the trails in order that their troops and wagons could traverse the area without making too much noise. They did not want to raise suspicions within the enemy forces. But despite their precautions some of the Federals still detected their movements. Unfortunately, General McCook would not react to the warnings of his commanders.

Joshua Sill, the commander of one of General Sheridan's brigades, became concerned with the sounds of troop movements on his front. At 2:00 A.M. he went to Phil Sheridan with his information and concerns. The two men visited Sill's front then proceeded to General McCook's headquarters near the Gresham house. Sheridan expressed his concerns about the movements and the possibility of a dawn attack on McCook's thin lines that virtually had no closely supporting reserves. He suggested that McCook could adjust his lines and move up supporting brigades to prevent a possible disaster. McCook claimed that he had explicit orders from Rosecrans that would prevent him from moving his lines. He would do nothing.

McCook was a courageous and able warrior, but he may have succeeded to a command much greater than his capabilities. By doing nothing to correct the possible flaws in the alignment of his lines, McCook unknowingly prepared his Right Wing for defeat. Phil Sheridan and Joshua Sill, the two old West Point classmates, sat for hours that night discussing the serious situation of the army. McCook made no attempt to make Rosecrans aware of the facts reported by his officers. He did not even warn his other division commanders to be prepared for an attack. [1]

After a night of light intermittent rain, it was now cold and windy; 1862 faced its final day. An eerie stillness prevailed over the battlefield in the pre-dawn hours. A mist floated along the course of the river. Colonel Sirwell stood quietly with his staff. He was anxious about the coming battle. A mile or so away, Rosecrans, Crittenden and their staff officers stood talking behind Crittenden's lines. Rosecrans was with the left wing where his army would make its initial attack at daybreak. His demeanor was that of confidence.

In the gray light of the early dawn, Rosey's army was not even vaguely aware of their fate. Some commanders had their men on alert. Others left their men to their morning mess and awaited the ordered time of attack. There were those that paced or stood anxiously peering into the fog toward the Rebel lines. There were those who rolled slowly out of their blankets and those who sat about and shivered in the morning cold. Clustered about bivouac fires that burned along their line in the thin forest some tried to warm themselves while others boiled coffee in small kettles. [2]

Unfortunately, Rosey had already made his greatest mistake. In the game of war it was not the trust of commanders, it was not the lay of the land, it was Rosey's method of operation. Rosecrans had ordered his attack to step off at seven o'clock; Bragg had

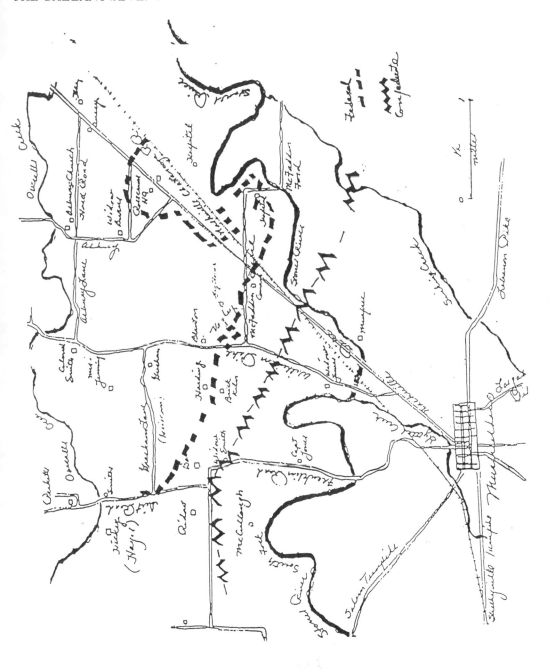

Full Battlefield Map

ordered his attack at first light. Rosecrans' right wing, key to the success of his plan, was not deep enough, not sufficiently supported and obviously staffed with officers not wholly alert to an attack. At the break of dawn, before the heavy fog had lifted, the battle of Stones River began with the attack on Rosecrans' right flank at 6:22 A.M. by thousands of Rebels, many warmed and fortified with corn liquor. They quietly crawled over breastworks and out of hiding to move forward ghost-like in the patchy fog. Their battle flags jerking from the rapid movement advance of the troops, not the morning breeze. Many broke into song as they neared the Federal lines. [3]

Inexplicably, Braxton Bragg chose Major General John Porter McCown to lead off the attack against McCook's rank and file. Bragg's decision was unusual in light of the fact that he considered McCown as being the sorriest leader in his Army of Tennessee. It could be argued that Bragg made his first mistake by using someone he could not trust to carry out his orders. General Bragg was correct in his original assessment. After McCown had positioned his lines on the 30th, General Hardee ordered him to change them. McCown did not comply with this order until the morning of the 31st. In finally executing Hardee's orders, he left a gap in his front line that had to be filled with Cleburne's reserves. As the Confederates stepped off for their attack, McCown's mistake left them with a weak, longer, sparse line instead of a strong attack formation. Although the Southrons drove McCook's Yankees from the field, the full weight of a hard hitting second assault prohibited them from capitalizing on their initial success. [4]

Years later, Sam Watkins remembered that morning very clearly. According to him many of the men and particularly the officers were still drinking excessively. [There had been so much drinking by the officers that] "...they couldn't see straight. It was said to be buckeye whisky. They couldn't tell our men from Yankees...But here they were-the Yankees-a battle had to be fought. We were ordered forward. I was on the skirmish line. We marched plumb into the Yankee lines..." [and their flags]. [5]   Although Sam Watkins embellished his stories a bit, the fog may have lifted enough by the time the First Tennessee set out so that the Yankee flags could be seen.

As was his habit every Wednesday and Sunday, Rosecrans had attended mass. He and Julius Garesché attended a high mass celebrated by Father Cooney of Indiana and Father Trecy. After the services Rosey left the cabin and joined his staff. He placed his rosary, the "talisman" of Roman Catholics, in his pocket. As they stood talking, they heard the first crackle and pop of musketry far to the right. The battle, Rosey thought, proceeded as he had planned. McCook was engaging the Confederates to permit Crittenden to cross Stones River, sweep Breckenridge from his path, and advance on Murfreesboro. [6]

Unknown to Rosecrans and his staff, the Federal right was not "engaging" the enemy; they were being vigorously attacked. The Confederate left moved on McCook's troops in a spectacular three-quarter mile long battle front. As the Rebels stepped off, their artillery opened on the enemy.

The Union soldiers protecting the far right portion of the Federal defenses were without the leadership of their brigade commander, General August Willich. The Prussian trained Willich had gone to division headquarters to express his concerns regarding the enemy movements to General Johnson. In his absence, the men were not fully prepared for the Rebel attack.

Willich's batteries, in compliance to orders, were incorrectly aimed. Furthermore, their horses were unleashed, making it virtually impossible to move the guns to more advantageous positions or to save them from the enemy. Many of the men were preparing what would be their last breakfast. At the first sign of the attack, General Willich hurried back to his brigade hoping to impede the onrushing, gray tide. Before he could reach his troops, Willich was unhorsed, wounded, and captured.

General Edward Kirk, another of Richard Johnson's brigade commanders, was mortally wounded. The Right Wing fell back firing, but it was apparent to the retreating soldiers that nothing could stem the Butternut tide sweeping over them in the early morning light. As the skirmishers of the Seventy-Seventh Pennsylvania fired into the attacking gray-butternut lines and fell back, they knew that they were in trouble. The confident Rebels sang as they moved forward. The Confederates drove the Yankees in the right wing out of their camps, overran gun emplacements, and killed hundreds of Union troops within the first half hour.

McCook's two right divisions, those commanded by Brigadier General Jefferson Davis and Brigadier General Richard Johnson, did little to insure their troops from the suspected attack. The insidious Davis endeavored to steady his division, but his excited manner and the impression that he was confused did little to inspire his fleeing troops. McCook's brigades melted like snow in a summer sun. The Yankees had quickly broken and fled in terror.

Supposedly, McCook and Johnson were aware of the extension of the Confederate lines to their right, but did nothing to support that section of their front. General Johnson in his after action report stated that he reported the over extension of the Rebel left. He claimed that McCook relayed the same fact to him. Some adjustments were made to the Union right, but obviously not enough. In spite of his report, with a dawn attack expected, and with the fearful possibility of a flank attack, Johnson did little to help the situation. He made his headquarters over a mile back from his division. This headquarter position made it impossible to direct his division when they needed him the most. [7]

Within an hour of Bragg's fierce assault, one of McCook's staff officers reported to Rosecrans that the Right Wing was under a full scale attack; however, Rosecrans was not told of Johnson's rout or the rapid succession of events that drove Davis from the field, too. Rosey sent word back to McCook to make a stubborn stand.

Even as the sounds of battle heightened on his right, Rosey was still confident in his plan. The sound of cannon and the battle cries did not yet indicate the degree of his problems; he continued pressing his attack on his left. Van Cleve's two brigades supported by Wood's division had forded Stones River. In Rosecrans' mind the plan was developing well, or so he thought. General McCook had engaged Bragg's left and Rosecrans' rank and file moved to engage Breckenridge on the Confederate right flank. Now another staff officer arrived from McCook to report that the right was collapsing. Rosecrans evaluated his situation and quickly abandoned his plan. Phil Sheridan recorded that the normal color of Rosey's ruddy face faded; he became anxious. His character was being tested to the limit. Nevertheless, Rosecrans quickly pulled himself together and went to work. He developed a defensive plan until he could counter stroke. He ordered the recall of Crittenden's troops, which Confederate intelligence failed to

Position on the Eve of Battle

notice. Rosey mounted his horse and galloped off to his right wing. He had to save his army. He was now on the defensive. [8]

Most of the right wing of Rosecrans' army was in flight by 10:00 A.M.. Wild eyed men poured back through the cedars in alarming numbers. The rapidly disintegrating lines of the Right Wing had been pushed into an acute angle with the Center and Left. Colonel Parkhurst of the Ninth Michigan, General Thomas' provost guard, in his after action report related that his regiment had been posted in the rear of the center of the line. His regiment was at the Overall's Creek bridge on the Nashville Pike. Parkhurst had his regiment fix bayonets and post themselves across the pike. The Ninth stopped many of the fleeing soldiers attempting to cross their path, save the wounded. Many of those that evaded the attacking Rebels and the Union rear guard became captives of the Confederates any way. Confederate boys under eighteen calling themselves "the Seed Corn Contingent" reportedly captured many Union troops running north along the Nashville, Murfreesboro Pike. However, a good number of Union officers and soldiers did make their way back to Nashville. [9]

Major Augustus B. Bonnaffon

"INTO LINE, MEN! INTO LINE!"

On this bitter cold Wednesday morning, Negley's division was aroused by the roar of artillery and the rattle of musketry at first light. The boys from the Keystone state along with their comrades had shivered through the night without fires and stood in line for hours in the tense expectation of an attack on their front. There had been no reveille blown; there had been no long roll of the drum, no call to arms. The sound of a spattering fire of musketry brought them to their lines. The command "Fall In!" quickened the beat of most hearts.

Hospitals had been set up, musicians, surgeons, and any other non-combatants stood at the ready with stretchers, medical supplies, and bandages. Many company and regimental officers sent their mounts to the rear. Rifles were at the set.

Some regiments stood at the ready; some were moved to defensive or support positions. The Tenth Wisconsin Infantry part of Rousseau's Division, Scribner's Brigade, encountered some Rebel soldiers among the rocks and dense thickets as they moved to the rear of Negley's Division as reserve. The few boys in gray had obviously been over run from the previous day's fighting. The badly scared Rebel stragglers were pulled from their hiding places and sent to the rear.

Sirwell's Pennsylvanians, as part of Thomas' Center Wing, did not receive an early morning, direct assault. The gun fire from the far right brought them promptly to attention. The Union troops had been waiting for the signal of their own attack, but there was no need of that now. The bugles that sounded were to bring the men into formation. The Seventy-Eighth held the same position as on the night of the Thirtieth. They were positioned to the left of Colonel Timothy Stanley's brigade [See Map, page 121]. Stanley's Brigade anchored James Negley's division on Phil Sheridan's left. Little Phil's division was the extreme left of McCook's Wing.

Colonel Sirwell boomed the commands for his battalion and company commanders. "Attention, Seventy-Eighth! Into line men! Into line!" The commands passed down through the ranks and eventually intermixed with the calls "Attention, Twenty-Onesters!, Attention, Thirty-Seventh!"

Sirwell advanced his regiment to a position on the right of a knoll at the intersection of McFadden's Lane and Wilkinson Turnpike where he faced south. He ordered his men down to escape the enemy's fire. "Battalion lie down!" passed down the lines.

Sirwell hurried to Marshall's Battery at the top of the knoll. He stood between the guns and directed their fire. The cannon fire was sporadic at first, but it rapidly increased until it became one deafening, thunderous roar of artillery along both lines. Continuous volleys of musketry were heard coming from the right. The fighting on that flank of the Federal line became desperate. McCook's Wing was being driven back. [1]

After making a gallant stand in the initial attack, Sheridan's men held tenaciously to their position. Phil Sheridan formed what was left of his division on the right of Negley's. Negley's line was facing south and east in the direction of the Wilkinson Pike and McFadden's Lane. Sheridan placed Robert's brigade essentially along Wilkinson Pike at a right angle with Negley's right, also facing southward. He then placed Colonel Frederick Schaefer's and General Joshua Sill's two brigades at right angles with Robert's line. These brigades now faced west extending northwesterly from the Blanton house and were deployed in a manner to protect the rear of Negley's combatants.

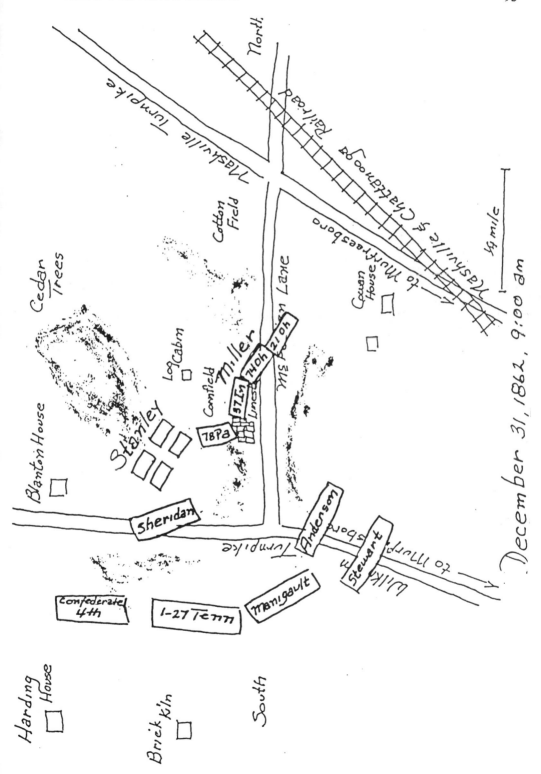

December 31, 1862, 9:00 am

Braxton Bragg's army now turned its attention to the Union center, which was virtually enfiladed. General Bragg hurled four brigades of Hardee's corps and four brigades of Polk's corps against the divisions of Sheridan and Negley. Three times the Rebels attacked these divisions en masse. Five batteries were posted with the two Federal divisions and they sparred within a two hundred yard range with Bragg's batteries. Many of Sheridan's and Negley's troops were wounded by Confederate projectiles that ricocheted off the limestone boulders.

Sheridan's men were exhausted. They had staved off Loomis' and Manigault's brigades in three separate attacks. The killing fire traded by the armies stacked the dead and wounded on both sides of the battlefield. Many of the nearby farm's cows, horses, sheep, and dogs were also killed. The casualties suffered by the opposing forces gave this area the well-deserved name of "the Slaughter Pens." [2]

Two of Sheridan's three brigade commanders were killed in early assaults. Roberts had been killed in "Marse Frank" Cheatham's attacks. Sill was killed while leading a counterattack against Arthur Manigault. With ammunition running low, Sheridan retreated, in the process losing eight guns. Schaefer, Sheridan's remaining brigade commander, would be killed later in the day in a counterattack while relieving Wood's division near the railroad.

The Confederate attacks had proceeded methodically along the Union line from the right. In the wake of McCook's retreating soldiers, pots, pans, kettles, camp stoves, and guns were thrown away. The surging Rebel lines either picked up what they wanted or crushed the spoils of war as they charged over them. None stopped to look or took note as they surged past the body of one insignificant Union Corporal holding the last letter from his mother. Corporal Frank Hale, Wisconsin Twenty-Fourth, Sill's Brigade, like his famed great-great uncle, Nathan Hale, had given up his life for his country. The boys in gray had a greater interest in their charge. They were now pushing Negley's division out of position. [3]

From the battle's first pop of musket fire, the men of the 78th, or at least Thompson Gibson, was "[confident] that McCook's troops would be able to hold their position." It quickly became evident that this was not the case. Negley's troops became more anxious and fearful as they watched the throng of Union blue retreating past their right flank. Riderless cavalry horses or artillery horses who had lost their masters or broken their traces bolted through the battlefield their reins and harnesses dancing wildly about their bodies. Teamsters with their wagons and Negro workers fled for safety out the Wilkinson Pike. But Negley's Division stayed its position.

The oppressive noise, musket fire, and the ever reverberating roll of the cannon's thunder panicked the wild animals that lived in the surrounding dense cedars and fields. Wild turkey bolted from their usually secret and protective hiding places and raced through the Union troops. The birds flew fearfully from their perches. Wild rabbits abandoned the safety of their hutches and sought shelter from the battle. In sheer terror, they found protection among the prone bodies of the soldiers. They huddled next to their saviors and shivered in fear. They "[nestled] under [the] coats [of the troops] and [crept] under their legs in a state of utter distraction."

In the din and smoke of battle, amid the screams of the wounded and dying, it was difficult to keep exact time, but Negley's Second Division had been engaged since mid

CONFEDERATE OPPONENTS OF THE SEVENTY-EIGHTH
DECEMBER 31, 1862
ARMY OF THE TENNESSEE AT STONES RIVER
General Braxton Bragg
BRAGG'S FIRST CORPS
Lieutenant General Leonidas Polk
POLK'S FIRST DIVISION
Major General Ben Franklin Cheatham
CHEATHAM'S SECOND BRIGADE
Brigadier General Alexander P. Stewart
4th Tennessee/5th Tennessee, Colonel Oscar F. Strahl
19th Tennessee, Colonel Francis M. Walker
24th Tennessee, Colonel H.L.W. Bratton [mw]
Major S.E. Shannon, Commanding
31st Tennessee/33rd Tennessee, Colonel E.E. Tansill
Stanford's Mississippi Battery, Captain T.J. Stanford
CHEATHAM'S THIRD BRIGADE
Brigadier General George Maney
1st Tennessee/27th Tennessee, Colonel Hume R. Feild
"Rock City Guards" Companies A-C, Captain W.D. Kelly
4th Tennessee, (Provisional Army) Colonel James A. McMurry
6th Tennessee/9th Tennessee, Colonel C.S. Hurt
Maney's Tennessee Sharpshooters, Captain Frank Maney
Smith's Mississippi Battery, Lieutenant William B. Turner
POLK'S SECOND DIVISION
Major General Jones M. Withers
WITHER'S THIRD BRIGADE
Brigadier General J. Patton Anderson, Commanding
45th Alabama Colonel James G. Gilcrest
24th Mississippi, Lieutenant Colonel R.P. McKelvaine
27th Mississippi, Colonel Thomas M. Jones [sick]
Lieutenant Colonel James L. Autry, Commanding [k]
Captain E.R. Neilson [w]
29th Mississippi, Colonel W.F. Brantly [w]
Lieutenant Colonel J.B. Morgan
30th Mississippi, Lieutenant Colonel Junius I. Scales
Barret's Missouri Battery, Captain O.W. Barret
WITHER'S FOURTH BRIGADE
Colonel Arthur M. Manigault, Commanding
24th Alabama, Colonel William A. Buck[w]
28th Alabama, Colonel John C. Reid
34th Alabama, Colonel Julius C.B. Mitchell
10th South Carolina/19th South Carolina, Colonel A.J.Lythgoe [k]
Lieutenant Colonel Pressley, Commanding
Waters' Alabama Battery, Captain D.D. Waters
Official Record

morning. Colonel Thomas Sedgewick of the Second Kentucky Infantry stationed to the left of Negley's Division noted that Negley was engaged at 8:00 A.M., but that does not indicate the Pennsylvanians were totally engaged. At 9:00 A.M., Anderson, Maney, Manigault and Stewart began their series of assaults to flank the center of Rosecrans' army.   Thus the full brunt of the attack probably fell on Negley's Division at approximately 9:00 or 9:30 A.M. with the retirement of Sheridan's division. Up to that point the Pennsylvanian's had been repelling all assaults.

Hume Feild's First/Twenty-Seventh Tennessee attacked Miller's Brigade from the direction of the brick kiln near the Harding house. As part of Maney's Brigade, they had originally been posted behind Manigault's Brigade.   However, in the right wheel movement, Maney had moved to the left of Manigault's Brigade and slightly ahead of it. The terror ridden retreat of the Union right flank had caused confusion in the Federal and Confederate formations, but Maney's new position would facilitate the continuing flank attack on the Yankees.

Initially, because Schultz's Battery stayed silent for some time, Feild assumed that it was a Confederate battery. When the battery opened on the Tennessee boys at a distance of 400 yards, Colonel Feild, still under the assumption that he was faced by friendly fire, sent two lieutenants forward at different intervals to notify "the Brown Jeans" battery to cease fire. The first messenger, Lieutenant R. Fred James, a lawyer from Murfreesboro, was killed within two miles of his widowed mother's farm also bordering the Wilkinson Pike; but Feild still persisted in the thought that he faced one of his own batteries. When Lieutenant John Marsh was fired upon, Feild finally began to realize he was sending messengers into the face of Union guns. Oddly enough even after he ordered his men to fire, they did so reluctantly. They still thought that they were firing on their brothers. The Tennesseans watched as two intrepid color bearers tested the field. Sergeant Oakley of the Fourth Tennessee Confederate stepped forward about eight to ten paces and unfurled his battle flag, while Sergeant Hooks of the Ninth Tennessee, placed his battle flag atop a nearby corn crib. They drew enough hot Union fire to prove a point.

General Maney, the Tennessee brigade commander, was determining his next offensive movements. Before the charge by his Tennessee troops, he had placed his guns on the knoll recently vacated by Houghtaling's battery, across the Wilkinson Pike and about 400 yards south of the Blanton house, near Harding's brick kiln. Like Colonel Feild, he was similarly deceived by Schultz's battery. He stood toe to toe with General Cheatham and argued that the guns were theirs, even though Marshall's Battery also opened fire. Eventually, he too realized that this was a Yankee battery, when his brigade standard continued to strangely draw enemy fire. After someone sighted the regimental battle flag of the 78th to the right of the battery, Maney ordered William Turner's battery to open on the position with simultaneous attacks by Feild, McMurry, and Hurt. A Rebel battery dropped an exploding shell into the artillery position. The battery captain screamed, "Give em hell, God damn em!"

The 1st and 27th Tennessee under Colonel Feild, 6th and 9th Tennessee, commanded by Colonel Hurt and the 4th Confederate Tennessee regiment commanded by Colonel McMurry heartily charged for the third time into the face of death. Colonel Feild shouted, "Forward First Tennessee Infantry!" With guns loaded and cocked the gray line sprang into action. The courageous Southern boys paid dearly for their courage; the First/Twenty-Seventh Tennessee alone losing 80 men. As manpower from Manigault's

Confederate brigades joined together with them they drove back the Yankees along with Sirwell's lads.

Bragg's troopers now exerted the utmost pressure on Negley's troops still ensconced among the thick cedars. They were attacking the Union division from the west across the Wilkinson Pike and from the south across McFadden's Lane. General Negley's division was virtually surrounded by swarms of rebels. There were several Confederate batteries to the right of the division playing hell on Negley's troops virtually caught in a fierce cross-fire.

The attack by the entire command of Cheatham's division and a portion of Whither's division fell upon Sheridan's remaining troops, Negley's two brigades, and the two brigades of Rousseau, who had been ordered into action on Negley's right rear. General Rousseau, the Kentuckian, who rode into battle on one of his state's famed, thoroughbred chestnuts, watched Sheridan's last troops break and head for the rear. Their retreat left a gaping hole between his men and Negley's. When the Confederates rushed into the gap, General Thomas quickly realized that Rousseau's brigades would be overrun. They would be spent uselessly. Thomas ordered Rousseau to fall back to cover Negley's eventual retrograde movement.

Cheatham's Confederates, along with Maney's Tennessee troops, advanced in line of battle over the ground vacated by the remnants of the Union right wing, coming in on Negley's right flank. They poured through the gap left by the retreat of Sheridan's men. The Confederates approaching from the left flank virtually attacked in tandem. The Tennessee native, Brigadier General Patton Anderson launched an attack against Negley, while Sheridan was still in position. The Confederates after being repelled, regrouped, and prepared to attack again. However, the second attack gave them the advantage. Negley's Division now stood alone and this time Anderson's troops were followed by the Tennessee troops of the West Point graduate, Brigadier General Alexander Stewart. [4]

In the attack, the fire of Negley's division had been effective and deadly. The cannonade of Marshall's and Ellsworth's Batteries combined with the hailstorm of bullets from Miller's Brigade tore into the charging Confederates. Anderson's soldiers faltered and fell back. Lieutenant Colonel James Autry commander of the 27th Mississippi fell from a bullet through his head. Colonel William Brantly, leading an attack with his 29th Mississippi along with his adjutant, Lieutenant John Campbell, were knocked unconscious by the impact of a shell that exploded close to them. The loss of these two regimental commanders was devastating; however, Anderson's troops were only stalled until Stewart's boys could join them and push the attack on Miller's Brigade. Sergeant Gibson stated in the regimental history that the Confederates could have been more effectively challenged if the Federal soldiers would have aimed and fired lower, but that is only speculation and it would appear to be faulty speculation.

Patton Anderson, whose brigade was essentially in combat only on the 31st, lost 730 men; 119 killed and another 548 wounded with 63 missing. The 30th Mississippi, coming in on the left of the division, alone lost 62 officers and men killed and 139 wounded on that morning. Colonel Neibling of the Twenty-First Ohio was heard to say, "My God boys! We gave 'em Hell; didn't we?" [5] He was right. The Confederate wounded and dead clad in gray, butternut, and denim littered the path of the attack.

"CUT YOUR WAY OUT!"

Soon the Rebels would crush the Union line. A renewed assault by the advancing Confederate regiments would be difficult to stave off. But James Negley was not prepared to "throw in the towel." Unlike General Richard Johnson, Negley did not make his headquarters a mile back from his men; he was with the troops. Negley said to be drunk half the time -- as most officers were accused -- seemed to be everywhere cheering and encouraging his men. But despite his reassuring presence, little by little with the retreat of the different Federal commands to his right his division began to waver.[1] The area occupied by Negley's Federals was virtually being destroyed. Wounded and dying troops lay about the ground newly plowed by shot and shell. The smoke hung low over the fields strewn with dead horses, wrecked wagons, and the boughs of cedar trees.

The two brigades under Stanley and Miller were formed in a line two columns deep across a corn field, a huge limestone out cropping, and a peach orchard; the division faced the corner of the Wilkinson Pike at a slight angle. Sirwell, Hull, Scott, Stoughton and Given stationed along the Wilkinson Pike poised their regiments for the impact.

Miller's other regiments waiting for the assault along McFadden's Lane prepared for the impact from that direction. The Reverend Colonel Moody thundered at his 74th Ohio, "Now, my boys, fight for your country and your God. Aim low!" James Neibling boomed at his Ohioans, "Twenty-Onesters, give 'em hell by the acre!" [2] With the retirement of Rousseau's and Sheridan's divisions to the rear of the cedars to form a new line, Negley's combatants found themselves virtually surrounded. [3]

From the history of The Nineteenth Illinois, a regiment within Timothy Stanley's brigade, James Haynie dramatically recorded his time in hell. "Our comrades were falling as wheat falls before the cradling machines at harvest time. We could hear the hoarse shriek of the shell, the swift rattle of musketry, the sound of buzzing bullets, the impact of solid shot, the 'chug' when human forms were hit hard, the yells of pain, the cries of agony, the fearful groans, the encouraging words of man to man and the death gasps of those who reported to the God of Battles...Struck horses, no longer neighing or whinnying, were agonizing in their frantic cries. Cannon balls cut down trees around and over us, which falling crushed living and dead alike...We hugged old Mother Earth, meanwhile firing low."

Greatly outnumbered from the south and now flanked on the west, Stanley's Second Brigade began to waver. The problem began with the 69th Ohio; its colonel, William Cassilly was supposedly so drunk as to be unfit for command. Colonel Cassilly, who had replaced the regiment's original commander, Colonel Lewis D. Campbell, after June 1862, had indulged in the spirits of rye whiskey so much that he was of little consequence on the field. Colonel Stanley ordered him to the rear and placed Major Hickcox in command. Hickcox was subsequently injured by a shell concussion. Captain Putnam and ultimately Captain Bingham, the senior captain, took command of the regiment. The 69th Ohio quit the field first followed by the remainder of the brigade.[4] Stanley's retreat brought the brunt of the battle to Third Brigade commander Colonel John Miller and his far right flank regiment, the Pennsylvania 78th.

General Negley directed a desperate order to Colonel Miller to hold his position. John Miller and his brigade now held the apex of the folding Federal line. He had arranged his brigade in convex order. Schultz's battery held his right, the Pennsylvania 78th next in line was the point regiment in the attack on his flank. Sirwell's Seventy-Eighth, was still deployed to receive an attack from the south across the Wilkinson Pike. The 37th Indiana center right regiment, the 74th Ohio center left, the Ohio 21st the far left regiment and Ellsworth's battery anchoring the far left remained set to receive an attack from the east. It was from the south, the crumbling Union right flank, that Miller's brigade was extremely vulnerable. [5]

Miller, from a vantage point in the cornfield behind his brigade, sat astride his horse near a log hut daubed with red mud. He attempted to repair his lines, but was not able to satisfactorily position his troops before the Confederates struck. His lines were barely formed when a heavy musketry and cannon fire opened upon his men, but they did not waver.

Schultz's and Ellsworth's batteries affected a terrible toll on the attacking Southerners. The brave men of the batteries sponged the throats of their heated cannon. They loaded the charges into the mouth of the guns, stepped back and watched the fiery explosion send steel, smoke, and death into the sky. They threw their shoulders into their guns to re-position them and repeated the process once again. The Rebel artillery posted by the Harding house worked their guns too; there was a resounding return fire. The engagement here was fierce and bloody. All along the front the dead and wounded lay in heaps, but the assaulting horde came over their bodies. [6]

Lieutenant Alban Ellsworth of Hewett's Kentucky Battery had placed his battery on the left of Miller's brigade next to the Ohio Twenty-Onesters. Early in the morning he sat almost directly west of the Cowan house, near McFadden's Lane. At times he delivered an oblique killing fire to his left into Chalmer's advancing troops and later, after repositioning, opened to his right into Stewart and Anderson's advancing brigades. His canister, double shot and shell drew a devastating return from Rebel artillery. A small rifled gun was disabled, numerous horses were crippled and Private Lewis Saegers, of the Pennsylvania 78th, Company C, on detached duty with the battery was mortally wounded.

The turbulent battle slowly destroyed Miller's regiments. The enemy was closing around to their rear, and there was a rapidly diminishing supply of ammunition. The original 60 rounds allotted per man was nearly exhausted. The teamsters bringing ammunition to the regiments broke and ran; that caused many regiments to go in search of a new supply. When the Thirty-Seventh Indiana pulled out of the line in search of ammunition, the 78th and the 74th Ohio closed up the gap.

The scene was becoming more chaotic, if that was possible. Men with powder-blackened faces were running in every which way. Smoke hung over the battlefield and the smell of saltpeter filled the air. Anxious soldiers fired blindly at the enemy. Officers shouted orders in an attempt to raise their voices over the continuous rolling thunder of the cannon and the pop of musketry. The charging Confederates were nearing the point where they would flood over Miller's position.

Despite the reversing fortunes, Captain Elwood, of the 78th's Company I, remained at the head of his command barking orders. He and his fellow commanders shouted encouragement to their troops. They cheered the boys and boomed the order to "Commence firing!" as if it was needed. In reality, there was little need for orders. As the fighting increased, each man assumed command of his own weapon and fired at will.

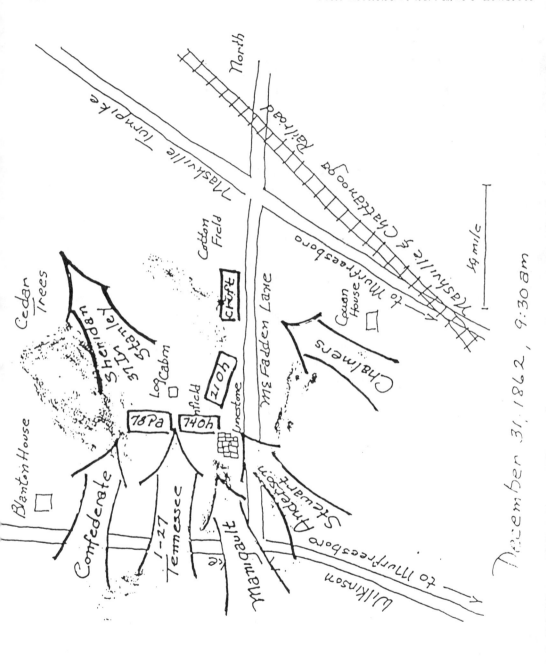

The Seventy-Eighth was boldly holding its position, but in the chaos and confusion of the fighting, Colonel Sirwell received an order to fall back. Reportedly the order came from Colonel Miller, through someone, who Sirwell supposed, "...was cloaked with authority." True to form, Sirwell immediately commenced his retrograde movement. [7]

Sirwell urged his men to keep their formation as they complied with Miller's supposed order. Bill Sirwell's secretary, Alfred Weir, his Adjutant, Lieutenant Henry Torbett, and Sergeant Major Franklin Mechling, his head bandaged from a slight wound, all stayed courageously at their chief's side. Sirwell's regiment had dropped back off the slight knoll and was slowly fighting its way back towards a huge limestone outcropping. The enormous, flat top limestone boulders varied in shape and size. They lay side by side and front to back like a large, rectangular checker board. The spaces between the boulders were large enough to protect a man and the naturally occurring trenches between the seemingly chiseled rocks were from two to five feet deep. Various parts of Miller's brigade had moved to or through this limestone maze during the morning; however, the ricocheting iron and lead made it difficult to hold. The heavy cedar thicket that blanketed the outcropping made it an ideal hiding place, but was likewise difficult to maneuver within. It would not be a good place for a stand. [8]

Colonel Miller, still in position near the log hut, was astounded at Sirwell's movement. He set out to rectify the inaccurate order by personally riding to the Seventy-Eighth and ordering them back into line. While galloping to correct this error he sustained a neck wound. But Colonel Miller would not be stopped. He considered that the wound was not severe enough to take him out of the fight. Later, Rosecrans' Medical Director, Dr. Swift, determined that Miller had received an "ugly" wound, but John Miller had stayed with his brigade.

The 78th, for the most part, regained the twenty rods they had retreated across and resumed their earlier position. Unfortunately, Bill Sirwell had lost one of his most courageous company commanders in the double movement. In falling back, Captain Jack, Company H, received a severe wound in his thigh. Bill Jack reeled from the horrible wound and was carried to the rear by his men. But Captain Jack was not Sirwell's only casualty. All about him his "boys" were taking a pounding. Private Jim Runyan was killed instantly. The German born, regimental teamster, Adam Shindler staggered back from his wound. He held his head as the blood seeped through his fingers, but he remained with the command. Comrades had to support Dallas Thompson and George Rose; both men had difficulty walking after suffering leg wounds.

Captain Jack would not be denied his place with his company. He appropriated a mount, returned to his command, and took his position at the head of his company as they moved forward once again. But his wound was too severe. He was forced to retire from the field, leaving the command of his company to First Sergeant Samuel McBride. Sam McBride admirably steadied the company, but was eventually wounded, too. Another young sergeant of the company, Henry Miller, courageously stepped into the responsibility of command. He remained in the front ranks of Company H, dealing death and destruction to the enemy. Blood seeped through his worn uniform from a wounded arm.

Irrespective of the effectiveness of the Union fire, Bragg's soldiers kept the pressure on John Miller's brigade. The troops of Maney, Manigault, Anderson and Stewart continued their flanking movement, charging up the rolling, low hills and through the limestone boulders. The 78th poured a terrific volley into their ranks, but as soon as one man was killed, another took his place. The Southrons may have wavered, but with heads down and bayonets glistening they affected a dauntless and desperate frontal assault. The Confederates totally cut off Negley's command from Rosecrans and Thomas.

Some of the men from the regiment detailed to man a cannon, captured by the 78th in the battle of Lavergne, reported to Sirwell that the gun had been captured by the Tennesseans. Not willing to give up this regimental prize, Sirwell immediately sent for Lieutenant Bill Maize to bring the piece back. Maize, of Company A, was commanding Company G. He affected his order, but not without casualties. Maize himself was wounded, and was compelled to leave the field. Sadly, the dead bodies of Private Hull and Corporal Arthur Myrtle were carried back along with the gun. Sergeant George Borland, the heel of his boot shot away exposing an ugly wound, hobbled back to the line using his spent rifle as a crutch. Jim Shannon was wounded and taken prisoner as the Rebels closed on the Federals. Sixteen year-old John Croyle took what was thought to be a mortal wound. He was seen falling, but could not be helped; his body was never found. Henry Weaver was killed instantly in a shower of bullets. He was the youngest man of the regiment ever killed in battle.

With the loss of Lieutenant Maize, Sergeant Sam Croyle then assumed command of Company G at Sirwell's order. Croyle expertly and bravely led his command. His company stood with the rest of the regiment methodically loading and firing at the advancing gray-butternut columns. Colonel Sirwell's Pennsylvanians gave as good as they received; however, they continued to be pushed back.

The full force of the battle collided with the soldiers in Sirwell's regiment. George Maney's Tennessee regiments rushed at their enemies. The Seventy-Fourth Ohio stood the ground from the limestone inlay to the middle of the cornfield. The 78th covered the turf from the center of the cornfield, behind the peach orchard to the edge of the cedars [See Map page 131]. It was at the point where the two regiments joined that the Rock City Guard of the First Tennessee struck.

Acting Captain Martin McCanna was the officer in charge of the skirmishers from Company B that dealt such destruction on Captain Kelly's combined three companies of the "Rock City Guards" as they charged. The courageous "Guard" crashed into the left of the 78th from the direction of the Wilkinson Pike. The destructive fire poured into their ranks by the Yankee skirmishers, nearly annihilated that proud group. Numerous Tennesseans fell in the lead storm near the cornfield held by Miller's Brigade. Rebel Privates Knight and Newsom were killed in their tracks. Al Hainey pitched forward in his charge, dead before he hit the ground. Bill Irwin and Bill Spain, of Company L, were killed instantly in the charge against Sirwell's regiment. The luck of Private Robert Bond, Company E, Ninth Tennessee, finally ran out. After surviving wounds at Shiloh and Perryville, he was killed in the charge.

Fifty-eight year-old, Private Charles Allen, the oldest member of the 78th, diligently worked his rifle to stop the Rebel approach. But they could not be stopped. Amos Dinger fell clutching an erupting gut wound. He and Elias Dibler disappeared in the wave of charging Confederates; never to be found.

In the one example of literary license in his after-action report, Sirwell reported the Rock City Guard "to be the best troops in the Rebel Army." Sirwell may have over stated the abilities of his adversary, but it should be pointed out that John Miller in his brigade report and Colonel Granville Moody of the Ohio Seventy-Fourth also credited the Rock City Guards with "outstanding efficiency and courage."

Mitchell Cobb and his brother Tom, members of Company L and Sam Watkins of Company H along with their comrades fearlessly followed their unit flag and drove the Federals from their position. The Cobb brothers and these Rock City Guards were part of Major General Benjamin Franklin Cheatham's First Division. As part of Brigadier General George Maney's Third Brigade, the combined First/Twenty-Seventh Tennessee commanded by Colonel Feild earned the grudging respect of the troops from the Buckeye and Keystone states.

Sirwell's officers, and enlisted alike, fell before the incessant Rebel fire; they fell thick and fast. Third Sergeant Bill Murphy, Company I, was wounded and taken prisoner. John Chapman, also of I Company, fell dead near the corn field. Acting Lieutenant Absolom Weaver, Company F, in command of the company, was severely wounded in the side and carried from the field. Mike Sullivan, Sam Slusser, and Jim Penman were carried from the field; their lives swiftly ebbing. Their buddies, Denny Conway, Phil Griffin, Jim Henry and Henry Weaver, had already "passed over the bar." Lieutenant Jim Anchors, of Company E, was overpowered and was taken prisoner. [9]

No matter how bravely they fought or the number of times they drove back the Rebels, the remainder of the brigade began to stagger. Stanley's brigade had entirely quit the field and the Confederates under Stewart and Maney were closing through the cedars on the rear of the brigade. The 37th Indiana, who had furthermore returned to their position at Miller's direction, broke once again and quickly retreated. Miller chose to let them go.

During a battle of this intensity most regimental and company commanders sent their horses to the rear. A mounted officer became too much of an appealing target for the enemy. The older Colonel Granville Moody needed his horse to get around, so he remained in the saddle. He quickly became a prime target. One of a hail of bullets found his right leg and felled the old colonel from his horse. The horse was hit simultaneously by three bullets. With help from his boys Moody staggered to the rear with his 74th Ohio. A shell exploded within the regimental lines and instantly killed three men. In falling back, the right of Colonel Moody's regiment swung against the left of Sirwell's, throwing it into confusion. Sirwell made a desperate effort to rally his men and partially succeeded in getting his regiment reformed.

One after another the Union regiments had pealed back; leaving the 78th with Neibling's stout hearted troopers to stand alone. The Ohio 21st, as gallant a regiment as any that stayed the field, remained positioned behind the Seventy-Eighth on a line in the direction of the Nashville Pike. The Pennsylvanians were still engaged on the left, right and in the front. The 78th and the 21st were the remnants of Miller's Brigade; the boys in butternut were about to seal the fate of these boys in blue. It was apparent to Miller, Sirwell, and Neibling that retreat was inevitable. [10]

Despite the fact that the regiment was soon to be over run, Father Christy stayed his post in the thickest of the battle. The spurned chaplain of the Seventy-Eighth earned the respect of his peers in the living hell along Stones River. The desperate life and death struggle swirled around him. The sound and fury of small arms fire had risen to a constant staccato. The cacophony of the combined roar of exploding cannon, the cries and screams of the wounded and dying men and horses mixed with the increasing haze of smoke, engulfed the battlefield. Amidst this blood and gore and insanity, Richard Christy aided and ministered to the wounded, while big tears rolled down his cheeks. He directed the movement of the wounded northward to the Nashville Pike. It no longer mattered what their religion; they were all his charge. The God of his fathers could not take away this living hell, but he would do whatever was possible to relieve their suffering. Private Bill Hosack, who joined Company G as a private, was a physician. A man of great courage, Dr. Hosack also ignored the battle and feverishly added his expertise to the care of the wounded and dying. [11] Christy and Hosack helped to evacuate all of the troops they could to the rear.

The remnant of Miller's Brigade was virtually surrounded. Comrades and relatives lay wounded and dead on the battlefield. Lack of ammunition now afflicted Sirwell's and Neibling's regiments as it had Sheridan's; forcing their retreat. Rousseau's Division, Timothy Stanley's Brigade, and part of Miller's Brigade had retreated along with part of Cruft's Brigade, originally posted to the left of Miller's Brigade. Wisely, Negley now concluded that it was useless to sacrifice his indomitable troops; he ordered them to cut their way back to the Union army forming on the Nashville Pike.

The profane and drunken many noted, yet courageous Major General Cheatham was now personally directing the advance of his Confederates. The Union forces apparently were crushed and Cheatham smelled victory. In the face of his crumbling lines and the onslaught of Cheatham's soldiers, Thomas bitterly ordered the movement, "Cut your way out!" [12]

The 78th and the 21st had held firmly until the ammunition of the killed and wounded was expended; the time had arrived for a retreat. Sirwell and Neibling knew that their regiments were about to be slaughtered and the cartridge boxes of the troops were virtually empty. The ammunition could only be replenished in the rear of Crittenden's lines, which still remained intact. Slowly, the Union lines fell back to reform in Palmer's rear. The charging Tennesseans passed over the corn field strewn with dead and dying. Many of the Yankees wounded sought shelter in the crevices of the large limestone boulders. Sirwell and Neibling both called out the command, "Fall back! Fall back, we are surrounded!" As the 78th retired, the Ohio 21st waited until they passed then fell in line between the 78th and the advancing Rebels. Colonel Neibling's Ohioans protected the brigade's retreat.

The picture of the fleeing Union right flank leaves little to the imagination. However, Miller's troops and many of the Yankee soldiers remained faithful to their charge. Thompson Gibson leaves the remembrance of one of those courageous Federals. As the 78th moved from the open cornfield into the cedar trees Sergeant Gibson surveyed the carnage they left behind. A lone artillery man was "trying to haul his gun off the field with one horse, the other five having been killed. One wheel of the gun carriage had become fastened between two rocks [in the limestone outcropping], and the brave artillery man was trying with a rail to pry it out." Of the 9 guns belonging to the brigade, 5 were lost and 1 was disabled, but it was not from lack of fight or courage. Of the 156 horses used by the artillery, 52 were killed and 18 wounded. "When [the regiment] entered the cedar woods, looking backward on the open [corn]field, there seemed to be nearly a regiment of [the] division left on the field killed and wounded."

The cedars provided a short-lived false sense of security. The hot lead cutting through the trees proved just as deadly. During their retreat Miller's regiments had to stop frequently and charge the Rebels between them and the Federal lines. The fighting literally surrounded them. They fought on all sides. Essentially, as the brigade fell back towards the north, they had to attack in a north and south direction, and continue to defend their flanks. At times the enemy lines became intermingled and they fought hand to hand.

The Confederates poured a destructive fire into Miller's column moving back through the forest. In all likelihood, the Confederates could have laid down a heavier fire screen, but they were having problems with their rifles. A number of Enfield rifles became so fouled that the balls had to be hammered down the barrel. This problem caused a much slower fire.

First Lieutenant L.D. Hinkley of the Tenth Wisconsin claimed that the Union troops caused more problems for the retreating Federals. Unaware that the troops pouring back through the cedars were Yanks, a few companies opened a "hesitating" fire on their own. With Hinkley's help the friendly fire ceased and along with Miller's soldiers they returned as much fire power that they could muster, aimed at the enemy. Despite the killing fire and confusion the men of Miller's brigade did not run.

Along with some original parts of Miller's brigade, other regiments now came to the aid of their fellow Union brethren. The Nineteenth Illinois and the "Twenty-Onesters" fixed bayonets and cleared the rearward path. The 10th Wisconsin and the 38th Indiana, also Benjamin Scribner's Brigade, took more pressure off of Miller's soldiers by wheeling into position to repulse the pursuing Rebels. But the Southerners pushed on, gaining hard fought for real estate, by the yard. The Western troops assured their retreating comrades that they could stem the Rebel tide. In all probability they may have stopped the Confederate advance, if they had only to contend with a frontal assault. However, the Western soldiers were attacked on three fronts and after twenty minutes fell back.

The victorious boys in gray wanted to continue their charge, but at this point it became impossible to advance further. The mere fact of moving through the dense thickets began to disrupt the integrity of their lines. A number of over exuberant Rebels were actually taken prisoner. And the Federal cannon that had been assembled on the Nashville Pike now opened a destructive fire upon them. One shot took off the head of a Confederate. The head with its hat still on landed in a tree. The exhausted gray line halted and began to reform. The pressure on Miller's brigade subsided. Of the retreat from the Wilkinson Pike to the railroad, John Miller proudly proclaimed in his after-action report, "My men did not run, but marched to the pike, carrying many of our wounded." [13]

The valiant stand by Sheridan's and Negley's soldiers undoubtedly saved Rosey's army that day. By ferociously maintaining their position as long as humanly possibly, they afforded Rosecrans and Thomas precious time to redeploy their battle lines and artillery to more effectively stave off the Confederate assault. If Miller's Brigade held for only thirty minutes, the dogged determination was worth the effort compared to the Rebels grit. Lt. Willis Nugent in a letter to his mother states that the regiment was engaged at 9:00 a.m. and fought until 2:00 p.m.

In the after-action reports of Sirwell, Miller, and Moody, they had praised the courage of the First/Twenty-Seventh Tennessee. Their determined adversary also praised the courage and tenacity of the men in Negley's Division and Sheridan's troops. Samuel

Robinson in writing the history of The First Tennessee Infantry for *The Military Annals of Tennessee. Confederate.* in 1886, stated his admiration for the staunch Union soldiers. He stated that the Yankees had stubbornly contested "every inch" of the battlefield on that New Year's Eve day. His proposition supports the conclusion that the time afforded Rosecrans by the desperate struggle of these troops saved the Union army from a fearful slaughter. The combined Confederate First and Twenty-Seventh Tennessee suffered heavy losses in the struggle at Stones River. Feild's combined regiment had eleven men killed and sixty-nine wounded. They also had 39 men taken prisoner. [14]

The Confederate charge now centered on the Union forces forming along the railroad. As their fury fell on the soldiers of John Palmer's division, the exhausted Seventy-Eighth retired to a hill near the Murfreesboro Pike where the weary troops reformed and received a supply of ammunition. A number of the men straggled into the rest area awkwardly limping from fatigue or wounds.

The regiment stacked arms and was permitted to rest for a while. The newly anointed Union Private Jim Champion lay on the ground fighting the pain from a wicked thigh wound. He was within three miles of the place where he was born.

The regiment had twelve killed and many, many more wounded while fighting in the late morning. Included in the roster of mortally wounded was Jimmy Bell, a musician from Company D, acting as a litter bearer. All companies reported missing comrades. Private Johnston McElroy, an ambulance attendant from Company I, was taken prisoner. Over thirty men from the regiment could not be accounted for; it was feared that many of them had also fallen into the Rebels hands. But the time to count noses and rest was short lived. Rosey rallied his troops and moved those troops that had fought during the morning into support positions for his left flank. A detachment from the Seventy-Eighth along with men from other regiments and divisions drove back an attack by the Rebels attempting to pierce through a section of Rosecrans' line that had a gap. A number from the regiment were also placed in support of the Chicago Board of Trade Battery.

From the vantage point on the hill near the railroad there was a good view of the Southern lines and the Federal lines nearby. There was no safe place to rest. Errant musket fire and cannon fire made it uncomfortable, at best. Many regiments had left their belongings in piles near their morning jump-off point. One regiment had piled their knapsacks near the position where the 10th Wisconsin rested. Lieutenant Hinkley could see a demoralized Union straggler hurriedly take refuge in the pile. A shell hit the pile directly scattering knapsacks in every direction. The soldier "was either stunned or killed" by the shock.

Sirwell soon received an order to advance his whole regiment and occupy a position on the right of the Nashville Pike as a reserve for Brigadier General Milo Hascall's Brigade of Crittenden's Corps. Rosecrans reined in his heaving mount and personally placed the 78th and the Twenty-First Ohio in this support position. At this juncture George Thomas again ordered that a terrific cannonade be opened on the Confederate lines. The boys of the regiment watched the spectacular scene as the cannon fire cut down the courageous, charging Rebels. Fire from the muzzle blasts, burning powder residue, and burning lint made the scene more dramatic by igniting fires in the cotton fields that eventually caught the fences on fire. [15]

HELL'S HALF ACRE

In the final afternoon hours of the day, Rosecrans' broken and beleaguered army prepared for the renewed assaults by Bragg's forces. The Union right and center had been forced back at right angles with the position they had held at dawn. The Confederate left had swung around to face the new position. Rosey issued orders reforming his scattered troops and shifted his artillery. After a brief lull the battle reopened. Bragg had still not blocked the road leading back to Nashville. He wanted to cut off the Union forces and crush them. Once again the grape shot and shell tore through the ranks of young men in blue and butternut.

Rosey's army was now in a formation similar to that of a wedge that straddled the Nashville Pike and Railroad; aimed at the Confederate lines. At the jointure of the "flying wedge" Colonel William Hazen's troops held the angle that anchored Rosecrans' army in dense woods known as the Round Forest. The wings of the wedge pointed roughly northwest to Nashville. Hazen's boys had maintained their position all morning, but General Polk now ordered an all out attack on that position. George Thomas had been moving batteries into defensive positions since noon and now he moved a number of cannon to support Hazen. Although the Rebels had routed the army easily during the morning fighting, most of Rosey's army was now relatively secure within the protection and fire power of the formation. They were also moved into position to support Hazen.

Old Rosey rode anxiously from one part of the battlefield to bolster Hazen; his faithful staff rode bravely with their leader. Rosecrans encouraged his troops and rallied his lines. He was the picture of the fearless, determined commander inspiring his army. With blood dripping from his cheek, he spurred his mount across the muddy, carnage-ridden battlefield. His light blue army cloak flapped furiously as he galloped through his lines followed by his loyal staff. Actually, the General had not been wounded as rumored or as it appeared. While riding through the storm of shot and shell, Garesché's big black mount had been shot in the nose. When the horse shook his head at the stinging pain, he splashed blood on Garesché and Rosecrans.

Rosecrans courageously ignored the shot and shell surrounding him. He dangerously exposed himself and his staff to the deadly enemy fire as he raced across the battlefield. Without warning, a ball thrown from a mile away by an Alabama battery blew off the head of Rosey's beloved chief-of-staff, Julius Garesché. The same shell killed one of his three orderly sergeants and a horse. Rosey was hit by the blood and tissue from his friend's exploding head, but he had no time to stop and change his blood bespattered cloak or to mourn a friend. The life of his army was at stake. He spurred his horse on; two more orderlies were killed in his wake. Unlike Bragg, who had not been seen on the battlefield by his officers all day, Rosecrans was everywhere cheering, chiding, and encouraging his men to hold fast.

Captain Bickham credits Rosey's ability to traverse the field swiftly to his high-spirited, war horse, Boney. Bickham claimed that Rosecrans' gray charger did not have the stamina for the day's work.[1] The picture of General Rosecrans, unlit cigar stump clamped in his teeth, charging across the battlefield on the magnificent, huge bay betwixt shot and shell, with his cloak flapping in the wind equals the picture of James Thomas Brudenell, Earl of Cardigan, charging with his Light Brigade through the "valley of

death" at Balaclava. Irrespective of his veiled reputation in history, on the last day of
1862, William Starke Rosecrans personal courage and attention to detail within the vortex
of a spectacular battle saved the Union army and strengthened its resolve.

From his headquarters, Braxton Bragg also reset his lines for his assault and called
for fresh soldiers. Breckenridge with a contingent of about seven thousand troops did not
answer Bragg's call for nearly three hours. Mistakenly, poor reconnaissance caused
Breckenridge to assume that gray-bearded Van Cleve's force of Crittenden's troops were
still in his front. Bragg would later report that Breckenridge's tardiness was the result of
being drunk. Whatever the truth, the Confederates would attack initially without this
small, but significant advantage.

Two mid-day assaults failed to carry the Union position in the Round Forest north of
the crossroads of the Nashville Pike and Nashville Railroad. The first attack began
slowly, but eventually became a full blown, Rebel-yell charge.   James Chalmers'
stouthearted Mississippi lads would tilt their shoulders to the storm of shot and shell and
attack. The Federal musket fire and cannon answered the charge by tearing ghastly holes
through the front ranks of the Southrons. The Rebels fell back, reformed and charged
again. Chalmers was wounded, and carried from the field. Dozens of young men leading
their regiments with the flag of Dixie fell in a hail of bullets. A regiment of Tennessee
boys captured two batteries, but they too could not pierce the Union line.

The second attack by the Confederates on the Round Forest was executed by General
Dan Donelson's brigade. Like their brothers before them, they marched into destruction.
Captain D.C. Spurlock, a native of the area who had visited his parents in the pre-dawn
hours of the day, was killed in the charge. Colonel John Savage accused Donelson of
leading his Tennessee boys to certain death. His brother, acting Lieutenant Colonel L.N.
Savage, fell with his comrades in the failed attack.

General Breckenridge's men arrived and made the last charge. Although Bragg would
blame Breckenridge for his tardiness in answering the call for support, General Bragg
also sent out and withdrew conflicting orders. As the day drew to an end, the brigades of
Adams, Jackson, Preston, and Palmer hurled themselves against the Federal formation
and failed.   General Polk's decision and General Bragg's sufferance in feeding
Breckenridge's brigades piecemeal into the attack had a lot to do with its failure.

The fighting in the Round Forest or "Hell's Half Acre" gave the vantage point to the
Union troops and their cannon. None of Bragg's forces or Breckenridge's valiant fellows,
who finally answered the call, could break through Rosecrans' determined lines or those
merciless, damn guns. [2]

"THIS ARMY DOES NOT RETREAT"

"The sun sank slowly to the west and the blaze of the guns showed red in the darkening air-an occasional shell rose like a shooting star above the woods-but the flashes grew less frequent-the rattle of the musketry and the roar of the cannon sank into silence, and tired men munched their crackers in the gloom of the evening, or dropped asleep blanketless on the frosty ground, uncertain of the results of the struggle of the day, and uncertain of the prospects of the near tomorrow." [1]

The darkness that had mercifully fallen brought down the curtain to the day's death and mayhem. Sirwell's boys lay near the knoll of a hill until about ten at night, when they were withdrawn to the foot of the hill for the purpose of kindling fires and bedding down till morning. Despite a warning from the commanding general himself the boys from the Twenty-First Ohio joined their comrades in building fires. [2]

For nearly eleven hours, the armies of North and South contested the field at Stones River. Bragg's men had clearly won the day. The right wing and center of Rosecrans' army were virtually folded back against its left. The Confederates had captured numerous prisoners, small arms, and cannon. Rosecrans' army had sustained extreme casualties. The blood of thousands seeped into the Tennessee fields. To many of the boys in blue, it was doubtful that they could fight another day. It would seem that Braxton Bragg had completely accomplished his goal. The Union forces were in a terrible state. However, the two prizes, the Nashville turnpike and railroad had eluded Bragg's grasp. When he wired his victory message to Richmond, he was well aware that his nose had also been severely bloodied.

The citizens of Nashville also celebrated the victory. The view of the horde of stragglers and wagons, many loaded with wounded, pouring back into the city gave rise to the news of Rosecrans' total defeat. Many inhabitants of Nashville went out into the streets and mounted their roof tops to cheer for the Confederate victory.

Although victory appeared in the grasp of Braxton Bragg, the issue was not settled in Rosey's mind. Both generals had sustained heavy losses: Bragg in his assault and Rosecrans in his defense. Colonel Urquhart of Bragg's staff wrote, "A bitter cold night was now on us. We were masters of the field. The sheen of a bright moon revealed the sad carnage of the day, and the horrors of war became vividly distinct." [3]

New Year's Eve on the Stones River battlefield, was cold and disagreeable. It snowed off and on during the night. No words could describe the terrible agony of the night. Many of the men and boys from little towns and villages like Kittanning and Murfreesboro lay mangled and dead among the rocks and trees along Stones River. Between the picket lines of the two armies lay hundreds of wounded men, away from home and friends, and with no one to minister to them as they passed through the Valley of the Shadow of Death in the cold, rain and darkness. They moaned and cried out for help. There were those with arms and legs torn, shattered, and shredded by shot and shell. There were those with jaws and faces blown away. Many had sustained fatal gut wounds. They slowly bled to death or were frozen into their final rest by the bitter cold. Chaplains, musicians, and comrades moved silently through the darkness searching for friends or comrades-in-arms in need of help. At the homes and cabins of the area that had been turned into field hospitals, piles of legs and arms mounted. Surgeons and hospital stewards worked tirelessly over their dying charges. Doctors Tom Blakeley and Bill McCullough worked over many of their friends and sons of friends. The maimed and torn flesh only became impersonal with the mounting number of casualties.

The waning hours of the old year were in reality to many a brave young soldier, North or South, their final hours at center stage. J.T. Gibson said, "Whether we look on the Union soldier or on the Confederate, the scene was unspeakably sad." The *Daily Richmond Examiner* reported that on New Year's Eve "Upon the battle field lay thousands of the enemy's dead and wounded, who froze stiff, presenting a ghastly scene by moonlight." [4] While celebrations of the coming new year occurred across the land, once young revelers now slept in eternal rest.

As his army struggled to regroup and care for itself, Rosecrans was meeting with his officers to determine the future of his army. The impulsive, decisive commander now wished for the consul of his general officers. Rosecrans' Corps commanders, their division officers, Eben Swift, Chief Surgeon General David Stanley and several staff officers assembled at General McCook's headquarters, a dismal little cabin on the battlefield. Crittenden, McCook and Thomas were polled on the direction the army should take. Whatever answers were given to the question it would seem that McCook and Stanley postured themselves for retreat, while Crittenden and Thomas opted for standing their ground.

Many biographers of George Thomas credit him with the steadfast reply, "This army does not retreat." John Lee Yaryan, who went to the meeting with General Wood, related that General Thomas responded to Rosecrans' question with his usual resolute and imposing demeanor. A compendium of personal accounts of the incident in *Rock of Chickamauga* by Freeman Cleaves is melodramatic to say the least: "Without a word of reply, Thomas slowly rose to his feet, buttoned his greatcoat from bottom to top, faced his comrades and stood there, a statue of courage chiseled out of black marble of midnight, by the firelight, and said, 'Gentlemen, I know of no better place to die than right here.' and walked out of the room into the dripping night." [5]

Irrespective of the account, William Rosecrans with a small entourage, rode his lines in the cold darkness to assess his options. He rode all the way to Overall's Creek. A number of torches seen by Rosecrans and his cadre were incorrectly presumed to be Confederates gaining the rear of the present Union lines. It was not until dawn that Rosecrans learned the torches had belonged to the Federal cavalry. Supposedly these fires helped sway his opinion to make a stand here or die. Nevertheless, he prepared for the next day.

The right side of the Union line was weak; Rosecrans drew his troops from the hard fought position in the Round Forest back into the V. He re-positioned his guns for maximum effect. Finally, Rosey once again drew on his ploy for signaling reinforced lines. He had numbers of men take positions on the right flank and boom out commands of company, regimental and division officers. These same men built fires to mimic the camps of their fabricated commands. Despite his courage and resolve, Rosey, as any competent commander, would practically consider the option of retreat, but in the end he made the ultimate decision to stand and fight. [6] General Crittenden stated that upon his return to the gathering of commanders Rosey announced, "...[return] to [your] commands and prepare to fight or die." [7]

NEW YEAR'S DAY, 1863

A comparative lull had settled over the battlefield. Battle weary soldiers in their respective companies on both sides of Stones River were regrouping on their own. J.E. Robuck of the 29th Mississippi told in his reminiscences that, "A temporary armistice was gotten up...to bury the dead, and to further care for the more seriously wounded. A few Federal surgeons had crossed the line under a flag of truce...to attend their wounded, who had been brought to our field hospital. The weather was bitter cold that morning. The dead on the field...were actually frozen." The wounded lay amidst the thick cedar trees, in the crevices of the limestone out-croppings, and upon the field. They cried out for help and mercy and death. [1]

J.T. Gibson of the 78th recorded his memories concerning the first day of 1863: "New Year's Day dawned clear and crisp. We expected an attack by the enemy in the early morning, but as the day grew older and only an occasional shot was heard from some battery, we began to suspect that Bragg's Army had suffered as severely as our own and that it was in no condition to attack. This conviction was very satisfactory, and the general sentiment of the men seemed to be in favor of letting well enough alone."

"During the day, stragglers from the ranks came in rapidly, and the regiments were filled up. Rations were distributed as far as possible, but in many cases, the commissary trains had been either delayed or destroyed by the enemy cavalry." In point of fact, the cavalry attacks were so threatening that troops heading for the battle had to remain behind and protect the Union supply lines. Colonel Moses Walker's Brigade, which had originally been the only part of General Fry's Division to actively enter the campaign under General Thomas, never reached the battlefield until January 1st. The brigade arrived at the jump-off point for the battle at Stewartsboro, but was ordered to fall back and attack the Rebel cavalry attempting to cut Rosecrans' supply lines to Nashville. Walker's Brigade had actually marched back as far as Nashville to engage the enemy. Walker's Brigade was not the only unit used in this fashion; various brigades and regiments pulled the same duty. It was imperative for Rosey to keep his supply lines open.

The road from Murfreesboro to Nashville was chaotic to say the least. The transfer of the wounded grew as the casualties were brought in. Unfortunately, teamsters, cowards, and slackers joined the procession back to the state capital. Wheeler and Wharton's Cavalry continued to harass wagons heading for Stones River, even to the point of capturing more supply trains near Lavergne. Nevertheless, some supplies were finding their way to the hungry soldiers. Food in any form was relished. "Flour was distributed instead of crackers. The facilities for turning flour into bread or anything edible were exceedingly primitive. Throughout the day men in the 78th mixed flour, water and salt to make dough. The "dough-boys" laid the dough on hot stones in the fire and made bread." [2]

Food had become a rare and precious commodity in both armies. Captain S.F. Horrall in the History of the Forty-Second Indiana Volunteer Infantry wrote that as his brigade lay in reserve "...late in the day an officer's horse was killed by a cannon ball..., and before the blood had ceased to circulate in the animal, so hungry were the boys that they cut steaks from the dead animal and broiled them for supper." [3]

There would be no champagne opened to celebrate the new year. There would be no oysters or steaming beef and pork roasts. The aroma of freshly baked bread would not permeate the trenches at Stones River. No candied yams basted in brown sugar or iced cakes and fruit pies would fill the bellies of holiday revelers. Meager catches of poor foodstuff would have to suffice for a majority of the volunteer soldiers waiting in the freezing weather.

The intense cold made warm blankets and clothing extremely valued items. There were a number of Union corpses stripped of their clothing. William Bickham wrote that after General Sill's death, "His body was plundered by the enemy." This act may seem somewhat barbaric, but the Southern boys needed clothing to fight off the frigid temperatures. James Mitchell of the 34th Alabama wrote, "There was a great deal of pilfering performed on the dead bodies of the Yankees by our men. Some of them were left as naked as they were born." General Alexander Stewart did ask that an order be issued forbidding this practice, but it is doubtful that it was followed, since General Stewart mentioned in his after action report that the Confederates even stripped their own brothers. [4]

As with the diary of Colonel John Beatty, everyone waited for the other shoe to drop; who would fight, who would stand. "At dawn we are all in line, expecting every moment the re-commencement of the fearful struggle. Occasionally, a battery engages a battery opposite, and the skirmishers keep up a continual roar of small arms. Here and there little parties are engaged in burying the dead which lie thick around us. Generals Rosecrans and Thomas are riding over the field, now halting to speak words of encouragement to the troops, then going to inspect portions of the line. A little before sundown all hell seems to break loose again, and for about an hour the thunder of the artillery and volleys of musketry are deafening. The darkness deepens; the weather is raw and disagreeable." [5]

Murfreesboro was a scene of extreme chaos. Guarded prisoners filled yards and fenced areas. Some were paroled; some sent South. Churches and homes had been turned into hospitals. The wounded and dying were everywhere. Surgeons cut away the torn and mangled parts of bodies. Limbs began to pile up outside makeshift hospitals. Bragg's "victory" had been costly. The Confederate did as best they could under the circumstances. One young Rebel, Jim Ellis of the 4th Arkansas heard a surgeon pronounce that Ellis' arm was too bad and would be amputated in the morning. When things quieted down, Ellis concealed his wound, left the hospital, and boarded the first train south. He was going home.

Sanford Williams of the Twenty-Fourth Wisconsin could not go home. He was a wounded captive of the Rebel forces. His recollections are vivid in their description of the appalling fate of many young men, both North and South. After being wounded in the leg on December 31st, he is picked up and taken to a Southern "hospital." "I am soon picked up, and carried in and laid on the floor of an old log house, which is covered with wounded and dying. The floor is swimming with slimy blood...The roar of the artillery makes the ground shake, and the moans of the wounded mix with other sounds. It is awful; and they die fast...Hundreds lie outside and have no shelter. I wonder if they know at home how we are spending New Year's Day in our own gore?"

The small town of Murfreesboro staggered under the abhorrent sights, sounds and confusion of battle. Prisoners seemed to be everywhere. Ambulances carried the dead, dying and wounded to the countless makeshift hospitals. Once peaceful churches were filled with the moans and screams of the wounded and dying. Instead of preachers ministering to their flock, surgeons stood in pools of blood amputating arms and legs. General Joshua Sill's body lay lifeless in the courthouse. The corpse of Lieutenant Frank Crosthwait, 20th Tennessee, lay on a nearby counter.

There were probably many young men in the Union army who, after being in battle and seeing its gruesome aftermath, waited for Old Rosey to begin his retreat to Nashville. Braxton Bragg had assumed the same train of thought, but, contrary to his beliefs, the blue army still clung desperately to its position. Good men high and low had enough of the cold, rain, blood and death. Alexander Stevenson and Henry Cist tell of an incident that purportedly took place during the early morning hours of 1863. A division commander discussed, with one of his brigade commanders, the possibility of deserting their Union comrades on New Year's Day and heading back to Nashville. The appalled brigade commander proposed to a peer the possibility of arresting their leader and taking him to Rosecrans. Word of his subaltern's feelings evidently passed back to the cowardly chieftain and nothing came of his plan. [6]

Colonel John Franklin Miller
Ronald S. Gancas, Collection

FIRST TO CROSS

First light broke on a dismal, dank and cold second day of 1863. Bragg ordered some of his batteries to open on Rosecrans' lines and skirmishers were sent out. The Federals were still in their positions. Much to the Southern commander's dismay, it was apparent that Rosecrans would stand and fight. The Union lines were well placed, supported, and entrenched. Bragg realized that only a determined assault could dislodge Rosecrans' army. He searched his lines and the fields around them. He needed a suitable place to resume the attack. Only Crittenden's Corps on Rosecrans' extreme left had not been tested to any degree. Bragg directed his trusted aide, Colonel George Brent, and the Captain Felix Robertson, a battery commander in Wither's division, generally scorned by the common troops, to find a good position to place artillery on the east bank of the river whereby the Federal lines could be enfiladed.

The two Confederates rode forward of Breckenridge's lines only to discover that Colonel Samuel Price, commander of Van Cleve's Third Brigade held the position best suited for their purpose. The hill was critical; from it either army could enfilade the other. It had to be taken, and despite Bragg's personal dislike of General Breckenridge, his was the only division available for the task. Bragg sent orders to the Kentuckian directing him to concentrate his entire command opposite Sam Beatty, now commanding Van Cleve's Third Division of Crittenden's Left Wing.

In the early afternoon, John Breckenridge appeared, as ordered, at General Bragg's headquarters along the Nashville Pike. He was to receive final direction for the assault. He had just reconnoitered his lines and the enemy's position. Breckenridge, with his son, Cabell, Colonel Theodore O'Hara, Breckenridge's acting Adjutant-General, and Major James Wilson, had ridden along the river bank. For a short time Breckenridge's party was joined by Generals Polk and Hardee; however, they were recalled to their own headquarters before being advised of the situation.

Back at Bragg's headquarters, Breckenridge alone, spent a great deal of time trying to dissuade Bragg from forcing him to make an attack that he felt was destined to fail. He discussed the circumstances as he saw them and from the viewpoint of the damning intelligence his men had gathered. He appealed to Bragg's sense of ethics and to the tactical realities of the terrain that the Kentuckians would be forced to attack. He drew a line in the dirt with a stick pointing out the high ground on the opposing bank of Stones River from which the Union could slaughter his boys with cannon fire. His common sense approach was to no avail. Apparently, without consultation of his corps commanders, Bragg ordered Breckenridge to proceed.

In light of the intelligence that Bragg had received from his cavalry along with Breckenridge's observations, it is puzzling as to why Bragg insisted upon the attack. The Federals were not retreating, and to Bragg's knowledge, the phony camps that Rosey had ordered were real reinforcements. In addition to these facts, Bragg rode to Polk's headquarters after Breckenridge left him. Bragg had ridden there not to see Polk, but to see the position he wished taken. Realizing Bragg's plan, Polk advised against the attack, but Bragg remained adamant. He asked for no consul from Hardee and accepted none from Polk or his attacking field commander. The only conclusion was that the Union left flank had not been tried. Once again Bragg would become his own worst enemy.

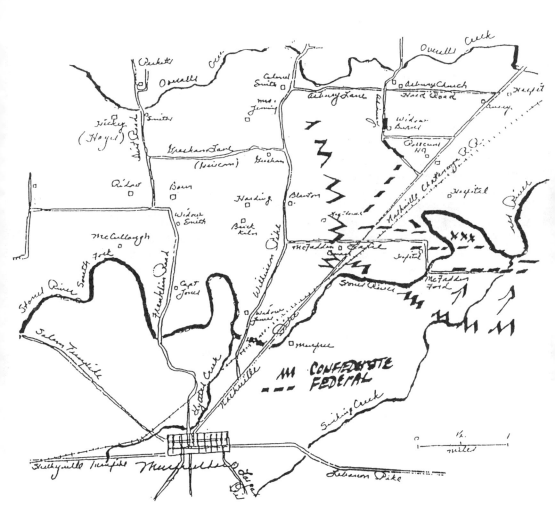

Battlefield positions on January 2, 1863

Breckenridge galloped unhappily back to his command. He made sure to confirm with General Preston that he thought the attack was utter folly. Nonetheless, he would do his duty. He added, "[General Preston]...If it [the attack] should result in disaster, and I be among the slain...I want you... [to] tell the people...[I] tried to prevent it." Brigadier General Roger Hanson, who would fall mortally wounded in the attack, was outraged at the prospect of the suicidal attack and wanted to go to Bragg's headquarters and kill him. Breckenridge and Preston persuaded him not to carry out his threat. [1]

From first light it appeared that the Confederates were ready to attack, but where? At 8:00 A.M. five Confederate batteries that General Polk had quietly moved into position below the Round Forest opened on the center of the Union lines. For a time it appeared that Bragg was once again directing his attack against the Nashville Turnpike in the hope of capturing the Nashville and Chattanooga Railroad salient. He then made a concerted demonstration on McCook's Wing. Rosecrans rode the lines puzzling over his adversary's next move. The Union command may have been attempting to determine the point of Bragg's attack, but General Crittenden's soldiers at the far left of the army felt they knew exactly where the impact would be.

Sam Beatty and his brigade commanders watched the flurry of activity within the Confederate lines. General Beatty suspected trouble long before any Confederate action and requested reinforcements. Brigadier General John Palmer, commander of Crittenden's Second Division, responded to Beatty's request. By noon, Rebel skirmishers opened on the Union position. General Beatty retaliated and at 1:00 P.M. Confederate artillery joined in with a barrage that continued intermittently for two hours.

Crittenden was keeping Rosecrans apprised of the ominous developments. Rosey would not take the Confederate actions and the sounds of a portending battle lightly as he had done with his Right Wing on the morning of the Thirty-First. He moved at once to shore up his left. In response to Palmer's request, he pulled Negley's division from the far right and placed it in reserve behind Beatty's Division at McFadden's Ford. With the increased activity in the front of his Left Wing, Rosecrans rode to that part of his line and directed the placement of cannon.

William Sirwell's regiment, along with the division, was ordered to support Crittenden's troops. During the morning, the 78th again took up a position as reserve to General Hascall, where they remained until approximately 1:00 P.M., when they were ordered to support General Crittenden. The boys of the 78th were still trying to turn flour, water and salt into something edible when they were again ordered from their position. Sirwell marched the remnants of his regiment across the Nashville Pike and rail tracks northward towards McFadden's Ford. It took almost an hour to cover the short distance to their new position in the left rear of a battery in a cornfield, posting themselves on a bluff overlooking the ford. Stones River flowed northward, but in front of the regiment at the bend the river was moving easterly. The regiment, along with the other Union reinforcements and support, was virtually concealed from Breckenridge's troops. It was 3:00 P.M. [2]

Jacob Adams of the Twenty-Onesters noted the movement of Negley's division in his diary. "On Friday, about 3 P.M. just after we had drawn part of a ration of flour and had mixed it into a dough preparatory to throwing it into the hot ashes to bake, we got orders

CONFEDERATE OPPONENTS OF THE SEVENTY-EIGHTH
JANUARY 2
ARMY OF THE TENNESSEE AT STONES RIVER
General Braxton Bragg
BRAGG'S SECOND CORPS
Lieutenant General William J. Hardee
HARDEE'S FIRST DIVISION
Major General John C. Breckenridge
BRECKENRIDGE'S SECOND BRIGADE
Colonel Joseph B. Palmer [w]
Brigadier General Gideon J. Pillow
18th Tennessee Colonel Joseph B. Palmer [w]
Lieutenant Colonel W.R. Butler
26th Tennessee, Colonel John M. Lillard
28th Tennessee, Colonel P.D. Cunningham [k]
32nd Tennessee, Colonel Ed. C. Cook
45th Tennessee, Colonel A. Searcy
ARTILLERY
S.A. Moses Georgia Battery   Lieutenant R.W. Anderson
BRECKENRIDGE'S THIRD BRIGADE
Brigadier General William Preston
1st Florida, 3rd Florida
Colonel William Miller [w]
4th Florida, Colonel William L.L. Bowen
60th North Carolina, Colonel Joseph A. McDowell
20th Tennessee Colonel T.B. Smith [w]
Lieutenant Colonel F.M. Lavender [w]
Major F. Claybrooke
ARTILLERY
Wright's Tennessee Battery
Captain E.E. Wright [k]
Lieutenant John W. Mebane

Official Record

to fall in and double-quick to the front. Here we took position to the left of our battle line with our brigade and the rest of our division on the west bank of Stones River, north of the railroad and pike, on the bend of the river below the ford." The Ohio 21st was at the far left of Miller's brigade. [3]

In total, two of General Negley's brigades, Miller's and Stanley's, along with Cruft's brigade from Palmer's division and Morton's Pioneer Brigade, plus eighteen guns were closely supporting Sam Beatty's Division from the east side of the railway, near the river's fords. [4]

The general attack on the Union would commence at 4:00 P.M. at the sound of a signal cannon. In Battles and Leaders, Colonel David Urquhart, a member of Bragg's staff, states that the assault by Breckenridge's troops began at 4:00 P.M. Bragg wanted very little daylight remaining after he carried the high ground on the east side of the river. Darkness at approximately 5 o'clock would halt the battle and give the Confederates an opportunity to entrench for the night. [5] During December in Rutherford County, the light of day begins to fade by 4:30 P.M.; by 5:00 it is almost dark.

Shortly after 4 o'clock in the afternoon, Beatty's division was assailed by Breckenridge's entire four brigades, strongly supported by artillery under Felix Robertson and cavalry supporting his right flank. Breckenridge hurled his division forward in two lines: the first line commanded by Generals Hanson and Pillow; the second, two hundred yards to the rear, commanded by General Preston and Colonel R.L. Gibson leading General D.W. Adams' Brigade. Roger Hanson boldly led his brigade forward while Pillow sought the safety of a large tree. Breckenridge personally ordered Pillow to move out with his brigade. Breckenridge's brigades, at the given signal, made their appearance and commenced a furious attack on General Beatty's division. [6]

The heavy cannonade that had opened on the left was followed by the Confederate battle cries and a deafening crash of musketry. The Rebel assault was so formidable that Colonel Grider's and Colonel Price's lines gave way. Its place was taken by the reserves composed of Ohio and Kentucky regiments. But Breckenridge's assault broke the remaining Union brigade belonging to Colonel James Fyffe; panic ensued. Beatty withdrew his troops across the river. The men of the Seventy-Eighth once again watched their terror stricken, wide-eyed brothers retreating through their lines to the rear. Many of the confused and frightened Federal troops took cover behind the house and fences of the "late" William Mitchell property. [7]

At McFadden's Ford, the Seventy-Eighth and their brothers in blue had waited patiently for the enemy. The days of rain, sleet and freezing temperatures only made the damp cold along the river more penetrating. The gentlest breeze made it most uncomfortable. Coughing, runny noses, burning nasal passages were the norm. The days of physical discomfort while sleeping on wet and frozen ground were virtually intolerable, but somehow these boys endured extreme hardship with little complaint. Sirwell's regiment anxiously awaited the howling enemy.

The Union troops retreated westward back over Stones River; heavily pressed, Beatty's troops scurried back to safety. The Rebels followed in hot pursuit, despite a deadly fire. General Negley had confronted the Confederates with compact lines of battle. He rode along the lines of his cheering troops. He called out, "Boys, you will now have an opportunity to pay them back for what they did on Wednesday."

Sergeant Welch of the 51st Ohio recorded the events of the retreat by Price's Brigade. "The river where we crossed was sixty feet wide and two feet deep. On the opposite side was a rocky bluff twenty feet high. As we were climbing up this bluff we could hear the enemy's bullets striking the rocks...When we reached the top of the bluff we found that General Negley's division was quietly laying in massed column in a cornfield, ready to move into action." [8]

The boys of the Pennsylvania 78th and the Ohio 21st along with their brothers in battle lay waiting for the enemy. Private Adams of the Twenty-First notes that Negley was not present and John Miller had taken command of the division, "Negley being in the rear." Negley left his command and joined Generals Rosecrans, Crittenden, and Palmer on the commanding ridge to the left of his division where Mendenhall had placed his batteries. Colonel Stanley states in his after action report that General Rosecrans, personally, ordered him to support and cover the retreating Federals. Irrespective of the command structure, when the last of Beatty's men had crossed, Colonel Miller within his own report states that he ordered the division to stand and give the enemy a volley. [9]

The Union soldiers supporting Sam Beatty's troops had watched the fight from their vantage point. With the retreat of Union forces the advancing Rebels could be fired upon without causing "friendly casualties." J.T. Gibson watched an Ohio regiment, possibly the 99th, advance, fire a volley and then inexplicably retire. Old Jim Neibling yelled out to his Twenty-Onesters, " Get up boys and give them Thunder." The 78th then advanced in line until they reached a rail fence where, along with their companion regiments, they poured a deadly volley into the Southerners, completely checking the advance of Breckenridge's boys.

From the bluff that dominated the area and overlooked Stones River, Captain John Mendenhall had posted 45 cannon. Along with an additional 12 cannon near the Nashville Pike and rail crossing they now began their slaughter of Bragg's right wing. Mendenhall's batteries opened such a destructive fire on the advancing Confederates that huge gaps were ripped in their lines. The murderous fire that Breckenridge feared was now a reality. In less than an hour, Breckenridge lost nearly one-third of his entire force. The withering, combined musket and cannon fire enfiladed the Rebel lines and literally staggered Bragg's attack. [10]

The rebels recoiled from the terrific, deadly fire storm and began to fall back. Only a few moments had elapsed when the cry passed through the Federal ranks, "They are retreating! They are retreating!" Miller and Sirwell instantly saw an opportunity to cross the river. Miller viewing the action from his war-horse rode to Colonel Joseph Scott of the 19th Illinois and requested that they make a joint charge upon the Rebels. Scott quickly replied in the affirmative. Sirwell pointed his battle sword at the opposite river bank and boomed the "Forward!" command.

Since Negley had not yet rejoined his command, Miller took the initiative and ordered his brigade and the whole division forward. While the men crossed the river, a staff officer reported to Miller that General Palmer had ordered that the men not cross. Palmer was not in Miller's direct line of command and the decision was made to ignore him. Furthermore, it was too late. The courageous Federals were in pursuit of Bragg's boys. Miller decided against ordering his men back; instead, showing a great deal of audacity, he ordered the remainder of his brigade to their support. [11]

Sirwell with no emotion and directly to the point reported in his after action report, "I now ordered my men to advance at a charge bayonet, which they did....My Regiment was the first to cross the river and pursue the retreating enemy, not, however, without being considerably scattered." Colonel Scott of the 19th Illinois saw Sirwell's troops wading the river and as agreed added the weight of his regiment to the charge. Colonel Scott sustained a severe and mortal thigh wound during the action. The bold Pennsylvanians had taken the lead and were closely followed by the 19th Illinois, 18th, 21st and 74th Ohio, the 11th Michigan, and the 37th Indiana. The water was ice-cold; it was almost waist high in some places. Brigade, regiment and company formations quickly ceased to exist; there was virtually no consistent battle line. But the anxious, shouting troops followed en masse. They forded the stream and for a time also obeyed Sirwell's commands. Color Bearer, Sergeant George Hamm, Company C of the 78th, who stoutly and bravely carried the colors through the numerous fights around Stones River, was once again at the front of the regiment. The men of the different regiments that had become intermixed held a tolerable line on the flag of Sirwell's 78th. Hamm miraculously remained unscathed, but the flag was riddled with numerous bullet holes and also a tear from a piece of shell. [12]

Bragg's weary soldiers had made a stand on the opposite side of the river in a narrow strip of timber, bounded by a rail fence. At this fence the rebels rallied, and as Miller's and Stanley's men ascended the bank they were greeted by a storm of bullets, which for a moment checked their advance.

Lieutenant Matthew Halstead was leading Company K into the face of the enemy. Urging his men forward with raised sword; he was hit by a rifle ball and killed instantly. Sergeant Bill Smith fell almost at the same time with a mortal head wound. Company K was experiencing severe losses. Privates Hollingsworth, John W. Hutchinson, Altman, Akins, and Mark Bowser fell mortally wounded at the Rebel fire. But the regiment pushed forward. Charge after charge was made, and gallantly repulsed by the Confederates, but the assistance of Negley's reserves proved insurmountable. By the exertions of Stanley and Miller, the division was formed rapidly upon the bank, and with a tremendous shout they charged the rebel lines. Jim Erwin, Company G, Reuben Latshaw, Company E, and Nat Keirn of Company D, all fell dead in the chase. Nathan Keirn had died instantly from a gut wound caused when a bullet pierced his waist belt plate.

The Union troops under Miller's command were charging in on Gideon Pillow's right flank. The surprise charge by Negley's Division threw this portion of Breckenridge's line into confusion. The galling fire from the Federal muskets and cannon raked the Rebel lines. The latter wavered and broke, retreating over the low, wooded ground. Miller's troops followed closely in pursuit. [13]

During this movement Rebel batteries were posted on a rise in the woods near a cornfield in front of the regiment. Colonel Miller ordered Sirwell to charge the battery 150 yards ahead. Closely supported by the 69th Ohio with its new commander, Captain Putnam, the 19th Illinois and various other regiments of the brigade, the Pennsylvania 78th broke the Confederate 26th Tennessee and captured a stand of its colors. Negley's troops also captured three pieces of artillery that were brought off the field in safety. Supposedly, these guns had been originally captured from the English by Andrew

Private Jimmy Thorne
Company A, Pennsylvania Seventy-Eighth
Frank Leslie's Magazine

Jackson's troops at the battle of New Orleans. Private Jimmy Thorne, a boy of sixteen from Tennessee, who had enlisted in Company A only a few weeks before the battle, sat astride a cannon, lovingly patted it and hollered to his company commander, "Here it is Captain!"

The History of Armstrong County states that the 78th also captured the guidon of the 4th Florida - Lieutenant Nugent of the 78th called it a streamer. Although they lost their guidon, the Florida regiment did not lose their colors. Sergeant L.N. Miller of Company H, and two other color bearers were shot down while bravely, and obstinately protecting their flag. The Fourth Florida, at one point, stood alone as their comrades on both flanks "abandoned" them and fell back. Major John Lesley stated that they were the last to leave the field.

Regarding the regimental colors of the 26th Rebel Tennessee, Sirwell writes in his after action report that Private Hughes, of Company B, and Private William J. Davis, of Company I, were most instrumental in the capture of the colors belonging to the 26th Tennessee Regiment. The fifty-six year-old, Davis closed so quickly on the Color Bearer that the young Rebel could not make his escape. When he did try, Davis shot him; another soldier bayoneted the faithful flag bearer and "he sank in a pool of blood." At this time Davis and Hughes advanced together, Davis seizing the flag staff and Hughes the colors. Hughes attempted to tear the flag from the staff, but was prevented from doing so by some members of the regiment. The valued prize was then turned over to Davis; Sirwell ordered the flag to the rear. An officer of the 78th carried the prize to Rosecrans. He rode to the command at break neck speed the Rebel colors fluttering from his hand. "The sight of the Rebel banner had an electric effect upon our men. Almost instantly the soldiers of the whole reserve sprang to their feet and cheered for the Union."

For their acts of bravery, Hughes and the middle-aged, Welshman Davis were both promoted to the rank of sergeant by Sirwell and Hughes was commended by General Rosecrans in his after action report. [14]

It is an interesting sidelight to history that whatever the source of the capture of the flag of the Tennessee regiment, to an extent, the history of the Seventy-Eighth is incorrect regarding the tenacious Twenty-Sixth Tennessee Rebel flag bearer. Color-bearer H.P. Green was struck by a shot; however, history does not record a bayonet wound. Green's comrades did fear that he was mortally wounded and carried him back to a safe place presumably to die. To their surprise they found that the projectile did not enter Green's body. The ball had "struck a daguerreotype of his sweetheart, in the coat-pocket just opposite his heart." [15]

The 26th Tennessee and the 4th Florida both fought in Hardee's (Second) Corps, General Breckenridge's First Division. The 26th Tennessee, commanded by Colonel John Lillard, was part of the Second Brigade commanded by the incompetent, chicken-hearted Brigadier General Gideon Pillow. General Thomas' gross hyperbole regarding the Twenty-Sixth in his after-action report noted its "complete annihilation." Lillard's Regiment had sustained casualties, but he left the field with 300 combatants.

The 4th Florida, commanded by Colonel W.L.L. Bowen and Major John T. Lesley, fought in the Third Brigade commanded by Brigadier General William Preston. It was as the Union forces pushed doggedly forward that Breckenridge, who had arrived at the front and realized the plight of his division, ordered Preston to begin his retreat back to Murfreesboro. [16]

The Rebels continued to run for their lives in a hailstorm of bullets. But for many the fatigue of battle left them with only the strength to stagger or make back to their lines in a "slow walk." The Federals had taken possession of the terrain so quickly that many of the wounded still lay upon the battlefield. Their dead and wounded littered the ground from the river and beyond a dense forest reaching to Murfreesboro. The 78th did not follow into this forest. After reaching the ridge running parallel with the river before turning north, they began to slow. It was about sunset. Miller ordered his troops to halt and hold the ground gained until reinforcements arrived. The whole Rebel line had fallen back leaving a large number of arms, cannon and men behind. The Union lines were greatly broken, and although the men were still recklessly enthusiastic, they were in no condition to either charge the enemy or resist a concerted counterattack.

The chase was becoming disorganized and was beginning to lag. Miller's soldiers were in total disorder and running out of ammunition. Sirwell rallied his men on a hill lately occupied by the enemy. He formed up his officers and reformed the regiment by the side of the river. A quick head count showed that along with Lieutenant Halstead of Company K, four privates had been killed, and there were a number of walking wounded. Union troops commanded by General Davis, Colonel Hazen, and Colonel Grose relieved their weary brethren. Jefferson Davis, the ranking officer on the east bank of the river, took command of the Federal forces. Stanley's Brigade, Miller's Brigade, and the 78th were ordered back across the river. Bill Sirwell reformed his regiment on the west side of the river into their original position. The cold, hungry, and tired, but victorious Pennsylvanians bivouacked for the night. [17]

One of James Negley's detractors claimed the General had earned his second star for Miller's heroic actions. When Miller took responsibility for the division and issued orders for it, he reportedly had become disgusted with Negley. [18] Contrary to this, Captain James St. Clair Morton, commander of the Pioneer Brigade, in his after action reports, indicates he had contact with Negley in a request for support of his division across the river. Captain John Mendenhall, although not noting a direct meeting with Negley, writes that nine of Negley's guns were mounted with the 45 guns overlooking McFadden's Ford. In The Nineteenth Illinois, Negley is credited with giving the order to charge across the river. An exact quote of Negley's, "Who'll save the Left?" appears in two places. However, in a third place in the same history Rosecrans is reported to have shouted the same question, "Who'll save the Left?" The presentation style of Reverend Gibson in the regimental history, shows that he would not give false information. He would say nothing at all before he would criticize one of his own. He did indicate that Negley was riding the line rallying his troops. And if Gibson is to be believed, he also states that neither Sirwell, Miller nor Negley gave the order to pursue the Confederates across the river. He claims the forward movement was spontaneous.[19] In all probability Negley was with Rosecrans at various times, and not continuously with his division.

In regard to the capture of the artillery and flag of the Twenty-Sixth Tennessee, it would seem that various regiments participated in the action. The men of the Seventy-Eighth definitely captured the Rebel flag. But the Pennsylvanians, along with Colonel Miller's other regiments and some of Stanley's regiments, combined an attack that broke the Rebel Tennessee and led to a concerted capture of the enemy guns. The 19th Illinois definitely got their hands on one piece. John Mendenhall reported that they brought a gun back across the river to replace one that had been knocked out of service. [20]

The Confederates were completely routed. Miller's decision to attack, Stanley's courage to follow, and the loyalty and courage of the soldiers along with Mendenhall's guns broke the back of the valiant Confederate army. Rosecrans' defensive position of the morning became offensive under Miller's leadership. The courage and fortitude of William Sirwell and his gallant soldiers began the wave of Union troops that enlarged and crested over their stout- hearted adversaries. It was a victory.

The Union troops exalted in that victory. Long after dark, in response to traded volleys by enemy pickets, the Federal soldiers would break into cheers that proceeded along the whole line. Bragg no longer held a commanding position within the battlefield, and the Yankees were closing in upon him. [21]

Darkness now shrouded the battlefield and it was deemed prudent not to advance further or enter the woods at that time. From the cornfields to the river the distance was about one mile, and within that space the evidence of the terrible carnage was visible. The woods resounded with the shrieks and groans of the wounded and dying. [22] After three days, the four thousand acres of gentle rolling Tennessee farm and dairy land had become a bivouac for the wounded and the dead.

> The muffled drum's sad roll shall beat the soldiers last tattoo.
> No more on life's parade shall meet that brave and fallen few.
> The neighing troop, the flashing blade, the bugles stirring blast,
> the charge, the dreadful cannonade, the din and shout are past.
>
> No vision of the morrows strife, the warrior's dread alarms,
> no braying horn, nor screaming fife at dawn shall call to arms.
> On fame's eternal camping ground their silent tents are spread,
> and glory guards with solemn round the bivouac of the dead.

Theodore O'Hara   1847 [23]

ASHES, ASHES! WE ALL FALL DOWN!

Nine days of marching and fighting had come to an end. The strategies and tactics of the commanding generals had disintegrated into children's games. Ring around Old Rosey had left everyone bone tired. The battle weary soldiers now searched for basic needs. As usual, food was a priority, but the boys had a difficult time getting anything substantial to eat. Money could not buy rations, since there were none to be had. Hungry soldiers still cut steaks from the slain horses. General Crittenden, whose wagon could not get to him, unknowingly enjoyed a "first-rate beefsteak." It was not until the morning after his fine meal that the General learned he had eaten horse meat. Among the troops, as much as twenty-five cents was offered for a single hard-tack, if they were available.

Eventually the boys realized they had survived the fighting and slaughter, and they became almost light-hearted. There was cheerful conversation among many of the men. They discussed the battle, the officers and each other, and at times actually broke into song. [1]

Sam Dumm of the 78th wrote home telling of the personal suffering during and after the battle. Dumm described the hardships suffered by the boys of the valley. He related the days with little sleep, sleeping with their rifles and very little food. He spoke of losing virtually all of his personal belongings when the Rebels captured Company K's wagons and knapsacks. Several of the regimental tents had also been lost. Most importantly Dumm lamented the great loss of his needle case. "[Now] I have nothing with which to mend my pants." Private Kipp wrote his mother after the battle, "We lay nine days on the field without blankets and a good many had no overcoats and the weather was wet and cold." [2] He neglected to inform her that he had sustained a leg wound.

The army was suffering, but many of the men and some noted officers found ways to put their sorrow behind them. John Beatty again records in his diary, "In the evening I met Rousseau, McCook and Crittenden. They are imbibing freely. On the way to Rousseau's headquarters, Crittenden sings 'Mary had a little lamb....' "

"General McCook complimented me by saying that my brigade fought well. He should know, for he sat behind it at the commencement of the second assault of the enemy in the cedars, on the first day, but very soon thereafter disappeared."

"At Rousseau's we found a large number of staff and line officers. The demijohn was introduced, and all paid their respects to it. Much merriment prevailed." [3]

On the morning of January 3rd, still positioned on the west side of McFadden's Ford, Sirwell was ordered to prepare for possible new fighting. He detailed men to throw up breast-works, which was speedily done, and placed cannon behind them. The rain had turned the field into a quagmire and mud was "shoe mouth" deep. Regimental quartermasters and commissary personnel took squads of men to secure ammunition and rations. Bunk mates searched for their "pards." Bill Sirwell presided over a small, despondent detail from Company K that buried their heroic commander, Matt Halstead.

About dusk, during a rain storm, the enemy commenced a threatening attack. Thomas threw Beatty's and Spear's Brigades plus the 85th Illinois into the fight. The Rebs were driven from the woods and their entrenchments on his front. The minor engagement became heated for a short time. The artillery the 78th was guarding helped drive them back. With the sudden Confederate pull-back, Sirwell reformed his regiment in a line of battle, and awaited orders.

Little did Sirwell know that Bragg was only testing the Union lines to determine if Rosecrans was still there in force. Bragg found the information he wished. It supported the decision he made at noon to abandon the field. One additional fact added to Bragg's decision, the constant rain. It was causing the water level in the river to rise. The high water could separate commands from the main army leaving them open to slaughter or capture.

The Rebel feint had been driven back and Bill Sirwell's boys rested on their arms, awaiting the next fight. The regiment remained all night in the same position. While the Union troops slept, Bragg's army retreated. By 11:00 P.M. the whole army except for the cavalry was in retreat. The bloodied and weary Southern troops trudged the muddy roads leading to Beech Grove, Shelbyville and Wartrace in a pelting storm. The battered, courageous First Tennessee waded through cold water and a shivering winter rain to begin their twenty-five mile hike to Shelbyville.

Along with the Rebel army, many of the citizens of Murfreesboro and the surrounding area, who celebrated the Confederate victory of the 31st, now fled in confusion with the Southrons. Buggies and wagons of every description laden with hastily gathered belongings hustled out of the Union path.

The citizens of the little town of Murfreesboro left with Bragg's army; knowing that their homes were still standing. This was not the same for the people of the surrounding farms. The stark reality of the inhabitants who populated the Nashville Basin for generations was much sadder. A reporter from The *St. Louis Republican* traveled the thirty miles from Nashville to Murfreesboro on the second of January. He left a description of the area in an article published almost a week after the battle. "What a scene of desolation is now presented the whole distance from Nashville to [Murfreesboro]. But two or three families now live at their homes...Fences are gone, houses are deserted, and a good share of them have been burned, their works smoldering, and their tall shafts of chimneys yet standing. Not a cornfield but has been stripped and trodden down." Juniper Wiggins left the same impression in the *Nashville Union*. "...winter quarters for every encampment looks as if it had once been a miniature village...[the houses and tents all gone], leaving the chimneys still there...Such a forlorn place, I have never before seen. The armies have ruined the place."

The aftermath of the battle left hundreds homeless or fleeing for their lives. It also left thousands of soldiers killed and wounded. Bragg left behind approximately 2500 of their wounded, 1200 of them in serious condition. They filled many of Murfreesboro's homes. The Confederate "victory" of New Year's Eve had turned to ashes. [4]

The next morning, the 78th took up the line of march and proceeded down the Murfreesboro Pike in strong force until approximately two miles from town they came to the entrenchment lately occupied by the enemy, which was found to be deserted. Here the regiment formed on the top of a hill outside the Confederate entrenchment and rested for the night. [5]

Other regiments spent the day burying the dead while Stanley's cavalry reconnoitered the area. All information from the infantry and cavalry showed that the Confederates had left the field. They had abandoned their posts; they had retreated. After sustaining over 10,000 casualties, Bragg fled with his army. He had lost the field, but captured around 77 field guns. In the retreat, his men threw away almost 4000 small arms. [6]

On the glorious morning of Monday, January 5, while Stanley's cavalry drove the last evidence of the Confederate rear-guard from the Manchester Pike, the victorious Army of the Cumberland led by Thomas' Corps marched into Murfreesboro. In celebration of the Union victory the gods of war brought a change in the weather. It became "beautiful and warm; [and] the birds sing..." The Union army entered the town in triumph; flags and guidons waving in the breeze and the bands playing. The Pennsylvania 78th, because of its gallantry was accorded the honor of entering Murfreesboro and raising the Stars and Stripes over the dome of Rutherford court house, scene of a Confederate Christmas ball eleven days earlier. The young boys, who cheered Governor Curtin on the Allegheny Commons so long ago, watched proudly as their flag was hoisted.

Thomas' Corps camped in a crescent shaped configuration from the Manchester Pike to the Shelbyville Road; because of their heroic actions the 78th bedded down in the court house; the first real roof over their heads in a long time. Eventually they were moved to homes within the town. There were few brigades in Rosey's army that were called upon to fight during both days of the hard fighting around Murfreesboro. The Seventy-Eighth and their sister regiments in Miller's Brigade saw heavy action on December 31st and January 2nd. The honor accorded to Negley's Division and the Seventy-Eighth was well deserved. [7]

According to Private Kipp, the day that the 78th marched into Murfreesboro, General Rosecrans rode up to General Negley hitting him slightly on the back. "With tears in his eyes he said, 'General Negley, your division saved my army both days of the hardest fighting.'" Robert Dinsmore related the same comment to his mother and added that the Seventy-Eighth and Negley's Division were cheered whenever they were seen and recognized.

Colonel Sirwell was appointed Provost Marshal and the Seventy-Eighth with Major Bonnaffon commanding was placed on provost guard. Sirwell placed Willis Nugent in command of an honor guard to stand watch over the now American flag draped body of General Sill. Working from the Court House the officers of the 78th also saw to the guarding and care of the prisoners. They attempted to make the crowded jail of Confederates somewhat comfortable and warm by giving blankets to the prisoners. Colonel Sirwell gave permission to the women of Murfreesboro to bring food to the prisoners. His kindness was returned by those women. They brought "biscuits, corn bread, meat, butter and everything you could ask." So while Sirwell and his officers enjoyed the Court House, the troops enjoyed the homes of Murfreesboro.

Unlike the mostly middle class homes in Kittanning, the great difference in economic status of the citizens of Murfreesboro was reflected by the humble shacks of the very poor or the grand homes of the wealthy. Sam Dumm noted that the regiment was quartered within the houses of the wealthy families of Murfreesboro. "We are quartered in a better house than most folks at home have to live in...[Although] the part of town we are...in is mostly filled with Sesesh Hospitals." Despite the prisoners and wounded, Sam Dumm liked his quarters. Anything had to be better than the cold ground.

The boys took whatever they could for comfort. And some looting did take place. One of the homes occupied by the Pennsylvanians was that of Charles Ready. Mattie Ready, the new missus John Hunt Morgan, and her family had already fled the town. During his stay at the Ready home, Private George Schaffner of Company H, "captured" a sword supposedly belonging to Mattie's father or her new husband, John Hunt Morgan. Private Schaffner used both versions in re-telling the story to his family.

There was still a poor supply of food, and the folks back home were trying to help. Lieutenant Wils Dinsmore, commended by Sirwell for his notable actions during the battle, got a letter from home with the sad news that his father had passed away on December 23. The boys in Company K also found out that George Monroe and John Barnhart from Slate Lick had attempted to get supplies to the regiment, but were not permitted to go any further than Louisville. [8]

Colonel Sirwell was very proud of the tenacity and courage of his lads. When he filed his after-action report on January 12, 1863, recording the events of the seven days of movements and the battle, he praised the men in his regiment for their bravery and valor in the fight at Murfreesboro.

Headquarters, Seventy-Eighth Pennsylvania Volunteers
Murfreesboro, Tennessee. January 12, 1863.

"...I cannot speak too highly of the bravery of the officers and men of the 78th Pennsylvania Volunteers, who were ready at any moment to obey any order.

Of my Secretary, Alfred L. Weir, Company F, I must not pass by without notice. He is an industrious young man, as all who have had dealings with the Regiment can testify. The only time he would leave his desk was when the Regiment was likely to have a fight. At the battles of Stone River, he was always by my side ready for any emergency. I bespeak for him higher honors than he now enjoys.

Of Lieutenant Henry W. Torbett, my Adjutant, a braver man never wore the straps of a First Lieutenant. I would respectfully recommend him for promotion.

Of my Sergeant Major Franklin Mechling, whom I have mentioned in the Reports of the Fights of Lavergne, and Neely's Bend, behaved himself gallantly in the battle of Stones' River; in the fight of Wednesday, he was struck in the forehead by a ball and slightly wounded; after getting his wounds dressed, he returned and faithfully discharged the duties of his office. I would respectfully recommend him for promotion.

Of my Major A.B. Bonnaffon, who is on Colonel Miller's Staff as Topographical Engineer, when not in discharge of his duties to Colonel Miller, rendered me valuable services. Major Bonnaffon, although a young man, is an old soldier with but few equals in the army; a higher position awaits him.

I would respectfully say a few words in behalf of Private Hosack, who joined Company G. as a private and since the Regiment entered the service, Private Hosack has been acting as a Private Physician for the Company of which he is a member. Of Dr. Hosack's services on the battle field and since the battle of Stone's River, the poor soldier who is now wounded or suffering from his wounds can speak. He has been and is all to my Regiment.

The Rev. Richard C. Christy, Chaplain of my Regiment, is a brave, good man, always to be found (although in feeble health), in the middle of danger and where duty called him. He has been and is of valuable service in attending to the sick and wounded.

All of which is Respectfully submitted,
William Sirwell, Colonel Commanding,
78th Regiment Pennsylvania Volunteers"

Although the after-action report of Colonel William Sirwell on the battle of Stones River was submitted properly, and in part used by Colonel Miller to fill out his own report, it was inadvertently left out of the Official Record. It is printed in total in the History of the Seventy-Eighth Pennsylvania Volunteer Infantry. [9]

In his after-action report General Rosecrans commended numerous officers for bravery, gallantry, skill, and courage; General Negley and five of his officers were on the list: Colonels Sirwell, 78th Pennsylvania, Moody, 74th Ohio, Hull, 37th Indiana, Lt. Colonel Neibling, 21st Ohio, Captain Brigham, 69th Ohio. In total 64 officers, virtually one third of his officers commanding a formal unit, were commended. Eleven officers that had no command and three surgeons were also commended.

The Seventy-Eighth was commended for its capture of the flag of the Twenty-Sixty [Rebel] Tennessee. Of the seven regiments or batteries commended, the Seventy-Eighth was listed first. Although the 78th is mentioned specifically, it should be noted that Negley's other regiments, although not listed, were also mentioned as to their assistance in this action.

Out of the thousands of enlisted soldiers taken into battle, twenty-three men were commended for gallant conduct; four already acclaimed by Colonel Sirwell were from the Seventy-Eighth. Sergeant Henry A. Miller [staff], Sergeant Absolom Weaver [Co. F], Sergeant Franklin Mechling[staff Sergeant Major, promoted to Second Lieutenant Co. B], and Corporal William L. Hughes [Co. B, the soldier actually responsible for the capture of the flag of the 26th Tennessee] were the ones mentioned in Rosecrans' report. Staff Assistant Surgeon of the Seventy-Eighth, Victor Miller of Franklin County, Pennsylvania, was the one glaring black mark against the regiment. Miller was chastised for desertion in battle by Chief Surgeon Eben Swift. Conceivably the worst accusation could come from your associates. John Hogan of Company K was branded a "Poor Coward" by his friends. It was the prevailing opinion that he left before the battle with no reason other than fear. In the coming campaign to Tullahoma and Chattanooga, he along with George Boney of Company K, would be left behind at Manchester because "[he was] not stout enough for the march."[10]

In Colonel Sirwell's after-action report he lauded many of the regiment, officers and enlisted alike. Naturally, kudos were in order for George Hamm, the regimental flag bearer. Captains Bill Jack, William Cummins, Martin McCanna, and Robert Elwood, Lieutenants Sam Lee, Matt Halstead, Robert Wilson Dinsmore, Robert Smith, Hugh Ayres, Bill Maize, and John Marlin all received the Colonel's praise. Sergeants Thompson Bell, John Keifer, Sam Croyle, Sam McBride, Bill Murphy, and Bill Smith, and Acting Sergeant Bill Davis also received marked commendations from Bill Sirwell.

A somber duty befell each and every regimental commander. Bill Sirwell dutifully sent a letter with a list of the killed, wounded or missing in action to the proper Pennsylvania state authorities and the area newspapers. In February, the sorrowful report appeared on the first page of the *Kittanning Mentor* along with Sirwell's comments.

To: Colonel John Boreland Finlay

Sir:

...We have had hard fighting for five days - three hard battles - two of them the most terrific battles that have been fought during the war. My poor boys did their duty.

I am sincerely,

William Sirwell, Col. 78th P.V.

The people of the Allegheny Valley anxiously scanned the report for the loved ones that had not written home, as yet. The report listed the names of approximately two hundred local boys. Many families shed tears for the fifty-eight men who were killed or died of wounds. Matilda Halstead grieved with her three children for her fallen husband. The hopes and prayers of families and friends went out to the ninety-seven boys who were in hospital from wounds. The uncertainty and anxiety that accompanies the missing in action or prisoners affected the families of fifty-one boys. In the final tally, luck played a hand in the number of casualties sustained by a company. Although the whole of Seventy-Eighth regiment had been engaged position in rank could affect losses. Indiana County's Company A took a greater pounding than Indiana County's Company D. Company D, according to Lieutenant Adam Braughler of Company D, ended up positioned in a ravine. In that location they did not take as much direct fire. [11]

The recognition of gallantry and bravery from commanding officers was an honor to cherish. A soldier could be proud if he was noted for his bravery in battle. It should be noted that if this army had been part of the Army of the Potomac men such as Sergeant Major Henry A. Miller, Acting Lieutenant Absolom Weaver, Second Lieutenant Franklin Mechling Acting Sergeant William L. Hughes and Acting Sergeant Bill Davis may have not only have received promotions but just may have been placed in nomination for the Congressional Medal of Honor. But it is possible that the greatest honor came to five men of Butler County's Company H; they were voted the five most courageous men in the company at the battle of Stones River: Sergeant Albert B. Hay, Corporal William H. Black, Private Gideon R. Allen, Private Nelson Elias, and Private Abram Richey.

The young men from Western Pennsylvania, Indiana, Michigan, and Ohio had faced their first great battle and now Colonel Miller reported his losses on January 6th. He showed that of the 2181 men in his brigade, 531 were either killed or wounded, or approximately 24 percent. The 78th Pennsylvania, the 37th Indiana, and the Ohio 21st took the brunt of the brigade losses. [12]

Of the 555 men of the Pennsylvania 78th that went into battle 178 were killed, mortally wounded, wounded, or missing in action never to be found, that is over thirty-two percent. Of the 18 men listed as killed in battle by the brigade commander, Colonel John Miller, only 16 were actually killed. One hundred and forty men were wounded; however, the records indicate that eventually 42 died of their wounds. Shortly after the battle, 52 men were still not accounted for; it would later be learned that many were captured and on their way to Southern prisons. Eight of those men listed as "missing in action" would never be found. Thirteen men had been taken prisoner, four of those would never be accounted for.   Of the men that died, one had been missing for a time and one had been a prisoner. The regiment also lost one wagon, one mule, one draught horse, and nine cavalry horses. [13]

For purposes of this book researching, checking and cross-referencing have made the battle casualty tally as close to exact as possible. In calculating battle wounds and deaths all of the figures are approximate to within ninety-eight percent. The difficulty came from the fact that Sirwell's report was incorrect to the spelling of a number of names. Miller's report, written on January 6th, still did not have enough information and was incorrect in its tally. In all likelihood, there were probably many superficial wounds that were never reported. In researching material for this book a number of twentieth century obituaries and a few tombstones stated that an old veteran was "wounded at Stones River," even though his name did not appear on Sirwell's list.

"William Rosecrans...was hailed as a hero, but the tales of dead and wounded silenced the clamor of rejoicing." [14]   Over 23,000 men, Union and Confederate, were killed, wounded or missing in action after the battle. The Union force had over 12,906 of those casualties. The Army of the Cumberland with around 43,400 effectives was approximately one-third as large in effectives as the 113,687 man Army of the Potomac that was defeated at Fredericksburg, Virginia two weeks earlier. Yet it had slightly more than the 12,653 Fredericksburg losses. [15]

One fact is clear, despite the severity of their wounds, many of those who died subsequent to the battle, died from poor medical care. Twenty-one men from the 78th died in battle or from wounds a few days later. Additionally, twenty-one men died from wounds in the weeks and months to follow.

Although doctors and hospital personnel labored diligently, it is evident that deaths resulted not from lack of care, but from lack of knowledge relating to battle wounds, and the lack of sanitary conditions. The Civil War was the last great war waged before the theories of viruses, bacteria and germs became part of medicine. Field hospitals were unsanitary places, to say the least. Surgeon W.W. Keen later described the field hospital operatory.

"We operated in old blood-stained and often pus-stained coats, the veterans of a hundred fights. We operated with clean hands in the social sense, but they were undisinfected hands....We used undisinfected instruments from undisinfected plush-lined cases....If a sponge or instrument fell on the floor it was washed and squeezed in a basin of tap water and used as if it were clean."

Amputation was the general consequence of wounds in the arms or legs; since nothing was known of antisepsis, an infection was almost inevitable. Abdominal wounds and major amputations meant probable death.[16] When surgeons wanted to amputate Henry Claypoole's leg he refused. Private Claypoole was transferred to a Nashville hospital where he slowly recovered.

The history of the Seventy-Eighth shows that the regiment was attending to its dead and wounded while struggling to return to normalcy. Surviving wounded were sent to Nashville, hopefully for better medical care.   The courageous Captain Jack died of his wounds in Nashville on February 5, 1863. The embalmed body of Sam Slusser was transported back to Freeport. He died on January 9, 1863. Acting Lieutenant Absolom

Weaver was returned to his home in Freeport. He struggled to regain his health for over a year. In late July of 1864, he passed away. He was laid to rest in Freeport Cemetery not far from his friend Sam Slusser.

Many men would be returned to good health by the tender care of female nurses in Nashville. These angels of mercy would add something to the care of a soldier that no man could. However, it is most interesting that Buck Simkins in a reply to a request to join the nursing corps by his sister, received an answer of "absolutely not." He chided her that she would become a "Hospital Whore" as the soldiers referred to these caring women.

Soldiers deemed to be missing returned to active company rosters while others were found within Murfreesboro. Thirty year-old, Mike Younkins, still "fat as a pig," was thrilled to see his younger brother John return. Lieutenant Anchors from Black Fox, Pennsylvania, thought to be in Rebel hands, returned to the regiment, and on April 27th was promoted to First Lieutenant. Henry Harrison Whitehill was found in a hospital in Murfreesboro. Young Harrison, as he was known to his comrades would succumb to his shoulder wound on January 9, 1963. His friend Levi Boyer, also of Company E, would bury him in the "Old School Presbyterian Church Yard" in Murfreesboro. Captain James Hosey would write to Whitehill's father and return his belongings: "[his] money and watch, a handsome pocket bible, a testament which was presented to him by the Young Men's Bible Society of Pittsburgh and a carefully preserved likeness [of] Miss Mary Thomson." [17]

Many of the Union soldiers captured during the battle took an extended tour of the Confederacy in the month of January. While the battle raged around them, the Yankees who were taken prisoner were whisked from their positions and hurried into town. Jailed in the area around the Rutherford County court house, the Union troops were instantly relieved of blankets, ponchos, and overcoats. They were moved south of town, and sent by flat car to Chattanooga. Some were spirited off to Vicksburg others were headed for Florida then rerouted to Richmond. In the next few weeks those that were taken to Virginia, traveled to Atlanta, Montgomery, Knoxville, and finally Richmond. After being marched through Richmond's streets of jeering and threatening crowds, they were put into the infamous Libby Prison. Any possession of value had been taken from the boys in blue at this point. There was little care afforded the prisoners and the food was meager. Fortunately, the Yankees were paroled by months end. They would never suffer the living hell of prison life similar to the Union soldiers as the war lengthened when soldiers were no longer paroled.

At the time when prisoners were paroled, it would appear that taking prisoners to Richmond was ridiculous. The Confederacy tied up numerous guards, much needed trains, and time to move prisoners hundreds of miles only to let them free. Seeing prisoners being herded down Grace, Broad or Main Streets may have given the locals a morale boost, but it was a foolish waste of manpower and resources. Of the thirteen men from the Seventy-Eighth taken prisoner, only nine returned to the regiment. Enoch Gilliam and Jerry Southworth, both wounded, were two men of the 78th who took the "guided tour" of the sunny south. They were later exchanged at Camp Chase in Columbus, Ohio. Jack Painter, the blacksmith from Slate Lick, returned in good condition despite the fact that three fingers and one half of his forefinger were gone from his left hand. The fingers had been shot off in the battle. The Confederate doctors treated his wounds. Surgeon Eben Swift interviewed a number of prisoners from Negley's Division who were able to escape or were freed before being transported south. According to Swift the men had been "well treated, and had no reason to complain." [18]

While the army settled in, the news of the spectacular battle filtered out to the country. Wheeler's cavalry raids, the weather and numerous misunderstandings stopped much of the information headed for the nation's newspapers on the battle at Murfreesboro. On January 2nd, a correspondent from the *Chicago Times* informed his paper that for seven days no mail or telegrams had passed between Nashville and Louisville.   A misunderstanding between the Post Office Department and the Louisville and Nashville Railroad halted all mail along the rail line during the battle. A midwestern blizzard on January 4th, brought wire service to a stop.

Many of the facts that originally appeared in newspapers around the country came from skulkers and cowards that had fled to Nashville. Allegedly, some of these ridiculous reports were attributed to cowardly officers who had fled Stones River also. There was a degree of indignation at Rosey's headquarters regarding ludicrous and outrageous reports sent to the Eastern press by many correspondents who had never seen the battlefield.

The lack of concrete information led to rumors and speculation and unfounded fears. W.B. Shaw, onetime chief Washington correspondent for the *New York Herald*, still posted in the nation's capital, notified New York's Senator Ira Harris that a bulletin was issued in New York stating that Rosecrans and thirty thousand of his officers and men had surrendered. [19]

The accuracy of field reporting in the *Cincinnati Daily Enquirer* and from information it reported from other newspaper sources would seem to be incorrect in a number of areas. Although news of the large battle at Stones River was reported essentially from the first to the seventh of January 1863, it is often reported out of order. Owing to the confusion of a large battle, and evaluating the eyewitness, first hand account versus the rumor and inaccuracy of word of mouth makes the source of historical facts questionable, especially as reported in this newspaper.

Within a column titled, "Telegraph News" or "Latest By Telegraph," the *Daily Enquirer* reported the Death of General Bragg, the deaths of Rebel Generals Hardee and Hanson, and the arrival of reinforcements from Richmond. [20]

The truth of the battle began to appear, when some reporters used couriers or carried their reports back to wire services or newspapers themselves. West of the Allegheny Mountains, Cincinnati was the center of news collection for the western armies. The *Enquirer* does not seem to be the most reliable source of news. However, many times during the war in all theaters of operation there were printed rumors in more reliable newspapers. The *Cincinnati Gazette* was a more prominent paper and the leading paper in the city. It was reputed to be a stable news reporting source and Whitelaw Reid was the paper's renowned war correspondent. However, the most popular paper with the soldiers was the *Cincinnati Commercial*. It was known as the "soldier's paper." [21] It was the Commercial that sent information to the *Pittsburgh Gazette*. What follows are articles from the front page of that newspaper.

PITTSBURGH GAZETTE
WEDNESDAY MORNING, JANUARY 7, 1863

We invite attention to a letter from the correspondent of the Cincinnati Commercial giving a graphic account of the advance of the army from Nashville to Murfreesboro. The reader will feel after perusing it that with such an army and such a leader victory, glorious and complete victory, was almost a matter of course; and he will sigh to think that other armies
equally brave failed because they had no such leader. Contrast the conduct of McClellan at Fair Oaks and Antietam, and that of Buell at Perryville with that of Rosecrans at Murfreesboro and then you will see why the Rebels are not subdued.

General Negley
In every dispatch from the battle field which we have seen, one Pennsylvania General and one Pennsylvania regiment have received honorable mention. General Negley, who commanded a division, bore himself with great skill and bravery, and did much to secure the glorious result. The regiment of which we speak, the 78th formed a part of Negley's division and is noticed more particularly in another place and in a letter which we give today.
This gallant regiment commanded by Colonel William Sirwell of Kittanning, distinguished itself in the late battle, and is most honorably mentioned by nearly every writer from the battlefield. It suffered severely, but we have not yet received the names of any of its killed and wounded. The regiment was organized at Kittanning in the autumn of 1861, and has been in active service ever since. Its members are mainly from Armstrong, Clarion and Butler counties. This county has some representatives in it. [22]

In each and every battle individual decisions or acts of valor change the ebb and flow of battle. In light of the killing fire of Mendenhall's batteries, were Bragg's troops finished? Could they have retrieved the offensive? Could Bragg have pulled this setback into a victory? Did Colonel Miller's command to follow the Rebels on January 2nd, break the resolve and determination of Braxton Bragg and his troops? Historical suppositions can be argued for years. Facts remain that Phil Sheridan's and James Negley's brigades fought a determined action on the battle's first day. Mendenhall's batteries performed exceptionally well. Colonel Miller ordered Negley's division forward at an opportune time. Colonel Sirwell makes a very simple statement in his after-action report. "I now ordered my men to advance at a charge bayonet, which they did...." Had this simple, dutiful command capitalized on the death and confusion within the Rebel soldiers? Did this order change the flow of victory to the Federal army?

Thomas Van Horne in his *History of the Army of the Cumberland* states that if not for the fortuitous charge of the Union troops of Negley's division on January 2nd, Breckenridge and subsequently Bragg could have regrouped on the Confederate right, held their position and possibly renewed the fight on the next day. [23] Bill Sirwell and his men performed gallantly on both days of the major fighting. Along with Rosecrans' attention to detail and his personal courage, their dauntless efforts were instrumental in the Union victory at Stones River.

It was now Rosecrans' turn to send a wire of victory to his capital. On January 5th, he wired Secretary of War, Stanton which read in part: "God has crowned our arms with victory. The enemy are badly beaten, and in full retreat." To General-in-Chief, Henry Halleck he wired: "We have fought one of the greatest battles of the war, and are victorious. Our entire success on the 31st was prevented by a surprise of the right flank; but have, nevertheless, beaten the enemy, after a three-days' battle. They fled with great precipitancy on Saturday night. The last of their columns of cavalry left this morning. Their loss has been very heavy. Generals Rains and Hanson killed. Chalmers, Adams, and Breckenridge are wounded."

Lincoln wired Rosecrans on the same day: "Your dispatch announcing retreat of enemy has just reached here. God bless you, and all with you! Please tender to all, and accept for yourself, the Nation's gratitude for yours, and their, skill, endurance, and dauntless courage." On the 9th of January, Halleck added after confirming the facts: "General: Rebel accounts fully confirm your telegrams from the battle-field. The victory was well earned and one of the most brilliant of the war. You and your brave army have won the gratitude of your country and the admiration of the world. The field of Murfreesborough is made historical, and future generations will point out the places where so many heroes fell, gloriously, in defense of the Constitution and the Union. All honor to the Army of the Cumberland - thanks to the living and tears for the lamented dead." Rosey's Army of the Cumberland paid dearly for Halleck's half-hearted congratulatory message. [24]

Different sources argue that Bragg was not defeated at Murfreesboro. The *Richmond Enquirer* reported a Confederate drifting into the world of delusion. On January 5, 1863, after Captain J.B. Smith's Silver Band serenaded the president with the popular "Mocking Bird," Jefferson Davis in a speech given to a "respectable audience" in Richmond stated, "In the West...at Murfreesboro, you have gained a victory over hosts vastly superior to our own in numbers. You have achieved a result there as important, as brilliant at that which occurred on the soil of [Fredericksburg] Virginia." History records a completely different conclusion by Bragg's countrymen. The Confederate House voted on a resolution to commend Bragg and his army for their "conduct" at the battle of Murfreesboro. The Confederate Senate held up the vote on the resolution. Newspapers throughout the South censured Bragg through scathing editorials. General Polk was actively campaigning for Bragg's removal. A series of written reports by Bragg's commanders showed that he had lost the confidence of those senior commanders. This phrase "lost the confidence" is a kind euphemism for vanquished. As with Shiloh and Perryville, when an army leaves the field of battle in the hands of their foe that equates to defeat.

Braxton Bragg almost lost his command, but circumstances changed his history. In early March, General Joe Johnston was directed by Secretary of War, James Seddon, to replace Bragg. Bragg was to be relegated to an advisory position in Richmond. When Johnston arrived at Tullahoma, he found Bragg totally consumed with the illness of his wife. Out of consideration for the situation, Johnston never informed Bragg of his orders. He did assume command of the Army of the Tennessee, while Bragg ministered to his frail, dying mate. Miraculously, Mrs. Bragg recovered, but as fate would have it

Johnston fell ill. In point of fact, General Johnston was so sick that he could not assume full command of the army. The mantel of leadership returned to Braxton Bragg. [25]

In the end, the facts support the proposition that William Starke Rosecrans and his army beat Bragg's forces, fair and square. Bragg's retrograde movement defines defeat. The Army of the Cumberland, put together by Don Carlos Buell and moved into action by William Rosecrans, had what some thought was a questionable victory. Nonetheless, Braxton Bragg's army no longer existed in force in Kentucky or middle and Western Tennessee. Unlike the Army of the Potomac which see-sawed back and forth over captured and lost ground. The armies in the west pushed slowly and persistently forward.

So, the official action at Stones River ended. The gray and blue clad boys of the nation paid a heavy price for their beliefs or what at some point was to be the great adventure. They had beaten each other to death. In the chronicles of the battle at Stones River many individuals and regiments of both the North and South showed particular courage. The charge of the Seventy-Eighth on January 2, 1863, was significant in terms of its incontestable effect on the Federal army. But what made these boys from Southwestern Pennsylvania take up the assault. They were similar to all of the other combatants present in that they were of the same age, occupations and beliefs. They had seen the carnage and death of battle and watched again as their comrades ran in fear for their lives. So what made them rise from their position and charge headlong into the face of death. Maybe it was the cold, and the long days without sleep or food. Maybe it was the fatigue of battle. Maybe it was the leadership and tenacity of their cherished Colonel William Sirwell. Whatever it was, when the boys and men of the Seventy-Eighth were summoned to the center stage of history, they fearlessly answered the call. Through determination and courage they helped change the course of history.

TENTING TONIGHT

For over six months Rosecrans and his army would camp around the small town of Murfreesboro; time was needed to heal, time was needed to refit, maybe too much time was taken. Rosecrans needed to accumulate supplies, and rebuild rail beds and bridges for the campaign ahead. Although his army still outnumbered Bragg's, sixteen thousand of the forty-one thousand Union troops available for duty had to be utilized in protecting the growing Federal lines of supply and communication. Rosey wanted more soldiers for a text book offensive campaign against Braxton Bragg's army centered only thirty miles away in a small rail town called Tullahoma.

Actually, the condition of the roads south would have hampered any campaign. The winter months with their rain and snow made the roads virtually impassable. Even the turnpikes that stretched from Nashville were torn up and made the movement of supplies slow going. Earthworks were constructed to encircle the town and protect its supply depot. Many of the regiments were assigned duties relating to road repair. The Seventy-Eighth worked on the repair of the Salem Pike. It was an arduous, mundane detail, but it was necessary. Irrespective of the work to be done so that future campaiguing could be effective, as always, Washington would accept no excuses. Rosey's tardiness, for whatever reason, would once again cause him trouble with his superiors. [1]

Regrouping may have been the order of the day, but the unpleasant task of clearing the battlefield of its dead still remained. The men of the 11th Michigan along with many others were detailed to the burial guard. Twenty-eight days after the battle had passed Corporal Gillaspie noted that they buried twenty-seven bodies, an extra leg and three arms. An entry in Gillaspie's diary made on February 10th, shows that the burial detail interred 48 more bodies. [2] Major Daniel Collier and his Third Kentucky Volunteers did not reach the battlefield until January 1st. The regiment did not participate in any engagement, but Major Collier notes in his after action report that his men spent all day Sunday burying the dead. Bragg had abandoned 1200 wounded in Murfreesboro and many of the Confederate dead remained unburied. The Union soldiers buried their own in individual graves. They buried about 2000 Confederates in a common grave. [3]

Many of the battle's survivors were astonished at what they had endured. Charles Bennett wrote in his diary: "January 25th, Our regiment went foraging last Tuesday and again Wednesday, passing through [the area] where our Right Wing (McCook's) was driven back and lost so heavily on the first day of the battle of Stone River. To see the effects of that battle one wonders how a single man escaped. The underbrush was literally mowed down by bullets, the large trees did not have a space as large as one's hand free from scars, and I saw trees from all sizes up to eighteen inches in diameter cut down by bullets, shot and shell." [4] Colonel John Beatty also recorded the aftermath of battle. "I ride over the battlefield. In one place a cassion and five horses are lying, the latter killed in harness, and all fallen together. Nationals and Confederates of all ages are scattered over the woods and fields for miles. We find men with legs shot off, one with brains scooped out with a cannon ball, another with half a face, another with entrails protruding. Many wounded horses are limping over the field." [5] In Lieutenant Nugent's diary he noted that the scene was "sickening. The were piles of mangled bodies - friend and foe alike. "The ground [was] covered with broken ordanance, dead animals, shot, shell, and fragments of wagons, arms and legs." Private Kipp wrote to his mother: "I tell you Mother, ...the trees and corn stalks are riddled by balls for miles around. It is one of the most horrible places I ever saw. Horses are lying on the field as high as six in a pile...killed...all together." The smell of the rotting horse flesh would become oppressive at times. In late February, hundreds of dead horses laid about the battlefield and near the long lines of rifle pits. The country around Stones River was also ravaged. Little if any fencing had survived and many houses had been torn down or burned. [6]

"Little" Phil Sheridan in his memoirs painted a vivid and horrifying picture of the battle's aftermath. "As soon as possible after the Confederate retreat I went over the battle-field to collect such of my wounded as had not been carried off to the South and to bury my dead. In the cedars and on the ground where I had been so fiercely assaulted when the battle opened on the morning of the 31st, evidences of the bloody struggle appeared on every hand in the form of broken fire-arms, fragments of accouterments, and splintered trees. The dead had nearly all been left unburied, but as there was likelihood of their mutilation by roving swine, the bodies had mostly been collected in piles at different points and enclosed by rail fences." [7]

Deaths from battle along with revisiting the scenes of their trial saddened, sickened and in some way numbed the men of the army. Future battles would be as bloody, but they would never have the same horrifying effect.

In February, an ailing, gaunt Colonel Sirwell spent three weeks at home on furlough. In all deference to the Colonel, although not wounded, he had been ill for some time. He also suffered a severe hearing loss while working with the cannon posted with his regiment during the battle. In later life he would virtually lose his hearing. Orders emanating from regimental command at this time were issued by Major Bonnaffon. Blakeley was placed on judge advocate duty in Nashville.

Father Richard Christy was also ordered home. In worsening and frail health, he needed to recuperate. [8] However, he returned to the Butler Valley with a new respect from the boys of the regiment. None questioned his religion now. The camps and battlefields had brought about a change in the regiment. Reverend Christy, the "Fighting Chaplain" as the boys now called him, was an acknowledged member of the Seventy-Eighth.

Along with logistical considerations, burial details, and supply shortages, there was also the problem of the wounded and dying. When the 78th entered Murfreesboro they found hundreds of wounded soldiers of both armies. Bragg had left 200 medical personnel and attendants to care for his wounded, but they lacked the necessary medical supplies to help their own let alone the Union soldiers brought into town during the battle. For many weeks following the fight, medical teams treated the wounded as best they could. Hundreds were sent to hospitals in Nashville. As the number of wounded grew, Nashville hotels, churches and schools were utilized as makeshift hospitals.

In the days after the battle, the casualties from the Seventy-Eighth, for the most part, were moved to Nashville. As their condition improved they were moved on to Louisville, then to Cincinnati and then home. Twenty-one year-old, Mark C. Bowser of Company K had sustained a chest wound and was on the mend. Private Bowser had stated to his doctor in Hospital #17 at Nashville that he was feeling fit and wished to be moved to Louisville. The doctor concurred and on March 12, 1863, Mark Bowser was sent with a group of men to the docks to board the boat for Louisville. Private Bowser was in good spirits on that Thursday morning.   He had walked the "80 perches" - a little over 400 yards - and sat talking with his buddies when he became suddenly ill.   Within minutes he dropped dead.   In writing to Bowser's father, Noah Bowser, Captain Joseph Smith, commanding Company K, said that "[the doctors] being so astonished at his death...held a post mortem Examination of his body..."   Evidently the wound in the right lung had developed an infection.   The sac containing "three pints of mater" had burst causing instant death.   Private Bowser was buried in his uniform with honors in the National Cemetery at Nashville.   Records today show that he was incorrectly listed as Mark C. Brown.   His family placed a monument at the Rogers Chapel Cemetery outside of Freeport, Pennsylvania.

During Colonel Sirwell's leave the 78th was relieved of provost duty in Murfreesboro by the 37th Indiana.   The boys were forced to leave their comfortable homes and were moved into Camp Sill near Miller's headquarters.   Colonel Stoughton of the 11th Michigan had been trying to replace the 78th with his men for some time.   With Sirwell's departure, he covertly affected his goal.   The 37th Indiana did not get the homes in Murfreesboro; the 11th Michigan did.   Major Bonnaffon did not have the power or politics to resist Stoughton.   When Sirwell returned from his leave he was incensed at the affront.   He angrily challenged Stoughton to a round or two of fisticuffs.   The fight never took place. Sam Dumm pronounced: "We left him alone in his glory," and "Old Bill's" boys remained in Camp Sill.

As time passed, conditions became more bearable.   The wounded were moved to hospitals in Nashville.   Warm quarters were erected.   The American soldier was introduced to the "pup" tent.   Originally the new shelter was christened the "dog" tent. On the night that the tents were issued, many the of the critical members of the Army of the Cumberland showed their scorn for their new quarters by barking at passing officers or posturing themselves at the tent opening and howling at the night skies.

It may not have been "home cookin'," but food also became more plentiful.   The regimental mess of the 78th reported daily to the division commissary and received allotments of bread and beef.   Usually, two cattle per battalion were issued daily.   When the weather became warmer, pudding served with raisins or peaches was a real treat.

Delicacies may have been available at times, but the lack of proper food or inattention to the requisitioning of proper food shows that the men in the army, three months after the battle of Stones River, were not being properly cared for; scurvy had appeared.   On April 7th, Colonel John Miller addressed the subject with his brigade.   Regimental commanders were apprised of the fact that beans, rice and corn were available through the commissaries, but that many companies were neglecting to make use of these vegetables supplied by the government.   Regimental Commanders were enjoined to examine the matter and remedy the situation immediately.   Company commanders were ordered to actually supervise the cooking and serving of vegetables.

In March the Tennessee spring returned to the Nashville Basin.   "[Murfreesboro began] to improve in appearance.   Several large stores [had] been opened.   There [were] now two or three large military stores, one large dry goods store, several Sutlers and a Jail.   And the latter generally [had] more customers than the former."   The fields began to return to their many hues of green.   The warm weather brought blossoms to the peach trees and the grass began to cover the multitude of graves.   Many of the Union troops fashioned fishing rods and equipment and supplemented their diets with fish. During

May the men would swim in the river. It is hard to conceive of soldiers passing a lazy, balmy day along the banks of Stones River where only months before they engaged in a struggle for their very lives.

Rosecrans' army of occupation began to build their own city around Murfreesboro. Fortifications and military storage houses sprung up. Regiments and companies tailored their camps and streets. Insignia and logos appeared on camp entrance ways. Flowers and trees were planted. The huge army quickly cut down a great percentage of the trees in and around the town to add to their quarters and cook their meals. The tents appearing white under the night sky could be seen for miles.

As their stay continued, the soldiers became more difficult to manage. The army continued to lose its discipline and military edge. The routine of guard duty, drilling, and monotonous camp life became abhorrent. Sutlers permeated the camps. People of all descriptions wandered in an out of the army. Some soldiers drifted off or just plain went home. Stealing was no better or worse, but the opportunities were greater. Alcohol consumption remained at its normal level. In March, alcohol was definitely the reason that Milton Welsh of Company H stabbed Hugh Morgan of the same company. Thankfully, Morgan survived and was none the worse for the attack. The Army of the Cumberland had won. Now they wanted to do as they "damn well" pleased.

A situation that caused great concern within the command structure was the unauthorized movement of people in the Union camps. The Army of the Cumberland was definitely a prime target of Confederates spies. Many persons in citizen's dress were in the habit of strolling through the camps with no other purpose than to make themselves familiar with Union strength and position. Spies in enlisted federal uniforms would wander through the camps supposedly in search of their command, but in reality they were gathering military information. General Rosecrans warned that many unauthorized persons passed into and out of the camps by uniting themselves with forage trains. Questionable soldiers were to be held in custody until they were identified by their immediate commanding officer. Confederate deserters were also suspect and normally were confined. In mid June, two spies were executed just outside the camp of the 78th, "Old Rosey [was]...prompt in punishing crime."

Camp followers, a welcome attraction for many lonely soldiers, were strictly forbidden. The command felt that they could also be spies and their activities would also lead to demoralization of the soldiers. Most troops didn't agree; they enjoyed the female companionship. The boys of the Seventy-Eighth took advantage of the goods being offered by the ladies and were know to have visited a few of the black girls in the area. Corporal Adam Beck, Company D, noted in his diary the fun he had at the "niggar dance near [his] quarters." The newly anointed lieutenant Robert Wilson "Wils" Dinsmore of Company K wrote to his brother Marion, who had been given a medical discharge from the Seventy-Eighth in June of 1862, extolling the satisfaction of the women in Murfreesboro. "[It is] a gay time...plenty of women and they all play cards and drink whiskey."

Bragg's army spread out thirty miles away was experiencing the same problem. There were simply a great number of women plying their "trade." John Harris of the 19th Louisiana advised his wife not to visit him. He felt there were too many lewd women in the area for decent women to be visiting. [9]

It was distressing to Sirwell that some of the men took advantage of their victorious-occupation status. In July two men of Company E attempted to rape a local woman. Colonel Sirwell, usually a benevolent commander, had the men brought before the brigade on dress parade; their crime and sentence were read aloud to the troops. Thirty days at hard labor with ball and chain was the punishment. [10]

Punishments for minor crimes were meted out as required, but, when the crime was more grievous, the punishment also became more severe. On June 5, 1863, at Camp Drake just outside of Murfreesboro one individual would pay for a crime of assault, torture and murder. The army would be taught the lesson of the criminal. In the morning, general orders came to every camp stating that the execution of a man by the name of William A. Selkirk was to take place at 12 noon that day. The whole army gathered at the spot where the scaffold was erected. Soldiers filled every tree for the best vantage point for viewing the execution. For miles around, the area was covered with one mass of people there to witness the scene.

Adam Johnston of the 79th Pennsylvania and Sergeant George H. Puntenney of the 37th Indiana both described the event also reported in the *Nashville Union*. "At 1 o'clock you could see two regiments moving from the Murfreesboro prison, slowly followed by a spring-wagon [being pulled by] four nice cream-colored horses, ornamented with ribbons of red, white and blue. The criminal [was] seated on his coffin. His consul and the hangman were seated in front of the coffin. The wagon was followed by the son, daughter and friends of the murdered man. A heavy escort followed. They all came along slowly and solemnly to the spot. [The wagon drove] through and under the scaffold...there was a final halt."

"Then you could see a fine looking and stout built man seated on the coffin soon to receive his mortal remains after being ushered into eternity. An awful death to die."

"It appeared by his capture and trial, that on...the 1st of March this year this man and two others [who would follow Selkirk to the gallows on June 28, 1863]...went to the house of Adam Weaver, of Williamson county, Tennessee, and did willfully beat him with clubs, and sticks, and stones, and brickbats, and with knives cut him and scarred and tortured him as long as life seemed visible, and then took a knife, and pulling his tongue out as far as possible cut it off...taking his money, [they] left this man dead, wallowing in blood..."

"[The daughter and son]..., stood close to the drop, [Weaver's daughter] adjusted the noose before the hanging. At six minutes past 2 o'clock the trap door was unlatched from under him, leaving him hang for twenty-six minutes without a struggle...and a smile played on [the daughter's] face as the man struggled in death." [11]

Sutlers descended upon the Union and Confederate soldiers now needing essentials and a little entertainment. In most regiments these nomadic merchants were received with mixed feelings. Their arrival promised news, rumors and precious goods that were normally unattainable. These underhanded peddlers filled a need and many of the soldiers were willing to pay the exorbitant prices for things that would ease their lives and make them happy. Tobacco, razors, fruits, vegetables, canned milk, canned meats, medicaments, and clothing were just some of the scarce articles or delicacies that were available from a sutler. But there was a price. One example was tobacco that sold for 5¢ a plug in Kittanning was sold by Mr. Reynolds, the brother of Tom Reynolds the original

78th sutler, for 20¢. Although mostly despised by the Union troops, the regimental history of the Seventy-Eighth gives the impression that the sutlers were enjoyed and did a thriving business with them.

After seeing the condition of the bodies strewn over the battlefield at Stones River, the men of the regiment came to the cold realization that they too could one day be one of those bodies. They did not want a common grave. They wanted to be sent home. So, they prepared for their possible fate. A number of men purchased a fore runner of the present day "dog tag" from the sutlers. A cheap metal coin with some character's face upon it was used. The soldier's name, regiment, company, and home addresses were stamped on the coin. A hole in the coin and a rough string held it around the trooper's neck. It was their ticket home, if dead.

The Confederates also delighted in their sutlers. There were luxuries that everyone enjoyed. A Texan wrote, "Our camp has been invaded by peddlers selling pies, ground peas, paper-envelopes, pins, needles, buttons &c. &c." [12]

The sutlers were a necessary evil in all armies; many regiments or brigades had their own. But their presence was not always welcomed. In the coming Chickamauga campaign one of the sutlers paid the ultimate price for earning the wrath of Sirwell's soldiers. While climbing Lookout Mountain, one of the sutlers traveling with Sirwell's Third Brigade overloaded his wagons and then stalled at the side of the road. His only alternative was to lighten his load by selling off some of his goods, at what the men perceived as an unfair profit. The men promptly pushed his wagon still loaded with his precious cargo over the side of the mountain. At times it was difficult to part the hard earned dollars of the soldier from him even for the best of luxuries.

Most of the sutlers "purchased" the right to sell regiments from the governor of a state, a cheap politician looking to line his pockets, or that of a regimental commander. One Israel Marienthal claimed that he "indirectly" paid $2000 for the right to sell his goods to the Twenty-First Ohio. To his ill fortune, Mr. Marienthal reported at headquarters that boots were stolen from his wagon when the Twenty-Onesters failed to provide a proper guard. Silas Canfield argued for the private to be court martialed for the oversight and won his case. But he would not forget or forgive Marienthal for causing him to punish one of his own.

A Council of Administration was convened to look into the dealings of Mr. Marienthal. It was found that Israel Marienthal had only a letter of appointment from Colonel Jessee Norton, the original regimental commander; he also was found to not have kept any records of his transactions. His penalty for poor record keeping and having never paid any of his profits into the Regimental Fund was a ten cent assessment for every man listed on the monthly roster of the regiment for the past eighteen months. His bill was $1290.30.

The total was reconsidered and the final penalty was $500 plus all outstanding debts by members of the regiment were canceled. Five days after his complaint, Marienthal was replaced by Sutler Thomas Richards, who paid a $200 fee for the privilege of sutling to the regiment.

Dr. Thomas Blakeley always held firm to the belief that if the sutlers had the whiskey, they would eventually have the money, and after that they would own the regiment. In the case of the Seventy-Eighth, a few men decided to compete with the sutlers. With opportunities all around them they cashed in on the needs of their fellow soldiers. They started their own businesses.   Adam Beck and Isaac Keirn sold apples and lemons. After buying apples for $20.00 a barrel, they sold them for 10¢ each. Some of the boys purchased oranges for $25.00 a box and sold them 2 for a quarter. Tom and Bill Sykes cleared about $70.00 profit each for their work in one week. David McQuiston's boys, Dave Junior and John cleared about $65.00 during the same time period. Abe Prosser was top salesman of a week with $80.00 in profit. [12]

The carnage of Stones River inevitably changed many of the lads from the farms and cities of the North. Diarist Ira Gillaspie was now writing of burial parties and body parts. On the last day of February, he stated that after eighteen months he was fully prepared to remain in the army as long as it would take to restore the Union. He finished his diary with, "My energy is with my country, heart with my friends." [13] Something had changed. If the huge battle had changed them, if they had become lazy, that did not matter: they had earned the right. Maybe they questioned the reasons for battles and death. But it angered some, when those at home questioned the war or refused to participate. The ultimate insult was the lack of sympathy for their efforts and sacrifice. A prevailing opinion was that these Northern men should be drafted or just sent to the Rebel South. There was little use for "Copperheads, slackers or quitters." Private Kipp expressed very strong feelings regarding these types to his mother. "I go for killing any man of them who is running us down, calling this Lincoln's Niger War...For my part, I would sooner kill such men as that, as I would the Rebels."

Musician Phineas Hatzell of Company C, months later would write to his foster parents relating to stories that had worked their way back to the boys in the army. Unlike Private Kipp, Phineas had no desire to kill anyone at home; however, he was more concerned with the treatment of former soldiers. "I can never harbor a thought of living in Pennsylvania [again], for I have become completely disgusted at the people of that state, with the treatment that crippled soldiers get who have no homes. [In] many places the people are turning up their noses at the soldiers. [They] are afraid that these soldiers will become a burden to them...to keep. [The] people of Pennsylvania are always making a g–d––d fuss about taxes and God knows what all." He had no desire to return to Pennsylvania. He stated that he would go to Arizona. [14]

During the long months in Murfreesboro, men began to build dreams for a better future in the army. A number of them wrote home asking if "political" connections could get them an officer's billet in another regiment. Will Lowery, Buck Simkins, Sam Steel all wished for advancement and officers straps. Lieutenant Robert Smith, Doctor William England and others made application to become officers in the new "colored" regiments. Only Will Lowery, over Sirwell's objection at losing a good soldier, got his commission in the Pennsylvania 103rd.

James Negley issued orders in early February that the system of passes and furloughs was breaking down. He ordered that no passes would be approved at headquarters unless the business and destination of the individual were clearly stated and time of absence specified. Necessity has always whetted the ingenuity of the American soldier; the lack of approved passes provided that forgery became a viable option. Therefore, Negley ordered that each Provost Marshal forward to his headquarters an autograph and official pass approving signature to enable the Division Provost Marshal to guard against fraudulent approvals.

Negley did not want to stop the granting of passes. He simply wanted his officers to be more judicious in granting them. However, if the men were permitted to return to their homes to take care of pressing business, they were charged a one-way fee for transportation of $4.53. At a pay rate of $13.00 per month that was a stiff price. Nonetheless, with or without permission, the men were willing to pay whatever the price for a visit to their home.

Leaving without permission, "deserting," was common in both armies. Evan Slater of Company E was known to have been wounded and taken prisoner during the battle. He was paroled by the Confederates and deserted. Banks Woodford and Robert Walker of Company D, and Michael Rowdybush and Abraham Bennett of Company G were all at home on legal furloughs. They all became listed as deserters, when they did not return on time. Woodford, Walker, and Rowdybush returned to the regiment. Bennett became a permanent deserter.

John Drum, of Company F, was captured December 31st and was sent to Libby Prison. Drum was paroled on January 27, 1863; however, did not return to the regiment until June 3, 1863. In all probability, John Drum took a "French Leave." He visited his home. It was not an official leave, the soldier was listed as a straggler or as deserted. Usually, upon his return he was never punished. Drum returned to serve as the company teamster for the remainder of the regiment's service time.

Lewis Hill of the Seventy-Eighth's Company I was typical of soldiers both Union and Confederate; he just plain went home to attend to business. Hill fought in the battle of Stones River and was taken prisoner. It is not quite clear of when, but Hill went home. After some time, Lieutenant Colonel Cross, from the office of the Deputy Quartermaster General in Pittsburgh, informed Colonel Sirwell that he had paid $30 for "the apprehension and delivery of Corporal Lewis T. Hill a deserter...[from the regiment]."

Corporal Hill was brought before a general court martial, charged with desertion, and found guilty of the specification and charge. He was sentenced to forfeit all pay and allowances for six months, to be reduced to the rank of private, and to make good the time lost by desertion.

Lewis Hill served faithfully with the regiment and transferred to the second organization upon its formation. He was mustered out, again at the rank of corporal, on April 12, 1865, at the end of the term prescribed by the Court. He along with the other Honorably Discharged veterans attended the Chickamauga Park dedication in 1897. [15]

Going home was one thing, but desertion in the face of the enemy was all together different. Some men were drummed out of the service after having their heads shaved and being branded on the face with a "D." The punishment was somewhat similar in the Confederate. However, the "D" was branded on the hip. Up to May of 1862, the lash was applied, sometimes up to 50 in number. Phil Sheridan, after investigation, found that four of his officers had abandoned their regiments and colors. He formed up his division and had the cowardly four men deliver their swords to his "colored" servant. Before they were drummed out of the service, that same servant then cut any vestige of insignia from their uniforms. Jones Withers and Pat Cleburne had officers drummed out of the service. Lieutenant John Davidson of the 25th Tennessee and Lieutenant I. W. Butler of the 9th Mississippi both disgraced themselves and paid the price for cowardice at Stones River.

Private Johnston described an execution for desertion on June 20, at Camp Drake. "A fine warm day...we fell into line and formed three side of a square at open order, double division, to see David Leisure, of Colonel Bushe's 4th Indiana Battery, shot dead for desertion...in the face of the enemy. At a quarter before 12 o'clock he was shot dead   on his coffin...So ends a traitor's doom." [16]

Colonel Stoughton issued an order, while Provost Marshall, on February 7th, leading to the belief that some soldiers were once again taking advantage of their conqueror role by taking property of the folks in and around Murfreesboro under the guise of official policy. Complaints were lodged with Colonel Stoughton by local citizens that unauthorized parties dressed in Federal uniforms had made searches at homes in the city and in some instances taken away property supposed to be contraband. None of these activities had been ordered by or reported to the proper officers, and was nothing less than plundering and robbery. Colonel Stoughton warned that any person making searches without authority and appropriating property to his own use would be dealt with as his crime deserved.

In all probability, many transgressions occurred during the occupation of Murfreesboro. Sam Dumm did not record any violations of common decency or military law; however, he did write to his sister describing the people of the area. "The warm weather [brought] out the Secesh ladies in their silks and furs and laces....They are all very much down on the 'blue bellied Yankees', as they call [us]. Some of them appear very independent, and will turn their heads if they see a Yankee approaching while others appear more cordial, and they will condescend to converse familiarly....There are a few families that profess to be Union, but I am afraid that they are milk and water ones, and change as the wind blows." In deference to the women of Murfreesboro, with most of their men away they used whatever means they had to "fight" the Union and realized that they had to survive in their war ravaged countryside.

The army in and around town was regaining its strength and resolve. Within the Seventy-Eighth many of the men were getting back to their former selves and things were returning to normal...or at least normal for an army in the field. Henry Claypoole was getting fat again. The leg that the doctors had wanted to take off had regained its strength. Lem Rea and Ham Smith still raced for the "pork and beans" call. Sam Dumm's health was excellent and he was enjoying the warm weather. John and Wash Doty, as usual, entertained the Slate Lick boys by playing the court jesters. Richard Christy and Sirwell's new friend, the Reverend, Colonel Granville Moody, of the 74th Ohio, held "well attended" services for the troops. Buck Simkins purchased a pair of boots that had been sent to John Hartman. Hartman had died of his wounds in mid January. Lieutenant Smith decided that it would be better to sell the boots and send the money to Hartman's mother.

Personal care and habits degenerated over a period of time. The Regiment was reported by the Medical Officer of the Day for not paying proper attention to policing of quarters. They were also cited for permitting bread, meat, and general garbage to accumulate and decompose in the latrines and ditches. The boys threw convention to the wind, they urinated in the company streets, between the tents, and on the parade ground. It became so frequent that Colonel Sirwell threatened his boys with punishments if their filthy habits persisted.

There was a growing loss of military discipline or respect, but again that disrespect for convention was the way of the American soldier. Nonetheless, some of the boys from the regiment, and evidently enough to require Sirwell's attention, were showing a growing disrespect for authority or military form. Colonel Sirwell's order follows.

Headquarters 78th Pennsylvania Volunteer Infantry.
Murfreesboro, Tennessee, April 8th, 1863.

Special Orders No 76.

Commanders of companies will instruct their sergeants to be more attentive in duties of the soldier.

The enlisted men and in some cases the Non Commissioned officers have a habit of blowing their noses, spitting and looking around in the ranks. Said habits being very disagreeable and unsoldier like, will not be tolerated any longer.

Sergeants should correct these habits. It is their duty. If they fail to do so they fail to perform the duties they are assigned to and may rest assured they will be attended to.

The next time any actions like the above are noticed the person or persons so offending will be sent to jail. This order will be read to the men.

By Command of Colonel William Sirwell
Henry W. Torbett, Acting Adjutant

If the Seventy-Eighth was having problems, the Ohio Twenty-First was gaining recognition for their problems. James Neibling was an affable man not really intent on command. He wanted nothing more than to be friends with his boys. Therefore, discipline was almost non existent in the regiment. When Silas Canfield or Dwella Stoughton were commanding in Neibling's absence, there was strict military discipline. But when "Colonel Jim" returned, the men threw rules and orders to the wind.

Bliss Morse of the 105th Ohio wrote home that a sergeant in the regiment was court martialed for calling his captain "a damned old piss pot." The offending sergeant lost his stripes and two months pay.

In March, Colonel John Miller noted in a directive to Colonel James Neibling that his sentinels "loafed" around camp fires, sat and wrote letters, and there was generally build up of garbage and offal in the kitchen sinks and cast off clothing lying in the company areas.

In May, General Negley addressed Colonel Jim with the complaint that the Ohio 21st was all too frequently on the report of the Department Inspector General for "neglect and non-performance of picket duty" and that an inspection of weapons showed them generally to be dirty and uncared for. In July, Captain Lord the Brigade Inspector General reported to Army Headquarters that the Twenty-Onesters kept the poorest records of any regiment in the brigade. General Rosecrans forwarded the report to Colonel Sirwell, then brigade commander, for his personal "attention and action." It is doubtful that Sirwell was able to rectify the problem, since the Twenty-First only reported the names of the forty-seven killed and mortally wounded at the battle of Stones River to Washington – two years after the battle.

Discipline did return, when Lieutenant Colonel Stoughton replaced Colonel Jim after he was sent back to Camp Chase, Ohio in August 1863, for "recruiting duty" by General Thomas. The boys would always keep James Neibling fondly in their memories. The regimental history relates the story that on a particular day Silas Canfield reprimanded a private walking post. Before Canfield was out of hearing, "...Colonel Jim came out [of his tent] and said, 'guard I'll be damned if I'd walk post, come here and sit down.'"

It was not always the enlisted men that broke regulations, Colonel Neibling and many other officers could also be faulted for laxity. Major General George Thomas on March 20th, noted that General Rosecrans, although pleased with the widespread good appearance of the men on review, noted some irregularities. Commissioned officers were not saluting the reviewing officer in passing. The troops ordered for review were not appearing under full arms and equipment. And all officers were not showing the insignia of their rank. [17]

Like his army, Rosecrans easily made himself insufferable to the high command. Secretary Stanton forwarded information that erroneously reported that "Fighting" Joe Hooker at the battle of Chancellorsville had inflicted as many casualties on Lee's Army of Northern Virginia as he had sustained. In response to the dispatch, in what seems to be a tongue in cheek reply Rosey stated, "Thanks for your dispatch. It relieved our great suspense."

Sergeant "Buck" Simkins was more scathing in his criticism. "[In the Army of the Potomac] they had better Enlist a new Set of men and then Discharge Generals...The news is here ...[that the] men run like Sons of Bitches...if I had Relatives in a Running Regiment...[I] Sooner would claim Kindred with a Negro for I consider them far away better than a Cowardly Soldier." [18] In Washington D.C., was the advancing Army of the Cumberland still held in less regard than the inept Army of the Potomac?

On the Confederate front it was not the army's reputation in question. General Bragg's leadership was still in question. Braxton Bragg also had problems, but they were still with his command and subordinates. General Polk was actively campaigning for Bragg's removal. [19]

Despite Washington's constant harping about Rosey's lack of movement, in reality, he and his staff were working constantly to put his army into motion. In the coming campaign against Bragg, his plans would be shown to be well worth the victory with very little loss in life. Nonetheless, Halleck wanted all of the Union armies to move. He came up with a plan to give the next victor in the field a promotion for his efforts. Rosecrans resented this trite offer.

Murfreesboro, 6th March, 1863.
To Major-General H.W. Halleck,

General: - Yours of the 1st instant, announcing the offer of a vacant major-generalship in the regular army to the general in the field who first wins an important and decisive victory, is at hand. As an officer and a citizen I feel degraded at such an auctioneering of honors. Have we a general who would fight for his own personal benefit when he would not [fight] for honor and his country? He would come by his commission basely in that case, and deserve to be despised by men of honor. But are all the brave and honorable generals on an equality as to chances? If not, it is unjust to those who probably deserve most.

    W.S. Rosecrans, Major-General [20]

Assuredly the army had stayed too long in Murfreesboro, but Rosey was the field commander and would move at his own time schedule. In reality, General Rosecrans was supported in his decision to remain in Murfreesboro and refit his army by all of his subordinate commanders except General Garfield. Naturally, Garfield had both military and political motives for his stance.

  Orders in the Company I Order Book, Pennsylvania Seventy-Eighth, show that Rosey was preparing to move. In mid May, Colonel Miller issued an order which would indicate that the army might be on the move, but as it turned out, it would be weeks away.

Headquarters, 3rd Brigade, 2nd Division, 14th Army Corps
Murfreesboro, Tennessee, May 14th, 1863.

General Order No 17

Enlisted men will carry in active campaign during the warm season in knapsacks the following articles and no more Viz: one shirt, two pair of socks, one pair shoes, one blanket, and one gum blanket, on top of knapsack if possible.

Before the march the men's overcoats and all other clothing of value not included in the Uniform Suit on the person and the above allowances [will be judged] as extra. [They] will be carefully inventoried and stored in a warehouse, either in Murfreesboro or Nashville.

Each Company Commander will draw and carry in the company wagon a number of pairs of pantaloons equal to one fifth of the number of men under his command. [These will] be issued in case of accident in that article of clothing.

All necessary preparation for the observance of these regulations will be immediately made and on the first intimation of a movement of the Army the boxes must be packed ready for transportation.

   By Command of Colonel John Franklin Miller
   Henry M. Cist, Acting Assistant Adjutant General

The citizens of Murfreesboro would be happy to see the Union troops leave. The land in and around the town had been devastated. Most of the trees had been cut down for shelter, forts or fire wood. Forts and entrenchments surrounded the city and the army supply depots were filled to capacity.

On June 1st, a warm and dry day, General Rosecrans had a grand review of all his divisions. He had to be evaluating his preparedness. Two days later it would appear from the following directive that Rosey's army was preparing to move, but he still would move only in his own time frame.

Headquarters, Department of the Cumberland
Murfreesboro, Tennessee, June 3rd, 1863.

The General Commanding directs that a minute and thorough company inspection of every company in your command be immediately made to ascertain that the men have everything ready for movements including: 3 days rations in haversacks and five days Bread, Sugar and Coffee in knapsacks. And that a report be made to these Headquarters that everything necessary has been provided as contemplated in this order. And [that a report be prepared] giving the actual effective strength of each brigade, that is, the number of men and officers who would march with it were our immediate move ordered.

I am Sir Very Respectfully, Your Obedient Servant
[William S. Rosecrans] (Signed) Calvin Goddard
Lt. Colonel & Assistant Adjutant General [21]

"WE ARE COMING, FATHER ABRA'AM"

On the 19th of June, Colonel Bill Sirwell assumed command of the third brigade, second division of the 14th Army Corps, replacing Colonel Miller. John Miller returned to his Twenty-Ninth Indiana and as senior officer took command of the brigade within which his regiment was posted. Colonel Miller would be seriously wounded in the coming campaign and sent home. He would one day return to the Army of the Cumberland. Appointed a Brigadier General of Volunteers, he would be breveted a Major General for his actions as a division commander in the battle of Nashville in 1864.

Sirwell led a brigade toward Tullahoma and Chickamauga that approximately equaled the original size of his regiment. He proudly wore a new presentation sword. The boys in the Seventy-Eighth had honored their commander with the second of swords awarded for their appreciation. The scabbard was heavily gold-plated and beautifully ornamented. The blade was of the finest steel and appropriately deviced. The handle was of solid silver with a mounted design of the Goddess of Liberty; it also contained 12 rubies. In the presentation speech, the speaker noted, "On the field at Stones River you carried a sword without a scabbard...we hope that this will be your motto, 'A sword without a sheath.'...Use [this sword] against those whom we came to punish and may the bright glittering steel prove as true as the heart of him who henceforth wields it." [1]

During April and May there was a prevailing belief within the ranks that part of Grant's and Burnside's armies would unite with Rosecrans for the push against Bragg. Second Lieutenant Franklin Mechling wrote home on May 3, 1863, confident in the fact that "...Old Rosy is biding his own time, when Burnsides and grant can co-operate and then strike a grand and effective blow." In the end Washington would be of little help and the Army of the Cumberland would be alone. Neither Grant or Burnside would send troops; however, Halleck would bring pressure to bear on Rosey. But regardless of Washington's pressure, the advance on the Confederate army was Rosecrans' decision. As June moved into its second two weeks, Washington stepped up pressure for Rosey to move against the Confederates. Lincoln was totally frustrated with his lack of action. Lincoln wanted that rail center in Chattanooga. Chattanooga rail lines connected with Vicksburg, Atlanta and Richmond. These rails carried a goodly percentage of the South's supplies, and Lincoln felt that taking and holding Chattanooga would choke the Southern war effort. Cutting off these supply lines from the west was equally if not more important than capturing Richmond.

On the 16th, via "Woodenhead" Halleck, a wire was sent to Bill Rosecrans. "Is it your intention to make an immediate movement forward? A definite yes or no is required." Rosey obstinately wired back, "If immediate means tonight or tomorrow, no. If it means as soon as things are ready, say five days, yes."

Rosecrans had spent a great deal of time and energy preparing his army to move. His army had to heal. Supplies and cavalry were needed. When the forward progress would begin, it was necessary to guard rail and supply lines along with Clarksville, Donelson and Nashville. Intelligence had to be gathered on terrain and Confederate positions. Groups of Union sympathizers that came into the Federal lines after the battle of Stones River had been formed into "scout" squads. They preceded the army into enemy territory and reported valuable information to Rosecrans.

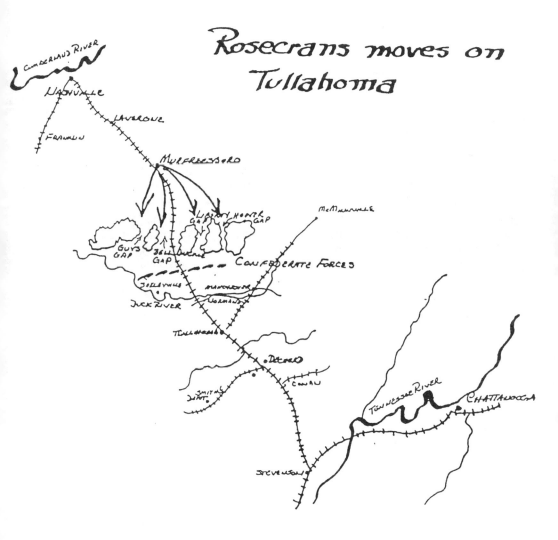

Rosecrans moves on Tullahoma

Lastly and most importantly Bill Rosecrans was evasive with Washington because he did not want his battle plan to be "leaked" to the enemy. It is evident from the orders posted in Company I's order book that the army was preparing to move, but Rosecrans kept his plan from superiors and subordinates alike. The element of surprise was the key.

Rosecrans wired Washington June 24th that he was advancing within the hour. This would be a covert operation; he did not detail his direction or strength to his superiors. It was not Rosey's recalcitrant character that caused him to keep information from his superiors. He did not want his plan known to General Bragg. Much of the information reported to Washington tended to leak to the media. The newspapers always seemed to report the movements of Northern armies in great detail. Early in the six month stay in Murfreesboro, General Rosecrans asked in an open letter to the *Nashville Union* that the Western newspapers cease from reporting shipments of supplies to the army. These reports only notified the Confederate forces of when and where to attack and or capture those supplies. Interestingly enough, Braxton Bragg subscribed to several Northern newspapers through a friend in Elizabethtown, Kentucky. These papers afforded better intelligence than his scouts.

At 9:00 A.M., on June 24, 1863, Sirwell led his brigade out the Manchester Pike with George Thomas' Fourteenth Army Corps. The advance proceeded with the virtually ever present, but now torrential rain fall which would persist for fifteen days. [2]

Rosey's army headed southeast toward Chattanooga, preceded by a group of "refugee Rebels" acting as scouts. A long ridge, the Cumberland Plateau, blocked the path of the Union army. There were four gaps in the ridge. From northeast to southwest the gaps were: Hoover's Gap, Liberty Gap, Bellbuckle Gap and Guy's Gap to the west through which Rosey's army could confront the Confederate army. Bragg with his army positioned along the Duck River line assumed that Rosecrans would attack the left of his position from the passes to the west that were easily more accessible to Rosey's right. Hoover's Gap, to the east, because of its mountainous terrain was of no consideration to Bragg. Bragg assumed incorrectly. [3] Actually a movement on Bragg's right, through the unpassable Hoover's Gap, was to be the body of the Union attack. If Rosey could cut off Bragg from Chattanooga by flanking his right, he could destroy the Southern army.

The Federal plan was set and movement began. Stanley's cavalry initiated the Union feint toward Shelbyville to Bragg's left. Crittenden moved his Twenty-First Corps to Guy's Gap. McCook's Twentieth Corps moved to Liberty Gap and Thomas moved to Hoover's Gap, the point of Rosey's attack. Bragg had taken the bait; he moved to defend his army against the feint to his left. When he realized the real threat was coming from his right, it was too late. The dangerous position of his army with the Union troops closing on his right forced him to begin a retreat. [4]

Bragg had been completely out foxed. It would seem that if not for the rain, Rosecrans could have fallen on his adversary and destroyed him, but the rain and mud hampered his movements and ultimately affected his overall plan, more so than Bragg. The mud was so bad that Crittenden's Corps struggled for four days, marching only seventeen miles. Horses and mules floundered while artillery and ammunition wagons had to be hauled by the men. Some "mules perished in the mud, unable to extricate themselves." If Crittenden had been able to join McCook and Thomas two days earlier... [5]

Sirwell's brigade and the 78th had skirmished and "mud marched" with most of Thomas' Corps through Hoover's Gap. Despite the horrid weather the campaign was virtually flawless. Rosey's series of adroit flanking movements drove Bragg army out of Tullahoma on June 30th. It was a virtual bloodless victory. [6]

A few days after Rosecrans' brilliant victory, Vicksburg finally fell under the pressure of General Grant's army and Marse Robert was defeated on the farm land near Gettysburg, Pennsylvania. Like a wolf closing on his prey, Lincoln could smell blood. If George Gordon Meade and William Starke Rosecrans could press their opposition and defeat these Confederate armies in the field, Lincoln felt the South would capitulate.

Through Stanton and Halleck, Lincoln conveyed his desires and Rosey reacted with his usual incensed manner. Stanton prodded General Rosecrans with the message, "You and your noble army now have the chance to give the finishing blow to the rebellion. Will you neglect the chance?" Rosey felt that his army had accomplished a feat by driving Bragg out of Tennessee. His terse reply told the administration what they feared, "I beg in behalf of this army that the War Department may not overlook so great an event because it is not written in letters of blood." He would take his time in moving. [7]

For the soldiers in the Army of the Cumberland it was back to camp life. Procuring food was always important. The boys in the regiment now acted the part of conquering invaders. Since Hoover's Gap, they had "killed, sheep, hogs and cattle and took everything [they] wanted." Albert Dougherty and Adam Beck were just two of the boys who picked blackberries. Many procured peaches, butter, milk, maple sugar and "roastin ears" from the area farms. Even though this was going to be a temporary camp the troops worked at making comfortable quarters and visited the farms and girls of the region. Visitors from home were a real delight. Letters, baked goods, warm under shirts, candied fruit and most of all -- news. For Abram Kipp visitors from home caused him a problem. His name was spelled incorrectly by the Kittanning paper when they reported Sirwell's casualties at Stones River. He had been able to keep the news of his wound a secret from his mother. The visitors from Leechburg noticed his limp. He wrote his mother immediately of his deception.

An army in camp is difficult to control and the boys instantly returned to their old habits developed and nurtured in Murfreesboro. Captain Findley described in his diary a trip on Monday, September 1, 1863. "Lieutenant [Edward A.] Ballard and I procured a pass and walked to Stevenson [Alabama] - three miles distant. Procured some whiskey for the march at Post Commissary. Got 6 quarts for $1.00." Sergeant Puntenney of Sirwell's Brigade noted that a few of the boys slipped out of their camps to find fun loving young ladies of the area or engage in another of their favorite pastimes. [8] "While at Decherd...the Regiment was put under strict army regulations- company and regimental drill, dress parade, policing grounds, guard duty, brightening guns, etc. "

"Strange as it may seem, here under strict discipline the troops developed such a affection for gambling that the officers felt it to be their duty to suppress it, if possible. Even after orders forbidding gambling had been issued, the men would slip out and throw dice by moonlight. Digging stumps was usually the punishment for being caught gambling."[9] Puntenney's brigade commander, William Sirwell, had issued orders regarding gambling, but nothing about local female companionship or drinking. The sutlers were selling as much beer as they could for 25¢ a pint.

Headquarters 2nd Division, 3rd Brigade
Decherd, Tennessee, August 1st, 1863.

General Order No. 29

 I. From this date all card playing of any kind is strictly forbidden. Officers and privates of this command caught or known to have been playing cards, hereafter within the limits of this Brigade, will be severely punished for disobedience of orders.
 II. Gambling for money by any games is strictly forbidden. All officers or privates in this command who may know of card playing or gambling within the limits of this command and fail to give information to the Regimental Provost or Brigade Provost Marshal will be arrested and tried as one of the guilty parties.
 III. Sutlers of this Brigade are strictly forbidden to sell cards to any officer or enlisted man of this command under penalty of being reported to the General Commanding with a view of having his commission as Sutler revoked.

By Command of Colonel William Sirwell
Commanding 3rd Brigade
W.F. Armstrong Captain & Provost Marshall

Although, as mentioned, Sirwell displayed a fatherly demeanor towards his boys, when the time came for punishment, it was just and swift. Sergeant Puntenney notes in his recollections of the war that before the battle of Chickamauga two men of the brigade were punished for their transgressions of the rules. "Our last camp before we crossed the Tennessee River was near the last of August. It was uncomfortably cold there for several nights. While at this camp we were called into line to witness the punishment of two artillery men, who, for some offense had the hair shaved off one side of their heads, and marched in front of the entire brigade with a fifer before them playing: 'Poor old soldier.' A file of soldiers behind them with bayonets fixed distressingly close to their seats. Those two men went on to perform conspicuously at the battle of Chickamauga." [10]

From his headquarters at Cave Spring, Alabama, on August 19th, Major General Negley complained about the numerous instances of straggling during the last march. The 37th Indiana and the 88th Indiana were condemned for having the most cases. Negley warned that if the straggling persisted he intended to report through Corps and Departmental Headquarters to the Governors of their States the name of every officer who failed to restrain his men from straggling. He added a warning to his order; he would prevent the further promotion of any such officer. [11]

Meanwhile, Rosecrans was receiving the old, familiar refrain from Washington, "Advance!" But Rosey used up three weeks repairing the one hundred and thirteen mile rail line reaching back to Nashville. He finished a 2700 foot span over the Tennessee River and collected twenty day rations and adequate ammunition. [12]

The Army of the Cumberland under Old Rosey was to meet its destiny on an obscure battlefield in Georgia; called Chickamauga. On August 16, the Union army took up the march to Chattanooga. Once again, Bragg fled fearing he would be cut off from his

Atlanta base. William Rosecrans, although not engaging the Rebels, had once again dexterously maneuvered his adversary out of position.   Bragg's retreat was quite a birthday gift for the big Dutchman who had turned forty-four on September 6th. Rosey's army had achieved Lincoln's goal of capturing the rail hub at Chattanooga on September 9, 1863. [13]

Understandably, over confidence and the politics of war now infected Rosecrans. The high command urged Rosecrans to move after Bragg, and this time he was in agreement. For the first time General Thomas was reluctant to go into battle; he felt the army needed more time to prepare for this battle. Chattanooga was now firmly in Federal hands; why not take time to plan the defeat of Bragg's army. Prudence was advisable; Bragg could be a worthy enemy. George Thomas did not protest strongly enough; his wise consul would be ignored.

William Starke Rosecrans in concert with the Union high command affected the eventual Federal defeat at Chickamauga. Rosey's cocksure attitude prohibited him from wisely evaluating his adversary. He advanced pell mell to his defeat and Sirwell's Brigade faithfully followed. Pap Thomas assigned James Negley's division to lead the center of the army through Pigeon Mountain. Major General Negley formed with his division Rosecrans' advanced guard in the forward movement from Tennessee against Bragg. Negley had chosen Bill Sirwell's Third Brigade to lead the way to McLemore's Cove. [14]

"WEEPING SAD AND LONELY"
CHICKAMAUGA

On a bright and crisp September morning, fully assured that Braxton Bragg's army was running away, Colonel William Sirwell, his staff and brigade led General Thomas' Corps through McLemore's Cove into the Dug Gap pass in the Pigeon Mountains. Intelligence on the enemy would be inadequate. No cavalry units were assigned to either Thomas, Negley or Sirwell. The troops labored every step of the way. They had to clear huge boulders and trees placed in their path by the retreating Confederates. Movement was slow over steep mountain roads and especially hampered by the four hundred wagons moving with the column.

The coming battle at Chickamauga was teeming with circumstances that could portend disaster in any battle. Aside from the growing cocksure attitude of the General-in-Command, there was the ever present danger of a wily and determined Confederate army that should have made caution a determinate precept. The rough terrain of the Cumberland Mountains rising before Rosey's army would present new problems. Simple movement would be difficult. Intelligence and reconnaissance would not be exacting. Communication and support between moving wings of the Union army would be encumbered by the rugged topography. Despite the obstacles presented to him, Rosey's ultimate goal was to move south and destroy Bragg's army.

Six weeks at Decherd had passed and on August 16, the Union army had moved out to pursue Bragg once again. Sirwell's Brigade, starting at Cave Spring, crossed the Tennessee River southeast of Stevenson, Alabama at Caperton's bridge. From the very beginning Sirwell's lads slogged through difficult countryside under unusual circumstances. Since Captain Joe Smith of Company K was acting Brigade Commissary Officer, Company K was detailed to drive 200 head of cattle on the trip. The hundreds of wagons slowed the movement of the division. At times Sirwell and Negley took off their coats and pulled ropes hauling wagons and cannon up steep slopes just like the enlisted troops.

Driving towards Chattanooga with the other tentacles of Rosey's army, Negley's troops at the summit of Lookout Mountain watched the dust clouds of Bragg's retreating army move once again to the south. The men in the field, like their commander, became more confident. The Rebels would run from a fight again. The rough roads presented the greatest problem now, or so they thought.

There were always trivial events during a tramp that could bring joy to a campaigning soldier. Projects and physical labor that had become arduous and mundane in the Western Pennsylvania valleys now brought a break from boredom. Colonel Sirwell's brigade was given an assignment to build a bridge across a deep ravine near Raccoon Mountain. Bill Sirwell assigned the task to the boys of the Seventy-Eighth and the Twenty-First Ohio. Colonel Blakeley posted the project to Lieutenant Brinker and a force from Company C. Captain Alban's Company F, Ohio 21st, began the project while Brinker and his men completed the 160 foot bridge in ten hours. A good part of the bridge came from the dismantled Warren's Sawmill. But hard work followed by a long rest break could be fun. The men dozed, wrote letters and swam. Unfortunately, two men from the Ohio company drowned while swimming in the river.

During a reconnaissance mission up Will's Valley a detail discovered a mill on Lookout Creek full of approximately five hundred bushels of wheat, corn and rye. Captain Marlin's detail from Company A and some fellows from the 21st Ohio ground up the grain in the mill and any that could be found in the area. They gave out the unsifted, coarse flour to the other passing troops. They made sure to send a bag of the unbolted flour to General Thomas. The troops also acquired some beef cattle in the area; making sure to leave some for the local residents, or so records Thompson Gibson. "Sweet" bread, fresh beef, agreeable toil and a retreating enemy...all the things that make the troops happy and confident. [1]

On September 10th, Negley and Thomas had the opportunity to interrogate a Rebel officer from the Thirty-Second Mississippi. Although he was reticent in giving out information, he boldly proclaimed that if Negley proceeded with his movement through the mountains he would be attacked and defeated. A few of the local citizens verified enemy troops moving in force to flank Negley's Division. Despite this information Rosey chided "Pap" Thomas for not pushing Negley harder with his forward movement. Negley pushed forward. Sirwell ordered that another forty rounds of ammunition be issued to his soldiers.

Either Rosey's over confidence was filtering down through the command or Thomas and his staff ignored the intelligence they had received. Colonel Blakeley the first of Sirwell's regiments leading Negley's division had been informed that there was no need for skirmishers. The undaunted army blundered forward, and with mild surprise met a force of what was initially thought to be only Confederate skirmishers at Dug Gap near Davis' Crossroads. Colonel Sirwell wheeled his mount and followed by his staff raced back to the Seventy-Eighth booming, "Into line, Colonel! Into line!" Hearts quickened as Lieutenant Colonel Blakeley hurried to form his regiment for battle. There was an intense Confederate fire that kept the Federals pinned down, and the Union position quickly became precarious. Holding on until dark and leaving his advanced pickets in position, Sirwell moved back about one half of a mile. With the early morning light, firing commenced along Sirwell's whole front and the attempt to sweep his left told him that the Rebel force was more than a skirmish line.

At about the same time as the Rebel fire began, Baird's division closed up on Negley's at the Widow Davis house. With the reinforcements from Baird's Division and in the face of a large attacking force, Sirwell and John Beatty ordered their cannon to open on the enemy. The Confederates quickly retreated back off the dangerous ridge. During the sporadic rifle fire of the whole day, Negley affected the westerly retrograde movement of his division to a stronger position in front of Steven's Gap without a loss of a single wagon. The Seventy-Eighth had lost their comrade Jake Wiant of Company C.

Negley's Division had been very fortunate. Bragg had three converging columns preparing to crush them and hopefully Thomas' whole Corps. [3] Confusion within Bragg's officers had helped the Union cause. Bragg, who knew that he had Thomas' Corps in a position for their destruction, was quite angry with Thomas Hindman for his indecisiveness. D. Harvey Hill was accused of insubordination for not moving to battle quickly enough to close the trap on Negley. General Buckner did not obey his orders either. He held a council of war that decided not to fight. [4]

Battle at Davis Crossroads

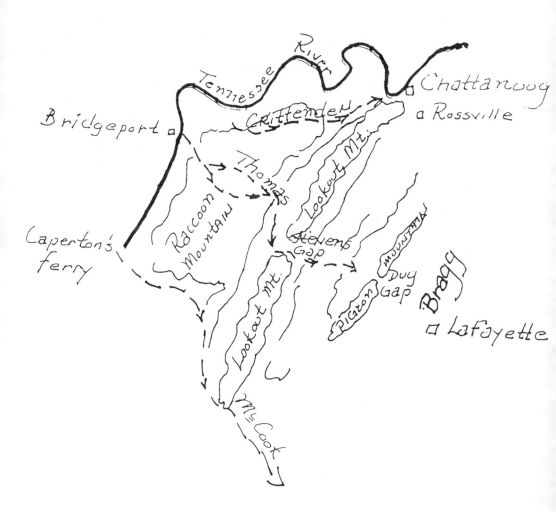

Another fascinating side light to history occurred before the battle of Chickamauga. While the men of the 78th were building the bridge and grinding grain in Lookout Valley, a number became ill. Private Bill Hosack, the doctor in G Company, was detailed to remain with these men. Hosack and his charges were over run during the ensuing battle. They were captured and sent either to Andersonville or Libby Prison in Richmond. John Irwin of Company D and Henry Marshal of Company E would die at Andersonville. Fortunately Dr. Hosack was sent to Libby.

During his imprisonment Dr. Hosack made the acquaintance of Major Harry White who was on the regimental staff of the Sixty-Seventh Pennsylvania and a member of the Pennsylvania State Senate. Major White had been captured by the Confederates in the Shenandoah Valley. While White had been at war, the power of the anti-war forces had increased in the Pennsylvania Senate, so much so that there was now a deadlock in voting on war issues. One of the nation's largest states was left virtually powerless on voting for appropriations, men and supplies for the war effort. The Confederates became aware of Pennsylvania's dilemma and refused to exchange White or permit him to correspond with anyone.

When White learned of Hosack's exchange, he wrote his resignation on tissue paper torn from his bible and sewed it into the back coat button of Hosack's uniform. Upon his release, Hosack headed for Indiana, Pennsylvania, and White's father. Thomas White delivered the resignation to Governor Curtin who immediately called for a special election. Dr. St. Clair, a strong war advocate, of the area was elected and broke the Senate deadlock. In Pennsylvania it was business as usual. [5]

The battle of Chickamauga was a failure for Rosey from start to finish. It actually took General Rosecrans some time to realize that he would have to do battle. On September 10th, Rosecrans was still under the impression that Bragg was retreating. From Sirwell's first contact with the Rebels, Rosecrans handled the battle improperly. Poor command decisions, confusing orders, and disorganization permeated the battle both Saturday and Sunday, the 19th and 20th of September. The one highlight of the battle was George Thomas' stubborn stand on Snodgrass Hill which literally preserved the Union army from total annihilation.

The saving grace for the Union was Bragg's lack of fortitude in following up his devastating defeat of Rosey's army. Charles Dana wired the War Department, "Chickamauga is as fatal a name in our history as Bull Run." Dana's assessment was ludicrous in light of the fact that, in the end, the Federals were able to hold the important rail center at Chattanooga. [6]

If the set of orders issued to Colonel Sirwell and Major General Negley from September 18, 1863, to September 20, are indicative of the consistency of orders to other divisions or brigades, it is little wonder that Rosecrans lost the battle along Chickamauga Creek.

In the late afternoon of September 18th, James Negley rode up to General Hazen's position, dismounted and proceeded to affect his orders to relieve Hazen. General Hazen who was lying on the ground nonchalantly refused to be relieved; he had not been ordered to be relieved. Later, General Beatty of Negley's Division again tried to relieve Hazen with the same result. Major Lowrie, Negley's Assistant Adjutant General, had to find General Thomas and report that Palmer's brigades refused to be relieved. General

CHAIN OF COMMAND
THE PENNSYLVANIA SEVENTY-EIGHTH [8]
ARMY OF THE CUMBERLAND
COMMAND
Major General William Rosecrans
XIV ARMY CORPS
Major General George Thomas
THOMAS' SECOND DIVISION
Major General James Scott Negley
NEGLEY'S FIRST BRIGADE
Brigadier General John Beatty
42nd Indiana, Lieutenant Colonel William T.B. McIntire
88th Indiana, Colonel George Humphrey
104th Illinois, Lieutenant Colonel Douglas Hapeman
15th Kentucky, Colonel Marion C. Taylor
ARTILLERY
Illinois Light, Bridge's Battery, Captain Lyman Bridges
NEGLEY'S SECOND BRIGADE
Colonel Timothy R. Stanley
Colonel William L. Stoughton
18th Ohio, Lieutenant Colonel Charles Grosvenor
19th Illinois, Lieutenant Colonel Alexander W. Raffen
11th Michigan, Colonel William L. Stoughton
Lieutenant Colonel Melvin Mudge
ARTILLERY
1st Ohio, Battery G, Captain Alexander Marshall
NEGLEY'S THIRD BRIGADE
Colonel William G. Sirwell
21st Ohio, Lieutenant Colonel Dwella M. Stoughton
Major Arnold McMahan
Captain Charles H. Vantine
37th Indiana, Lieutenant Colonel William D. Ward
74th Ohio, Captain Joseph Fisher
78th Pennsylvania, Lieutenant Colonel Archibald Blakeley
ARTILLERY
1st Ohio, Battery "M", Captain Fredrick Schultz

Official Record

Palmer again sent an order to his brigades [Hazen's included] that they were to be relieved. Sirwell was to relieve Hazen; and did. This was an example of the tenor of the battle communications to come on the 19th and 20th. [7]

One of the most devastating factors in the battle of Chickamauga was the addition of General Longstreet's Corps of Lee's Army of Northern Virginia to Bragg's forces. James Longstreet's Confederate reinforcements dramatically affected the eventual Federal defeat at Chickamauga. Additionally, other reinforcements sent to Bragg from Joe Johnston gave Bragg a superior troop strength of over 14,000 men, 71,000 to Rosecrans 57,000. Oddly enough, The *Kittanning Mentor* reported in early February of 1863, "General Longstreet is reported to be about attacking General Rosecrans." Although this report was probably rumor or conjecture, it is interesting in the light of newspaper information sources. [9]

Official and unofficial sources disagreed on the whereabouts of James Longstreet's Corps. Richmond and Baltimore buzzed with rumors of an impending large troop movement. Henry Halleck's faulty intelligence sources caused him to incorrectly notify Rosecrans on September 11, that part of Bragg's army was being sent to General Lee in Virginia. Reports from Fortress Monroe on September 13th and 14th indicated that Longstreet was moving his Corps to Bragg. General Meade reported the disappearance of Longstreet's army from his front at the same time.

Unfortunately, even after Washington reversed their report, Rosecrans would not believe the information regarding his old West Point roommate. Halleck properly ordered Burnside to re-enforce Rosecrans from Knoxville, but Burnside failed to carry out his assignment. Telegraphs to Grant at Vicksburg and General Hurlbut at Memphis could not be affected. Any federal support was too far away to help the Army of the Cumberland now in the face of battle. [10]

On the evening of September 18th, Braxton Bragg's army was centrally concentrated in the neighborhood of Lee and Gordon's Mill, south of the Chickamauga Creek. He had hoped to cross the Chickamauga below the mill and attack Rosey's left flank. If the gods of war were with him, he could intersperse himself between Chattanooga and the Union army and retake the city. To Bragg's dismay, Rosecrans changed the positions of his Corps, but still left the opportunity for the Confederates to recapture Chattanooga.

Four days earlier, two different "Negro women" relayed the disposition of Bragg's troops to Major General Thomas. One that had been taken prisoner by Buckner and released reported to Thomas that Rebel forces were at Catlett's Gap while the other from Dug Gap reported forces between Dug Gap and Lafayette. This information may have helped in final placement of Rosey's foot soldiers.

For the story of the Pennsylvania Seventy-Eighth, the battle at Chickamauga was never the fight as seen at Stones River. Sam Dumm wrote to his parents: "Our Regiment was providentially dealt with, for we were moved from one part of the field to another, almost under the enemies guns...and not a man was hurt." The story of Chickamauga was William Sirwell's. His adventures during the two day battle were a virtual reflection of Rosey's army. Simultaneous and conflicting orders fractured his brigade. Parts of his brigade moved at Negley's orders, part via Rosecrans' or Thomas' command, some because of General Brannan and damn few at Sirwell's command. Unlike Rosey and many of his corps commanders, Sirwell remained on the field to the last. In the end with his brigade shattered, Bill Sirwell did the only thing left to him. He took a position on the line of battle and fought.

On a bright, clear autumn day of September 19th, the battlefield at Chickamauga saw a series of charges and counter charges. About 9:00 A.M., Bragg, who was preparing to attack Crittenden's Corps that he supposed was the end of the Union left flank, was astonished by Thomas' attack on his right near Reed's Bridge. Thomas' Corps had surprisingly moved three to four miles from where he was reported to be on the evening of the 18th. Bragg now found his army fighting for Chattanooga with the Union army between himself and his goal. Attacking forces charged each other for the better part of the day. Troops on both sides were broken then rallied by officers. At times the Union initiative succeeded and again failed. Dashing strokes of victory were displayed by the Confederate soldiers. Negley's division reached its final position near the Widow Glenn's house at about 4:30. They prepared for an immediate assault, but the Rebel Generals Cleburne and Walker made a furious assault on Johnson's Division of McCook's Corps. Despite the sever pounding at the hands of the Confederates, at day's end the battle saw no real advantage on either side. Most importantly Rosecrans' army still controlled the Dry Valley and Rossville roads, pathways back to Chattanooga. [11]

On September 20, the second day of hard fighting at Chickamauga, Rosecrans, Sheridan, Davis, Negley, and McCook fled the battlefield with their frightened and bewildered soldiers. Rosey did not leave from cowardice. With General Garfield, and Majors McClintock and Bond, he hoped to save his army after setting up headquarters in Chattanooga. But he was still confused to his next move. Sirwell stayed the field with part of his brigade standing off the Rebel charges on Horseshoe Ridge.

Many of the soldiers assumed that Rosey would not fight on the Sabbath, but James Negley's Second Division had been ordered early on the morning of the 20th to join with General Thomas where the Union left was being hotly tested. Thomas became anxious when Negley did not arrive. He sent an aid to hurry up the errant division. When Captain Willard of Thomas' staff located Negley, Negley's skirmishers were being attacked and it was impossible to move the division. The second request by Thomas found Negley still waiting for his replacement, General McCook. Rosecrans, upset with McCook's tardiness, now personally ordered Crittenden to send General Thomas Wood. Negley ordered John Beatty's brigade to support Thomas at once. A new request by Thomas was finally acted upon. Negley with Stanley's Brigade pressed toward Thomas leaving Sirwell's small brigade and artillery to follow when relieved. Negley's Division had just pulled out of the Brotherton Woods moving eastward to the Snodgrass House when the Confederates hit the position just vacated.

It was about the same time that Negley was ordered through Thomas' aide, Captain Gaw, to mass his artillery at the Dyre farm when Negley learned that no troops had relieved Sirwell's position. Lieutenant Moody, of Negley's staff, carried orders from Negley to Sirwell to notify him he was to be relieved of his position and join the main division. Unknown to Negley, because of the Rebel assault Sirwell and Colonel Stanley had been ordered by General Rosecrans personally to return to their positions until relieved. Sirwell finally moved his brigade to Negley's aid when he was relieved by a portion of Wood's division. [12]

The Seventy-Eighth, at one point during the late morning, was posted alone, but in a strong position. Colonel Blakeley chided Augustus Bonnaffon his Battalion commander:

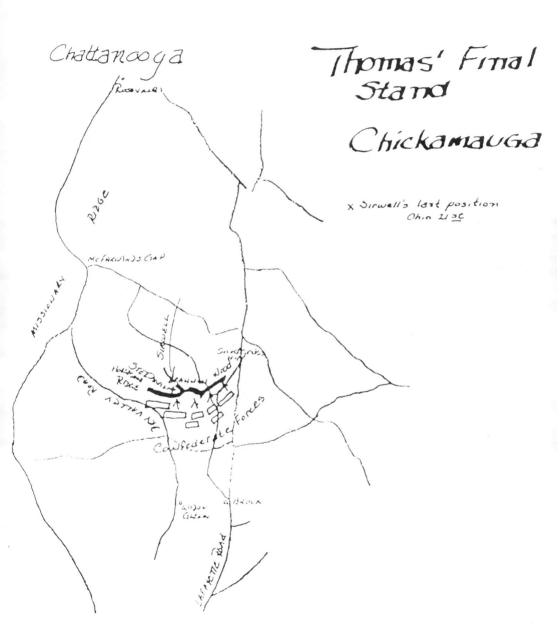

Thomas' Final Stand

Chickamauga

x Dirwell's last position
Ohio 21∞C

"Hold your line Major till we die unless ordered back." Bonnaffon quickly shouted his usual blasphemous reply: "Then we'll all go to hell..." There was no reason for Bonnaffon to fear the fiery bowels of the earth, the Seventy-Eighth would retire.

It was becoming more important to shore up the left of the Federal line. If the Rebels were successful in defeating Thomas' troops, they would shut the door of retreat into Chattanooga. They could annihilate Rosey's army. Brigadier General John Brannan of Thomas' Third Division who was making a bold stand on Snodgrass Hill requested a regiment from Bill Sirwell. Sirwell decided to send the Seventy-Eighth, but Negley ordered him to send the Twenty-First to re-enforce General Brannan. Negley kept the 78th at his command attempting to save the Union guns. Negley, Sirwell and their staffs all valiantly attempted to rally "fugitives" to protect the Union guns. However, Major Lowrie states in his after-action report that "As soon as a detachment brought to the front to support the batteries heard the sound of the enemy's muskets in their front, they disappeared like smoke."

When Colonel Sirwell eventually took the remaining part of the Seventy-Fourth Ohio to the right of Thomas' line to protect a battery, it became immediately apparent that the left flank needed more troops on the line. Colonel Sirwell followed by his orderly, Alfred Weir, rode off to bring up the bulk of his brigade. Upon returning to the position where he had placed the Pennsylvania 78th, a portion of the 37th Indiana, and a fragment of the 74th Ohio, Sirwell could not find them. Lieutenant Weir learned that they had been ordered to other parts of the field.

Unknown to Sirwell, the Seventy-Eighth had been ordered by General Negley to hold a chasm totally out of line and virtually surrounded. Colonel Blakeley was not aware of his precarious position and as luck would have it, their position in the woods was not realized by the Confederates. An aide to General Thomas accidentally discovered them and directed the regiment back to the Dry Valley Road. Actually, at 2 o'clock, Negley with the remnants of Sirwell's brigade saw that he was virtually surrounded and had quit the field; there was no time to find the Pennsylvanians. Furthermore, Generals Rosecrans, McCook and Crittenden had already left the field. [13]

The increased pressure on Thomas' assembled mass of troops became greater with the disintegration of the right wing of the Union line. In concert with an incorrectly worded order, General Thomas Wood more than anyone sealed the fate of Rosey's army. Wood had held a crucial point in the center of the Union front. He received an order from Rosecrans that directed him to take an action that made little sense. The rapscallion Wood, in all likelihood, purposely misinterpreted the order. He had been openly chastised and embarrassed earlier by Rosecrans for not relieving Negley on a more expeditious basis. Now he would follow the letter of the order and leave a gap in the Union line. Without taking the 3-5 minutes to ride and check with Rosey, he affected his order...with alacrity. The open space left by his division was hit by the Confederate assault.

The Rebel attack split the Union line. The right side of the line, Sheridan and Jeff Davis' Divisions, were left high and dry. The fierce Confederate assault drove them from the field. The day could only be saved by Thomas and those that gathered around him.

One of the many units gathered on Snodgrass Hill was the dauntless "Twenty Onesters." The 21st Ohio had stood at everyone's call. Sirwell was on another part of the hill with the 74th Ohio, and the Twenty-First now answered to many other officers. History would show that the boys from the Ohio Twenty-First were an invaluable asset.

Armed with Colt five-shot repeating rifles the Ohio lads constituted a devastating force. Their small regiment had the fire power of a brigade or greater. [14]

After holding off a number of fierce charges, the Ohio Twenty-First was overwhelmed. One hundred and fifteen men, their regimental and state flags and the precious Colt rapid fire revolving rifles were captured by Kelley's Brigade of the Seventh Florida. Without any notice to Sirwell or the Ohio 21st, General Walter Whittaker of Major General Granger's Reserve Corps had withdrawn his brigade from the line, leaving the Ohio regiment without any support on its right. About one hundred members of the Ohio regiment did evade capture. They slipped out in the darkness and battle smoke through a 90 foot gap in the Rebel lines that were closing in upon them. [15]

It is perplexing as to exactly how the men of the Ohio 21st were captured and sent off to Libby Prison. But in the History of the Twenty-First Regiment, Ohio Volunteer Infantry, Captain Silas Canfield writes bitterly, thirty years after the fact, that without ammunition the regiment was ordered to occupy a position on the extreme right of the hill and then abandoned. This devastating order that Canfield credits with causing their capture was given by an officer who "wore colored glasses." As with many confusing orders carried by aides, no name is attached to this courier, but an aide to General Brannan wore colored glasses. Still in all, when the order was given to the Twenty-Onesters to hold the line, Captain Isaac Cusac, their commander, responded, "Colonel, we have no more ammunition!" Brannan's colonel shouted, "It does not make a gawddamn bit of difference. Have the men fix bayonets and hold that line." The recalcitrant, courageous boys from the Buckeye State did just that. [16]

Although Silas Canfield writes harshly of the lack of command support during the Chickamauga campaign, many noted the bravery of the "Twenty-Onesters" for posterity. Colonel Sirwell wrote in his after-action report: "The Twenty-First Ohio faithfully remained at its post the whole of that dreadful afternoon [September 20th]. The men fought as heroes; almost unsupported...they fought gallantly on; their ammunition giving out, they gathered the cartridges of the dead and wounded...Their loss is terrible." [17]

General Thomas who directed the battle about 400 yards from the fire line had many generals around him in the late afternoon. "Pap" could have used a few more plain soldiers. However, he did draw troops from other sources. "Brigade commanders fought much like privates, among them Sirwell, Stoughton, and John Beatty...and Lieutenant Colonel Charles Grosvenor...all of Negley's division." Thomas' soldiers staved off three separate attacks, Kershaw's, Bushrod Johnson's and Longstreet's. [18]

At the battle's end Sirwell rode alone along the Dry Valley Road in darkness attempting to reform his shattered brigade. After he positioned the remnants of his brigade in line, he was ordered to station some of his troops as a rear guard unit. With part of his brigade, he was posted on the Rossville and Lafayette road. The command consisted of two companies each from the 78th Pennsylvania, and the 74th Ohio, and the Thirty-Seventh Indiana. The 37th Indiana acting as rear guard for the brigade was the last to enter Chattanooga. Sirwell's brigade was hotly pursued by the First Tennessee along with a detail of Confederate Cavalry. [19]

The Confederates won and now commanded the field. Sam Watkins wrote, "We remained upon the battlefield of Chickamauga all night. Everything had fallen into our hands. We had captured a great many prisoners and small arms, and many pieces of artillery and wagons and provisions. The Confederate and Federal dead, wounded and dying were everywhere scattered over the battlefield. Men were lying where they fell, shot in every conceivable part of the body. Some with their entrails torn out and still hanging to them and piled up on the ground beside them, and they still alive. Some with their under jaw torn off, and hanging by a fragment of skin to their cheeks, with their tongues lolling from their mouth, and they trying to talk. Some with both eyes shot out, with one eye hanging down their cheek." In many places the dead were piled in groups. [20]

Ira Owens recorded a visit to the battlefield of Chickamauga shortly after the Union victory at Lookout Mountain and Missionary Ridge, over two months after the battle. "There we saw many horrors of still unburied dead and decaying carcasses of men and animals. Two of us saw on a stump the partly decayed head of a Union soldier, which had been stuck up on a pole, and had been denuded of flesh by carrion crows. We gave burial to the awful spectacle of southern brutality, and this was said to be but one of many cases of the kind seen by those who first revisited the field." Surgeons went out after the battle to care for the Union wounded. After the task was completed, they were sent to Libby prison. One of these surgeons informed Ira Owens that on a part of the field there was a Yankee's head on every stump. [21]

The Union army was crushed, and retired from the field into the safety of Chattanooga. They still controlled the important rail center; however, they were virtually surrounded.

The casualties of the Union army strained the medical corps to the utmost. Surgeon Israel Moses and his staff of 43 surgeons, four of them Confederate surgeons, worked feverishly to provide care for the wounded. On September 18th, Moses was notified to be prepared for 5000 casualties; he had "a partial supply of medicine, blankets, furniture and dressings...[for an] estimated 1000 men..." Within the next two days he received approximately 10,000 casualties. To accommodate his charges, Dr. Moses set up hospitals in buildings, hotels, churches and private homes. It is interesting to note that Dr. Moses assumed that the Confederates had "employed little artillery." There were very few wounds caused by shell or round shot. [22]

The lack of supplies was evident within a few weeks. Food became scarce and even the animals suffered from the lack of forage and corn. The "horse" corn was eaten by the hungry troops. The savior of the Union army, now christened the "Rock of Chickamauga", was forced in early October to cut the rations of his army.

Headquarters 14th Army Corps
Chattanooga, Tennessee, October 3rd, 1863.

Circular:

Division Commanders are directed to issue hereafter until further orders, no more than two thirds rations and where they may think it Sufficient only half rations.

By Command of Major General George Thomas
(Signed) B.H. Polk Captain and A.A.A.G.
Official A.S. Hough Captain and A.A.D.C. [23]

The food rations must have run very low at times, since the men began to eat acorns. Some of the boys took to calling themselves "the Acorn Boys." To commemorate the hard times in Chattanooga, the acorn device was officially adopted as the insignia of the Army of the Cumberland. Many soldiers claimed the acorn was a fair portion of their diet, when under siege at Chattanooga. Buck Simkins confided to his father that the men were starving, but asked him to "keep it quiet." Sam Watkins claimed that he and his Rebel friends surrounding the city were suffering from hunger just as much as their enemy.

But once again old enemies would trade for their needs. The blue and gray officers agreed that their pickets would not fire on each other. However, the Union pickets were ordered not to talk to the enemy. So...the boys communicated with each other in writing. The Rebs would trade a plug of tobacco worth a dollar for canteens or useful articles. The citizen-soldier always found a way to survive. [24]

James Negley, who had been made a major general for his bravery at Stones River, was censured by the quick-tempered Rosecrans' for his actions at Chickamauga. Oddly enough, General Thomas Wood, a leading contributor in the Union defeat, pushed for Negley's court martial. Instead of supporting General Negley, Rosecrans advised him to demand a court of inquiry. Negley requested a formal court of inquiry. He was tried and exonerated, but he was removed from active command. Negley contended that not being part of the West Point clique caused his removal.

In early October of 1863, James Scott Negley took his leave of the Army of the Cumberland. The day before he left, Negley and all of his staff rode into the regimental camp of the Seventy-Eighth about 10:00 a.m. In a cheerful style Negley dismounted at regimental headquarters and shook Sirwell's hand. Then he and his staff made the rounds shaking the hands of the remainder of Sirwell's officers. As the compliment of regimental soldiers gathered, Negley took off his hat and addressed the boys that had left Pittsburgh with him seemingly so long ago. At the conclusion of his speech, Negley mounted his horse and to the hearty cheers of his Pennsylvanians he cantered out of the camp followed by his staff.

General John Turchin wrote of Negley, "Gen. Negley, at the time, was blamed for his conduct. Remembering what blunders and omissions have been made by some regular-army officers, it seems as if Gen. Negley, who was only a volunteer officer, by saving eight batteries of artillery, at the time when fifty guns had been lost in the rout, and gathering and organizing several thousands of stragglers at McFarland's Gap...ought to have been praised than blamed for what he had done during the Chickamauga battle." [25]

Rosey's career fared no better that Negley's. The loss to Braxton Bragg and the reports of two sly antagonists finished his military career. The future president, Brigadier General James A. Garfield, who had replaced Julius Garesché, had not displayed the same loyalty as Rosecrans' former chief of staff. The politically adroit, young general would enhance his career path at Rosey's expense. Rosecrans could not read the aspirations of his ambitious, new staff member. In one of the few existing letters written to his wife, Sirwell only refers to Garfield as the "Fighting Preacher," but John Beatty's witty, intuitive observation on Garfield's handshake was, "Vote early, vote right."

Garfield had become Rosecrans' confidant and one of his principal advisors. "James Garfield said once the he 'loved every bone in [Rosecrans'] body.'" But in the final chapter, he would betray his superior's trust.   He secretly forwarded his unfavorable perceptions of Rosey to his fellow Ohioan, Secretary of the Treasury, Salmon P. Chase. His assumptions of his commander would provide Washington with fact and conjecture that would be detrimental to Rosecrans' career.

In June, the second "Judas", Charles A. Dana, Jr., the Assistant Secretary of War, had been attached to headquarters for the sole purpose of reporting back to Stanton on Rosecrans' public and private behavior. Emulating Garfield's work as a spy, Dana did not have to search far for things to report.   Bill Rosecrans had a very bad habit of speaking disparagingly of the Washington establishment around any man who would listen. This lack of discretion regarding his perceived shortcomings of his superiors was uppermost in his undoing. Assuredly, these opinions were reported back to Washington by both Garfield and Dana.

In reality, Dana and Garfield did not have to feed Washington much information unfavorable to Rosecrans. Rosecrans had earned the antipathy of Edwin Stanton long before Chickamauga. In the early days of the war Rosecrans had complained about the fact that George McClellan had received the credit for the West Virginia victory earned by Rosecrans. He had the poor judgment to balk at being demoted and the unmitigated gall to criticize Secretary Stanton's plan to neutralize Stonewall Jackson in the Shenandoah Valley. Stanton never forgot. [26]

William Rosecrans never received the credit or adulation from the nation that other Union generals received. Old Rosey won his battles in West Virginia, Iuka, Stones River and Tullahoma. At this point in the war, unlike Grant and most of Lincoln's generals in the East, he had won his battles fighting superior or equal forces at best, but he lost at Chickamauga. Maybe more importantly, Grant, Sherman and Sheridan, men who had fought with the western army and were leaders at the war's end, wrote major works on the war that were self-serving and meant to build their own reputations.   Grant in particular, whom had a propensity for altering his hindsight evaluations to fit the present, had no regard for Rosecrans.

If one is to win good publicity, he needs good press and a mentor or two. Rosecrans had good press relations, but the power of the press was centered in Washington, far from Tennessee and Georgia. Secretary Chase had given support to Rosecrans and other Ohioans. However, Rosecrans continued castigation of Washington and Chase's own mounting political problems brought about the loss of that support. Eventually William Rosecrans would have no real mentor in the Capitol. When a commander is winning battles and has good press, but has no mentors, arrogance is acceptable. With the same arrogance, battle losses and no champion, a general can get fired. Rosecrans got fired.

By War Department order of October 16th, 1863, the Departments of the Ohio, the Cumberland, and the Tennessee were constituted "The Military Division of the Mississippi," under the Command of General Ulysses Grant. By the same order, William Rosecrans was relieved of command and replaced by George Thomas. When Rosecrans returned to his headquarters on the 19th of October, Halleck's orders were waiting for him. That evening he wrote out his farewell order and without saying good-bye to his staff placed Thomas in command. A dejected Rosecrans left for his home in Cincinnati. [27]

So, an intelligent, energetic, aggressive soldier would leave America's center stage. He would serve in the House of Representatives from 1881 until 1885, and grow in stature in the hearts of the veterans of the Army of the Cumberland. A great general would be relegated to the footnotes of history. If not for his rebellious personality, he could have become the leader of his country.

Long before the presidential campaign of 1864, it was a desire of some within the Republican party to advance a new candidate other than Lincoln. Rosecrans was considered a good possibility for the high office, but he chose not to oppose his commander-in-chief. Abraham Lincoln, an astute politician, needed support within his party. He wired Rosey an offer of the number two spot on the ticket. William Rosecrans at the time was with his troops in the field. He would have enjoyed the Vice Presidency and wired the president so. Regrettably, Secretary of War, Stanton controlled the wartime telegraph; he kept the favorable response to himself. Lincoln assuming that Rosecrans did not want to run with him offered the spot to Andrew Johnson. [28]

Maybe the one person most responsible of the defeat at Chickamauga was never censured. Henry Halleck's tardy and irresponsible lack of action in moving troops from Grant, Hurlbut and Burnside would have saved the day. In the face of mounting evidence that Bragg was being reinforced Halleck waited too long to affect troop movements. With additional forces Rosey may have carried the battle.

William Sirwell would admit to Nellie Bly in her interview with him shortly before his death that he and Negley also had a "misunderstanding" [Sirwell's word]. No person could question Sirwell's whereabouts during the battle and none could question his courage. Since Sirwell and Negley, for the most part, always had a stormy working relationship it is possible, General Negley did just that. Bill Sirwell's reasons for resigning are shrouded in history, but he was relieved of his brigade command then resigned command of his beloved Pennsylvania Seventy-Eighth. [29] Chickamauga was a defeat for Rosecrans' army. The loss cost many officers their careers; however, Bill Sirwell would return to his boys some day.

General Braxton Bragg, the victor, truly became the vanquished. He too lost his command. The stunning defeat of the Confederate army in November at Missionary Ridge spelled the end for Bragg. He stepped down on December 1, 1863. He was returned to Richmond and succeeded by General Joe Johnston seventeen days later. Oddly enough, he was promoted to military adviser to President Jefferson Davis. He was the area commander at Wilmington, North Carolina when Fort Fisher fell to the Federals. He fought in the last battle of the war at Bentonville, North Carolina. In the years after the war he scratched out a meager living employed in railroads, municipal works projects and the insurance industry. He constantly bordered on abject poverty. On September 27, 1876, at age fifty-nine, Braxton Bragg dropped dead on a Galveston, Texas, street. [30]

In late October, Fightin' Joe Hooker, and his "cracker line" broke the siege and hunger at Chattanooga. On November 22nd, Colonel Sirwell left his command for his home in Kittanning. The night before Old Bill had stood before his regiment to say good-bye, but that is all he could say. He was too overcome by emotion to give the speech his boys requested. The troops formed in line and each shook their Colonel's hand. Whatever his attitude at the time, Sirwell left his boys carrying the belief with him that General Grant, now commanding the army, "had the iron will and strong nerve to accomplish wonders. He [would] be victorious." Lieutenant Colonel Blakeley assumed command of the Seventy-Eighth.

In late November of 1863, the capture of Lookout Mountain and Missionary Ridge by the Union forces broke the Confederate resolve. Much to Grant's chagrin the Army of the Cumberland, who he held in some contempt because of what he thought was their failure at Chickamauga, would bring him his Lieutenant Generalship. An unordered action by the Army of the Cumberland at Missionary Ridge and their subsequent courageous charge and victory put Chattanooga firmly in the hands of the Federals. Braxton Bragg pulled back, again. The 78th did not participate in the battle. They were posted in Fort Negley near the city under the watchful eye of their commander, Archibald Blakeley.

After a time, the camp of the Seventy-Eighth was moved to the top of Lookout Mountain. The troops spent a miserable winter on this mountain top retreat. They spent time clearing the refuse of battle and trying to get warm and comfortable. In December, some boys in the 78th found the body of a Johnnie Reb who had apparently died of smallpox. The troops opted to burn the body instead of bury it for fear that they would be infected if they touched it. Small pox was growing into an epidemic level. In January, the army would begin vaccinations against the disease.

For their third Christmas away from home, the men would make do. Samuel Dumm lamented only the fact that there would be no snow for the holiday, but he did admit that it had been cold and blustery. On Christmas Day, Colonel Blakeley relieved the regiment of duty. Tongue in cheek Sam Dumm wrote his sister, "I suppose he wanted to give us time to prepare for Christmas, get the turkey roasted and the plum pudding baked, etc." Many of the troops had weak coffee and crackers for their Christmas feast. Decorations were sparse, but the command raised a huge flag on the mountain that could be seen from Chattanooga. In the afternoon "a ball convened....with thirteen women present...there to spend the day." The men in Company K had hoped to see Reverend W.M. Kane, pastor of the Slatelick Presbyterian church. It would be good to hear news from home and visit with an old friend; but he never came. The men enjoyed the day to the utmost. Tomorrow it would be back to building fortifications and blasting rock to cut roads in the mountain.

The food supply in the Seventy-Eighth fluctuated in quantity and quality. Many of the women of families that now returned to their nearby homes supported themselves by taking in washing and selling baked goods. The men purchased cakes and dodgers, a kind of corn bread, from these women, but they were of poor quality. "The women down here either never paid much attention to the baker's art or else served under very poor masters," so wrote Private Dumm.

There were clothes to be had; however, shoes and clothing were quickly wearing out. The lack of clothing actually prohibited some soldiers from performing their regular duties. The weather atop Lookout Mountain was erratic, and drastic, but bitter cold for the most part. On New Year's Eve the day was so hot that Major Bonnaffon permitted the men to remove their coats during skirmish drills. That night a howling winter storm moved into the area. Many of the pickets and camp guards dropped their rifles during their watch because their hands became numb. The lack of gloves and shoes caused many cases of severe frostbite.

With William Sirwell no longer in the chain of command, Lt. Colonel Archibald Blakeley assumed total control over the Seventy-Eighth. Unfortunately, despite his Christmas relief, he was disliked by many of the boys in the regiment. They carried the perception, during the war, that Blakeley was too severe in his discipline. During his tenure as regimental commander, Blakeley instituted a punishment unit. A squad called the "Sink Squad" was organized in the regiment to consist of persons assigned to it for bad conduct or disobedience of orders. This punishment was inflicted for five successive days. The men in the squad had to perform all other regular duties not interfering with their punishment.

To prevent straggling, Blakeley would order surprise roll calls. When these roll calls were ordered, assembly was sounded at regimental headquarters and the roll called ten minutes thereafter. All personnel absent at such roll calls without written permission from headquarters were punished. In light of Negley's old threat to pass names of stragglers to the governor, Blakeley's order was not out of line.

It is possible that Blakeley's punishments were severe or unfair, and the public "loss of face" could be devastating for young men who now called themselves "veterans." However, Blakeley was also known to give wrong commands during regimental drills and then proceed to curse the men for their stupidity. In all probability these punishments and tongue lashings brought more resentment for Blakeley.

In January, Blakeley severely reprimanded several non commissioned officers for breaking general orders concerning use of wood from the area and picket rules. The offenders, boys of the 78th, were slacking off on military protocol and were using wood for make-shift lodgings and camp fires and their non-coms permitted the transgressions. Corporal Sullivan of Company B was reprimanded for gross neglect of duty while on picket. He permitted two adjoining sentinels under his charge to sit together and talk. Sullivan also sat with them. He was also reprimanded for disobedience to orders in allowing men under his command to cut lumber belonging to the Mountain Saw Mill. Corporal Jim Morehead also of B Company was reprimanded for the same offense. In the same order, Corporal Hepler of C Company was reprimanded for gross neglect of duty while on guard in permitting one post on his relief to be unfilled for two hours. Sergeant William Kerr of Company I was reprimanded for disobedience of orders in permitting boards to be carried through the camp guard lines under his immediate observation and sanction. Corporal Drummond of B Company was reprimanded for directing his men to cut down a tree.

The conduct of Sergeant Kerr, Corporals Sullivan, and Drummond is without explanation, other than the fact that they were thinking of the comfort of their comrades. No punishment was listed other than Blakeley's command that his order was to be read at dress parade, dinner roll call of each company and recorded in the Regimental and Company Order Books. The offenses were in all likelihood minor, the punishment, was light, and to many the non-coms were "bully fellows" and had achieved champion status. In defense of Blakeley's actions, Major General Palmer had issued orders against the "burning of fence rails, parts of houses, sheds, or other improvements."

During the winter months on Lookout Mountain it took ingenuity and creativity to keep warm, but at least an adequate amount of food was now coming through. The government issue was coming through and Father Christy was working his connections in Chattanooga. "Hard Tack, Sowbelly, Coffee, Tea, Sugar and Saeur Kreaut" were all in good supply. Sugar rarely available in any quantity could cause severe sickness if once again taken in huge quantities. Jim Burford stood on line to get the sugar ration for him and his mess mates, Sam Dumm and Henry Claypoole. The table spoon per man for five days was a real treat. Normally, as soon as the bearer of the sweet ration returned, "[the boys] would take [their share] in [their] hands, and sit down in a corner and lick [it] up, like a cat licking out a cream crock." On this day Jimmy returned with "two pounds of sugar." Needless to say there were three very sick fellows who spent three days recovering after eating all two pounds. [31]

Archibald Blakeley was an enigma to his troops. All of the men agreed that Blakeley was too strict. It was a commonly held opinion that he favored and promoted the men in his "Click." However, they also knew that at times he was a "good egg." He was known to offer a loan to boys from Butler that he knew were broke. On one occasion he stood for a court martial and was fined rather than give up two of his men to the Provost Martial in Chattanooga for what he felt were unjust reasons.

Sam Boreland of Company F, who still seemed better off in the service than cooped up teaching his class in Easley's Hollow, and Charles Smith of Company H had no shoes. When they approached Colonel Blakeley about their problem, he sent them off to Chattanooga for new ones. Everyone knew that passes were necessary to enter the city, but Blakeley could not give them one. He had no paper or pencil. With a pat on the back he promised that he would support them if trouble arose. As luck would have it, the Provost Marshall stopped them and took their names with the threat to arrest them. When the guard appeared at the camp of the 78th to collect Boreland and Smith, Archibald Blakeley refused to turn them over. Bonnaffon refused the same order. Both Blakeley and Bonnaffon were court martialed and assessed a month's pay. But Blakeley backed up his troops and neither Boreland or Smith were arrested.

It was well known that Blakeley could change in a minute and mete out severe discipline. For reasons lost to history he had twenty men tied up to trees as punishment for some transgression. Feelings against Blakeley ran high within the regiment. One night ten men cut their buddies loose and were caught. Blakeley had those men tried for mutiny and confined to hard labor with ball and chain. The men and officers of the Seventy-Eighth signed a petition and forwarded it to the War Department and to Sirwell requesting his return. The morale was at a low ebb in the regiment. Where was "Old Bill?" [32]

General Grant could not be concerned with petty regimental problems. He had bigger fish to fry. He made no attempt to intervene in the Seventy-Eighth's problems or to follow up on the Union victory for that matter. He moved his headquarters to Nashville. There he and his wife spent the winter months waiting for his promotion to Lieutenant General. No telegrams urging him to move came from Washington. [33]

Bill Sirwell spent about two months at home with his wife Elizabeth and family. He was in frail health and Elizabeth forced him to rest during most of his stay. The *Kittanning Mentor*, a Copperhead newspaper, made no mention of the reasons why the Colonel was home. They only reported that Colonel Sirwell had "been sojourning with his family in Kittanning for some time past, [and] left to rejoin and take command of his regiment." [34]

Bill Sirwell did rejoin the regiment on March 10th, 1864. He rejoined a regiment that now feared the stern, unreasonable discipline of their commander. In the years after the war Lieutenant Colonel Blakeley became revered and loved by the veterans of the Seventy-Eighth, but at this point he was extremely disliked by most.

Sirwell & Staff ≅ March 11, 1864
Lookout Mountain
Colonel Sirwell - slightly left center - walrus mustache, no hat
Lt. Colonel Blakeley - in front of Sirwell's right
Father Christy with X
Major Augustus Bonnaffon in front of Christy's left

John Meredith, Battalion Commissary, saw Colonel Sirwell while in Chattanooga on March 8th and cheerfully spread the word of his return to the regiment. As Sirwell approached the regimental camp on Lookout Mountain his "boys" recognized him in the distance from his familiar walk. Three wild and lusty cheers rolled through the mountains. Sirwell answered by waving his hat. Virtually every man of the regiment gathered on the rocks, near the bluff overlooking his path of ascent and cheered him for a half a mile. The hills echoed with the cheers, "Old Bill's come back! We've got a Colonel now!"

"...they formed on each side of the road, and cheered him as he passed them, and then closed around him in mass, and escorted him to camp."

To further show their appreciation, the regimental officers took up a collection among the troops to purchase Sirwell a new horse. The huge bay costing $550 - $171 collected from Apollo's Company I alone - was presented to the Colonel the day after Blakeley left for home.

On April 8th, 1864, Lieutenant Colonel Blakeley resigned and the regimental command returned to Colonel Sirwell, who had been re-commissioned. Blakeley had actually gone on furlough the day after Sirwell returned until the end of March. Upon Sirwell's return, the thirty men of the regiment were still under arrest for mutiny. Sirwell released all of the "boys" with a strong reprimand. Ostensibly, Blakeley resigned because of illness in his family. [36]

Nothing written or even in legend exists indicating Bill Sirwell's or Arch Blakeley's feelings on the change of command. Just as they had done when Sirwell originally resigned, the officers of the Seventy-Eighth, headed by Major Augustus Bonnaffon, presented Lieutenant Colonel Blakeley with a written testimonial. Resolutions to Blakeley's "strict discipline...governing without tyranny or partiality...a nobel fellow and a gallant hero..." were signed by all of the officers. [37]

Archibald Blakeley never returned to an active command. The boys had Old Bill back and they were happy. However with the end of the war and the passage of time old wounds healed. Colonel Blakeley became active in the army and regimental reunion organizations. He became a respected member in the Society of the Army of the Cumberland, but maybe more importantly to him, he came to be the beloved old soldier to the boys of the Seventy-Eighth.

ON TO ATLANTA

William Sirwell returned to a restructured Union command. The original Army of the Cumberland now served under George Thomas, while General William Tecumseh Sherman held overall command of the Western army. It had been over two years since Negley, Sirwell, Stambaugh, and Hambright had joined their commander, General Sherman, for dinner at the Galt House in Louisville. Now only Sirwell and Hambright remained in an active command.

Over the years the national press had haunted Grant and Sherman with innuendoes. But the "drunken" Grant wanted the "crazy" Bill Sherman, his trusted friend, back. In March of 1864, Ulysses Grant was promoted to the new rank of Lieutenant General and command of all Federal armies. He was not just another Major General who had been appointed General-in-Chief, his new rank gave him command of all Federal armies. Unlike the past, Grant's new position would enable a well planned, concerted effort by all Union forces to crush the South.

The Federal armies would never again fight independent of each other; co-ordination would be the by word. This unified effort would prevent Robert E. Lee from ever again dispatching parts of his armies to other theaters of operation, as he had done with Longstreet's Corps at Chickamauga. The diminishing forces of the Confederacy would have to face their respective enemy on their own. General Winfield Scott's original "Anaconda Plan" of 1861, was in some form coming to its final phase. The Northern forces had slowly squeezed the life blood out of their adversary. Grant, in the field with General Meade's Army of the Potomac, would move against Lee in May. Sherman immediately set in motion his plan to move against Joe Johnston, the new commander of the Confederates.

In early January and February of 1864, before Sherman's appointment, the army began to prepare for the coming campaign. Brigadier General Johnson, from his headquarters at Tyners Station, Tennessee, issued orders that he felt would "preserve and if possible increase the proficiency of the troops in [the coming] military exercises." Richard Johnson directed regimental commanders to conduct daily drills of all officers and enlisted men. In addition to their drills enlisted men of each company were required to spend one hour in shooting target. Unlike the initial stages of the war, regimental commanders were directed to drill their battalions in simulated battle drills. Skirmish Drills "by the bugle" were to be a considerable portion of each day's drill hours. One bugler was assigned to two companies. At this time the ranks of the Seventy-Eighth swelled by 65 troops. These men from the Pennsylvania Seventy-Ninth did not re-enlist with their old regiment; they finished out their original term with Colonel Sirwell.

In preparation for the campaign a new supply of rifles was acquired for the troops. All arms in possession of infantry regiments other than the Springfield and Enfield Rifles had to be turned over to the Division Ordnance Officer. Rifles other than those prescribed were replaced with either a new Enfield or Springfield musket.

But everything was not all work. On the cool, windy Monday night of April 4th, Father Christy married Private Billie Wolff of Company K to his beloved Biddy. His brother Jack stood up as his best man. Biddy remained with her new husband until after April 12th, accepting visitors to their "private" quarters just as any newly married couple

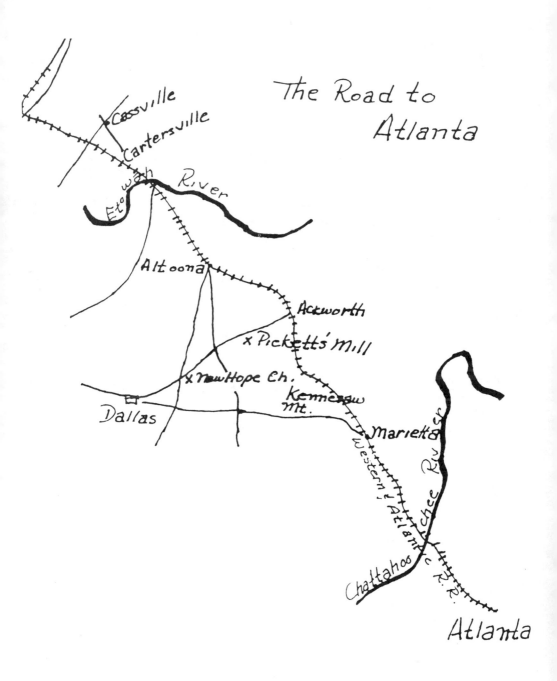

The Road to Atlanta

would entertain well wishers. However, during the honeymoon, drills, guard mounting, and picket duty went on as usual.

When Grant received his new command, he promoted Bill Sherman to the commander of the newly created Military Division of the Mississippi, over the senior George Thomas. Sherman would prove equal to the command. Uncle Billy planned his campaign with the same meticulous style that Rosecrans did. He revived Thomas' plan for the campaign against Atlanta, and modified it. He was beginning to develop his "total warfare" strategy.

For almost one hundred and thirty years it has been accepted fact, accusingly by the South and reluctantly by the North, that the destructive policies carried out by Sherman in the Atlanta Campaign and Sheridan in the Shenandoah Valley were of their own making. However, Dr. Jay Luvaas reported the finding of an obscure order drafted by Lieutenant General Ulysses Grant that shows he developed the scorched earth policy. The order "not to be copied" gave the commanding generals the charge to destroy as much property and goods as possible, thus enabling the total subjugation of the Confederacy.

Along with this harsh policy and the troops to carry them out, Sherman would utilize some of the newest technology in this campaign. There were pre-built, bridge parts for river crossings. Telegraphers would keep the commanding general in contact with far parts of his battlefield, and area maps would be reproduced for field commanders in the "dark wagons" of photographers. He instituted trained and drilled railroad repairmen; he seized trains and rolling stock for his use. He studied tax documents and census reports, in the event his supplies could not keep up with his army. He knew where he could live off the land. [1]   The army that had not moved for seven months would go into battle prepared.

The Army of the Cumberland commanded by Major General George Thomas was now just one part of Major General Sherman's huge force. Uncle Billy's army was much larger than the one that he relinquished to Don Carlos Buell in 1861. In fact the army of approximately 100,000 men was larger than the one left by Rosecrans. Sherman's army also included the Army of the Ohio under Major General John Schofield and the Army of the Tennessee commanded by his young protege' Major General James McPherson.

In April, Sherman's army prepared to break camp and begin their push against their foe. General Johnson conveyed Sherman's desire to lighten the excess baggage for the strike against Joe Johnston. He also ordered the regiments of his First Division to supply themselves for the coming campaign. Bill Sirwell requisitioned the supplies he needed; in recopying Johnson's orders, the news quickly spread from the company scribes that they were headed into a bloody campaign once again.

CHAIN OF COMMAND
THE PENNSYLVANIA SEVENTY-EIGHTH
COMMAND
William Tecumseh Sherman
ARMY OF THE CUMBERLAND
Major General George H. Thomas
XIV ARMY CORPS
Major General John M. Palmer
PALMER'S FIRST DIVISION
Brigadier General Richard W. Johnson
JOHNSON'S THIRD BRIGADE
Colonel Benjamin F. Scribner
21st Ohio, Colonel James M. Neibling
Lieutenant Colonel Arnold McMahan
37th Indiana, Lieutenant Colonel William D. Ward
38th Indiana, Lieutenant Colonel Daniel F. Griffin
74th Ohio, Colonel Josiah Given
Major Joseph Fisher
78th Pennsylvania, Colonel William Sirwell
79th Pennsylvania, Colonel Henry A. Hambright
Major Michael Locher
1st Wisconsin, Lieutenant Colonel George B. Bingham
ARTILLERY
Captain Lucius H. Drury, 1st Illinois, Battery "C"
Captain Mark H. Prescott 1st Ohio, Battery "I"
Captain Hubert Dilger

Official Record

Headquarters 1st Division, 14th Army Corps
Graysville, Georgia, April 16th, 1864.

General Order No 56

I. In accordance with instructions received from the Headquarters of the Corps it is announced that immediate preparations are necessary to rid the command of everything not indispensable on an active campaign. It is intended to confine the Army wagons on hand mainly to transportation of rations, forage and ammunition. The Major General Commanding the Corps announces that at the commencement of active operations each Division must be prepared to transport: Twenty [20] days Bread, Ten [10] days Salt Meat, Twenty [20] days Coffee, Thirty [30] days Salt, Ten [10] days Forage [Grain], and the ammunition required to existing orders.

With the present allowances of transportation to transport this amount of Supplies will require that in addition to the supply train each Regimental wagon shall carry near 2000 lbs of Rations and Forage independent of baggage. Regimental Commanders will therefore at once turn in store or in some other way dispose everything not indispensably necessary in an active Campaign.

It is enjoined on Brigade Commanders to see that these orders are promptly carried out.
> *By Command of Brigadier General*
> *Richard W. Johnson [Signed]*
> *E.F. Wells Captain and A.A.A.G.* [2]

During May and June of 1864, the Seventy-Eighth followed "Pap" Thomas to battle once again. As part of Major General John Palmer's Fourteenth Army Corps and Brigadier General Richard W. Johnson's First Division, Sirwell's Regiment served in Colonel Benjamin Scribner's Third Brigade.[3] The regiment added the names of more hard fought battles in Georgia to their regimental history on the road to Atlanta: Buzzard's Roost, Resaca, Cassville, and the last great fight of Sirwell's regiment, Pickett's Mill. It was another long campaign in cold, heat, mud, and rain.

In the first week of Sherman's campaign for Atlanta, Bill Sirwell led his regiment into the face of the Rebel guns planted in the heights of Bald Face Ridge at Buzzard Roost Gap. Once again the Seventy-Eighth was the first to cross the field in formation. J.T. Gibson notes in the regimental record that this time it was an advantage. From their high perch it was difficult for the Rebs to get the range on the attacking Federals. By the time they corrected their cannon for range and effect the Pennsylvanians were at the base of the Ridge. However, the succeeding regiments paid dearly. From this first battle the Union army doggedly pushed Joe Johnston and his Army of the Tennessee slowly to Atlanta.[4]

Lieutenant Colonel Archibald Blakeley
Courtesy of Harry Blakeley, Lower Burrell, Pennsylvania

"I AM IN THE FRONT RANKS YET"

Just as Ulysses Grant pushed Robert Lee through the Wilderness southward toward Richmond, Uncle Billy Sherman pushed Joe Johnston south, easterly through Georgia. Both Union armies used the hit and flank movement. The diminished forces of the South could not stave off the growing numbers of Yankees soldiers. It no longer mattered how much the Rebels punished the "invaders;" they kept coming. After the heavy fighting at Buzzard's Roost and Resaca, Sherman once again attempted to flank Johnston's army at New Hope Church, near Dallas, Georgia.

During the last few days the Seventy-Eighth had moved with the Union army through heat and thunder storms of the Georgia Spring. They closed in on Johnston's troops and on the morning of May 26th, the Union army was spread through the woods and rough terrain north and west of Dallas. Sporadic firing and skirmishing took place as the opponents positioned themselves for battle.

George Thomas' Army of the Cumberland would assault the Confederated right flank. Major General Oliver Otis Howard, the victim of Jackson's flanking movement at Chancellorsville, would lead the attack. In preparation for the attack on what Sherman hoped was Joe Johnston's right flank, George Thomas shifted Richard Johnson's Division, over the objection of John Palmer, from Major General Palmer's Corps to O.O. Howard' Corps. Richard Johnson's Division, in which the Pennsylvania Seventy-Eighth remained, was to support General Thomas Wood's Division.

On the morning of May 27th, the Union soldiers moved to battle. Howard's, Hooker's and Schofield's artillery open a duel with the Confederate batteries. About 11:00 A.M., the sanctimonious General O.O. Howard led his small army off to victory.

A perfect flank attack is comprised of intelligence, surprise, speed and determination. The attacking Union force only had determination. The Federal regiments moving into a line of battle struggled through across ground, with gentle slopes and deep ravines, populated with low hanging trees, dense thickets, and thick bushes to a place Howard's reconnaissance made him "think" was the end of the Confederate line. They slowly groped their way toward the enemy while brigade commander Colonel William Gibson had his buglers blow short, frequent blasts so that the men would know by sound the direction to go. Howard had learned nothing from Chancellorsville. He had been defeated by a surprise attack; now he concocted the scheme for an assaulting force to be defeated.

After an hour and a half the Federals came in sight of the enemy over a relatively clear field, they were entrenching. Howard leading the movement made the assumption that he had passed the right flank of Joe Johnston's Rebel army about two miles northeast of New Hope Church. After tramping through the red Georgia clay under a blazing sun the exhausted Federals began to take up their jump off position at approximately 3:30 P.M.

Thomas Wood's Division was assigned the center, two of Johnson's brigades [Colonel Benjamin Scribner's being one of them] were positioned to Wood's left and Brigadier General Nat McLean's First Brigade, Army of the Ohio, XXIII Corps, Second Division, covered Wood's right flank. McClean's Brigade would never get into the coming battle. He would be reticent in moving.

Around four o'clock, after crossing the "Little" Pumpkin Vine Creek Wood's Brigades took the line for the attack and Howard sent General Thomas the positively indecisive note: "I am now turning the enemy's right flank, I think."

Wood's brigades were to lead off the attack. General Bill Hazen moved out first at roughly 5:00 P.M., not knowing that Sherman was sending orders to halt the attack. He would supposedly be followed by Colonel Gibson's Brigade then Colonel Knefler's Brigade. Stepping off through thickets with flags furled Hazen's 1500 troops headed for the enemy trenches. As soon as they hit open ground the flags were unfurled and they quickened the pace. Victory over the small force was inevitable; they thought. The Federals were surprised when they did not encounter the Confederate right flank, but instead blundered head on into General Pat Cleburne's well-entrenched and reinforced division at the top of a steep rise. Granbury's Texans pour a galling fire into the advancing blue line. Unbelievably, Hazen's boys held a position for almost an hour within rods of the Rebel line. Repeated calls for Gibson's and Knefler's troops went unheeded. After it was too late Howard and Wood sent them forward. [1]

To the immediate left of Wood's Division, the Seventy-Eighth moved onto the battlefield at Pickett's Mill in the face of heavy Rebel musket and artillery fire from the front and a galling fire from dismounted Rebel cavalry to their left. The fact that Johnson stalled his line to protect his flanks left Wood's Brigades out on their own. Scribner's Brigade had been ordered to move to battle on the left of General King's Second Brigade, also of Palmer's Corps. After passing through the Wheat Field south of the creek, Scribner's men met the Rebels on a wooded ridge barricaded behind breast-works. From right to left Scribner's regiments were the 78th Pennsylvania, the 37th Indiana, the 38th Indiana, the First Wisconsin and the Ohio Twenty-First.

Many of Johnson's regiments fell back in the initial fire fight. Colonel Scribner remained back of the lines supposedly getting drunk. The 37th Indiana and Sirwell's soldiers stayed their position and paid the price. Colonel Frederick Knefler noted in his after-action report that "the left of the line was further strengthened by the Seventy-eighth Pennsylvania... [who] rendered valuable assistance." Knefler's men had gone out in the darkness and retrieved wounded soldiers. Unfortunately, Wood's troops fell back on General Howard's orders and left Sirwell's flank exposed. Sirwell changed front to rear on the tenth company to now protect his own flank. In the fight that followed, the regiment was severely punished. Sirwell and his boys were once again in the thick of the fighting. James Little of Company A, died in Father Christy's arms with the words, "Tell Mother I am in the front ranks yet." His dying words described the position of his regiment, also. Pinned down in an open field at Pickett's Mill, they held on for four hours "in the front ranks." [2]

At 10:00 P.M. the Confederates exercised an unusual night attack, but were driven back with a thunderous volley of gun fire. The Thirty-Seventh Indiana and the Pennsylvania Seventy-Eighth left the field at midnight. These two regiments suffered the bulk of Scribner's 125 casualties. The regiment suffered forty-nine casualties; 5 men were killed in battle, and 13 others subsequently died of their wounds. Samuel Dumm sustained a wound. J. Thompson Gibson, the future historian for the regiment, was also wounded. He lost the diary he had kept since the beginning of the war. Eighteen year-old, veteran, Albert Gibson of Kittanning wounded at Stones River, would sustain another wound at Pickett's Mill. George D. Smith of Company B would receive his second wound

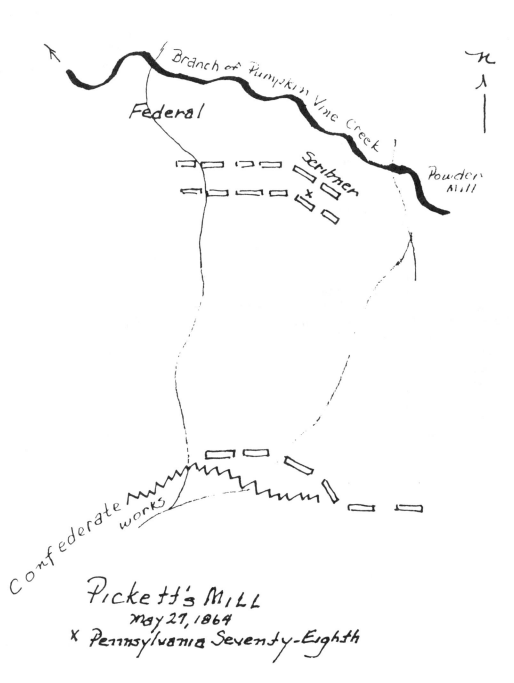

Pickett's Mill
May 27, 1864
x Pennsylvania Seventy-Eighth

in the war. The Thirty-Seventh sustained 53 casualties. James Neibling of the 21st Ohio lost his arm and Colonel Bill Ward of the 37th Indiana sustained a face wound. The Federals suffered approximately 1600 casualties in the fight. Richard Johnson was seriously wounded and relinquished his command. The Confederates lost approximately 450 men. [3]

So marked was the gallantry of Colonel Sirwell and his boys at the battle of Pickett's Mill that he was commended by his brigade commander and General George Thomas. Brigade commander, Colonel Benjamin Scribner wrote, the Seventy-Eighth had a "persistency and heroism worthy of all praise." The Seventy-Eighth, temporarily serving with Colonel Stoughton in command of King's Brigade, was relieved of front line duty by Colonel Josiah Given's Seventy-Fourth Ohio on June 2nd. The battered and depleted Pennsylvania regiment pushed toward Atlanta with Sherman's conquering army.

Maybe because of his losses or the plain fact that New Hope Church was just another "skirmish" on the road to Atlanta, General Sherman would make no mention of Pickett's Mill in his after-action report or in his memoirs. But to the ground troops, the few days spent along the battle line of Pumpkin Vine Creek were horrifying. Heat, the stench of the dead, the moaning and screams of the wounded and dying, lack of food, and the ever present fear of death from sniper fire made it a wretched time. [4]

Union successes in its push to Atlanta paradoxically created new problems for the Federal command. The invading armies had to drop off large numbers of troops to guard their supply lines against cavalry and guerrilla raids. Many divisions were detached as occupation forces to police 100,000 square miles of conquered territory. In Sherman's campaign for Atlanta, the number of men protecting his rail communications 450 miles back to Louisville nearly equaled the number of front-line soldiers. [5] Consequently the 78th was pulled out of the battle line at Kennesaw Mountain on June 27, 1864, to become one of the many regiments placed on guard duty on rail lines back to Nashville.

Although guarding rail lines and lines of communication was still mundane work, it was not without its dangers. George Adams of Indiana County's Company A was wounded shortly after the regiment was pulled off of Kennesaw Mountain. The twenty-two year-old Corporal Adams was shot by a "bushwacker" near Centerville, Georgia, while guarding a prisoner train. The bullet tore through his left shoulder and shattered his jaw.

General Maney's Brigade was still part of the retreating Confederate defenses. The battered Tennessee brigade had engaged the Yankees at New Hope Church and was now entrenched on Kennesaw Mountain. The First and Twenty-Seventh Tennessee still commanded by Colonel Feild remained on Kennesaw through the battles fought there. Twenty-seven men were killed or wounded on Kennesaw. Colonel Feild and Captain Kelly of the Rock City Guard were both wounded defending a portion of that mountain called the "Dead Angle." [6]

In the final campaigns of the war for the Seventy-Eighth, Sirwell commanded another brigade. Lieutenant Colonel Joseph Good and his 108th Ohio, and Lt. Colonel Espy and his 68th Indiana filled Sirwell's brigade of 627 effectives. The combined unit performed the mundane task, at few times hazardous, of guarding trains and railroad track. Their greatest excitement came at chasing General Joe Wheeler throughout Tennessee as a mounted infantry unit. Years later legends of the Seventy-Eighth added Nathan Bedford Forrest's name and sometimes replaced that of Wheeler's as the object of their mounted hunt.   There was no contact with either famed cavalry leader, but campaigning as a unique mounted infantry unit was exhilarating. Sirwell's last fight came at an old battle ground, Buzzard's Roost. In mid August, 1864, Sirwell's brigade, in concert with troops from the Fourteenth U.S. Colored Troops, fought a small battle against a force of Confederates. There were no losses. [7]

With the prospect of going home looming nearer, the men of the regiment began to enjoy themselves more.   In late September, Sirwell and a number of men from the regiment took a train to Atlanta to see the now-fallen Confederate rail center. Even after years of war and destruction, the Union men were still appalled at the devastation. The Union siege guns and hundreds of fires had gutted the city. Miles of barricades with deep trenches covered the fields and surrounded some large estates. Broken and useless wagons and camp equipage was everywhere. Along the rail lines wheels and burned out rolling stock lay in heaps. Atlanta still housed thousands of wounded and dying soldiers. The wreckage of Atlanta left in the wake of days of bombardment and battle left a lasting impression. [8]

Lieutenant Franklin Mechling
Courtesy of Ronn Palm

GOIN' HOME

Bill Sirwell and his regiment had traveled many miles over the past three years. Rain, sleet, cold, and southern heat had toughened the skin of many a young boy that followed the paths of the western Union army. Young boys had grown up and men had grown older. Death, wounds, disease, starvation, and discomfort had been their constant companions. Many members of the Seventy-Eighth had already returned home to their final rest in family plots and hometown cemeteries. One hundred and seven of these gallant Pennsylvanians rested in national cemeteries at Louisville, Nashville, Murfreesboro and Chattanooga. There were also those whose unmarked graves or bleached bones lay hidden in the tangle of grass and weeds that already covered once bloody battlefields. Attitudes had changed and bonds of friendship had been forged. And now large groups of men routinely attended Father Christy's "eloquent" services; "he [Father Christy] never [saying] a word that would arouse the feelings or excite the passions of the members of any [religious belief]." But some things never changed. Colonel Sirwell's last order entered in the Company I Order Book addressed drill and deportment.

Headquarters 78th Pennsylvania Volunteer Infantry.
Chattanooga, Tennessee, September 13th, 1864.

...II. It is therefore ordered that each company and Battalion drill at least two hours a day [Sunday excepted]. That guard mounting be kept up regular as directed by military discipline.
...IIIII. Officers and privates will not be allowed to leave their companies without permission from the officers in command of the company and approved by the commanding officer of this regiment. Officers & Privates arriving at these Headquarters are required to report themselves at once. Officers in command of the Battalion and companies will be strictly held responsible for the conduct of troops under their command.

      By Order of Colonel William Sirwell
      Commanding J. W. Powell, Adjutant [1]

On the 18th of October, 1864, 250 members of the Pennsylvania Seventy-Eighth Volunteer Infantry boarded one steam boat at Nashville for the long journey home. The *Caroline* carried them home via the Cumberland and Ohio Rivers. It had been three years since they had traveled south in the autumn of 1861.

The Seventy-Eighth arrived in Pittsburgh on October 29, 1864. After being feted at a noon-day dinner served by the Subsistence Committee at Pittsburgh's Soldier's Home, with accompanying speeches by General Negley and Mayor James Lowry, the men boarded a train for the four hour trip home. The weary travelers rolled through the darkened, autumn river valleys, arriving in Kittanning at 9:30 P.M. On November 4th, at a large convention, the regiment was mustered out in Kittanning.

A number of men from the regiment joined or formed other groups that returned to the war. Martin McCanna, who went off to war in April of 1861 with Sirwell's Company

B and was mentioned for bravery in his fight against the Rock City Guards at Stones River, formed a company that joined the Pennsylvania 104th. Captain McCanna's Company K, made up exclusively of men from Armstrong County, remained on active service until August 25th, 1865. Eight veterans from the Seventy-Eighth accompanied Captain McCanna: Hoof Benhough, Joel Crawford, Georgie Drake, Bill Graham, Jim Jack, Bill Martin, Jack Unger and John Young. Private John Shettler joined the 206th Pennsylvania Infantry. John Fiscus joined the 204th Heavy Artillery.

During his tenure as regimental commander, Bill Sirwell commanded approximately 1230 men. Two hundred and fifty proudly marched through the streets of Pittsburgh when they returned home; 233 stayed on in the reorganization of the regiment, two of those men were drafted into the regiment and Emmuel Rafennacht was a paid substitute. Considering the material written about paid substitutes, one substitute out of twelve-hundred is extremely low.

Not counting the replacements, the regiment lost approximately seventy percent of their original roster in three years through death, resignation, medical discharges, transfers and desertions.

Two hundred and sixty-four men would never return to the Allegheny River Valley. Two hundred and twenty-four men lost their lives in the three years of war: thirty men were killed, fifty-four were mortally wounded, and one hundred and four died of various causes. Twenty-one men were reported as missing in action or captured. Eighteen men deserted over the course of the war. One man was totally overwhelmed by the death and hardships of war. John Bradin, the young gold miner from Butler, Pennsylvania, who survived the Atlanta Campaign would commit suicide by slitting his throat with his straight razor on July 2, 1865.

Colonel Sirwell's selection for the new commander of the 78th regiment's second organization, Lieutenant Colonel Augustus Bonnaffon, through politics now lost to history, did not originally lead the Second Seventy-Eighth. Lieutenants Henry W. Torbett, Company F, and Robert M. Smith, Company K, led 233 veterans to garrison duty in Nashville. Of the 233 men to follow Torbett 40 were re-enlistees from the original October 1861 roster; the remaining 197 veterans were fulfilling their original 3-year commitment. First Lieutenant Bill McCue returned to a promotion of Regimental Quarter Master. McCue had resigned on November 29, 1862, to return to Freeport and marry Captain Charles Gillespie's widowed sister-in-law.

After about a month a newly-anointed Colonel Bonnaffon took command of the regiment. Many of the veterans were pleased that the regiment was placed in the command of their old brigade commander, now General John Miller. The officers may have been to the men's liking, but the duty was not. The Second Seventy-Eighth returned to train guard duty.

In early December the regiment was returned to Nashville and placed on provost guard duty. Nashville had changed a great deal since mid-1862. The city had rebounded from the fall siege of 1862; business was brisk. Merchants had goods to sell and bargains to be made. Bars, theaters and ballrooms flourished. Gamblers, prostitutes and toughs filled the city streets at night. Sam Dumm states that it was a common occurrence that some "rowdy" would be shot every other night. But one more grand battle would upset the lives of the pleasure seekers.

After a Confederate attack at Franklin, Tennessee on November 30th, General George Thomas with almost 50,000 troops attacked General John Bell Hood's approximate 23,000 men south of Nashville, on the 15th of December 1864. A decisive Federal victory virtually sealed the fate of the Tennessee region. The Second Seventy-Eighth did not participate in the battle.

During the battle of Nashville, the Seventy-Eighth protected the city streets and guarded the "prisoners that came into Nashville almost by regiments...[The Confederates] were in bad condition for want of clothing. Some were entirely barefoot, while others...[tied their uppers and soles together with string]...Many had their pants stitched off at the knees and pieces of blankets bound around their legs." A very few of the prisoners indicated to Sergeant Major Dumm that "they were ready to try it again. "

The differences between Civil War combatants now became pronounced. If a few Rebels were eager to carry on the fight, more were ready to go home. The men, money and manufactured goods of the Union had virtually closed the door on a crumbling Confederacy. The Second Seventy-Eighth gave Lincoln the edge in voting for his presidency and the legitimacy to pursue the war to its end, but it was close. Company A votes gave Abe Lincoln the majority; however Company B almost gave George McClellan the edge. Supposedly, the "old line Democrats" from Clarion County found it hard to vote for anything Republican.

The last man of the Seventy-Eighth killed in battle was Private James McKelvey of Company A. Having served for two weeks short of one year, Private McKelvey was killed in Spring Hill, Tennessee. He had been guarding a train that was attacked by guerrillas and was killed in the skirmish.

In February, 1865, 900 new recruits joined the regiment, but they were obviously a different lot. Many young boys finally got their chance to be in the war, but never saw a battle. The regiment now slept in barracks. Rations were cooked and kept in a kitchen. There was a place behind a soldier's numbered bunk to hang his haversack, rifle, canteen and accouterments. New clothing and underdrawers were obtainable when needed. Even blacking was available to shine new shoes. The supplies and food were in abundance. Sanitary commissions and medical services were at an all time high. After the war, in a reply to Sergeant Major Dumm's question regarding the old and new 78th, Colonel Sirwell "smiled" and said, "It was the same regiment, only a transfer. There was but one, could only be one 78th Pennsylvania...[From] its birth [at] Camp Orr, Kittanning, in 1861, and its muster out of service at Harrisburg in 1865, after four years of faithful service." As always Bill Sirwell was being diplomatic. There was a significant difference between war hardened veterans and those 900 who did guard duty in Nashville. During the three years of the original regiment 12 men deserted; 52 of the men who served from February 1865 until September of 1865 deserted. It was time for the war to be over.

On April 9, 1865, unofficial word was received that Robert E. Lee had surrendered. General Thomas told some officers, "...There is nothing official, but if [they felt] like celebrating the occasion by getting drunk, [they would] be safe enough by going ahead." Officers and men became drunk or went crazy. The night was filled with the sounds of drums, tin horns and pans; "anything to make a noise." It was on April 15, that during preparations for a grand review that word came of Lincoln's assassination. Sam Dumm relates that the men became fearful again. They traveled in threes or squads. The night before the funeral services small printed pieces of paper were found on the streets of

Nashville. "Tomorrow will be the funeral of our beloved President. Any one failing to display the usual badge of mourning from the windows along the line of march, May expect a visit from, Soldiers who are in earnest." On the day of the funeral flags were seen from all windows along the parade and the power of the Union was sounded out from every cannon that surrounded the city for the whole of the day.

The Regiment spent the remainder of the war on provost guard duty in Nashville. From the middle of June until early September men were ordered home. The Seventy-Eighth Pennsylvania Volunteer Infantry Regiment passed into history on September 11th, 1865. [2]

The worthy opponents of the Seventy-Eighth, the First Tennessee continued on in the closing campaigns of the war. Many of the Tennessee Confederates were with General Joe Johnston at the last battle in Bentonville, North Carolina and the surrender on April 26, 1865. Private Robinson described the attrition of the regiment during its life. Of the 1167 men that courageously marched off to war in 1861 and 1862, a mere 125 remained with their "tattered flag" at the surrender. The vaunted Rock City Guard presented themselves with 27 men at the surrender; 334 had formed the "Guard" in April 1861. [3] Many of their records were destroyed in fear of retribution for their enlistment in the Confederate cause.

Third Lieutenant Thomas Cobb was present at Johnston's surrender; his brother was not. Mitchell had died shortly after the battle of Murfreesboro. Mitchell Cobb had been sent home on furlough after the battle of Stones River. He returned to his regiment in February of 1863. He died in an Atlanta hospital about a month later. He left behind his young wife and two year-old son, George. He had seen his son for the last time during his February furlough. His brother Thomas passed away at age 47 in 1871. Sam Watkins would return to his home in Columbia, Tennessee. He married his sweetheart, Jennie. He raised a family and passed away at age 62 in 1901. Martha "Mattie" Ready Morgan, with her younger sister, Alice, would return to the family home in Murfreesboro after a more than two year absence. Mattie would care for her baby girl, Johnnie, alone. She was a widow at twenty-one. Her Hero, General John Hunt Morgan, had been killed while trying to avoid capture during a night raid on his headquarters near Greenville, Tennessee on September 4, 1864. He was shot in the back. [4]

The First Tennessee left High Point, North Carolina on May 3, 1865. They arrived in the Tennessee state capitol eighteen days later; home at last. [5]

BLOOD OF THE DYING SUN

The men of the Seventy-Eighth had returned to their homes. They took up their lives once more. As Theodore Roosevelt would say years later, these were the men who had stood in the arena. They were not those who chose the cloistered life. They were the men who knew the pride of accomplishment and of victory. They had quelled the storm and ridden the thunder.

Many of the men like Abram Kipp and Christian Hinchberger, had returned to their homes and farms; however, Hinchberger eventually opened a grocery store in Butler. Many more returned to the valley, but gave up the farm life. They were drawn to the life of a laborer. Within twenty years of the war the men of the Seventy-Eighth populated the mills and factories that sprung up along the Allegheny River. South of Kittanning the borough of Ford City grew around the Ford Glass Plant. Bill Sproul and Sam Dumm moved to Parnassus, Pennsylvania, where Alcoa would build its first large aluminum manufacturing plant. The town of New Kensington would grow around the plant that spread for miles along the river.

The adventure of the Civil War put the wanderlust in many men who did not wish to return to the Alley-Kiski Valley. Two of the members of Sirwell's staff and one company officer joined the regular army at the war's end. Augustus Bonnaffon, First Lieutenant Regular U.S. Army, commanding a troop, died of Yellow Fever in Indianola, Texas in 1867. Henry Torbett, commended for bravery at Stones River by Bill Sirwell, also accepted a commission as a First Lieutenant in the 11th U.S. regiment, regular army. During his tour in Texas in 1869, he caught a "southern miasma" similar to malaria. He returned to his home in Freeport, Pennsylvania, where he died on June 8, 1871. His burial site at Freeport Cemetery overlooks that of his companions from Company F. William R. Maize of Indiana would take a commission of Second Lieutenant in the US Army. He rose to the rank of major and in 1914, was living in the US Grant Hotel in San Diego, California.

Albert Buell Hay lived not far from George McCandless. He entered Allegheny County politics. He served as County Solicitor from 1906 to 1916. He served as Allegheny County Assistant District Attorney from 1918 until his death on September 23, 1936. Robert Elwood, Captain of Company I, would move to Verona, Pennsylvania, and become the President of the First National Bank of Verona. Robert Boreland opened a shoe store in Freeport, Pennsylvania. Levi Step would open a hotel in Worthington, Pennsylvania. Evan Lewis would serve as a school director and make a living as a stone mason. His 13 children from his three wives would produce hundreds of descendants. Will Lowery would serve as Prothonotary of Butler County.

Archibald Blakeley moved his law practice to Pittsburgh, while his brother Thomas opened a medical practice in St. Louis. Colonel Blakeley would head the Pennsylvania delegation to the Chickamauga dedication in 1897. William Sirwell's boisterous nephew George McCandless moved to Pittsburgh and began the life of a traveling salesman selling Pabtz Blue Ribbon Beer. He would settle in the Bellevue section of what is today Pittsburgh and become a Justice of the Peace. Father Christy was assigned to a parish in Ebensburg, Pennsylvania. Dr. Hosack opened a medical practice in Allegheny City. Private David McElroy of Company A, opened McElroy Iron works in Keokuk, Iowa. Major Robert Smith went into real estate in New Mexico. Fred Wiehl of Butler spent the remainder of his life in the shadow of Lookout Mountain. He passed away in 1900 in Chattanooga. "Old Bill" received letters from Illinois, Kansas, California, Indiana, Arizona and South Dakota. Phineas Hatzell of Company C, as he wrote to his parents, did not go home to Pennsylvania. Although he did not carry out his plan to go to the Arizona Territory, he made his home in Lafayette, Indiana after the war. For unknown reasons many of the boys moved to Kansas. They would spread their stories and history of the Seventy-Eighth throughout the United States.

The war did eventually take its toll on many members and their families. Many drank hard, they left their wives and for many the remainder of their lives were troubled. Elijah Snyder Barrackman of Butler, Pennsylvania was "sickly" for the rest of his life. He spent a great deal of time in "veterans hospitals." Sarah Springer Foy, his wife Jane's sister married to George Foy also in the regiment, was widowed at 28 years-old. George Foy taken by the Rebels along with Dr. Hosack at McLemore's Cove in 1863, died at Libby Prison in Richmond, Virginia a month after his capture. Jane and Sarah's brother John Springer of the Pennsylvania 103rd, died at Andersonville Prison in August of 1864, four months after his capture at Plymouth, North Carolina. George Adams wounded by a sniper on June 27, 1864, lived a life of misery until the age of 87. He died in 1929. He was collecting a $90.00 per month, 75% disability pension. Half of his jaw had been shot away.

Clarion County's Company E Private Reuben George of East Brady and owner of the Monterey House committed suicide on January 19, 1909, at age 72. When just twenty-one years-old Philip Harman of Company A was captured at Chickamauga. He was held in Andersonville Prison for 15 months. In 1923, he would commit suicide in his home in Dayton, Borough, Pennsylvania.

There would be times that old soldiers would be called upon to defend their deeds on the battlefield. William Rosecrans mildly defended his actions at Chickamauga. At a reunion of the Society of the Army of the Cumberland in 1870, Rosey adopted the position that his prime objective in that campaign was to capture Chattanooga. Which his army did. However, his claim that he achieved that objective is shallow in light of the fact that he had captured Chattanooga before the battle of Chickamauga. Rosecrans' defeat in Northern Georgia remains a fact. [1]

William Sirwell, as "Mister Military" in Armstrong County was widely criticized for not bringing his prominence to bear and not seeing that all Civil War veterans of the county received equal acclaim for their Civil War deeds. Since Sirwell had been instrumental in writing the Civil War history for Smith's History of Armstrong County, he was naturally open to such attacks. Sirwell had persevered in writing an overall history of the 44 companies that were formed in Armstrong, despite the fact that Robert Smith died two years before his history was published. Smith had originally planned to have a much smaller chapter on the war, because his book was to be a history of the county, not of the Civil War. It was only at the insistence of the publishers that Sirwell, Blakeley and Captain Andrew Scott Warner, Company E, Pennsylvania 139th, of Freeport expanded the chapter.

Nonetheless, it was Sirwell, not Smith, who came under fire. In one particular instance, Brevet Major David Marshall angrily wrote to Sirwell and essentially accused him of seeking glory only for his vaunted Seventy-Eighth. Marshall commanded Company K of the 155th Pennsylvania Zouaves, an Armstrong County unit that he felt deserved greater recognition. A few letters were exchanged and Sirwell finally resolved the problem. He challenged Marshall to rectify the oversight by writing a history of the company. Sirwell's sympathy and suggestion healed the personal feelings between the two old soldiers. Almost twenty-six years after their muster, David Porter Marshall wrote the first unit history of an Armstrong county company or regiment. [2]

In 1907, forty-five years after the battle at Stones River, an article appeared in the National Tribune stating that the flag of the 26th Tennessee was not captured by the Seventy-Eighth, but by Company E of the 69th Ohio. Lieutenant Frederick Wilson of Company E claimed that his men captured the flag then threw it away. Wilson's statement is preposterous, since any captured national, regimental or company ensign was extremely valued. Its possession usually brought a commendation from the commanding general and a promotion for the holder. David Ake of Company D, in responding to the ridiculous charge, incorrectly assumed that the flag had been burned in a fire at Color Bearer George Hamm's home.[3] The flag of the Twenty-Sixth Tennessee still remains in the Pennsylvania State Capital.

For the most part, the petty bickering would diminish over time. The years would pass and the veterans would grow older. At Regimental reunions, battlefield dedications and within organizations like the Society of the Army of the Cumberland, and the Grand Army of the Republic the boys of Sirwell's regiment would remember the past. They would retell the stories of battles that took the lives of their comrades and strengthened their brotherhood. They would pass values to their children and grand children of patriotism, duty, and love of the Union. Volumes of books on famous Civil War leaders would fill library shelves and grand equestrian statues of generals would dominate national parks and battlefields. But the soldiers would be relegated to common battlefield regimental and state markers, or generic statues in city parks. Grant and Lee's courage, Longstreet and Thomas' steadfast determination, Sheridan and Hood's fearlessness would fill volumes of books.

The fiber of the citizen-soldiers would fade into obscurity, but they would be remembered. Corporal Herbert "Hoof" Bengough of Company K moved to Pittsburgh. He served as the secretary of the committee that raised Soldiers and Sailors Memorial Hall to commemorate the men of the Civil War. His secretary/clerk was Mame Sirwell, the Colonel's daughter. But the men would also be remembered by the Sons of Veterans, both Union and Confederate. They would be remembered by families. And eventually they would be remembered by historians. It is unique that Braxton Bragg, the general that history remembers as being excessively hard on his men, would be the man to recognize the value of the volunteer. After the battle of Stones River, Bragg would write. "We have had in a great measure to trust to the individuality and self reliance of the private soldier. Without the incentive or the motive which controls the officer, who hopes to live in history; without the hope of reward, and actuated only by a sense of duty and of patriotism, he has, in this great contest, justly judged that the cause was his own, and gone into it with a determination to conquer or die. [Irrespective of the officer] history will yet award the main honor where it is due - to the private soldier." [4]

William Sirwell would take up his life again, but the Civil War years would always affect his life. He re-opened his jeweler's shop and became the exclusive franchise for Elgin watches and clocks. In September of 1865, he would run for the Pennsylvania State Senate. Sirwell had no designs on the state office. He supported Colonel Sam

Jackson of Apollo.   Samuel Jackson, who commanded the Eleventh Pennsylvania Reserves was the soldiers candidate in the district that covered Armstrong, Lawrence and Butler counties. However, in his bid for the nomination in the Union party he was denied the position and "received the cold shoulder" by "shoddy, corrupt political tricksters." The immense power of the Grand Army of the Republic had not yet grown to the proportions it would someday achieve. Both Sirwell and Jackson had hoped for a candidate "who looked...to the rewarding of the noble soldier." Upon Jackson's loss, he and a number of friends and old veterans urged Sirwell to run for the Senate seat. Running on the Democratic ticket, Sirwell was defeated. The soldiers would have to wait for their day.

In 1866, Sirwell engaged in an oil digging operation. The "Sirwell Well" did produce oil at 550 feet, but could never become profitable. Not so many years after, in Oil City, Pennsylvania, the process for drilling for oil and its refinement would be developed.

In 1870, William Lowry of Butler drove to Kittanning and at a meeting in Colonel Sirwell's home they formed the Regimental Organization. Sirwell was the first president and Lowry served as Secretary for thirty-one years. It is interesting that the year after Sirwell's death, the Organization voted to keep membership to comrades of the "Old 78th," meaning those from the original regiment. Those that formed their bonds amid the death and destruction of the years of campaigning in the field and in the many bloody battles.

In 1873, Sirwell headed up the committee of the Kittanning Bridge Company that sold stock that was used in re-building the bridge across the Allegheny River from Kittanning to West Kittanning. As always, he would be active in the church and school affairs. He was a member of the Grand Army of the Republic, the Eagle Volunteer Fire Company, the Red Men and the Marshal of the German Benefit Union, an organization for the benefit of persons descended from the "Fatherland." He served as Kittanning Postmaster and Justice of the Peace. In 1881, he lost a race for a position as a school director by 11 votes. Perhaps it was just possible that the fame of members of the vaunted 78th was fading. Twenty years after the war, many men of the regiment had moved away. And many of the boys that had trudged over the roads of Kentucky, Tennessee, Alabama and Georgia now were interred in the cemeteries throughout the Allegheny-Kiski Valley.

Those veterans in the valley still honored their old colonel. He was the president of their regimental reunion association. They bestowed the honorary title of General on "Old Bill," the rank that politics had kept from him during the war. Private Andrew Johnson of Kittanning named his son "Sirwell Johnson." Colonel Sirwell spoke at many of the cemetery dedications in the county during each Spring when the graves of fallen soldiers were covered with flowers. He would attend any function that honored his regiment.

Bill Sirwell remained generous to a fault. Although his nephew George went to Pittsburgh to make his way in the world, Sam McCandless, Sirwell's brother-in-law, opened a tailor shop in the Sirwell residence on South Jefferson Street. Sam would outlive his revered relative and friend, and would remain with his sister until his death. Old veterans in need of a hand-out always knew that their old commander was good for a hot meal or a quick "loan." He attempted to see that all veterans were given their due. The unassuming Colonel considered it an honor and duty to compile the section on the

William Sirwell
1876
Picture and "wood–cut"
Courtesy of H.R. "Hap" Fleming of Kittanning

Civil War for the *Armstrong County History*. Sirwell received honors for his leadership and accomplishments until his death.

In late July of 1885, Nellie Bly, who would become world famous in 1890, by completing a 72 day trip around the world, a week less than Jules Verne's fictional Phileas Fogg, interviewed a dying Colonel William Sirwell. The twenty-one year-old Miss Bly, was a relatively new feature reporter at the *Pittsburgh Dispatch* from where she would someday move to the *New York World*, investigative journalism and fame. She picked Colonel Sirwell to interview because of the recent death of President Grant. As a native of Apollo, Pennsylvania, Miss Bly, nee Elizabeth Jane Cochran, was familiar with the exploits of Colonel Sirwell and his renowned Seventy-Eighth for most of her life. [5]

In her lengthy article, Miss Bly constructed the parallel lives of Ulysses Grant and William Sirwell. Although never achieving Grant's station in life, Sirwell had been a soldier for the better part of his life. Like Grant, financially Sirwell was virtually a failure. His generosity with his family, friends, and old comrades probably led to his lack of substantial funds in his old age. Like his one time chief in the Union army, Sirwell was dying of throat cancer. The disease had progressed so far that he had difficulty in speaking. He responded to most of Miss Bly's questions in scrawled writings. But like any old soldier he had to have enjoyed the attention and admiration of a beautiful young lady from a new generation.

Looking through the extensive collection of books, papers and memorabilia the young woman was able to see and report on the life of Kittanning's war time "hero." William Sirwell was an incomparable collector, maybe even a "pack rat." He collected and saved anything that was of interest to him. He had a piece of scaffolding from John Brown's gallows, an Indian tomahawk from Kittanning's early inhabitants, many coins aged from 50 to 500 years old, and his father's 150 year old watch. Through some means, Bill Sirwell had acquired a piece of an apple tree from the yard of Wilmer McLean's Appomattox home. The residence used by Grant and Lee to sign the surrender papers that brought the Civil War to an end. He proudly showed "Miss Cochran" a small meteor and a large pure amethyst that changed daily in color from purple to yellow to white. These were just a few of the treasurers Sirwell showed the reporter. Sadly, many years after Sirwell died the old home at the corner of Jacob and South Jefferson Streets was destroyed by fire. Bill Sirwell, Jr. and his wife, Nancy, barely escaped with their children. Colonel Sirwell's prized battle and presentation swords were saved.

At the end of what had to be a very long interview for the dying veteran, Miss Bly completed her article with one of Sirwell's written messages, "I was born a soldier, have always lived one and hope to die the same." [6] Nellie Bly's "hero" lived only six more weeks. On September 9, 1885, William Sirwell, like his famed regiment, passed into history.

O CAPTAIN! MY CAPTAIN

"At last, after more than one year's intense suffering, the order to surrender came to Colonel William Sirwell. At half past 9 o'clock on Wednesday night last, the gallant, old commander laid down his arms. His was an eventful life, but no matter what station in it he was called to fill, the summons always met with a ready response."

"In the days when the future of the Union looked gloomy and dangerous, he was one of the first to offer his services to his country, and throughout the four years that followed, was a conspicuous character in his country's history."

"But although he was able to successfully combat the attacks of his country's foes, yet like all mortals, when the dread enemy, death, laid its icy hand upon him, he was powerless to resist. He is dead and the loving hearts in his community, in sympathy with his immediate family and the comrades who fought with him, weep in sorrow over the death of the gallant hero. He will be buried with the honors of war by the Grand Army." [1]

What makes young men go off to war? The adventure, peer pressure, and duty are certainly factors, but patriotism was definitely a certainty. Throughout the letters and diaries of members of the Seventy-Eighth used or studied for this book, even after the Civil War had dragged on for years, there are comments of patriotism. Sirwell's comments in Smith's *History of Armstrong County* lead to the belief that he and his boys had fought only for the preservation of the Union. Like the veterans of wars before and wars after, maybe only they understood their motivation. And like all wars before, the carnage and death faded. The smell of gun powder, the screams and sobs of dying men, and the smell of rotting horse flesh were replaced by picnics, reunions and parades. Old comrades now met for the funeral of their fallen commander.

"The men of his renowned and glorious old regiment [had always] ardently supported the commander who fought with them through so many hard battles, who encouraged them in sickness and privation, and was ever kind, humane and generous to them. And who can blame them? The ties which connect a soldier with his Colonel, after the battle fought and won, cannon be sundered. They are of an almost sacred character."

On Monday, September 14, 1885, the remains of Colonel William Graham Sirwell were laid to rest in the land he had given to Saint Mary's Catholic Church. In the bright autumn sun, his family and old comrades of the Seventy-Eighth, took "Old Bill" home. The funeral was most impressive and in the spirit for a fallen hero.

Promptly at 11:00 A.M., the procession started. The Kittanning Cornet Band played a funeral march. They were followed by over 100 Grand Army members, members of the 78th Regiment, and old soldiers. Each member wore a badge of mourning designed by Colonel Sirwell. The old warriors were commanded by Sirwell's friend, First Lieutenant Samuel Lee of the old Seventy-Eighth's Company B. They wanted no cassion to transport Sirwell's remains. Just as Sirwell had walked with his boys down Penn Avenue to Governor Curtin's ceremony on that cloudy October day almost twenty-four years ago, his comrades now carried his flag draped coffin to its final rest. Eight pall bearers carried the coffin flanked by another eight uniformed men carrying reversed rifles. Twenty carriages and buggies carried Elizabeth Sirwell, her family, relatives, and friends. The caravan proceeded through Kittanning to St. Mary's Church.

At the church Colonel Sirwell's coffin was placed near the altar and opened for the service. Father Brady standing in the haze of burning incense began the Roman Catholic mass for the dead solemnly intoning in Latin, "I go unto the altar of God, to God who gives joy to my youth...." At the end of the ceremony, the coffin was closed and removed to the hearse.

The procession of mourners headed for the cemetery, one mile north of town. The column of friends and family climbed the steep hill to St. Mary's Cemetery. They stood silently as the eight guards fired a three volley salute to their comrade. Sirwell was laid to rest in a plot overlooking the old fair ground that was Camp Orr, home of the converging companies entering the service of the 78th Regiment in 1861. The landscape was once again blanketed with the reds, yellows, oranges, purples and greens of the fall foliage.

Today a tall obelisk cut from marble excavated at Resaca, Georgia, marks Sirwell's grave. It is virtually surrounded by trees and the graves of his wife and children.

In 1885, without those monstrous trees, invariably, a few old soldiers gazed down at the old camp grounds below and the Allegheny River beyond remembering the days of their youth. And just for a short time they fondly remembered only the joyful, adventuresome times and the smiling faces of young soldiers tramping the battlefields of the South with their comrades in the Gallant Seventy-Eighth. [2]

In the years that followed Sirwell's death many of the old soldiers would continue to gather at other reunions, but their ranks diminished with each passing year. Fifty to one hundred men could be counted on for the regimental reunions held on an annual basis. One hundred and sixty-five men from the Seventy-Eighth attended the dedication of the Chickamauga battlefield in 1897. In 1927, Sam Steel and George McCracken attended a dinner in Tarentum, Pennsylvania, in honor of old Civil War soldiers. By 1936, Sam Steel would be the last survivor in the valley of the original Seventy-Eighth. A cane-pipe combination, made on Lookout Mountain in 1864, and dubbed "The Staff of the Regiment" has disappeared in time. The cane originally presented to Colonel Sirwell was to pass after each death to the next oldest member of the regiment. It should have gone to Sam Steele. On December 27, 1936, almost seventy-four years to the day after the battle at Stones River, Private Steele mustered out. Sam was laid to rest in the Slatelick Cemetery not far from the huge granite stone of his old friend George McCracken. McCracken's massive stone emblazoned with his name under two crossed rifles has the inscription, "Company F, Pennsylvania Seventy-Eighth." His family was one of the few to remember his days of service to the Union. In 1940, Private William Cypher, Company F, who joined the regiment under Sirwell in the Fall of 1864, but served most of his time in the Second Organization of the regiment, would end the line of veterans of the Seventy-Eighth in the Alle-Kiski Valley with his death at age 94.

Over the many years that the regiment held reunions, it was commonplace to receive letters from members that could not attend or letters from luminaries that had been invited to the reunion. In 1901, Confederate General James Longstreet in responded to a letter from Theodore Barrett. Although he could not attend, he hoped that as they once again gathered around the camp fire "in patriotic remembrances of the daring and endurance by the soldiers of Pennsylvania in defense of the old flag which today symbolizes a united and happy people," that he wished to extend his fraternal greetings to comrades of the *"gallant 78th Pennsylvania."* Earlier in 1891, General Rosecrans in response to an invitation to the reunion of the Seventy-Eighth, obviously not aware of Colonel Sirwell's death, sent his regrets along with his best wishes, "Greetings and love to Colonel Sirwell and all the boys." Old Rosey reminisced about the war years and the struggles of each soldier. He stated in his letter that each of the boys of the Seventy-Eighth should have "Stones River" carved on their grave stone in remembrance of their deeds at that far off battlefield.

It is true that Colonel William Graham Sirwell and his courageous Pennsylvania Seventy-Eighth met and overcame their greatest challenge at Murfreesboro. When they were summoned to the center stage of history, they fearlessly answered the call. Through determination and courage they helped change the course of American history. Nonetheless, few families, if any, etched the inscription suggested by General Rosecrans on the grave markers of deceased soldiers. Even the committee that placed the tall, gun-metal gray, marble obelisk on Sirwell's grave did not have the name carved on it. In all probability, the inscription on Bill Sirwell's monument would have been more to his liking.

Colonel William Sirwell
Our Beloved Commander

"The apples are ripe in the orchard,
The work of the soldier is done,
And the golden woodlands redden
In the blood of the dying sun."

FOOTNOTES

RALLY ROUND THE FLAG!
  1. Morison, Samuel Eliot, *The Oxford History of the American People*,
     Oxford University Press, New York, 1965, p. 685.

TO ARMS, TO ARMS!
  1. Smith, Robert Walter, Esq., *History of Armstrong County, Pennsylvania*,
     Waterman, Watkins & Co., Chicago, 1883,   pp. 60-62, 598.
     Frederic, Harold and William J. McMaster Sr., *Civil War Stories Old and New*, Volume I,
     The John Crawford Memorial History of Armstrong County, Pennsylvania,
     Sponsor: Camp #43, Sons of Union Veterans of the Civil War,
     Printer: The Print Shop, Havelock, North Carolina, 1991, p. 69.
     U.S. Census 1820 - 1860
     Armstrong County Genealogy Club Quarterly, The Armstrong County Historical Society,
     300 N. McKean Street, PO Box 735, Kittanning, Pennsylvania 16201-1345. Fall 1996, p. 16
  2. Grigg, Elliot & Company, *General Scott and his Staff*,   Philadelphia, 1849, pp. 145, 146.
  3. Bates, Samuel P., *History of the Pennsylvania Volunteers, 1861-5*.
     B. Singerly, State Printer, Harrisburg, Volume I, 1869, pp. 86-88.
  4. Buel, Clarence C. and Johnson, Robert U., eds., *Battles and Leaders of the Civil War*,
     Volume I, New York, 1888, pp. 172-183. Hereafter: Battles and Leaders.
  5. Bates, Volume I, p. 87.
  6. Battles and Leaders, Volume I, pp. 172-183.   Smith, pp. 60-62.

"THE KID HAS GONE TO THE COLORS"
  1. Gibson, Joseph, *History of the Seventy-Eighth Pennsylvania Volunteer Infantry*,
     J.T. Gibson/Historical Committee of the Regimental Association,
     Press of the Pittsburgh Printing Co., Pittsburgh, Penn'a. 1905, pp. 15-23.
     Dickey, L.S., *History of the 103d Regiment Pennsylvania Veteran Volunteer Infantry.
     1861-1865*. Chicago. 1910, p. 2.
     ORIGINAL ROSTER and DESCRIPTIVE LIST of the 78TH PENNSYLVANIA
     VOLUNTEER INFANTRY. Soldiers and Sailors Memorial Library,
     Pittsburgh, Pennsylvania.
  2. Frederic, Volume I, p. 69.
  3. Gibson, pp. 24, 25.
  4. Smith, pp. 60, 70-76. Gibson, pp. 24, 25. *Pittsburgh Gazette*, Pittsburgh, Pennsylvania,
     October 12, 14, 1861, p. 1.
  5. Fleming, George T., "Flem's" Views of Old Pittsburgh," Published by George T.
     ("Flem") Fleming, Pittsburgh, 1905, p. 40.
     Jenkins, Howard M., Editor, *Pennsylvania, Colonial and Federal, A History: 1608-1903*,
     Volume III, Pennsylvania Historical Publishing Association, Philadelphia, 1905, p. 466.
     Pittsburgh Gazette, October 18, 1861, p. 1.
  6. Gibson, pp. 24, 25.   *Seventy-Seventh Pennsylvania at Shiloh, History of the Regiment.*
     Harrisburg Publishing Co., State Printers, Harrisburg, Pennsylvania, 1905, p. 69.
     Pittsburgh Gazette, October 15, 1861.
  7. Jordan, John W., of the Historical Society of Pennsylvania, *A Century and a Half of
     Pittsburg and Her People*, Volume III, The Lewis Publishing Company, 1908, p. 116-118.
     Fitch, John, *Annals of the Army of the Cumberland*, J.B. Lippincott & Co., Philadelphia,
     1864, pp. 91, 110. *Pittsburgh Gazette*, February 12, 14, 1861.
     Baldwin, Leland D., *Pittsburgh, The Story of a City*, University of Pittsburgh Press, 1937, p. 314.
  8. *Pittsburgh Gazette*, October 17, 1861. Jenkins, p. 467.
  9. *History of Butler County, Pennsylvania*, Robert C. Brown & Co. Publishers, 1895, pp. 156, 157.
  10. Gibson, p. 19, 23. *Pittsburgh Gazette*, "Official Paper of the City", October 17-19, 1861.
     History of Butler County, Pennsylvania, Waterman, Watkins & Co., Chicago, 1883, p. 61.
     United States Census, 1860. Roster and Descriptive List. Beers, J.H., *Armstrong County*,

Pennsylvania, Her People Past and Present, J.H.Beers & Co., Chicago, 1914, p. 125.
Brown's History of Butler County, Pennsylvania, p. 237

THE BONNIE BLUE FLAG
1. Watkins, Samuel, *"CO. AYTCH" Maury Grays, First   Tennessee Regiment.* Introduction by
   Bell Irvin Wiley. Nashville, 1882. Reprinted 1952 by McCowat-Mercer Press, 1987, 1990 by
   Broadfoot Publishing Company, Wilmington, North Carolina, pp. 11, 13.
   Daniel, Larry J., *Soldiering in the Army of Tennessee*, The University of North Carolina
   Press, Chapel Hill & London, 1991, p. 40.
   Lindsley, John Berrien, M.D., D.D., *The Military Annals of Tennessee. Confederate.* J.M.
   Lindsley & Co., Publishers, Nashville, 1886, pp. 156, 159.
   Womack, Bob, *Call Forth the Mighty Men*, Colonial Press, Nashville, 1986, pp. 30, 31.
   Clayton, Prof. W.W., History of Davidson County, Tennessee, J.W. Lewis & Co.,
   Philadelphia, 1880. Reproduced by Charles Elder - Bookseller, Publisher,
   Nashville, 1971, p. 170.
2. Lindsley, pp. 156, 167, 411, 412, 415, 416.   *Tennesseans in The Civil War, A Military History
   of Confederate and Union Units*, Published by the Civil War Centennial Commission,
   Nashville, 1964, pp. 163, 172. Hereafter: Tennesseans.   Carol Kaplan Letter, 1992.
   Manigault, Arthur Middleton, *A Carolinian Goes to War*, edited by R. Lockwood Tower,
   University of South Carolina   Press, Columbia, South Carolina, 1983, p. 64.

CAMP FIRES IN KENTUCKY
1. Gibson, p. 20, 23.
2. Simkins, Albert P., Letters & Diary.   Courtesy of Bill May, Butler, PA
3. *Pittsburgh Gazette*, October, 1861. Fleming, p. 76.
4. Roster and Descriptive List.
5. Johnston, Adam S., *Soldier Boy's Diary Book*, kept by Adam S. Johnston [Private in the 79th
   Regiment of Pennsylvania Volunteer Infantry of Turtle Creek, Pennsylvania] From
   September 14, 1861, to October 2, 1864. Pittsburgh: 1867, p. 9.
   Bates, Volume II, p. 1083.
6. *Louisville Daily Journal*, Louisville, Kentucky, October 21, 22, 1861.
7. Roster and Descriptive List. United States Census, 1860.
8. *Pittsburgh Gazette*, October, 1861.
9. *Pittsburgh Gazette*, October 22, 1861. Gibson, pp. 24, 25. *Louisville Daily Journal*,
   October 22, 1861.
   Louisville Daily Courier, Bowling Green, Kentucky, October 29, 1861.
10. Gibson, pp. 24, 25.   The Pennsylvania Seventy-Seventh at Shiloh, p. 70.
    Louisville Daily Courier, October 29, 1861.
    Cist, Henry M. *The Army of the Cumberland.* New York, Charles Scribner's Sons, 1882, pp. 1-5.
    Horn, Stanley F., *The Army of the Tennessee,* The Bobbs-Merrill Company,
    Publishers, Indianapolis/New York, 1941, p. 44.
11. COMPANY ORDERS, Company I, Seventy-Eighth Pennsylvania, 1861-1864.
    R. S. Gancas Library. Hereafter: Company I.
12. Gibson, p. 26.
13. Company I, General Order No. 3, December 16th, 1862, was included here to indicate the
    musical calls used to bring   the men to order.
14. Luvaas, Jay, "Tramping the battle fields of the Civil War," 1977-1994.
15. Canfield, Silas S., *History of the 21ST Regiment Ohio Volunteer Infantry in the War of the
    Rebellion* by Captain S.S. Canfield, Toledo, O. Vrooman, Anderson & Bateman, Printers, 1893, p. 70.
16. Company I

DON CARLOS THE FIRST
1. Cist, pp. 21, 22.
   Cleaves, Freeman, *Rock of Chickamauga*, The Life of General George H. Thomas,
   University of Oklahoma Press, Norman and London, 1948, p. 74, 78.

2. Street, James R., and the Editors of Time-Life Books, *The Civil War, The Struggle for Tennessee, Tupelo to Stones River*, Time-Life Books, Alexandria, Virginia, pp. 14, 15. Battles and Leaders, I, p. 482.

3. Morison, p. 622.

4. Gibson, p. 30.

5. Bates, Volume II, p. 1029.

6. *The Daily Dispatch*, New Kensington, Pa., *"Civil War Echoes"* by Edward S. Osheskie, A Series of Articles Based on Letters of Pvt. Abram E. Kipp (1840-78) of Allegheny Township, Westmoreland County and History of the 78TH Regiment, Pennsylvania Volunteer Infantry. April 11-May 25, 1961, p. 10. Hereafter: Osheskie. Simkins Letters & Diary.   Gibson, pp. 195-236.

7. Gillaspie, Ira, *The Diary of Ira Gillaspie of the Eleventh Michigan Infantry*, Edited with an Introduction by Daniel B. Weber. Central Michigan University Press, Mount Pleasant, Clarke Historical Library, Copyright 1965, pp. 13, 17.

8. Diary of Dr. Thomas Blakeley Diary, Hospital Steward, PA 78th.

9. Andrews, J. Cutler, *The North Reports the Civil War*, University of Pittsburgh Press, Pittsburgh, Pa, 1955, p. 117. Hereafter: Andrews [North]

10. Company I

11. Gibson, p. 26. Original letter of George Washington Black, Company I, Pennsylvania 78th Regiment, to his wife in Apollo, PA. Speech of Archibald Blakeley, 1880 Regimental Reunion. Simkins Letters & Diary.

12. Bates, Volume II, p. 1077. Gibson, pp. 24, 25. O.R., XVI, Part II, p. 8.

13. Gibson, pp. 30-32. Roster and Descriptive List. Simkins Letters & Diary.

"TRAMP! TRAMP! TRAMP"

1. Letters of William Lowry

2. Gibson, p. 36.

3. Black Letters

4. Jones, Katharine M., Editor, *Heroines of Dixie*, The Bobbs-Merrill Company, Inc., 1955, p. 84. Henry, Robert Selph, *"First With the Most" Forrest*,   Mallard Press, New York, 1991, p. 69. Foote, Shelby, *The Civil War, A Narrative*, Random House, New York, 1963, Volume I, p. 216.

5. Gibson, p. 36.

6. Street, pp. 12-14. Canfield, p. 60.

7. Diary of Thomas G. Blakeley

8. Gibson, pp. 37, 38. Fitch, p. 103.

9. Company I, Order Book. Albert P. Simkins Letters & Diary.

10. Gibson, p. 37.

11. Osheskie, pp. 20, 21. Nashville Union, October 3-29, 1862.

12. Bennett, Charles W., *Historical Sketches of the Ninth Michigan Infantry*, by Charles W. Bennett of Company G, Daily Courier Print, Coldwater, Mich., 1913, pp. 11, 12. O.R., XX, Part II, pp. 162, 163.

13. Smith, pp. 70-76. Lowry Letters.

"THE CITY BIDES THE FOE"

1. Cist, pp. 56-58. Gibson, p. 42. Fitch, p. 102. *Nashville Union*, October 29,   1862. Haynie, J. Henry, *The Nineteenth Illinois*, M.A. Donohue & Co., Chicago, 1912, p. 180. *Chattanooga Rebel*, October 8, 1862.   Henry, Robert, pp. 86-90.

2. Andrews, p. 643. *Nashville Union*, October 26-29, 1862.   *The Picket Line and Camp Fire Stories*, by a Member of the G.A.R., Hurst & Co., Publishers, New York, 1903, pp. 47, 48. Cist, pp. 56-58. Gibson, p. 42.

SEEING THE ELEPHANT

1. Fitch, pp. 104, 105. Gibson, pp. 44, 45.   Smith, pp. 70-76, 598. *Nashville Union*, October 8, 1862. *Chattanooga Rebel*, October 12, 1862. Funk, Arville L., *A HOOSIER REGIMENT IN DIXIE, A History of the Thirty-eighth Indiana Volunteer Infantry Regiment*,   Adams Press, Chicago, Illinois, 1978, p. 117.

Van Horne, Thomas B., *History of the Army of the Cumberland*, Volume I, Written at the request of
Major-General George H. Thomas, Robert Clarke & Co., Cincinnati, 1875, p. 210.
Dodge, William Sumner, *History of the Old Second Division, Army of the Cumberland*,
Church and Goodman, Chicago, 1864, p. 12.   Canfield, p. 63.
2. Daniel, p. 13, 17. *Nashville Union*, October 8, 1862.
3. Fitch, pp. 104, 105. Gibson, pp. 44, 45.
Smith, pp. 70-76, 598. Henry, Robert, pp. 102-104.
Canfield, p. 64. *Nashville Union*, October 8, 1862.   *Chattanooga Rebel*, October 12, 1862.
Cumming, Kate, *Kate: The Journal of a Confederate Nurse*, Edited by Richard Barksdale
Harwell, Louisiana State University Press, Baton Rouge, 1959, p. 71.
4. Company I. *Nashville Union*, October 1, 1862.
5. Gibson, pp. 43, 44.
6. Gillaspie, pp. 13, 17, 36. William Lowry Letters
7. Osheskie, p. 16. William Lowry Letters, Blakeley Diary.
8. Gibson, p. 45.
9. Fitch, p. 105.   Dumm, Samuel, Diary, Letters & History. Courtesy of James Coulson,
Lower Burrell, PA. Great Grandson.

OLD ROSEY TAKES COMMAND

1. Cist, pp. 71, 72. *Louisville Journal*, October 27, 1862.   *Nashville Union*, October 29, 1862.
2. Cozzens, Peter, *The Battle of Stones River, No Better Place to Die*. University of Illinois Press,
Urbana and Chicago, 1990, pp. 13, 14. Lindsley, p. 160.
McDonough, James Lee, *Stones River - Bloody Winter in Tennessee*, The University of
Tennessee Press/Knoxville. 1980, p. 31.
3. Tucker, Glenn, *Chickamauga, Bloody Battle in the West*. The Bobbs-Merrill Company, Inc.,
1961. Morningside Bookshop, Dayton, 1976, pp. 32-41.   *Nashville Union*, November 4, 1862. Bly, p. 2.
Duyckinck, Evert A., National Portrait Gallery of Eminent Americans, Volume II, Johnson,
Fry & Company, New York, 1862, p. 451.
Catton, Bruce, *Never Call Retreat*, Doubleday & Company, Inc., Garden City, New York, 1965, p. 37.
4. Greeley, Horace, *The American Conflict*, Volume II,   Published by the National Tribune,
Washington, D.C., 1899, p. 270.   Quiner, E.B., Esq., *The Military History of Wisconsin*,
Clarke & Co., Publishers, Chicago, 1866, p. 326.
5. Osheskie, p. 25. *Nashville Union*, November 11, 1862.
Bickham, "W.D.B.", *Rosecrans' Campaigns with the Fourteenth Army Corp or the Army of the
Cumberland*, Moore, Wilstach, Keys & Co., Cincinnati, 1863, p. 30.
Tucker, p. 65. Cozzens, p. 16.
6. Gibson, p. 195-236. Simkins Letters & Diary.
7. Company I
8. Cist, p. 79.
9. Company I
10. W.D.B., pp. 62-65.
11. Luvaas, p. 349.
12. National Archives, Washington D.C., Casualty Sheet submitted by
Brigadier John F. Reynolds, November 2,   1862.
National Archives, Washington D.C., Casualty Sheet   submitted by Major General G.G. Meade.
Luvaas, Dr. Jay and Colonel Harold W. Nelson, *The U.S. Army War College Guide to the
Battles of Chancellorsville and Fredericksburg*, South Mountain Press, Inc.,   Publishers,
Carlisle, Pennsylvania, 1988, p. 41. Gibson, p. 224.
Brown's History of Butler County, Pennsylvania, p. 157.
13. Catton, Never Call Retreat, p. 34. Greeley, p. 287.

ONWARD CHRISTIAN SOLDIERS

1. Cist, p. 87. Jordan, 116-118. O.R., XX, Part I, p. 441.
2. W.D.B., pp. 31, 78, 128, 136, 143. Army of the Cumberland, 1869, p. 74, 75.
3. W.D.B., pp. 80, 129.
4. O.R., XX, Part I, pp. 174-178

5. O.R., XX, Part I, pp. 416-420.
6. Gibson, pp. 20-23. United States Census, 1860.   Simkins Letters & Diary.
7. Cist, p. 78.
8. Catton, Never Call Retreat, p. 37. W.D.B., p. 120.
9. Cist, p. 78.
10. O.R., XX, Part I, p. 206. McDonough, p. 37.   Manigault, p. 61.
11. Sheridan, Philip Henry, *Personal Memoirs of P.H. Sheridan, General United States Army,* In
    Two Volumes,   Volume I, New York, Charles L. Webster & Company, 1888, pp. 247, 248.
    W.D.B., p. 65. Lindsley, p. 156.
12. Cist, p. 97. Van Horne, Volume I, p. 219. Confederate Military History, p. 57.
13. Catton, Never Call Retreat, pp. 35, 36.
14. Gibson, pp. 47, 48.
15. W.D.B., pp. 120, 121. Andrews [North], p. 305.
16. Gibson, pp. 195-236. O.R., XX, Part I, p. 436. *Louisville Daily* Journal, December 29, 1862.
17. Roster and Descriptive List.   Frank Leslie's Magazine, New York Public Library.
    1860 U.S. Census, Giles County Tennessee.
    Tennessee in the Civil War - Union, pp. 490, 591. O.R., XXXII, Part I, p. 102.
18. Service Records, John L. Tanner, 1861-1864.   Tennessee State Library and Archives

"WE MOVE TOMORROW, GENTLEMEN"

1. McDonough, pp. 57, 58.
   Catton, Bruce, *This Hallowed Ground,* Doubleday & Company,   Inc.,
   Garden City, New York, 1956, pp. 190-194. Gibson, p. 70.
   Samuel Dumm Letters & Diary.   Simkins Letters & Diary.
2. Gillaspie, p. 40.
3. Catton, Never Call Retreat, p. 38.   Manigault, p. 52. Daniel, p. 97.
   Ridley, Lieutenant General Bromfield L., *Battles and Sketches of the Army of the Tennessee,*
   Missouri Printing & Publishing Co. Mexico, Missouri, 1906, p. 149.
   McMurray, W.J. M.D., *History of the Twentieth Tennessee Regiment of Volunteer Infantry,*
   C.S.A., Nashville, 1904, p. 224. Samuel Dumm Letters & Diary.
4. Daniel, pp. 111, 112.
   Holmes, Robert Masten, C.S.A., *Kemper County Rebel, The Civil War Diary*
   of Robert Masten Holmes, C.S.A. Edited by Frank Allen Dennis, forward by Thomas L.
   Connelly, University and College Press of Mississippi, Jackson,   1973, p. 36.
5. Watkins, p. 93.
6. W.J. McMurray, *History of the Twentieth Tennessee Regiment of Volunteer Infantry, C.S.A*
   (Nashville, 1904),   p. 224.
7. Losson, Christopher, *Tennesse's Forgotten Warriors,* The University of Tennessee Press,
   Knoxville, 1989, p. 79.
8. Daniel, p. 12. Cozzens, pp. 8-11, 33-35.
9. McDonough, p. 33.   Battles and Leaders, Volume III, pp. 604, 605.
10. Blue & Gray. Catton, Never Call Retreat, p. 50.
11. Love, William DeLoss, *Wisconsin in the War of the Rebellion,* Church and Goodman,
    Publishers, Chicago. A. Whittemore, Milwaukee. Sheldon & Co., New York. 1866, p. 621.
    Gibson, p. 178. 12. Gibson, pp. 49, 178-184. W.D.B., p. 164.
13. Cist, p. 92. Van Horne, Volume I, p. 219. Canfield, p. 72.
14. Gibson, pp. 49, 178-184. Samuel Dumm Letters & Diary. Haynie, pp. 181, 188.
15. Cist, p. 92.
16. O.R., XX, Part II, p. 247.
17. O.R., XX, Part I, p. 705. W.D.B., pp. 76, 157-163.
    Louisville Daily Journal, December 29, 1862.
18. Catton, Never Call Retreat, p. 38.
19. Gillaspie, p. 41.
20. Gibson, pp. 178-184.
21. Cist, pp. 89, 90.
22. Manigault, p. 54. Haynie, p. 202.

23. Logsdon, David R., *Eyewitnesses at the Battle of Stones River*, Nashville,
    Tennessee, 1989, p. 8.
24. Blackburn, Theodore W., *Letters from the Front, A Union "Preacher" Regiment (74TH
    OHIO) in the Civil War*. Press of Morningside Bookshop, Division of Morningside House,
    Inc., Publishers and Booksellers, Dayton, Ohio, 45410, p. 93.
25. Manigault, p. 54. Cist, pp. 89, 125, 126.
26. Van Horne, Volume I, p. 221. Evans, p. 60.
27. Gibson, pp. 178-184. Cist, p. 92. Haynie, p. 199.
28. W.D.B., p. 172. Battles and Leaders, Volume III, p. 605.
    Andrews, J. Cutler, *The South Reports the Civil War*, Princeton University Press, Princeton,
    New Jersey, 1970, p. 257. Hereafter: Andrews [South].
29. Owens, Ira, *Greene County Soldiers in the Late War, Ira S. Owens, Company C, Seventy-fourth
    Ohio*, Christian Publishing House Print Dayton, Ohio, 1884, p. 28.   Cist, p. 92.
30. Gibson, pp. 178-184. O.R., XX, Part I, p. 413, 448, 459.   Gillaspie, p. 42.
31. O.R., XX, Part I, pp. 412, 435.   National Archives Records.
32. Greeley, p. 288.
33. *The Kittanning Mentor*, February 1863, p. 1.

"THE BALL OPENED"
 1. Stones River Tramp, 12/3-4/1991.
    Beatty, John, *The Citizen-Soldier or Memoirs of a Volunteer*.
    Wilstach, Baldwin & Co., Publishers, Cincinnati 1879, p. 214. O.R., XX, Part I, p. 164.
 2. Roster and Descriptive List
 3. Gibson, pp. 178-184. Sheridan, p. 205-218. Haynie, pp. 181, 202.
    O.R., XX, Part I, pp. 191, 369, 407, 421,   431, 432, 439, 769.
 4. Logsdon, p. 10.
 5. Gibson, pp. 49-50, 196-228. O.R., XX, Part I, p. 431.
 6. Cist, p. 90. W.D.B., p. 195.
 7. Stones River Tramp, 12/3-4/1991.   O.R., XX, Part I, p. 432. Sheridan, p. 205-218.
 8. Cist, pp. 92, 100. Foote, Volume II, pp. 85, 86.   Battles and Leaders, Volume III, p. 617.
 9. Cist, pp. 97. Foote, Volume II, pp. 85, 86.
10. Cist, pp. 99, 100.
11. Foote, Volume II, pp. 85, 86. Logsdon, p. 13.   Tennesseans, p. 183.

SHOUT! SHOUT! THE BATTLE CRY OF FREEDOM
 1. Stevenson, Alexander F., *The Battle of Stone's River near   Murfreesboro, Tenn.*, [1884],
    Press of Morningside Bookshop, Dayton, Ohio, 1983, pp. 29-33.   Sheridan, p. 205-218.
 2. Catton, Never Call Retreat, p. 41. Sheridan, p. 205-218.   W.D.B., p, 205.
    Tenth Wisconsin Infantry, Tenth Annual Reunion, First Lieutenant L.D. Hinkley, Tenth
    Wisconsin Infantry, p. 15.
 3. O.R., XX, Part I, pp. 364, 407. Cist, p. 101.   Seventy-Seventh Pennsylvania, p. 104.
 4. Cist, pp. 104, 105.
 5. Watkins, p. 93.
 6. W.D.B., p. 143. Cist, p. 102. McDonough, p. 38.
 7. Cist, p. 133. O.R., XX, Part I, pp. 295, 296.
    The Pennsylvania Seventy-Seventh at Shiloh, p. 104.
 8. Cist, p. 104. McDonough, p. 83.   Sheridan, p. 205-218.
 9. Bennett, p. 28. W.D.B., p. 248.   Ridley, p. 149

"INTO LINE, MEN! INTO LINE!"

 1. Gibson, pp. 178-184. National Archives.   Hinkley, p. 16. Love, p. 622.
 2. Cist, pp. 110, 111. McDonough, pp. 101, 107, 122. Stevenson, p. 58. Sheridan, p. 205-218.
 3. Cist, pp. 110, 111. McDonough, pp. 101, 107, 122. Stevenson, p. 58.
    O.R., XX, Part I, 349, 350.
    Daniel, p. 23. Love, pp. 633, 634.

4. Battles and Leaders, Volume III, pp. 621, 622.   Cist, pp. 110, 111.
   McDonough, pp. 101, 107, 122.
   Van Horne, Volume I, p. 237. O.R., XX, Part I, pp. 407, 537, 688, 706.
   W.D.B., pp. 42, 215, 249-251, 362, 363. Ridley, pp. 155, 156.   Womack, p. 205.
5. O.R., XX, Part I, pp. 411-416, 688, 756, 764.   Gibson, p. 52. Simkins Letters & Diary.

"CUT YOUR WAY OUT!"
1. W.D.B., p. 250. Gibson, p. 52.
2. Cist, pp. 111. O.R., XX, Part I, p. 407.
3. Cozzens, p. 142. Gillaspie, p. 43.   O.R., XX, Pt. I, p. 421. O.R., XVI, Pt. II, p. 8.
   Cleaves, p. 127. Haynie, p. 186.
4. Battles and Leaders, Volume III, p. 621. O.R., XX, Pt. I, p. 432. Blue & Gray Magazine,
   The Battle of Stones River, By Charles M. Spearman, Blue & Gray Enterprises, Inc.,
   Columbus, Ohio, February 1989.
5. Battles and Leaders, Volume III, pp. 621, 622.   O.R., XX, Part I, p. 732.
6. O.R., XX, Part I. pp. 411, 412.
7. Gibson, pp. 178-184. O.R., XX, Pt. I, pp. 408, 432, 439,   658, 659. Stevenson, p. 82.
8. Stones River Tramp, 12/3-4/1991.
9. Gibson, pp. 178-184. O.R., XX, Pt. I, pp. 408, 432,   439, 658, 659, 688, 756, 757, 733-737.
   Stevenson, p. 82. Carol Kaplan, Nashville Public Library, 12/17/91.
   Watkins, p. 93. Jackman, John S., Diary of a Confederate Soldier, John S.
   Jackman of the Orphan Brigade. Edited with an introduction by William C. Davis. Published
   in Columbia, South Carolina, by the University of South Carolina Press, 1990, p. 31.
10. Cozzens, p. 143. Gibson, pp. 178-184.
11. Frederic, Harold, Civil War Soldier's Own Stories, Volume II, The John Crawford Memorial
    History of Armstrong County, Pennsylvania, Sponsor: Camp #43, Sons of Union Veterans of
    the Civil War, Printer: The Print Shop, Havelock, North Carolina, 1991, p. 133.
    Gibson, pp. 178-184.
12. W.D.B., p. 251. Van Horne, Volume I, p. 237. O.R., XX, Part I, pp. 432, 532, 735.
    Stevenson, p. 90.
13. Battles and Leaders, Volume III, pp. 622-624.
    O.R., XX, Pt. I, pp. 383, 384, 408, 421, 433, 739.
    W.D.B., p. 251, 252. Gibson, p. 53. Van Horne, Volume I, p. 238. Blue & Gray, p. 26.
    Canfield, p. 74. Hinkley, p. 17.
14. Lindsley, p. 161. O.R., XX, Part I, p. 231.
15. Gibson, pp. 56, 178-184. O.R., XX, Part I, p. 245.   Lindsley, pp. 171-173. Hinkley, p. 20.

HELL'S HALF ACRE
1. Cist, p. 117. W.D.B., p. 216.
2. Catton, Never Call Retreat, p. 43.   McDonough, pp. 132-149.

"THIS ARMY DOES NOT RETREAT"
1. Hinkley, p. 21.
2. Gibson, pp. 178-184. Canfield, p. 74.
3. Battles and Leaders, Volume III, p. 607. Van Horne, Volume I, p. 246.
   W.D.B., pp. 304, 305. Andrews [South], p. 258.
4. Gibson, pp. 57, 58.
5. McDonough, pp. 160, 161. Cleaves, pp. 129-132.   Gibson, p. 58.
6. Stevenson, p. 144.
7. Battles and Leaders, III, p. 634.

NEW YEAR'S DAY, 1863
1. Logsdon, pp. 51, 52.
2. Gibson, pp. 58-61. O.R., XX, Part I, pp. 441-443. Van Horne, Volume I, p. 247.
   Haynie, p. 188.
3. Logsdon, p. 51.
4. Stevenson, p. 8. Logsdon, p. 52. W.D.B., p. 237.

5. Beatty, p. 205.
6. Stevenson, pp. 125, 126. Cist, p. 128.   Love, p. 631. Ridley, p. 154.

FIRST TO CROSS
1. McDonough, pp. 175-177. Stevenson, pp. 131, 132.   Stanley Horn, p. 207.
2. Gibson, pp. 61, 178-184. Cist, pp. 120, 121. O.R., XX, Part I, p. 808. Van Horne,
   Volume I, p. 249.
3. Adams, Jacob, *Diary of Jacob Adams, Private in Company F 21st O.V.V.I.*. Reprinted from
   the Ohio Archaeological and   Historical Quarterly for October, 1929. The F.J. Heer
   Printing Co., Columbus, Ohio, 1930, pp. 21, 22.
4. Stevenson, pp. 130, 131. McDonough p. 180.
5. Battles and Leaders, Volume III, p. 609. Cist, p. 121.
6. Gibson, pp. 178-184. Cist, p. 121. McDonough, p. 185.
7. Bradley, Stanley, *The Soldier in our Civil War*, Vol. II, Stanley Bradley Publishing Co., New
   York, 1890, p. 97.   Gibson p. 62. Cist, p. 121.   O.R., XX, Part I, p. 806.
8. Gibson, p. 62.
9. Adams, pp. 21, 22. O.R., XX, Pt. I, p. 424.   Cist, p. 122.
10. Bradley, p. 97. Gibson, pp. 62, 178-184.
11. Owens, pp. 36, 37. O.R., XX, Pt. I, p. 434.   Cist, p. 123.
12. Gibson, pp. 178-184. Cozzens, p. 193.   Bradley, p. 97. O.R., XX, Part I, p. 434.
    Stevenson, p. 140.
13. Owens, pp. 36, 37 . Bradley, p. 97. O.R., XX, Pt. I,   pp. 434, 808-810. Frederic II, p. 133.
14. Gibson, pp. 63, 178-184. Owens, pp. 36, 37. W.D.B., p. 314. Smith, p. 598.   *Butler*
    Eagle, Butler, Pennsylvania, November 1923   O.R., XX, Part I, pp. 204, 434, 817, 818.
    Nashville Union, January 20, 1863.
15. Lindsley, p. 412.
16. Stevenson, pp. 177-179. Cozzens, p. 186.   O.R., XX, Part I, pp. 374, 813.
    Confederate Military History, p. 73.
17. Owens, pp. 36, 37. Gibson, pp. 64, 178-184.   O.R., XX, Part I, p. 435. Cist, p. 123.
    Van Horne, Volume I, p. 250.
18. Tucker, pp. 287, 416.
19. O.R., XX, Part I, pp. 244, 456. Gibson, 62, 63.   Haynie, pp. 191, 194, 206.
20. O.R., XX, Part I, p. 456
21. Fitch, p. 405.
22. Owens, pp. 36, 37. O.R., XX, Part I, p. 422.
23. Green/McDonough, Tour.

ASHES! WE ALL FALL DOWN!
1. Beatty, p. 207. Owens, p. 55.   Battles and Leaders, Volume III, p. 633.
2. Osheskie, p. 27. Samuel Dumm Letters & Diary
3. Beatty, pp. 210-212.
4. Gibson, pp. 68, 178-184. Cist, pp. 127, 214.   Lindsley, p. 161. O.R., XX, Part I, p. 669.
   Van Horne, Volume I, p. 251. Fitch, p. 406.   Andrews [North], p. 311.
   Simkins Letters & Diary.   *Nashville Union*, January 20, 1863.
5. Gibson, pp. 178-184. Samuel Dumm Letters & Diary.
6. Cist, p. 125. Smith, p. 46, 49. Horn, p. 11.
7. Walker, p. 72. Cist, 125, 127. Love, p. 631.   O.R., XX, Part I, p. 669. W.D.B., p. 327.
8. Osheskie, p. 29. Samuel Dumm Letters & Diary.   *Butler Eagle*, November 1923.
9. Gibson, pp. 178-184.
10. O.R., XX, Part I, pp. 201-205, 221. Samuel Dumm Letters & Diary
11. O.R., XX, Pt. I, pp. 228, 436.   *Kittanning Mentor* February 1863. Gibson, pp. 195-267
    United States Census, 1860.
12. O.R., XX, Part I, p. 436.
13. O.R., XX, Pt. I, pp. 228, 436. Cist, p. 133.   *Kittanning Mentor* February 1863.
    Gibson, pp. 195-267
14. Leech, Margaret, *Reveille in Washington*, Harper &   Brothers, New York,
    New York, 1941, p. 280.

15. Stevenson, pp. 191, 197. O.R., XX, Part I, pp. 197, 201. Luvaas, p. 349.
16. Dobell, Byron, Editor, <u>American Heritage</u>, October/November 1984. *"Military Medicine,"* by Jane Colihan with the help of Dr Robert J.T. Joy, M.D., American Heritage Publishing Company, New York, NY. pp. 65, 66. Morison, p. 624.
17. Gibson, pp. 212, 224. Samuel Dumm Letters & Diary.
18. Barnes, James A., *The Eighty-Sixth Regiment, Indiana Volunteer Infantry,* The Journal Company, Printers, Crawfordsville, Indiana, 1895, pp. 117-122.
    Marks, Rev. J.J., D.D., *The Peninsular Campaign in Virginia,* J.B. Lippencot Co., Philadelphia, 1864, p. 421. O.R., XX, Part I, p. 221.
19. Andrews [North], pp. 312, 313.
20. *Cincinnati Daily Enquirer*: Reports on the battle at Murfreesboro, Tennessee. January 1 to January 7, 1863. Cincinnati Public Library.
21. Andrews [North], pp. 27, 28.
22. *The Pittsburgh Gazette,* January 7, 1863. The Carnegie Library, Microfilm, Pittsburgh.
23. Van Horne, Volume I, p. 251.
24. O.R., XX, Part I, pp. 186, 187.
25. Horn, Stanley, pp. 222-227. *Nashville Union,* January 9, 1863.
    Richmond Enquirer, January 7, 1863.

TENTING TONIGHT

1. Meredith, John, Diary, Co. F. 78th Penna. Vols., 1st Battalion, Army of the Cumberland, p. 1. Canfield, p. 95.
2. Gillaspie, pp. 46, 47.
3. Daniel, p. 71, 163. O.R., XX, Part I, p. 490.
4. Bennett, p. 30.
5. Beatty, pp. 210-212.
6. Osheskie, pp. 31, 32, 37.
7. Sheridan, p. 239.
8. National Archives, Washington DC, Field and Staff Muster Roll Special Order #38. Dept of the Cumberland February 10th, 1863 The *Kittanning Mentor*, p. 1. Osheskie, p. 34.
9. Company I. Daniel, p. 98. Canfield, p. 97. Samuel Dumm Letters & Diary.
    Armstrong County Genealogy Club Quarterly, The Armstrong County Historical Society, 300 N. McKean Street, PO Box 735, Kittanning, Pennsylvania 16201-1345. Volume 1, Number 2, Winter 1995, p. 35. Letter of Captain Joseph Smith, Company K, by Kathy Marcinek from D. Norton of Kittanning, PA.
10. Meredith Diary, p. 10.
11. Johnston, pp. 37-39. Puntenney, George H., *History of the Thirty-Seventh Regiment of Indiana Infantry Volunteers,* Written by Sergeant George H. Puntenney, Jacksonian Book and Job Department, Rushville, Indiana, 1896, p. 40. *Nashville Union,* June 7, 1863.
12. "Dog Tag" owned by Ronn Palm, Kittanning, Pennsylvania. Daniel, p. 90. Puntenney, p. 48.
    Canfield, pp. 88-93. Thomas Blakeley Diary.
13. Gillaspie, pp. 46-48.
14. Osheskie, p. 32, 33.
15. Company I. Gibson, p. 229, 242.
16. Osheskie, p. 33. Daniel, p. 108. Sheridan, p. 240. Daniel, p. 105. Johnston, p. 41.
17. Company I. Canfield, pp. 82-87. Samuel Dumm Letters & Diary.
    Morse, Loren J., *Civil War Diaries & Letters of Bliss Morse,* Printed by Heritage Printing, Talequah, Oklahoma, 1985, p. 64.
18. Foote, Volume II, p. 663. Simkins Letters & Diary.
19. Horn, Stanley, p. 226.
20. McCabe, James D., *The Life of James A. Garfield our Martyred President,* P. W. Ziegler & Co., Publishers, Philadelphia and Chicago, 1881. pp. 95, 96.
21. Company I

"WE ARE COMING, FATHER ABRA'AM"
1. Smith, pp. 70-76. Nellie Bly, 1885   O.R.. Middle Tennessee Campaign, p. 412.
    The Seventy-Seventh Pennsylvania at Shiloh, p. 115.   Dodge, p. 13.
2. Foote, Volume II, pp. 664-667, 675.   Horn, Stanley, p. 234.
    Nashville Union, January 28, 1863 Cleaves, pp. 144, 154.
    Armstrong County Genealogy Club Quarterly, The Armstrong County Historical Society,
        300 N. McKean Street, PO Box 735, Kittanning, Pennsylvania 16201-1345. Summer 1996, p. 12.
    Letter of Lieutenant Franklin Mechling; Newspaper article from the scrapbook of John Englert.
3. Samuel Dumm Letters & Diary.
4. Cleaves, p. 144, 145.
5. Battles and Leaders, Volume III, p. 637.
6. Gibson, p. 72.
7. Gibson, p. 72. Catton, Never Call Retreat, p. 210.
8. Blackburn, p. 145. Puntenney, p. 44.
9. Puntenney, p. 43.
10. Company I. Puntenney, pp. 45, 46. Meredith, p. 22.
11. Company I
12. Cleaves, p. 148.
13. Cleaves, p. 149. Puntenney, p. 48. Blackburn, p. 146.   Duyckinck, p. 451.
14. *Pennsylvania at Chickamauga and Chattanooga*, William Stanley Ray, State
        Printer of Pennsylvania, Harrisburg, Pennsylvania. 1901, p. 219

"WEEPING SAD AND LONELY"
1. Gibson, p. 89, 90. Meredith, p. 26. Canfield, pp. 104.
2. Atlas, Plate
3. Gibson, p. 89, 90. Meredith, p. 26. Canfield, pp. 104.
4. Foote, Volume II, p. 693. Cleaves, p. 153.
5. Pennsylvania at Chickamauga, pp. 217-220.   Gibson, p. 84-86. Cleaves, pp. 149, 152, 153.
    Belknap, Charles Eugene, *History of the Michigan Organizations at Chickamauga,*
    Chattanooga and Missionary Ridge, 1863. Robert Smith Printing Co.,
    Lansing, Michigan, 1899, pp. 111, 112.
    Puntenney, p. 48. Blackburn, p. 146. Duyckinck, p.   451.
6. Gibson, p. 3, 113.   Pennsylvania at Chickamauga, pp. 217-220.
    Turchin, John B., *CHICKAMAUGA*, Fergus Printing Company, Chicago, 1888, p. 126.
7. O.R., XXX, Pt. I, pp. 336, 385.
8. Battles and Leaders, Volume III, p. 672.
9. Blackburn, p. 143. Adams, p. 30. Cist, p. 217.   Battles and Leaders, Volume III, p. 669.
10. Blackburn, p. 143. Adams, p. 30. Cist, p. 217.   Battles and Leaders, Volume III, p. 669.
    The *Kittanning Mentor*, February 2, 1863.
11. Cist, pp. 200, 201. Gibson, pp. 92-99.   O.R., XXX, Pt. I, p. 248.
12. Puntenney, pp. 55-57. Indiana at Chickamauga, p. 175. Gibson, pp. 105, 114. O.R., XXX, Pt. I, 338.
13. Blackburn, p. 142, 143, 273, 274. Gibson, p. 113. Turchin, p. 126. Smith, p. 73.
    O.R., XXX, Pt. I, 339.
14. Blackburn, p. 143. Adams, p. 30. Turchin 126.
15. Adams, p. 30, 31. Blackburn, p. 144, 156.
16. Canfield, pp. 4, 136, 137
17. O.R., XXX, Pt. I, 385.
18. Tucker, p. 332-334.
19. Puntenney, p. 60. O.R., XXX, Pt. I, p. 386.   Lindsley, p. 161.
20. Watkins, pp. 118-119.
21. Owens, p. 163.
22. O.R., XXX, Pt. I, pp. 244, 245
23. Company I. Gibson, p. 114. Society, p. 85.
24. Blackburn, p. 157. Funk, p. 70. Watkins, p. 121.   Simkins Letters & Diary.
25. Blackburn, p. 144, 275, 276. Turchin, p. 127.
26. Tucker, pp. 46, 47. McDonough, p. 40.

27. Cist, p. 234. Davis, Burke, *Our Incredible Civil War*, Holt, Rinehart and Winston, 1960.
 Published by Ballantine Books, New York, 1974, pp. 144-146.
28. Peters, James Edward, Arlington National Cemetery, *"Shrine to American Heroes,"*
 Woodbine House, 1986, pp. 198, 199.
29. Nellie Bly Interview, 1885.
30. Horn, pp. 305-307. Foote, III, p. 1052.
 Gragg, Rod, *Confederate Goliath, The Battle of Fort Fisher*,
 Harper Collins, Publishers, New York, 1991, p. 26.
31. Company I. Samuel Dumm Letters & Diary.
 Meredith, p. 34, 37. Simkins Letters & Diary.
32. Osheskie, p. 53.
33. McFeely, William S., *Grant, a Biography*, W.W. Norton & Company, New York . London,
 1981, pp. 143-151. The Army of the Cumberland, 1896, p. 80.
34. *The Kittanning Mentor* February, 1864
35. Osheskie, pp. 53, 54. Meredith Diary, p. 41. Dumm Letters & Diary.
 Simkins Letters & Diary.
36. Beers History, p. 1034. Butler, p. 61. Simkins Letters & Diary.
37. Gibson, p. 142.

ON TO ATLANTA

1. Gibson, p. 142. Catton, Never Call Retreat, p. 322.
 Davis, Burke, *Sherman's March*, Random House, New York, 1980, p. 19.
 Meredith Diary, p. 37. Luvaas, M.J./1993.
 2. Company I. Simkins Letters & Diary.
 3. O.R., XXXVIII, Part I, pp. 94, 95.
 4. Gibson, pp. 143-149, 195-236.

"I AM IN THE FRONT RANKS YET"

1. Castel, Albert, *Decision in the West*, Published by the University Press of Kansas, Lawrence,
 Kansas, 1992, pp. 228-241.
 Civil War Times, June 1971, *"Scenes of Awful Carnage"*, Phillip L. Secrist.
 pp. 5-9, 45-48. vis, William C., Editor,
 Civil War Times Illustrated, February 1973, *"The Hell Hole"*, Richard M. McMurry.
 Historical Times, Inc., Harrisburg, PA, pp. 32-43.
 Battle & Leaders, Vol. IV, pp. 284-288.
 2. O.R., XXXVIII, Part I, pp. 445-447, 593-596, 604-607. Van Horne, Vol. II, p. 79.
 Gibson, pp. 147-149. Castel, pp. 228-241.
 3. O.R., XXXVIII, Part I, pp. 445-447, 593-596, 604-607. Van Horne, Vol. II, p. 80.
 4. Beers, p. 623. Funk, p. 69. O.R., XXXVIII, Part I, p. 615.
 5. Luvaas, M.J./1989.
 6. Lindsley, p. 163.
 7. O.R., XXXVIII, 38, Part I, pp. 619, 620.
 8. Osheskie, p. 62.

GOIN' HOME

1. Company I. Samuel Dumm Letters & Diary.
 2. Dumm, Samuel, *History of the Seventy-Eighth Pennsylvania Veteran Volunteer Infantry*.
 Unpublished, p. 1. Gibson, pp. 194-236. Smith, p. 88.
 ORIGINAL ROSTER and DESCRIPTIVE LIST of the 78TH PENNSYLVANIA
 VOLUNTEER INFANTRY, Second Organization. National Archieves, Washington D.C.
 3. Lindsley, p. 166. Simkins Letters & Diary.
 4. Carol Kaplan. Jones, Katharine M., pp. 92, 210, 211.
 5. Tennesseans, p. 174

BLOOD OF THE DYING SUN
  1. Army of the Cumberland, Reunion 1870, p. 72.   Paraphrased from a speech given by
     Teddy Roosevelt, Paris, April, 1910.
     Dumm, History of the Seventy-Eighth Pennsylvania, p. 17.
  2. Frederic, Volume II, pp. 10, 27, 29.
  3. National Tribune, 1907.
  4. Robertson, James I. Jr., and the Editors of Time-Life Books, *The Civil War, Tenting Tonight,*
     The Soldier's Life, Time-Life Books, Alexandria, Virginia, p. 161.
  5. *Kittanning Leader Times*, 1990. *The Pittsburgh Dispatch*, 1885.
     Kittanning Times, February 18, 1881. *The Butler Union Herald*, September 27, 1865
  6. *Pittsburgh Dispatch* July 1885.

O CAPTAIN! MY CAPTAIN
  1. *The Kittanning Times* Friday, September 11, 1885.
  2. *The Kittanning Times* Friday, September 18, 1885.
  3. Report of the Pennsylvania Seventy-Eighth Regimental Association, 1907.

BIBLIOGRAPHY

UNIT HISTORIES

Barnes, James A., *The Eighty-Sixth Regiment, Indiana Volunteer Infantry*, The Journal Company, Printers, Crawfordsville, Indiana, 1895.

Bennett, Charles W., *Historical Sketches of the Ninth Michigan Infantry*, by Charles W. Bennett of Company G, Daily Courier Print, Coldwater, Mich., 1913.

Canfield, Silas S. *History of the 21ST Regiment Ohio Volunteer Infantry in the War of the Rebellion* by Captain S. S. Canfield, Toledo, O. Vrooman, Anderson & Bateman, Printers, 1893.

Dickey, L.S., *History of the 103d Regiment Pennsylvania Veteran Volunteer Infantry.* 1861-1865. Chicago. 1910.

Dumm, Samuel, *History of the Seventy-Eighth Pennsylvania Veteran Volunteer Infantry.* Unpublished.

Funk, Arville L., *A HOOSIER REGIMENT IN DIXIE, A History of the Thirty-eighth Indiana Volunteer Infantry Regiment,* Adams Press, Chicago, Illinois, 1978.

Gibson, Joseph, *History of the Seventy-Eighth Pennsylvania Volunteer Infantry*, J.T. Gibson/Historical Committee of the Regimental Association, Press of the Pittsburgh Printing Co., Pittsburgh, Penn'a. 1905.

Haynie, J. Henry, *The Nineteenth Illinois*, M.A. Donohue & Co., Chicago, 1912.

Hinkley, First Lieutenant L.D., *Tenth Wisconsin Infantry, Tenth Annual Reunion,* 1904

Owens, Ira, *Greene County Soldiers in the Late War, Ira S Owens, Company C, Seventy-fourth Ohio,* Christian Publishing House Print Dayton, Ohio, 1884.

McMurray, W.J. M.D., *History of the Twentieth Tennessee Regiment of Volunteer Infantry, C.S.A.,* Nashville, 1904.

Puntenney, George H., *History of the Thirty-Seventh Regiment of Indiana Infantry Volunteers,* Written by Sergeant George H. Puntenney, Jacksonian Book and Job Department, Rushville, Indiana, 1896.

MEMOIRS

Adams, Jacob, *Diary of Jacob Adams, 21st O.V.V.I.*. From the Ohio Archaeological and Historical Quarterly for October, 1929. The F.J. Heer Printing Co., Columbus, Ohio, 1930.

Beatty, John, *The Citizen-Soldier or Memoirs of a Volunteer.* Wilstach, Baldwin & Co., Publishers, Cincinnati 1879.

Blakeley, Dr. Thomas G., Diary. Courtesy of the Harry Blakeley Family, Lower Burrell, PA

Cumming, Kate, Kate: The Journal of a Confederate Nurse, Edited by Richard Barksdale Harwell, Louisiana State University Press, Baton Rouge, 1959.

Dumm, Samuel, Diary. Courtesy of James Coulson, Lower Burrell, PA. Great Grandson.

Simkins, Albert P., Diary. Courtesy of Bill May, Butler, PA

Gillaspie, Ira, *The Diary of Ira Gillaspie of the Eleventh Michigan Infantry,* Edited with an introduction by Daniel B. Weber. Central Michigan University Press, Mount Pleasant, Clarke Historical Library, Copyright 1965.

Holmes, Robert Masten, C.S.A., *Kemper County Rebel, The Civil War Diary of Robert Masten Holmes, C.S.A.* Edited by Frank Allen Dennis, forward by Thomas L. Connelly, University and College Press of Mississippi, Jackson, 1973.

Jackman, John S., *Diary of a Confederate Soldier, John S. Jackman of the Orphan Brigade.* Edited with an introduction by William C. Davis. Published in Columbia, South Carolina, by the University of South Carolina Press, 1990.

Johnston, Adam S., *Soldier Boy's Diary Book,* The 79th Regiment of Pennsylvania Volunteer Infantry of Turtle Creek, Pennsylvania. Pittsburgh: 1867.

Manigault, Arthur Middleton, *A Carolinian Goes to War*, edited by R. Lockwood Tower, University of South Carolina Press, Columbia, South Carolina, 1983.

Marks, Rev. J.J., D.D., *The Peninsular Campaign in Virginia*, J.B. Lippincott & Co., Philadelphia, 1864.

Meredith, John, Diary, Co. F. 78th Penna. Vols., 1st Battalion, Army of the Cumberland.

Morse, Loren J., Civil War Diaries & Letters of Bliss Morse, Printed by Heritage Printing, Talequah, Oklahoma, 1985

Sheridan, Philip Henry, *Personal Memoirs of P.H. Sheridan, General United States Army,* IN TWO VOLUMES, Volume I, New York, Charles L. Webster & Company, 1888

Watkins, Samuel, *"CO. AYTCH" Maury Grays, First Tennessee Regiment.* Introduction by Bell Irvin Wiley. Nashville, 1882. Reprinted 1952 by McCowat-Mercer Press, 1987, 1990 by Broadfoot Publishing Company, Wilmington, North Carolina.
Womack, Bob, *Call Forth the Mighty Men*, Colonial Press, Nashville, 1986.
Woodward, C. Vann, *Mary Chestnut's Civil War*, Yale University Press, New Haven and London, 1981.

SPECIAL EDITIONS

ANNUAL REPORT OF THE ADJUTANT GENERAL OF PENNSYLVANIA, Harrisburg, Singerly & Myers, State Printers, 1867.
Pennsylvania at Chickamauga and Chattanooga, William Stanley Ray, State Printer of Pennsylvania, Harrisburg, Pennsylvania. 1901.
Seventy-Seventh Pennsylvania at Shiloh, History of the Regiment. Harrisburg Publishing Co., State Printers, Harrisburg, Pennsylvania, 1905.
Society of the Army of the Cumberland, Third Reunion, Published by Order of the Society, Robert Clarke & Co., Cincinnati, 1870.
Society of the Army of the Cumberland, Twenty-Third Reunion, Published by Order of the Society, Robert Clarke & Co., Cincinnati, 1892.
Reunion of the 78th Regiment of Pennsylvania Volunteers, Address by Comrade Archibald Blakeley, Leechburg, PA, September 1880. Courtesy of Eric McCandless
Reunion of the 78th Regiment of Pennsylvania Volunteers, Indiana, PA, August 1908.
Tennesseans in The Civil War, A Military History of Confederate and Union Units, Published by the Civil War Centennial Commission, Nashville, 1964.
OFFICIAL RECORDS The War of the Rebellion: A Compilation of the Official Records of the Union and Confederate Armies, Washington, D.C., U.S. Government Printing Office, 1902.
The Atlas, Maps to accompany the Official Records of the Union and Confederate Armies, Washington, D.C., U.S. Government Printing Office, 1895.
National Archives: Documents, Letters, Reports and Muster Rolls.
Official Army Register of the Volunteer Force of the United States Army, 1861-1865. Adjutant General's Office, Published by order of the Secretary of War. 1865.
Revised Regulations for the Army of the United States, 1861. J G. L. Brown, Printer, Philadelphia, Republished by The National Historical Society, Harrisburg, PA, 1980.
Company Orders, Company I, Seventy-Eighth Pennsylvania, 1861- 1864. R. S. Gancas Library
Cemetery Records and Burial List of the Seventy-Eighth Pennsylvania Volunteer Infantry at Stones River and Nashville, Stones River National Park Service, Murfreesboro, Tennessee.
Original Roster and Descriptive List of the 78th Pennsylvania Volunteer Infantry. Soldiers and Sailors Memorial Library, Pittsburgh, Pennsylvania.
Original Roster and Descriptive List of the 78th Pennsylvania Volunteer Infantry, Second Organization. National Archives, Washington D.C.

ARMY HISTORIES

Bickham, "W.D.B.", *Rosecrans' Campaigns with the Fourteenth Army Corp or the Army of the Cumberland*, Moore, Wilstach, Keys & Co., Cincinnati, 1863.
Cist, Henry M. *The Army of the Cumberland.* New York, Charles Scribner's Sons, 1882.
Daniel, Larry J., *Soldiering in the Army of Tennessee*, The University of North Carolina Press, Chapel Hill & London, 1991.
Dodge, William Sumner, *History of the Old Second Division, Army of the Cumberland*, Church and Goodman, Chicago, 1864.
Drake, Dr. Edwin L., *The Annals of the Army of the Tennessee*, Printed by A.D. Haynes, Nashville, 1878.
Evans, Clement A., Editor, *Confederate Military History*, Volume VIII, The Blue & Grey Press.
Fitch, John, *Annals of the Army of the Cumberland*, J.B. Lippincott & Co., Philadelphia, 1864.
Horn, Stanley F., *The Army of the Tennessee*, The Bobbs-Merrill Company, Publishers, Indianapolis/New York, 1941.
Losson, Christopher, *Tennesse's Forgotten Warriors*, The University of Tennessee Press, Knoxville, 1989.
Love, William DeLoss, *Wisconsin in the War of the Rebellion*, Church and Goodman, Publishers, Chicago. A. Whittemore, Milwaukee. Sheldon & Co., New York. 1866.

Lindsley, John Berrien, M.D., D.D., *The Military Annals of Tennessee. Confederate.* J.M. Lindsley & Co., Publishers, Nashville, 1886.

Quiner, E.B., Esq., *The Military History of Wisconsin,* Clarke & Co., Publishers, Chicago, 1866.

Ridley, Lieutenant General Bromfield L., *Battles and Sketches of the Army of the Tennessee,* Missouri Printing & Publishing Co. Mexico, Missouri, 1906.

Van Horne, Thomas B., *History of the Army of the Cumberland,* Volume I & II, Written at the request of Major-General George H. Thomas, Robert Clarke & Co., Cincinnati, 1875.

AREA HISTORIES

Baldwin, Leland D., *Pittsburgh, The Story of a City,* University of Pittsburgh Press, 1937.

Beers, J.H., *Armstrong County, Pennsylvania, Her People Past and Present,* J.H. Beers & Co., Chicago, 1914.

Clayton, Prof. W.W., *History of Davidson County, Tennessee,* J.W. Lewis & Co., Philadelphia, 1880. Reproduced by Charles Elder - Bookseller, Publisher, Nashville, 1971.

Jenkins, Howard M., Editor, *Pennsylvania, Colonial and Federal, A History: 1608-1905,* Volume III, Pennsylvania Historical Publishing Association, Philadelphia, 1905.

Jordan, John W., of the Historical Society of Pennsylvania, *A Century and a Half of Pittsburg and Her People,* Volume III, The Lewis Publishing Company, 1908.

Smith, Robert Walter, Esq., *History of Armstrong County, Pennsylvania,* Waterman, Watkins & Co., Chicago, 1883.

History of Butler County, Pennsylvania, Robert C. Brown & Co. Publishers, 1895.

History of Butler County, Pennsylvania, Waterman, Watkins & Co., Chicago, 1883.

CIVIL WAR SPECIALS

King, William C., and W.P. Derby of the 27th Massachusetts Regiment, *Camp Fire Sketches and Battlefield Echoes of the Rebellion,* King, Richardson and Co., Springfield, MA, 1886.

The Picket Line and Camp Fire Stories, by a Member of the G.A.R., Hurst & Co., Publishers, New York, 1903.

CIVIL WAR HISTORIES

Andrews, J. Cutler, *The North Reports the Civil War,* University of Pittsburgh Press, Pittsburgh, Pa, 1955.

Andrews, J. Cutler, The South Reports the Civil War, Princeton University Press, Princeton, New Jersey, 1970.

Bates, Samuel P., *History of the Pennsylvania Volunteers,* 1861-5. B. Singerly, State Printer, Harrisburg, Volume I and II, 1869.

Bradley, Stanley, *The Soldier in our Civil War,* Vol. II, Stanley Bradley Publishing Co., New York, 1890.

Buel, Clarence C. and Johnson, Robert U., eds., Battles and Leaders of the Civil War, Volume I, From Sumter to Shiloh, New York, 1888.

Buel, Clarence C. and Johnson, Robert U., eds., Battles and Leaders of the Civil War, Volume III, Retreat from Gettysburg, New York, 1888.

Buel, Clarence C. and Johnson, Robert U., eds., Battles and Leaders of the Civil War, Volume IV, The Way to Appomattox, New York, 1888.

Castel, Albert, *Decision in the West,* University Press of Kansas, Lawrence, Kansas, 1984.

Catton, Bruce, *This Hallowed Ground,* Doubleday & Company, Inc., Garden City, New York, 1956.

Catton, Bruce, *Never Call Retreat,* Doubleday & Company, Inc., Garden City, New York, 1965.

Davis, Burke, *Our Incredible Civil War,* Holt, Rinehart and Winston, 1960. Published by Ballantine Books, New York, 1974.

Davis, Burke, *Sherman's March,* Random House, New York, 1980.

Frederic, Harold and William J. McMaster Sr., *Civil War Stories Old and New,* Volume I, The John Crawford Memorial History of Armstrong County, Pennsylvania, Sponsor: Camp #43, Sons of Union Veterans of the Civil War, Printer: The Print Shop, Havelock, North Carolina, 1991

Frederic, Harold, *Civil War Soldier's Own Stories*, Volume II, The John Crawford Memorial History of Armstrong County, Pennsylvania, Sponsor: Camp #43, Sons of Union Veterans of the Civil War, Printer: The Print Shop, Havelock, North Carolina, 1991.
Foote, Shelby, *The Civil War, A Narrative*, Volume II, Fredericksburg to Meridian, Random House, New York, 1963.
Gragg, Rod, *Confederate Goliath, The Battle of Fort Fisher*, Harper Collins, Publishers, New York, 1991.
Greeley, Horace, *The American Conflict*, Volume II, Published by the National Tribune, Washington, D.C., 1899.
Jones, Katharine M., Editor, *Heroines of Dixie*, The Bobbs-Merrill Company, Inc., 1955.
Leech, Margaret, *Reveille in Washington*, Harper & Brothers, New York, New York, 1941.
Luvaas, Dr. Jay and Nelson, Col. Harold W., *The U.S. Army War College Guide to the Battles of Chancellorsville and Fredericksburg*, South Mountain Press, Inc., Publishers, Carlisle, Pennsylvania, 1988.

NEWSPAPERS

The *Butler Eagle*, Butler, Pennsylvania, November 1923
The *Chattanooga Rebel*, Chattanooga, Tennessee, 1862. Micro film, The Ben West Library, Nashville.
The *Cincinnati Daily Enquirer*, Cincinnati, Ohio, Reports on the battle at Murfreesboro, Tennessee. January 1 to January 7, 1863. Cincinnati Public Library.
The *Murfreesboro Rebel*, Murfreesboro, Tennessee, 1862. Micro film, The Ben West Library, Nashville.
The *Nashville Union*, Nashville, Tennessee, 1862. Micro film, The Ben West Library, Nashville.
The *Pittsburgh Gazette*, Pittsburgh, Pennsylvania, 1861-1863. Originals, Western Pennsylvania Genealogy Society; Micro film, Carnegie Library, Pittsburgh.
The *Pittsburgh Dispatch*, Pittsburgh, Pennsylvania, 1885. Micro film, Carnegie Library, Pittsburgh.
The *Daily Dispatch*, New Kensington, Pa., "Civil War Echoes" by Edward S. Osheskie, A Series of Articles Based on Letters of Pvt. Abram E. Kipp (1840-78) of Allegheny Township, Westmoreland County and History of the 78TH Regiment, Pennsylvania Volunteer Infantry.
April 11-May 25, 1961.
The *Kittanning Leader-Times*, Kittanning, Pennsylvania, "Nellie Bly" by John F. Englert, May 5, 1990.
The *Kittanning Times*, Kittanning, Pennsylvania, 1885.
The *Mentor*, Kittanning, Pennsylvania, 1861-1863, Kittanning Public Library.
The *Richmond Enquirer*, Richmond, Virginia 1863. Micro film, The Ben West Library, Nashville.
The *Union Herald*, Butler, Pennsylvania, September 1865

LETTERS

Black, George Washington, Original letters of George Washington Black, Company I, Pennsylvania 78th Regiment, to his wife in Apollo, PA., R.S. Gancas Library.
Blackburn, Theodore W., Letters from the Front, A Union "Preacher" Regiment (74TH OHIO) in the Civil War. Press of Morningside Bookshop, Division of Morningside House, Inc., Publishers and Booksellers, Dayton, Ohio, 45410.
Dinsmore, Marion, Letters to his family
Hatzell, Phineas, Letters home.
Lowry, William A., Letters. Courtesy Bill May, Butler, PA
Dumm, Samuel, Letters to his sister. Courtesy of James Coulson, Lower Burrell, PA. Great Grandson.
Simkins, Albert P., Letters. Courtesy Bill May, Butler, PA

STONES RIVER HISTORIES

Cozzens, Peter, *The Battle of Stones River, No Better Place to Die*. University of Illinois Press, Urbana and Chicago, 1990.
Logsdon, David R., *Eyewitnesses at the Battle of Stones River*, Nashville, Tennessee, 1989.
McDonough, James Lee, *Stones River - Bloody Winter in Tennessee*, The University of Tennessee Press/Knoxville. 1980.

Stevenson, Alexander F., *The Battle of Stone's River near Murfreesboro, Tenn.*, [1884], Press of
Morningside Bookshop, Dayton, Ohio, 1983.

CHICKAMAUGA HISTORIES

Belknap, Charles Eugene, *History of the Michigan Organizations at Chickamauga, Chattanooga and Missionary
Ridge,* 1863. Robert Smith Printing Co., Lansing, Michigan, 1899.
Tucker, Glenn, *Chickamauga, Bloody Battle in the West.* The Bobbs-Merrill Company, Inc., 1961. Morningside
Bookshop, Dayton, 1976.
Turchin, John B., *CHICKAMAUGA*, Fergus Printing Company, Chicago, 1888.

MAGAZINES

Dobell, Byron, Editor, <u>American Heritage</u>, October/November 1984. *Military Medicine,* by Jane
    Colihan with the help of Dr Robert J.T. Joy, M.D., American Heritage Publishing Company, New York, NY.
Fleming, George T., "Flem's" Views of Old Pittsburgh", Published by George T. ("Flem") Fleming, Pittsburgh,
1905.
Folwer, Robert W., Editor, <u>Civil War Times Illustrated</u>, June 1971, *"Scenes of Awful Carnage",* Phillip L. Secrist.
Historical Times, Inc., Harrisburg, PA.
Davis, William C., Editor, <u>Civil War Times Illustrated,</u> February 1973, *"The Hell Hole",* Richard M. McMurry.
Historical Times, Inc., Harrisburg, PA.
<u>Blue & Gray Magazine</u>, *The Battle of Stones River*, By Charles M. Spearman, Blue & Gray Enterprises, Inc.,
Columbus, Ohio, obruary 1989.
National Tribune, 26 September, 1907, The Flag of the 26th Tennessee, David S. Ake, Co. D, 78th Pennsylvania,
Hillsdale, Pa. Courtesy of Bill May, Butler, PA

AUTOBIOGRAPHY/BIOGRAPHY

Cleaves, Freeman, *Rock of Chickamauga, The Life of General George H. Thomas,* University of
Oklahoma Press, Norman and London, 1948.
McCabe, James D., *The Life of James A. Garfield our Martyred President,* P.W. Ziegler & Co.,
Publishers, Philadelphia and Chicago, 1881.
McFeely, William S., Grant, a Biography, W.W. Norton & Company, New York . London, 1981.
Grigg, Elliot & Company, *General Scott and his Staff,* Philadelphia, 1849.
Henry, Robert Selph, *"First With the Most" Forrest,* Mallard Press, New York, 1991.

GENERAL HISTORIES

Blake, W.G., The History of Slavery and the Slave Trade,Published and Sold Exclusively by
Subscription, J.& H. Miller, Columbus, Ohio, 1859.
Morison, Samuel Eliot, The Oxford History of the American People, Oxford University Press, New York, 1965.

GENERAL WORKS

Duyckinck, Evert A., National Portrait Gallery of Eminent Americans, Volume II, Johnson, Fry & Company, New
York, 1862.
Peters, James Edward, Arlington National Cemetery, "Shrine to American Heroes," Woodbine House, 1986.

REFERENCES

Boatner, Mark Mayo III, The Civil War Dictionary, David McKay Company, Inc., New York, 1987.
Bowman, John S., The Civil War Day by Day, Published by Dorset Press a division of Marboro Books Corp by
arrangement with Brompton Books Corporation, Greenwich, CT, 1989.
Robertson, James I. Jr., and the Editors of Time-Life Books, The Civil War, Tenting Tonight, The Soldier's Life,
Time-Life Books, Alexandria, Virginia.
Street, James R., and the Editors of Time-Life Books, The Civil War, The Struggle for Tennessee, Tupelo to
Stones River, Time-Life Books, Alexandria, Virginia,

INDEX

Acorn Boys, 167.
Adams, General Daniel W., CSA, 108, 118, 135.
Alabama Cavalry, Colonel John T. Morgan's, 47.
Alabama, Twenty-Fourth Infantry, 95.
       Buck, Colonel William A., 95.
Alabama, Twenty-Eighth Infantry, 95.
       Reid, Colonel John C., 95.
Alabama Thirty-Second Infantry, 47.
       Murray, Lieutenant Colonel James, 47.
       Sanford, Lieutenant Colonel, 47.
       Smith, J. Morgan, 47.
Alabama, Thirty-Fourth Infantry, 95, 112.
       Mitchell, Colonel Julius C.B., 95.
       Mitchell, James, 112.
Alabama, Forty-Fifth Infantry, 95.
       Gilcrest, Colonel James G., 95.
Alabama, Waters' Alabama Battery, 95.
       Waters, Captain D.D., 95.
Allegheny Arsenal, 13.
American Party, "Know Nothings," 16, 20.
Anaconda Plan, 175.
Anderson, General J. Patton, CSA, 95-97, 99, 101.
Anderson, General Robert, US, 24, 29, 63.
Anderson, General S.R., CSA, 45, 48.
Andersonville Prison, 58, 159, 191.
Antietam, 2, 134.
Arkansas, Fourth Infantry, 112.
       Ellis, Private Jim, 112.
Armstrong, W.F., Captain & Provost Marshall, US, 154.
Army of the Cumberland [Fourteenth Army Corps], 1, 2, 29, 30, 36, 37, 42, 52, 56, 58, 61, 62.
       64, 69, 131, 134, 136, 139, 140, 147, 148, 150, 152-154, 161, 166, 167, 168, 170, 175, 177,
       179, 181.
Army of Northern Virginia, 161.
Army of the Ohio, 29, 30, 52, 60, 177, 181.
Army of the Potomac, 2, 3, 42, 55, 58, 131, 147.
Army of the Tennessee, Confederate, 1, 54, 64, 73, 135, 179.
Army of the Tennessee, US, 78, 177.
Baird, Brigadier General Absalom, US, 157.
Barnhart, John of Slate Lick, 128.
Barrackman, Jane Springer, 191.
Beauregard, General Pierre G.T., CSA, 7, 8, 71.
Beatty, Colonel Sam, US, 118, 119.
Bentonville, battle of, 169.
Bickham, Captain William, US, 73, 84, 107, 112.
Black, Ruth, 32.
Black, Sarah, 32.
Black, Annabelle, 32.

Blacks/Negroes, 6, 40, 41, 43, 44, 68, 69, 143, 147.
    Hannibal Guards, "First Colored Unit", 6.
    Pie Boys, 69.
    Dinahs, 69.
    Slave sale, 72.
Blakeley, Harry, 155.
Blanton House, 92, 96.
Bly, Nellie "Cochran, Elizabeth Jane", 54, 169, 195.
Bond, Major Frank S., US, 162.
Bowser, Noah, 139.
Brady Alpines, 4, 6, 7, 8, 10, 18, 58.
Brady, Matthew, 3.
Bragg, General Braxton, 1, 3, 19, 43, 44, 52, 54, 58, 60, 64, 65, 69, 70, 71, 137, 138, 140, 147,
    150, 152-154, 156, 157, 167, 169, 170, 192.
    Battle of Chickamauga, 159, 161, 162.
    Battle of Stones River, 72-74, 76, 77, 84-86, 88, 89, 94, 95, 97, 101, 107-109, 113-115,
    117-120, 124, 126, 133-136.
Brannan, Brigadier General John, US, 161, 164, 165.
Breckenridge, Cabell, 114.
Breckenridge, US Vice President, General John, CSA, 19, 54, 70, 71, 84, 89, 108, 114, 115,
    117-119, 122, 134, 135.
Brent, Colonel George, 114.
Brooklyn Bridge, 21.
Brudenell, James Thomas, Earl of Cardigan, 107.
Brunker, Sue, 13.
Buchannan, President James, 71.
Buckner, Major General Simon, CSA, 33, 157.
Buell, General Don Carlos, US, 29, 33, 36, 38, 42-44, 52, 54, 57, 60, 61, 63, 71, 134, 136, 177.
Bull Run-First [Manassas Junction], 7, 8, 18, 20, 61.
Burns, Ken, 2.
Burnside, Major General Ambrose, US, 2, 150, 161, 169.
Butler, Major General Ben, US, 39.
Buzzard, Elizabeth of Apollo, PA, 34.
Card, James, spy, US, 65.
Camp Andy Johnson, Nashville, TN, 39.
Camp Chase, Columbus, Ohio, 132, 147.
Camp Cheatham, Nashville, TN, 18.
Camp, Drake, Murfreesboro, TN, 141.
Camp Hamilton, Nashville, TN, 68, 72.
Camp Curtin, Harrisburg, PA, 6.
Camp Lucinda, Nashville, TN, 41.
Camp Negley, Kentucky, 33, 35.
Camp Nevin, Nolin Creek, KY, 24-26, 28, 30, 32, 33.
Camp Oakland, Louisville, KY, 24.
Camp Orr, Kittanning, PA, 9, 10, 11, 188, 197.
Camp Sherman, Louisville, KY, 24.
Camp Sill, Murfreesboro, TN, 139.
Camp Bill Sirwell, Columbia, TN, 39.
Camp Wilkens, Pittsburgh, PA, 13, 14, 20, 21.
Camp Wood, Green River, Kentucky, 35, 36.
Catton, Bruce, 59.

Chalmers, Brigadier General James Ronald, CSA, 99, 108, 135.
Chase, Salmon P., Treasury Secretary, 78, 168.
Cheatham, Major General Benjamin F., CSA, 19, 70, 94, 95, 96, 97, 103, 104.
Chicago Board of Trade Battery, 106.
Chicago *Times*, 133.
Chickamauga, battle of, 159-166.
Chickasaw Bluffs, 2, 78.
Chickasaw Bayou, 78.
Christmas, 35, 59, 66, 68, 69, 71, 74, 170.
Cincinnati *Commercial*, 44, 73, 133, 134.
Cincinnati *Daily Enquirer*, 133.
Cincinnati *Gazette*, 32, 133.
City Blues, 5.
Cleaves, Freeman, 110.
Cleburne, General Patrick Ronayne, CSA, 54, 71, 85, 88, 144, 162, 182.
Cobb, George, 189.
Cooney, Father, 88.
Cozzens, Peter, 2.
Crittenden, US Senator John Jordan, 61.
Crittenden, Major General George, CSA, 61.
Crittenden, Major General Thomas L., US, 42, 56, 60, 61, 63, 152, 162, 164.
        Battle of Stones River, 72-74, 76, 78, 84-86, 89, 110, 114, 115, 119, 125.
Crittenden, US General Thomas T., 42.
Cruft, Brigadier General Charles, US, 104, 118.
Curtin, Governor Andrew, 4, 20, 21, 159, 196.
Dana, Charles, 5, 159, 168.
Davis Crossroads, battle of, 156-158.
Davis, President Jefferson, 4, 64, 65, 70, 71, 135, 169.
Davis, Major General Jefferson, US, 60, 63, 89, 123, 162, 164.
Dennison, Ohio Governor William, 54.
dog tag, 142.
Don Carlos I of Spain, 29.
Donelson, General Dan, CSA, 108.
Douglas' Battalion, Major Douglas' Battalion, CSA, 47.
Duquesne Grays, 14.
Eagle Volunteer Fire Company, 193.
Emancipation Proclamation, 2, 79.
Finlay, Colonel J.B., 130.
Fleming, H.R. Hap, 194.
Florida, First/Third Infantry, 117.
        Miller, Colonel William, 117.
Florida, Fourth Infantry, 117, 122.
        Bowen, Colonel William L.L., 117, 122.
        Lesley, Major John, 122.
        Miller, Sergeant L.N., 122.
Florida, Seventh Infantry, 165.
Forrest, Lieutenant General Nathan Bedford, CSA, 37, 38, 42, 43, 48, 73, 184.
Fort Casino, Nashville, TN, 43.
Fort Confiscation, Nashville, TN, 43.
Fort Donelson, Tennessee, 19, 37.
Fort Fisher, North Carolina, 169.

Fort Andrew Johnson, Nashville, TN, 43.
Fort Negley, Nashville, TN, 43.
Fort Sumter, Charleston, SC, 4, 24, 54, 63.
Fortress Monroe, Virginia, 161.
Fourth U.S. Cavalry, 66.
      Watson, Sergeant John, of Sarver, 66.
Fourteenth U.S. Colored Troops, 185.
Foy, Sarah Springer, 191.
Fredericksburg, battle at, 58, 68, 78, 131, 135.
French Leave, 144.
Fry, Colonel James B., 51.
Fry, General Speed, 60, 111.
Fyffe, Colonel James, US, 118.
Galt House, 24, 63, 175.
Garesché, Colonel Julius, 63, 88, 107, 167.
Garfield, General/President James A., 148, 162, 167, 168.
Gaw, Captain, Thomas' aide, US, 162.
Georgia, Forty-First, 52.
Georgia, S.A. Moses Georgia Battery, 117.
      Anderson, Lieutenant R.W., 117
German Benefit Union, 193.
Gibson, Colonel R.L., CSA, 118.
Gibson, Colonel William, US, 182.
Gilmore, General Quincy A., US, 40, 41.
Given, Lieutenant Colonel Josiah, US, 98.
Goddard, Lt. Colonel & Assistant Adjutant General, Calvin, 149.
Granbury, Brigadier General Hiram B., CSA, 182.
Grand Army of the Republic, 192, 193, 196.
Granger, Major General Gordon, US, 165.
Grant, Lieutenant General Ulysses, 2, 9, 29, 36, 150, 153, 161, 168, 169, 170, 172, 175, 177, 181,
      192, 195.
Greeley, Horace, 5, 59.
Gresham House, 86.
Grider, Colonel Benjamin C., US, 118.
Grose, Colonel William, US, 123.
Halbert, Mrs. Marshall, Louisville, KY, 24.
Hale, Nathan, 94.
Halleck, Major General Henry Wager, US, 36, 52, 61, 64, 135, 147, 148, 150, 153, 161, 168, 169.
Halstead, Matilda, 130.
Hannibal Guards, "First Colored Unit", 6.
Hanson, General Roger, CSA, 76, 115, 118, 133, 135.
Hardee, General William, CSA, 54, 71, 77, 84, 85, 88, 94, 114, 117, 122, 133.
Harding, Giles, "Harding House," 82, 84, 96.
Harris, Senator Ira, New York, 133.
Hascall, Brigadier General Milo, US, 106, 115.
Hayes, President Rutherford B., 54.
Hays, Captain A.B., US, 11.
Hazen, Colonel William, US, 107, 123, 159, 161, 182.
Hervey, Kate, 16.
Hill, Lieutenant General D. Harvey, CSA, 157.
Hindman, Major General Thomas, CSA, 157.
Holly Springs, 2, 59.
Hood, General John Bell, CSA, 188, 192.

Hooker, Major General Joseph, US, 59, 76, 147, 169, 181.
Hough, A.S., Captain and A.A.D.C., US, 166.
Howard, Major General Oliver O, US, 181, 182.
Hurlbut, Major General Stephen, US, 161, 169.
Illinois Battery, Houghtaling's, 45, 47, 96.
        Houghtaling, Charles, 47.
Illinois Nineteenth Infantry, 38, 50, 62, 74, 80, 82, 98, 105, 119, 120, 123, 160.
        Haynie, James, 98.
        Raffen, Colonel Alexander W., 160.
        Scott, Colonel Joseph R., 62, 98, 119, 120.
Illinois Twenty-First, 45.
Illinois Twenty-Second, 48.
Illinois Twenty-Fourth, 67.
        Mihalotzy, Colonel Geza, 67.
Illinois, Eighty-Fifth Infantry, 125.
Illinois, 104th Infantry, 160.
        Hapeman, Lieutenant Colonel Douglas, 160.
Illinois, First, Battery "C", 178.
        Drury, Captain Lucius H., 178.
Illinois Light, Bridge's Battery, 160.
        Bridges, Captain Lyman, 160.
Indiana Twenty-Ninth Infantry, 150.
Indiana Thirty-Seventh Infantry, 40, 62, 80, 82, 99, 103, 120, 129, 130, 139, 141, 160, 164, 165,
        178, 182, 183.
        Hull, Colonel James S., 62, 82, 98, 129.
        Lozier, Chaplain J.H. Lozier, 40.
        Puntenney, Sergeant George, 141, 153, 154.
        Ward, Lieutenant Colonel William D., 160, 178, 183.
Indiana Thirty-Eighth Infantry, 105, 178, 182.
        Griffin, Lieutenant Colonel Daniel F., 178.
Indiana, Forty-Second Volunteer Infantry, 111, 160.
        Horrall, Captain S.F., 111.
        McIntire, Lieutenant Colonel William T.B., 160.
Indiana, Sixty-Eighth Infantry, 184.
        Espy, Lt. Colonel, 184.
Indiana, Eighty-Eighth Infantry, 160.
        Humphrey, Colonel George, 160.
Indiana, Colonel Bushe's 4th Indiana Battery, 145.
        Leisure, David, 145.
Jack, Andrew, 6.
Jackson Blues, 14.
Jackson, President Andrew, 120-122.
Jackson, General, John K., 108.
Jackson, Major General Thomas Stonewall, 42, 58, 59, 168, 181.
Jefferson County Republican, 39.
Johnson, Governor & Vice President Andrew, 43, 48, 52, 72, 169.
Johnson, Brigadier General Bushrod, CSA, 165.
Johnson, Brigadier General Richard, US, 60, 63, 88, 89, 98, 162, 175, 177, 178, 179, 181, 183.
Johnson, Sirwell, 193.
Johnston, General Albert Sidney, 36, 37.
Johnston, General Joseph E., 7, 8, 64, 70, 135, 136, 169, 175, 177, 179, 181, 182, 189.
Kane, Reverend W.M. Kane, pastor of the Slatelick Presbyterian church, 170.
Keen, Surgeon W.W., 131.

Kentucky First Battery, B, US, Ellsworth's [Hewett's] , 45, 62, 78, 97, 99.
 Ellsworth, Lieutenant Alban A., 62, 99.
Kentucky, Second Infantry, US, 96.
 Sedgewick, Colonel Thomas, 96.
Kentucky Third Volunteers, 137.
 Collier, Major Daniel, 137.
Kentucky Sixth Infantry, CSA, 70.
 Lewis, Private Asa, 70.
Kentucky Ninth Infantry, CSA, 76.
 Green, Johnny, 76.
 Hunt, Colonel Thomas H., 76.
Kentucky, Fifteenth Infantry, US, 160.
 Taylor, Colonel Marion C., 160.
Kershaw, Brigadier General Joseph, CSA, 165.
King, General, John H., US, 182, 184.
Kirk, General Edward, 89.
Kittanning Cornet Band, 196.
Kittanning *Mentor*, 78, 79, 129, 161, 172.
Kittanning Yeagers [German Yeagers], 4, 6, 10.
Knefler, Colonel Frederick, US, 182.
Lancaster Brass Band, 20, 21.
 Clemens, Dan, 21.
Latshaw, Elizabeth, 23.
Latshaw, John, 23.
Lavergne, Battle of, 45-48, 68, 102.
Lee, Custis, 64.
Lee, General Robert E., 2, 58, 59, 64, 153, 161, 175, 181, 188, 192, 195.
Leslie, Frank, Frank Leslie's Magazine, 67.
Libby Prison, 159, 165, 166, 191.
Lincoln, President Abraham, 2, 3, 4, 7, 14, 25, 29, 44, 52, 54, 61, 72, 78, 79, 135, 143, 150, 153, 168, 169, 188.
 Mrs. Lincoln's Pies, 35.
Longnecker, Colonel Henry C., 7.
Longstreet, Lieutenant General James, CSA, 59, 161, 165, 175, 192, 197.
Lookout Mountain, 170.
Loomis, Colonel J.Q., 94.
Louisiana, Nineteenth Infantry, 140.
 Harris, John, 140.
Louisville Daily Courier, 24.
Louisville Daily Journal, 24, 44, 72.
Lowrie, Major James, Negley's Assistant Adjutant General, 14, 28, 32, 159, 164.
Lowrie, Pennsylvania Chief Justice W.H. Lowrie, 14.
Lowry, Pittsburgh Mayor James, 186.
Luvaas, Dr. M. Jay, 177.
McCandless, Judge Wilson, 14.
McClellan, Major General George, US, 2, 3, 36, 42, 54, 76, 134, 168, 188.
McClintock, Major M., US, 162.
McCook, General Alexander, US, 32, 33, 56, 60, 61, 63, 65, 137, 152, 164.
 Battle of Stones River, 72, 74, 76, 77, 84-86, 88, 89, 92, 94, 110, 115, 125.
McCook, Colonel Daniel, 61.
McCown, General John P., 43, 65, 71, 85, 88.
McDonough, Professor James Lee, 2, 71.
McDowell, General Irvin, 7, 8.

McFadden's Lane, 84.
McKinley, President William, 54.
McLean, General Nat, US, 181.
McLean, Wilmer, 195.
McPherson, General James, 177.
Magilton, Colonel Albert L., 58.
Maney, General George, 18, 19, 52, 71, 95, 96, 101-103, 184.
Manigault, General Arthur Middleton, 69, 74, 94-97, 101.
Marshall, James, 76.
Massachusetts Fifty-Fourth "Colored" Infantry Regiment, 6.
May, Bill of Butler Pennsylvania, 17, 22.
Meade, Major General George Gordon, US, 58, 161, 175.
Mendenhall, Captain John, US, 119, 123, 124, 134.
Mexican War, 4, 14, 19, 63.
Michigan Ninth Infantry, 40, 41, 91.
        Bennett, Charles W., 40, 137.
        Parkhurst, Colonel John G., 40, 91.
Michigan Tenth Infantry, 48.
Michigan Eleventh Infantry, 30, 48, 50, 62, 120, 137, 139, 160.
        Gillaspie, Corporal Ira, 30, 50, 68, 74, 137, 143.
        Stoughton, Colonel William L., 62, 98, 139, 145, 160, 165, 184.
        Mudge, Lieutenant Colonel Melvin, 160.
Michigan, Fourteenth Infantry, 45.
Miller, Brigadier General John Franklin, 40, 45-51, 62, 63, 139, 146, 148, 150.
        Battle of Stones River, 77, 78, 80, 84, 96-99, 101, 103-105, 118-120, 123, 124, 127-131,
        134, 187.
Minty, Colonel Robert, 76.
Missionary Ridge, 170.
Mississippi, Smith's Mississippi Battery, 95.
        Turner, Lieutenant William B., 95, 96.
Mississippi, Stanford's Mississippi Battery, 95.
        Stanford, Captain T.J., 95.
Mississippi, Ninth Infantry, 145.
        Butler, Lieutenant I. W., 145.
Mississippi, Twenty-Fourth Infantry, 95.
        McKelvaine, Lieutenant Colonel R.P., 95.
Mississippi, Twenty-Seventh Infantry, 95, 97.
        Autry, Lieutenant Colonel James L., 95, 97.
        Jones, Colonel Thomas, 95.
        Neilson, Captain E.R., 95.
Mississippi, Twenty-Ninth Infantry, 95, 97, 111.
        Brantly, Colonel W.F., 95, 97.
        Campbell, Lieutenant John, 97.
        Morgan, Lieutenant Colonel J.B., 95.
        Robuck, J.E., 111.
Mississippi, Thirtieth Infantry, 97.
        Scales, Lieutenant Colonel Junius I., 97.
Mississippi, Thirty-Second Infantry, 157.
Missouri, Barret's Missouri Battery, 95.
        Barret, Captain O.W., 95.
Mitchell, General Robert, 60.
Monitor, USS, 78.
Monongahela House, 20.

Monroe, George, of Slate Lick, 128.
Morgan, General John Hunt, 42, 43, 56, 69, 73, 127, 128, 189.
    Morgan's Cavalry, 42.
Morgan, "Johnnie," 189.
Morgan, Mattie Ready, 69, 127, 128, 189.
Morison, Samuel Eliot, 3.
Morton, Captain James St. Clair , 43, 63, 118, 123.
    Pioneer Brigade, 66, 78, 118, 123.
Morton, Governor Oliver P., 52, 63.
Moses, Surgeon Israel, US, 166.
Muehler's Light Artillery Battery, 14.
    Muehler, Captain Charles F., 14.
Nashville Insane Asylum, 48.
Nashville National Cemetery, 67.
Nashville *Union*, 44, 45, 49, 126, 141, 152.
National Tribune, 192.
Nelson, General William "Bull," US, 63.
Negley, Major General James Scott, 11, 13-15, 18, 20, 21, 24, 27-30, 32, 33, 35, 36, 39, 42-48,
    50-52, 55, 56, 57, 60, 62, 63, 143, 144, 146, 154-157, 167, 169, 170, 175, 186.
    Battle of Chickamauga, 159-162, 164.
    Battle of Stones River, 72, 77, 78, 80, 82, 84, 85, 92, 94, 96-98, 102, 105, 115, 118-120, 123,
    127, 129, 133, 134.
New Orleans, battle of, 122.
New York *Herald*, 66, 133.
New York *Tribune*, 5.
New York *World*, 195.
Nicholson, Sam, 67.
North Carolina, Sixtieth, 117.
    McDowell, Colonel Joseph A., 117.
O'Hara, Theodore, Poet, 124.
O'Hara, Colonel Theodore, CSA, 114.
Ohio Third Infantry, 38.
    Beatty, Brigadier General John, 38, 112, 125, 137, 157, 159, 160, 162, 165, 167.
Ohio Sixth Infantry Regiment, 78.
    Anderson, Colonel Nicholas, 78.
Ohio Eighteenth Infantry, 40, 45, 62, 120, 160.
    Dillon, Reverend Chaplain John, 40.
    Given, Lt. Colonel Josiah, 62.
    Grosvenor, Lieutenant Colonel Charles, 160, 165.
Ohio Twenty-First Infantry, 27, 45, 62, 82, 146, 147, 156, 182, 183.
    Battle of Stones River, 97-99, 103-106, 109, 115, 118-120, 129, 130.
    Battle of Chickamauga, 160, 164, 165.
    Adams, Private Jacob, 115.
    Alban, Captain, 156.
    Canfield, Captain Silas, 27, 142, 146, 147, 165.
    Cusac, Captain Isaac, 165.
    McMahan, Major Arnold, 160, 178.
    Marienthal, Israel, Sutler, 142.
    Neibling, Colonel James M., 62, 97, 98, 103, 104, 119, 129, 146, 147, 178, 183.
    Norton, Colonel Jessee, 142.
    Richards, Thomas, Sutler, 142.
    Stoughton, Lieutenant Colonel Dwella, 146, 147, 160.
    Vantine, Captain Charles H., 160.

Ohio Twenty-Third Infantry, 54.
Ohio Fifty-First Infantry, 119.
    Welch, Sergeant, 119.
Ohio Sixty-Ninth Infantry, 62, 98, 120, 169, 192.
    Bingham, Captain, 98, 129.
    Campbell, Colonel Lewis D., 98,
    Cassily, Colonel William B., 62, 98.
    Hickcox, Major Eli, 98.
    Putnam, Captain David, 98, 120.
    Wilson, Lieutenant Frederick, 192.
Ohio Seventy-Fourth Infantry, 27, 40, 49, 57, 62, 160, 164, 165, 178, 184.
    Battle of Stones River, 98, 99, 102, 103, 120, 129.
    Cist, Lieutenant Henry M., 49, 52, 77, 113, 148.
    Fisher, Major Joseph, 160, 178.
    Given, Lt. Colonel Josiah, 178, 184.
    Owens, Ira Owens, 166.
    Moody, Colonel Granville, 27, 40, 62, 98, 103, 105, 129, 145.
    Von Schrader, Colonel Alexander, 57.
Ohio Ninety-Ninth Infantry, 119.
Ohio, 105th Infantry, 146.
    Morse, Bliss, 146.
Ohio, 108th Infantry, 184.
    Good, Lieutenant Colonel Joseph, 184.
Ohio, First Battery G, Marshall's, 62, 78, 92, 96, 97, 160.
    Marshall, Lieutenant Alexander, 62, 78, 160.
Ohio First Battery I, 178.
    Dilger, Captain Hubert, 178.
    Prescott, Captain Mark H., 178.
Ohio, First Battery M, Schultz's, 62, 96, 99, 160.
    Schultz, Captain Fredrick, 62, 160.
Otey, Lieutenant W.N. Mercer, 82.
Palmer, General John, US, 43, 45, 47, 63, 159, 161, 171, 178. 179, 181, 182.
    Battle of Stones River, 80, 85, 106, 115, 118, 119, 120.
Palmer, Joseph B., CSA, 108, 117.
Patterson, General Robert, 7, 8, 10, 14, 18, 29.
Pemberton, General John C., 64.
Pennsylvania Dragoons, 14.
Pennsylvania Seventh Cavalry, 45, 47.
Pennsylvania Fourteenth Cavalry, 58.
    Blakeley, Lieutenant Colonel William, 15, 58.
Pennsylvania Eighth Reserve Infantry, 58.
    McCandless, Lieutenant Samuel, 58, 193.
Pennsylvania Eleventh Reserve Infantry, 192.
    Jackson, Colonel Samuel, 192, 193.
Pennsylvania Ninth Infantry, 6, 7, 18, 20.
Pennsylvania Sixty-Seventh Infantry, 159.
    White, Major Harry, 159.
Pennsylvania Seventy-Seventh Infantry, 13, 33, 89.
    Stambaugh, Colonel Frederick, 13, 20, 24, 175.
    Blakeley, Corporal Harvey, 58.

Pennsylvania Seventy-Eighth Infantry, 1-3, 18-22, 25-28, 32, 33, 35, 37, 38, 41, 42, 50-52, 56-58,
    62-68, 137-139, 141, 142, 145, 146, 150, 153, 156, 167, 169, 170, 172, 175, 178, 181, 186,
    190, 192, 197, 198.
    Company I, Order Book, 9, 25, 26, 32, 33, 148, 152, 179, 186.
    Formation, 9-11,
    Pennsylvania Volunteer Rail Road Guards, 36, 60.
    Regiment Commended, 48, 51, 127, 129, 134, 182, 183.
    Battle of Chickamauga, 160-162, 164, 165.
    Battle of Lavergne, 45-48.
    Battle of Neeley's Bend, 51.
    Battle of Pickett's Mill, 181-183.
    Battle of Stones River, 72, 76-80, 82, 84, 85, 92, 94, 96-99, 101-104, 106, 109, 115,
        118-120, 122, 123, 126, 127, 129, 130, 134, 136.
Pennsylvania Seventy-Ninth Infantry, 13, 21, 33, 141, 175, 178.
    Frailey, Lieutenant Charles, 21.
    Hambright, Colonel Henry, 14, 20, 21, 24, 175, 178.
    Johnston, Private Adam, 21, 141, 145.
    Landis, Private Dan, 21.
    Sutman, Private Aaron, 14, 23.
    Locher, Major Michael, 178.
Pennsylvania 103rd Infantry Regiment, 10, 191.
    Springer, Private Springer, 191.
Pennsylvania 104th Infantry Regiment, 187.
Pennsylvania 134th Infantry Regiment, 66.
Pennsylvania 139th Infantry Regiment, 191.
    Warner, Captain Andrew Scott, 191.
Pennsylvania 155th Pennsylvania Zouaves, 191.
    Marshall, Major David, 191, 192.
Pennsylvania 206th Infantry Regiment, 187.
Pennsylvania 204th Heavy Artillery, 187.
Pennsylvania State Senate, 159.
Perryville, battle of, 52, 54, 60, 70, 135.
Pickett's Mill, battle of, 182-184.
Pillow, General Gideon, CSA, 19, 117, 118, 120, 122.
Pittsburgh *Dispatch*, 195.
Pittsburgh *Gazette*, 15, 16, 133, 134.
Polk, B.H., US, Captain and A.A.A.G., US, 166.
Polk, General Leonidas, 24, 43, 54, 65, 69, 70, 135, 147.
    Battle of Stones River, 76, 77, 82, 84, 94, 95, 107, 108, 114, 115.
Pope, General John, 76.
Preston, General William, CSA, 108, 115, 117, 118, 122, 123.
Price, Colonel Samuel, US, 114, 118, 119.
prostitutes, 68, 132, 140.
    "Smokey Row," 68.
    "Hospital Whore," 132.
"pup" tent, 139.
Rains, General James E., CSA, 135.
Ready, Alice, 189.
Ready, Charles, 127, 128.
Reid, Whitelaw, 32.
Reynolds, General Joseph, 60.
Richmond, Lieutenant William B., CSA, 82.
Richmond *Dispatch*, 59.

Richmond *Enquirer*, 135.
Richmond *Examiner*, 110.
Roberts, Colonel George, US, 82, 84, 92, 94.
Robertson, Captain Felix, CSA, 114, 118.
Roebling, John, 20.
Roebling, Washington, 20.
Rosecrans, Major General William Starke, 1-3, 33, 52, 54-58, 60-66, 68, 69, 71, 137, 140, 147,
    148, 150, 152-157, 167-169, 177, 191, 197, 198.
    Battle of Chickamauga, 159-162, 164.
    Battle of Stones River, 73, 74, 76-80, 84-86, 88, 89, 91, 96, 101, 102, 105-110, 112-115,
    119, 122-125, 127, 129, 131, 134-136.
Roosevelt, Theodore, 190.
Rousseau, General Lovell, US, 60, 63, 92, 97, 98, 104, 125.
St. Louis *Republican*, 126.
Savage, Colonel John, CSA, 108.
Savage, Lieutenant Colonel L.N., CSA, 108.
Schaefer, Colonel Frederick, US, 92, 94.
Schofield, General John, US, 177, 181.
Scott, Dred Scott Decision, 5.
Scott, Lieutenant General Winfield, 7, 8, 14, 175.
Scribner, Colonel Benjamin, 92, 105, 178, 179, 181-183.
Seddon, James, Secretary of War, CSA, 135.
Seed Corn Contingent, 91.
Selkirk, William A., 141.
Seward, Secretary of War, William, 78.
Shanks, William, 66.
Sheridan, General Phil, 9, 60, 63, 65, 138, 144, 162, 164, 177, 192.
    Battle of Stones River, 80, 84, 86, 89, 92, 96-98, 104, 105, 134, 168.
Sherman, Major General William, US, 2, 9, 24, 29, 71, 78, 82, 94, 168, 175, 177, 178, 181-183.
Shaw, W.B., 133.
Shiloh-Pittsburg Landing, 18, 19, 36, 61, 135.
Sill, General Joshua, US, 74, 86, 92, 94, 112, 113, 127.
Simkins, Lida, 20.
Sirwell, Elizabeth, 6.
Sirwell, Elizabeth Graham, 5
Sirwell, Elizabeth McCandless, 6, 30, 54, 172, 196.
Sirwell, Emma, 6.
Sirwell, Lucinda, 6, 41.
Sirwell, Mary "Mame," 6, 192.
Sirwell, Nancy Hemphill, 195.
Sirwell, Richard, 5
Sirwell, Sarah, 6.
Sirwell, Colonel William, 1, 3, 4, 10, 14-16, 18-21, 24-30, 33, 36, 38, 39, 49, 50, 56, 57, 59, 62, 64,
    66-68, 71, 138, 139, 142, 143, 145-147, 150, 153-157, 167, 169, 170, 172, 174, 175, 177,
    178, 179, 185-188, 190-198.
    Personal: 5-8, 11, 13, 20, 39, 50, 54, 55, 139, 141, 156, 157, 174, 193.
    Commended, 48, 127, 129, 134, 165, 182, 183.
    Battle of Chickamauga, 159-162, 164, 165.
    Battle of Lavergne, 45-48.
    Battle of Pickett's Mill, 182, 183.
    Battle of Stones River, 72, 74, 76-78, 80-82, 86, 92, 98, 99, 101-105, 115, 119, 120,
    122-131, 134, 136.
Sirwell, William Mitchell, 6, 30, 195.

Sirwell Blues, 6.
Sirwell's Watch Making Shop, 6.
Smith, Captain J.B., Silver Band, 135.
Smith, General Kirby, 43, 54, 71.
Smith, Robert W., 191.
Society of the Army of the Cumberland, 17, 174, 191, 192.
Soldiers and Sailors Memorial Hall, Pittsburgh, PA, 192.
Sons of Confederate Veterans, 192.
Sons of Union Veterans of the Civil War, 192.
South Carolina, Tenth/Nineteenth Infantry, 95.
     Lythgoe, Colonel A.J., 95.
     Pressley, Lieutenant Colonel, 95.
South Mountain, battle of,
Spears, General James, US, 63, 125.
Spurlock, Captain D.C., CSA, 108.
Stanley General David, US, 63, 76, 110, 126, 127.
Stanley, Colonel Timothy R., US, 62, 63, 84, 85, 92, 98, 103, 104, 118-120, 123, 160.
Stanton, Edwin, Secretary of War, 56, 134, 147, 153, 168, 169.
Starkweather, General John, US, 33.
Steamboat: Caroline, 186.
Steele, Isaac & Mary, 23.
Stevenson, Alexander, 2, 113.
Stevenson, General Carter, CSA, 64.
Stewart, General Alexander P., CSA, 95-97, 99, 101, 103, 112.
Stones River, Battle of, 2, 18, 19, 60-136.
Stuart, General Jeb, US, 42, 65.
Swift, Doctor Eben, US, 101, 110, 129, 133.
Taylor, President Zachary, 63, 71.
Tennesseans, Biffle's Tennesseans, CSA, 47.
Tennessee, First Cavalry, CSA, 76.
     Carter, Colonel James, 76.
Tennessee, First Middle Tennessee Cavalry, US, 45.
     Stokes, Colonel, 48.
Tennessee, First Infantry Regiment, CSA, 18, 19, 52, 65, 70, 71, 165, 189.
     Battle of Stones River, 85, 102, 106, 126.
     Rock City Guard, 18, 85, 95, 102, 103, 184, 186, 189.
     Rock City Volunteers, 19.
     Rutherford Rifles, 65.
     Maury Grays, 18.
     Cobb, Private Mitchell, 18, 19, 103, 189.
     Cobb, Corporal Thomas, 18, 19, 103, 189.
     Field, Colonel Hume, 3, 19, 52, 71, 95, 96, 103, 106, 184.
     Fulcher, Captain Joseph, 19.
     Hainey, Private Al, 102.
     Hawkins, Major James M., 19.
     Irwin, Private Bill, 102.
     Kelly, Captain W.D., 95, 102, 184.
     Knight, Private W.K., 102.
     Newsom, Private W.M., 102.
     Robinson, Samuel, 106, 189.
     Seay, Private Sam, 85.
     Spain, Private Bill, 102.
     Watkins, Private Sam, 18, 19, 70, 88, 165, 167, 189.

Tennessee, First/ Twenty-Seventh Infantry Regiment, CSA, 71, 73, 95, 96, 103, 105, 106, 184.
    James, Lieutenant R. Fred, 96.
    Marsh, Lieutenant John, 96.
Tennessee, Fourth (Provisional Army), CSA, 95.
    McMurry, Colonel James A., 95, 96.
Tennessee, Fourth/Fifth Infantry, CSA, 95, 96.
    Strahl, Colonel Oscar F., 95.
    Oakley, Sergeant, 96.
Tennessee, Sixth Infantry Regiment, CSA, 52.
Tennessee, Ninth Infantry Regiment, CSA, 52, 102.
    Bond, Private Robert, 102.
Tennessee, Sixth/Ninth Infantry, CSA, 95, 96.
    Hurt, Colonel C.S., 95, 96.
    Hooks, Sergeant, 96.
Tennessee, Tenth Union Volunteers Infantry, 67.
Tennessee, Thirteenth Infantry, CSA, 70.
    Rogers, Private Bill, 70.
Tennessee, Sixteenth Infantry Regiment, CSA, 67.
Tennessee, Eighteenth Infantry Regiment, CSA, 117.
    Butler, Lieutenant Colonel W.R., 117.
Tennessee, Nineteenth Infantry Regiment, CSA, 95.
    Walker, Colonel Francis M., 95.
Tennessee, Twentieth Infantry, CSA, 70, 113, 117.
    Crosthwait, Lieutenant Frank, 113.
    Smith, Colonel T.B., 117.
    Lavender, Lieutenant Colonel F.M., 117.
    Claybrooke, Major F., 117.
Tennessee, Twenty-Fourth Infantry, CSA, 95.
    Bratton, Colonel H.L.W., 95.
    Shannon, Major S.E., 95.
Tennessee, Twenty-Fifth Infantry, CSA, 144.
    Davidson, Lieutenant John, 144.
Tennessee, Twenty-Sixth Infantry Regiment, CSA, 19, 117, 120, 122, 129, 192.
    Lillard, Colonel John, 3, 19, 117, 122.
    Green, Color-bearer H.P., 122.
Tennessee, Twenty-Seventh Infantry Regiment, CSA, 19, 52, 71.
    Williams, Kit, 19.
Tennessee, Twenty-Eighth Infantry Regiment, CSA, 117.
    Cunningham, Colonel P.D., 117.
Tennessee, Thirty-First/Thirty Third Infantry, CSA, 95.
    Tansill, Colonel E.E., 95.
Tennessee, Thirty-Second Infantry, CSA, 117.
    Cook, Colonel Ed. C., 117.
Tennessee, Forty-Fifth Infantry, CSA, 117.
    Searcy, Colonel A., 117.
Tennessee, Eighthy-Fourth Infantry, CSA,
    Stanton, Colonel S.S., 82.
Tennessee, Wright's Tennessee Battery, CSA, 117.
    Wright, Captain E.E., 117.
    Mebane, Lieutenant John W., 117.
Tennessee, Maney's Tennessee Sharpshooters, 95.
    Maney, Captain Frank, 95.

Texas Rangers, CSA, 48.
    Sparks, Major, 48.
Thomas, Major General George, US, 29, 43, 52, 60-63, 66, 71, 147, 152, 156, 157, 168, 175, 177, 178, 179, 181, 183, 188, 192.
    Battle of Chickamauga, 159-162, 164, 165, 166.
    Battle of Stones River, 72, 84, 91, 92, 97, 102, 106, 107, 110-112, 122, 127.
Trecy, Father, 54, 88.
Truesdail, Chief of Army Police, Colonel William, 65.
Turchin, Colonel John, 38, 167.
Twentieth Corps, 152.
Twenty-First Corps, 152.
Urquhart, Colonel David, 109, 118.
Van Cleve, General Horatio P., 63, 78, 84, 89, 108, 114.
Van Dorn, General Earl, 59.
Van Horne, Thomas, 134.
Veteran Reserve, 66.
Walker, Major General W.H.T., CSA, 162.
Walker, Colonel Moses B., 60, 111.
Washington, President George, 61.
Washington Blues, 4, 6.
Washington Infantry, 14.
Watkins, Jennie, 189.
Weaver, Adam of Williamson county, TN, 141.
Wells, Captain and A.A.A.G. E.F., US, 179.
Wharton, General John A.,
Wheeler, Major General Joseph, CSA, 65, 73, 74, 76, 184.
White, Thomas of Indiana, PA, 159.
Whittaker, General Walter, US, 165.
Wiggins, Juniper, 126.
Wiles, Captain William, 58.
Willard, Captain L.S., US, 162.
Willich, General August, US, 76, 88, 89.
Wilson, Major James, 114.
Wisconsin First Infantry, 178, 182.
    Bingham, Lieutenant Colonel George B., 178.
Wisconsin Eighth Infantry, 59.
    Murphy, Colonel R.C., 59.
Wisconsin Tenth Infantry, 92, 105, 106.
    Hinkley, First Lieutenant L.D., 105, 106.
Wisconsin Twenty-Fourth Infantry, 74, 94, 112.
    Silsby, Amandus, 74, 76.
    Hale, Corporal Frank Hale, 94.
    Williams, Private Sanford, 112.
Withers, Major General Jones, CSA, 70, 95, 97, 144.
Wood, Brigadier General Thomas, US, 33, 63, 85, 89, 110, 162, 164, 167, 181, 182.
Yaryan, John Lee, 110.
Zahm, Colonel Lewis, 76.

Members of the Pennsylvania Seventy-Eighth Regiment

Adams, Private George, 35, 184, 191.
Allen, Private Charles, 23, 102.
Allen, Private Gideon R., 130.
Altman, Private Hamilton, 120.
Altman, Private Solomon, 22.
Ake, Private David, 192.
Akins, Private Adam, 120.
Anchors, Lieutenant Jim, 103, 132.
Angless, Private Jacob J., 67.
Ayres, Lieutenant Alfred, 78, 129.
Barclay, Lieutenant Colonel David, 13, 15, 21.
Barrackman, Private Elijah Snyder, 191.
Barrett, Private Teddy, 6, 197.
Bartlebaugh, Private Mathais, 23.
Bartlebaugh, Private Sam, 23.
Beck, Corporal Adam, 140, 143, 153.
Bell, Musician Jimmy, 106.
Bell, Sergeant Thompson, 129.
Benhough, Corporal Herbert "Hoof," 187, 192.
Bennett, Private Abraham, 144.
Black, Lieutenant George Washington, 32-34, 37, 40.
Black, Corporal William H., 130.
Blakeley, Lt. Colonel Archibald, 15, 33, 58, 66, 82, 138, 155-157, 160, 162, 164, 169-172, 174,
     190, 191.
Blakeley, Doctor Thomas, 41, 110, 142.
Boney, Private George, 129.
Boney, Private Wilson, 51.
Bonnaffon, Major Augustus, 11, 20, 36, 45, 47, 48, 50, 76, 78, 127, 128, 138, 139, 162, 172, 174,
     187, 190.
Boreland, Corporal Robert, 36, 190.
Boreland, Sergeant Samuel, 172.
Borland, Sergeant George, 102.
Bowser [Brown], Private Mark, 67, 120, 138, 139.
Boyd, Corporal Bill, 48.
Boyer, Private Levi, 132.
Bradin, Private John, 187.
Braughler, Lieutenant Adam, 130.
Brinker, Captain John M., 63, 81, 156.
Brown, Private John G., 21.
Burford, Private Jim, 171, 172.
Butler, Private Eplenia, 21.
Carnahan, Private James, 66.
Champion, Private James A., 67, 106.
Chapman, Private John, 103.
Christy, Father Richard, 16, 17, 25, 40, 54, 103, 104, 128, 138, 145, 171, 175, 182, 186, 190.
Claypoole, Private Henry, 131, 145, 171.
Colbert, Private Daniel, 51.
Conway, Private Denny, 103.
Cook, Private Jeremiah, 23.

Crawford, First Sergeant Joel, 187.
Crosby, Lt. Samuel, 56.
Croyle, Private John, 22, 102.
Croyle, Sergeant Sam, 102, 129.
Cummins, Captain William, 20, 63, 81, 82, 129.
Cypher, Private William, 197.
Daniels, Private David, 23.
Daniels, Private Harrison, 23.
Davis, Private Michael, 48.
Davis Acting Sergeant William J., 23, 122, 129, 130.
Devlin, Private John, 35.
Dibler, Private Elias, 102.
Dinger, Private Amos, 102.
Dinsmore, Private Marion, 140.
Dinsmore, Lieutenant Robert Wilson, 127-129, 140.
Doty, Private John, 51, 145.
Doty, Private Washington, 51, 145.
Dougherty, Private Albert, 153.
Drake, Private George, 187.
Drum, Private John, 144.
Drummond, Corporal James,
Dumm, Sergeant Samuel, 40, 51, 69, 125, 127, 139, 145, 161, 170, 171, 182, 187, 188, 190.
Dunnington, Frank "Dudley," Negro Cook, DDS, 41.
Edmonson, Corporal George, 21.
Elias, Private Nelson, 130.
Elwood, Captain R. D., 33, 57, 64, 81, 99, 129, 190.
England, Doctor William, 143.
Erwin, Private Jim, 120.
Fiscus, John, 187.
Forbes, Captain Michael, 63, 81.
Fox, Private George, 67.
Foy, Private George, 191.
Gap, Private Silas, 21.
Geary, Private John W., Jr, 23.
Geary, Private John W., Sr, 23.
George, Private Reuben, 191.
Gibson, Private Albert, 182.
Gibson, Sergeant J. Thompson, 9, 24, 30, 35, 38, 41, 49, 50, 84, 94, 97, 104, 110, 111, 119, 123, 157, 182.
Gilliam, Private Enoch, 132.
Gillam, Private James, 51.
Gillespie, Captain Charles B., 13, 63, 82, 187.
Golden, Musician Dennis "Danny," 6, 20, 22.
Graham, Private Bill, 187.
Griffin, Private Phil, 103.
Halstead, Lieutenant Matthew, 64, 81, 120, 123, 125, 129.
Hamm, Color Bearer, Sergeant George, 81, 120, 192.
Harman, Private Phillip, 191.
Hartman, Private John, 145.
Hastings, Privates John, 35.
Hatzell, Private Phineas, 143, 191.
Hay, Sergeant Albert B. , 130, 190.

Hays, Private William, 37.
Henry, Private Jim, 103.
Henry, Private L.P., 67.
Hepler, Corporal Samuel, 171.
Hervey, Captain DeWitt, 9, 16, 40, 56, 57, 64.
Hilberry, Captain James, 20, 64, 80.
Hill, Corporal Lewis, 144.
Hinchberger, Private Christian, 22, 189.
Hollingsworth, Private Benjamin F., 120.
Hogan, Private John, 129.
Holben, Private Solomon, 22.
Hosack, Doctor Bill, 104, 128, 159, 190, 191.
Hosey, Captain James N., 33, 63, 81, 132.
Hughes, Sergeant William, 122, 129, 130.
Hull, Private Morrison, 102.
Huff, Private Bill, 10.
Hutchinson, Private John W., 23, 120.
Hutchinson, Private Samuel A., 23.
Irwin, Private John, 159.
Jack, Private James, 187.
Jack, Captain William, 20, 63, 80-82, 101, 129, 131.
Johnson, Private Andrew, 193.
Jordan, Captain John, 64.
Keifer, Sergeant John, 129.
Keirn, Private Isaac, 143.
Keirn, Private Nat, 120.
Kenniston, Private David, 39.
Kerr, Sergeant William, 171.
Kipp, Private Abram, 30, 40, 50, 56, 125, 127, 137, 143, 153, 190.
Knox, Assistant Surgeon William, 50.
Langdon, Corporal George, 47.
Latshaw, Private Ebenezer, 23.
Latshaw, Private Reuben, 23, 120.
Lee, Lieutenant Sam, 11, 129, 196.
Little, Private James, 182.
Lloyd, Private Absalom, 10.
Lowry, Private Alexander, 23.
Lowry, Commissary Sergeant Joseph, 22.
Lowry, Corporal William, 40, 50, 143, 190, 193.
McBride, First Sergeant Samuel, 101, 129.
McCandless, Private George Washington, 6, 50, 58, 66, 78, 190.
McCanna, Lieutenant Martin, 64, 80, 81, 102, 129, 186, 187.
McCracken, Private George, 197.
McCue, First Lieutenant Bill, 187.
McCullough, Doctor William, 11, 110.
McElroy, Private Johnston, 106, 190.
McKelvey, Private James, 188.
McQuiston, Private David, Sr, 23, 143.
McQuiston, Private David, Jr, 23, 143.
McQuiston, Private John, 143.
Maize, Lieutenant William, 81, 102, 129, 190.
Marlin, Lieutenant John, 129, 157.
Marshal, Private Henry, 159.

Martin, Sergeant Bill, 187.
Mechling, Sergeant Major Franklin, 101, 128-130, 150.
Mechling, Lieutenant Joseph, 50, 56, 57.
Meredith, John, Battalion Commissary, 174.
Minteer, Private Sam, 51.
Miller, Sergeant Henry, 101, 129, 130.
Miller, Victor, Staff Assistant Surgeon, 129.
Morehead, Corporal Jim, 171.
Morgan, Private Hugh, 50, 140.
Murphy, Third Sergeant Bill, 103, 129.
Myers, Private James, 82.
Myrtle, Corporal Arthur, 102.
Nugent, Lt. Willis, 105, 122, 127.
Painter, Private Jack, 132.
Penman, Private Jim, 103.
Powell, Lieutenant Joseph, 25, 186.
Prosser, Private Abe, 143.
Rafennacht, Private Emmuel, 187.
Rea, Private Lemuel, 51, 145.
Reed, Sergeant Alfred, 55, 56, 59, 66.
Rettinger, Private Elias, 66.
Reynolds, "Captain" Thomas Hamilton, sutler, 39.
Richey, Private Abram, 130.
Ritchey, Private William, 51.
Rose, Private George, 101.
Roth, Private George, 35.
Rowdybush, Private Michael, 144.
Runyan, Private Jim, 101.
Ryers, Private Valentine, 67.
Saegers, Private Lewis, 78, 99.
Schaffner, Private George, 127, 128.
Schrecengost, Private Alfred, 21.
Shaffer, Private Sam, Sr, 23.
Shaffer, Private Sam, Jr, 23.
Shannon, Private Jim, 102.
Sheilds, Private John, 67.
Shettler, Private John, 187.
Shindler, Private Adam, 101.
Simkins, Sergeant Albert "Buck", 20, 47, 132, 143, 145, 147, 167.
Slater, Private Evan, 144.
Slusser, Private Sam, 103, 131, 132.
Smith, Sergeant Bill, 120, 129.
Smith, Sergeant Charles, 172.
Smith, Corporal George D., 182.
Smith, Private George H., 22.
Smith, Private Hamilton, 51, 145.
Smith, Captain Joe, 139, 156.
Smith, Lieutenant Robert, 129, 143, 145, 187.
Southworth, Private Jerry, 132.
Sproul, Private Bill, 190.
Stahl, Private Sam, I., 58.
Stahl, Private Sam, II., 58.
Stark Private Bob, 35.

Steele, Private Sam, 22, 23, 143, 197.
Step, Private Levi, 190.
Sullivan, Corporal Mark, 171.
Sullivan, Private Mike, 103.
Sykes, Private Bill, 143.
Sykes, Private Tom, 143.
Tanner, John L., 67.
Thompson, Private Dallas, 101.
Tittle, Private Richard, 37.
Thorn, Private Samuel, 33.
Thorne, Private James, 66, 122.
Torbett, Lieutenant Henry, 57, 101, 128, 146, 187, 190.
Truxall, Corporal Ben, 35.
Unger, Private Jack, 187.
Walker, Private Robert, 144.
Weaver, Lieutenant Absolom, 81, 82, 103, 129-132.
Weaver, Private Henry, 22, 102, 103.
Wallace, Private Sam, Jr.,
Wallace, Private Sam, Sr.,
Weir, Lieutenant Alfred, 101, 128, 164.
Welsh, Private Milton, 50, 140.
Wheeler, Private Bill, 21.
Whitehill, Private Henry Harrison, 132.
Wiant, Private Jake, 157.
Wiehl, Lieutenant Fred, 190.
Wilson, Private James, [James Wilson Reed], 41.
Wilson, Private Thomas, 23.
Wissa, Private F., 67.
Wolff, Private Bill, 175.
Wolff, Private Jack, 175.
Woodford, Private Banks, 144.
Young, Private John, 187.
Younkins, Private Mike, 132.
Younkins, Private John,
Zerby, Private Daniel, 51.

THE PENNSYLVANIA SEVENTY-EIGHTH REGIMENTAL ROSTER

Within the list of members of the Seventy-Eighth, there are many instances when a soldier has two or more names listed. This occurred when distinct records used contrasting names. It was only after verifying and cross checking the identity of each soldier that these differences were noted.

Grave registrations are listed in the most recent government numerical designation for Stones River and Nashville.

Information was compiled from:
1. History of the Pennsylvania Seventy-Eighth
2. Pennsylvania at Chickamauga
3. Bates History
4. Descriptive List of the Pennsylvania Seventy-Eighth
5. Descriptive List of the Second 78th Pennsylvania Volunteer Infantry
6. Letters and Diaries
7. Kittanning Newspapers
8. Louisville Newspapers
9. Regimental Reunion Records
10. Smith's History of Armstrong County
11. Annual Report of the Adjutant General of Pennsylvania,
12. Burial Records for Stones River and Nashville, Tennessee.
13. Tombstone information from Western Pennsylvania Cemeteries.
14. Nashville Union
15. 1890 Veterans Census
16. 1914 Regimental Reunion Roster
17. Reunion Records of Secretary/Treasurer Will Lowry
18. County histories: Clarion, Butler, Indiana, Westmoreland and Allegheny.
19. Official Records of the Union and Confederate Armies.
12. Dedication of the Pennsylvania Monument at Andersonville
13. Dedication of the Pennsylvania Monument at Chickamauga

CODE MEANING:
1. There are instances where a soldier is noted as an enlistee of Armstrong County and Allegheny County. The Armstrong County Enlistee was listed in Smith's History of Armstrong County. The Allegheny County Enlistee is listed on the memorials at the Soldiers & Sailors Hall in Pittsburgh, PA.
2. Sworn: OCT 12, 1861 YRS signifies the regiment or a soldier was sworn in on that date. Company enlistment dates differ.
3. /3 indicates the number of years of contracted service.
4. Muster is the date mustered out of the service.
5. AGE: is the age of enlistment.
6. # indicates that the soldier was not listed in original regimental history, however, his membership in the regiment was verified from other sources.
7. Ninth Regiment, Company B was Sirwell's original company.
8. VRC indicates the Veteran Reserve. Unhealthy men not able to campaign were placed in this unit.
9. "Briefly Missing in Action" @ Stones River could mean returned within days or imprisonment and return after months.
10. Veteran is indicative of a soldier having the honorable distinction of having served two enlistments.

 * Noted in History of Armstrong County as a county enlistee
 ** Noted at Soldiers & Sailors Hall, Pittsburgh, PA as an Allegheny County enlistee
*** Noted as an enlistee of both sources

"Died before 1905" comes from the original regimental history where it was noted that the soldier was dead. No date was given for his death.

Home: Info garnered from 1890 Census, 1914 Regimental Reunion Records, Pension records and various other sources.

Recruitment:

First Regiment
Company A recruited in Indiana County
Company B recruited in Armstrong County
Company C recruited in Clarion County
Company D recruited in Indiana County and Cambria County
Company E recruited in Clarion County
Company F recruited in Armstrong County
Company G recruited in Armstrong County
Company H recruited in Butler County
Company I recruited in Armstrong County
Company K recruited in Armstrong County
Second Regiment
Company A recruited from First Regiment
Company B recruited from First Regiment
Company C recruited in Mifflin County
Company D recruited in Cumberland County
Company E recruited in Butler County
Company F recruited in Allegheny County
Company G recruited in Beaver County
Company H recruited in Allegheny County
Company I recruited in Allegheny County
Company K recruited in Huntington County

Battles:
Lavergne, October 8, 1862.
Hermitage Ford, October 20, 1862.
Stones River, December 31, 1862–January 2, 1863.
Tullahoma, June 23-30, 1863.
McLemore's Cove, Davis' Crossroads, September 10-11, 1863.
Chickamauga, September 18-20, 1863
Buzzard's Roost Gap, Bald Face Ridge, GA, May 7-8, 1864
Resaca, May 14, 1864.
Pickett's Mill, GA, May 27, 1864
Buzzard's Roost Gap, August 15, 1864.

Roster of the Pennsylvania Seventy-Eighth Volunteer Infantry

STONES RIVER TO PICKETT'S MILL 1861-1865

ADAMS, DUNCAN ***   PVT   CO. F   AGE:19
    SWORN: OCT 12, 1861/3 YRS   MUSTER: NOV 4, 1864
    BORN: TARENTUM, PA   OCCUPATION: LABORER
    HEIGHT: 5' 4½"   COMPLEXION: FRESH   EYES: BLUE   HAIR: BROWN
    HOME 1914: SOLDIER'S HOME, SANDUSKY, OHIO
    BURIED: PROSPECT CEMETERY, TARENTUM, PA; DIED: MAR 30, 1930 @ 87

ADAMS, GEORGE   CPL   CO. A   AGE:19
ADAM, GEORGE A.   INDIANA COUNTY ENLISTEE: HOME, PA
    SWORN: OCT 12, 1861/3 YRS   MUSTER: NOV 4, 1864
    BORN: ARMSTRONG COUNTY   OCCUPATION: SHOEMAKER
    HEIGHT: 5' 11"   HAIR: BROWN   EYES: GREY   COMPLEXION: DARK
    ENLISTED AS 4TH CPL; WOUNDED JUN 27, 1864/KENESAW MOUNTAIN
    HOME: 1876-1927: SMICKSBURG, INDIANA COUNTY, PA
    PENSION: $90.00/MO ON 75% DISABILITY IN 1927
    REUNION CHICKAMAUGA 1897, INDIANA 1908
    BURIED: INDIANA COUNTY, PA, GREENWOOD CEMETERY, WHITE TWP., 1842-1929

ADAMS, GEORGE *   PVT   CO. B   AGE:18
ADAM, GEORGE
    SWORN: OCT 12, 1861/3 YRS   DIED: DEC 8, 1861 AT CAMP NEGLEY, KY
    BORN: ARMSTRONG COUNTY   OCCUPATION: FARMER
    HEIGHT: 5' 3"   COMPLEXION: DARK   EYES: BROWN   HAIR: LIGHT

ADAMS, HARRISON   CPL   CO. E   AGE:26
    SWORN: OCT 12, 1861/3 YRS   MUSTER: NOV 4, 1864
    BORN: JEFFERSON COUNTY   OCCUPATION: LABORER
    HEIGHT: 5' 7"   COMPLEXION: DARK   EYES: BLUE   HAIR: BROWN
    PROMOTED TO CPL APR 6, 1863

ADAMS, JAMES ***   PVT   CO. F   AGE:24
    SWORN: OCT 12, 1861/3 YRS   MUSTER: NOV 4, 1864/ABSENT, iLL
    BORN: TARENTUM, PA   OCCUPATION: OIL BORER
    HEIGHT: 5' 7"   COMPLEXION: FRESH   EYES: BLUE   HAIR: BROWN
    CAPTURED @ STONES RIVER; RETURNED TO REGT JUN 6, 1863
    REUNION IN FREEPORT 1886, KITTANNING 1901
    HOME 1886, 1901-1914: TARENTUM, PA
    HOME 1897: WEST VALLEY, ARMSTRONG COUNTY, PA
    BURIED: PROSPECT CEMETERY, TARENTUM, PA, DIED: JUL 24, 1920

ADAMS, JAMES*   PVT   CO. K   AGE: 25
    NATIVE OF TARENTUM, ALLEGHENY COUNTY, PA
    SWORN: OCT 12, 1861/3 YRS   MUSTER: NOV 4, 1864
    BORN: COUNTY DOWN, IRELAND   OCCUPATION: FARMER
    HEIGHT: 5' 11"   COMPLEXION: FAIR   EYES: GREY   HAIR: FAIR
    CAPTURED AT STONES RIVER, PAROLED AND RETURNED JUNE 6, 1863
    1890 CENSUS: GREENDALE, ARMSTRONG COUNTY, PA
    1894 SOLDIERS PENSION: $6/mo   HOME 1894: GREENDALE
    HOME 1914: RD #2, KITTANNING, PA
    BUREID: SLATE LICK CEMETERY, SLATE LICK, PA [1842-1917]

ADAMS, JOHN B.*   CPL   CO. B   AGE:32
    SWORN: OCT 12, 1861/3 YRS   MEDICAL: APR 20, 1862
    BORN: ARMSTRONG COUNTY   OCCUPATION: FARMER
    HEIGHT: 6' 2"   COMPLEXION: DARK   EYES: GREY   HAIR: BLACK
    1890 CENSUS: DELANCY, JEFFERSON COUNTY, PA

ADAMS, JOHN L.   PVT   CO. A   AGE: 18
    SWORN: OCT 12, 1861/3 YRS   TRANS: SIG CORPS, OCT 22, 1863
    BORN: INDIANA COUNTY   OCCUPATION: FARMER
    HEIGHT: 5' 5"   COMPLEXION: FAIR   EYES: BLUE   HAIR: BROWN

ADAMS, THOMAS B.*   PVT   CO. B   AGE:21
    SWORN: OCT 12, 1861/3 YRS   MEDICAL: DEC 12, 1863.
    BORN: ARMSTRONG COUNTY   OCCUPATION: FARMER

HEIGHT: 5' 10"   COMPLEXION: DARK   EYES: BROWN   HAIR: LIGHT
REUNION INDIANA 1908; HOME 1890-1914: PORTER, JEFFERSON COUNTY, PA

ADEN, CHARLES R./B.   PVT   CO. A   AGE:32
SWORN: OCT 12, 1861/3 YRS   DIED: JUN 5, 1864 AT CHATTANOOGA
BORN: INDIANA COUNTY   OCCUPATION: LABORER
HEIGHT: 5' 11"   COMPLEXION: DARK   EYES: GREY   HAIR: BROWN
MORTALLY WOUNDED MAY 27, 1864/PICKETT'S MILL

AIKINS, ADAM*   PVT   CO. K   AGE: 41
AIKENS, ADAM
SWORN: OCT 12, 1861/3 YRS   DIED: JAN 20, 1863
BORN: ARMSTRONG COUNTY   , JUN 20, 1820 OCCUPATION: LABORER
HEIGHT: 5' 5¾"   COMPLEXION: DARK   EYES: BLUE   HAIR: DARK
MORTALLY WOUNDED AT STONES RIVER/HEAD
BURIED AT NATIONAL CEMETERY NASHVILLE, GRAVE #B-478
TOMBSTONE ALSO IN APPLEBY MANOR PRESBYTERIAN CEMETERY, FORD CITY, PA
1890 CENSUS: FORD CITY, ARMSTRONG COUNTY, PA; WIDOW ESTHER

AKE, DAVID S.   PVT   CO. D   AGE:18
SWORN: OCT 12, 1861/3 YRS   MUSTER: NOV 4, 1864
BORN: INDIANA COUNTY, HILLSDALE   OCCUPATION: FARMER
HEIGHT: 5' 5"   COMPLEXION: DARK   EYES: BLACK   HAIR: BLACK
HOME 1890-1897: HILLSDALE, INDIANA COUNTY, PA
REUNION CHICKAMAUGA 1897, INDIANA 1908.
BURIED: INDIANA COUNTY, PA, THOMPSON HILLSDALE CEM, MONTGOMERY TWP.,
OCT 2, 1842-MAR 1, 1913

ALCORN, JESSEE *   PVT   CO. B   AGE:30
SWORN: OCT 12, 1861/3 YRS   MUSTER: NOV 4, 1864
BORN: ARMSTRONG COUNTY   OCCUPATION: CARPENTER
HEIGHT: 5' 8"   COMPLEXION: LIGHT   EYES: BLACK   HAIR: DARK
HOME 1890-1897: BROOKVILLE, JEFFERSON COUNTY, PA

ALLEBACH, CALEB W.   CPL   CO. C   AGE:18
ALBACH, CALEB
SWORN: OCT 12, 1861/3 YRS   MUSTER: NOV 4, 1864
BORN: CLARION COUNTY
HEIGHT: 5' 5"   COMPLEXION: DARK   EYES: BLACK   HAIR: BLACK

ALLEN, ARCHIBALD B.*   CPL   CO. B   AGE:28
ALLAN, ARCHIBALD   OCCUPATION: FARMER
BORN: MAR 1, 1832, W. MAHONING TWP. INDIANA COUNTY
SWORN: OCT 12, 1861/3 YRS   MUSTER: NOV 4, 1864
HEIGHT: 5' 9"   COMPLEXION: LIGHT   EYES: BLACK   HAIR: DARK
PROMOTED TO CPL DEC 11, 1863
BROTHER WILLIAM SERVED IN CO. M, U.S. 1st CAVALRY
HOME 1890-1897: PHOENIX, ARMSTRONG COUNTY, PA
MEMBER OF J. EDWARD TURK G.A.R. POST #321
REUNION CHICKAMAUGA 1897, INDIANA 1908
DIED: NOV 29, 1912; NEVER MARRIED; LIVING WITH BROTHER WILLIAM AT DEATH
BURIED: GLADE RUN PRESBYTERIAN CEMETERY, DAYTON, PA
BROTHER: ROBERT ALLEN IN 78th

ALLEN, CHARLES ***   PVT   CO. B   AGE: 58
SWORN: OCT 12, 1861/4 YRS   MUSTER: SEP 11, 1865   VETERAN
BORN: ARMSTRONG COUNTY   OCCUPATION: MINER
HEIGHT: 5' 6"   COMPLEXION: LIGHT   EYES: BLUE   HAIR: GRAY

ALLEN, GIDEON R.   PVT   CO. H   AGE:22
ORIGIN: BUTLER COUNTY   HEIGHT: 5' 11½"
SWORN: OCT 12, 1861/3YRS   MUSTER: NOV 4, 1864   BOUNTY: $100.
BORN: CLARION COUNTY   OCCUPATION: FARMER
HEIGHT: 5' 10½"   COMPLEXION: FAIR   EYES: BLUE   HAIR: BROWN
HOME IN NOV 1897-1914: EUCLID, BUTLER COUNTY, PA; REUNION KITTANNING 1901

ALLEN, ROBERT M. *   CPL   CO. B   AGE:25
BORN: APR 15, 1836, W. MAHONING TWP, INDIANA COUNTY, PA
SWORN: OCT 12, 1861/3 YRS   MUSTER: NOV 4, 1864
BORN: INDIANA COUNTY   OCCUPATION: FARMER
HEIGHT: 6'   COMPLEXION: LIGHT   EYES: DARK   HAIR: DARK

PROMOTED TO CPL: JUN 30, 1862
BROTHER WILLIAM SERVED IN CO. M, U.S. 1st CAVALRY
1890 CENSUS: RED BANK, ARMSTRONG COUNTY. PA
1894 SOLDIERS PENSION: $4/mo
HOME 1894-1901: PHOENIX, ARMSTRONG COUNTY, PA
REUNION CHICKAMAUGA 1897, KITTANNING 1901, INDIANA 1908
DIED: 1912   WIFE: AMANDA GASTON ALLEN
BURIED: PHOENIX, ARMSTRONG COUNTY, PA   BROTHER: ARCHIBALD ALLEN

ALTER, DAVID *   PVT   CO. F   AGE:26
SWORN: OCT 12, 1861/3 YRS   MUSTER: NOV 4, 1864
BORN: FREEPORT, PA   OCCUPATION: LABORER
HEIGHT: 5' 5"   COMPLEXION: DARK   EYES: GREY   HAIR: BLACK
SEVERLY WOUNDED/FACE AT STONES RIVER ON DEC 31, 1862

ALTER, JOHN M. "MILTON" *   2ND CPL   CO. F   AGE:22
SWORN: OCT 12, 1861/3 YRS   MUSTER: NOV 4, 1864
BORN: FREEPORT, PA   OCCUPATION: TINNER
HEIGHT: 5' 11½"   COMPLEXION: LIGHT   EYES: BLUE   HAIR: LIGHT
REUNION FREEPORT 1886   HOME 1886-1890: EAST BRADY, PA
BECAME HE WAS AN INVALID; THE 1900 REGIMENTAL REUNION PURCHASED AN
"INVALID CHAIR" FOR MILTON ALTER.

ALTMAN, HAMILTON*   PVT   CO. K   AGE: 21
SWORN: OCT 12, 1861/3 YRS   DIED: JAN 3, 1863
BORN: ARMSTRONG COUNTY   OCCUPATION: FARMER
HEIGHT: 6' ¾"   COMPLEXION: FAIR   EYES: GREY HAIR: FAIR
MORTALLY WOUNDED AT STONES RIVER/THIGH

ALTMAN, LEVI   PVT   CO. C   AGE: 21
SWORN: OCT 12, 1861/3 YRS   MEDICAL: DEC 4, 1862
BORN: ARMSTRONG COUNTY
HEIGHT: 5' 5"   COMPLEXION: DARK   EYES: BROWN   HAIR: BLACK

ALTMAN, SOLOMON*   3RD CPL CO. C   AGE: 42
SWORN: OCT 12, 1861/3 YRS   MEDICAL: JUN 27, 1862   VETERAN
BORN: CLARION COUNTY
HEIGHT: 6' 4"   COMPLEXION: DARK   EYES: GREY
SOLOMON ALTMAN JOINED CO. K OF THE 14th Cav AS A PVT.
SWORN: FEB 23, 1864   DISCHARGED: ≅MAY 31, 1865

ALWINE, FRANCIS*   PVT   CO. K   AGE: 19
SWORN: OCT 12, 1861/3 YRS   MUSTER: NOV 4, 1864
BORN: ADAMS COUNTY   OCCUPATION: MILLER IN BUTLER COUNTY
HEIGHT: 5' 10"   COMPLEXION: FAIR   EYES: GREY HAIR: FAIR
BURIED: ST. MARY'S OF THE ASSUMPTION CEMETERY, HERMAN, PA: 1842-1912
FRANCIS ALWINE'S FIRST WIFE WAS MARY M. HINCHBERGER THE SISTER OF
CHRISTIAN HINCHBERGER, CO. H.
1886 REUNION IN FREEPORT   HOME 1886: SAXONBURG, PA

ALWINE, LEWIS ***   PVT   CO. K   AGE: 20
SWORN: FEB 24, 1864/3 YRS   MUSTER: SEP 11, 1865
HEIGHT: 5' 9"   COMPLEXION: FAIR   EYES: BLUE   HAIR: FAIR
BORN: BUTLER COUNTY   OCCUPATION: BLACKSMITH
JOINED TO BE WITH HIS BROTHER FRANCIS ALWINE ALSO OF CO. K

AMES, JAMES **   PVT   CO. C
SWORN: OCT 12, 1861/3 YRS   NOT AT FINAL MUSTER

ANCHORS, ALLEN   CPL   CO. E   AGE:25
SWORN: OCT 12, 1861/3 YRS   MUSTER: NOV 4, 1864
BORN: CLARION COUNTY   OCCUPATION: FARMER
HEIGHT: 5' 11"   COMPLEXION: SANDY   EYES: BLUE   HAIR: SANDY
PROMOTED TO CPL, NOV 1, 1862
BRIEFLY MISSING IN ACTION AT STONES RIVER

ANCHORS, JAMES H.   1LT   CO. E   AGE:27
SWORN: OCT 12, 1861/3 YRS   MUSTER: NOV 4, 1864
BORN: CLARION COUNTY   OCCUPATION: FARMER
HEIGHT: 5' 10"   COMPLEXION: SANDY   EYES: BLUE   HAIR: SANDY
WOUNDED, TAKEN PRISONER AT STONES RIVER/LEG; PAROLED
PROMOTED FROM 2LT, APR 27, 1863

1886 REUNION IN FREEPORT: HOME, EMLENTON, PA
HOME 1897: CROTHERS, WASHINGTON COUNTY, PA
HIS WOUNDS MADE HIM LAME FOR THE REST OF HIS LIFE   DIED: CROTHERS, PA
ANDERSON, JONATHAN   PVT   CO. D   AGE:40
   SWORN: OCT 12, 1861/3 YRS   MEDICAL: JAN 20, 1863
   BORN: CAMBRIA COUNTY   OCCUPATION: LABORER
   HEIGHT: 5' 7½"   COMPLEXION: FAIR   EYES: BLUE   HAIR: SANDY
   1890 CENSUS: KIMMEL, INDIANA COUNTY, PA
   BURIED: INDIANA COUNTY, PA, McDOWELL CEMETERY, GREEN TWP., 1822-FEB 14, 1898
ANDERSON, WILLIAM G.   PVT   CO. H   AGE:29
   BORN: MERCER COUNTY   OCCUPATION: WAGON MAKER
   HEIGHT: 5' 11¼"   COMPLEXION: FAIR   EYES: DARK   HAIR: BLACK
   SWORN: OCT 12, 1861/3YRS   DIED: MAY 9, 1864
   DIED AT CHATTANOOGA, TN OF HEART DISEASE
ANGLES, JACOB J.   PVT   CO. H   AGE: 18
   ORIGIN: NEW BETHLEHEM; ENLISTED BY CAPTAIN BRINKER
   SWORN: MAR 14, 1863/3 YRS   TRANS:JUL 27, 1863 TO VRC
   BORN: ELK COUNTY   OCCUPATION: MINER   BOUNTY $29
   HEIGHT: 5' 6½"   COMPLEXION: LIGHT EYES: GREY   HAIR: LIGHT
   DIED AT CLARION, PA BEFORE THE REGIMENTAL HISTORY WAS PUBLISHED IN 1905
ANGLESS, JACOB J. #   PVT
   BURIAL RECORDS AT NASHVILLE INDICATE THAT THIS SOLDIER DIED AUG 5, 1863,
   AND IS BURIED AT NATIONAL CEMETERY IN NASHVILLE, GRAVE #E-141
   NOT LISTED IN THE REGIMENTAL HISTORY OF 1905
ARMSTRONG, CHARLES   PVT   CO. E   AGE:19
   SWORN: OCT 12, 1861/3 YRS   MUSTER: NOV 4, 1864
   HEIGHT: 6'   COMPLEXION: FAIR   EYES: BLUE   HAIR: DARK
ARMSTRONG, CHARLES JACKSON
ANDERSON, JACKSON   PVT   CO. E   AGE: 19
   SWORN: AUG 28, 1862/3 YRS   DISCHARGED: JUN 19, 1865
   BORN: JEFFERSON COUNTY   OCCUPATION: LABORER
   HEIGHT: 6'   COMPLEXION: FAIR   EYES: BLUE   HAIR: DARK
   1886 REUNION IN FREEPORT: HOME, PETROLIA, PA
   HOME IN NOV 1897: MAGIC, BUTLER COUNTY, PA
ASH, MICHAEL ***   PVT   CO. F   AGE: 42
   ORIGIN: BUTLER COUNTY
   SWORN: FEB 26, 1864/3 YRS   DISCHARGED: MAY 13, 1865
   BORN: IRELAND   OCCUPATION: LABORER
   HEIGHT: 5' 7"   COMPLEXION: DARK   EYES: BLUE   HAIR: DARK
ASHBAUGH, HEZEKIAH V.*   SGT   CO. I   AGE:21
   SWORN: OCT 12, 1861/3 YRS   MUSTER: NOV 4, 1864
   BORN: LEECHBURG, PA   OCCUPATION: FARMER
   HEIGHT: 6'   COMPLEXION: DARK   EYES: BROWN   HAIR: BLACK
   BRIEFLY MISSING IN ACTION AT STONES RIVER
   PROMOTED FROM 6TH CPL APR 30, 1863
   P0 BOX 1886-1914: BOX #835, LEECHBURG, ARMSTRONG COUNTY, PA
   1890 CENSUS, ASHBAUGH WESTMORELAND COUNTY, PA
   REUNION IN FREEPORT 1886, CHICKAMAUGA 1897, PUNXSUTAWNEY 1899,
   KITTANNING 1900, 1901 INDIANA 1908
   SERVED AS PRESIDENT OF THE REUNION ASSOCIATION
AYRES, HUGH ALFRED "ALF"   CPT   CO. H   AGE:22
AYERS, HUGH A.   ORIGIN: BUTLER COUNTY
   SWORN: OCT 12, 1861/3YRS   MUSTER: NOV 4, 1864
   BORN: BUTLER COUNTY   OCCUPATION: ARTIST
   HEIGHT: 5' 10¾"   COMPLEXION: LIGHT   EYES: HAZEL   HAIR: LIGHT
   SUFFERED FROM FEVER IN EARLY 1862
   MEN OF HIS CO. PURCHASED HIM A SWORD WHEN HE WAS STILL A LIEUTENANT
   COMMENDED BY COL JOHN MILLER FOR COURAGE WHILE ACTING AS
   BRIGADE VOLUNTEER AIDE-DE-CAMP AT THE BATTLE OF STONES RIVER.
   PROMOTED FOR BRAVERY AT STONES RIVER TO FIRST LT   FEB 17, 1863.
   PROMOTED TO CPT APR 16, 1863
   COMMENDED BY BLAKELEY FOR BRAVERY AT CHICKAMAUGA

REUNION IN FREEPORT 1886, KITTANNING 1900, 1901
HOME 1886: HARRISVILLE, PA, 1897: BUTLER, PA

BAILEY, WILLIAM C. *   PVT   CO. K   AGE: 36
SWORN: OCT 12, 1861/3 YRS   DESERTED: DEC 14, 1862
BORN: ALLEGHENY COUNTY   OCCUPATION: BAKER
HEIGHT: 5' 6½"   COMPLEXION: DARK   EYES: BROWN   HAIR: BLACK

BAILEY, WILLIAM D.   SURGEON
REGIMENTAL STAFF   ORIGIN: YORK COUNTY
SWORN: MAR 14, 1863/3 YRS   MUSTER: NOV 4, 1864
PROMOTED FROM ASSISTANT SURGEON JUL 26, 1864
HOME 1886: DILLSBURG, PA

BAIR, JAMES C.*   CPL   CO. I   AGE: 21
SWORN: OCT 12, 1861/3 YRS   MUSTER: NOV 4, 1864
BORN: APOLLO, PA   OCCUPATION: BLACKSMITH
HEIGHT: 5' 10"   COMPLEXION: FAIR   EYES: GREY   HAIR: LIGHT
PROMOTED TO CPL, MAR 1, 1863
1890 CENSUS: LONG RUN, ARMSTRONG COUNTY, PA
HOME 1911: OLIVET, ARMSTRONG COUNTY, PA
BURIED EVERGREEN CEMETERY, LEECHBURG, PA

BAIR, GEORGE *   PVT   CO. I   AGE: 18
SWORN: OCT 12, 1861/3 YRS   MUSTER: NOV 4, 1864
BORN: APOLLO, PA   OCCUPATION: LABORER
HEIGHT: 5' 9"   COMPLEXION: SANDY   EYES: GREY   HAIR: LIGHT
BURIED EVERGREEN CEMETERY, LEECHBURG, PA; DIED BEFORE 1905

BAIRD, WILLIAM   PVT   CO. C   AGE:22
BAID, WILLIAM
SWORN: OCT 12, 1861/3 YRS   MUSTER: NOV 4, 1864
BORN: IRELAND
HEIGHT: 5' 7½"   COMPLEXION: FAIR   EYES: GREY   HAIR: SANDY

BAKER, MARION M.   PVT   CO. I   AGE: 18
SWORN: OCT 12, 1861/3 YRS   MUSTER: NOV 4, 1864
ORIGINAL ENLISTMENT IN CO. E
BORN: CLARION COUNTY   OCCUPATION: FARMER
HEIGHT: 5' 10"   COMPLEXION: DARK   EYES: BLUE   HAIR: DARK

BAKER, MORRISON M.*   PVT   CO. I
BAKER, MARION M.   BORN: CLARION, PA
SWORN: OCT 12, 1861/3 YRS   DESERTED: OCT 14, 1864 AT MADISON

BALLENTINE THEODORE J.   PVT   CO. A   AGE:18
SWORN: OCT 12, 1861/3 YRS   MUSTER: NOV 4, 1864
BORN: CAMBRIA COUNTY   OCCUPATION: FARMER
HEIGHT: 5' 7"   COMPLEXION: DARK   EYES: BLACK   HAIR: BLACK
REUNION IN FREEPORT 1886
HOME 1897: EAST LIBERTY, PITTSBURGH, PA
HOME 1914: 145 MAYFLOWER ST, PITTSBURGH, PA

BARKEY, DAVID *   5th SGT   CO. D   AGE:25
SWORN: OCT 12, 1861/3 YRS   TRANS: JAN 30, 1864 TO VRC
BORN: INDIANA COUNTY, HILLSDALE   OCCUPATION: FARMER
HEIGHT: 5' 4"   COMPLEXION: FAIR   EYES: GREY
DIED BEFORE THE REGIMENTAL HISTORY WAS PUBLISHED IN 1905

BARKEY, ROBERT A.   PVT   CO. D   AGE:19
SWORN: OCT 12, 1861/3 YRS   MUSTER: APR 27, 1864
BORN: INDIANA COUNTY, HILLSDALE   OCCUPATION: FARMER
HEIGHT: 5' 2"   COMPLEXION: DARK   EYES: GREY   HAIR: FAIR
BURIED: INDIANA COUNTY, OLD FAIRVIEW CEMETERY, GRANT TWP.
BORN: 1842 DIED: APR 27, 1864

BARKLEY, DAVID   LT COL   STAFF
REGIMENTAL STAFF   OCCUPATION: LAWYER, FROM BUTLER
SWORN: OCT 12, 1861/3 YRS   RESIGNED: OCT 19, 1861
RESIGNED BECAUSE OF A DISPUTE WITH COLONEL SIRWELL
U.S. CONGRESSMAN [XXXIV CONGRESS] FROM PUNXSUTAWNEY, JEFFERSON COUNTY.
DIED: FREEPORT, PA, SEP 10, 1889

BARNABY, ALBIN M.   HOSP STEW   STAFF   AGE: 40

HEIGHT: 5' 8"   COMPLEXION: DARK   EYES: BLUE   HAIR: BROWN
SWORN: OCT 12, 1861/3 YRS   MUSTER: NOV 4, 1864
BORN: SALOP, ENGLAND   OCCUPATION: CLERK
ENLISTED AS A 1st MUSICIAN IN CO. E;   PROMOTED FROM PVT NOV 1, 1863
1886 REUNION IN FREEPORT, HOME: VANBUREN, PA

BARNETT, DANIEL   PVT   CO. E   AGE: 19
BORN: AUG 13, 1845 IN BEAVER TWP., CLARION COUNTY TO JOSEPH AND
MARY BENNETT BARNETT
SWORN: MAR 31, 1864/3 YRS   MUSTER: SEP 11, 1865
BORN: CLARION COUNTY   OCCUPATION: FARMER
HEIGHT: 5'3"   COMPLEXION: DARK   EYES: BLUE   HAIR: BROWN
1890 CENSUS: KNOX, CLARION COUNTY, PA; WIFE: MARY ALBERT STANFORD

BARNETT, DANIEL H. *   CPL   CO. B   AGE:19
SWORN: OCT 12, 1861/3 YRS   MUSTER: NOV 4, 1864
BORN: ARMSTRONG COUNTY   OCCUPATION: FARMER
HEIGHT: 5' 7"   COMPLEXION: DARK   EYES: BLACK   HAIR: BLACK
PROMOTED TO CPL, JUN 26, 1863
HOME 1897-1914: OLANTA, CLEARFIELD COUNTY, PA
REUNION CHICKAMAUGA 1897, INDIANA 1908

BARNETT, WILLIAM C. *   SGT   CO. K   AGE: 21
SWORN: OCT 12, 1861/3 YRS   MUSTER: NOV 4, 1864
BORN: ARMSTRONG COUNTY   OCCUPATION: FARMER
HEIGHT: 5' 5¼"   COMPLEXION: FAIR   EYES: BROWN   HAIR: AUBURN
BORN: 1839   DIED: 1925   WIFE: SARAH
BURIED: WORTHINGTON PRESBYTERIAN CEMETERY, WORTHINGTON, PA
PROMOTED FROM CPL, MAY 26, 1862,
REUNION CHICKAMAUGA 1897, KITTANNING 1901
HOME 1890-1914: KITTANNING, PA

BARNHARD, HUBER*   4TH SGT   CO. G   AGE:44
HUBER, BERNARD   ORDERLY SERGEANT
BORN: WURTEMBERG, GERMANY NOV 6, 1819
SERVED 5 YEARS IN THE GERMAN ARMY
BORN: RURAL VALLEY, PA   OCCUPATION: TAILOR
HEIGHT: 5' 8"   COMPLEXION: FAIR   EYES: BLUE   HAIR: SANDY
SWORN: OCT 12, 1861/3 YRS   MUSTER: NOV 4, 1864
SON LEWIS: PA 55th, CO. G; DIED @ BEAUFORT, S.C. ON JAN 5, 1863
DIED: JULY OF 1891 @ RURAL VALLEY

BARR, GEORGE #   PVT   CO. I
SWORN: OCT 12, 1861/3 YRS   MUSTER: NOV 4, 1864
POSSIBLY GEORGE BAIR
1890 CENSUS: IRWIN, WESTMORELAND COUNTY, PA

BARR, JOHN T. *   PVT   CO. F   AGE:24
SWORN: OCT 12, 1861/3 YRS   MUSTER: NOV 4, 1864
BORN: FREEPORT, PA   OCCUPATION: LABORER
HEIGHT: 6' 1"   COMPLEXION: LIGHT   EYES: GREY   HAIR: LIGHT
CAPTURED @ STONES RIVER; RETURNED TO REGT JUN 6, 1863
DIED BEFORE THE REGIMENTAL HISTORY WAS PUBLISHED IN 1905
1886 REUNION IN FREEPORT
HOME, NORRISVILLE, PA

BARRACKMAN, E.S.   PVT   CO. E   AGE: 38
BARRACKMAN, ELIJAH SNYDER
SWORN: SEP 1862/3 YRS   TRANS: MAY 1, 1864 TO VRC
BORN: CLARION COUNTY   OCCUPATION: LABORER
HEIGHT: 5' 9"   COMPLEXION: DARK   EYES: BLUE   HAIR: DARK
HOME 1890-1897: BUTLER, PA   DIED: NOV 4, 1898
WIFE: JANE SPRINGER
ELIJAH'S BROTHER DAVID R.P. BARRACKMAN WAS A PVT IN CO. C,   PA 139th INFANTRY;
WHO SAW ACTION @ BATTLES: FREDERICKSBURG, CHANCELLORSVILLE, GETTYSBURG,
WILDERNESS, SPOTTSYLVANIA, COLD HARBOR,   PETERSBURG, WINCHESTER,
CEDAR CREEK

BARRETT, THEODORE "TEDDIE"* MUS   CO. I   AGE:14
SWORN: APR 22, 1861/3 MONTHS, CO B, NINTH PENNSYLVANIA

SWORN: OCT 12, 1861/3 YRS   MUSTER: NOV 4, 1864   VETERAN
BORN: KITTANNING, PA   OCCUPATION: STUDENT
HEIGHT: 5' 4½"   COMPLEXION: LIGHT   EYES: GREY   HAIR: LIGHT
HOME 1914: BELTZ BLDG., PHILADELPHIA, PA
REUNION KITTANNING 1900, 1901

BARTLEBAUGH, MATHIAS   PVT   CO. D   AGE:50
ORIGIN: GREEN TWP., INDIANA COUNTY
SWORN: OCT 12, 1861/3 YRS   MEDICAL: APR 29, 1863
BORN: INDIANA COUNTY, COOKPORT   OCCUPATION: FARMER
HEIGHT: 5' 9½"   COMPLEXION: DARK   EYES: BLUE   HAIR: GREY
DIED BEFORE THE REGIMENTAL HISTORY WAS PUBLISHED IN 1905
ENLISTED WITH HIS GRANDSON, JEREMIAH COOK [ALSO CO. D] OF THE 78TH
BURIED: INDIANA COUNTY, UNIONTOWN CEMETERY, GREEN TWP.

BARTLEBAUGH, SAMUEL   PVT   CO. D   AGE:18
BRATTLEBAUGH, SAMUEL
SWORN: OCT 12, 1861/3 YRS   MUSTER: NOV 4, 1864
BORN: INDIANA COUNTY, HILLSDALE   OCCUPATION: LABORER
HEIGHT: 5' 5"   COMPLEXION: FAIR   EYES: BROWN   HAIR: SANDY
1890 CENSUS: PURCHASE LINE, INDIANA COUNTY, PA
DIED: APR or MAY 1907 AT GLEN CAMPBELL, PA

BARTLEY, DANIEL W.   PVT   CO. E   AGE: 21
BARKLEY, DANIEL
SWORN: OCT 12, 1861/3 YRS   MUSTER: NOV 4, 1864
BORN: CLARION COUNTY   OCCUPATION: FARMER
HEIGHT: 5' 7"   COMPLEXION: LIGHT   EYES: BLUE   HAIR: LIGHT
1890 CENSUS: POLLOCK, CLARION COUNTY, PA

BARTLEY, WILLIAM   PVT   CO. C   AGE: 19
SWORN: AUG 28, 1862/3 YRS   DISCHARGED: JUN 19, 1865.
BORN: CLARION COUNTY   OCCUPATION: FARMER
HEIGHT: 5' 6"   COMPLEXION: FAIR   EYES: BROWN   HAIR: DARK

BATHELL, DANIEL   3RD SGT   CO. A   AGE: 23
BOTHELL, DANIEL
SWORN: OCT 12, 1861/3 YRS   MEDICAL: MAR 21, 1863.
BORN: INDIANA COUNTY   OCCUPATION: FARMER
HEIGHT: 5' 9"   HAIR: RED   EYES: BLUE   COMPLEXION: LIGHT

BAYLOR, LEANDER H.   PVT   CO. A   AGE:19
BAILOR, LEANDER   ORIGIN: INDIANA COUNTY, PA
SWORN: OCT 12, 1861/3 YRS   TRANS: 4TH CAV, DEC 1, 1862.
BORN: INDIANA COUNTY   OCCUPATION: LABORER
HEIGHT: 5' 6"   COMPLEXION: FAIR   EYES: GREY   HAIR: DARK
WOUNDED AT ROME, GA
REUNION IN FREEPORT 1886, INDIANA 1908   HOME 1886: INDIANA, PA

BAYNE, JOHN *   PVT   CO. B   AGE:25
BAIN, JOHN
SWORN: OCT 12, 1861/3 YRS   MUSTER: NOV 4, 1864
BORN: ARMSTRONG COUNTY   OCCUPATION: FARMER
HEIGHT: 5' 7"   COMPLEXION: LIGHT   EYES: BLUE   HAIR: RED
1890 CENSUS: MAHONING, ARMSTRONG COUNTY, PA
HOME 1897-1901: KITTANNING, PA   REUNION IN KITTANNING 1901

BEAL, PETER *   PVT   CO. B   AGE: 25
BEED, PETER   BEAR, PETER   BEER, PETER
SWORN: FEB 27, 1864/3 YRS   MUSTER: SEP 11, 1865
BORN: ARMSTRONG COUNTY   OCCUPATION: FARMER
HEIGHT: 6' 2"   COMPLEXION: LIGHT   EYES: BLACK   HAIR: LIGHT
1890 CENSUS: BETHEL TWP., ARMSTRONG COUNTY, PA

BEALL, PETER*   PVT   CO. K   AGE:22
SWORN: FEB 24, 1864/3 YRS   MUSTER: SEP 11, 1865
BORN: VENANGO COUNTY   OCCUPATION: FARMER
HEIGHT: 5' 6"   COMPLEXION: DARK   EYES: HAZEL   HAIR: DARK

BEAR, GEORGE *   PVT   CO. B   AGE:19
BIER, GEORGE
SWORN: OCT 12, 1861/3 YRS   DIED: NOV, 16, 1863 AT CHATTANOOGA

BORN: ARMSTRONG COUNTY   OCCUPATION: FARMER
HEIGHT: 5' 7"   COMPLEXION: LIGHT   EYES: LIGHT   HAIR: LIGHT
BECK, ADAM   CPL   CO. D   AGE:20
    SWORN: OCT 12, 1861/3 YRS   MUSTER: NOV 4, 1864
    PROMOTED FROM PVT
    BORN: INDIANA COUNTY, COOKPORT   OCCUPATION: LABORER
    HEIGHT: 5' 7½"   COMPLEXION: FAIR   EYES: GREY   HAIR: DARK
    REUNION FREEPORT 1886, CHICKAMAUGA 1897, INDIANA 1908
    HOME 1886-1914: SYLVIS, CLEARFIELD COUNTY, PA
BECK, MATTHIAS   PVT   CO. D   AGE: 28
    SWORN: AUG 25, 1862/3 YRS   MEDICAL: OCT 3, 1863
    BORN: INDIANA COUNTY, NEW SALEM   OCCUPATION: FARMER
    HEIGHT: 5' 9"   COMPLEXION: FAIR   EYES: BLUE   HAIR: DARK
    1890 CENSUS: RED BANK, ARMSTRONG COUNTY, PA, DIED BEFORE 1905
BECKET, WILLIAM *   PVT   CO. G   AGE:24
BERKET, WILLIAM
    SWORN: OCT 12, 1861/3 YRS   TRANS: NOV 30, 1862 TO 4th CAV
    BORN: KITTANNING, PA   OCCUPATION: FARMER
    HEIGHT: 5' 9"   COMPLEXION: DARK   EYES: BLUE   HAIR: BROWN
BEIGHLEY, JOSEPH H. #   PVT78th   CO. B
    SWORN: AUG 12, 1861/3 YRS   MUSTERED: NOV 4, 1864
    1890 CENSUS: WEST VALLEY, ARMSTRONG COUNTY, PA; WIDOW MARY
BELL, JAMES S.   2 MUSICIAN   CO. D   AGE: 18
    SWORN: OCT 12, 1861/3 YRS   DIED: JAN 3, 1863 AT MURFREESBORO
    BORN: BRADY BEND   OCCUPATION: FARMER
    HEIGHT: 5' 6½"   COMPLEXION: FAIR   EYES: BLUE   HAIR: BROWN
    MORTALLY WOUNDED AT STONES RIVER
BELL, LEANDER   PVT   CO. C
    SWORN: FEB 24, 1864/3 YRS   MUSTER: SEP 11, 1865
BELL, THOMPSON M.   2ND SGT   CO. D   AGE:26
BELL, THOMAS
    SWORN: OCT 12, 1861/3 YRS   DIED: MAR 20, 1863 AT MURFREESBORO AT 10:30 AM
    BORN: INDIANA COUNTY, CHAMBERSVILLE   OCCUPATION: TEACHER
    HEIGHT: 5' 8½"   COMPLEXION: FAIR   EYES: BROWN
    MORTALLY WOUNDED STONES RIVER
    COMMENDED BY SIRWELL FOR BRAVERY AT STONES RIVER
    BURIED AT NATIONAL CEMETERY STONES RIVER, GRAVE #M-5049
BELL, WILLIAM *   PVT   CO. B   AGE:30
    SWORN: APR 22, 1861/3 MONTHS, CO B, NINTH PENNSYLVANIA
    SIRWELL'S BRADY ALPINES
    SWORN: OCT 12, 1861/3 YRS   MUSTER: NOV 4, 1864   VETERAN
    BORN: INDIANA COUNTY   OCCUPATION: FARMER
    HEIGHT: 6'   COMPLEXION: DARK   EYES: BLACK   HAIR: BLACK
    1890 CENSUS: DEE, ARMSTRONG COUNTY, PA
    HOME 1897: TEMPLETON, ARMSTRONG COUNTY, PA
    HOME 1914: HORTON, PA   REUNION CHICKAMAUGA 1897
BELL, WILLIAM W.   1ST CPL   CO. A   AGE:22
    SWORN: OCT 12, 1861/3 YRS   MEDICAL: MAR 23, 1863.
    HEIGHT: 5' 10"   HAIR: SANDY   EYES: GREY   COMPLEXION: LIGHT
BELTZ, ANDREW J. *   PVT   CO. A   AGE:20
BETZ, ANDREW J.
    SWORN: OCT 12, 1861/3 YRS   MUSTER: NOV 4, 1864
    BORN: INDIANA COUNTY   OCCUPATION: FARMER
    HEIGHT: 5' 9"   COMPLEXION: DARK   EYES: BROWN   HAIR: DARK
    HOME 1897-1914: PLUMVILLE, INDIANA COUNTY, PA
    REUNION CHICKAMAUGA 1897, INDIANA 1908.
    BURIED: INDIANA COUNTY, BARACHA CEMETERY, SOUTH MAHONING TWP.,
    APR 1, 1841-NOV 18, 1915
BENGOUGH, HERBERT H. "HOOF"   CPL***   CO. K   AGE:18
    SWORN: OCT 12, 1861/3 YRS   MUSTER: NOV 4, 1864   VETERAN
    BORN: ALLEGHENY COUNTY   OCCUPATION: PRINTER
    HEIGHT: 5' 4"   COMPLEXION: FAIR   EYES: GREY   HAIR: FAIR

PROMOTED TO CPL MAY 27, 1862   WOUNDED AT STONES RIVER
SERVED WITH PA 104TH, CO. K: MAR 18-AUG 25, 1865 NEAR   PETERSBURG, VA.
HOME IN NOV 1897/1914: 7724 HAMILTON AVE., PITTSBURGH, PA
SERVED AS SECRETARY OF THE COMMITTEE THAT ERECTED THE SOLDIERS AND
SAILORS MEMORIAL IN PITTSBURGH, PA
SERVED AS A CIVIL WAR PENSION COMMISSIONER
ELECTED SECRETARY OF THE 78th REUNION COMMITTEE IN 1886
REUNION FREEPORT 1886, CHICKAMAUGA 1897, PUNXSUTAWNEY 1899,
KITTANNING 1900-1901, INDIANA 1908   HOME 1886-1901: PITTSBURGH, PA
MAME SIRWELL, COLONEL SIRWELL'S DAUGHTER, SERVED AS HIS CLERK IN NOV 1890

BENNETT, ABRAHAM   PVT   CO. G   AGE:40
    SWORN: OCT 12, 1861/3 YRS   DESERTED: MAR 30, 1864   VETERAN
    BORN: PITTSBURGH, PA   OCCUPATION: LABORER
    HEIGHT: 5' 8½"   COMPLEXION: DARK   EYES: BROWN   HAIR: SANDY
    RE-ENLISTED AND DESERTED WHILE AT HOME IN GRATIOT, OHIO - NEAR NEWARK -
    WHILE ON VETERAN FURLOUGH

BERGER, WILLIAM   PVT   CO. E   AGE: 25
BARGER, WILLIAM   BARGER, W.
    SWORN: OCT 12, 1861/3 YRS   DIED: DEC 10, 1861 AT LOUISVILLE
    BORN: CLARION COUNTY   OCCUPATION: LUMBERMAN
    HEIGHT: 5' 7"   COMPLEXION: SANDY   EYES: BLUE   HAIR: SANDY
    BURIED @ CAVE HILL CEMETERY, LOUISVILLE, KY

BEST, MICHAEL B.   PVT   CO. B   AGE:24
    SWORN: AUG 25, 1863/3 YRS   DISCHARGED: JUL 29, 1865.
    BORN: ARMSTRONG COUNTY   OCCUPATION: FARMER
    HEIGHT: 5' 6"   COMPLEXION: FAIR   EYES: GREY   HAIR: DARK

BIER, PETER   PVT   CO. B
BEED, PETER
    SWORN: OCT 12, 1861/3 YRS   TRANS: VRC, JUN 27, 1863

BIEREY, JEREMIAH   PVT   CO. E   AGE: 19
BEERY, JEREMIAH
    SWORN: OCT 12, 1861/3 YRS   NOT AT FINAL MUSTER
    BORN: CLARION COUNTY   OCCUPATION: LUMBERMAN
    HEIGHT: 5' 7"   COMPLEXION: DARK   EYES: BROWN   HAIR: DARK

BIGELOW, LORENZO D. *   CPL   CO. A   AGE:47
    SWORN: OCT 12, 1861/3 YRS   MUSTER: NOV 4, 1864
    BORN: INDIANA COUNTY   OCCUPATION: CARPENTER
    HEIGHT: 5' 6"   COMPLEXION: DARK   EYES: GREY   HAIR: DARK
    PROMOTED FROM PVT   1886 REUNION IN FREEPORT
    HOME 1886: PLUMVILLE, PA
    BURIED: INDIANA COUNTY, PLUMVILLE PRESBYTERIAN CEMETERY, SOUTH MAHONING
    SEP 10, 1834-FEB 23, 1892

BIRCH, JOHN   PVT   CO. H   AGE:24
    SWORN: OCT 12, 1861/3YRS   DIED: APR 22, 1862 AT LOUISVILLE OF CONSUMPTION
    BORN: BUTLER COUNTY   OCCUPATION: LABORER
    HEIGHT: 5' 11"   COMPLEXION: FAIR   EYES: BLUE   HAIR: LIGHT
    DATE OF DEATH CORRECTED FROM LOWRY LETTERS
    BURIED: NATIONAL CEMETERY LOUISVILLE; SECTION.A, RANGE.21, GRAVE.1

BIRCH, WILLIAM   PVT   CO. H   AGE:28
BORCH, WILLIAM   BOUNTY: $100
    SWORN: OCT 12, 1861/3YRS   MUSTER: NOV 4, 1864
    BORN: BUTLER COUNTY   OCCUPATION: MASON
    HEIGHT: 5' 8½"   COMPLEXION: FAIR   EYES: GREY   HAIR: LIGHT
    DETAILED TO FIRST KY BATTERY AT STONES RIVER.

BLACK, GEORGE WASHINGTON   1LT   CO. I   AGE:43
    SWORN: OCT 12, 1861/3 YRS   MUSTER: NOV 4, 1864
    BORN: APOLLO, PA   OCCUPATION: GROCER
    HEIGHT: 5' 8"   COMPLEXION: DARK   EYES: GREY   HAIR: BLACK
    COMMANDED COMPANY FROM AUG 1863-NOV 1864
    DIED BEFORE 1905 @ SOUTH BEND, PA; NO INFORMATION; GOVERNMENT STONE
    U.S. PENSION, 1894: $12.00   HOME: GIRTY
    1890 CENSUS: GIRTY, ARMSTRONG COUNTY, PA

BURIED: MT. ZION UNITED METHODIST CEMETERY, GIRTY FLATS, PA
GRANDAUGHTER ELIZABETH BUZZARD SUPPLIED INFORMATION FOR THIS BOOK

BLACK, JOHN A. *   PVT   CO. H   AGE:20

BLACK, JOHN C.   BOUNTY: $100.
SWORN: FEB 26, 1862/3 YRS   DISCHARGED: FEB 26, 1865
BORN: BUTLER COUNTY   OCCUPATION: MINER
HEIGHT: 6' 1½"   COMPLEXION: FAIR EYES: GREY   HAIR: LIGHT
SEPARATED FROM UNIT AT STONES RIVER 12/31/1862
WOUNDED/BREAST & ARM[S] AT STONES RIVER

BLACK, JOHN C.   PVT   CO. H   AGE:18
SWORN: OCT 12, 1861/3YRS   MUSTER: NOV 4, 1864
BORN: MERCER COUNTY   OCCUPATION: BLACKSMITH
HEIGHT: 5' 8¼"   COMPLEXION: FAIR EYES: BROWN   HAIR: DARK
WOUNDED/SHOULDER AT STONES RIVER; DEC 31, 1862
SENT NORTH TO CINCINNATI HOSPITAL ON STEAM SHIP UNDINE
DIED IN MISSOURI BEFORE THE REGIMENTAL HISTORY WAS PUBLISHED IN 1905

BLACK, JOSEPH M.*   PVT   CO. B   AGE:28
SWORN: OCT 12, 1861/3 YRS   MUSTER: NOV 4, 1864
BORN: ARMSTRONG COUNTY   OCCUPATION: FARMER
HEIGHT: 5' 10"   COMPLEXION: DARK EYES: BLUE   HAIR: DARK

BLACK, SAMUEL C. *   PVT   CO. B   AGE:45
SWORN: OCT 12, 1861/3 YRS   DIED: FEB 22, 1862 AT MUNFORDSVILLE, KY
BORN: ARMSTRONG COUNTY   OCCUPATION: FARMER
HEIGHT: 5' 10"   COMPLEXION: DARK EYES: BLACK   HAIR: GREY
1890 CENSUS: DAYTON BOROUGH, ARMSTRONG COUNTY, PA; WIDOW RACHEL

BLACK, WILLIAM H.   2ND CPL   CO. H   AGE:18
SWORN: OCT 12, 1861/3YRS   MUSTER: NOV 4, 1864
BORN: MERCER COUNTY   OCCUPATION: STUDENT
HEIGHT: 5' 7¹/₈"   COMPLEXION: SANDY EYES: HAZEL   HAIR: DARK
BOUNTY: $100.   PROMOTED TO CPL MAY 1, 1863

BLAIR, ISAIAH   PVT   CO. E   AGE: 19
SWORN: OCT 12, 1861/3 YRS   MEDICAL: OCT 20, 1862
BORN: BUTLER COUNTY   OCCUPATION: LABORER
HEIGHT: 5' 8"   COMPLEXION: FAIR   EYES: BLUE   HAIR: BROWN

BLAIR, JOHN W.P.***   CPL   CO. G   AGE:18
SWORN: OCT 12, 1861/4 YRS   MUSTER: SEP 11, 1865   VETERAN
BORN: PITTSBURGH, PA   OCCUPATION: LABORER
HEIGHT: 5' 8"   COMPLEXION: DARK   EYES: BROWN   HAIR: BROWN
PROMOTED FROM PVT
1886 REUNION IN FREEPORT: HOME, MANORVILLE, PA
HOME 1890-1897: MARIASVILLE, VENANGO COUNTY, PA
REUNION CHICKAMAUGA 1897

BLAIR, MILTON *   PVT   CO. K   AGE: 18
SWORN: OCT 12, 1861/3 YRS   MUSTER: NOV 4, 1864
BORN: ARMSTRONG COUNTY   OCCUPATION: FARMER
HEIGHT: 6' 1"   COMPLEXION: FAIR   EYES: GREY   HAIR: FAIR

BLAKELEY, ARCHIBALD   LT COL   STAFF   AGE:34
ORIGIN: BUTLER COUNTY   OCCUPATION: LAWYER
BORN: FORWARD TOWNSHIP, BUTLER COUNTY, PA.
1855 DELEGATE TO FIRST REPUBLICAN CONVENTION IN PITTSBURGH.
BUTLER COUNTY DISTRICT ATTORNEY 1853.
SWORN: OCT 12, 1861/3 YRS   RESIGNED: APR 8, 1864
APPOINTED BY GENERAL BUELL; SERVED AS THE PRESIDENT OF THE GENERAL COURT
MARTIAL & MILITARY COMMISSION DURING APR-AUG, 1862.
BROTHER THOMAS IN PA 78th.
BROTHER HARVEY IN PA 77TH [died 1864]; HE FOUGHT AT SHILOH, STONES RIVER,
TULLAHOMA, MCLEMORE'S COVE, CHICKAMAUGA.
BROTHER WILLIAM LT. COLONEL IN PA 14th CAVALRY; HE HELPED ENLIST MEN FOR
COMPANIES L & M OF THE 14TH; HE FOUGHT @ SKIRMISHES/BATTLES: BEVERLY,
ROCKY GAP RAID, WHITE SULPHUR SPRING, SALEM, MOOREFIELD, CEDAR CREEK,
WINCHESTER, MILLWOOD, ASHBY'S GAP, WOODSTOCK
NOV 1862, ARCHIBALD RETURNED HOME FOR HEALTH REASONS

ALSO COMMANDED 21st WISCONSIN DURING 1863-1864
REUNION IN FREEPORT 1886, CHICKAMAUGA 1897, KITTANNING 1901, INDIANA 1908
HOME 1886-1914: PITTSBURGH, PA   PRESIDENT REGIMENTAL ASSOCIATION IN 1908
PRESIDENT OF PENNSYLVANIA DELEGATION TO CHICKAMAUGA DEDICATION, NOV 1897
COMMANDER U.N.L.   BURIED: SOUTH CEMETERY, BUTLER, PA
BORN: JUL 16/24, 1827   DIED; AUG 27, 1915
WIFE: SUSAN DRUM MECHLING; SEP 27, 1825- AUG 27, 1893

BLAKELEY, THOMAS A.   1LT   STAFF   AGE:25
BLAKELEY, THOMAS G.
    ORIGIN: ARMSTRONG COUNTY   ARCHIBALD BLAKELEY'S BROTHER
    SWORN: OCT 12, 1861/3 YRS   MUSTER: NOV 4, 1864
    BORN: KITTANNING, PA   OCCUPATION: PHYSICIAN
    HEIGHT: 6'   COMPLEXION: FAIR   EYES: BLUE   HAIR: LIGHT
    REGIMENTAL QUARTERMASTER   PROMOTED FROM PVT CO. G
    PROMOTED FROM HOSPITAL STEWARD, NOV 1, 1863.
    HOME 1886-1914: AVALON, MO   DIED: ST. LOUIS, MO

BLUE, DAVID   SGT   CO. A   AGE:25
    BORN: IRELAND FEB 14, 1831; HOME: INDIANA COUNTY
    SWORN: OCT 12, 1861/3 YRS   MUSTER: NOV 4, 1864
    BORN: INDIANA COUNTY   OCCUPATION: FARMER
    HEIGHT: 5' 8"   HAIR: BLACK   EYES: DARK   COMPLEXION: DARK
    PROMOTED FROM 2ND CPL SEP 1, 1863   WIFE: MARGARET SWAN
    HOME 1886-1914: CHAMBERSVILLE, INDIANA COUNTY, PA
    REUNION CHICKAMAUGA 1897, INDIANA 1908
    BURIED: INDIANA COUNTY, WASHINGTON CEMETERY, RAYNE TWP., 1831 APR 30, 1915

BOICE, JOHN   PVT   CO. D   AGE:22
    SWORN: OCT 12, 1861/3 YRS   DIED: SEP 17, 1863 AT MURFREESBORO
    BORN: CLEARFIELD COUNTY   OCCUPATION: FARMER
    HEIGHT: 5' 10"   COMPLEXION: FAIR   EYES: BROWN   HAIR: DARK
    REUNION CHICKAMAUGA 1897

BONEY, GEORGE H.   PVT   CO. K   AGE: 23
    SWORN: OCT 12, 1861/3 YRS   MUSTER: NOV 4, 1864
    BORN: ARMSTRONG COUNTY   OCCUPATION: FARMER
    HEIGHT: 5' 7¾"   COMPLEXION: FAIR   EYES: BLACK   HAIR: FAIR
    LEFT BEHIND AT MANCHESTER, JUN 1863, "NOT STOUT ENOUGH FOR THE MARCH"
    HOME IN NOV 1897-1901:EBENSBURG, CAMBRIA COUNTY, PA
    REUNION CHICKAMAUGA 1897, KITTANNING 1901

BONEY, WILLIAM WILSON*   PVT   CO. K   AGE: 26
BANEY, WILLIAM WILSON   BONEY, W.C.   BOUNTY: $29
    SWORN: SEP 10, 1862/3 YRS   DISCHARGED: JUN 19, 1865
    BORN: ARMSTRONG COUNTY   OCCUPATION: FARMER
    HEIGHT: 5' 8"   COMPLEXION: FAIR   EYES: BLUE   HAIR: DARK
    WOUNDED AT STONES RIVER/FOOT   U.S. PENSION, 1894: $8.00
    HOME 1886-1901: SLATE LICK, ARMSTRONG COUNTY, PA
    REUNION FREEPORT 1886, CHICKAMAUGA 1897, KITTANNING 1901

BOND, RICHARD *   PVT   CO. I   AGE: 22
    SWORN: OCT 12, 1861/3 YRS   MUSTER: NOV 4, 1864
    BORN: SMICKSBURG   OCCUPATION: LABORER
    HEIGHT: 5' 10"   COMPLEXION: SANDY   EYES: GREY   HAIR: DARK
    REUNION IN FREEPORT 1886   HOME 1886: PITTSBURGH, PA

BONNAFFON, AUGUSTUS B. **   LT COL   STAFF   VETERAN
    SWORN: APR 25, 1861   MUSTER: AUG 5, 1861
    4TH SGT, PA 12th; RECRUITED IN PITTSBURGH, SERVED UNDER NEGLEY
    SWORN: OCT 12, 1861/4 YRS   MUSTER: DEC 14, 1865
    SERVED AS MAJOR UNDER SIRWELL; CAPTURED AT LAVERGNE AND EXCHANGED;
    SERVED ON MILLER'S STAFF AT STONES RIVER COMMENDED BY COL JOHN MILLER   AND
    COL SIRWELL FOR BRAVERY AT   STONES RIVER.
    COMMENDED BY BLAKELEY FOR BRAVERY AT CHICKAMAUGA.
    PROMOTED TO LT COLONEL JUL 25, 1864
    PROMOTED TO REGIMENTAL COMMANDER/COLONEL MAR 26, 1865
    JOINED REGULAR ARMY AS FIRST LT   PROMOTED TO TROOP COMMAND
    DIED: 1867 IN INDIANOLA, TEXAS FROM YELLOW FEVER

BONNER, JAMES   PVT   CO. K   AGE: 22
    SWORN: OCT 12, 1861/3 YRS   DIED: JAN 5, 1862 AT LOUISVILLE
    BORN: ARMSTRONG COUNTY   OCCUPATION: FARMER
    HEIGHT: 5' 11"   COMPLEXION: FAIR   EYES: GREY   HAIR: FAIR
    BURIED: UNITED BRETHEREN CHURCH, SLATE LICK, PA
    IN ALL PROBABILITY THIS IS SAMUEL BONNER
BONNER, SAMUEL C.*   PVT   CO. K
BONER, SAMUEL C.
    SWORN: OCT 12, 1861/3 YRS   DIED: JAN 5, 1862 AT LOUISVILLE
    1894 SOLDIERS PENSION: $6/mo HOME: WORTHINGTON/WIDOW
BORLAND, GEORGE G. *   SGT   CO. G   AGE:24
BORELAND, GEORGE G.
    SWORN: OCT 12, 1861/3 YRS   MUSTER: NOV 4, 1864
    BORN: DAYTON, PA   OCCUPATION: FARMER
    HEIGHT: 5' 9"   COMPLEXION: DARK   EYES: BLUE   HAIR: BLACK
    PROMOTED FROM 3RD CPL   WOUNDED AT STONES RIVER DEC 31, 1862/HEEL
    1890 CENSUS: DAYTON BOROUGH, ARMSTRONG COUNTY, PA
    DIED: DAYTON, PA BEFORE 1905
BORLAND, ROBERT C.   5TH CPL   CO. H   AGE:24
BORELAND, ROBERT C.   BOUNTY: $100
    SWORN: OCT 12, 1861/3YRS   MUSTER: NOV 4, 1864
    BORN: BUTLER COUNTY   OCCUPATION: SHOEMAKER
    HEIGHT: 5" 8"   COMPLEXION: DARK   EYES: BROWN   HAIR: BROWN
    PROMOTED TO SGT MAY 1, 1863   DEMOTED SEP 23. 1864, PVT AT MUSTER
    U.S. PENSION, 1894: $6.00   HOME: FREERORT [LISTED AS BORLANK]
    REUNION IN FREEPORT 1886, CHICKAMAUGA 1897
    HOME 1886-1894: FREEPORT, PA
    OWNED A SHOE STORE IN FREEPORT: 1894
    HOME 1897: RENFREW, BUTLER COUNTY, PA
    DIED/ 1903 AT SOLDIERS HOME, MARION, INDIANA
    BROTHER SAMUEL, CPL CO. F.
    BROTHER A.M. BORLAND IN PA 134th AND PA 4th CAVALRY
BORLAND, SAMUEL *   5TH CPL CO. F   AGE:31
BORELAND, SAMUEL
    BORN: FREEPORT   OCCUPATION: SHOEMAKER
    HEIGHT: 5' 8"   COMPLEXION: DARK   EYES: DARK BROWN   HAIR: BLACK
    SWORN: OCT 12, 1861/3 YRS   MUSTER: NOV 4, 1864
    U.S. PENSION, 1894: $12.00
    REUNION IN FREEPORT 1886, CHICKAMAUGA 1897, KITTANNING 1901
    HOME 1886: FREEPORT, PA   HOME 1894: DAYTON, ARMSTRONG COUNTY, PA
    HOME 1897-1914: BUTLER, PA;   BROTHER ROBERT, CPL CO. H.
    BROTHER A.M. BORLAND IN PA 134th AND PA 4th CAVALRY
BORLAND, SAMUEL *   PVI   CO. G   AGE:22
    SWORN: OCT 12, 1861/3 YRS   MUSTER: NOV 4, 1864
    BORN: DAYTON, PA   OCCUPATION: TEACHER
    HEIGHT: 5' 8"   COMPLEXION: FAIR   EYES: BLUE   HAIR: SANDY
    HOME 1890-1901: DAYTON, ARMSTRONG COUNTY, PA
    REUNION CHICKAMAUGA 1897, KITTANNING 1901
BOUGHTON, THOMAS   PVT   CO. D   AGE:40
    SWORN: OCT 12, 1861/3 YRS   MEDICAL: FEB 28, 1863
    BORN: INDIANA COUNTY, ANSONVILLE   OCCUPATION: FARMER
    HEIGHT: 5' 10"   COMPLEXION: DARK   EYES: BROWN   HAIR: BROWN
    DIED BEFORE 1905
BOWERS, ADAM   PVT   CO. D   AGE:20
    SWORN: OCT 12, 1861/3 YRS   MEDICAL: DATE UNKNOWN
    BORN: CAMBRIA COUNTY   OCCUPATION: SHOEMAKER
    HEIGHT: 5' 5½"   COMPLEXION: DARK   EYES: GREY   HAIR: LIGHT
    HOME 1901-1914: GRANT, PA   REUNION KITTANNING 1901
BOWERS, LEWIS *   PVT   CO. F   AGE:22
    SWORN: OCT 12, 1861/3 YRS   MUSTER: NOV 4, 1864
    BORN: LEECHBURG, PA   OCCUPATION: PLASTERER
    HEIGHT: 5' 7"   COMPLEXION: DARK   EYES: BROWN   HAIR: DARK BROWN

SERVED ON LEECHBURG SCHOOL BOARD
BURIED: LEECHBURG CEMETERY, LEECHBURG, PA
BOWSER, HEZEKIAH *   PVT   CO. K   AGE:35
   SWORN: OCT 12, 1861/3 YRS   MEDICAL: JAN 10, 1862
   BORN: ARMSTRONG COUNTY   OCCUPATION: FARMER
   HEIGHT: 5' 6"   COMPLEXION: DARK   EYES: BLACK   HAIR: BLACK
BOWSER, JOHN G. *   PVT   CO. G
   SWORN: SEP 13, 1862/3 YRS   MEDICAL: JUN 29, 1863
   1886 REUNION IN FREEPORT: HOME, TARENTUM, PA
BOWSER, MARK C. *   PVT   CO. K   AGE: 19
   SWORN: OCT 12, 1861/3 YRS   DIED: MAR 12, 1863
   BORN: ARMSTRONG COUNTY   OCCUPATION: FARMER
   HEIGHT: 5' 4½"   COMPLEXION: DARK   EYES: BROWN   HAIR: DARK
   MORTALLY WOUNDED/ SIDE-LUNG AT STONES RIVER
   BURIED AT NATIONAL CEMETERY NASHVILLE, GRAVE #E-865 UNDER MARK C. BROWN
   BURIED: ROGERS CHAPEL CEMETERY, CLINTON, PA
   [MEMORIAL TOMBSTONE OR NEW GRAVE]
   BORN: AUG 9, 1842   DIED; MAR 12, 1863
BOWSER, MATTHAIS A. ***   PVT   CO. B/CO. I   AGE:42
BOWSER, MATTHAIS P.   SERVED AS A TEAMSTER
   CAPTAIN IN STATE MILITIA BEFORE THE WAR
   SWORN: MAR 4, 1862/3 YRS   DISCHARGED: MAR 13, 1865
   BORN: ARMSTRONG COUNTY   OCCUPATION: FARMER
   HEIGHT: 5' 5"   COMPLEXION: FAIR   EYES: BROWN   HAIR: DARK
   REPORTEDLY CAPTURED AND PAROLED [BEERS]
   U.S. PENSION, 1894: $12.00   HOME 1894-1901: MOSGROVE, PA
   REUNION KITTANNING 1901   WIFE: SARAH ANN BAUM
BOWSER, PETER O. *   SGT   CO. G   AGE:31
   SWORN: OCT 12, 1861/3 YRS   DISCHARGED: OCT 12, 1864
   BORN: KITTANNING, PA   OCCUPATION: FARMER
   HEIGHT: 6'   COMPLEXION: DARK   EYES: BLUE   HAIR: SANDY
   PROMOTED FROM 2ND CPL   DIED: KITTANNING, PA
   REUNION IN FREEPORT 1886   1894 SOLDIERS PENSION: $12/mo
   HOME 1886-1890: KITTANNING, ARMSTRONG COUNTY. PA; DIED BEFORE 1905
BOWSER, WASHINGTON R. *   PVT   CO. G   AGE: 17
BOWZER, WASHINGTON R.
   SWORN: AUG 27, 1862/3 YRS   DISCHARGED: JUN 19, 1865
   HOME 1886-1901: KITTANNING, ARMSTRONG COUNTY, PA
   1894 SOLDIERS PENSION: $8/mo   HOME: KITTANNING
   REUNION IN FREEPORT 1886, KITTANNING 1901
   BURIED: KITTANNING CEMETERY 1844-1917; WIFE: CAROLINE JACK
BOWSER, WILLIAM *   PVT   CO. K   AGE: 21
   SWORN: OCT 12, 1861/4 YRS   MUSTER: SEP 11, 1865   VETERAN
   BORN: ARMSTRONG COUNTY   OCCUPATION: LABORER
   HEIGHT: 5' 6"   COMPLEXION: DARK   EYES: BROWN   HAIR: AUBURN
BOWSER, WILLIAM J. *   PVT   CO. G   AGE: 26
   SWORN: OCT 12, 1861/3 YRS   MUSTER: NOV 4, 1864
   BORN: KITTANNING, PA   OCCUPATION: LABORER
   HEIGHT: 5' 7½"   COMPLEXION: FAIR   EYES: BLUE   HAIR: SANDY
   HOME 1897-1901: IRWIN, WESTMORELAND COUNTY, PA
   REUNION CHICKAMAUGA 1897, KITTANNING 1901
BOYD, WILLIAM J.   1ST CPL   CO. H   AGE:19
   ORIGIN: BUTLER COUNTY   BOUNTY: $100.
   SWORN: OCT 12, 1861/3YRS   MUSTER: NOV 4, 1864
   BORN: BUTLER COUNTY   OCCUPATION: CLERK
   HEIGHT: 5' 7$^{1}/_{3}$"   COMPLEXION: FAIR   EYES: BLUE   HAIR: LIGHT
   PROMOTED TO CPL OCT 16, 1862
   CAPTURED BY REBEL GUERRILLAS, NOV 1862; ESCAPED
   HOME 1897-1914: 332 CENTER AVE., BUTLER, PA;   REUNION CHICKAMAUGA 1897
   BURIED: NORTH CEMETERY, BUTLER, PA; 1842-1924
BOYER, LEVI M.   PVT   CO. E   AGE: 19
   SWORN: OCT 12, 1861/3 YRS   MUSTER: NOV 4, 1864

BORN: CLARION COUNTY   OCCUPATION: LABORER
HEIGHT: 5' 8"   COMPLEXION: LIGHT   EYES: BLUE   HAIR: LIGHT
SERVED AS A CPL AT CAMP ORR
HOME 1901-1908: COLUMBUS, OHIO
DID NOT FIGHT AT STONES RIVER ON DEC 31, 1862
BECAME A MINISTER   REUNION KITTANNING 1901
BOYER, MARTIN L.   PVT   CO. E   AGE: 26
　　SWORN: OCT 12, 1861/3 YRS   DIED: DEC 13, 1861 AT LOUISVILLE
　　BORN: UNION COUNTY   OCCUPATION: TEACHER
　　HEIGHT: 5' 8"   COMPLEXION: FAIR   EYES: BLUE   HAIR: DARK
　　BURIED: NATIONAL CEMETERY LOUISVILLE; SECTION.A, RANGE.2, GRAVE.4
BOYER, RALPH   PVT   CO. E   AGE:27
　　SWORN: OCT 12, 1861/3 YRS   MEDICAL: AUG 13, 1863
　　BORN: CLARION COUNTY   OCCUPATION: TEACHER
　　HEIGHT: 5' 7"   COMPLEXION: FAIR   EYES: BLUE   HAIR: BLACK
　　DEMOTED FROM SEVENTH CPL; APPOINTED REGIMENTAL BLACKSMITH
BOYLE, JOHN *   PVT   CO. F   AGE:23
　　SWORN: OCT 12, 1861/3 YRS   MUSTER: NOV 4, 1864
　　BORN: SHEARERS CROSS RDS   OCCUPATION: LABORER
　　HEIGHT: 5' 7"   COMPLEXION: FRESH   EYES: GREY   HAIR: DARK BROWN
BOYLE, MICHAEL *   PVT   CO. F   AGE:25
　　SWORN: OCT 12, 1861/3 YRS   DISCHARGED: MAY 23, 1865
　　BORN: BRADY BEND   OCCUPATION: COLLIER
　　HEIGHT: 5' 9"   COMPLEXION: FRESH   EYES: BLUE   HAIR: DARK BROWN
　　CAPTURED: SEP 20, 1863 AT CHICKAMAUGA; IMPRISONED @ ANDERSONVILLE
BOYLE, PATRICK *   CPL   CO. B   AGE:26
BAYLE, PATRICK
　　SWORN: OCT 12, 1861/3 YRS   TRANS: TO 15 U.S., DATE UNKNOWN
　　BORN: BUTLER COUNTY   OCCUPATION: COLLIER
　　HEIGHT: 6' 1"   COMPLEXION: DARK   EYES: BLACK   HAIR: BLACK
　　BURIED: ST. JOHN'S, COYESVILLE
BOYLE, PETER *   PVT   CO. F   AGE: 19
　　SWORN: OCT 12, 1861/3 YRS   TRANS: AUG 1, 1863 TO VRC
　　BORN: BRADY BEND   OCCUPATION: COLLIER
　　HEIGHT: 5' 9"   COMPLEXION: FAIR   EYES: GREY   HAIR: DARK BROWN
　　WOUNDED AT STONES RIVER/THIGH
BRADEN, ALEXANDER C.   PVT   CO. H   AGE:20
　　SWORN: OCT 12, 1861/3YRS   MUSTER: NOV 4. 1864
　　BOUNTY: $100   DEMOTED FROM FIRST MUSICIAN
　　BORN: LAWRENCE COUNTY   OCCUPATION: FARMER
　　HEIGHT: 5' 9"   COMPLEXION: DARK   EYES: GREY   HAIR: BLACK
　　HOME 1914: 624 LULU ST., PARKERSBURG, WVA
BRADIN, JOHN ***   PVT   CO. F   AGE: 32
BREDIU, JNO.   BRAYDON, JOHN
　　ORIGIN: BUTLER COUNTY; BORN IN BUTLER COUNTY
　　OCCUPATION: GOLD MINER   BOUNTY: $27.75
　　HEIGHT: 5' 8½"   COMPLEXION: SANDY   EYES: BLUE   HAIR: SANDY
　　SWORN: SEP 15, 1863/3 YRS   COMMITTED SUICIDE: JUL 2, 1865
　　SLIT HIS THROAT WITH A RAZOR
　　BURIED @ NASHVILLE, SEC J, GRAVE# 789, BATES
BRADY, JOHN   PVT   CO. E   AGE:19
　　SWORN: OCT 12, 1861/3 YRS   MUSTER: NOV 4, 1864
　　BORN: CLARION COUNTY   OCCUPATION: FARMER/PEDDLER
　　HEIGHT: 5' 7"   COMPLEXION: DARK   EYES: BROWN   HAIR: DARK
BRANTHOOVER, DANIEL *   PVT   CO. B   AGE:40
BRADHOOVER, DANIEL
　　SWORN: OCT 12, 1861/3 YRS   DIED: MAR 16, 1862 AT LOUISVILLE, KY
　　BORN: ARMSTRONG COUNTY   OCCUPATION: FARMER
　　HEIGHT: 5' 10"   COMPLEXION: LIGHT   EYES: GREY   HAIR: GRAY
　　BURIED: NATIONAL CEMETERY LOUISVILLE; SECTION.A, RANGE.21, GRAVE.19
BRAUGHLER, ADAM C.   1LT   CO. D   AGE:23
　　ORIGIN: INDIANA COUNTY   WIFE: SARAH C.

SWORN: OCT 12, 1861/3 YRS   MUSTER: NOV 4, 1864
BORN: INDIANA COUNTY, HILLSDALE   OCCUPATION: CARPENTER
HEIGHT: 5' 8"   COMPLEXION: FAIR   EYES: GREY
PROMOTED APR 16, 1863 FROM FIRST SGT
REUNION IN FREEPORT 1886, CHICKAMAUGA 1897, INDIANA 1908
HOME 1886-1914: INDIANA, INDIANA COUNTY, PA
DIED: JUL 10, 1923, E. PHILADELPHIA ST., INDIANA, PA
BURIED: OAKLAND CEMETERY, INDIANA, PA   1838-1923

BRIDGET, HAMILTON *   PVT   CO. G   AGE: 38
BRIDGES, HAMILTON
SWORN: SEP 13, 1862/3 YRS   DISCHARGED: JUN 19, 1865
BORN: ARMSTRONG COUNTY   OCCUPATION: BOATMAN
HEIGHT: 5' 9¼"   COMPLEXION: FAIR   EYES: GREY   HAIR: FAIR

BRIGGS, JAMES G.   1ST SGT   CO. F   AGE:36
SWORN: OCT 12, 1861/3 YRS   MUSTER: NOV 4, 1864
BORN: HUNTINGTON COUNTY   OCCUPATION: CARPENTER
HEIGHT: 5' 10"   COMPLEXION: DARK   EYES: DARK   HAIR: DARK
WOUNDED AT STONES RIVER/LEG
ADMITTED TO HOSPITAL #12, LOUISVILLE MAR 1, 1863
PROMOTED FROM SGT SEP 1, 1863
1890 CENSUS: POLLOCK, CLARION COUNTY, PA

BRINK, ANDREW   PVT   CO. B   AGE:30
SWORN: OCT 12, 1861/3 YRS   MUSTER: NOV 4, 1864
BORN: ARMSTRONG COUNTY   OCCUPATION: FARMER
HEIGHT: 6' 2"   COMPLEXION: LIGHT   EYES: GREY   HAIR: LIGHT
1890 CENSUS: CRETE, INDIANA COUNTY, PA
BURIED: GREENWOOD CEMETERY, INDIANA; DIED AUG 8, 1891

BRINK, GEORGE W, # *   PVT   CO. A
SWORN: AUG 1, 1864/1 YEAR   DISCHARGED: JUN 19, 1865
INDIANA HISTORY RECORDS INDICATE SERVICE FROM
SWORN: OCT 21, 1861   DISCHARGED: NOV 4, 1864
NOT LISTED IN THE REGIMENTAL HISTORY OF 1905
BURIED: INDIANA COUNTY, GREENWOOD CEMETERY, DIED: AUG 6, 1891

BRINKER, DAVID R.   1LT   CO. C   AGE:22
BORN: CLARION COUNTY   OCCUPATION: FARMER
HEIGHT: 5' 7½"   COMPLEXION: DARK   EYES: GREY   HAIR: DARK
SWORN: OCT 12, 1861/3 YRS   MUSTER: NOV 4, 1864
PROMOTED: APR 23, 1863, SGT TO 2ND LT; TO 1LT/ 78th JUL 22, 1863

BRINKER, JOHN "JACK" M.   CPT   CO. C   AGE:26
SWORN: OCT 12, 1861/3 YRS   MUSTER: NOV 4, 1864
OCCUPATION: BUSINESSMAN, NEW BETHLEHEM, CLARION COUNTY, PA
HEIGHT: 5' 8"   COMPLEXION: LIGHT   EYES: GREY
RECRUITING OFFICER 1862
REUNION FREEPORT 1886, PUNXSUTAWNEY 1899, KITTANNING 1900
SERVED AS VP OF REUNION ASSOCIATION
HOME 1886: BUFFALO, NY   DIED: JUN 9, 1903

BRINKER, WILLIAM M. *   PVT   CO. C   AGE:18
SWORN: OCT 12, 1861/3 YRS   MUSTER: NOV 4, 1864
BORN: CLARION COUNTY
HEIGHT: 5' 5"   COMPLEXION: FAIR   EYES: BROWN   HAIR: BROWN
HOME 1914: WILKENSBURG, PA

BROWN, ALLEN *   PVT   CO. I   AGE:28
SWORN: MAR 31, 1864/3 YRS   MUSTER: SEP 11, 1865   VETERAN
BORN: ALLEGHENY COUNTY   OCCUPATION: FARMER
HEIGHT: 5' 7"   COMPLEXION: SANDY   EYES: BLUE   HAIR: SANDY

BROWN, ANDREW *   CPT   CO. C   AGE:20
SWORN: OCT 12, 1861/4 YRS   RESIGNED: JUL 26, 1865   VETERAN
HEIGHT: 5' 9"   COMPLEXION: FAIR
WOUNDED AT STONES RIVER/LEG
PROMOTED: 1ST SGT TO 1ST LT, DEC 3, 1864; TO CAPTAIN CO. B II; MAR 15, 1865

BROWN, JOHN G.   PVT   CO. G   AGE:27
SWORN: OCT 12, 1861/3 YRS   DESERTED: OCT 18, 1861, NEVER REPORTED IN

BORN: TEXAS, PA
HEIGHT: 6' 1"   COMPLEXION: DARK   EYES: BLUE   HAIR: DARK
BROWN, JOHN M.   CPL   CO. A   AGE: 27
    ENLISTED AS SEVENTH CPL
    SWORN: OCT 12, 1861/3 YRS   MUSTER: OCT 19, 1864
    TRANS: VRC, JAN 30, 1864
    BORN: INDIANA COUNTY   OCCUPATION: FARMER
    HEIGHT: 5' 9"   COMPLEXION: DARK   EYES: GREY   HAIR: BROWN
    REUNION AT INDIANA 1908   HOME 1886-1914: WILLETT, PA
    BURIED: INDIANA COUNTY, LUTHERAN CEMETERY, WASHINGTON TWP., 1834-1924
BROWN, JOSEPH   PVT   CO. H   AGE:25
    BORN: BUTLER COUNTY, MAY 1, 1836   BOUNTY: $100
    SWORN: OCT 12, 1861/3YRS   MUSTER: NOV 4, 1864
    BORN: BUTLER COUNTY   OCCUPATION: MILLER
    HEIGHT: 5' 6^{1}/$_{3}$" COMPLEXION: DARK   EYES: DARK   HAIR: BLACK
    HOME 1897-1904: BROWNSDALE, BUTLER COUNTY, PA
    DIED JUL 24, 1904 AT BROWNSDALE
    ATTENDED THE DEDICATION OF THE CHICKAMAUGA BATTLEFIELD, NOV 1897
    BROTHERS NATHAN AND WILLIAM SERVED IN THE CIVIL WAR
    WIFE: CHRISTY ANN GREY
BRUMBAUGH, FREDERICK *   PVT   CO. A/B   AGE:39
BUMBAUGH, FREDERICK   BROOMBAUGH, FREDERICK   BRUMBAUGH, F.D.
    SWORN: SEP 25, 1863/3 YRS   DISCHARGED: MAY 20, 1865
    BORN: HUNTINGTON COUNTY   OCCUPATION: LABORER
    HEIGHT: 5' 11½"   COMPLEXION: DARK   EYES: BLACK   HAIR: DARK
    ENLISTED AT EDDYVILLE; AUG, 28, 1862
    1890 CENSUS: RED BANK, ARMSTRONG COUNTY, PA
    HOME 1897-1914: EDDYVILLE, ARMSTRONG COUNTY, PA
    REUNION IN KITTANNING 1901
BRUMBAUGH, SAMUEL   PVT   CO. D
    SWORN: OCT 12, 1861/4 YRS   MUSTER: SEP 11, 1865   VETERAN
    U.S. PENSION, 1894: $12.00
    HOME 1890-1914: PHOENIX, ARMSTRONG COUNTY, PA
BRYAN, NATHANIEL S. *   PVT   CO. A   AGE:19
    SWORN: OCT 12, 1861/3 YRS   MUSTER: NOV 4, 1864
    BORN: INDIANA COUNTY   OCCUPATION: FARMER
    HEIGHT: 5' 8"   COMPLEXION: LIGHT   EYES: GREY   HAIR: BROWN
BRYSON, DANIEL ***   PVT   CO. I   AGE:21
    SWORN: OCT 12, 1861/3 YRS   MUSTER: NOV 4, 1864
    BORN: KITTANNING, PA   OCCUPATION: FARMER
    HEIGHT: 5' 7"   COMPLEXION: DARK   EYES: GREY   HAIR: DARK
    DEMOTED FROM FOURTH SGT SEP 1, 1862
    HOME IN NOV 1897: SHARON, MERCER COUNTY, PA
BUCHANAN, JAMES   PVT   CO. A   AGE:19
BUCHANAN, JAMES S.
    SWORN: OCT 12, 1861/3 YRS   MUSTER: NOV 4, 1864
    BORN: INDIANA COUNTY   OCCUPATION: FARMER
    HEIGHT: 5' 7"   COMPLEXION: LIGHT   EYES: GREY   HAIR: BROWN
    BRIEFLY MISSING IN ACTION AT STONES RIVER; DEATH NOTICE CLAIMS HE WAS A
    CAPTIVE FOR 7 MONTHS
    REGIMENTAL REUNION FREEPORT 1886, CHICKAMAUGA 1897, INDIANA 1908
    HOME 1886: DIXONVILLE, PA
    HOME 1897: TANOMA, INDIANA COUNTY, PA
    HOME 1914: CLYMER, PA [RD 1]
    DIED: MAY 11, 1926, RAYNE TWP, INDIANA COUNTY
    BURIED: INDIANA COUNTY, TWO LICK BAPTIST CEMETERY, DIXONVILLE, 1842-1926
BURDETT, JAMES *   PVT   CO. B   AGE:37
BIRDETT, JAMES
    SWORN: OCT 12, 1861/3 YRS   MEDICAL: JUN 30, 1862
    BORN: ARMSTRONG COUNTY   OCCUPATION: BLACKSMITH
    HEIGHT: 6'   COMPLEXION: DARK   EYES: GREY   HAIR: BLACK
BURFORD, HENRY H. ***   PVT   CO. A

```
        SWORN: JUL 24, 1864/1 YEAR      DISCHARGED: JUN 12, 1865
BURFORD, JAMES C. *              CPL              CO. K              AGE:22
BUFORD, J.C.
        SWORN: OCT 12, 1861/3 YRS      MUSTER: NOV 4, 1864
        BORN: ARMSTRONG COUNTY              OCCUPATION: LABORER
        HEIGHT: 5' 10"   COMPLEXION: DARK   EYES: GREY   HAIR: BLACK
        PROMOTED TO CPL MAY 27, 1862
        REUNION IN FREEPORT 1886
        1886-1914: WALK CHALK, EAST FRANKLIN TWP., ARMSTRONG COUNTY, PA
        1890 CENSUS CLAIMS THAT ONLY HIS WIDOW ELIZABETH WAS ALIVE
BURFORD, SAMUEL                  PVT              CO. E              AGE: 28
BURLORD, SAMUEL
        SWORN: OCT 12, 1861/3 YRS      DIED: JAN 8, 1863
        BORN: ARMSTRONG COUNTY      OCCUPATION: PEDDLER
        HEIGHT: 5' 8"    COMPLEXION: SANDY   EYES: DARK     HAIR: LIGHT
        MORTALLY WOUNDED AT STONES RIVER/ARM
        BURIED: NATIONAL CEMETERY STONES RIVER, GRAVE #D-1594
BURKET, JOHN *                   PVT              CO. B/G            AGE:41
BURKET, WILLIAM
        SWORN: OCT 12, 1861/3 YRS      DIED: MAR 16, 1862 AT LOUISVILLE
        BORN: KITTANNING, PA           OCCUPATION: TEAMSTER
        HEIGHT: 5' 7¼"   COMPLEXION: DARK   EYES· BROWN   HAIR: GREY
        SURGEON'S REPORT "DIED OF OLD AGE" @ CAMP ANDREW JOHNSON
        BURIED: NATIONAL CEMETERY LOUISVILLE; SECTION.A, RANGE.18, GRAVE.5
        1890 CENSUS: KITTANNING, ARMSTRONG COUNTY, PA; WIDOW LEAH
        DANIEL RARAH, CO. A, SON-IN-LAW; SON HENRY CO. B
BURKET, HENRY WILLIAM *          PVT              CO. B              AGE:20
        SWORN: OCT 12, 1861/3 YRS      MUSTER: NOV 4, 1864
        BORN: ARMSTRONG COUNTY              OCCUPATION: FARMER
        HEIGHT: 5' 11"   COMPLEXION: LIGHT   EYES: GREY        HAIR: LIGHT
        JOHN BURKET'S SON; HWB DIED NOV 24, 1905 @ YOUNGSTOWN OHIO
BURKET, PETER ***                PVT              CO. C
        SWORN: SEP 30, 1864/1 YR       MEDICAL: AUG 5, 1865
BURKHOUSE, SOLOMON               PVT              CO. C              AGE: 22
        SWORN: AUG 28, 1862/4 YRS      DISCHARGED: JUN 19, 1865
        BORN: CLARION COUNTY               OCCUPATION: BLACKSMITH
        HEIGHT: 5' 10"   COMPLEXION: FAIR   EYES: BROWN   HAIR: LIGHT
        WOUNDED AT STONES RIVER/KNEE
        1890 CENSUS: EMERACKVILLE, JEFFERSON COUNTY, PA, DIED BEFORE 1905
        DIED: [EURICKVILLE]
BURNHEIMER, AARON                PVT              CO. B              AGE:18
BURNHINSER, AARON                BERNHEIMER, AARON
BURSHINER, A.                    BURNHAMMER, AARON
        SWORN: OCT 12, 1861/3 YRS      MUSTER: NOV 4, 1864
        BORN: INDIANA COUNTY, COOKPORT         OCCUPATION: LABORER
        HEIGHT: 5' 8"   COMPLEXION: FAIR   EYES: GREY   HAIR: LIGHT
        ORIGINALLY ENLISTED IN CO. D.
        HOME 1886: DIXONVILLE, PA
        HOME 1890-1897: TANOMA, INDIANA COUNTY, PA
        REUNION AT FREEPORT 1886, CHICKAMAUGA 1897, INDIANA 1908.
        BURIED: INDIANA COUNTY, DUNKARD CEMETERY, RAYNE TWP., 1844-1916
BURNS, THOMAS L.                 PVT              CO. E              AGE: 27
        SWORN: OCT 12, 1861/3 YRS      TRANS: NOV 10,1864 VRC
        BORN: CLARION COUNTY           OCCUPATION: LABORER
        HEIGHT: 5' 10"   COMPLEXION: DARK   EYES: BLUE   HAIR: DARK
BUTERBAUGH, JOSEPH L.            4th SGT          CO. D              AGE:21
BUTTERBAUGH, JOSEPH L.
        SWORN: OCT 12, 1861/3 YRS      MEDICAL: JUN 9, 1862
        BORN: INDIANA COUNTY, INDIANA      OCCUPATION: FARMER
        HEIGHT: 5' 8"   COMPLEXION: DARK   EYES: BROWN
        HOME: 1876: SMICKSBURG, INDIANA COUNTY, PA
BUTLER, EPLENIA                  PVT              CO. G              AGE:18
```

    SWORN: OCT 12, 1861/3 YRS   DESERTED: OCT 18, 1861, NEVER REPORTED IN
    BORN: DAYTON, PA
    HEIGHT: 5' 7"   COMPLEXION: FAIR   EYES: GREY   HAIR: SANDY
BYERS, DANIEL *   PVT   CO. A   AGE:18
BEYERS, DANIEL
    SWORN: OCT 12, 1861/3 YRS   MUSTER: NOV 4, 1864
    BORN: INDIANA COUNTY   OCCUPATION: FARMER
    HEIGHT: 5' 10"   COMPLEXION: DARK EYES: BLACK   HAIR: BROWN
CABLE, JOHN W. *   PVT   CO. G   AGE:18
    SWORN: OCT 12, 1861/3 YRS   DIED: DEC 14, 1861 AT CAMP WOOD
    BORN: DAYTON, PA   OCCUPATION: LABORER
    HEIGHT: 5' 10"   COMPLEXION: FAIR   EYES: BLUE   HAIR: FAIR
CALHOUN, JAMES W. #   PVT   CO. G
    SWORN: AUG 27, 1861/3 YRS   MUSTER: SEP 11, 1865   VETERAN
    1890 CENSUS: PARKWOOD, INDIANA COUNTY, PA
CALLENDER, JAMES   PVT   CO. E   AGE:26
    BORN: ADAMS TWP., BUTLER COUNTY, MAR 22, 1835
    SWORN: OCT 12, 1861/3 YRS   MUSTER: NOV 4, 1864
    BORN: BUTLER COUNTY   OCCUPATION: FARMER
    HEIGHT: 6'   COMPLEXION: FAIR   EYES: BLUE   HAIR: BROWN
    REDUCED FROM SECOND CPL AT HIS OWN REQUEST
    BROTHER, BUTERMORE SERVED IN THE ARMY OF THE POTOMAC
    BROTHER, WILLIAM SERVED IN THE 91st OHIO; HOME 1892: ZENO, BUTLER COUNTY
CALLENDER, JAMES ***   PVT   CO. K   AGE: 28
    SWORN: OCT 12, 1861/3 YRS   MUSTER: NOV 4, 1864
    BORN: ALLEGHENY COUNTY   OCCUPATION: MILLER
    HEIGHT: 5' 10"   COMPLEXION: SANDY EYES: BLUE   HAIR: SANDY
    HOME 1897: PITTSBURGH, PA
CALLENDER, ROBERT ***   MUS   CO. K   AGE: 20
    SWORN: OCT 12, 1861/3 YRS   MUSTER: NOV 4, 1864
    BORN: ALLEGHENY COUNTY   OCCUPATION: FARMER
    HEIGHT: 5' 10"   COMPLEXION: DARK   EYES: GREY   HAIR: BLACK
    HOME IN NOV 1897-1901: HOMESTEAD, ALLEGHENY COUNTY, PA
    REUNION KITTANNING 1901
CALLENDER, THOMAS ***   CPL   CO. K   AGE:31
    SWORN: OCT 12, 1861/3 YRS   MEDICAL: NOV 10, 1862
    BORN: ALLEGHENY COUNTY   OCCUPATION: MILLER DIED BEFORE 1905
    HEIGHT: 5' 7¼"   COMPLEXION: DARK   EYES: GREY HAIR: BLACK
CAMPBELL, F.W.   CPL   CO. C   AGE:19
CAMAPBELL, F.W.   CAMPBELL, FRANCIS W.   VETERAN
    SWORN: OCT 12, 1861/4 YRS   MUSTER: SEP 11, 1865
    BORN: CLARION COUNTY
    HEIGHT: 5' 7"   COMPLEXION: DARK   EYES: BROWN   HAIR: BROWN
    PROMOTED FROM PVT TO CPL CO. B IN SECOND REGIMENT
    1890 CENSUS: FAIRMOUNT, CLARION COUNTY, PA
    HOME 1914: MOON RUN, PA
CAMPBELL, JAMES   PVT   CO. A   AGE:43
    BORN IN PETROLIA, BUTLER COUNTY, TO ROBERT AND ELIZABETH GIBSON CAMPBELL
    SWORN: OCT 12, 1861/3 YRS   MEDICAL: MAR 23, 1863.
    INDIANA COUNTY ENLISTEE   OCCUPATION: FARMER
    HEIGHT: 5' 5"   COMPLEXION: DARK   EYES: BLUE   HAIR: GRAY
    BROTHER ROBERT D. SERVED IN CO. H, PA 78th, ANDREW IN PA 14th CAV
CAMPBELL, JAMES **   PVT   CO. A
    SWORN: JUL 21, 1863/1 YRS   MUSTER: SICK AT MUSTER
CAMPBELL, JOHN O.   PVT   CO. A   AGE:21
    SWORN: OCT 12, 1861/3 YRS   MUSTER: NOV 4, 1864
    BORN: INDIANA COUNTY   OCCUPATION: FARMER
    HEIGHT: 5' 9½"   COMPLEXION: FAIR   EYES: GREY   HAIR: SANDY
    1890 CENSUS: SOUTH BEND, ARMSTRONG COUNTY, PA
    HOME 1897: SHELOCTA, INDIANA COUNTY, PA
    HOME 1914: PARKWOOD, INDIANA COUNTY, PA
    ATTENDED THE DEDICATION OF THE CHICKAMAUGA BATTLEFIELD, NOV 1897

BURIED: INDIANA COUNTY, UNITED PRESBYTERIAN CEMETERY, SHELOCTA, AUG 3, 1840–NOV 16, 1929

CAMPBELL, MARK *   PVT   CO. G   AGE:31
SWORN: OCT 12, 1861/3 YRS   MUSTER: NOV 4, 1864
BORN: RURAL VALLEY, PA   OCCUPATION: FARMER
HEIGHT: 5' 7½"   COMPLEXION: DARK   EYES: BLUE   HAIR: SANDY
DIED: AT LONG RUN, PA; 1830–MAY 17, 1895
BURIED: INDIANA COUNTY, RIDGEVIEW CEMETERY, ELDERS RIDGE

CAMPBELL, ROBERT D.   PVT   CO. H   AGE:27
BORN IN PETROLIA, BUTLER COUNTY, TO ROBERT AND ELIZABETH GIBSON CAMPBELL
SWORN: OCT 12, 1861/3YRS   MUSTER: NOV 4, 1864   BOUNTY: $100
BORN: BUTLER COUNTY   OCCUPATION: CARPENTER
HEIGHT: 5' 9$^{1}/_{3}$"   COMPLEXION: DARK   EYES: GREY   HAIR: LIGHT
BROTHER JAMES G. SERVED IN CO. A, PA 78th, ANDREW IN PA 14th CAV
ATTENDED THE DEDICATION OF THE CHICKAMAUGA BATTLEFIELD, NOV 1897
HOME 1897: MOUNT CHESTNUT, BUTLER COUNTY, PA, DIED BEFORE 1905

CARNAHAN, JAMES   PVT   CO. A   AGE:24
SWORN: AUG 28, 1862/3 YRS   DIED: FEB 11, 1863 AT MURFREESBORO
BORN: INDIANA COUNTY   OCCUPATION: FARMER   BOUNTY: $29
HEIGHT: 5' 8"   COMPLEXION: SANDY   EYES: GREY   HAIR: BROWN
MORTALLY WOUNDED AT STONES RIVER
BURIED AT NATIONAL CEMETERY STONES RIVER, GRAVE #G-2761

CARROLL, JAMES A.   CPL   CO. A   AGE: 21
SWORN: OCT 12, 1861/3 YRS   DIED: JAN 4, 1863 AT MURFREESBORO
BORN: INDIANA COUNTY   OCCUPATION: FARMER
HEIGHT: 6' 2"   HAIR: BROWN   EYES: BLUE   ENLISTED AS SIXTH CPL
MORTALLY WOUNDED/LEG AT STONES RIVER
BURIED AT NATIONAL CEMETERY STONES RIVER, GRAVE #D-1690

CASSIDY, THOMAS **   PVT   CO. H   AGE:18
CASSIDAY, THOMAS   BOUNTY $29   ORIGIN: BUTLER COUNTY
SWORN: MAR 14, 1863/3 YRS   MEDICAL: JUL 27, 1863
BORN: PITTSBURGH, PA   OCCUPATION: TEAMSTER
HEIGHT: 5' 6"   COMPLEXION: LIGHT   EYES: BLUE   HAIR: LIGHT
DISCHARGED FROM NASHVILLE   DIED IN CLARION, PA

CASTERLINE, ELIJAH T. *   PVT   CO. F   AGE:37
CASTERLON, ELIJAG T.   CASTERLINE, ELISHA T.   DIED: OCT 1901
SWORN: OCT 12, 1861 / 3 YRS   MEDICAL: MAY 18, 1862
BORN: UTICA, NY   OCCUPATION: CARPENTER
HEIGHT: 5' 11½"   COMPLEXION: FAIR   EYES: BLUE   HAIR: LIGHT
U.S. PENSION, 1894: $8.00   HOME: FREEPORT

CHAMBER, JAMES B.   PVT   CO. E   AGE:18
CHAMBERS, JAMES B.
SWORN: OCT 12, 1861/3 YRS   MEDICAL: DEC 14, 1862
BORN: CLARION COUNTY   OCCUPATION: FARMER
HEIGHT: 5' 9"   COMPLEXION: FAIR   EYES: BLUE   HAIR: BLACK

CHAMPION, JAMES A.   PVT   CO. I   AGE:19
SWORN: DEC 17, 1862/3 YRS   MUSTER: SEP 11, 1865
BORN: MURFREESBORO, TN   OCCUPATION: LABORER
HEIGHT: 6'   COMPLEXION: DARK   EYES: BROWN   HAIR: DARK
WOUNDED AT STONES RIVER/THIGH   ENLISTED BY COL SIRWELL

CHAPMAN, JOHN C. *   PVT   CO. I   AGE: 22
SWORN: OCT 12, 1861/3 YRS   KILLED DEC 31, 1862 AT STONES RIVER
BORN: APOLLO, PA   OCCUPATION: NAILER
HEIGHT: 5' 9½"   COMPLEXION: SANDY   EYES: GREY   HAIR: LIGHT

CHARLES, WILLIAM   PVT   CO. D   AGE:40
SWORN: OCT 12, 1861/3 YRS   DIED: MAR 16, 1863 AT NASHVILLE
BORN: INDIANA COUNTY, TYLERSBURG   OCCUPATION: SADDLER
HEIGHT: 5' 9½"   COMPLEXION: FAIR   EYES: BROWN   HAIR: SANDY
BURIED @ NASHVILLE, ROW E, GRAVE #435

CHERRY, JOHN***   PVT   CO. A   AGE: 39
SWORN: MAR 3, 1864/3 YRS   MUSTER: SEP 11, 1865.
BURIED: LUTHERAN CEMETERY, WORTHINGTON, PA, SEP 28, 1865 @ AGE 43

CHRISTLEY, NEYMAN   PVT   CO. H   AGE:18
CHRISTLEY, WYMAN   CHRISTLEY, WILLIAM
    BORN: SLIPPERY ROCK, BUTLER COUNTY, MAY 10, 1844
    SWORN: OCT 12, 1861/3YRS   MUSTER: NOV 4, 1864
    BORN: BUTLER COUNTY   OCCUPATION: FARMER
    HEIGHT: 5' 7¼"   COMPLEXION: LIGHT   EYES: GREY   HAIR: LIGHT
    HOME IN NOV 1897: SLIPPERY ROCK, BUTLER COUNTY, PA, DIED 1903
    REUNION CHICKAMAUGA 1897, KITTANNING 1901   WIFE: MARY ROBB
CHRISTLEY, WILLIAM   PVT   CO. H   AGE:19
CHRISTY, WILLIAM   BOUNTY: $100
    ORIGIN: BUTLER COUNTY   HEIGHT: 5' 6"
    SWORN: OCT 12, 1861/3YRS   MUSTER: NOV 4, 1864
    BORN: BUTLER COUNTY   OCCUPATION: FARMER
    HEIGHT: 5' 6"   COMPLEXION: LIGHT   EYES: BLUE   HAIR: LIGHT
    WOUNDED/SHOULDER AT STONES RIVER
    NOV 8, 1863: "CHRISTIE WOUNDED BY A NIGGER MAN"
    1886 REUNION IN FREEPORT
    HOME 1886-1914: EUCLID, BUTLER COUNTY, PA
CHRISTLEY, WILLIAM C.   PVT   CO. H   AGE:19
    SWORN: OCT 12, 1861/3YRS   MUSTER: DEC 4, 1864   BOUNTY: $100
    BORN: NEW AMSTERDAM, PA   OCCUPATION: FARMER
    HEIGHT: 5' 6⅓"   COMPLEXION: LIGHT   EYES: GREY   HAIR: SANDY
    DIED AT SLIPPERY ROCK, PA BEFORE 1905
CHRISTMAN, MICHAEL*   PVT   CO. G
    SWORN: SEP 13, 1862/3 YRS   DIED: FEB 25, 1863 AT NASHVILLE
    BURIED @ NASHVILLE, ROW E, GRAVE #509, BATES
CHRISTY, FATHER RICHARD C.   REGIMENTAL CHAPLAIN
    BORN IN LORETTO, PA   ORIGIN: BUTLER COUNTY
    SWORN: OCT 12, 1861/3 YRS   MUSTER: NOV 4, 1864
    OCCUPATION: PASTOR, SAINT JOHN'S RCC, CLEARFIELD TWP., BUTLER COUNTY
    COMMENDED BY COL SIRWELL FOR BRAVERY AT STONES RIVER
    APPOINTED ASST. PASTOR ST. MARY'S RCC IN KITTANNING; 1873
    LECTURED IN FREEPORT OCTOBER 4, 1876
    DIED IN COLUMBUS, OHIO, OCTOBER 16, 1878
    BURIED: EBENSBURG, CAMBRIA COUNTY, PA
CHURCHILL, JOHN W.*   PVT   CO. F   AGE:21
    SWORN: OCT 12, 1861/3 YRS   MUSTER: NOV 4, 1864
    BORN: FREEPORT, PA   OCCUPATION: SHOEMAKER
    HEIGHT: 5' 8"   COMPLEXION: DARK   EYES: BROWN   HAIR: DARK
CLARK, DAVID*   PVT   CO. K   AGE: 38
    SWORN: OCT 12, 1861/4 YRS   MUSTER: SEP 11, 1865   VETERAN
    BORN: WESTMORELAND COUNTY   OCCUPATION: FARMER
    HEIGHT: 5' 11½"   COMPLEXION: DARK   EYES: BLUE   HAIR: BLACK
CLARK, JAMES B.   PVT   CO. H   AGE:20
    SWORN: OCT 12, 1861/3YRS   MEDICAL: JUL 29, 1863
    BORN: LAWRENCE COUNTY   OCCUPATION: STUDENT
    HEIGHT: 5' 10½"   COMPLEXION: LIGHT   EYES: GREY   HAIR: BLACK
    DISCHARGED FROM BOWLING GREEN, KY.
    REUNION KITTANNING 1901; HOME 1901: SYDNEY, WA
CLARK, WILLIAM*   PVT   CO. G
CLARK, W.C.
    SWORN: SEP 13, 1862/3 YRS   MUSTER: SEP 11, 1865
    RESIDENT OF HAMILTON, NB IN 1886
CLAWSON, ALBERT H.*   PVT   CO. F   AGE:18
    SWORN: OCT 12, 1861/3 YRS   MUSTER: NOV 4, 1864
    BORN: FREEPORT, PA   OCCUPATION: LABORER
    HEIGHT: 5' 8"   COMPLEXION: SHALLOW   EYES: BROWN   HAIR: DARK BROWN
    SOME FAMILIES RECEIVED $100 BOUNTY UPON ENLISTMENT
    HOME 1886-1901: FREEPORT, ARMSTRONG COUNTY, PA
    REUNION KITTANNING 1901, INDIANA 1908
CLAYPOOL, AMOS*   CPL   CO. K   AGE: 18
    SWORN: OCT 12, 1861/3 YRS   MUSTER: NOV 4, 1864

BORN: ARMSTRONG COUNTY   OCCUPATION: FARMER
HEIGHT: 5' 8½"   COMPLEXION: FAIR   EYES: GREY   HAIR: RED
PROMOTED TO CPL MAY 27, 1862
CLAYPOOL, HENRY*   PVT   CO. K   AGE: 21
SWORN: OCT 12, 1861/3 YRS   MUSTER: NOV 4, 1864
BORN: ARMSTRONG COUNTY   OCCUPATION: FARMER
HEIGHT: 5' 11"   COMPLEXION: FAIR   EYES: BLACK   HAIR: BLACK
BRIEFLY MISSING IN ACTION AT STONES RIVER
REUNION IN FREEPORT 1886, CHICKAMAUGA 1897, KITTANNING 1901
HOME 1886-1901: WORTHINGTON, ARMSTRONG COUNTY, PA
HOME 1914: 170 GRANT AVE., VANDERGRIFT, PA
BURIED: FRANKLIN UNION BAPTIST CHURCH, WORTHINGTON, PA
BORN: NOV 9, 1839; DIED: AUG 31, 1922;   WIFE: MARGARET; FEB 9, 1847 - MAR 23, 1913
CLEMENTS, JESSE A.*   PVT   CO. I   AGE:17
CLEMENTS, JESSE ALLEN   CLEMENTS, ALLEN
BORN JUL 31, 1844 IN WASHINGTON TWP., WESTMORELAND COUNTY
PARENTS: JESSE AND ANN BARR [ARMSTRONG COUNTY] CLEMENTS.
SWORN: OCT 12, 1861/3 YRS   MUSTER: NOV 4, 1864
BORN: N. WASHINGTON, PA   OCCUPATION: FARMER
HEIGHT: 5' 7"   COMPLEXION: LIGHT   EYES: BROWN   HAIR: DARK
WOUNDED AT STONES RIVER/LEG, JUST BELOW THE KNEE; 6 MONTHS RECUPERATION
REUNION IN FREEPORT 1886, CHICKAMAUGA 1897
HOME 1886-1897: MERWIN, WESTMORELAND COUNTY, PA
WIFE: MARGARET EWER; HOME 1914: APOLLO, PA; MEMBER OF THE GAR POST #243
BURIED: POKE RUN PRESBYTERIAN CEMETERY, APOLLO, PA
CLEVER, WILLIAM H.H.*   PVT   CO. G   AGE:20
CLEAVER, WILLIAM H.
SWORN: OCT 12, 1861/3 YRS   DIED: DEC 1, 1861 AT NASHVILLE
BORN: KITTANNING, PA   OCCUPATION: LABORER
HEIGHT: 5' 7"   COMPLEXION: FAIR   EYES: GREY   HAIR: LIGHT
BURIED AT NATIONAL CEMETERY NASHVILLE, GRAVE #B-237
CLINE, RUDOLPHUS M.*   PVT/ORDERLY   STAFF   AGE: 18
KLINE, RUDOLPHUS "DOLF"
SWORN: OCT 12, 1861/3 YRS   MUSTER: NOV 4, 1864
BORN: LEECHBURG, PA   OCCUPATION: LABORER
HEIGHT: 5' 5½"   COMPLEXION: DARK   EYES: GREY   HAIR: DARK
U.S. PENSION, 1894: $10.00   1886 REUNION IN FREEPORT
HOME 1861-1915: LEECHBURG, ARMSTRONG COUNTY, PA
BURIED: PLEASANT HILLS CEMETERY, LEECHBURG, PA; SEP 19, 1843-MAR 25, 1915
CLINGENSMITH, FRANK*   PVT   CO. B   AGE:19
KLINGENSMITH, FRANKLIN   KLINGENSMITH, F.
SWORN: OCT 12, 1861/3 YRS   TRANS: 4TH CAV, DEC 1, 1862
BORN: ARMSTRONG COUNTY   OCCUPATION: BOATMAN
HEIGHT: 5' 10"   COMPLEXION: LIGHT   EYES: GREY   HAIR: DARK
BURIED: APOLLO CEMETERY, APOLLO, PA
CLOWES, DAVID   PVT   CO. A   AGE:23
SWORN: SEP 10, 1862/3 YRS   DISCHARGED: JUN 19, 1865   BOUNTY: $29
BORN: INDIANA COUNTY   OCCUPATION: FARMER
HEIGHT: 5' 11½"   COMPLEXION: LIGHT   EYES: GREY   HAIR: BROWN
HOME 1890-1914: WILLET, INDIANA COUNTY, PA
CLOWES, JOHN W.*   PVT   CO. F   AGE:26
SWORN: OCT 12, 1861/3 YRS   MUSTER: NOV 4, 1864
BORN: BLAIRSVILLE, PA   OCCUPATION: BOAT MAKER
HEIGHT: 5' 10½"   COMPLEXION: SHALLOW   EYES: GREY   HAIR: DARK BROWN
BORN: OCT 2, 1835
WIFE: MARY SHEARER
DIED: JUN 14, 1915
REUNION KITTANNING 1901   HOME 1914: SLATE LICK, PA
BURIED: ST. PAUL'S LUTHERAN CEMETERY, SARVER, PA
COBBETT, WILLIAM   PVT   CO. E   AGE:19
SWORN: OCT 12, 1861/3 YRS   MUSTER: NOV 4, 1864
BORN: BUTLER COUNTY   OCCUPATION: FARMER

HEIGHT: 5' 7"   COMPLEXION: DARK   EYES: BLUE   HAIR: LIGHT
HOME IN NOV 1897: RIMERSBURG, CLARION COUNTY, PA
COCHLIN, JAMES*   PVT   CO. I   AGE: 26
SWORN: OCT 12, 1861/3 YRS   MUSTER: NOV 4, 1864
BORN: APOLLO, PA   OCCUPATION: LABORER
HEIGHT: 5' 5¼"   COMPLEXION: DARK   EYES: BLUE   HAIR: LIGHT
1890 CENSUS, BELL WESTMORELAND COUNTY, PA
DIED: AT SALTSBURG, PA, JAN 26. 1895
BURIED IN ST. MATTHEWS RCC CEMETERY, SALTSBURG
COCHRAN, DAVID S.*   CPL   CO. G   AGE: 26
SWORN: OCT 12, 1861/3 YRS   MUSTER: NOV 4, 1864
PROMOTED FROM PVT
BORN: DAYTON, PA   OCCUPATION: PLASTERER
HEIGHT: 5' 8"   COMPLEXION: FAIR   EYES: BLUE   HAIR: FAIR
HOME 1890-1901: DAYTON BOROUGH, ARMSTRONG COUNTY, PA
REUNION CHICKAMAUGA 1897, KITTANNING 1901, INDIANA 1908
COCHRAN, WILLIAM   PVT   CO. A   AGE:22
SWORN: OCT 12, 1861/3 YRS   MEDICAL: MAR 20, 1863 AT MURFREESBORO
BORN: FEB 16, 1840 IN INDIANA COUNTY . OCCUPATION: FARMER
HEIGHT: 5' 7"   COMPLEXION: DARK   EYES: GREY   HAIR: BROWN
WOUNDED/RIGHT ANKLE AT STONES RIVER & LEFT SIDE
SOME RECORDS SHOW HIM MORTALLY WOUNDED AND DYING MAR 20, 1863
AT MURFREESBORO; THEY HAVE BEEN PROVEN INCORRECT.
1890 CENSUS:COWANSHANNOCK TWP., ARMSTRONG COUNTY, PA
DIED: FEB 21, 1900   WIFE: MARY J. HENDERSON
COLBERT, DANIEL*   PVT   CO. K   AGE: 18
COBERT, DANIEL   COSERT, DANIEL BOUNTY: $29
SWORN: SEP 10, 1862/3 YRS   DISCHARGED: JUN 19, 1865
BORN: CENTER COUNTY   OCCUPATION: FARMER
HEIGHT: 5'   COMPLEXION: FAIR   EYES: GREY   HAIR: DARK
HOSPITAL ORDERLY DURING 1864
COLLAR, GEORGE   PVT   CO. E   AGE:19
CELLAR, GEORGE
SWORN: OCT 12, 1861/3 YRS   MEDICAL: JUN 28, 1862
BORN: CLARION COUNTY   OCCUPATION: FARMER
HEIGHT: 6'   COMPLEXION: LIGHT   EYES: BLUE   HAIR: BLACK
REUNION KITTANNING 1901   HOME 1901: SANDY POINT, PA
COLLINS, BERNARD*   PVT   CO. A/B   AGE:19
COLLINS, BARNARD
SWORN: OCT 12, 1861/3 YRS   DEMOTED FROM CPL OCT 31, 1861
DISHONORABLE DISCHARGE: SEP 1, 1862
BORN: ARMSTRONG COUNTY   OCCUPATION: RR BREAKMAN
HEIGHT: 5' 3"   COMPLEXION: LIGHT   EYES: BLACK   HAIR: LIGHT
CONDER, ANDREW J. *   PVT   CO. A
COUDER, ANDREW J.
SWORN: OCT 12, 1861/3 YRS   MUSTER: NOV 4, 1864
CONLEY, GEORGE W. *   PVT   CO. F   AGE:21
CONNELLY, GEORGE
SWORN: OCT 12, 1861/3 YRS   MUSTER: NOV 4, 1864
BORN: FREEPORT, PA   OCCUPATION: LABORER
HEIGHT: 5' 7"   COMPLEXION: DARK   EYES: DARK BROWN   HAIR: DARK BROWN
SOME FAMILIES RECEIVED $100 BOUNTY UPON ENLISTMENT
HOME 1890-1897: FREEPORT, ARMSTRONG COUNTY, PA
HOME 1914: CHESWICK, PA   REUNION CHICKAMAUGA 1897, INDIANA 1908.
CONNELL, OWEN   PVT   CO. C   AGE:43
SWORN: OCT 12, 1861/3 YRS   MUSTER: NOV 4, 1864
BORN: IRELAND
HEIGHT: 5' 5"   COMPLEXION: DARK   EYES: BROWN   HAIR: BROWN
CONWAY, DENNIS *   PVT   CO. F   AGE:29
SWORN: OCT 12, 1861/3 YRS   KILLED: DEC 31, 1863 AT STONES RIVER
BORN: BRADY BEND, PA   OCCUPATION: COLLIER
HEIGHT: 5' 3"   COMPLEXION: DARK   EYES: BROWN   HAIR: DARK

BURIED AT NATIONAL CEMETERY STONES RIVER, GRAVE #L-4669

CONWAY, JOHN *   PVT   CO. A   AGE:40
CONAWAY, JOHN
    SWORN: OCT 12, 1861/3 YRS   MEDICAL: JUN 28, 1862.
    BORN: INDIANA COUNTY   OCCUPATION: FARMER
    HEIGHT: 5' 9"   COMPLEXION: DARK   EYES: BLUE   HAIR: GRAY

COOK, JEREMIAH "JERRY"   PVT   CO. D   AGE:19
    BORN: 1841 IN GREEN TWP., INDIANA COUNTY TO HEZEKIAH
    AND LUCINDA BARTLEBAUGH
    SWORN: OCT 12, 1861/3 YRS   TRANS: AUG 1, 1863 TO VRC
    BORN: INDIANA COUNTY, COOKPORT   OCCUPATION: FARMER
    HEIGHT: 5' 8½"   COMPLEXION: FAIR   EYES: GREY   HAIR: BROWN
    WOUNDED AT STONES RIVER
    LIVED IN PITTSBURGH FROM 1871-1918
    HOME 1914: 815 BLUFF ST., PITTSBURGH, PA
    DIED: OCT 24, 1918 IN GREEN TWP.   WIFE: LENA WAGONER
    ENLISTED WITH HIS GRANDFATHER, MATHIAS BARTLEBAUGH [ALSO CO.D]

COOPER, STEPHEN   PVT   CO. H   AGE:24
    SWORN: OCT 12, 1861/3YRS   MUSTER: NOV 4, 1864   BOUNTY: $100
    BORN: BUTLER COUNTY   OCCUPATION: FARMER
    HEIGHT: 5' 8"   COMPLEXION: LIGHT   EYES: BROWN   HAIR: BROWN
    HOME IN NOV 1897:ANANDALE, BUTLER COUNTY, PA
    ATTENDED THE DEDICATION OF THE CHICKAMAUGA BATTLEFIELD, NOV 1897
    DIED AT SLIPPERY ROCK, PA, BEFORE 1905; OBVIOUSLY THIS IS INCORRECT
    HOME 1914: RD #58, SLIPPERY ROCK, PA

COPENHAVER, JOHN *   PVT   CO. C   AGE: 21
COPENHAUER, JOHN
    SWORN: FEB 2, 1864/3 YRS   DIED: FEB 8, 1865 AT NASHVILLE
    BORN: CLARION COUNTY
    HEIGHT: 5' 6"   COMPLEXION: DARK   EYES: BLUE   HAIR: BROWN

COPENHAVER, JOHN J. *   PVT   CO. B/C
COPENHAUER, JOHN J.
    SWORN: SEP 13, 1864/3 YRS   DISCHARGED: AUG 5, 1865
    1890 CENSUS: RED BANK, ARMSTRONG COUNTY, PA

COPLEY, ALBERT ***   PVT   CO. K   AGE: 27
COPLEY, DAVID
    SWORN: OCT 12, 1861/3 YRS   DIED: JAN 21, 1863
    BORN: ARMSTRONG COUNTY   OCCUPATION: FARMER
    HEIGHT: 5' 5½"   COMPLEXION: DARK   EYES: GREY   HAIR: DARK
    SERVED AS A CPL AT CAMP ORR   MORTALLY WOUNDED AT STONES RIVER
    TAKEN PRISONER AT STONES RIVER, DIED AT KNOXVILLE
    ALBERT WAS GIVEN HELP BY HIS COUSIN, CPT SMITH OF THE 7th FLORIDA -
    CONFEDERATE
    PARENTS: JOSIAH & MARGARET CHADWICK HAAS
    JOSIAH FOUNDED THE KITTANNING GAZETTE;
    EVENTUALLY WORKED FOR THE PITTSBURGH GAZETTE
    BROTHER: JOHN SIBBET COPLEY DIED @ THE BATTLE OF SOUTH MOUNTAIN
    AS MEMBER OF THE PA 9th RESERVES; SEP 14,1862
    BROTHER: JOSIAH Jr. TAKEN PRISONER AT CHICKAMAUGA

COUSINS, JAMES H. *   PVT   CO. G   AGE: 22
COURSINS, JAMES H.
    SWORN: SEP 13, 1862/3 YRS   DISCHARGED: MAY 23, 1865
    BORN: ARMSTRONG COUNTY   OCCUPATION: LABORER
    HEIGHT: 5' 7½"   COMPLEXION: FAIR   EYES: GREY   HAIR: FAIR
    WOUNDED AT STONES RIVER/HAND
    DESERTED: MAY 1864, RETURNED: APR 13, 1865
    WIFE: MARY HOOKS, DAUGHTER OF HUGH HOOKS, SR., JOHN A. COUSINS BROTHER

COUSINS, JOHN A. *   PVT   CO. H   AGE:19
COUSSINS, JOHN A.   CAUSSINS, JOHN A.   CUSSINS, JOHN A.
    SWORN: AUG 28, 1862   DISCHARGED: JUN 19, 1865
    BORN: ARMSTRONG COUNTY   OCCUPATION: LABORER
    HEIGHT: 5' 9"   COMPLEXION: FAIR EYES: GREY HAIR: AUBURN

HOME IN NOV 1897: DEE, ARMSTRONG COUNTY, PA; JAMES H. COUSINS BROTHER
COUSINS, SIMON *   PVT   CO. G   AGE: 26
COURSINS, SIMON
    SWORN: SEP 13, 1862/3 YRS   MUSTER: SEP 11, 1865
    BORN: ARMSTRONG COUNTY   OCCUPATION: LABORER
    HEIGHT: 5' 8"   COMPLEXION: FAIR   EYES: GREY   HAIR: FAIR
    BRIEFLY MISSING IN ACTION AT STONES RIVER
COWAN, ANDREW J   PVT   CO. B   AGE:19
DOWAN, A. J.
    SWORN: OCT 12, 1861/3 YRS   MUSTER: NOV 4, 1864
    BORN: ARMSTRONG COUNTY   OCCUPATION: FARMER
    HEIGHT: 5' 11"   COMPLEXION: DARK   EYES: BLUE   HAIR: BLACK
    WOUNDED/BACK AT STONES RIVER
CRAFT, JAMES S. *   CPL   CO. B   AGE:29
CROFT, JAMES S.
    SWORN: OCT 12, 1861/3 YRS   MEDICAL: FEB 16, 1863
    BORN: ARMSTRONG COUNTY   OCCUPATION: FARMER
    HEIGHT: 5' 10"   COMPLEXION: LIGHT   EYES: BLUE   HAIR: DARK
CRAFT, JOHN # *   PVT   CO. B
    SWORN: JUN 13, 1863/3 YRS   MEDICAL: AUG 13, 1864
    1890 CENSUS: ELDERTON, PLUM CREEK TWP., ARMSTRONG COUNTY, PA
CRAMER, MARTIN V. *   PVT   CO. C   AGE:19
    SWORN: OCT 12, 1861/3 YRS   MUSTER: NOV 4, 1864   HEIGHT: 5' 8"
    BORN: HUNTINGTON COUNTY
    HEIGHT: 5' 8"   COMPLEXION: FAIR   EYES: HAZEL   HAIR: LIGHT
    REUNION FREEPORT 1886, KITTANNING 1901
    HOME 1886-1914: KITTANNING, PA
CRAWFORD, JOEL *   1ST SGT   CO. K   AGE: 19
    SWORN: OCT 12, 1861/4 YRS   MUSTER: NOV 4, 1864   VETERAN
    BORN: ARMSTRONG COUNTY   OCCUPATION: PAINTER
    HEIGHT: 5' 9"   COMPLEXION: DARK   EYES: GREY   HAIR: BLACK
    PROMOTED TO CPL OCT 18, 1862; TO SGT FEB 1, 1864
    SERVED WITH PA 104TH, CO. K: MAR 18-AUG 25, 1865;
    LIEUTENANT IN 104TH
    1894 SOLDIERS PENSION: $12/mo
    HOME 1890-1901: KITTANNING, PA
    REUNION CHICKAMAUGA 1897, KITTANNING 1900, 1901
    SERVED AS VP OF REUNION ASSOCIATION
    BATTLES/DUTY: PETERSBURG, FORTRESS MONROE, PORTSMOUTH
CRICK, HENRY A.   SGT   CO. E   AGE:23
    SWORN: OCT 12, 1861/3 YRS   MUSTER: NOV 4, 1864
    BORN: CLARION COUNTY   OCCUPATION: FARMER
    HEIGHT: 5' 10"   COMPLEXION: SANDY   EYES: BLUE   HAIR: SANDY
    PROMOTED FROM FIRST CPL MAR 1, 1863
CRITZER, DANIEL *   PVT   CO. F   AGE:35
    SWORN: OCT 12, 1861/3 YRS   MEDICAL: FEB 22, 1862
    BORN: FREEPORT, PA   OCCUPATION: ENGINEER
    HEIGHT: 5' 6"   COMPLEXION: DARK   EYES: BROWN   HAIR: BLACK
    SOME FAMILIES RECEIVED $100 BOUNTY UPON ENLISTMENT
    BURIED: FREEPORT CEMETERY, FREEPORT, PA
CROCKER, EDWARD S.   PVT   CO. H   AGE:19
    ORIGIN: BUTLER COUNTY, CENTERVILLE
    SWORN: OCT 12, 1861/3YRS   DIED: FEB 23, 62, CAMP WOOD OF MEASLES
    BORN: LAWRENCE COUNTY   OCCUPATION: FARMER
    HEIGHT: 5' 9½"   COMPLEXION: LIGHT   EYES: GREY   HAIR: LIGHT
    BURIED: NATIONAL CEMETERY LOUISVILLE; SECTION.D, RANGE.6, GRAVE.16
CROLL, FRANKLIN *   SGT   CO. B
    SWORN: OCT 12, 1861/3 YRS   MUSTER: NOV 4, 1864
    PROMOTED TO CPL, OCT 31, 1861; TO SGT: JUL 1, 1863
CROOKS, JOSEPH M.   PVT   CO. A   AGE:18
    SWORN: OCT 12, 1861/3 YRS   DIED: JAN 5, 1862 AT LOUISVILLE, KY OF TYPHOID
    BORN: INDIANA COUNTY   OCCUPATION: FARMER

HEIGHT: 5' 10"   COMPLEXION: FAIR   EYES: GREY   HAIR: BLACK
BURIED: NATIONAL CEMETERY LOUISVILLE; SECTION.A, RANGE.5, GRAVE.18

CROSBY, SAMUEL M. *   2ND LT   CO. I   AGE:27
SWORN: OCT 12, 1861/3 YRS   DISCHARGED: DEC 9, 1862
BORN: LEECHBURG, PA   OCCUPATION: TEACHER
HEIGHT: 5' 9"   COMPLEXION: DARK   EYES: GREY   HAIR: BLACK
DISMISSED BY GENERAL ROSECRANS   HOME 1861-1911: LEECHBURG, PA
1886 REUNION IN FREEPORT

CROSS, BOSTON B.   PVT   CO. H   AGE: 17
SWORN: OCT 12, 1861/4 YRS   DISCHARGED: MAR 29, 1865   VETERAN
BORN: BUTLER COUNTY   OCCUPATION: MOULDER   BOUNTY: $100
HEIGHT: 5' 8½"   COMPLEXION: LIGHT   EYES: GREY   HAIR: LIGHT
TAKEN PRISONER [LEFT SICK] AT CHICKAMAUGA SEP 20, 1863
HELD BY CONFEDERATES UNTIL NOV 20, 1864

CROYLE, JOHN *   PVT   CO. G   AGE:16
SWORN: SEP 13, 1862/3 YRS   KILLED: DEC 31, 1862
BORN: ARMSTRONG COUNTY   OCCUPATION: FARMER
HEIGHT: 5' 10"   COMPLEXION: FAIR   EYES: GREY   HAIR: LIGHT
MISSING IN ACTION AT STONES RIVER/PRESUMED DEAD

CROYLE, SAMUEL H. *   1ST SGT   CO. G   AGE: 25
SWORN: OCT 12, 1861/3 YRS   MUSTER: NOV 4, 1864
BORN: KITTANNING, PA   OCCUPATION: FARMER
HEIGHT: 5' 9"   HAIR: BROWN   EYES: BLUE   COMPLEXION: FAIR
PROMOTED FROM SECOND SGT
COMMENDED BY SIRWELL FOR BRAVERY AT STONES RIVER
HOME 1890-1897: JEANNETTE, WESTMORELAND COUNTY, PA
HOME 1914: 5824 RIPPEY ST., PITTSBURGH, PA

CUMMINS, LYCURGUS R.   3RD SGT   CO. H   AGE:27
SWORN: OCT 12, 1861/3YRS   MUSTER: NOV 4, 1864   BOUNTY: $100.
BORN: BUTLER COUNTY   OCCUPATION: FARMER
HEIGHT: 6' ¾"   COMPLEXION: LIGHT   EYES: BROWN   HAIR: BLACK
PROMOTED FROM SIXTH CPL NOV 3, 1863;
HOME 1897-1914:HARRISVILLE, BUTLER COUNTY, PA
ATTENDED THE DEDICATION OF THE CHICKAMAUGA BATTLEFIELD, NOV 1897

CUMMINS, WILLIAM   CPT   CO. A   AGE:27
ORIGIN: INDIANA COUNTY   OCCUPATION: MERCHANT
HEIGHT: 5' 10"   COMPLECTION: DARK HAIR: BLACK   EYES: GREY
SWORN: OCT 12, 1861/3 YRS   RESIGNED: AUG 1, 1863
RESIGNED BECAUSE OF DISABILITY
COMMENDED BY SIRWELL FOR BRAVERY AT STONES RIVER
PRESENTED A $100 SWORD AND SASH MAR 1863 BY MEN OF COMPANY
HOME 1886: SHELBY, OHIO

CUNNINGHAM, THOMAS A. *   MUS   CO. I   AGE: 23
SWORN: OCT 12, 1861/3 YRS   MUSTER: NOV 4, 1864
BORN: INDIANA COUNTY   OCCUPATION: CHAIRMAKER
HEIGHT: 5' 7½"   COMPLEXION: FAIR   EYES: GREY   HAIR: LIGHT
ORIGINALLY ENLISTED IN CO. H

CURREN, JAMES *   CPL   CO. I
SWORN: MAR 4, 1862/3 YRS   DISCHARGED: MAR 13, 1865
ARMSTRONG COUNTY, PINE CREEK NATIVE
INADVERTANTLY LISTED AS KILLED AT STONES RIVER.
PROMOTED TO CPL OCT 1, 1864
1894 SOLDIERS PENSION: $8/mo
HOME 1886-1897: KITTANNING, ARMSTRONG COUNTY, PA
REUNION IN FREEPORT 1886, KITTANNING 1901

CURRIE, GEORGE F. *   PVT   CO. A   AGE:18
CURRIER, GEORGE F.
SWORN: OCT 12, 1861/3 YRS   MUSTER: NOV 4, 1864
BORN: INDIANA COUNTY   OCCUPATION: FARMER
HEIGHT: 5' 8"   COMPLEXION: FAIR   EYES: GREY   HAIR: BLACK
BRIEFLY MISSING IN ACTION AT STONES RIVER
HOME 1890-1914: DAYTON, ARMSTRONG COUNTY, PA

REUNION KITTANNING 1901

CURRY, WILLIAM B.   PVT   CO. C   AGE:24
    SWORN: OCT 12, 1861/3 YRS   DIED: JUN 22, 1863 AT CLARION, PA
    BORN: CLARION COUNTY
    HEIGHT: 5' 11"   COMPLEXION: FAIR   EYES: BLUE   HAIR: LIGHT

CYPHER, JAMES S. *   PVT   CO. F   AGE:19
    ORIGIN: BUTLER COUNTY
    SWORN: OCT 12, 1861/3 YRS   MEDICAL: MAY 13, 1862
    BORN: DOUBLE SALE   OCCUPATION: LABORER
    HEIGHT: 5' 7"   COMPLEXION: DARK   EYES: DARK BROWN   HAIR: BLACK

CYPHER, WILLIAM H.   PVT   CO. F   AGE: 18
    ORIGIN: BUTLER COUNTY
    SWORN: FALL OF 1864   MUSTER: SEP 11, 1865
    BURIED: ST. PAUL'S LUTHERAN CEMETERY, SARVER, PA [1846-1940]
    WIFE: LOUISA   SERVICE: GUARD DUTY, NASHVILLE 1865

CYPHER, REUBEN A. ***   PVT   CO. F
    SWORN: FEB 29, 1864/3 YRS   NOT AT MUSTER

DANIELS, DAVID   PVT   CO. E   AGE:26
    SWORN: OCT 12, 1861/3 YRS   DIED: FEB 25, 1863
    BORN: VENANGO COUNTY   OCCUPATION: FARMER
    HEIGHT: 5' 9"   COMPLEXION: FAIR   EYES: BLUE   HAIR: BROWN
    MORTALLY WOUNDED AT STONES RIVER/LEG

DANIELS, HARRISON   PVT   CO. E   AGE:18
    SWORN: OCT 12, 1861/3 YRS   MUSTER: NOV 4, 1864
    BORN: CLARION COUNTY   OCCUPATION: FARMER
    HEIGHT: 5' 6"   COMPLEXION: SANDY   EYES: GREY   HAIR: DARK

DARIN, JOHN ***   PVT   CO. I   AGE: 45
    SWORN: OCT 12, 1861/3 YRS   MEDICAL: JUN 6, 1863
    BORN: PITTSBURGH, PA   OCCUPATION: TAILOR
    HEIGHT: 5' 5½"   COMPLEXION: LIGHT   EYES: GREY   HAIR: GREY
    DIED BEFORE THE REGIMENTAL HISTORY WAS PUBLISHED IN 1905

DAUGHERTY, ALBERT   PVT   CO. D   AGE:19
DOUGHERTY, ALBERT
    SWORN: OCT 12, 1861/3 YRS   MUSTER: NOV 4, 1864
    BORN: INDIANA COUNTY, HILLSDALE   OCCUPATION: LABORER
    HEIGHT: 5' 9"   COMPLEXION: DARK   EYES: BROWN   HAIR: FAIR
    HOME 1914: LIBERTY, TN

DAUGHERTY, CYRUS   CPL   CO. D   AGE:21
DIUGHERTY, CYRUS   DOUGHERTY, CYRUS
    SWORN: OCT 12, 1861/3 YRS   MUSTER: NOV 4, 1864
    BORN: INDIANA COUNTY, HILLSDALE   OCCUPATION: LABORER
    HEIGHT: 5' 7"   COMPLEXION: FAIR   EYES: GREY   HAIR: FAIR
    PROMOTED FROM PVT
    HOME 1890-1897: PURCHASE LINE, INDIANA COUNTY, PA
    REUNION CHICKAMAUGA 1897, INDIANA 1908.
    BURIED: E. MAHONING BAPTIST, GRANT TWP., INDIANA COUNTY 1840-1909

DAUGHERTY, JOHN W.   PVT   CO. D/CO. G   AGE: 24
DOUGHERTY, JOHN W.   DOUGHERTY, JOHN N.
    BORN: SALTSBURG, JUL 4, 1837 TO JOHN AND ELIZABETH
    CARPENTER   WIFE: ANNIE FERNSWORTH
    SWORN: OCT 12, 1861/3 YRS   DESERTED: JAN 3, 1864
    BORN: INDIANA COUNTY   OCCUPATION: BLACKSMITH
    HEIGHT: 5' 8"   COMPLEXION: FAIR   EYES: BLUE   HAIR: DARK
    ORIGINAL ENLISTMENT AGE STATES 32
    IN ALL PROBABILITY DESERTION WAS "FRENCH LEAVE"
    RESWORN: MAR 6, 1865   MUSTER: SEP 11, 1865
    1890 CENSUS: DIXONVILLE, INDIANA COUNTY, PA; WIDOW MARGARET
    REUNION KITTANNING 1900   HOME 1914: INDIANA, PA
    BURIED: GREENWOOD CEMETERY, INDIANA, PA [JUL 25, 1840-OCT 4, 1902]

DAVIDSON, JOHN S. *   CPL   CO. F   AGE:22
DAVIDSON, JOHN L.
    SWORN: OCT 12, 1861/3 YRS   MUSTER: NOV 4, 1864

BORN: FREEPORT, PA   OCCUPATION: DRUGGIST
HEIGHT: 5' 8½"   COMPLEXION: DARK   EYES: GREY   HAIR: DARK BROWN
PROMOTED TO CPL DEC 1, 1861   WOUNDED AT STONES RIVER/BACK

DAVIS, DAVID *   PVT   CO. K   AGE:18
    SWORN: OCT 12, 1861/3 YRS   DIED: OCT 1,1862 AT NASHVILLE
    BORN: ARMSTRONG COUNTY   OCCUPATION: TINNER
    HEIGHT: 5' 4"   COMPLEXION: DARK   EYES: BROWN   HAIR: BLACK
    BURIED @ NASHVILLE, ROW A, GRAVE #648, BATES

DAVIS, MICHAEL *   PVT   CO. K   AGE: 20
    HOME IN BUTLER COUNTY, PA
    SWORN: OCT 12, 1861/3 YRS   DIED: DEC 19, 1863 AT NASHVILLE
    BORN: BUTLER COUNTY   OCCUPATION: FARMER
    HEIGHT: 5' 8"   COMPLEXION: FAIR   EYES: GREY   HAIR: FAIR
    CAPTURED: JUL 1862 AT COLUMBIA, TN; SWORN & PAROLED
    TAKEN PRISONER AT STONES RIVER/PAROLED AT VICKSBURG
    BURIED @ NASHVILLE, ROW D, GRAVE #225, BATES

DAVIS, ORLANDO P. *   PVT   CO. G   AGE: 33
    SWORN: JUL 8, 1863/3 YRS   DISCHARGED: JUL 20, 1865
    BORN: OSWEGO, NY   OCCUPATION: FARMER
    HEIGHT: 5' 7"   COMPLEXION: LIGHT   EYES: BLUE   HAIR: GREY
    DESERTED AND RETURNED

DAVIS, WILLIAM I. *   PVT   CO. I   AGE:39
DAVIS, WILLIAM P.   DAVIS, WILLIAM D.
    SWORN: OCT 12, 1861/3 YRS   DIED: NOV 5, 1862 AT NASHVILLE
    BORN: LEECHBURG, PA   OCCUPATION: FARMER
    HEIGHT: 5' 8"   COMPLEXION: DARK   EYES: BROWN   HAIR: DARK
    BURIED @ NASHVILLE, ROW A, GRAVE #1166, BATES

DAVIS, WILLIAM J. *   SGT   CO. I   AGE:54
    SWORN: OCT 12, 1861/3 YRS   MUSTER: NOV 4, 1864
    BORN: WALES   OCCUPATION: LABORER
    HEIGHT: 5' 9"   COMPLEXION: FAIR   EYES: BLUE   HAIR: SANDY
    ENLISTED IN CO. E.   PROMOTED FROM PVT FEB 17, 1863
    COMMENDED BY SIRWELL FOR BRAVERY AT STONES RIVER
    FIELD PROMOTION BY SIRWELL; WOUNDED RIGHT LUNG
    ATTENDED 1886 REUNION IN FREEPORT
    HOME 1886-1890: CLARKSBURG, INDIANA COUNTY, PA   DIED: DEC 17, 1893
    BURIED: CLARKSBURG PRESBYTERIAN CEMETERY, CLARKSBURG, INDIANA COUNTY, PA

DEAN, BENJAMIN F.   PRINCIPAL MUSICIAN
    ORIGIN: BUTLER COUNTY   REGIMENTAL STAFF   AGE:29
    SWORN: OCT 12, 1861/3 YRS   MUSTER: NOV 4, 1864
    BORN: BUTLER COUNTY   OCCUPATION: FARMER
    HEIGHT: 5' 8"   COMPLEXION: LIGHT   EYES: GREY   HAIR: LIGHT
    HAD ORIGINALLY BEEN PRINCIPAL MUSICIAN; BUT REDUCED TO MUSICIAN
    PROMOTED FROM 2ND MUSICIAN CO. H, FEB 1, 1864
    HOME IN 1897: NEW CASTLE, PA   REUNION CHICKAMAUGA 1897

DEBO, SIMON A.   CPL   CO. E   AGE: 18
DELO, SIMEON
    SWORN: MAR 3, 1864/3 YRS   MUSTER: SEP 11, 1865
    BORN: CLARION COUNTY   OCCUPATION: FARMER
    HEIGHT: 5' 4"   COMPLEXION: DARK   EYES: BLACK   HAIR: DARK
    PROMOTED TO CPL IN 2ND REGIMENT
    1890 CENSUS: KNOX, CLARION COUNTY, PA

DELP, PETER #   PVT   CO. E
    SWORN: FEB 25, 1864/3 YRS   DISCHARGED: JAN 25, 1865
    1890 CENSUS: WEST FREEDOM, CLARION COUNTY, PA

DENNY, JAMES W. *   PVT   CO. F   AGE:25
    SWORN: OCT 12, 1861/3 YRS   MUSTER: NOV 4, 1864
    BORN: COYLESVILLE, PA   OCCUPATION: CARPENTER
    HEIGHT: 5' 7½"   COMPLEXION: FLORID   EYES: BLUE   HAIR: DARK BROWN
    HOME IN 1897: TARENTUM, PA   DIED: APR 1909
    SOME FAMILIES RECEIVED $100 BOUNTY UPON ENLISTMENT
    BURIED: ST. MARY'S, FREEPORT, PA

DENNY, JOHN F.   4TH CPL   CO. H   AGE:19
    SWORN: OCT 12, 1861/3YRS   MUSTER: NOV 4, 1864   BOUNTY: $100
    BORN: BUTLER COUNTY   OCCUPATION: PAINTER
    HEIGHT: 5' 11½"   COMPLEXION: LIGHT   EYES: GREY   HAIR: BROWN
    SUFFERED WITH MEASLES, DEC 1861
    PROMOTED TO CPL AUG 22, 1863
    HOME 1914: 14 OAKLAND AVE., SHARON, PA

DEPP, GEORGE *   PVT   CO. I   AGE:18
DEFF, GEORGE   DEPP, JOHN
    SWORN: MAR 31, 1864/3 YRS   MUSTER: SEP 11, 1865
    BORN: JEFFERSON COUNTY   OCCUPATION: LABORER
    HEIGHT: 5' 9"   COMPLEXION: LIGHT   EYES: GREY   HAIR: LIGHT
    1890 CENSUS: BIG RUN, JEFFERSON COUNTY, PA

DERR, FREDERICK   PVT   CO. B
    SWORN: SEP 19, 1864/1 YRS   DISCHARGED: SEP 2, 1865

DERRIMORE, JOHN   PVT   CO. H
    ORIGIN: BUTLER COUNTY
    SWORN: FEB 29, 1864/3 YRS   DIED: MAR 30, 1864
    BURIED IN ALLEGHENY CEMETERY, PITTSBURGH, PA

DERVIER, JOHN *   PVT   CO. C   AGE:29
DEWIRE, JOHN
    SWORN: OCT 12, 1861/3 YRS   MUSTER: NOV 4, 1864
    BORN: CLARION COUNTY
    HEIGHT: 5' 7"   COMPLEXION: DARK   EYES: GREY   HAIR: BROWN

DEVERS, NEAL *   PVT   CO. I   AGE:26
    SWORN: OCT 12, 1861/3 YRS   MUSTER: NOV 4, 1864
    BORN: KITTANNING, PA   OCCUPATION: ROLLER
    HEIGHT: 5' 7"   COMPLEXION: LIGHT   EYES: GREY   HAIR: DARK
    DIED BEFORE 1905

DEVLIN, JAMES R.   PVT   CO. A   AGE:21
DERLIN, JAMES R.
    SWORN: OCT 12, 1861/3 YRS   DIED: DEC 4, 1862 AT NASHVILLE
    BORN: INDIANA COUNTY   OCCUPATION: FARMER
    HEIGHT: 5' 8½"   COMPLEXION: FAIR   EYES: BLUE   HAIR: BROWN
    DIED OF PNEUMONIA
    BURIED AT NATIONAL CEMETERY NASHVILLE, GRAVE #A-986

DEVLIN, JOHN   PVT   CO. A   AGE:25
    SWORN: OCT 12, 1861/3 YRS   DIED: DEC 4, 1861 AT CAMP NEGLEY, KY
    BORN: INDIANA COUNTY   OCCUPATION: FARMER
    HEIGHT: 5' 9"   COMPLEXION: DARK   EYES: BROWN   HAIR: DARK
    DIED OF TYPHOID

DIBLER, ELIAS *   PVT   CO. B   AGE:19
    SWORN: OCT 12, 1861/3 YRS   MIA: @ STONES RIVER 12/31/62
    BORN: ARMSTRONG COUNTY   OCCUPATION: FARMER
    HEIGHT: 5' 10"   COMPLEXION: LIGHT   EYES: GREY   HAIR: LIGHT

DIBLER, HENRY **   PVT   CO. A
    SWORN: SEP 14, 1864/1 YEAR   DISCHARGED: MAY 27, 1865
    HOME 1890-1914: RINGGOLD, JEFFERSON COUNTY, PA/POSSIBLE

DICKIE, WILLIAM H.   PVT   CO. A   AGE:22
DICKEY, WILLIAM H.
    SWORN: OCT 12, 1861/3 YRS   TRANS: SIG CORPS, JAN 26, 1864
    BORN: INDIANA COUNTY   OCCUPATION: FARMER
    HEIGHT: 5' 5½"   COMPLEXION: DARK   EYES: BROWN   HAIR: BROWN
    DIARY USED IN WRITING REGIMENTAL HISTORY
    REUNION AT FREEPORT 1886; INDIANA 1908.
    HOME 1886-1914: BLACK LICK, PA

DICKSON, JOHN ***   PVT   CO. G/A
    SWORN: SEP 12, 1864/3 YRS   DISCHARGED: MAY 27, 1865

DINGER, AMOS   PVT   CO. B   AGE: 33
    SWORN: OCT 12, 1861/3 YRS   MIA: @ STONES RIVER 12/31/62
    BORN: SKUYLKILL COUNTY   OCCUPATION: FARMER
    HEIGHT: 5' 8"   COMPLEXION: FLORID   EYES: BROWN   HAIR: DARK

DINGER, JOHN   SGT   CO. D   AGE: 18
    SWORN: SEP 20, 1862/3 YRS   DISCHARGE: JUN 19, 1865
    BORN: ARMSTRONG COUNTY   OCCUPATION: FARMER
    HEIGHT: 5' 7"   COMPLEXION: FAIR   EYES: BLUE   HAIR: AUBURN
    HOME IN 1897-1901: OAK RIDGE STATION, ARMSTRONG COUNTY, PA
    REUNION CHICKAMAUGA 1897, KITTANNING 1901   HOME 1914: HOMER, PA
DINLANE, SAMUEL A. #   PVT   CO. K   AGE: 25
    SWORN: APR 1, 1862/3 YRS   NOT ON MUSTER OUT LIST
    BORN: WESTMORELAND COUNTY   OCCUPATION: FARMER
    HEIGHT: 5' 5"   COMPLEXION: FAIR   EYES: BLUE   HAIR: FAIR
    LISTER IN ORIGINAL ROSTER
DINSMORE, MARION J. *   SGT   CO. K   AGE: 24
DINSMORE, MARVIN J.
    SWORN: OCT 12, 1861/3 YRS   MEDICAL: JUN 1, 1862 @ CAMP DUGAN
    BORN: HUNTINGTON COUNTY   OCCUPATION: FARMER
    HEIGHT: 5' 7½"   COMPLEXION: DARK   EYES: BROWN HAIR: DARK
    MARION & ROBERT WERE BROTHERS
    SENT HOME [HOLIDAYSBURG, PA] WITH TYPHOID
    HOME: 1890-1899: PUNXSUTAWNEY, JEFFERSON COUNTY, PA
    REUNION PUNXSUTAWNEY 1899
    DIED: DEC 28, 1899 AT PITTSBURGH, PA
DINSMORE, ROBERT WILSON *   1LT   CO. K   AGE:22
DINSMORE, "WILS"
    SWORN: OCT 12, 1861/3 YRS   MUSTER: NOV 4, 1864
    BORN: HUNTINGTON COUNTY   OCCUPATION: FARMER
    HEIGHT: 5' 8½"   COMPLEXION: FAIR   EYES: GREY   HAIR: DARK
    MARION & ROBERT WERE BROTHERS
    COMMENDED BY SIRWELL FOR BRAVERY AT STONES RIVER
    PROMOTED FROM PVT; TO 1LT FEB 17, 1863; COMMANDED CO. DURING 1863
    HOME 1886-1914: PUNXSUTAWNEY, JEFFERSON COUNTY, PA
    REUNION AT FREEPORT 1886, CHICKAMAUGA 1897, KITTANNING 1900, INDIANA 1908.
DINSMORE, THOMAS J. *   PVT   CO. K   AGE: 18
DINSMORE, "BOB"
    SWORN: APR 1, 1862/3 YRS   DISCHARGED: MAR 31, 1865
    BORN: JEFFERSON COUNTY   OCCUPATION: FARMER
    HEIGHT: 5' 8"   COMPLEXION: FAIR   EYES: HAZEL   HAIR: DARK
    WOUNDED AT PICKETT'S MILL MAY 27, 1864   DIED: JAN 2, 1904
DISLER, JOSEPH M.   PVT   CO. E   AGE:20
    SWORN: OCT 12, 1861/3 YRS   MUSTER: NOV 4, 1864
    BORN: CLARION COUNTY   OCCUPATION: FARMER
    HEIGHT: 5' 9"   COMPLEXION: DARK   EYES: BLUE   HAIR: BLACK
    WOUNDED AT STONES RIVER/HEAD
DIXON, JOHN #   PVT   CO. A
    SWORN: SEP 21, 1864   MUSTER: MAY 27, 1865
    BURIED: METHODIST CEMETERY, RURAL VALLEY, PA
    NO INFORMATION; GOVERNMENT STONE LISTS 78th REGIMENT
    1890 CENSUS:COWANSHANNOCK TWP., ARMSTRONG COUNTY, PA; WIDOW HANNAH
DONLEY, GEORGE   PVT   CO. D   AGE: 42
    SWORN: OCT 12, 1861/3 YRS   DIED: JUL 27, 1863 AT NASHVILLE
    BORN: INDIANA COUNTY, CHERRY TREE   OCCUPATION: FARMER
    HEIGHT: 5' 9"   COMPLEXION: DARK   EYES: GREY   HAIR: GREY
    BURIED AT NATIONAL CEMETERY NASHVILLE, GRAVE #E-791
DOTTY, GEORGE "WASH" *   PVT   CO. K   AGE: 21
DOTY, GEORGE W.   BOUNTY $29
    SWORN: SEP 10, 1862/3 YRS   DIED: MAR 28, 1864 AT LOUISVILLE
    BORN: CLARION COUNTY   OCCUPATION: LABORER
    HEIGHT: 5' 9½"   COMPLEXION: DARK   EYES: BLACK HAIR: DARK
    JOHN & GEORGE "WASH" DOTY WERE BROTHERS
DOTTY, JOHN C. *   PVT   CO. K   AGE: 27
DOTY, JOHN C.   BOUNTY $29
    SWORN: SEP 10, 1862/3 YRS   DISCHARGED: JUN 19, 1865
    BORN: WESTMORELAND COUNTY   OCCUPATION: LABORER

HEIGHT: 5' 11½"   COMPLEXION: DARK   EYES: GREY   HAIR: DARK
WOUNDED AT STONES RIVER
1886 REUNION IN FREEPORT: HOME, WALK CHALK, PA; U.S. PENSION, 1894: $6.00

DOUGHERTY, HARRISON *   PVT   CO. I   AGE:18
SWORN: OCT 12, 1861/3 YRS   DIED: MAY 6, 1863
BORN: APOLLO, PA   OCCUPATION: LABORER
HEIGHT: 5' 5½"   COMPLEXION: LIGHT   EYES: GREY   HAIR: DARK
MORTALLY WOUNDED AT STONES RIVER/HEAD, HAND

DOUTHETT, WILLIAM S.   PVT   CO. D   AGE: 25
SWORN: SEP 20, 1862   DIED: FEB 25, 1863 AT NASHVILLE
BORN: INDIANA COUNTY, NEW SALEM   OCCUPATION: FARMER
HEIGHT: 5'   COMPLEXION: FAIR   EYES: GREY   HAIR: BROWN

DOVERSPIKE, DANIEL *   PVT   CO. B   AGE:18
DAVERSPIKE, DANIEL
SWORN: AUG 25, 1862/3 YRS   DISCHARGED: MAY 27, 1865
BORN: ARMSTRONG COUNTY   OCCUPATION: FARMER
HEIGHT: 5' 6"   COMPLEXION: DARK   EYES: BLACK   HAIR: BLACK
1890 CENSUS: RED BANK, ARMSTRONG COUNTY, PA

DOVERSPIKE, GEORGE W.   PVT   CO. B
SWORN: OCT 12, 1861/3 YRS   MUSTER: NOV 4, 1864 WOUNDED/HEAD AT STONES RIVER
BORN: ARMSTRONG COUNTY   OCCUPATION: FARMER
HEIGHT: 6'   COMPLEXION: DARK   EYES: BLUE   HAIR: BLACK
1890 CENSUS: RED BANK, ARMSTRONG COUNTY, PA
HOME 1914: PIERCE, PA; 1894: NORTH FREEDOM; U.S. PENSION, 1894: $12.00

DOWAN, A.J.   PVT   CO. B   AGE:19
COWAN, ANDREW J.
SWORN: OCT 12, 1861/3 YRS   MUSTER: NOV 4, 1864
WOUNDED/BACK AT STONES RIVER

DOWNEY, JAMES   PVT   CO. B   AGE: 48
DOWNRY, JAMES
SWORN: DEC 25, 1861/3 YRS   MEDICAL: AUG 18, 1862
BORN: IRELAND   OCCUPATION: FARMER
HEIGHT: 5' 8"   COMPLEXION: DARK   EYES: BLUE   HAIR: GRAY

DOWNEY, JOSEPH B.   SUR/78th   REGIMENTAL STAFF
ORIGIN: LANCASTER COUNTY
SWORN: AUG 2, 1862/3 YRS   RESIGNED: APR 5, 1864
PROMOTED FROM ASSISTANT SURGEON MAY 31, 1863.
AWOL SEP 1, 1863 - SEP 10, 1863

DRAKE, GEORGE S. *   PVT   CO. I   AGE: 22
SWORN: OCT 12, 1861/3 YRS   MUSTER: NOV 4, 1864
BORN: KITTANNING, PA   OCCUPATION: LABORER
HEIGHT: 5' 9"   COMPLEXION: LIGHT   EYES: BROWN   HAIR: LIGHT
SERVED AS A TEAMSTER
SERVED WITH PA 104TH, CO. K: MAR 18-AUG 25, 1865/SGT   VETERAN
1890 CENSUS: KITTANNING, ARMSTRONG COUNTY, PA; DIED BEFORE 1905
BATTLES/DUTY: PETERSBURG, FORTRESS MONROE, PORTSMOUTH

DRUM, JOHN KARNES*   PVT   CO. F   AGE:22
DRUMM, JOHN K.   DRUMM, J.K.
DUNN, JOHN K.   DEUM, JOHN K.
SWORN: OCT 12, 1861/3 YRS   MUSTER: NOV 4, 1864
BORN: FREEPORT, PA   OCCUPATION: LABORER
HEIGHT: 5' 8½"   COMPLEXION: SHALLOW   EYES: GREY   HAIR: DARK BROWN
BORN: FREEPORT, NOV 19, 1839   DIED: OCT 27, 1918
WOUNDED & CAPTURED @ STONES RIVER DEC 31, 1862: 7" SABRE CUT ON RIGHT SIDE OF
HEAD ALSO ON LEFT HAND. SENT TO LIBBY PRISON 1/19/1863:
EXCHANGED AT CITY POINT, VA. 1/26/1863; SENT TO CAMP PAROLE, MARYLAND 1/27/1863.
RECORDS SHOW 3 MONTH TIME IN LIBBY PRISON; HOWEVER, OTHER RECORDS
INDICATE ONE WEEK. NAME ON A LIST OF STRAGGLERS AND DESERTERS, PVT DRUM
COULD HAVE TAKEN "FRENCH LEAVE."   RETURNED TO REGIMENT: JUN 3, 1863,
SERVED AS A TEAMSTER; "WAGONEER" FOR COMPANY
1886 REUNION IN FREEPORT: HOME, NATRONA, PA
1894 SOLDIERS PENSION: $24/mo, HOME: FREEPORT

HOME 1914: BIRDVILLE, ALLEGHENY COUNTY, PA
BURIED: MT AIRY CEMETERY, NATRONA HEIGHTS, PA
DRUMMOND, JAMES A. *   8TH CPL   CO. I   AGE:22
   SWORN: OCT 12, 1861/3 YRS   MUSTER: NOV 4, 1864
   BORN: LIVERMONT, PA   OCCUPATION: FARMER
   HEIGHT: 6' 3"   COMPLEXION: LIGHT   EYES: GREY   HAIR: DARK
   CENSURED BY LT COL BLAKELEY
   ATTENDED THE REGIMENTAL REUNION AT INDIANA, PA, IN 1908.
   BURIED: EDGEWOOD CEMETERY, SALTSBURG, INDIANA COUNTY, PA 1839-1926
DUFF, ANDREW J. *   PVT   CO. F   AGE:27
   SWORN: OCT 12, 1861/3 YRS   DIED: JUN 19, 1864 AT CHATTANOOGA
   BORN: COYLESVILLE, PA   OCCUPATION: FARMER
   HEIGHT: 5' 7"   COMPLEXION: FAIR   EYES: BLUE   HAIR: DARK
   MORTALLY WOUNDED JUN 1, 1864 NEAR DALLAS, GA.
   BURIED: NATIONAL CEMETERY CHATTANOOGA, GRAVE: 230
DUGAN, DENNIS *   PVT   CO. F   AGE:39
DUJAN, DENNIS
   SWORN: OCT 12, 1861/3 YRS   DIED: FEB 23, 1863 OF TYPHOID AT NASHVILLE
   BORN: COYLESVILLE, PA   OCCUPATION: FARMER
   HEIGHT: 5' 11½"   COMPLEXION: FRESH   EYES: BROWN   HAIR: BLACK
   BURIED AT NATIONAL CEMETERY NASHVILLE, GRAVE #E-602
DUMM, SAMUEL M. *   SGT MAJ/78th   CO. K   AGE:23
DUNN, SAMUEL M.
   SWORN: SEP 10, 1862/3 YRS   DISCHARGED: JUN 19, 1865
   OCCUPATION: TEACHER   BOUNTY: $29
   WOUNDED AT PICKETT'S MILL MAY 27, 1864
   PROMOTED CPL TO SGT, CO. B II, DEC 1, 1864: TO 1SGT MAR 15, 1865;
   PROMOTED TO SGT MAJOR MAY 1, 1865; REGIMENTAL STAFF II
   HOME 1886-1890: SLATE LICK, ARMSTRONG COUNTY, PA
   HOME 1897-1914: PARNASSUS, WESTMORELAND COUNTY, PA
   WROTE UNPUBLISHED HISTORY OF SECOND REGIMENT
   REUNION IN FREEPORT 1886, CHICKAMAUGA 1897
   BURIED: SLATE LICK CEMETERY, SOUTH BUFFALO TWP.
DUNCAN, HARRISON   PVT   CO. D   AGE: 18
   SWORN: OCT 12, 1861/3 YRS DIED: MAR 4, 1862
   BORN: INDIANA COUNTY, HILLSDALE   OCCUPATION: CARPENTER
   HEIGHT: 5' 8"   COMPLEXION: FAIR   EYES: GREY   HAIR: DARK
DUNCAN, WILLIAM   PVT   CO. D   AGE:21
   SWORN: OCT 12, 1861/3 YRS   MUSTER: NOV 4, 1864
   BORN: INDIANA COUNTY, CHERRY TREE   OCCUPATION: FARMER
   HEIGHT: 5' 10"   COMPLEXION: FAIR   EYES: BROWN   HAIR: FAIR
   HOME 1886: BERINGER, PA
   REUNION AT FREEPORT 1886, INDIANA 1908.
   BURIED: INDIANA COUNTY, GREENWOOD CEMETERY, 1840-OCT 16, 1914
DUNLAP, JOHN W.   PVT   CO. H   AGE:26
   SWORN: OCT 12, 1861/3YRS   MUSTER: NOV 4, 1864   BOUNTY: $100.
   BORN: MERCER COUNTY   OCCUPATION: FARMER
   HEIGHT: 5' 8"   COMPLEXION: SANDY   EYES: GREY   HAIR: SANDY
DUNLAP, ROBERT W.   PVT   CO. D   AGE:20
DUNLAP, CHARLES [CHANGED NAME AFTER THE WAR]
   SWORN: OCT 12, 1861/3 YRS   MEDICAL: MAY 27, 1863
   BORN: CAMBRIA COUNTY   OCCUPATION: LABORER
   HEIGHT: 5' 6¾"   COMPLEXION: DARK   EYES: BLUE   HAIR: DARK
   1890 CENSUS: CAMBRIA COUNTY, PA
DUNLAP, THOMAS *   PVT   CO. I   AGE:45
   SWORN: OCT 12, 1861/3 YRS   MUSTER: NOV 4, 1864
   BORN: N. WASHINGTON, PA   OCCUPATION: LABORER
   HEIGHT: 5' 8"   COMPLEXION: DARK   EYES: BROWN   HAIR: DARK
   TAKEN PRISONER AT STONES RIVER/PAROLED
DUNMIRE, ADAM #   PVT   CO. K
   SWORN: UNKNOWN   MUSTER: UNKNOWN SERVICE: 18 MONTHS
   DIED: @ IDEAL REST HOME, BLACKLICK, PA @ 93

DUNMIRE, JACOB   1st CPL   CO. D   AGE:25
DURNMEYER, JACOB
    SWORN: OCT 12, 1861/3 YRS   MUSTER: NOV 4, 1864
    BORN: INDIANA COUNTY, CHERRY TREE   OCCUPATION: WAGON MAKER
    HEIGHT: 5' 9½"   COMPLEXION: FAIR   EYES: GREY
EAKMAN, AARON *   PVT   CO. I   AGE:26
    SWORN: OCT 12, 1861/3 YRS   DIED: JAN 24, 1863
    BORN: APOLLO, PA   OCCUPATION: LABORER
    HEIGHT: 5' 9½"   COMPLEXION: FAIR   EYES: GREY   HAIR: LIGHT
    MORTALLY WOUNDED AT STONES RIVER/LEG
    BURIED AT NATIONAL CEMETERY NASHVILLE, GRAVE #B-910
EASTLEY, RAYMOND E. ***   PVT   CO. B
    SWORN: AUG 12, 1864/1 YEAR   DISCHARGED: JUN 19, 1865
    1886 REUNION IN FREEPORT: HOME, RUSHVILLE, IL
    HOME 1914: COLERIDGE & McKEE STS, PITTSBURGH, PA
EDDINGER, HENRY   PVT   CO. E   AGE:18
EDINGER, HENRY
    SWORN: OCT 12, 1861/3 YRS   CAPTURED: SEP 8, 1863 NEAR CHATTANOOGA
    BORN: CLARION COUNTY   OCCUPATION: FARMER
    HEIGHT: 5' 7"   COMPLEXION: LIGHT   EYES: GREY   HAIR: SANDY
    NO INFORMATION AFTER CAPTURE   DIED: MAY 5, 1909 IN WEST VIRGINIA
    1890 CENSUS: ST. PETERSBURG, CLARION COUNTY, PA
    BURIED: ST. PETERSBURG, CLARION COUNTY, PA
EDMONSON, GEORGE *   CPL   CO. I   AGE:22
    SWORN: OCT 12, 1861/3 YRS   DESERTED: OCT 17, 1861
    BORN: ARMSTRONG COUNTY   OCCUPATION: FARMER
    HEIGHT: 5' 8"   COMPLEXION: LIGHT   EYES: DARK   HAIR: FAIR
EDWARDS, ADAM *   PVT   CO. K   AGE:21
    SWORN: OCT 12, 1861/3 YRS   MEDICAL: JUN 26, 1862
    BORN: ARMSTRONG COUNTY   OCCUPATION: FARMER
    HEIGHT: 5' 8"   COMPLEXION: DARK   EYES: BROWN   HAIR: AUBURN
    1890 CENSUS: EAST FRANKLIN TWP., ARMSTRONG COUNTY, PA
    HOME 1901-1914: KITTANNING, PA   REUNION KITTANNING 1901
EDWARDS, ALBERT *   PVT   CO. K   AGE:30
    SWORN: OCT 12, 1861/3 YRS   MEDICAL: JUN 26, 1862
    BORN: ARMSTRONG COUNTY   OCCUPATION: FARMER
    HEIGHT: 5' 7"   COMPLEXION: DARK   EYES: GREY   HAIR: AUBURN
    1890 CENSUS: EAST FRANKLIN TWP., ARMSTRONG COUNTY, PA
    HOME 1901: MOSGROVE, PA; REUNION KITTANNING 1901
EDWARDS, PHILIP *   PVT   CO. F   AGE:31
EDWARDS, PHILLIP   VETERAN
    SWORN: APR 22, 1861/3 MONTHS, CO B, NINTH PA; BRADY ALPINES
    SERVED IN SIRWELL'S ORIGINAL THREE MONTH CO.
    SWORN: OCT 12, 1861/3 YRS   MUSTER: NOV 4, 1864
    BORN: ORRSVILLE, PA   OCCUPATION: ENGINEER
    HEIGHT: 5' 5"   COMPLEXION: DARK   EYES: BLACK   HAIR: DARK
EKAS, ADAM *   CPL   CO. F   AGE:22
    SWORN: OCT 12, 1861/3 YRS   MUSTER: NOV 4, 1864
    BORN: SARVERSVILLE, PA, DEC 27, 1838   OCCUPATION: FARMER
    HEIGHT: 6' 1"   COMPLEXION: LIGHT   EYES: BLUE   HAIR: LIGHT
    PROMOTED TO CPL APR 1, 1864
    HOME 1861-1886: SARVERSVILLE, PA
    HOME 1897-1901: EKASTOWN, BUTLER COUNTY, PA   HOME 1914: SARVER, PA
    BURIED IN ST. PAUL'S LUTHERAN CEMETERY, SARVER, PA. [1839-1926]
    WIFE: MARY J. KIRKPATRICK
    REUNION FREEPORT 1886, CHICKAMAUGA 1897, KITTANNING 1901
ELLENBERGER, LEVI *   PVT   CO. B   AGE:20
ELENBARGER, LEVI
    SWORN: OCT 12, 1861/3 YRS   MUSTER: NOV 4, 1864
    BORN: ARMSTRONG COUNTY   OCCUPATION: FARMER
    HEIGHT: 5' 10"   COMPLEXION: DARK   EYES: BLUE   HAIR: BLACK
    1890 CENSUS: REYNOLDSVILLE, JEFFERSON COUNTY, PA; WIDOW HANNAH

ELLIOTT, DAVID R.   PVT   CO. E   AGE: 21
    SWORN: FEB 19, 1864/3 YRS   DISCHARGED: SEP 12, 1865
    BORN: CLARION COUNTY   OCCUPATION: FARMER
    HEIGHT: 5' 8"   COMPLEXION: DARK   EYES: HAZEL   HAIR: DARK
    TRANS: FEB 2, 1865 TO 1ST BATTERY, 5TH REGIMENT VRC
    1886 REUNION IN FREEPORT: WEST FREEDOM, PA
    1890 CENSUS: POLLOCK, CLARION COUNTY, PA;   HOME 1914: WEST FREEDOM, PA
ELLIOTT, THOMAS J.   1LT   CO. E   AGE:30
    ORIGIN: CLARION COUNTY   LICENSED PHYSICIAN
    SWORN: OCT 12, 1861/3 YRS   RESIGNED: AUG 30, 1862
    BORN: CLARION COUNTY   OCCUPATION: PHYSICIAN
    HEIGHT: 5' 10"   COMPLEXION: DARK EYES: BROWN   HAIR: BLACK
    PRACTICE IN RIMERSBURG, BUTLER COUNTY, PA
    ALLEGHENY COLLEGE GRADUATE, MEADVILLE, PA
ELLIOTT, WILLIAM   PVT   CO. I   AGE:18
    SWORN: OCT 12, 1861/3 YRS   MUSTER: NOV 4, 1864
    BORN: FREEPORT, PA   OCCUPATION: BOATMAN
    HEIGHT: 5' 4½"   COMPLEXION: LIGHT   EYES: GREY   HAIR: DARK
    HOME IN 1897-1901: ALLEGHENY CITY, PA
    REUNION CHICKAMAUGA 1897, KITTANNING 1901
ELLIOTT, WILLIAM F.   2LT   CO. E   AGE:26
    SWORN: OCT 12, 1861/3 YRS   MUSTER: NOV 4, 1864
    BORN: CLARION COUNTY   OCCUPATION: FARMER
    HEIGHT: 6'   COMPLEXION: SANDY   EYES: BLUE   HAIR: DARK
    PROMOTED FROM 1ST SGT SEP 1, 1863
ELWOOD, ROBERT D. ***   CPT   CO. I   AGE:26
    SWORN: OCT 12, 1861/3 YRS   MUSTER: NOV 4, 1864
    BORN: APOLLO, PA
    HEIGHT: 5' 9"   COMPLEXION: SANDY   EYES: GREY   HAIR: RED
    OCCUPATION: CAPTAIN OF A PACKET BOAT IN APOLLO, ARMSTRONG COUNTY, PA
    COMMENDED BY SIRWELL FOR BRAVERY AT STONES RIVER
    FROM AUG 1863 TO NOV 1864, WAS THE COMMANDER OF CAMP COPELAND IN
    PITTSBURGH UNTIL MUSTERED OUT.
    HOME 1886: PITTSBURGH, PA   HOME 1897-1921: VERONA, PA
    REUNION FREEPORT 1886, CHICKAMAUGA 1897, KITTANNING 1901, INDIANA 1908.
    PRESIDENT FIRST NATIONAL BANK, VERONA, PA
    ELECTED PRESIDENT OF THE REUNION COMMITTEE IN 1886, TREASURER 1908
    BURIED: ALLEGHENY CEMETERY, PITTSBURGH, PA - 1836-1921
    WIFE: MARY 1835-1916
    MEMBER OF CORPORAL MURRAY G.A.R. POST # 243
ENBODY, DAVIS   PVT   CO. E   AGE: 28
    SWORN: FEB 19, 1864/3 YRS   MUSTER: SEP 11, 1865
    BORN: BERKS COUNTY   OCCUPATION: STONE MASON
    HEIGHT: 5' 8"   COMPLEXION: SANDY   EYES: BROWN   HAIR: DARK
ENGLAND, WILLIAM P. *   CPL   CO. K   AGE: 33
    SWORN: OCT 12, 1861/3 YRS   MUSTER: NOV 4, 1864
    BORN: CLEARFIELD COUNTY   OCCUPATION: PHYSICIAN
    HEIGHT: 5' 7"   COMPLEXION: LIGHT   EYES: BLUE   HAIR: FAIR
    PRACTICING PHYSICIAN FROM WORTHINGTON, PA
    PROMOTED TO CPL MAR 1, 1863   DIED: IN LYCOMING COUNTY, PA
ERB, URIAH F. *   PVT   CO. I   AGE:21
    SWORN: OCT 12, 1861/3 YRS   MUSTER: NOV 4, 1864
    BORN: FREEPORT, PA   OCCUPATION: LABORER
    HEIGHT: 5' 5½"   COMPLEXION: FAIR   EYES: DARK   HAIR: DARK
    HOME 1897-1901: MILLIGANTOWN, WESTMORELAND COUNTY, PA
    HOME 1914: RD #1, PARNASSUS, WESTMORELAND COUNTY, PA
    REUNION CHICKAMAUGA 1897, KITTANNING 1901, INDIANA 1908.
ERWIN, JAMES *   PVT   CO. G   AGE:19
    SWORN: OCT 12, 1861/3 YRS   KILLED: JAN 2,1863 AT STONES RIVER
    BORN: BELKNAP, PA   OCCUPATION: BLACKSMITH
    HEIGHT: 6'   COMPLEXION: FAIR   EYES: GREY   HAIR: LIGHT
ESHENBAUGH, JOSEPH P.   PVT   CO. H   AGE:22

SWORN: OCT 12, 1861/3YRS   DESERTED: JUL 17, 1862 FROM CAMP
KITTANNING [CULLEOKA, TN]
BORN: BUTLER COUNTY   OCCUPATION: ENGINEER
HEIGHT: 5' 9"   COMPLEXION: LIGHT   EYES: GREY   HAIR: FAIR
EVANS, THOMAS   SGT   CO. C   AGE:21
SWORN: OCT 12, 1861/4 YRS   MUSTER: SEP 11, 1865   VETERAN
BORN: CLARION COUNTY
HEIGHT: 5' 10"   COMPLEXION: FAIR   EYES: BLUE   HAIR: BROWN
PROMOTED FROM PVT TO SGT; CO. B Π
HOME 1914: BRANDY CAMP, PA
EVENSELL, ROBERT #   PVT   CO. A
WOUNDED AT STONES RIVER/SHOULDER
EVENSELL IS AMONG THE LIST OF CASUALTIES AT STONES RIVER IN
1T IS POSSIBLE THAT THIS SOLDIER IS PVT EVAN W. SLATER.
NOT LISTED IN THE REGIMENTAL HISTORY OF 1905
FAIRMAN, FRANCIS M.   PVT   CO. D   AGE:29
FAIRMAN, FRANCIS S.
SWORN: OCT 12, 1861/3 YRS   DISCHARGED: OCT 17, 1864
BORN: INDIANA COUNTY   OCCUPATION: FARMER
HEIGHT: 5' 8½"   COMPLEXION: FAIR   EYES: BROWN   HAIR: DARK
DIED BEFORE THE REGIMENTAL HISTORY WAS PUBLISHED IN 1905
FAIRMAN, ROBERT J.   PVT   CO. D   AGE: 28
SWORN: SEP 20, 1862/3 YRS   DIED: APR 7, 1863 AT MURFREESBORO OF SCURVEY
BORN: INDIANA COUNTY, NEW SALEM   OCCUPATION: LABORER
HEIGHT: 5' 5"   COMPLEXION: FAIR   EYES: BLUE   HAIR: DARK
MORTALLY WOUNDED AT STONES RIVER
BURIED AT NATIONAL CEMETERY STONES RIVER, GRAVE #K-4352
INDIANA COUNTY, WASHINGTON TWP., 1860 CENSUS
FAIRMAN, SAMUEL L.   PVT   CO. D   AGE:19
FAIRMAN, SAMUEL S.
SWORN: OCT 12, 1861/3 YRS   DIED: JAN 2, 1862 AT CAMP WOOD
BORN: INDIANA COUNTY   OCCUPATION: FARMER
HEIGHT: 5' 8"   COMPLEXION: SANDY   EYES: GREY   HAIR: SANDY
FARR, GEORGE W.   PVT   CO. C   AGE: 18
SWORN: MAR 24, 1864/ 3 YRS   MUSTER: SEP 11, 1865
BORN: JEFFERSON COUNTY   OCCUPATION: LABORER
HEIGHT: 5' 7"   COMPLEXION: DARK   EYES: BROWN   HAIR: BLACK
FAWSER, EDWARD ***   PVT   CO. A/B   AGE: 18
FAWZER, EDWARD   FOWZER, EDWARD   FOWSER, EDWARD
SWORN: FEB 28, 1864/3 YRS   MUSTER: SEP 11, 1865
BORN: ARMSTRONG COUNTY
HEIGHT: 5' 4"   COMPLEXION: DARK   EYES: BROWN   HAIR: DARK
1890 CENSUS: KITTANNING, ARMSTRONG COUNTY, PA
FENNELL, JOHN M. *   PVT   CO. I
SWORN: OCT 12, 1861/3 YRS   MUSTER: NOV 4, 1864
BORN: APOLLO, PA   OCCUPATION: LABORER
HEIGHT: 5' 7½"   COMPLEXION: DARK   EYES: BLACK   HAIR: DARK
DIED BEFORE THE REGIMENTAL HISTORY WAS PUBLISHED IN 1905
FERGUSON, D. CLAYTON   PVT   CO. E   AGE: 18
FURGASM, C.D.   FURGASM, CLAYTON D.   FERGASM, C.D.
SWORN: MAR 31, 1864/3 YRS   MUSTER: SEP 11, 1865
BORN: CLARION COUNTY   OCCUPATION: FARMER
HEIGHT: 5' 3"   COMPLEXION: DARK   EYES: BLACK   HAIR: BROWN
FERRY, PATRICK T. ***   PVT   CO. C   AGE: 27
FERRY, PATRICK S.
SWORN: SEP 15, 1863/3 YRS   MUSTER: SEP 11, 1865, SICK AT MUSTER
BORN: IRELAND   OCCUPATION: CARPENTER
HEIGHT: 5' 7"   COMPLEXION: FAIR   EYES: GREY   HAIR: LIGHT
FETTER, JOHN   PVT   CO. D   AGE: 26
KETTER, JOHN
SWORN: SEP 20, 1862/3 YRS   DISCHARGED: JUN 9, 1865
BORN: INDIANA COUNTY   OCCUPATION: LABORER

HEIGHT: 5' 11¼"   COMPLEXION: FAIR   EYES: BROWN   HAIR: DARK
FETTER, HENRY *   PVT   CO. B   AGE:21
FETTERS, HENRY
    SWORN: OCT 12, 1861/3 YRS   DIED: AUG 3, 1864
    BORN: ARMSTRONG COUNTY   OCCUPATION: FARMER
    HEIGHT: 5' 9"   COMPLEXION: LIGHT   EYES: BLUE   HAIR: RED
    MORTALLY WOUNDED IN ACTION DURING THE ATLANTA CAMPAIGN
    DIED IN HOSPITAL AT JEFFERSONVILLE, IN
    BURIED: NATIONAL CEMETERY JEFFERSONVILLE, IN; SECTION.1, GRAVE.152
FISCUS, ABRAHAM K. *   PVT   CO. B   AGE:37
    SWORN: OCT 12, 1861/3 YRS   MUSTER: NOV 4, 1864
    BORN: ARMSTRONG COUNTY   OCCUPATION: FARMER
    HEIGHT: 5' 8"   COMPLEXION: DARK   EYES: BLUE   HAIR: BLACK
FISCUS, JAMES A. *   PVT   CO. B   AGE:20
    SWORN: OCT 12, 1861/3 YRS   MUSTER: NOV 4, 1864
    BORN: ARMSTRONG COUNTY   OCCUPATION: FARMER
    HEIGHT: 5' 11"   COMPLEXION: LIGHT   EYES: BLACK   HAIR: BLACK
    ATTENDED 1886 REUNION IN FREEPORT; HOME 1886-1890: KITTANNING, PA
FISCUS, JOHN W./M. *   PVT   CO. K   AGE: 20
    SWORN: OCT 12, 1861/3 YRS   MEDICAL: MAR 1863   VETERAN
    BORN: ARMSTRONG COUNTY   OCCUPATION: FARMER
    HEIGHT: 5' 6¾"   COMPLEXION: SANDY   EYES: GREY   HAIR: AUBURN
    WOUNDED AT STONES RIVER DEC 31, 1862
    SWORN: SEP 3, 1864   MUSTER: JUN 30, 1865
    PA 204th HEAVY ARTILLERY, SGT
    U.S. PENSION, 1894: $6.00   HOME 1890-1914: APOLLO, PA
    ONE OF "THE LAST DOZEN" LIVING IN ARMSTRONG COUNTY IN 1936
    BURIED: APOLLO CEMETERY, APOLLO, PA; DEC11, 1841-NOV 14, 1936
FITZPATRICK, THOMAS #   PVT   CO. F
    SWORN: UNKNOWN   MUSTER: UNKNOWN
    BURIED: PROSPECT CEMETERY, TARENTUM, PA; DIED DEC 13, 1903
FITZSIMMONS, JOHN   PVT   CO. H   AGE:18
    SWORN: OCT 12, 1861/3YRS   DIED: FEB 11, 1863 AT LOUISVILLE OF TYPHOID
    BORN: BUTLER COUNTY   OCCUPATION: FARMER
    HEIGHT: 5' 8½"   COMPLEXION: LIGHT   EYES: GREY   HAIR: BROWN
    BURIED: NATIONAL CEMETERY LOUISVILLE; SECTION.A, RANGE.6, GRAVE.27
FLANIGAN, JOHN *   3RD SGT   CO. F   AGE: 42
FLANNIGAN, JOHN   FLANIGAN, JOHN
    SWORN: OCT 12, 1861/3 YRS   MUSTER: NOV 4, 1864
    BORN: PITTSBURGH, PA   OCCUPATION: MOULDER
    HEIGHT: 5' 5"   COMPLEXION: FRESH   EYES: BLUE   HAIR: BROWN
    HOME IN 1897: INGRAM, ALLEGHENY COUNTY, PA
    1886 REUNION IN FREEPORT: HOME, BEAVER, PA
FLECK, MARTIN L. *   PVT   CO. I   AGE:18
    SWORN: MAR 31, 1864/3 YRS   MUSTER: SEP 11, 1865
    BORN: INDIANA COUNTY   OCCUPATION: LABORER
    HEIGHT: 5' 7"   COMPLEXION: LIGHT   EYES: GREY   HAIR: LIGHT
FLEMING, BARTHOLEMEW *   CPL   CO. D   AGE:22
    SWORN: OCT 12, 1861/3 YRS   DIED: MAY 1, 1863
    BORN: INDIANA COUNTY, COOKPORT   OCCUPATION: FARMER
    HEIGHT: 5' 9½"   COMPLEXION: DARK   EYES: BROWN   HAIR: DARK
    PROMOTED FROM PVT   MORTALLY WOUNDED AT STONES RIVER
    BURIED: INDIANA COUNTY, COOKPORT METHODIST CEMETERY, GREEN TWP.,
    BORN: 1839-DIED: MAY 1, 1863
FLEMING, JAMES B. *   2ND SGT   CO. B
    SWORN: OCT 12, 1861/3 YRS   MUSTER: NOV 4, 1864
    BORN: ARMSTRONG COUNTY   OCCUPATION: FARMER
    HEIGHT: 5' 10"   COMPLEXION: LIGHT   EYES: GREY   HAIR: DARK
    PROMOTED FROM SGT, AUG 29, 1862; HOME 1914: PORT ANGLES, WASHINGTON
FLEMING, JOHN M. *   1LT   CO. B   AGE:21
    SWORN: JUL 20, 1863/3 YRS   MUSTER: SEP 11, 1865
    BORN: ARMSTRONG COUNTY   OCCUPATION: FARMER

HEIGHT: 5' 10"   COMPLEXION: FAIR   EYES: BLUE   HAIR: LIGHT
PROMOTED FROM SGT TO 2LT, MAR 31, 1865; TO 1LT: JUL 17, 1865
1890 CENSUS: RED BANK, ARMSTRONG COUNTY, PA
HOME IN 1897: KITTANNING, PA
ATTENDED THE DEDICATION OF THE CHICKAMAUGA BATTLEFIELD, NOV 1897
BURIED: INDIANA COUNTY, PRESBYTERIAN CEMETERY, COVODE, 1835-NOV 12, 1898

FLEMING, RICHARD DANIEL   PVT   CO. A
FLEMING, R.B.
 SWORN: AUG 16, 1864/1 YEAR   DISCHARGED: JUN 19, 1865
 HOME 1886: EMLENTON, PA
 REUNION IN FREEPORT 1886; INDIANA 1908.

FLEMING, SAMUEL J.   SGT   CO. A   AGE:23
 SWORN: OCT 12, 1861/3 YRS   MUSTER: NOV 4, 1864
 BORN: ARMSTRONG COUNTY   OCCUPATION: CARPENTER
 HEIGHT: 5' 10" COMPLEXION: DARK   EYES: GREY   HAIR: BLACK
 PROMOTED FROM MUSICIAN JAN 1, 1862.
 1886 REUNION IN FREEPORT   HOME 1886: CHAMBERSVILLE, PA
 HOME 1890-1914: CREEKSIDE, INDIANA COUNTY, PA [RD 2]
 BURIED: INDIANA COUNTY, WASHINGTON CEMETERY, RAYNE TWP.

FLEMING, THOMAS M.   PVT   CO. A   AGE:21
 SWORN: OCT 12, 1861/3 YRS   MUSTER: NOV 4, 1864
 BORN: INDIANA COUNTY   OCCUPATION: FARMER
 HEIGHT: 6'   COMPLEXION: DARK   EYES: BLACK   HAIR: BROWN
 COMPANY TEAMSTER   HOME 1914: ROCHESTER MILLS, PA
 BURIED: INDIANA COUNTY, CURRY RUN CEMETERY, ARMSTRONG TWP.,
 AUG 22, 1840-MAR 21, 1927

FLEMING, WILLIAM A.   CPL   CO. A   AGE:19
 SWORN: OCT 12, 1861/3 YRS   MUSTER: NOV 4, 1864
 BORN: INDIANA COUNTY   OCCUPATION: FARMER
 HEIGHT: 5' 10" COMPLEXION: LIGHT   EYES: GREY   HAIR: FAIR

FLENNER, ELIJAH *   PVT   CO. G   AGE: 37
FUNNER, E.   FLINNER, E.
 SWORN: SEP 12, 1862/3 YRS   DIED: MAR 10, 1863
 BORN: ARMSTRONG COUNTY   OCCUPATION: FARMER
 HEIGHT: 5' 7"   COMPLEXION: DARK   EYES: BLUE   HAIR: DARK
 BURIED AT NATIONAL CEMETERY NASHVILLE, GRAVE #E-761

FLICK, DAVID R.   PVT   CO. E   AGE:28
 SWORN: OCT 12, 1861/3 YRS   MEDICAL: JUL 2, 1862 - HERNIA
 BORN: CLARION COUNTY   OCCUPATION: TEACHER
 HEIGHT: 6'   COMPLEXION: DARK   EYES: DARK   HAIR: BLACK
 1890 CENSUS: RIMERSBURG, CLARION COUNTY, PA

FLICK, JOHN R. #   PVT   CO. C
 SWORN: OCT 12, 1861/3 YRS   MUSTER: UNKNOWN
 1890 CENSUS: OAK RIDGE, ARMSTRONG COUNTY, PA; WIDOW CATE BISH

FOLWER, FRANCIS *   PVT   CO. G   AGE:42
FOWLER, FRANCIS
 SWORN: OCT 12, 1861/3 YRS   MEDICAL: MAY 18, 1862
 BORN: ARMSTRONG COUNTY   OCCUPATION: LABORER
 HEIGHT: 5' 8"   COMPLEXION: FAIR   EYES: BLUE   HAIR: GREY
 DIED BEFORE THE REGIMENTAL HISTORY WAS PUBLISHED IN 1905

FORBES, MICHAEL   CPT   CO. D   AGE:36
 BORN: INDIANA COUNTY, CHERRY TREE TWP.
 OCCUPATION: CARPENTER IN INDIANA COUNTY
 HEIGHT: 6'   COMPLEXION: SANDY   EYES: BROWN
 SWORN: OCT 12, 1861/3 YRS   RESIGNED: JAN 23, 1863
 DIED BEFORE THE REGIMENTAL HISTORY WAS PUBLISHED IN 1905

FORCHT, HENRY   PVT   CO. H   AGE: 18
FORK, HENRY   FORT, HENRY
 ORIGIN: BUTLER COUNTY   BOUNTY $100
 SWORN: OCT 12, 1861/3YRS   MUSTER: NOV 4, 1864
 BORN: ALLEGHENY COUNTY   OCCUPATION: FARMER
 HEIGHT: 5' 9½"   COMPLEXION: FAIR EYES: BLUE   HAIR: SANDY

SEPARATED FROM UNIT AT STONES RIVER
WOUNDED/HIP AT DALLAS, GA, AUG 14, 1864
HOME IN 1897: BUTLER, PA
BORN: FEB 20, 1843   DIED IN BUTLER, PA, JUN 24, 1904
BURIED: NORTH CEMETERY, BUTLER, PA WIFE: MARY R.

FORNEY, ABRAHAM   PVT/78th   CO. C   AGE:43
TORNEY, ABRAHAM
SWORN: OCT 12, 1861/3 YRS   MUSTER: NOV 4, 1864
HEIGHT: 5' 10"   COMPLEXION: DARK   EYES: DARK   HAIR: BROWN
BRIEFLY MISSING IN ACTION AT STONES RIVER
1890 CENSUS: MAHONING, ARMSTRONG COUNTY, PA; WIDOW CHRISTINA

FORNEY, CHARLES #   COOK/78th   STAFF   AGE: 13
TORNEY, CHARLES
SWORN: OCT 12, 1861/3 YRS   MUSTER: MAY 19, 1864
BORN: DEC 15, 1847 @ KITTANNING, PA
VOLUNTEER COOK FOR OFFICERS MESS IN 78th
SWORN: JUN 9, 1864   MUSTER: SEPT 15, 1864   KNAPP'S BATTERY/BATE'S
MOVED TO CLARION COUNTY IN 1884;   BURIED EMLENTON, PA

FOX, GEORGE   PVT   CO. E   AGE:22
SWORN: OCT 12, 1861/3 YRS   MUSTER: NOV 4, 1864
BORN: GERMANY   OCCUPATION: PUDDLER
HEIGHT: 5' 8"   COMPLEXION: SANDY   EYES: BLUE   HAIR: FAIR
ALSO INFORMATION THAT PVT FOX IS BURIED AT ANDERSONVILLE, GRAVE 2261

FOX, JOHN L.   PVT   CO. E   AGE:22
SWORN: OCT 12, 1861/3 YRS   MUSTER: NOV 4, 1864
BORN: CLARION COUNTY   OCCUPATION: FARMER
HEIGHT: 6'   COMPLEXION: DARK   EYES: DARK   HAIR: DARK
ATTENDED 1886 REUNION IN FREEPORT
HOME 1886-1897: POLLOCK, CLARION COUNTY, PA

FOX, WILLIAM C.   PVT   CO. E
SWORN: AUG 19, 1861/3 YRS   MUSTER: JUL 11, 1865   VETERAN
1890 CENSUS: POLLOCK, CLARION COUNTY, PA

FOY, GEORGE CLINTON   CPL   CO. A   AGE:26
FOY, GEORGE E.
SWORN: OCT 12, 1861/3 YRS   DIED: NOV 19, 1863
BORN: ELDERTON, ARMSTRONG COUNTY   OCCUPATION: FARMER
HEIGHT: 5' 9"   COMPLEXION: LIGHT   EYES: BLUE   HAIR: BROWN
PROMOTED TO 5th CPL, OCT 1862
WIFE: LAVINA RARICH MARRIED 9/8/1857 @ PLUM CREEK TWP.
FOY WAS CAPTURED NEAR CHICKAMAUGA 9/23/63 ALONG WITH DR. HOSACK
DIED AT LIBBY PRISON, RICHMOND

FRANK, EDWARD   PVT   CO. H   AGE:20
SWORN: OCT 12, 1861/3YRS   MEDICAL: APR 28, 1863
BORN: BUTLER COUNTY   OCCUPATION: CARPENTER
HEIGHT: 5' 7"   COMPLEXION: FAIR   EYES: BROWN   HAIR: DARK
WOUNDED/ARM AT STONES RIVER

FRANKLIN, ADAM   PVT   CO. C
SWORN: FEB 14, 1864/3 YRS   MUSTER: SEP 11, 1865

FRAUNTZ, JACOB *   PVT   CO. A   AGE:25
FRANTZ, JACOB
SWORN: AUG 24, 1863/1 YEAR   MUSTER: SEP 11, 1865.
BORN: UNION COUNTY
HEIGHT: 5' 8½"   COMPLEXION: SANDY   EYES: BLUE   HAIR: SANDY
1890 CENSUS: GEORGEVILLE, INDIANA COUNTY, PA
HOME 1914: ROSSMOYNE, PA   REUNION IN KITTANNING 1901

FRANTZ, LOUIS *   PVT   CO. E
FRANTZ, LEWIS
SWORN: FIRST INFANTRY BATTILION
SWORN: AUG 24, 1863/1 YEAR   MUSTER: SEP 11, 1865.
PROBABLY THE SAME MAN AS JACOB FRANTZ

FRASIER, JOHN   PVT   CO. C   AGE: 18
FRAZIER, JOHN

SWORN: OCT 12, 1861/3 YRS   MUSTER: NOV 4, 1864
BORN: CLARION COUNTY
HEIGHT: 5' 9"   COMPLEXION: FAIR   EYES: BLUE   HAIR: BROWN
FRAZIER, WILLIAM H.   PVT   CO. C   AGE: 23
FREASIER, WILLIAM H.
BORN: IN NEW BETHLEHEM TO HENRY AND MARGARET
SWORN: AUG 28, 1862/3 YRS   DISCHARGED: OCT 26, 1863 BECAUSE OF
WOUNDS RECEIVED AT STONES RIVER, LOST TWO FINGERS FROM RIGHT HAND
BORN: CLARION COUNTY   OCCUPATION: CARPENTER
HEIGHT: 5' 10"   COMPLEXION: FAIR   EYES: GREY   HAIR: AUBURN
TEMPORARILY MISSING IN ACTION AT STONES RIVER
HOME 1886-1897: NEW BETHLEHEM, CLARION COUNTY, PA
BROTHER, THOMAS IN PA 63:   BROTHER GEORGE W. IN 11th PA RESERVE
FIRST WIFE: RACHEL SHANKLE SECOND WIFE: CATHARINE SHANKLE
REUNION FREEPORT 1886, CHICKAMAUGA 1897
FRIEL, ADAM   PVT   CO. C
SWORN: FEB 27, 1864/3 YRS   MUSTER: SEP 11, 1865
FRIEL, DANIEL **   PVT   CO. B   AGE: 18
SWORN: JAN 27, 1864/3 YRS   MUSTER: SEP 11, 1865
BORN: BUTLER COUNTY   OCCUPATION: FARMER
HEIGHT: 5' 5"   COMPLEXION: FAIR   EYES: BROWN HAIR: BROWN
FULLER, FREDERICK   PVT   CO. D   AGE:18
SWORN: OCT 12, 1861/3 YRS   MUSTER: NOV 4, 1864
BORN: INDIANA COUNTY   OCCUPATION: FARMER
HEIGHT: 5' 6"   COMPLEXION: DARK   EYES: GREY   HAIR: DARK
HOME IN 1897: BURNSIDE, CLEARFIELD COUNTY, PA
FREDERICK FULLER & JOHN FULLER WERE BROTHERS
REUNION CHICKAMAUGA 1897, INDIANA 1908.
FULLER, JOHN   PVT   CO. D   AGE:21
SWORN: OCT 12, 1861/3 YRS   DIED: MAR 21, 1862 AT LOUISVILLE
BORN: INDIANA COUNTY   OCCUPATION: FARMER
HEIGHT: 5' 10½"   COMPLEXION: DARK   EYES: GREY   HAIR: DARK
FREDERICK FULLER & JOHN FULLER WERE BROTHERS
BURIED: NATIONAL CEMETERY LOUISVILLE; SECTION.A, RANGE.14, GRAVE.26
FULTON, SAMUEL T. *   PVT   CO. B   AGE:45
SWORN: OCT 12, 1861/3 YRS   MEDICAL: JUN 30, 1863
BORN: ARMSTRONG COUNTY   OCCUPATION: FARMER
HEIGHT: 5' 9"   COMPLEXION: LIGHT   EYES: BLUE   HAIR: GRAY
1890 CENSUS: SMICKSBURG, INDIANA COUNTY, PA
BURIED: METHODIST CEMETERY, SMICKSBURG
GABLE, MARTIN ***   PVT   CO. F   AGE: 21
SWORN: MAR 31, 1864/3 YRS   MUSTER: SEP 11, 1865
BORN: ALLEGHENY COUNTY   OCCUPATION: BLACKSMITH
HEIGHT: 5' 6"   COMPLEXION: FAIR   EYES: BLUE   HAIR: DARK
GALBRAITH, WILLIAM J. *   1LT   CO. G   AGE:24
GALBRAITH, SAMUEL   ORIGIN: ARMSTRONG COUNTY
BORN: FREEPORT, PA   OCCUPATION: ATTORNEY
HEIGHT: 6'   COMPLEXION: FAIR   EYES: GREY   HAIR: BROWN
SWORN: OCT 12, 1861/3 YRS   TRANS: JUN 20,1863 TO U.S.SIGNAL CORPS
GAMBLE, ROBERT *   PVT   CO. B   AGE:18
SWORN: OCT 12, 1861/3 YRS   MUSTER: NOV 4, 1864
BORN: ARMSTRONG COUNTY   OCCUPATION: FARMER
HEIGHT: 5' 5"   COMPLEXION: LIGHT   EYES: GREY   HAIR: LIGHT
1886 REUNION IN FREEPORT: HOME, LEECHBURG, PA
1890 CENSUS: KIRTLAND, WESTMORELAND COUNTY, PA
HOME IN 1897: BAGDAD, WESTMORELAND COUNTY, PA
HOME 1914: TARENTUM, PA
GAMBLE, WILLIAM *   PVT   CO. B   AGE: 19
SWORN: OCT 12, 1861/3 YRS   DIED: SEP 15, 1864
BORN: ARMSTRONG COUNTY   OCCUPATION: FARMER
HEIGHT: 5' 5"   COMPLEXION: LIGHT   EYES: GREY   HAIR: BLACK
DIED AT MARIETTA, GA, ACCIDENTLY WOUNDED

        BURIED @ MARIETTA, ROW G, GRAVE #1626, BATES
GAP, SILAS   PVT   CO. G   AGE:20
        SWORN: OCT 12, 1861/3 YRS   DESERTED: OCT 18, 1861
        BORN: DAYTON, PA
        HEIGHT: 5' 6"   COMPLEXION: FAIR   EYES: BLUE   HAIR: LIGHT
        NEVER REPORTED IN/AWOL
GARRETT, WILLIAM **   4th SGT   CO. A   AGE:22
GARRET, WILLIAM
        SWORN: OCT 12, 1861/3 YRS   MUSTER: NOV 4, 1864
        BORN: INDIANA COUNTY   OCCUPATION: FARMER
        HEIGHT: 5' 6"   HAIR: BROWN   EYES: GREY   COMPLEXION: FAIR
        BURIED: BROOKLAND CEMETERY, ALLEGHENY TWP. [1837-1903]
GARRISON, ROBERT R. *   PVT   CO. F   AGE: 26
        SWORN: OCT 12, 1861/3 YRS   MEDICAL: JUN 3, 1862
        BORN: FREEPORT, PA   OCCUPATION: NAIL CUTTER
        HEIGHT: 5' 7"   COMPLEXION: DARK   EYES: BLACK   HAIR: DARK
GATES, JOHN *   MUS   CO. B   AGE: 14
        SWORN: OCT 12, 1861/3 YRS   MUSTER: NOV 4, 1864
        BORN: ALLEGHENY COUNTY   OCCUPATION: "DRUMMER"
        HEIGHT: 4' 8"   COMPLEXION: LIGHT   EYES: LIGHT   HAIR: LIGHT
        HOME IN 1897: PITTSBURGH, PA   HOME/1908: LOS ANGLES, CA
        ATTENDED THE DEDICATION OF THE CHICKAMAUGA BATTLEFIELD, NOV 1897
        HOME 1914: 420 HARVARD BLDG, LOS ANGELES, CA
GEARY, JOHN W.   PVT   CO. K   AGE:35
        SWORN: OCT 12, 1861/3 YRS   MUSTER: NOV 4, 1864
        BORN: ARMSTRONG COUNTY   OCCUPATION: COLLIER
        HEIGHT: 5' 9½"   COMPLEXION: SANDY   EYES: BLUE   HAIR: FAIR
        DIED: IN KITTANNING IN 1871
        BURIED: UNION BAPTIST CEMETERY, SLATE LICK, PA
        PAGE 75 OF THE ARMSTRONG COUNTY HISTORY ALONG WITH THE 1886 REUNION
        RECORDS AND THE DEATH NOTICE AT UNION BAPTIST CEMETERY INDICATE THAT
        THERE WERE TWO JOHN GEARYs; FATHER AND SON
GEARY, JOHN W.   PVT   CO. K   AGE:15
        SWORN: OCT 12, 1861/3 YRS   MUSTER: NOV 4, 1864
        HOME 1890-1901: KITTANNING, PA
        REUNION FREEPORT 1886, KITTANNING 1901
        PAGE 75 OF THE ARMSTRONG COUNTY HISTORY ALONG WITH THE 1886 REUNION
        RECORDS AND THE DEATH NOTICE AT UNION BAPTIST CEMETERY INDICATE THAT
        THERE WERE TWO JOHN GEARYs; FATHER AND SON
GEORGE, CHRISTIAN H.   PVT   CO. E   AGE:20
        SWORN: OCT 12, 1861/3 YRS   MUSTER: NOV 4, 1864
        BORN: CLARION COUNTY   OCCUPATION: FARMER
        HEIGHT: 6'   COMPLEXION: DARK   EYES: DARK   HAIR: BLACK
        REDUCED IN RANK FROM 5TH SGT
GEORGE, JOHN *   PVT   CO. I   AGE:36
        SWORN: SEP 13, 1862/3 YRS   MUSTER: SEP 11, 1865
        BORN: CLARION, PA   OCCUPATION: LABORER
        HEIGHT: 5' 10"   COMPLEXION: DARK   EYES: GREY   HAIR: DARK
        DIED BEFORE THE REGIMENTAL HISTORY WAS PUBLISHED IN 1905
GEORGE, MARTIN W.   PVT   CO. E   AGE:18
        SWORN: OCT 12, 1861/3 YRS   MUSTER: NOV 4, 1864
        BORN: ARMSTRONG COUNTY   OCCUPATION: LABORER
        HEIGHT: 5' 4"   COMPLEXION: FAIR   EYES: BROWN   HAIR: BLACK
GEORGE, REUBEN *   PVT   CO. E   AGE: 25
        BORN: 1837 IN MERCER COUNTY TO MARTIN AND ANNA DAVIS GEORGE
        SWORN: AUG 28, 1862/3 YRS   MUSTER: SEP 11, 1865
        BORN: MERCER COUNTY   OCCUPATION: LABORER
        HEIGHT: 5' 8"   COMPLEXION: FAIR   EYES: BROWN   HAIR: DARK
        HOME 1890-1901: EAST BRADY, CLARION COUNTY, PA
        WIFE: MARY JANE MILLER   OWNED: MONTEREY HOUSE
        REUNION CHICKAMAUGA 1897, KITTANNING 1901
        COMMITTED SUICIDE: JAN 19, 1909

GEORGE, SAMUEL *   PVT   CO. I   AGE: 20
   SWORN: OCT 12, 1861/3 YRS   MUSTER: NOV 4, 1864
   BORN: LONG RUN, PA   OCCUPATION: LABORER
   HEIGHT: 5' 8½"   COMPLEXION: DARK   EYES: BLACK   HAIR: LIGHT
   1886 REUNION IN FREEPORT   HOME 1886-1897: APOLLO, PA
   BURIED: APOLLO CEMETERY, APOLLO, PA
GETTY, THOMAS C. *   PVT   CO. I   AGE:19
   SWORN: OCT 12, 1861/3 YRS   MUSTER: NOV 4, 1864
   BORN: BLANKET HILL, PA   OCCUPATION: LABORER
   HEIGHT: 5' 9½"   COMPLEXION: SANDY   EYES: GREY   HAIR: LIGHT
   DIED BEFORE THE REGIMENTAL HISTORY WAS PUBLISHED IN 1905
GIBSON, ALBERT S.***   PVT   CO. K   AGE: 21
   BORN: MAY 1, 1840 [BEERS]
   SWORN: OCT 12, 1861/3 YRS   MUSTER: NOV 4, 1864
   BORN: ALLEGHENY COUNTY   OCCUPATION: FARMER
   HEIGHT: 5' 6"   COMPLEXION: LIGHT   EYES: GREY   HAIR: LIGHT
   ENLISTED FROM NORTH BUFFALO
   HOME IN 1897: LOGANSPORT, ARMSTRONG COUNTY, PA
   WOUNDED ANKLE/STONES RIVER AND IN THE BACK AT PICKETT'S MILL
   U.S. PENSION, 1894: $8.00   HOME 1897: NORTH BUFFALO
   HOME 1901: LOGANSPORT, PA   HOME 1914: ROSSTON, PITTSBURGH, PA
   REUNION KITTANNING 1901
   BURIED: BETHEL LUTHERAN CHURCH CEMETERY, CROOKED CREEK 1840-1915
GIBSON, ANDREW   PVT   CO. A   VETERAN
   SWORN: OCT 12, 1861/4 YRS   MUSTER: SEP 11, 1865
   ATTENDED REUNION IN FREEPORT 1886
   HOME 1886-1890: CREEKSIDE, INDIANA COUNTY, PA
   BURIED: INDIANA COUNTY, PRESBYTERIAN CEMETERY, CREEKSIDE,
   WASHINGTON TWP., MAR 22, 1842-AUG 23, 1898
GIBSON, ELIJAH *   PVT   CO. F   AGE:31
   SWORN: OCT 12, 1861/3 YRS   MUSTER: NOV 4, 1864
   BORN: FREEPORT, PA   OCCUPATION: CARPENTER
   HEIGHT: 5' 11"   COMPLEXION: SHALLOW   EYES: GREY   HAIR: DARK BROWN
GIBSON, GEORGE W. *   PVT   CO. F   AGE:19
   SWORN: OCT 12, 1861/3 YRS   MUSTER: NOV 4, 1864
   BORN: SLATE LICK, PA   OCCUPATION: CARPENTER
   HEIGHT: 5' 10½"   COMPLEXION: SHALLOW   EYES: GREY   HAIR: DARK BROWN
   HOME 1914: CABOT, PA
GIBSON, J. THOMPSON   5th SGT   CO. A   AGE:18
   SWORN: OCT 12, 1861/3 YRS   MUSTER: NOV 4, 1864
   BORN: JEFFERSON COUNTY   OCCUPATION: STUDENT
   HEIGHT: 5' 8"   HAIR: BROWN   EYES: DARK   COMPLEXION: DARK
   BECAUSE OF WOUNDS NEVER DISCHARGED UNTIL DEC 28, 1864.
   WOUNDED AT PICKETT'S MILL MAY 27, 1864
   EDITOR OF REGIMENTAL HISTORY   BECAME A MINISTER
   REUNION IN FREEPORT 1886, INDIANA 1908
   HOME 1886: SHARPSBURG, PA   ; 1914: 6356 MARCHAND ST, PITTSBURGH, PA
GIBSON, WILLIAM R. *   PVT   CO. A   AGE:20
GIBSON, WILLIAM K.   BORN: AUG 15, 1841 IN PLUM CREEK TWP.
   SWORN: OCT 12, 1861/3 YRS   MUSTER: NOV 4, 1864
   BORN: ARMSTRONG COUNTY   OCCUPATION: LABORER
   HEIGHT: 5' 10"   COMPLEXION: LIGHT   EYES: BLUE   HAIR: BROWN
   HOSPITALIZED SIX WEEKS IN BRIDGEPORT, ALABAMA WITH SMALL POX
   REUNION IN FREEPORT 1886; INDIANA 1908
   HOME 1886: GOHEENVILLE, PA; 1890: NEW BETHLEHEM, CLARION COUNTY, PA
   HOME 1914: MOSGROVE, PA
GILCREST, JOHN C. *   PVT   CO. B   AGE:20
GILCREST, JOHN E.
   SWORN: OCT 12, 1861/3 YRS   MORTALLY WOUNDED: PICKETT'S MILL MAY 27, 1864
   BORN: ARMSTRONG COUNTY   OCCUPATION: FARMER
   HEIGHT: 5' 11"   COMPLEXION: DARK   EYES: BLUE   HAIR: BLACK
   DIED: JUN 4, 1864 IN FIELD HOSPITAL

BURIED @ MARIETTA, ROW G, GRAVE #785, BATES

GILLAM, ENOCH ***   PVT   CO. K   AGE: 27
GILLIAM, ENOCH   GILLAN, ENOCH
     SWORN: OCT 12, 1861/3 YRS   MUSTER: NOV 4, 1864
     BORN: ARMSTRONG COUNTY   OCCUPATION: FARMER
     HEIGHT: 5' 9½"   COMPLEXION: DARK   EYES: GREY   HAIR: BLACK
     SERVED AS A CPL AT CAMP ORR   WOUNDED AT STONES RIVER/THIGH
     TAKEN PRISONER AT STONES RIVER/PAROLED
     1890 CENSUS: SLATELICK, ARMSTRONG COUNTY, PA
     HOME IN 1897-1901: McVILL, ARMSTRONG COUNTY, PA
     HOME 1914: SHELOCTA, PA
     REUNION KITTANNING 1901, INDIANA 1908.
     BURIED: ROGERS CHAPEL, SOUTH BUFFALO TWP.

GILLAM, JAMES W. *   PVT   CO. K   AGE:21
GILLIAM, JAMES
     SWORN: SEP 10, 1862/3 YRS   TRANS: MAY 1, 1864 TO VRC
     BORN: ARMSTRONG COUNTY   OCCUPATION: FARMER
     HEIGHT: 5' 10½"   COMPLEXION: DARK   EYES: GREY   HAIR: BLACK
     BORN: ARMSTRONG COUNTY   BOUNTY: $29
     1890 CENSUS: INDIANA, INDIANA COUNTY, PA
     BURIED: UNION BAPTIST CEMETERY, SLATE LICK, PA [1840-1884] WIFE: EMILY

GILLESPIE, CHARLES B. *   CPT   CO. F   AGE:40
     BORN: DONEGAL, BUTLER COUNTY, 1820. PARENTS FROM IRELAND
     GRADUATE OF PHILADELPHIA MEDICAL COLLEGE
     TRAVELED TO CALIFORNIA GOLD FIELDS IN 1849
     RAISED AND TRAINED THE "FREEPORT CADETS"/COMPANY F.
     MARRIED SUE BRUNKER AT THE SUGAR CREEK RCC ON OCT 13, 1861
     CPT GILLESPIE'S WIFE STAYED WITH HIM IN NASHVILLE AND HAD HER SON THERE.
     GILLESPIE REQUESTED LEAVE ON OCT 2, 1863, TO TAKE HER HOME SINCE SHE HAD
     BECOME "DERANGED."
     SWORN: OCT 12, 1861/3 YRS   MUSTER: NOV 4, 1864
     BORN: FREEPORT, PA   OCCUPATION: PHYSICIAN
     HEIGHT: 5' 7"   COMPLEXION: LIGHT   EYES: GREY   HAIR: GRAY
     SOME FAMILIES RECEIVED $100 BOUNTY UPON ENLISTMENT
     SERVED AS PROVOST MARSHALL IN PULASKI, TN MAY-AUG 1862
     SERVED ON GENERAL COURT MARTIAL [NASHVILLE] NOV-DEC 1862
     SERVED AS SIRWELL'S BRIGADE A.A.A.G. DURING 1863
     ELECTED TREASURER OF THE REUNION COMMITTEE 1886
     REUNION FREEPORT 1886, CHICKAMAUGA 1897, PUNXSUTAWNEY 1899, KITTANNING 1901
     U.S. PENSION, 1894: $12.00
     HOME 1886-1907: FREEPORT, ARMSTRONG COUNTY, PA
     CO. ORDER BOOK USED IN WRITING REGIMENTAL HISTORY
     DIED: AUG 3, 1907, BURIED: ST. MARY'S CEMETERY, FREEPORT, PA

GILMORE, JAMES A.   1ST SGT   CO. H   AGE:20
GILMER, JAMES A.   GILMAN, JAMES A.
     SWORN: OCT 12, 1861/3YRS   MUSTER: NOV 4, 1864   BOUNTY: $100
     BORN: MERCER COUNTY   OCCUPATION: FARMER
     HEIGHT: 6'   COMPLEXION: LIGHT   EYES: GREY   HAIR: BROWN
     PROMOTED CPL TO 2ND SGT, SEP 1, 1862; TO 1ST SGT MAY 1, 1863
     HOME IN 1897-1901: MERCER, PA   HOME 1914: GILMORE AVE., GROVE CITY, PA
     REUNION CHICKAMAUGA 1897, KITTANNING 1901

GIRTS, JAMES R.   PVT   CO. C
     SWORN: OCT 12, 1861/3 YRS   DIED: APR 13/14, 1862 AT NASHVILLE
     BURIED AT NATIONAL CEMETERY NASHVILLE, GRAVE #A-210

GIRTS, JOHN   1LT   CO. C   AGE:36
GIRTZ, JOHN   ORIGIN: CLARION COUNTY
     HEIGHT: 5' 8"   COMPLEXION: DARK   EYES: GREY
     SWORN: OCT 12, 1861/3 YRS   RESIGNED: JUN 13, 1863 BECAUSE OF DISABILITY
     PROMOTED: APR 16, 1863, FROM 2LT
     1890 CENSUS: NEW BETHLEHEM, CLARION COUNTY, PA

GIRTS, JOHN B.   PVT   CO. C   AGE:25
     SWORN: AUG 28, 1862/3 YRS   DIED: SEP 15, 1863

BORN: CLARION COUNTY   OCCUPATION: LABORER
HEIGHT: 5' 9" COMPLEXION: DARK EYES: BROWN   HAIR: DARK
MORTALLY WOUNDED McLEMORE'S COVE, GA
GIRTS, JOHN M.   PVT   CO. C   AGE:34
   SWORN: OCT 12, 1861/3 YRS   MUSTER: NOV 4, 1864
   BORN: CLARION COUNTY
   HEIGHT: 6'   COMPLEXION: SANDY   EYES: BROWN   HAIR: SANDY
   1890 CENSUS: SCOTCH HILL, CLARION COUNTY, PA; WIDOW ALICE
GIRT, JOHN #   PVT   CO. F
   SWORN: UNKNOWN   MUSTER: UNKNOWN
   BURIED: PROSPECT CEMETERY, TARENTUM, PA; DIED APR 18, 1926
GIRTS, JOSEPH ***   PVT   CO. F   AGE:19
GIRT, JOSEPH P.
   SWORN: OCT 12, 1861/3 YRS   TRANS: APR 10,1864 TO VRC
   BORN: TARENTUM, PA   OCCUPATION: FERRYMAN
   HEIGHT: 5' 6"   COMPLEXION: SHALLOW   EYES: BROWN   HAIR: DARK BROWN
   HOME IN 1897-1901: STURGEON, ALLEGHENY COUNTY, PA
   HOME 1914: SPRINGDALE, PA
   BURIED: PROSPECT CEMETERY, TARENTUM, PA [1841-1924]: WIFE: MARGARET F.
   REUNION CHICKAMAUGA 1897, KITTANNING 1901, INDIANA 1908.
GIRTS, REED A.   PVT   CO. C   AGE:20
   SWORN: OCT 12, 1861/3 YRS   MUSTER: NOV 4, 1864
   BORN: CLARION COUNTY
   HEIGHT: 5' 6"   COMPLEXION: DARK   EYES: GREY   HAIR: BROWN
GLENN, ABRAHAM ROCKEY*   PVT   CO. B   AGE:29
   SWORN: OCT 12, 1861/3 YRS   MUSTER: NOV 4, 1864
   BORN: ARMSTRONG COUNTY   , 1832   OCCUPATION: FARMER
   HEIGHT: 5' 8" COMPLEXION: LIGHT   EYES: GREY   HAIR: RED
   APR-SEP 1862, SERVED AS HOSPITAL NURSE IN BOWLING GREEN & NASHVILLE
   FEB 2, 1863 ASSIGNED TO ESCORT OF PALMER, NEGLEY & GRANT
   HOME 1890-1910: SMICKSBURG, INDIANA COUNTY, PA
   REUNION CHICKAMAUGA 1897, INDIANA 1908.
   BROTHERS: ABRAHAM, ARCHIBALD AND ELIJAH
   BROTHER JAMES ALEXANDER GLENN JOINED PA 62nd
   BROTHER WILLIAM TURNER GLENN JOINED PA 48th
   BURIED: INDIANA COUNTY, UNION CEMETERY, SMICKSBURG
   DIED: APR 1910 [MAY 1911] @ SMICKSBURG, INDIANA COUNTY, PA
GLENN, ARCHIBALD DAVID*   SGT   CO. B   AGE:19
   SWORN: OCT 12, 1861/3 YRS   MEDICAL: FEB 16, 1863   BORN: JAN 30, 1842
   BORN: ARMSTRONG COUNTY   OCCUPATION: FARMER/TEACHER
   HEIGHT: 5' 11"   COMPLEXION: DARK   EYES: BLACK   HAIR: DARK
   ENLISTED AS FIFTH SGT; REGIMENTAL HISTORY SHOWS ENLISTMENT AS PVT
   HOWEVER, REDUCED IN RANK APR 30, 1862 AFTER MEDICAL
   RE-SWORN: JUL 1863   MUSTER: NOV 4, 1864
   PROMOTED TO CPL, JUN 30, 1862; TO SGT, JAN 12, 1864
   BROTHERS: ABRAHAM AND ELIJAH IN 78th; JAMES ALEXANDER GLENN JOINED PA 62nd
   BROTHER WILLIAM TURNER GLENN JOINED PA 48th
   EDITOR: KITTANNING UNION FREE PRESS
   REPUBLICAN: ELECTED TO THE STATE ASSEMBLY IN 1882
   ATTENDED 1886 REUNION IN FREEPORT: HOME, KITTANNING, PA
GLENN, ELIJAH C.T. *   PVT   CO. B   AGE:27
   SWORN: OCT 12, 1861/3 YRS   MUSTER: NOV 4, 1864
   BORN: ARMSTRONG COUNTY   OCCUPATION: FARMER
   HEIGHT: 6'   COMPLEXION: LIGHT   EYES: GREY   HAIR: RED
   APR 8, 1864-AUG 19, 1864; SERVED AS GENERAL JOHN PALMER'S ESCORT
   BROTHERS: ABRAHAM AND ELIJAH IN 78th; JAMES ALEXANDER GLENN JOINED PA 62nd
   BROTHER WILLIAM TURNER GLENN JOINED PA 48th
   PARENTS: ARCHIBALD & SUSANNA BARNES COURSIN; ECTG DIED: FEB 1871
   1890 CENSUS: DAYTON BOROUGH, ARMSTRONG COUNTY, PA; WIDOW LOUISA
GOLDEN, J. DENNIS *   MUS   CO. B   AGE:12
GOLDEN, DANNY A.   VETERAN
   SWORN: APR 22, 1861/3 MONTHS, CO B, NINTH PA

SWORN: OCT 12, 1861/4 YRS   MUSTER: SEP 11, 1865
BORN: ARMSTRONG COUNTY   OCCUPATION: "BOY"
HEIGHT: 4' 8"   COMPLEXION: LIGHT   EYES: BLUE   HAIR: LIGHT
YOUNGEST MEMBER OF THE REGIMENT
REUNION IN FREEPORT 1886, KITTANNING 1901
HOME 1886: KITTANNING, PA;   HOME 1897-1901: PITTSBURGH, PA

GOODMAN, DAVID   SGT   CO. C   AGE:22
SWORN: OCT 12, 1861/4 YRS   MUSTER: SEP 11, 1865   VETERAN
BORN: CLARION COUNTY
HEIGHT: 5' 10"   COMPLEXION: FAIR   EYES: GREY   HAIR: BROWN
PROMOTED FROM CORPORAL TO SGT; CO. B Π
HOME 1890-1897: NEW BETHLEHEM, PA; HOME 1914: FAIRMONT CITY, PA

GOSS, GEORGE   PVT   CO. D   AGE:18
GASS, GEORGE
SWORN: OCT 12, 1861/3 YRS   DIED: MAY 25, 1862 AT LOUISVILLE
BORN: INDIANA COUNTY, HILLSDALE   OCCUPATION: FARMER
HEIGHT: 5' 5"   COMPLEXION: DARK   EYES: BROWN   HAIR: FAIR
BURIED: NATIONAL CEMETERY LOUISVILLE; SECTION.A, RANGE.26, GRAVE.3

GOULD, HENRY *   PVT   CO. C   VETERAN
SWORN: OCT 12, 1861/4 YRS   MUSTER: SEP 11, 1865
BORN: ARMSRTONG COUNTY   HAIR: BLACK
1890 CENSUS: TEMPLETON, ARMSTRONG COUNTY, PA

GRADEN, JAMES M. *   PVT   CO. A   AGE:22
GRADER, JAMES N.
SWORN: OCT 12, 1861/3 YRS   DIED: NOV 1, 1862 @ NASHVILLE OF DYSENTERY
BORN: ARMSTRONG COUNTY   OCCUPATION: FARMER
HEIGHT: 5' 8½"   COMPLEXION: DARK   EYES: BROWN   HAIR: BROWN
BURIED AT NATIONAL CEMETERY NASHVILLE, GRAVE #A-450

GRAHAM, OLIVER   PVT   CO. E   AGE:18
SWORN: OCT 12, 1861/3 YRS   MUSTER: NOV 4, 1864
BORN: CLARION COUNTY   OCCUPATION: WARF MASTER
HEIGHT: 5' 4"   COMPLEXION: FAIR   EYES: BROWN   HAIR: SANDY
HOME 1914: MT. MORRIS, PA

GRAHAM. SAMUEL *   PVT   CO. B   AGE:22
SWORN: OCT 12, 1861/3 YRS   MUSTER: NOV 4, 1864
BORN: ARMSTRONG COUNTY   OCCUPATION: FARMER
HEIGHT: 5' 5"   COMPLEXION: LIGHT   EYES: BLUE   HAIR: BLACK

GRAHAM. THOMAS M.   4TH SGT   CO. E   AGE:30
SWORN: OCT 12, 1861/3 YRS   MUSTER: NOV 4, 1864
BORN: CLARION COUNTY   OCCUPATION: FARMER
HEIGHT: 6'   COMPLEXION: SANDY   EYES: BLUE   HAIR: SANDY
WOUNDED/ARM AT STONES RIVER/TAKEN PRISONER; PAROLED
REUNION IN FREEPORT 1886, CHICKAMAUGA 1897
HOME/ 1886-1897: WEST FREEDOM, CLARION COUNTY, PA
HOME/1908: SAN LUIS OBISPO, CA   HOME 1914: WEST FREEDOM, PA

GRAHAM, WILLIAM W. *   PVT   CO. A   AGE:18
SWORN: OCT 12, 1861/3 YRS   MUSTER: AUG 25, 1865.   VETERAN
BORN: ARMSTRONG COUNTY   OCCUPATION: FARMER
HEIGHT: 5' 9½"   COMPLEXION: DARK   EYES: BLACK   HAIR: BROWN
SERVED WITH PA 104TH, CO. K: MAR 18-AUG 25, 1865/CPL
DUTY: FORTRESS MONROE, PORTSMOUTH
HOME 1914: YATES CENTER, KANSAS

GRANT, JOSEPH L.   PVT   CO. E   AGE:25
GRANT, J.G.
SWORN: OCT 12, 1861/3 YRS   MUSTER: NOV 4, 1864
BORN: ARMSTRONG COUNTY   OCCUPATION: FARMER
HEIGHT: 5' 10"   COMPLEXION: SANDY   EYES: BLUE   HAIR: SANDY
ATTENDED 1886 REUNION IN FREEPORT
HOME 1886-1890: WEST FREEDOM, CLARION COUNTY, PA

GRANT, JOHN L. #   PVT   CO. E   AGE: 21
SWORN: OCT 12, 1861/3 YRS   DIED: DEC 14, 1863 IN CONFEDERATE PRISON, VA

GRAY, HENRY J. *   2ND CPL   CO. C   AGE:23

GREY, HENRY S.
    SWORN: OCT 12, 1861/3 YRS   MEDICAL: FEB 12, 1864
    BORN: CLARION COUNTY
    HEIGHT: 5' 6"   COMPLEXION: FAIR   EYES: BROWN
GRAY, SAMUEL A. *   PVT   CO. I   AGE: 24
    SWORN: SEP 13, 1862/3 YRS   DIED: FEB 24, 1863
    BORN: HUNTINGTON, PA   OCCUPATION: LABORER
    HEIGHT: 5' 5½" COMPLEXION: DARK   EYES: GREY   HAIR: DARK
    MORTALLY WOUNDED AT STONES RIVER/THIGH
    BURIED AT NATIONAL CEMETERY STONES RIVER, GRAVE #O-5937
GRAY, WILLIAM H. *   PVT   CO. I   AGE:22
    SWORN: SEP 13, 1862/3 YRS   MUSTER: SEP 11, 1865
    BORN: HUNTINGTON, PA   OCCUPATION: LABORER
    HEIGHT: 5' 6" COMPLEXION: DARK   EYES: GREY   HAIR: DARK
    WOUNDED AT STONES RIVER/LEG
GREEN, WILLIAM H. *   SGT   CO. K   AGE: 23
GREEN, H.W. "HARRISON"
    SWORN: OCT 12, 1861/3 YRS   DIED: JUL 6, 1863 AT MANCHESTER, TN
    BORN: ARMSTRONG COUNTY   OCCUPATION: FARMER
    HEIGHT: 5' 9½" COMPLEXION: SANDY   EYES: BLUE   HAIR: FAIR
    BURIED AT NATIONAL CEMETERY STONES RIVER, GRAVE #J-3971
GRIFFITH, PHILIP *   PVT   CO. F   AGE:18
GRIFFIN, PHILIP
    SWORN: OCT 12, 1861/3 YRS   KILLED: DEC 31, 1862 AT STONES RIVER
    BORN: JOHNSTOWN, PA   OCCUPATION: COLLIER
    HEIGHT: 5' 4"   COMPLEXION: FRESH   EYES: BLUE   HAIR: DARK BROWN
    BURIED AT NATIONAL CEMETERY STONES RIVER, GRAVE #L-4612
GROVER, PETER #   PVT   CO. H
    SWORN: UNKNOWN   DIED: MAR 9, 1862
    BURIED @ LOUISVILLE, KY, DIV 12, ROW A, GRAVE #20, BATES
GROVES, GEORGE #   PVT   CO. UNKNOWN
    SWORN: UNKNOWN   DIED: MAR 9, 1862
    BURIED @ NASHVILLE, BATES
GRUNDEN, JOHN   8TH CPL   CO. E   AGE:20
    SWORN: OCT 12, 1861/3 YRS   MUSTER: NOV 4, 1864
    BORN: LANCASTER COUNTY   OCCUPATION: CARPENTER
    HEIGHT: 5' 7" COMPLEXION: DARK EYES: BROWN   HAIR: BROWN
    1890 CENSUS: LARMARTINE, CLARION COUNTY. PA
GUINTER, GEORGE   PVT   CO. D   AGE:19
GUITER, GEORGE
    SWORN: OCT 12, 1861/3 YRS   MUSTER: NOV 4, 1864
    BORN: INDIANA COUNTY, CHERRY TREE   OCCUPATION: LABORER
    HEIGHT: 5' 6½" COMPLEXION: FAIR   EYES: BLUE   HAIR: BROWN
    HOME 1914: RD #1, BOX 70, LYONS, KANSAS
GUTHRIE, JAMES A. *   PVT   CO. A   AGE:20
    SWORN: OCT 12, 1861/3 YRS   DIED: JAN 23, 1863 AT MURFREESBORO
    BORN: ARMSTRONG COUNTY   OCCUPATION: LABORER
    HEIGHT: 5' 8"   COMPLEXION: FAIR   EYES: BLUE   HAIR: BROWN
    MORTALLY WOUNDED/SHOULDER AT STONES RIVER
    BURIED AT NATIONAL CEMETERY STONES RIVER, GRAVE #N-5592
GUTHRIE, JAMES D. *   PVT   CO. B   AGE: 21
    BORN: ARMSTRONG COUNTY   OCCUPATION: FARMER
    HEIGHT: 5' 11"   COMPLEXION: LIGHT   EYES: BLUE   HAIR: LIGHT
    SWORN: AUG 25, 1862/3 YRS   MUSTER: SEP 11, 1865
GUYER, JOHN   PVT   CO. C   AGE:20
GUIRE, JOHN
    SWORN: OCT 12, 1861/3 YRS   MUSTER: NOV 4, 1864
    BORN: CLARION COUNTY
    HEIGHT: 5' 8"   COMPLEXION: DARK   EYES: GREY   HAIR: BLACK
GUYER, WILLIAM W.*   PVT   CO. G
    SWORN: APR 1, 1862/3 YRS   MEDICAL: MAY 18, 1862
HAGAN, JAMES   PVT   CO. E   AGE:22

SWORN: OCT 12, 1861/3 YRS   MUSTER: NOV 5, 1865
TRANS: NOV 1, 1862 TO VRC
BORN: CLARION COUNTY   OCCUPATION: FARMER
HEIGHT: 6'   COMPLEXION: DARK   EYES: BROWN   HAIR: BLACK
HOME 1890: WEST FREEDOM, CLARION COUNTY, PA

HAGERTY, WILLIAM A. *   PVT   CO. G   AGE:18
HAGGERTY, WILLIAM
SWORN: OCT 12, 1861/3 YRS   ABSENT/SICK AT FINAL MUSTER
BORN: BUTLER, PA   OCCUPATION: FARMER
HEIGHT: 5' 6½"   COMPLEXION: FAIR   EYES: GREY   HAIR: BROWN
WOUNDED AT STONES RIVER DEC 31, 1862/LEG
RESIDENT OF DAYTON [PA] SOLDIER'S HOME IN 1886

HAGINS, JOHN *   PVT   CO. F   AGE: 22
HAGEN, JOHN   HAGIUS, JOHN   HAGANS, JNO.
SWORN: OCT 12, 1861/3 YRS   DIED: DEC 18, 1861 AT LOUISVILLE
BORN: DOUBLE SALE   OCCUPATION: FARMER
HEIGHT: 5' 7½"   COMPLEXION: DARK   EYES: BLUE   HAIR: AUBURN
ACCIDENTLY CRUSHED BETWEEN RAIL CARS

HALBEN, JACOB   PVT   CO. A   AGE: 30
HOLBEN, JACOB
SWORN: AUG 25, 1862/1 YEAR   DISCHARGED: JUN 19, 1865.
BORN: ARMSTRONG COUNTY   OCCUPATION: FARMER
HEIGHT: 5' 8½"   COMPLEXION: DARK   EYES: BLUE   HAIR: BLACK
1890 CENSUS: RED BANK, ARMSTRONG COUNTY, PA
HOME IN 1897: OAK RIDGE STATION, ARMSTRONG COUNTY, PA
ATTENDED THE DEDICATION OF THE CHICKAMAUGA BATTLEFIELD, NOV 1897

HALL, JAMES   PVT   CO. A   AGE:22
SWORN: OCT 12, 1861/3 YRS   MUSTER: NOV 4, 1864
BORN: INDIANA COUNTY   OCCUPATION: FARMER
HEIGHT: 6'   COMPLEXION: DARK   EYES: DARK   HAIR: BROWN

HALL, JOHN **   PVT   CO. G   AGE:23
SWORN: OCT 12, 1861/3 YRS   ABSENT AT FINAL MUSTER
BORN: PITTSBURGH, PA   OCCUPATION: MECHANIC
HEIGHT: 5' 6"   COMPLEXION: SANDY   EYES: GREY   HAIR: BLACK
CAPTURED: DEC 31, 1862 AT STONES RIVER

HALL, JOHN D. *   5TH SGT CO. I   AGE:18
SWORN: OCT 12, 1861/3 YRS   MEDICAL: MAR 26, 1863
BORN: N. WASHINGTON, PA   OCCUPATION: LABORER
HEIGHT: 5' 8"   COMPLEXION: LIGHT   EYES: GREY   HAIR: DARK
WOUNDED AT STONES RIVER, DEC 30th/KNEE; SENT TO HOSPITAL # 18 IN NASHVILLE

HALSTEAD, MATTHEW J. *   2LT   CO. K   AGE:41
ORIGIN: ARMSTRONG COUNTY, SLATELICK
SWORN: OCT 12, 1861/3 YRS   KILLED: JAN 2, 1863 AT STONES RIVER
COMMANDED CO. AT STONES RIVER
COMMENDED BY SIRWELL FOR BRAVERY AT STONES RIVER

HAMILTON, WILLIAM W.   SGT   CO. D   AGE: 26
SWORN: OCT 12, 1861/3 YRS   MEDICAL: JAN 14, 1863
BORN: INDIANA COUNTY, CHERRY TREE   OCCUPATION: FARMER
HEIGHT: 5' 8½"   COMPLEXION: FAIR   EYES: BLUE   HAIR: SANDY
ENLISTED AS FIRST MUSICIAN
1890 CENSUS: HILLSDALE, INDIANA COUNTY, PA
DIED AT HILLSDALE, PA BEFORE 1905
BURIED: INDIANA COUNTY, THOMPSON CEMETERY, HILLSDALE, MONTGOMERY TWP.,
SEP 23, 1835-NOV 7, 1891

HAMM, GEORGE D.   SGT   REGIMENTAL STAFF   AGE:27
SWORN: OCT 12, 1861/3 YRS   MUSTER: NOV 4, 1864
BORN: CLARION COUNTY
HEIGHT: 5' 9"   COMPLEXION: DARK   EYES: BLUE   HAIR: BROWN
ORIGINAL ENLISTMENT IN CO. C.   REGIMENTAL COLOR SGT
COMMENDED BY COLONEL SIRWELL FOR BRAVERY AT STONES RIVER
HOME 1890-1901: FROGTOWN, CLARION COUNTY, PA
REUNION CHICKAMAUGA 1897, KITTANNING 1901

HAMMOND, CHAMBERS O. *   CPL   CO. B   AGE: 20
    SWORN: AUG 25, 1862/3 YRS   DISCHARGED: JUN 19, 1865
     BORN: ARMSTRONG COUNTY   OCCUPATION: SHOEMAKER
     HEIGHT: 5' 8½"   COMPLEXION: LIGHT   EYES: BLUE   HAIR: DARK
    PROMOTED TO SGT, DEC 4, 1864
    1890 CENSUS: DAYTON BOROUGH, ARMSTRONG COUNTY, PA

HARDY, FREDERICK *   PVT   CO. F   AGE: 28
    SWORN: OCT 12, 1861/3 YRS   TRANS: DEC 1, 1862 TO 4TH CAV
    BORN: UA OIL WORKS, PA   OCCUPATION: COLLIER
    HEIGHT: 5' 10½"   COMPLEXION: DARK   EYES: GREY   HAIR: BROWN

HARMAN, ANDREW J.   PVT   CO. A   AGE: 32
HARMON, A.J.
    SWORN: MAR 31, 1864/1 YRS   MUSTER: ABSENT, SICK AT MUSTER
    ATTENDED REUNION IN FREEPORT 1886
    HOME 1886-1890: WILLET, INDIANA COUNTY, PA   JAN 9, 1832-JUN 25, 1909
    BURIED: INDIANA COUNTY, WASHINGTON CEMETERY, RAYNE TWP.,

HARMAN, PHILIP *   PVT   CO. A   AGE:19
HANNON, PHILLIP   HARMON, PHILLIP   VETERAN
HARMOND, PHILIP
    SWORN: OCT 12, 1861/3 YRS   DISCHARGED: MAR 15, 1865
    BORN: INDIANA COUNTY   OCCUPATION: LABORER
    HEIGHT: 5' 6"   COMPLEXION: DARK   EYES: GREY   HAIR: BROWN
    CAPTURED SEP 20, 1863 AT CHICKAMAUGA
    IMPRISONED @ ANDERSONVILLE FROM SEP 20 TO DEC 10, 1864
    HOME 1886-1897/1914: DAYTON BOROUGH, ARMSTRONG COUNTY, PA
    BURIED: KITTANNING CEMETERY [1842-1923] WIFE: ISABELLE
    PHILIP HARMAN COMMITTED SUICIDE
    REUNION CHICKAMAUGA 1897, INDIANA 1908.

HARRIS, HORATIO *   PVT   CO. F   AGE:34
    SWORN: OCT 12, 1861/3 YRS   DIED: APR 4, 1863
    BORN: WASHINGTON, D.C.   OCCUPATION: CARPENTER
    HEIGHT: 5' 11"   COMPLEXION: FAIR   EYES: GREY   HAIR: LIGHT
    ACCIDENTLY KILLED: APR 4, 1863 AT DECHERD, TN; RAN OVER BY A TRAIN
    BURIED @ NASHVILLE, BATES

HARRISON, ADAM H. *   PVT   CO. E
    SWORN: OCT 12, 1861/3 YRS   MUSTER: NOV 4, 1864
    1890 CENSUS: RIMER, ARMSTRONG COUNTY, PA

HARTMAN, JOHN P. *   PVT   CO. K   AGE:19
HARMAN, JOHN P.
    SWORN: OCT 12, 1861/3 YRS   DIED: JAN 16, 1863 IN NASHVILLE
    BORN: ARMSTRONG COUNTY   OCCUPATION: LABORER
    HEIGHT: 5' 9"   COMPLEXION: DARK   EYES: GREY   HAIR: DARK
    MORTALLY WOUNDED AT STONES RIVER/HEAD; BURIED @ NASHVILLE, BATES

HARTMAN, ROBERT *   PVT   CO. A
HARMAN, JOHN P.
    SWORN: SEP 1864/1 YRS   DIED: APR 20, 1865, NASHVILLE OF SMALL POX
    ALSO LISTED IN UNASSIGNED COMPANY IN BATES
    BURIED @ NASHVILLE, BATES

HASLETT, REUBEN A. *   PVT   CO. F   AGE: 30
    SWORN: OCT 12, 1861/3 YRS   MEDICAL: JUN 2, 1863
    BORN: SARVERSVILLE, PA   OCCUPATION: FARMER
    HEIGHT: 5' 9"   COMPLEXION: LIGHT   EYES: BLUE   HAIR: AUBURN

HASTINGS, ABRAHAM JUDSON *   PVT   CO. K   AGE:21
    SWORN: OCT 12, 1861/3 YRS   MUSTER: NOV 4, 1864
    BORN: ARMSTRONG COUNTY   OCCUPATION: FARMER
    HEIGHT: 5' 10"   COMPLEXION: FAIR   EYES: HAZEL   HAIR: DARK

HASTINGS, ADONIRAM J.   SGT   CO. K
    SWORN: OCT 12, 1861/3 YRS   TRANS: JUN 27, 1864
    ORDERED TO SIGNAL CORPS, JAN 27, 1864

HASTINGS, ENOCH *   PVT   CO. K
    SWORN: OCT 12, 1861/3 YRS   MUSTER: NOV 4, 1864
    BORN: ARMSTRONG COUNTY   OCCUPATION: FARMER

HEIGHT: 5' 7"   COMPLEXION: DARK   EYES: BROWN   HAIR: DARK
WOUNDED AT STONES RIVER
HASTINGS, JOHN S. *   PVT   CO. G   AGE:41
    SWORN: OCT 12, 1861/3 YRS   DIED: DEC 11, 1861 AT CAMP NEGLEY
    BORN: DAYTON, PA   OCCUPATION: LABORER
    HEIGHT: 5' 6"   COMPLEXION: DARK   EYES: DARK   HAIR: DARK
HATZELL, PHINEAS F.   1ST MUC   CO. C   AGE:21
HARTSELL, PHINEAS F.
    SWORN: OCT 12, 1861/3 YRS   MUSTER: NOV 4, 1864
    BORN: CLARION COUNTY
    HEIGHT: 5' 8½"   COMPLEXION: LIGHT   EYES: GREY
    ORPHAN RAISED BY NEIGHBORS   HOME 1886: LAFAYETTE, INDIANA
HAWK, AARON *   2CPL   CO. I   AGE:29
    SWORN: OCT 12, 1861/3 YRS   MUSTER: NOV 4, 1864
    BORN: LEECHBURG, PA   OCCUPATION: FARMER
    HEIGHT: 5' 9"   COMPLEXION: DARK   EYES: BLUE   HAIR: BLACK
    HOME 1886: SPRING CHURCH, PA
    HOME 1890-1901: LEECHBURG, ARMSTRONG COUNTY, PA
    REUNION FREEPORT 1886, CHICKAMAUGA 1897, KITTANNING 1901; DIED BEFORE 1905
HAWK, JAMES M. *   MUC   CO. G
    SWORN: MAR 12, 1862/3 YRS   MUSTER: SEP 11, 1865
    HOME IN 1897-1914: PETROLIA, BUTLER COUNTY, PA
    REUNION CHICKAMAUGA 1897, KITTANNING 1901, INDIANA 1908.
HAWS, BENJAMIN F. *   PVT   CO. F   AGE:30
    SWORN: OCT 12, 1861/3 YRS   MUSTER: NOV 4, 1864
    BORN: FREEPORT, PA   OCCUPATION: FARMER
    HEIGHT: 5' 5"   COMPLEXION: FAIR   EYES: GREY   HAIR: LIGHT
    BRIEFLY MISSING IN ACTION AT STONES RIVER
    WOUNDED AT NEW HOPE CHURCH: MAY 30, 1864   DIED: AT BARBERTON, OH
    BURIED: PROSPECT CEMETERY, TARENTUM, PA; JUL 28, 1831-MAR 21, 1902
HAY, ALBERT BUELL**   2SGT   CO. H   AGE:18
HAY, ALBERT BUELL
    SWORN: OCT 12, 1861/3YRS   MUSTER: NOV 4, 1864   BOUNTY: $100.
    BORN: DEC 13, 1844   ORIGIN: ZELIONOPLE
    BORN: BUTLER COUNTY   OCCUPATION: STUDENT
    HEIGHT: 5' 7½"   COMPLEXION: LIGHT   EYES: GREY   HAIR: LIGHT
    PROMOTED FROM PVT, MAY 1, 1863
    ATTENDED CONNOQUENESSING ACADEMY IN CANNONSBURG; EVENTUALLY
    WASHINGTON & JEFFERSON COLLEGE IN WASHINGTON, PA; MEMBER OF SIGMA CHI
    HOME 1897-1901: 937 BEECH AVE., [NORTHSIDE], PITTSBURGH, PA
    HOME 1914: 1623 OLIVER BLDG., PITTSBURGH, PA
    REUNION CHICKAMAUGA 1897, KITTANNING 1901
    ALLEGHENY COUNTY SOLICITOR: 1906-1916; ALLEGHENY COUNTY ASST. D.A.: 1918-1934
    "MAJOR" HAY HELPED FOUND THE UNION VETERAN LEGION
    DIED: SEP 23, 1934   BURIED: UNIONDALE CEMETERY
HAYNES, SOLOMON   PVT   CO. B   AGE: 31
HAINES, SOLOMON
    SWORN: AUG 25, 1862/3 YRS   DISCHARGED: JUN 19, 1865
    BORN: HUNTINGDON COUNTY   OCCUPATION: LABORER
    HEIGHT: 5' 11"   COMPLEXION: DARK   EYES: BLACK   HAIR: BLACK
    1890 CENSUS: BROCKWAYVILLE, JEFFERSON COUNTY, PA
HAYS, WILLIAM   PVT   CO. E   AGE: 22
    SWORN: OCT 12, 1861/3 YRS   DIED: JAN 24, 1863
    BORN: DONEGAL, IRELAND   OCCUPATION: LABORER
    HEIGHT: 5' 9"   COMPLEXION: SANDY   EYES: GREY   HAIR: SANDY
    SISTER: SUSAN HAYS   MORTALLY WOUNDED AT STONES RIVER
HEATH, JOSHUA *   PVT   CO. G   AGE:21
    SWORN: OCT 12, 1861/4 YRS   MUSTER: SEP 11, 1865   VETERAN
    BORN: CLARION, PA   OCCUPATION: LABORER
    HEIGHT: 5' 6"   COMPLEXION: DARK   EYES: GREY   HAIR: LIGHT
HECK, PETER   COM SGT   CO. C   AGE:21
KECK, PETER

SWORN: FEB 8, 1864/3 YRS   MUSTER: SEP 11, 1865
ENLISTED AS 7TH CORPORAL   HEIGHT: 5' 8"; PROMOTED TO SERGEANT; CO. B ∏
COMMISSIONED 2LT, JUL 27, 1865 - NEVER MUSTERED AT RANK
PROMOTED TO COMMISSARY SGT, AUG 2, 1865; REGIMENTAL STAFF ∏.

HEFELFINGER, JOHN   PVT   CO. A   AGE:22
HEFFELFINGER, JOHN
SWORN: OCT 12, 1861/3 YRS   MEDICAL: DEC 19, 1862.
BORN: INDIANA COUNTY   OCCUPATION: CARPENTER
HEIGHT: 6' 1"   COMPLEXION: SANDY   EYES: GREY   HAIR: BROWN
DIED AT HOME SHORTLY AFTER DISCHARGE
BURIED: INDIANA COUNTY, CURRY RUN CEMETERY, ARMSTRONG TWP.,

HELM, JOHN *   PVT   CO. F   AGE: 18
HELLAN, JOHN
SWORN: MAY 21, 1863/3 YRS   MUSTER: SEP 11, 1865
BORN: LEBANON COUNTY, PA   OCCUPATION: LABORER
HEIGHT: 5' 3"   COMPLEXION: LIGHT   EYES: GREY   HAIR: LIGHT

HELMAN, GEORGE   PVT   CO. A   AGE:23
HELLMAN, GEORGE
SWORN: OCT 12, 1861/3 YRS   DIED: DEC 31, 1861 AT LOUISVILLE OF TYPHOID
BORN: INDIANA COUNTY   OCCUPATION: FARMER
HEIGHT: 6' 1"   COMPLEXION: DARK   EYES: GREY   HAIR: BROWN
BURIED: NATIONAL CEMETERY LOUISVILLE; SECTION.A, RANGE.5, GRAVE.13

HENDERSON, WILLIAM A. *   3SGT   CO. G   AGE:26
SWORN: OCT 12, 1861/3 YRS   MEDICAL: MAY 18, 1862   DIED BEFORE 1905
BORN: DAYTON, PA   OCCUPATION: PLASTERER
HEIGHT: 6'   COMPLEXION: FAIR   EYES: BLUE   HAIR: BROWN

HENDRICKS, ELIAS *   PVT   CO. B   AGE:20
SWORN: OCT 12, 1861/3 YRS   MUSTER: NOV 4, 1864
BORN: ARMSTRONG COUNTY   OCCUPATION: FARMER
HEIGHT: 5' 8"   COMPLEXION: LIGHT   EYES: BLUE   HAIR: DARK
WOUNDED/ARM AT STONES RIVER
1890 CENSUS: RINGGOLD, JEFFERSON COUNTY, PA
HOME 1897: PIERCE, ARMSTRONG COUNTY, PA; 1914: DuBOIS, PA

HENRY, CHARLES *   PVT   CO. G   AGE:46
HENESY, CHARLES   DIED BEFORE 1905
SWORN: OCT 12, 1861/3 YRS   MUSTER: NOV 4, 1864
BORN: KITTANNING, PA   OCCUPATION: LABORER
HEIGHT: 5' 7½"   COMPLEXION: FAIR   EYES: GREY   HAIR: LIGHT

HENRY, EBENEZER   PVT   CO. B   AGE:19
SWORN: OCT 12, 1861/3 YRS   DIED: FEB 20, 1862 AT LOUISVILLE OF PNEUMONIA
BORN: ARMSTRONG COUNTY   OCCUPATION: FARMER
HEIGHT: 6'   COMPLEXION: DARK   EYES: BLUE   HAIR: LIGHT
BURIED: NATIONAL CEMETERY LOUISVILLE; SECTION.A, RANGE.13, GRAVE.3

HENRY, JAMES *   PVT   CO. F   AGE: 21
ORIGIN: BUTLER COUNTY
SWORN: OCT 12, 1861/3 YRS   KILLED: DEC 31, 1862 AT STONES RIVER
BORN: RED BANK, PA   OCCUPATION: LABORER
HEIGHT: 5' 7"   COMPLEXION: DARK   EYES: BLUE   HAIR: BROWN
BURIED AT NATIONAL CEMETERY STONES RIVER, GRAVE #L-4695
ALSO SHOWING A GRAVE IN UNION BAPTIST CEMETERY, SLATE LICK, PA.

HENRY, JEFFERSON B.   SGT   CO. E   AGE:27
SWORN: OCT 12, 1861/3 YRS   MUSTER: NOV 4, 1864
BORN: BUTLER COUNTY   OCCUPATION: CARPENTER
HEIGHT: 5' 10"   COMPLEXION: DARK   EYES: GREY   HAIR: BROWN
PROMOTED FROM 2ND MUC TO PVT; TO CPL NOV 1, 1863; TO SGT OCT 31, 1864

HENRY, L.P. #   PVT/78th   CO. K
NO INFORMATION EXITS ON THIS SOLDIER OTHER THAN THE BURIAL RECORDS
BURIED AT NATIONAL CEMETERY NASHVILLE, GRAVE #B-1096; DIED: JAN 24, 1864

HENRY, OLIVER *   PVT   CO. G   AGE:33
HENESY, OLIVER
SWORN: OCT 12, 1861/3 YRS   MUSTER: NOV 4, 1864
BORN: DAYTON, PA   OCCUPATION: LABORER

HEIGHT: 5' 3"   COMPLEXION: DARK   EYES: DARK   HAIR: DARK
U.S. PENSION, 1894: $12.00; HOME 1890-1914: DAYTON, ARMSTRONG COUNTY, PA
REUNION CHICKAMAUGA 1897, KITTANNING 1901
BURIED: DAYTON CEMETERY, DAYTON, PA

HENRY, PATRICK   PVT   CO. C   AGE: 21
SWORN: AUG 28, 1862/3 YRS   DIED: JUL 15, 1864 AT CHATTANOOGA
BORN: CLARION COUNTY   OCCUPATION: BLACKSMITH
HEIGHT: 5' 6"   COMPLEXION: DARK   EYES: BROWN   HAIR: DARK
MORTALLY WOUNDED AT PICKETT'S MILL

HENRY, STUART P. *   CPL   CO. K   AGE:21
HENRY, STEWART P.   STEWART, L.P.
SWORN: OCT 12, 1861/3 YRS   DIED: JAN 24, 1863
BORN: ARMSTRONG COUNTY   OCCUPATION: CARPENTER
HEIGHT: 5' 10½"   COMPLEXION: DARK   EYES: GREY   HAIR: DARK
MORTALLY WOUNDED AT STONES RIVER/FOOT
BURIED AT NATIONAL CEMETERY NASHVILLE. GRAVE #B-1096

HENRY, WILLIAM, H., JR. *   1ST SGT   CO. I   AGE:20
SWORN: OCT 12, 1861/3 YRS   MUSTER: NOV 4, 1864
BORN: KITTANNING, PA   OCCUPATION: STUDENT
HEIGHT: 5' 9"   COMPLEXION: DARK   EYES: BROWN   HAIR: DARK
PROMOTED FROM 4TH CPL, MAR 1, 1863
DIED: JUN 18, 1882   BURIED: APOLLO CEMETERY, APOLLO, PA
WIFE MARY LISTED AS WIDOW IN 1890 CENSUS, IN APOLLO

HEPLER, SAMUEL   8TH CPL   CO. C   AGE:22
SWORN: OCT 12, 1861/3 YRS   MUSTER: NOV 4, 1864
BORN: CLARION COUNTY
HEIGHT: 5' 7"   COMPLEXION: DARK   EYES: GREY
REPRIMANDED BY COLONEL BLAKELEY
1890 CENSUS: FROGTOWN, CLARION COUNTY, PA

HEPLER, THOMAS   PVT   CO. C   AGE:24
SWORN: OCT 12, 1861/3 YRS   MEDICAL: APR 27, 1863
BORN: CLARION COUNTY
HEIGHT: 5' 9"   COMPLEXION: DARK   EYES: BROWN   HAIR: BROWN
WOUNDED AT STONES RIVER/LEG
1890 CENSUS: WEST MILLVILLE, CLARION COUNTY, PA

HERVEY, DeWITT C. *   CPT   CO. K   AGE:31
SWORN: OCT 12, 1861/3 YRS   RESIGNED: NOV 17, 1862
OCCUPATION: BAPTIST MINISTER, UNION BAPTIST CHURCH, SLATELICK,
ARMSRONG COUNTY, PA   INITIALLY RESIGNED IN JUN 1862

HETRICK, ADAM *   PVT   CO. C   AGE: 24
SWORN: AUG 28, 1862/3 YRS   MUSTER: SEP 11, 1865
BORN: CLARION COUNTY   OCCUPATION: LABORER
HEIGHT: 5' 7"   COMPLEXION: FAIR EYES: GREY   HAIR: LIGHT
1890 CENSUS: FAIRMOUNT, CLARION COUNTY, PA

HILBERRY, JAMES S.   CPT   CO. B   AGE: 24
HILLBERRY, J. S.
SWORN: APR 22, 1861/3 MONTHS, CO B, NINTH PA   VETERAN
SWORN: OCT 12, 1861/3 YRS   RESIGNED: DEC 25, 1862
BORN: ARMSTRONG COUNTY
HEIGHT: 6'   COMPLEXION: DARK   EYES: DARK
SERVED WITH SIRWELL'S ORIGINAL CO. B.
REUNION IN FREEPORT 1886
HOME 1886-1890: INDIANA, INDIANA COUNTY, PA; 1914: OBERLIN, OHIO

HILL, LEWIS T. *   3RD CPL   CO. I   AGE:29
SWORN: OCT 12, 1861/4 YRS   MUSTER: APR 12, 1865
BORN: KITTANNING, PA   OCCUPATION: PUDDLER
HEIGHT: 5' 9"   HAIR: LIGHT   EYES: GREY   COMPLEXION: DARK
DESERTED AND RETURNED; SERVED IN CO. B IN THE SECOND REGIMENT TO REPAY
DESERTION TIME LEVIED BY A GENERAL COURT MARTIAL,
HOME 1890-1897: KITTANNING, PA; DIED IN KITTANNING BEFORE 1905
ATTENDED THE DEDICATION OF THE CHICKAMAUGA BATTLEFIELD, NOV 1897

HILL, THOMAS T.   CPL   CO. D   AGE:19

SWORN: OCT 12, 1861/3 YRS   PROMOTED FROM PVT, APR 11, 1863
BORN: INDIANA COUNTY, HILLSDALE   OCCUPATION: FARMER
HEIGHT: 5' 7"   COMPLEXION: DARK   EYES: GREY   HAIR: DARK
DIED/NO OTHER INFORMATION   CAVALRY SERVICE DURING 1863

HILL, WILLIAM #   PVT/78th   CO. B
ORIGIN: ARMSTRONG COUNTY   SIRWELL'S BRADY ALPINES
SWORN: APR 22, 1861   MUSTER: JUL 22, 1861/9th
SWORN: OCT 12, 1861/3 YRS   DISCHARGED: 1863   VETERAN
1890 CENSUS: REYNOLDSVILLE, JEFFERSON COUNTY, PA

HILLBERRY, MARTIN   PVT   CO. A   AGE:18
SWORN: OCT 12, 1861/3 YRS   MUSTER: NOV 4, 1864
BORN: INDIANA COUNTY   OCCUPATION: LABORER
HEIGHT: 5' 8½"   COMPLEXION: DARK   EYES: DARK BROWN   HAIR: BROWN

HILLIARD, JOSIAH   3RD CPL   CO. H   AGE:19
SWORN: OCT 12, 1861/3YRS   MUSTER: NOV 4, 1864
BORN: BUTLER COUNTY   OCCUPATION: FARMER
HEIGHT: 5' 5^{1}/3"   COMPLEXION: DARK   EYES: BROWN   HAIR: LIGHT
PROMOTED TO CPL, MAY 1, 1863   BOUNTY: $100

HILLIARD, REUBEN   PVT   CO. C   AGE:22
SWORN: OCT 12, 1861/3 YRS   MEDICAL: OCT 2, 1863
BORN: CLARION COUNTY
HEIGHT: 5' 9"   COMPLEXION: DARK   EYES: BLUE   HAIR: BROWN
WOUNDED AT STONES RIVER/THIGHS

HIMES, ISRAEL *   PVT   CO. B   AGE:28
SWORN: AUG 25, 1862/3 YRS   DIED: JUN 4, 1864
BORN: ARMSTRONG COUNTY   OCCUPATION: MILLER
HEIGHT: 6' ½"   COMPLEXION: DARK   EYES: DARK   HAIR: DARK
MORTALLY WOUNDED @ PICKETT'S MILL; BURIED @ MARIETTA, ROW H, GRAVE #503
1890 CENSUS: RED BANK, ARMSTRONG COUNTY, PA; WIDOW SUSANNAH

HIMES, JACOB *   PVT   CO. B   AGE:53
SWORN: OCT 12, 1861/3 YRS   TRANS: VRC, AUG 1, 1863
BORN: ARMSTRONG COUNTY   OCCUPATION: FARMER
HEIGHT: 5' 7"   COMPLEXION: DARK   EYES: BROWN   HAIR: GRAY

HIMES, JOSEPH *   PVT   CO. B   AGE:21
SWORN: OCT 12, 1861/3 YRS   MUSTER: NOV 4, 1864
BORN: ARMSTRONG COUNTY   OCCUPATION: FARMER
HEIGHT: 5' 11"   COMPLEXION: DARK   EYES: BLACK   HAIR: BLACK
PROMOTED TO CPL, DATE UNKNOWN;   HOME 1914: BROCKWAYVILLE, PA

HIMES, JOSEPH C.   PVT   CO. C   AGE: 18
SWORN: MAY 7, 1863/3 YRS   MUSTER: SEP 11, 1865   DIED: OCT 10, 1908
BORN: CLARION COUNTY, JUN 8, 1846   OCCUPATION: LABORER
HEIGHT: 5' 8"   COMPLEXION: FAIR   EYES: GREY   HAIR: BROWN
ATTENDED 1886 REUNION IN FREEPORT; HOME 1886-1897: NEW BETHLEHEM, PA

HIMES, LEVI *   PVT   CO. C   AGE: 20
SWORN: AUG 28, 1862/3 YRS   TRANS: APR 13,1865 VRC,
BORN: CLARION COUNTY   OCCUPATION: FARMER
HEIGHT: 5' 7"   COMPLEXION: DARK   EYES: BROWN   HAIR: DARK
DISCHARGED: JUN 19, 1865   WIFE: MARGARET RUTHERFORD
PROMOTED TO CORPORAL [BEERS]

HIMES, MATTHEW *   PVT   CO. B   AGE:18
SWORN: OCT 12, 1861/3 YRS   MUSTER: NOV 4, 1864
BORN: ARMSTRONG COUNTY   OCCUPATION: FARMER
HEIGHT: 5' 4"   COMPLEXION: DARK   EYES: GREY   HAIR: DARK
REUNION IN KITTANNING 1901; HOME 1901: EDDYVILLE, ARMSTRONG COUNTY, PA

HIMES, SOLOMON   PVT   CO. B   AGE: 25
HINIES, SOLOMON   HEIMES, SOLOMON
SWORN: AUG 25, 1862/3 YRS   DISCHARGED: JUN 19, 1865
BORN: CLARION COUNTY   OCCUPATION: FARMER
HEIGHT: 5' 11"   COMPLEXION: LIGHT   EYES: BLUE   HAIR: LIGHT
WOUNDED AT STONES RIVER, HALF OF RIGHT THUMB TAKEN OFF [TO FIRST JOINT]
RECOVERED IN A NASHVILLE HOSPITAL; WIFE: ELIZABETH FETTER
BURIED: NORTH FREEDOM, JEFFERSON COUNTY, PA

U.S. PENSION, 1894: $6.00   HOME: NORTH FREEDOM
1890 CENSUS: RED BANK, ARMSTRONG COUNTY, PA
HINCHBERGER, CHRISTIAN   PVT   CO. H   AGE: 17
HINCHBURGER, CHRISTIAN
   BORN IN FRANCE   BOUNTY: $100.
   SWORN: OCT 12, 1861/3YRS   MUSTER: NOV 4, 1864
   BORN: BUTLER COUNTY   OCCUPATION: FARMER
   HEIGHT: 5' 6"   COMPLEXION: LIGHT   EYES: GREY   HAIR: LIGHT
   HOME IN 1886-1901: BUTLER, PA; 1914: 402 FRANKLIN ST., BUTLER, PA
   REUNION FREEPORT 1886, CHICKAMAUGA 1897, KITTANNING 1901
   BROTHERS, JOSEPH AND NICHOLAS SERVED IN THE CIVIL WAR
   BURIED: CAVALRY CEMETERY, BUTLER, PA
HINDMAN, CHARLES *   PVT   CO. K   AGE:18
   SWORN: OCT 12, 1861/3 YRS   MUSTER: NOV 4, 1864
   BORN: BUTLER COUNTY   OCCUPATION: LABORER
   HEIGHT: 5' 9½"   COMPLEXION: FAIR   EYES: GREY   HAIR: LIGHT
HINDMAN, JOHN McCLELLAND *   PVT   CO. B   AGE: 16/18
   SWORN: OCT 12, 1861/3 YRS   DIED: JUL 29, 1864 AT NASHVILLE
   BORN: BUTLER COUNTY/1845   OCCUPATION: FARMER
   HEIGHT: 5' 4"   COMPLEXION: DARK   EYES: BLACK   HAIR: LIGHT
   MORTALLY WOUNDED DURING THE ATLANTA CAMPAIGN
   BURIED AT NATIONAL CEMETERY NASHVILLE, GRAVE #J-368
HINSHAW, ELIAS H. *   PVT   CO. B   AGE:18
HENSHEN, ELIAS H.   HENSHAW, ELI H.
   SWORN: OCT 12, 1861/3 YRS   DIED: OCT 16, 1862 AT NASHVILLE
   BORN: BUTLER COUNTY   OCCUPATION: FARMER
   HEIGHT: 5' 3"   COMPLEXION: LIGHT   EYES: GREY   HAIR: RED
   BURIED AT NATIONAL CEMETERY NASHVILLE, GRAVE #A-813
HIPMAN, CONRAD *   PVT   CO. F   AGE: 45
HIPSMAN, CONRAD
   SWORN: OCT 12, 1861/3 YRS   DIED: MAY 1, 1863 AT NASHVILLE
   BORN: FREEPORT, PA   OCCUPATION: LABORER
   HEIGHT: 5' 10"   COMPLEXION: LIGHT   EYES: BLUE   HAIR: LIGHT
   BURIED AT NATIONAL CEMETERY NASHVILLE, GRAVE #E-323
HOBBIN, SOLOMON *   PVT   CO. B   AGE:22
HOLBEN, SOLOMON
   SWORN: OCT 12, 1861/3 YRS   DIED: MAR 21, 1862 AT LOUISVILLE OF TYPHOID
   BORN: ARMSTRONG COUNTY   OCCUPATION: FARMER
   HEIGHT: 6' 4"   COMPLEXION: LIGHT   EYES: BLUE   HAIR: LIGHT
HODIL, JACOB D. *   PVT   CO. I   AGE:19
   SWORN: JAN 4, 1864/3 YRS   MUSTER: SEP 11, 1865
   BORN: ALLEGHENY COUNTY   OCCUPATION: FARMER
   HEIGHT: 5' 4"   COMPLEXION: DARK   EYES: BROWN HAIR: DARK
   HOME 1914: HARMONY, PA
HOERR, JOHN   PVT   CO. H   AGE:19
HOOVER, JOHN   HOOVET, JOHN   HOEN, JOHN
   SWORN: OCT 12, 1861/3YRS   MUSTER: NOV 4, 1864   BOUNTY: $100.
   BORN: ALLEGHENY COUNTY   OCCUPATION: FARMER
   HEIGHT: 5' 9"   COMPLEXION: DARK   EYES: HAZEL   HAIR: BLACK
   PROMOTED TO CPL, MAY 1, 1863   DEMOTED NOV 4, 1863
   HOME 1886-1914: 270 FISKE ST., PITTSBURGH, PA
   REUNION FREEPORT 1886, CHICKAMAUGA 1897, KITTANNING 1901, INDIANA 1908.
HOFF, SAMUEL   PVT
   DRAFTED: OCT 16, 1862/3 YRS   MUSTER: NOV 4, 1864
HOFFER, JOHN   PVT   CO. C   AGE: 18
   SWORN: JAN 15, 1864/3 YRS   MUSTER: SEP 11, 1865
   BORN: ARMSTRONG COUNTY   OCCUPATION: FARMER
   HEIGHT: 5' 5"   COMPLEXION: FAIR   EYES: BROWN HAIR: BLACK
HOFFER, WILLIAM W.   PVT   CO. C   AGE:20
   SWORN: OCT 12, 1861/3 YRS   MUSTER: NOV 4, 1864
   BORN: ARMSTRONG OR CLARION COUNTY
   HEIGHT: 5' 7"   COMPLEXION: DARK   EYES: BROWN   HAIR: BROWN

HOFFER, SAMUEL A.   PVT   CO. C   AGE: 22
    SWORN: OCT 12, 1861/3 YRS   MUSTER: NOV 4, 1864
    BORN: ARMSTRONG COUNTY
    HEIGHT: 5' 8"   COMPLEXION: DARK   EYES: BROWN   HAIR: BROWN
HOFFMAN, FRANCIS S.   1SGT   CO. C   AGE:18
    SWORN: OCT 12, 1861/4 YRS   MUSTER: SEP 11, 1865   VETERAN
    BORN: CLARION COUNTY
    HEIGHT: 5' 7"   COMPLEXION: FAIR   EYES: BROWN   HAIR: BROWN
    PROMOTED FROM CORPORAL; CO. B I1
HOFFMAN, JOHN   PVT   CO. H   AGE:17
    SWORN: OCT 12, 1861/3YRS   MUSTER: NOV 4, 1864
    BORN: BUTLER COUNTY   OCCUPATION: FARMER
    HEIGHT: 5' 10" COMPLEXION: LIGHT EYES: HAZEL   HAIR: BROWN
    HOME 1914: STUART, NEBRASKA
HOFFMAN, ZEP'H H.   PVT   CO. C
    SWORN: SEP 21, 1864/1 YR   DISCHARGED: AUG 5, 1865
HOGAN, BENJAMIN F.   PVT   CO. E   AGE:20
HAGAN, BENJAMIN F.
    SWORN: OCT 12, 1861/3 YRS   MUSTER: NOV 4, 1864
    BORN: CLARION COUNTY   OCCUPATION: FARMER
    HEIGHT: 6'   COMPLEXION: FAIR   EYES: BLUE   HAIR: LIGHT
    1890 CENSUS: POLLOCK, CLARION COUNTY, PA
HOGAN, GEORGE W.   PVT   CO. E   AGE: 18
    SWORN: OCT 12, 1861/3 YRS   MUSTER: NOV 4, 1864
    BORN: CLARION COUNTY   OCCUPATION: LAWYER
    HEIGHT: 5' 8"   COMPLEXION: SANDY   EYES: GREY   HAIR: SANDY
HOGAN, JOHN W. *   PVT   CO. K   AGE:18
    SWORN: OCT 12, 1861/4 YRS   DISCHARGED: JUL 20, 1865   VETERAN
    BORN: CLARION COUNTY   OCCUPATION: FARMER
    HEIGHT: 5' 9½"   COMPLEXION: FAIR   EYES: BROWN HAIR: AUBURN
HOLBIN, JACOB *   PVT   CO. B   AGE:30
HOLBEN, JACOB
    SWORN: AUG 25, 1862/3 YRS   MUSTER: SEP 11, 1865
    HEIGHT: 5' 8½"   COMPLEXION: DARK
    HOME 1914: OAK RIDGE, PA
HOLLINGSWORTH, BENJAMIN FRANKLIN, PVT   CO. K   AGE:20***
    SWORN: OCT 12, 1861/3 YRS   DIED: JAN 16, 1863
    BORN: ALLEGHENY COUNTY   OCCUPATION: FARMER
    HEIGHT: 5' 4"   COMPLEXION: DARK   EYES: BROWN HAIR: BLACK
    MORTALLY WOUNDED AT STONES RIVER
HOLLISTER, LEONARD A.   MUC   CO. D   AGE:22
HOLLISTER, LEONARD D.
    SWORN: OCT 12, 1861/3 YRS   MUSTER: NOV 4, 1864
    BORN: INDIANA COUNTY, CHERRY TREE   OCCUPATION: CLERK
    HEIGHT: 5' 7"   COMPLEXION: FAIR   EYES: BROWN
    REDUCED IN RANK FROM 3RD SGT
    HOME 1890-1914: INDIANA, INDIANA COUNTY, PA
    ASSISTANT SECRETARY OF 1908 REUNION COMMITTEE
    REUNION CHICKAMAUGA 1897, KITTANNING 1901, INDIANA 1908
    BURIED: INDIANA COUNTY, GREENWOOD CEMETERY, 1838-MAY 20, 1917
HOLSAPPIE, GEORGE   PVT   CO. D   AGE: 22
HOLSAPPLE, GEORGE
    DRAFTED: OCT 16, 1862/9 MO   MUSTER: JAN 2, 1864
    BORN: SNYDER COUNTY, PENNSYLVANIA   OCCUPATION: CARPENTER
    HEIGHT: 5' 11"   COMPLEXION: SANDY EYES: BLACK   HAIR: BLACK
HOOKS, HUGH A. *   PVT   CO. G   AGE:18
    SWORN: OCT 12, 1861/3 YRS   MUSTER: NOV 4, 1864
    BORN: KITTANNING, PA, SEP 4, 1843   OCCUPATION: FARMER
    HEIGHT: 5' 5"   COMPLEXION: FAIR   EYES: BLUE   HAIR: DARK
    WOUNDED MOUTH/ AT STONES RIVER JAN 2, 1863
    GUT WOUND AT CHICKAMAUGA; RAN OVER BY TRAIN, SEP 29, 1864 LOST LEG
    1890 CENSUS: EAST FRANKLIN TWP., ARMSTRONG COUNTY, PA

JAMES H. COUSINS' BROTHER-IN-LAW;   ENUMERATOR FOR 1890 CENSUS
HOME 1897-1901: ADRIAN, ARMSTRONG COUNTY, PA
HOME 1914: GUNTOWN, PA,   REUNION KITTANNING 1901
BURIED: CROYLE CEMETERY, EAST FRANKLIN TWP.
HOOKS, HUGH F.*   PVT   CO. K   AGE:50
    SWORN: OCT 12, 1861/3 YRS   MEDICAL: NOV 10, 1862
    BORN: ARMSTRONG COUNTY   OCCUPATION: LABORER
    HEIGHT: 5' 7"   COMPLEXION: DARK   EYES: BROWN   HAIR: BLACK
    1890 CENSUS: EAST FRANKLIN TWP., ARMSTRONG COUNTY, PA
    HUGH A. HOOKS' FATHER, JAMES H. COUSINS' FATHER-IN-LAW
HOOVER, JACOB *   PVT   CO. G   AGE:34
    SWORN: OCT 12, 1861/3 YRS   MUSTER: NOV 4, 1864
    BORN: KITTANNING, PA   OCCUPATION: LABORER
    HEIGHT: 5' 11"   COMPLEXION: FAIR   EYES: BLUE   HAIR: LIGHT
HOPKINS, JOHN A.   PVT   CO. G   AGE:18
    SWORN: OCT 12, 1861/3 YRS   MUSTER: NOV 4, 1864
    BORN: KITTANNING, PA   OCCUPATION: LABORER
    HEIGHT: 5' 7"   COMPLEXION: DARK   EYES: DARK   HAIR: DARK
    HOME 1890-1914: REYNOLDSVILLE, PA
    ATTENDED THE DEDICATION OF THE CHICKAMAUGA BATTLEFIELD, NOV 1897
HORN, JOHN L. *   PVT   CO. C
    SWORN: SEP 21, 1864/3 YRS   NOT AT FINAL MUSTER
    1890 CENSUS: RED BANK, ARMSTRONG COUNTY, PA
HOSACK, WILLIAM S., M.D. *   PVT   CO. G   AGE:36
HOSICK, WILLIAM S.   DAYTON RESIDENT
    SWORN: OCT 12, 1861/3 YRS   MUSTER: NOV 4, 1864
    BORN: WESTMORELAND COUNTY   OCCUPATION: PHYSICIAN
    HEIGHT: 5' 7½"   COMPLEXION: FAIR   EYES: BLUE·   HAIR: BLACK
    COMMENDED BY SIRWELL FOR BRAVERY AT STONES RIVER
    CAPTURED AT McLEMORE'S COVE/PAROLED
    COMMENDED BY BLAKELEY FOR BRAVERY AT CHICKAMAUGA.
    HOME 1897: ALLEGHENY CITY, PA; 1914: 44 TAGGART ST., PITTSBURGH, PA
HOSEY, JAMES K.   MAJ   CO. E   AGE:29
    COMMISSIONED AS CAPTAIN OF CO. E
    SWORN: OCT 12, 1861/3 YRS   MUSTER: NOV 4, 1864
    BORN: CLARION COUNTY   OCCUPATION: TEACHER
    HEIGHT: 6'   COMPLEXION: DARK EYES: BLUE   HAIR: BLACK
    ALLEGHENY COLLEGE GRADUATE, MEADVILLE, PA
    COMMENDED BY GENERAL STARKWEATHER
    PROMOTED TO MAJOR APR 9, 1864
HOWE, HORATIO S.   PVT   CO. E
    SWORN: MAR 31, 1864/3 YRS   DISCHARGED: MAY 20, 1865
    ASSIGNED TO MUC BILLET IN 2ND REGIMENT
HOWSER, ISAAC *   PVT   CO. G   AGE:32
HOUSER, ISAAC
    SWORN: OCT 12, 1861/3 YRS   MEDICAL: MAY 18, 1862
    BORN: KITTANNING, PA   OCCUPATION: LABORER
    HEIGHT: 5' 7½"   COMPLEXION: DARK   EYES: DARK   HAIR: BROWN
    1890 CENSUS: BOGGS TWP., ARMSTRONG COUNTY, PA; WIDOW ELEANOR
HUBER, BERNARD *   4TH SGT   CO. G   AGE:44
BARNHARD, HUBER   ORDERLY SERGEANT
    BORN: WURTEMBERG, GERMANY NOV 6, 1819
    SERVED 5 YEARS IN THE GERMAN ARMY
    SWORN: OCT 12, 1861/3 YRS   MUSTER: NOV 4, 1864
    SON LEWIS: PA 55th, CO. G; DIED @ BEAUFORT, S.C. ON JAN 5, 1863
    1890 CENSUS:COWANSHANNOCK TWP., ARMSTRONG COUNTY, PA
    DIED: JULY OF 1891 @ RURAL VALLEY
HUDSON, JOHN   PVT   CO. D   AGE:19
    SWORN: OCT 12, 1861/3 YRS   MUSTER: NOV 4, 1864
    BORN: INDIANA COUNTY, COOKPORT   OCCUPATION: FARMER
    HEIGHT: 5' 4½"   COMPLEXION: DARK   EYES: GREY   HAIR: BROWN
    HOME IN 1897: UHL, CAMBRIA COUNTY, PA

ATTENDED THE DEDICATION OF THE CHICKAMAUGA BATTLEFIELD, NOV 1897

HUEY, DANIEL *   CPL   CO. F   AGE: 36
    SWORN: OCT 12, 1861/3 YRS   MUSTER: NOV 4, 1864
    BORN: SARVERSVILLE, PA   OCCUPATION: LABORER
    HEIGHT: 5' 9"   COMPLEXION: DARK   EYES: BROWN   HAIR: DARK
    PROMOTED TO CPL, MAR 1, 1863   WOUNDED AT PICKETT'S MILL
    HOME 1886-1897: SARVERSVILLE, BUTLER COUNTY, PA
    REUNION IN FREEPORT 1886, CHICKAMAUGA 1897

HUFF, JAMES EDDY#   PVT   CO. E
    SWORN: UNKNOWN   MUSTER: UNKNOWN
    BURIED: PROSPECT CEMETERY, TARENTUM, PA; DIED AUG 23, 1891

HUFF, JAMES S.K. *   2ND MUC   CO. F   AGE:18
    SWORN: OCT 12, 1861/3 YRS   MUSTER: NOV 4, 1864
    BORN: FREEPORT, PA   OCCUPATION: LABORER
    HEIGHT: 5' 9"   COMPLEXION: LIGHT   EYES: BLUE   HAIR: LIGHT

HUFF, SAMUEL   PVT   CO. D   AGE: 27
    DRAFTED: OCT 16, 1862/9 MO   MUSTER: JAN 2, 1864
    BORN: SNYDER COUNTY, PENNSYLVANIA   OCCUPATION: SHOEMAKER
    HEIGHT: 5' 4"   COMPLEXION: FAIR   EYES: DARK   HAIR: DARK

HUFF, WILLIAM H. *   SGT   CO. F   AGE:23
    SWORN: OCT 12, 1861/3 YRS   MUSTER: NOV 4, 1864
    OCCUPATION: GENTLEMAN   BORN: FREEPORT
    HEIGHT: 5' 8"   COMPLEXION: LIGHT   EYES: BLUE   HAIR: DARK BROWN
    PROMOTED FROM 7TH CPL, AUG 1, 1863
    HOME 1897-1901: McKEES ROCKS, PA   REUNION KITTANNING 1901

HUGHES, JOHN A.   PVT   CO. A   AGE:18
HUFHAN, JOHN A.
    SWORN: OCT 12, 1861/3 YRS   DIED: JAN 13, 1864 AT NASHVILLE
    BORN: ARMSTRONG COUNTY   OCCUPATION: LABORER
    HEIGHT: 5' 7"   COMPLEXION: FAIR   EYES: BLUE   HAIR: BLOND
    BURIED AT NATIONAL CEMETERY NASHVILLE, GRAVE #D-222

HUFFMAN, JOHN F.   PVT   CO. A
    SWORN: OCT 12, 1861/3 YRS   DIED:DEC 27, 1864, JEFFERSONVILLE, IN.
    BURIED: NATIONAL CEMETERY LOUISVILLE; SECTION.1, GRAVE.123

HUFFMAN, JOHN F.   PVT   CO. E   AGE: 22
    SWORN: FEB 29, 1864/3 YRS   MUSTER: SEP 11, 1865
    BORN: CLARION COUNTY   OCCUPATION: LABORER
    HEIGHT: 5' 3"   COMPLEXION: DARK   EYES: GREY   HAIR: BROWN

HUFFMAN, ZEFANIA #   PVT   CO. C
    SWORN: SEP 21, 1864/3 YRS   DISCHARGED: AUG 5, 1865
    1890 CENSUS: BROOKVILLE, JEFFERSON COUNTY, PA

HUGHES, GEORGE *   PVT   CO. G   AGE:30
    SWORN: OCT 12, 1861/3 YRS   MUSTER: NOV 4, 1864
    BORN: ARMSTRONG COUNTY   ; OCCUPATION: LABORER   DEMOTED FROM 5TH CPL
    HEIGHT: 5' 10"   COMPLEXION: FAIR   EYES: BROWN   HAIR: BROWN

HUGHES, WILLIAM   PVT   CO. B   AGE: 16
    SWORN: FEB 2, 1864   MUSTER: SEP 11, 1865
    1890 CENSUS: FORD CITY, ARMSTRONG COUNTY, PA; DIED: 1906 @ FORD CITY

HUGHES, WILLIAM L.*   ACTING SGT   CO. B   AGE:20
    SWORN: OCT 12, 1861/4 YRS   MUSTER: SEP 11, 1865   VETERAN
    SERVED AS A 7th CPL AT CAMP ORR
    BORN: ARMSTRONG COUNTY   OCCUPATION: RR ENGINEER
    HEIGHT: 5' 5"   COMPLEXION: DARK   EYES: BLACK   HAIR: DARK
    COMMENDED BY SIRWELL AND ROSECRANS FOR BRAVERY AT STONES RIVER
    PROMOTED BY SIRWELL FOR CAPTURE OF ENEMY FLAG; HOME 1890-1897: FORD CITY, PA
    REUNION CHICKAMAUGA 1897, KITTANNING 1901

HUGHES, WILLIAM W. *   CPL   CO. F
    SWORN: OCT 12, 1861/3 YRS   DIED: JAN 20, 1862 AT CAMP WOOD
    BORN IN FREEPORT
    HEIGHT: 5' 11½"   COMPLEXION: LIGHT   EYES: BLUE   HAIR: LIGHT

HULL, MORRISON *   PVT   CO. G   AGE:26
    SWORN: OCT 12, 1861/3 YRS   KILLED: DEC 31, 1862 AT STONES RIVER

BORN: DAYTON, PA   OCCUPATION: SADDLER
HEIGHT: 5' 8½"   COMPLEXION: DARK   EYES: BROWN   HAIR: BROWN
HUMMEL, JEREMIAH   5TH CPL   CO. E   AGE:27
HURMEL, JEREMIAH
     SWORN: OCT 12, 1861/3 YRS   MUSTER: NOV 4, 1864
     BORN: CLARION COUNTY   OCCUPATION: LABORER
     HEIGHT: 5' 9"   COMPLEXION: SANDY   EYES: BLUE   HAIR: DARK
     WOUNDED AT STONES RIVER/LEG
     HOME IN 1897: MONITEAU, BUTLER COUNTY, PA
HUMMEL, SAMUEL   PVT   CO. E   AGE: 19
     SWORN: OCT 12, 1861/3 YRS   MUSTER: NOV 4, 1864
     BORN: CLARION COUNTY   OCCUPATION: MILLER
     HEIGHT: 5' 7"   COMPLEXION: DARK   EYES: BLUE   HAIR: BLACK
     1886 REUNION IN FREEPORT: HOME, MONITEAU, PA
     HOME/1908: CLIFF MINE, PA   HOME 1914: RD #3, BURGETTSTOWN, PA
HUMPHRIES, JOSEPH   5TH CPL   CO. H   AGE:19
HUMPHREYS, DAVID W.
     SWORN: OCT 12, 1861/3YRS   MUSTER: NOV 4, 1864   BOUNTY: $100
     BORN: BUTLER COUNTY   OCCUPATION: FARMER
     HEIGHT: 5' 10¼"   COMPLEXION: LIGHT EYES: BROWN   HAIR: BLACK
     PROMOTED TO CPL, DEC 17, 1863   DIED AT NEW CASTLE, PA BEFORE 1905
HUNTER, MARTIN V. *   PVT   CO. I   AGE: 25
     SWORN: OCT 12, 1861/3 YRS   MUSTER: NOV 4, 1864
     BORN: APOLLO, PA   OCCUPATION: LABORER
     HEIGHT: 5' 9½"   COMPLEXION: DARK   EYES: BLUE   HAIR: DARK
     HOME 1914: PEARL, VENANGO COUNTY, PA
HUNTER, WILLIAM M.   PVT   CO. E   AGE: 21
     SWORN: OCT 12, 1861/3 YRS   MUSTER: NOV 4, 1864
     BORN: VENANGO COUNTY   OCCUPATION: FARMER
     HEIGHT: 5' 9"   COMPLEXION: LIGHT   EYES: GREY   HAIR: LIGHT
     HOME 1897 1914: CORYDON, WARREN COUNTY, PA
     ATTENDED THE DEDICATION OF THE CHICKAMAUGA BATTLEFIELD, NOV 1897
HUTCHISON, JOHN W. *   PVT   CO. K   AGE:21
     SWORN: OCT 12, 1861/3 YRS   DIED: APR 13, 1863
     BORN: BUTLER COUNTY   OCCUPATION: SADDLER
     HEIGHT: 5' 6"   COMPLEXION: FAIR   EYES: GREY   HAIR: LIGHT
     MORTALLY WOUNDED AT STONES RIVER
     BURIED AT NATIONAL CEMETERY STONES RIVER, GRAVE #J-3786
     TWIN BROTHERS JOHN W. & SAMUEL A.; PARENTS: DAVID AND MARY
HUTCHISON, SAMUEL A.   PVT   CO. K   AGE:21
     SWORN: OCT 12, 1861/3 YRS   DIED: FEB 6, 1862 AT CAMP WOOD
     BORN: BUTLER COUNTY   OCCUPATION: SHOEMAKER
     HEIGHT: 5' 6"   COMPLEXION: FAIR   EYES: GREY   HAIR: LIGHT
     TWIN BROTHERS JOHN W. & SAMUEL A.; PARENTS: DAVID AND MARY
IRVIN, JOSEPH   PVT   CO. E   AGE: 18
     SWORN: OCT 12, 1861/3 YRS   MUSTER: NOV 4, 1864
     BORN: CLARION COUNTY   OCCUPATION: FARMER
     HEIGHT: 5' 4"   COMPLEXION: FAIR   EYES: BLUE   HAIR: LIGHT
     DIED: AT BALDWIN, BUTLER COUNTY, PA BEFORE 1905
IRWIN, JOHN *   PVT   CO. I   AGE:35
     SWORN: OCT 12, 1861/3 YRS   DIED: AUG 23, 1864 AT CHATTANOOGA
     BORN: ARMSTRONG COUNTY   OCCUPATION: LABORER
     HEIGHT: 5' 4"   COMPLEXION: DARK   EYES: BROWN   HAIR: DARK
     SERVED AS A NURSE AT STONES RIVER
     BURIED AT NATIONAL CEMETERY, GRAVE #482
IRWIN, JOHN CALVIN   PVT   CO. D   AGE:19
     SWORN: OCT 12, 1861/3 YRS   DIED: JUL 8, 1864 AT ANDERSONVILLE, GA
     BORN: INDIANA COUNTY, HILLSDALE   OCCUPATION: LUMBERMAN
     HEIGHT: 5' 10"   COMPLEXION: DARK   EYES: BROWN   HAIR: DARK
     CAPTURED AT McLEMORE'S COVE; IMPRISONED @ ANDERSONVILLE
     BURIED: ANDERSONVILLE, GRAVE #3038
IRWIN, SAMUEL THOMAS   PVT   CO. D   AGE:48

SWORN: OCT 12, 1861/3 YRS   MEDICAL: JAN 8. 1863
BORN: INDIANA COUNTY. HILLSDALE   OCCUPATION: FARMER
HEIGHT: 5' 9"   COMPLEXION: DARK   EYES: BROWN
DEMOTED FROM 4TH CPL.; SON JOHN CALVIN IRWIN ALSO IN CO. D
1890 CENSUS: HILLSDALE, INDIANA COUNTY, PA; WIDOW MARY A.
BURIED: INDIANA COUNTY, THOMPSON CEMETERY, HILLSDALE, MONTGOMERY TWP.,
SEP 8, 1813–JAN 15, 1871
IRWIN, WILLIAM B. *   1LT   CO. B   AGE:22
SWORN: OCT 12, 1861/3 YRS   RESIGNED: JUN 24, 1865   VETERAN
BORN: BUTLER COUNTY   OCCUPATION: FARMER
HEIGHT: 5' 9"   COMPLEXION: LIGHT   EYES: GREY   HAIR: BLACK
PROMOTED CPL TO 1ST SGT: TO 1LT: MAR 15, 1865
REUNION IN FREEPORT 1886
HOME 1886-1890 CENSUS: MAHONING, ARMSTRONG COUNTY, PA
JACK, JAMES W. *   PVT   CO. K   AGE:19
SWORN: OCT 12, 1861/3 YRS   MEDICAL: JUN 30, 1862   VETERAN
BORN: ARMSTRONG COUNTY   OCCUPATION: LABORER
HEIGHT: 5' 9½"   COMPLEXION: DARK   EYES: BROWN   HAIR: DARK
SERVED WITH PA 104TH, CO. K: MAR 18-AUG 25, 1865, SERGEANT
BURIED: UNION BAPTIST CEMETERY, SLATE LICK, PA [1842-1921], WIFE: MARY A.
1890 CENSUS: SLATE LICK, ARMSTRONG COUNTY, PA
HOME 1886: NORTH BUFFALO TWP, PA
HOME 1901: McHADDON   HOME 1914: MARWOOD, PA
REUNION FREEPORT 1886, KITTANNING 1901
BATTLES/DUTY: PETERSBURG, FORTRESS MONROE, PORTSMOUTH
JACK, SAMUEL MAURICE *   PVT   CO. K   AGE:18
SWORN: OCT 12, 1861/3 YRS   MUSTER: NOV 4, 1864
BORN: ARMSTRONG COUNTY   OCCUPATION: FARMER
HEIGHT: 5' 5½"   COMPLEXION: DARK   EYES: GREY   HAIR: BLACK
1886 REUNION IN FREEPORT: HOME, NORTH BUFFALO TWP, PA
1890 CENSUS: FORD CITY, ARMSTRONG COUNTY, PA
JACK, WILLIAM H.   PRINCIPAL MUC   REGIMENTAL STAFF
SWORN: OCT 12, 1861/3 YRS   DISCHARGED: FEB 22, 1863.
HOME 1886-1901: LEECHBURG, PA   ATTENDED REUNION IN KITTANNING 1901
JACK, WILLIAM STEWART   CPT   CO. H   AGE: 27 [28]
ORIGIN: BUTLER COUNTY   VETERAN
OCCUPATION: CLERK TO THE [BUTLER] COUNTY COMMISSION
RECEIVED $170 FOR RECRUITING THE COMPANY
BORN: AUG 1, 1833 TO S. JACK AND ANNA ARMSTRONG JACK IN WORTH TWP.
SWORN: APR 25, 1861/3 MOS   MUSTER: ≅JUL 25, 1861
13th PENNSYLVANIA, PVT, CO. H
SWORN: OCT 12, 1861/3 YRS   DIED: FEB 5, 1863 IN NASHVILLE HOSPITAL
BORN: BUTLER COUNTY   OCCUPATION: CLERK
HEIGHT: 5' 10¼"   COMPLEXION: DARK   EYES: HAZEL   HAIR: BLACK
MORTALLY WOUNDED: DEC 31, 1862/LEG, THIGH
COMMENDED BY COLONEL SIRWELL FOR BRAVERY AT STONES RIVER
BURIED IN PLAIN GROVE CEMETERY [ROUTE #108] NEAR SLIPPERY ROCK.
JEWART, ROBERT *   PVT   CO. A   AGE:37
SWORN: OCT 12, 1861/3 YRS   MUSTER: NOV 4, 1864
BORN: ARMSTRONG COUNTY   OCCUPATION: FARMER
HEIGHT: 5' 9"   COMPLEXION: DARK   EYES: GREY   HAIR: BROWN
1890 CENSUS:COWANSHANNOCK TWP., ARMSTRONG COUNTY, PA; WIDOW SUSAN
JEWELL, THOMAS M. *   PVT   CO. G
SWORN: OCT 12, 1861/3 YRS   MUSTER: NOV 4, 1864
ATTENDED THE REGIMENTAL REUNION AT INDIANA, PA, IN 1908.
JOHN, DANIEL *   PVT   CO. K   AGE:18
SWORN: OCT 12, 1861/3 YRS   DIED: JAN 28, 1862 AT GREEN RIVER
BORN: ARMSTRONG COUNTY   OCCUPATION: FARMER
HEIGHT: 6'   COMPLEXION: DARK   EYES: BLACK   HAIR: DARK
JOHNSON, ANDREW   PVT   CO. B   AGE:19
JOHNSTON, ANDREW
SWORN: JUL 6, 1863/3 YRS   MUSTER: SEP 11, 1865

BORN: SOMERSET COUNTY   OCCUPATION: FARMER
HEIGHT: 5' 8½"   COMPLEXION: LIGHT   EYES: BLUE   HAIR: DARK

JOHNSON, BETHUEL   PVT   CO. D   AGE:24
JOHNSTON, BETHEREL   JOHNSTON, BETHEUL
SWORN: OCT 12, 1861/3 YRS   DISHONORABLY DISCHARGED: OCT 28, 1862
BORN: INDIANA COUNTY, CHERRY TREE   OCCUPATION: LABORER
HEIGHT: 5' 9½"   COMPLEXION: FAIR   EYES: GREY
REDUCED IN RANK FROM 7TH CPL
SWORN: JUL 2, 1863/3 YRS   MUSTER: UNKNOWN [PA 46th - ORDERLY SGT]
NO RECORD OF 46th SERVICE IN BATES #
1890 CENSUS: INDIANA, INDIANA COUNTY, PA
DIED: HILLSDALE, INDIANA COUNTY, PA; 1838-FEB 9, 1902
BURIED: INDIANA COUNTY, THOMPSON CEMETERY, HILLSDALE, MONTGOMERY TWP.,

JOHNSTON, THOMAS *   PVT   CO. G
SWORN: OCT 12, 1861/3 YRS   MEDICAL: MAY 18, 1862

JOHNSTON, WILLIAM #   PVT   CO. D
SWORN: OCT 12, 1861/3 YRS   MUSTER: NOV 12, 1861
1890 CENSUS: BIG RUN, JEFFERSON COUNTY, PA

JOHNSTON, WILLIAM C.*   PVT   CO. G
SWORN: OCT 12, 1861/3 YRS   MUSTER: NOV 4, 1864

JOHNSTON, WILLIAM J.   6TH CPL   CO. H   AGE:23
SWORN: OCT 12, 1861/3YRS   MUSTER: NOV 4, 1864   BOUNTY: $100.
BORN: MERCER COUNTY   OCCUPATION: FARMER
HEIGHT: 5' 8¾"   COMPLEXION: LIGHT   EYES: BROWN   HAIR: DARK
PROMOTED TO CPL, DEC 17, 1863   WOUNDED/HIP PICKETT'S MILL, MAY 27, 1864

JONES, THOMAS   PVT   CO. C   AGE:44
SWORN: OCT 12, 1861/3 YRS   MUSTER: NOV 4, 1864
BORN: CLARION COUNTY
HEIGHT: 5' 7½"   COMPLEXION: SANDY   EYES: GREY   HAIR: BROWN
SWORN: JAN 25, 1865   DESERTED: FEB 11, 1865
DESCRIPTIVE LIST OF 2ND REGIMENT SHOWS JONES DESERTED
AT WHEELING, WVA ON FEB 11, 1865

JORDAN, JOHN *   CPT   CO. G   AGE:37
SWORN: OCT 12, 1861/3 YRS   RESIGNED: APR 12, 1864
BORN: KITTANNING, PA   OCCUPATION: MANAGER
HEIGHT: 5' 9½"   COMPLEXION: FAIR   EYES: GREY   HAIR: GREY
DIED: IN LEADVILLE, COLORADO BEFORE 1905

KARNES, ALEXANDER   PVT   CO. E   AGE: 20
KARNS, ALEXANDER
SWORN: AUG 23, 1862/3 YRS   DISCHARGED: JUN 19, 1865
HEIGHT: 6'   COMPLEXION: SANDY   EYES: DARK   HAIR: DARK
HOME IN 1897: WEST FREEDOM, CLARION COUNTY, PA
ATTENDED CHICKAMAUGA BATTLEFIELD, NOV 1897
HOME 1914: PARKER'S LANDING, PA

KARNES, GODFREY C.*   PVT   CO. K   AGE:17
SWORN: FEB 29, 1864   MUSTER: SEP 11, 1865
BORN: VENANGO COUNTY   OCCUPATION: LABORER
HEIGHT: 5' 7¼"   COMPLEXION: DARK   EYES: HAZEL   HAIR: BROWN

KECK, PETER   COMM SGT   CO. C   AGE:21
HECK, PETER   ENLISTED AS 7TH CORPORAL
SWORN: FEB 8, 1864/3 YRS   MUSTER: SEP 11, 1865
BORN: CLARION COUNTY
HEIGHT: 5' 8"   COMPLEXION: DARK   EYES: GREY
PROMOTED TO SERGEANT; CO. B Π
COMMISSIONED 2LT, JUL 27, 1865 - NEVER MUSTERED AT RANK
PROMOTED TO COMMISSARY SGT, AUG 2, 1865; REGIMENTAL STAFF Π.

KEIBLER, ANDREW J. *   PVT   CO. F   AGE: 32
SWORN: OCT 12, 1861/3 YRS   MUSTER: NOV 4, 1864
BORN: FREEPORT, PA   OCCUPATION: FARMER
HEIGHT: 5' 8½"   COMPLEXION: FAIR   EYES: GREY   HAIR: BROWN
BRIEFLY MISSING IN ACTION AT STONES RIVER
1890 CENSUS: IRWIN, WESTMORELAND COUNTY, PA; WIDOW MAGGIE

KEIBLER, JOSEPH *   PVT   CO. F   AGE: 19
    SWORN: OCT 12, 1861/3 YRS   MUSTER: NOV 4, 1864
    BORN: SALEM CROSS RDS   OCCUPATION: FARMER
    HEIGHT: 5' 8"   COMPLEXION: DARK   EYES: BROWN   HAIR: DARK
    WOUNDED AT PICKETT'S MILL
KEIBLER, SAMUEL *   PVT   CO. F   AGE: 17
    SWORN: OCT 12, 1861/3 YRS   MEDICAL: JUN 23, 1862
    BORN: WESTMORELAND COUNTY   OCCUPATION: LABORER
    HEIGHT: 5' 11"   COMPLEXION: DARK   EYES: GREY   HAIR: LIGHT
    1890 CENSUS: CONGRUITY, WESTMORELAND COUNTY, PA
KEIFER, JOHN MILTON*   2ND SGT   CO. F   AGE:27
    SWORN: OCT 12, 1861/3 YRS   MUSTER: NOV 4, 1864
    BORN IN GERMANY IN 1834 BADEN-BADEN;   OCCUPATION: COLLIER
    HEIGHT: 5' 8"   COMPLEXION: SALLOW   EYES: DARK BROWN   HAIR: BLACK
    LED COMPANY @ STONES RIVER, JAN 2, 1863
    COMMENDED BY SIRWELL FOR BRAVERY AT STONES RIVER
    PROMOTED TO SERGEANT SEPTEMBER 13, 1863
    BLACKSMITH AFTER THE WAR; WIFE: BARBARA JANE KING DIED: 1923
    DIED: IN SMITHTON, WESTMORELAND COUNTY, PA, 1898
    BURIED: HOFFMAN CEMETERY, SMITHTON
KEIGAN, BERNARD   CPT   CO. C   AGE:19
    SWORN: OCT 12, 1861/4 YRS   MUSTER: SEP 11, 1865   VETERAN
    BORN: CLARION COUNTY
    HEIGHT: 5' 10"   COMPLEXION: FAIR   EYES: BLUE   HAIR: BROWN
    PROMOTED CO. B Π SGT TO 2LT, DEC 4, 1864; TO 1LT, MAR 15, 1865;
    TO CAPTAIN; AUG 7, 1865   DIED: JUN 14, 1896
    BURIED: INDIANA COUNTY, OAKLAND CEMETERY, WHITE TWP., 1843-JUN 14, 1896
KEIRN, HENRY   PVT   CO. D   AGE:22
KIERN, HENRY
    SWORN: OCT 12, 1861/3 YRS   MUSTER: NOV 4, 1864
    BORN: CLEARFIELD COUNTY   OCCUPATION: LUMBERMAN
    HEIGHT: 5' 9½"   COMPLEXION: DARK   EYES: BROWN   HAIR: DARK
    CAVALRY SERVICE DURING 1863   DIED BEFORE 1905
KEIRN, ISSAC   SGT   CO. D   AGE:23
KIEM, ISSAC
    SWORN: OCT 12, 1861/3 YRS   MUSTER: NOV 4, 1864
    BORN: CAMBRIA COUNTY   OCCUPATION: LUMBERMAN
    HEIGHT: 5' 6½"   COMPLEXION: DARK   EYES: GREY
    WOUNDED BY SHELL FRAGMENT AT STONES RIVER
    PROMOTED FROM 2ND CPL, MAY 29, 1863; CAVALRY SERVICE DURING 1863
KEIRN, MATTHEW   PVT   CO. D   AGE: 18
KIERN, MATTHEW
    SWORN: OCT 12, 1861/3 YRS   MUSTER: NOV 4, 1864
    BORN: CLEARFIELD COUNTY   OCCUPATION: LUMBERMAN
    HEIGHT: 5' 7½"   COMPLEXION: DARK   EYES: GREY   HAIR: DARK
KEIRN, NATHAN   PVT   CO. D
KIEM, NATHAN
    SWORN: OCT 12, 1861/3 YRS   KILLED AT STONES RIVER JAN 2, 1863
    BURIED AT NATIONAL CEMETERY STONES RIVER, GRAVE #D-1581
KELL, HENRY   PVT   CO. C   AGE: 20
KEEL, HENRY
    SWORN: MAR 31, 1864/3 YRS   MUSTER: SEP 11, 1865
    BORN: WESTMORELAND COUNTY   OCCUPATION: LABORER
    HEIGHT: 6'   COMPLEXION: FAIR   EYES: BLACK   HAIR: BLACK
KELLER, ELIJAH   PVT   CO. C   AGE: 19
    SWORN: MAR 24, 1864/3 YRS   MUSTER: SEP 11, 1865
    BORN: JEFFERSON COUNTY   OCCUPATION: FARMER
    HEIGHT: 5' 8"   COMPLEXION: FAIR   EYES: GREY   HAIR: DARK
KELLER, JOHN H.   PVT   CO. C   AGE: 25
    SWORN: OCT 12, 1861/3 YRS   MUSTER: NOV 4, 1864
    BORN: PENNSYLVANIA
    HEIGHT: 5' 7"   COMPLEXION: DARK   EYES: GREY   HAIR: BROWN

HOME IN 1890-1901: DEE, ARMSTRONG COUNTY, PA
REUNION KITTANNING 1901

KELLER, SAMUEL W.   PVT   CO. C   AGE: 23
ENLISTED @ CALDWELL FURNACE, PA
BECAME THE JUSTICE OF THE PEACE IN FORD CITY
SWORN: OCT 12, 1861/3 YRS   MEDICAL: FEB 12, 1864
BORN: PENNSYLVANIA, AUG 4, 1838
HEIGHT: 5' 8½"   COMPLEXION: DARK   EYES: HAZEL HAIR: BROWN
1890 CENSUS: DEE, ARMSTRONG COUNTY, PA
HOME 1914: FORD CITY, PA   MARRIED: SARAH CONWAY

KELLEY, ANDREW   PVT   CO. D   AGE:38
KELLY, ANDREW
SWORN: OCT 12, 1861/3 YRS   DIED: FEB 23, 1862 AT CAMP HAMBRIGHT
BORN: INDIANA COUNTY, COOKPORT   OCCUPATION: FARMER
HEIGHT: 5' 9"   COMPLEXION: DARK   EYES: GREY   HAIR: DARK

KELLEY, OLIVER   PVT   CO. C
KELLY, OLIVER
SWORN: FEB 29, 1864/3 YRS   NOT AT FINAL MUSTER

KELLY, PORTER   PVT   CO. A   AGE:21
KELLEY, PORTER T.
SWORN: OCT 12, 1861/3 YRS   MUSTER: NOV 4, 1864
BORN: INDIANA COUNTY   OCCUPATION: CARPENTER
HEIGHT: 5' 9"   COMPLEXION: DARK   EYES: BLUE   HAIR: BROWN
1890 CENSUS: PLUMVILLE, INDIANA COUNTY, PA
BURIED: INDIANA CTY, BARACHA CEMETERY, S. MAHONING, MAR 12, 1840-FEB 3, 1889

KELLEY, SAMUEL   PVT   CO. E   AGE:31
SWORN: OCT 12, 1861/3 YRS   MUSTER: NOV 4, 1864
BORN: CLARION COUNTY   OCCUPATION: FARMER
HEIGHT: 5' 10"   COMPLEXION: SANDY   EYES: BLUE   HAIR: DARK
SERVED AS A 3RD SGT AT CAMP ORR
REDUCED IN RANK FOR "INABILITY" BY ORDER OF COLONEL SIRWELL

KELLEY, THOMPSON   PVT   CO. A   AGE:25
KELLY, THOMPSON
SWORN: OCT 12, 1861/3 YRS   DIED: AT LOUISVILLE, APR 6, 1863
BORN: INDIANA COUNTY   OCCUPATION: CARPENTER
HEIGHT: 5' 9"   COMPLEXION: DARK   EYES: BLACK   HAIR: BLACK
MORTALLY WOUNDED/SHOULDER AT STONES RIVER
TRANSFERRED FROM NASHVILLE TO LOUISVILLE HOSPITAL, MAR 9, 1863
BURIED: NATIONAL CEMETERY LOUISVILLE; SECTION.B, RANGE.8, GRAVE.38

KENNEDY, GEORGE F. *   PVT   CO. I   AGE:18
SWORN: OCT 12, 1861/3 YRS   DIED: JUL 27, 1862 AT PULASKI, TN
BORN: SALTSBURG, PA   OCCUPATION: FARMER
HEIGHT: 5' 7"   COMPLEXION: DARK   EYES: BLUE   HAIR: DARK
BURIED AT NATIONAL CEMETERY STONES RIVER, GRAVE #J-4145

KENNEDY, PHILIP   PVT   CO. C   AGE: 18
SWORN: FEB 4, 1862/3 YRS   DISCHARGED: FEB 3, 1865
BORN: CLARION COUNTY   OCCUPATION: BLACKSMITH
HEIGHT: 5' 7"   COMPLEXION: FAIR   EYES: BLUE   HAIR: LIGHT

KENNEDY, ROBERT E.   PVT   CO. C   AGE: 21
KENNEDY, ROBERT EVANS III
SWORN: OCT 12, 1861/3 YRS   MUSTER: NOV 4, 1864
BORN: JUN 11, 1840 TO ROBERT E. & ELIZABETH KENNEDY, MAYPORT, CLARION CTY.
FARMER & BLACKSMITH
HEIGHT: 5'8"   COMPLECTION: SANDY   EYES: BLUE   HAIR: LIGHT
AT THE BATTLE OF STONES RIVER WAS ON DETACHED SERVICE TO BATTERY G, 1st OHIO
WIFE: SARAH AMELIA BARNES KENNEDY 1850-1926
1890 CENSUS: RED BANK TWP., CLARION COUNTY. PA
HOME IN 1897-1914: 265 MONTEREY AVE., RIDGEWAY, ELK COUNTY, PA
ATTENDED THE DEDICATION OF CHICKAMAUGA, NOV 1897; DIED: SEP 24, 1824

KENNISTON, DAVID *   PVT   CO. F   AGE: 31
KINSTON, DAVID
SWORN: OCT 12, 1861/3 YRS   DIED: AUG 9, 1862

BORN: FREEPORT, PA   OCCUPATION: BOAT BUILDER
HEIGHT: 5' 9½"   COMPLEXION: SALLOW EYES: BLUE   HAIR: DARK BROWN
ACCIDENTLY KILLED BY A TRAIN: AUG 9, 1862 AT PULASKI, TN
BURIED: NATIONAL CEMETERY LOUISVILLE; SECTION.A, RANGE.4, GRAVE.5
KENNISTON, JOSEPH A. *   PVT   CO. I   AGE: 18
KENSINGTON, JOSEPH A.   ENLISTED AS 1ST MUSICIAN
SWORN: OCT 12, 1861/3 YRS   MUSTER: NOV 4, 1864
BORN: FREPORT, PA   OCCUPATION: DRUMMER
HEIGHT: 5' 6½" COMPLEXION: LIGHT EYES: BLUE   HAIR: LIGHT
KERR, CHARLES B.   PVT   CO. D   AGE:21
SWORN: OCT 12, 1861/3 YRS   MUSTER: NOV 4, 1864
BORN: INDIANA COUNTY, UTAH   OCCUPATION: LABORER
HEIGHT: 6' 1" COMPLEXION: FAIR   EYES: BLUE   HAIR: DARK
KERR, JAMES #   PVT
SWORN: OCT 12, 1861/3 YRS   DIED: 1863
KERR, JOHN   PVT   CO. H   AGE:19
SWORN: OCT 12, 1861/3YRS   MEDICAL: JAN 10, 1862
BORN: BUTLER COUNTY   OCCUPATION: FARMER
HEIGHT: 5' 10¾" COMPLEXION: LIGHT EYES: BLUE   HAIR: BROWN
DIED BEFORE THE REGIMENTAL HISTORY WAS PUBLISHED IN 1905
KERR, JOSEPH L. *   7TH CPL   CO. I   AGE:24
SWORN: OCT 12, 1861/3 YRS   MUSTER: NOV 4, 1864
BORN: APOLLO, PA   OCCUPATION: LABORER
HEIGHT: 5' 11" COMPLEXION: DARK   EYES: BROWN   HAIR: BLACK
1890 CENSUS: APOLLO, PA
KERR, JOSEPH, PATRICK, ROBERT, SAMUEL AND WILLIAM [CO.I] WERE BROTHERS
BURIED: APOLLO CEMETERY, APOLLO, PA, DIED BEFORE 1905
KERR, PATRICK *   PVT   CO. I   AGE:26
SWORN: OCT 12, 1861/3 YRS   MUSTER: NOV 4, 1864
BORN: KITTANNING, PA   OCCUPATION: LABORER
HEIGHT: 5' 6½"   COMPLEXION: LIGHT   EYES: BLUE   HAIR: LIGHT
KERR, JOSEPH, PATRICK, ROBERT, SAMUEL AND WILLIAM [CO.I] WERE BROTHERS
DIED BEFORE THE REGIMENTAL HISTORY WAS PUBLISHED IN 1905
KERR, ROBERT *   PVT   CO. I   AGE:21
SWORN: OCT 12, 1861/3 YRS   MUSTER: NOV 4, 1864
BORN: APOLLO, PA   OCCUPATION: FARMER
HEIGHT: 5' 11½"   COMPLEXION: LIGHT   EYES: BLUE   HAIR: LIGHT
KERR, JOSEPH, PATRICK, ROBERT, SAMUEL AND WILLIAM [CO.I] WERE BROTHERS
KERR, SAMUEL H. *   1LT   CO. I   AGE:26
SWORN: OCT 12, 1861/3 YRS   MEDICAL: JAN 12, 1863   VETERAN
BORN: APOLLO, PA   OCCUPATION: FARMER
HEIGHT: 5' 9½" COMPLEXION: SANDY EYES: GREY   HAIR: DARK
PROMOTED FROM 1ST SGT
RE-ENLISTED IN THE PA 14th CAVALRY, PVT: PROMOTED TO SGT
SWORN: FEB 14, 1864/3 YRS   MUSTER: AUG 24, 1865
HONORABLY DISCHARGED @ FORT LEAVENWORTH, KS
CHARTER MEMBER OF WITWORTH G.A.R. POST #89
BORN: AUG 15, 1833   DIED: APR 14, 1907
KERR, JOSEPH, PATRICK, ROBERT, SAMUEL AND WILLIAM [CO.I] WERE BROTHERS
BURIED: APOLLO CEMETERY, APOLLO, PA   WIFE: NANCY
SKIRMISHES/BATTLES: WHITE SULPHUR SPRING, SALEM, MOOREFIELD, CEDAR CREEK,
WINCHESTER, MILLWOOD, ASHBY'S GAP, WOODSTOCK
KERR, THOMAS C.   PVT   CO. A   AGE:21
SWORN: OCT 12, 1861/3 YRS   KILLED AT PICKETT'S MILL, MAY 27, 1864
BORN: INDIANA COUNTY   OCCUPATION: CARPENTER
HEIGHT: 5' 9½"   COMPLEXION: FAIR   EYES: GREY   HAIR: FAIR
BURIED @ MARIETTA, ROW G, GRAVE # 1118, BATES
KERR, WILLIAM B. *   2ND SGT   CO. I   AGE:32
SWORN: OCT 12, 1861/3 YRS   MUSTER: NOV 4, 1864
BORN: KITTANNING, PA   OCCUPATION: LABORER
HEIGHT: 5' 11" COMPLEXION: SANDY EYES: GREY   HAIR: DARK
CENSURED BY LT COLONEL BLAKELEY

1890 CENSUS: KITTANNING, ARMSTRONG COUNTY, PA
KERR, JOSEPH, PATRICK, ROBERT, SAMUEL AND WILLIAM [CO.I] WERE BROTHERS
BURIED: KITTANNING CEMETERY [1828-1901]   WIFE: MARY
1886 REUNION IN FREEPORT: HOME, KITTANNING, PA

KETCHAM, JEFFERSON *   PVT   CO. I   AGE: 21
   SWORN: OCT 12, 1861/3 YRS   DIED: MAR 9, 1862 AT LOUISVILLE
   BORN: APOLLO, PA   OCCUPATION: FARMER
   HEIGHT: 6' 1½"   COMPLEXION: LIGHT   EYES: BLUE   HAIR: FAIR
   BURIED: NATIONAL CEMETERY LOUISVILLE; SECTION.A, RANGE.14, GRAVE.10

KIDD, JOHN C.   PVT   CO. H
   SWORN: FEB 15, 1864   NOT ON FINAL REGIMENTAL MUSTER ROLL

KILGON, JOHN *   PVT   CO. B   AGE:20
KILGORE, JOHN   GILGORE, JOHN W.
   SWORN: OCT 12, 1861/3 YRS   DIED: DEC 28, 1861 AT CAMP WOOD, KY
   BORN: ARMSTRONG COUNTY   OCCUPATION: FARMER
   HEIGHT: 5' 9"   COMPLEXION: LIGHT   EYES: BLUE   HAIR: RED

KING, EDWARD   SGT   CO. D   AGE:18
   SWORN: OCT 12, 1861/3 YRS   MUSTER: NOV 4, 1864
   BORN: INDIANA CTY, CHAMBERSVILLE, PA   OCCUPATION: FARMER
   HEIGHT: 5' 6½"   COMPLEXION: FAIR   EYES: BROWN   HAIR: DARK
   PROMOTED FROM PVT; FROM CPL, MAR 25, 1863
   WOUNDED LEFT FACE JUN 9, 1864; SENT TO JEFFERSONVILLE, IN HOSPITAL
   HOME 1897-1914: GRANT, INDIANA CTY; REUNION CHICKAMAUGA 1897, INDIANA 1908.
   BURIED: INDIANA COUNTY, IOOF CEM, CHERRY TREE, MONTGOMERY TWP., 1844-1933

KING, FRANCIS M. *   PVT   CO. I   AGE:22
   SWORN: SEP 5, 1862/3 YRS   DISCHARGED: JUN 19, 1865
   BORN: ARMSTRONG COUNTY   OCCUPATION: LABORER
   HEIGHT: 5' 2½"   COMPLEXION: DARK   EYES: GREY   HAIR: DARK
   BURIED: PRESBYTERIAN CEMETERY, PARKER'S LANDING, PA 1838-1894

KING, JAMES B. *   PVT   CO. K   AGE:22
   SWORN: OCT 12, 1861/3 YRS   MUSTER: NOV 4, 1864
   BORN: ARMSTRONG COUNTY   OCCUPATION: LABORER
   HEIGHT: 5' 6¼"   COMPLEXION: DARK   EYES: GREY   HAIR: DARK
   1890 CENSUS: SHENETT, ARMSTRONG COUNTY, PA; WIDOW SARAH
   BURIED: APPLEBY PRESBYTERIAN CEMETERY, FORD CITY, DIED: AUG 3, 1865

KIPP, ABRAM E.   PVT   CO. F   AGE: 22
KIPP, ABRAHAM   KEEPP, ADAM   WESTMORELAND COUNTY ENLISTEE
   SWORN: OCT 12, 1861/3 YRS   MUSTER: NOV 4, 1864
   BORN: SHEARER'S CROSS ROADS   OCCUPATION: LABORER
   HEIGHT: 5' 8½"   COMPLEXION: FAIR   EYES: BROWN   HAIR: LIGHT
   HOME 1897: ALLEGHENY TOWNSHIP, WESTMORELAND COUNTY
   WOUNDED AT STONES RIVER/LEG; DIED: JAN 9, 1879 AT AGE 38.   TOMBSTONE/1878.
   WIFE: REBECCA 1841-1919   BURIED: PLEASANT HILLS CEMETERY, LEECHBURG, PA.
   ABRAM, WALTER & DANIEL KIPP WERE BROTHERS; SONS OF ELIZA BAWN, ALLEGHENY
   TWP. WESTMORELAND COUNTY. DANIEL K. KIPP A SGT IN THE 123rd WAS KILLED ON   DEC
   13, 1862 @ FREDERICKSBURG; WALTER WAS ALSO IN THE 123rd

KIRKPATRICK, JAMES H.   PVT   CO. A   AGE: 19
   SWORN: OCT 12, 1861/3 YRS   MUSTER: NOV 4, 1864   HOME 1914: GANA, ILL
   BORN: ARMSTRONG COUNTY   OCCUPATION: FARMER
   HEIGHT: 5' 5½"   COMPLEXION: FAIR   EYES: BROWN   HAIR: BROWN

KIRKPATRICK, ROBERT B.   PVT   CO. A   AGE:25
   SWORN: OCT 12, 1861/3 YRS   MUSTER: NOV 4, 1864
   BORN: ARMSTRONG COUNTY   OCCUPATION: CARPENTER
   HEIGHT: 5' 5½"   COMPLEXION: FAIR   EYES: BROWN   HAIR: BROWN
   HOME 1890-1901: DAYTON, PA; REUNION CHICKAMAUGA 1897, KITTANNING 1901

KISTLER, ANDREW J. *   PVT   CO. F
   SWORN: OCT 12, 1861/3 YRS   MUSTER: NOV 4, 1864
   BRIEFLY MISSING IN ACTION AT STONES RIVER
   1890 CENSUS: IRWIN, WESTMORELAND COUNTY, PA; WIDOW MAGGIE

KLINGENSMITH, F. *   PVT   CO. B   AGE:19
KLINGENSMITH, FRANKLIN   CLINGENSMITH, FRANK   VETERAN
   SWORN: OCT 12, 1861/3 YRS   MUSTER: DEC 15, 1865

HEIGHT: 5' 10"   COMPLEXION: LIGHT   EYES: GREY   HAIR: DARK
TRANS: 4TH CAV, DEC 1, 1862
1890 CENSUS: KITTANNING, ARMSTRONG COUNTY, PA
BURIED: APOLLO CEMETERY, APOLLO, PA

KLUGH, SAMUEL, *   5TH SGT   CO. G   AGE: 26
SWORN: OCT 12, 1861/3 YRS   MEDICAL: MAY 18, 1862
BORN: MIFFLIN, PA   OCCUPATION: FARMER
HEIGHT: 6' ½" COMPLEXION: DARK   EYES: GREY   HAIR: BLACK
1890 CENSUS: FORD CITY, ARMSTRONG COUNTY, PA; DIED BEFORE 1905

KLUTZ, GEORGE   PVT   CO. C   AGE: 44
SWORN: OCT 12, 1861/3 YRS   DESERTED: DEC 9, 1861
BORN: GERMANY
HEIGHT: 5' 6"   COMPLEXION: DARK   EYES: GREY HAIR: BROWN

KNAFF, HENRY   PVT   CO. A   AGE:33
SWORN: JAN 5, 1864/3 YRS   TRANS: VRC, DATE UNKNOWN
BORN: BUTLER COUNTY   OCCUPATION: FARMER
HEIGHT: 5' 7½"   COMPLEXION: FAIR   EYES: GREY   HAIR: BROWN

KNAUFF, HENRY   PVT   CO. A
SWORN: JAN 5, 1864/3 YRS   DISCHARGED: OCT 4, 1865.
PROBABLY THE SAME MAN AS HENRY KNAFF

KNOX, JAMES   PVT   CO. E   AGE: 21
SWORN: OCT 12, 1861/3 YRS   MEDICAL: JUN 30, 1862
BORN: ARMSTRONG COUNTY   OCCUPATION: FARMER
HEIGHT: 5' 10"   COMPLEXION: LIGHT   EYES: GREY   HAIR: LIGHT

KNOX, WILLIAM M.   ASSISTANT SURGEON   REGIMENTAL STAFF
ORIGIN: BERKS COUNTY
SWORN: OCT 18, 1861/3 YRS   KILLED: APR 27, 1862 ACCIDENTLY
AT LOUISVILLE; WHILE INTOXICATED

KOPP, ANDREW A.   PVT   CO. D   AGE:24
KIPP, ANDREW A
SWORN: OCT 12, 1861/3 YRS   DISCHARGED: OCT 12, 1864
BORN: CLEARFIELD COUNTY   OCCUPATION: FARMER
HEIGHT: 5' 8½"   COMPLEXION: DARK   EYES: GREY   HAIR: DARK

KUNKLE, PHILIP   PVT   CO. A   AGE:19
SWORN: SEP 10, 1862/3 YRS   DISCHARGED: JUN 19, 1865   BOUNTY: $29
BORN: INDIANA COUNTY   OCCUPATION: FARMER
HEIGHT: 6'   COMPLEXION: DARK   EYES: BROWN   HAIR: BROWN
HOME 1890-1914: CREEKSIDE, INDIANA COUNTY, PA
ATTENDED THE REGIMENTAL REUNION AT INDIANA, PA, IN 1908.
BURIED: INDIANA COUNTY, GREENWOOD, APR 13, 1842-JAN 2, 1933

LACOCK, JOHN A. **   PVT   CO. A
SWORN: APR 1, 1864/3 YRS   DIED: FEB 21, 1865, NASHVILLE OF CHRONIC DIARRHEA
BURIED @ NASHVILLE, ROW H. GRAVE # 138, BATES

LAKE, HORACE   PVT   CO. H   AGE:22
SWORN: OCT 12 1861/3YRS   TRANS: 4TH U.S. CAV, DEC 1, 1862.
BORN: MICHIGAN   OCCUPATION: SAILOR
HEIGHT: 5' 9¼"   COMPLEXION: LIGHT   EYES: BLUE   HAIR: BROWN

LAMBING, GEORGE W. *   PVT   CO. I   AGE:19
SWORN: OCT 12, 1861/3 YRS   MUSTER: SEP 11, 1865   VETERAN
BORN: MAYSVILLE, PA   OCCUPATION: LABORER
HEIGHT: 5' 9½"   COMPLEXION: LIGHT   EYES: GREY   HAIR: LIGHT
DETAILED AS TEAMSTER, HQ 2nd DIV. MAY/JUN 1863
WIFE: ANNA ELIZA HUNTER
BORN: 1841; DIED: KILLED IN WPRR ACCIDENT, DEC 3, 1880 IN ARMSTRONG COUNTY

LAMBING, JOSEPH B. *   PVT   CO. I   AGE: 26
BORN AUG 1834, TO JOSEPH & MARY E. CUNNINGHAM LAMBING
SWORN: OCT 12, 1861/3 YRS   MEDICAL: JUN 27, 1862
BORN: MAYSVILLE, PA   OCCUPATION: LABORER
HEIGHT: 5' 11½"   COMPLEXION: SANDY   EYES: GRAY   HAIR: LIGHT
PENSION: $10, WIFE: [RETA] RETTIE GARRIS THE WIDOW OF JOHN DERRIMORE
MARRIED "MR. SIMS" OF BLAIRSVILLE, PA AFTER JBL DIED
1886 REUNION IN FREEPORT: HOME, LONG RUN, PA

DIED: MAR 17, 1907 - FOUND DEAD ALONG A ROAD NEAR AVENMORE, PA
FAMILY CLAIMS HE DIED IN BED.

LANEY, JOHN   PVT   CO. D   AGE: 19
LANCY, JOHN
    SWORN: OCT 12, 1861/3 YRS   MUSTER: NOV 4, 1864
    BORN: INDIANA COUNTY, CHERRY TREE   OCCUPATION: FARMER
    HEIGHT: 6' 1"   COMPLEXION: FAIR   EYES: BLUE   HAIR: DARK
    HOME 1886: COOKPORT, PA;   HOME 1897: HOMER CITY, INDIANA COUNTY, PA
    REUNION FREEPORT 1886, CHICKAMAUGA 1897, INDIANA 1908.
    BURIED: INDIANA COUNTY, GREENWOOD CEMETERY, FEB 14, 1842-FEB 23, 1915

LANGDON, DAVID   PVT   CO. D   AGE: 21
    SWORN: OCT 12, 1861/3 YRS   MUSTER: NOV 4, 1864
    BORN: CLEARFIELD COUNTY   OCCUPATION: LUMBERMAN
    HEIGHT: 5' 9½"   COMPLEXION: FAIR   EYES: GREY   HAIR: DARK
    1890 CENSUS: GRANT, INDIANA COUNTY, PA
    BURIED: INDIANA COUNTY, IOOF CEMETERY, CHERRY TREE, MONTGOMERY TWP.,

LANGDON, GEORGE   6TH CPL   CO. D   AGE: 25
    SWORN: OCT 12, 1861/3 YRS   DIED: NOV 12, 1862 AT NASHVILLE
    BORN: CLEARFIELD COUNTY   OCCUPATION: LABORER
    HEIGHT: 5' 9"   COMPLEXION: FAIR   EYES: GREY
    MORTALLY WOUNDED AT LAVERGNE
    1ST MEMBER OF THE REGIMENT TO DIE FROM BATTLE WOUNDS
    BURIED AT NATIONAL CEMETERY NASHVILLE, GRAVE #C-98
    RE-BURIED: INDIANA COUNTY, IOOF CEMETERY, CHERRY TREE, MONTGOMERY TWP.,
    MAR 1836-NOV 12, 1862

LANKARD, SAMUEL   5TH CPL   CO. C   AGE: 22
    SWORN: OCT 12, 1861/3 YRS   DIED: JAN 27, 1864 AT CHATTANOOGA
    BORN: CLARION COUNTY
    HEIGHT: 5' 10"   COMPLEXION: FAIR   EYES: BROWN

LATTIMER, WILLIAM G.   PVT   CO. C/D   AGE: 28
    SWORN: SEP 18, 1862/3 YRS   MUSTER: NOV 4, 1864
    HEIGHT: 5' 10"   COMPLEXION: FAIR
    DEMOTED FROM 5TH SGT; BRIEFLY MISSING IN ACTION AT STONES RIVER
    1886 REUNION IN FREEPORT: HOME, TARENTUM, PA
    BURIED: PROSPECT CEMETERY, TARENTUM, PA; DIED APR 11, 1894

LATSHAW, ABNER J.   2LT   CO. E   AGE: 23
    SWORN: OCT 12, 1861/3 YRS   RESIGNED: OCT 12, 1861, POOR HEALTH
    ENLISTED AS A PRIVATE WAS ELECTED TO 2 LT
    BORN: CLARION COUNTY   OCCUPATION: FARMER
    HEIGHT: 5' 11"   COMPLEXION: DARK   EYES: BROWN   HAIR: DARK

LATSHAW, EBERNEZER JULIAN   PVT   CO. E   AGE: 18
    SWORN: OCT 12, 1861/3 YRS   DIED: AUG 2, 1862 IN CLARION, PA
    PARENTS: JOHN AND ELIZABETH
    HOME 1860: MATILDAVILLE, PERRY TWP., CLARION COUNTY, PA

LATSHAW, REUBEN   SGT   CO. E   AGE: 20
    SWORN: OCT 12, 1861/3 YRS   KILLED: JAN 2, 1863 AT STONES RIVER
    BORN: CLARION COUNTY   OCCUPATION: FARMER
    HEIGHT: 5' 9"   COMPLEXION: SANDY   EYES: DARK   HAIR: DARK
    PROMOTED FROM FOURTH CPL
    BURIED: NATIONAL CEMETERY STONES RIVER, GRAVE #N-5591
    PARENTS: JOHN AND ELIZABETH
    HOME 1860: MATILDAVILLE, PERRY TWP., CLARION COUNTY, PA

LAWSON, WESLEY *   PVT   CO. A   AGE: 22
LOOSEN, WESTLEY
    SWORN: OCT 12, 1861/3 YRS   TRANS: SIG CORPS, OCT 22, 1863
    BORN: INDIANA COUNTY   OCCUPATION: TEACHER
    HEIGHT: 6' 1"   COMPLEXION: LIGHT   EYES: GREY   HAIR: AUBURN
    REUNION AT INDIANA, PA, 1908. HOME 1914: HOMER, ILL

LEAR, WILLIAM #   PVT   CO. A   AGE: 40
    SWORN: MAR 31, 1864/3 YRS MUSTER: UNKNOWN
    BORN: BUCKS COUNTY   OCCUPATION: LABORER
    HEIGHT: 5' 5¼"   COMPLEXION: RUDDY   EYES: BROWN   HAIR: DARK

LISTED IN ORIGINAL DISCRIPTIVE LIST; NOT IN ORIGINAL HISTORY

LECK, ADAM *   PVT   CO. B   AGE:18
     SWORN: OCT 12, 1861/3 YRS   MUSTER: NOV 4, 1864
     BORN: ARMSTRONG COUNTY   OCCUPATION: FARMER
     HEIGHT: 5' 9"   COMPLEXION: DARK   EYES: LIGHT   HAIR: LIGHT

LEE, SAMUEL N. *   1LT   CO. B   AGE:18
     SWORN: OCT 12, 1861/3 YRS   MUSTER: NOV 4, 1864
     HEIGHT: 5' 10"   COMPLEXION: FAIR   EYES: HAZEL
     PROMOTED FROM 2LT, DEC 26, 1862
     COMMENDED BY SIRWELL FOR ACTION AT STONES RIVER
     HOME 1890-1897: KITTANNING, ARMSTRONG COUNTY, PA

LEMMON, JOHN H. *   PVT   CO. G   AGE: 43
LEMON, JOHN H.
     SWORN: OCT 12, 1861/3 YRS   MEDICAL: AUG 1862
     DIED: AT KITTANNING, 1897   BURIED: KITTANNING CEMETERY [1818-1897]
     WIFE: ROSANNE
     1890 CENSUS: KITTANNING, ARMSTRONG COUNTY, PA

LEMON, LOBIN *   PVT   CO. K   AGE:25
LEMMON, LOBEN
     SWORN: OCT 12, 1861/3 YRS   MUSTER: NOV 4, 1864
     BORN: ARMSTRONG COUNTY   OCCUPATION: BLACKSMITH
     HEIGHT: 5' 11¼"   COMPLEXION: DARK   EYES: BROWN   HAIR: DARK

LEMON, ROBERT   PVT   CO. H   AGE:34
LEMMON, ROBERT   ENLISTED @ BUTLER, PA
     SWORN: FEB 16, 1864/3 YRS   DISCHARGED: JUN 19, 1865
     1890 CENSUS: PARKER'S LANDING, ARMSTRONG COUNTY, PA
     DIED AT BUTLER, PA BEFORE 1905
     BROTHER, ANDREW, PVT IN CO. K, 104th; BROTHER, JOHN, 2LT IN CO. F, PA 137th

LENKARD, JOHN   PVT   CO. H   AGE:25
LENKERD, JOHN   LENKIRK, JOHN
     BUTLER COUNTY ENLISTEE   BOUNTY $29
     SWORN: MAR 1, 1863/3 YRS   DISHONORABLE DISCHARGE: JUNE 5, 1865
     BORN: ALLEGHENY COUNTY   OCCUPATION: BLACKSMITH
     HEIGHT: 5' 7"   COMPLEXION: DARK   EYES: DARK   HAIR: BROWN
     DIED AT BUTLER, PA BEFORE THE REGIMENTAL HISTORY WAS PUBLISHED IN 1905

LEWIS, EVEN   2LT   CO. A   AGE:32
LEWIS, EVAN
     BORN: FEB 21, 1829 TO SAMUEL AND ABIGALE HALLOWELL LEWIS
     RAISED BY MATERNAL GRANDFATHER
     BORN: INDIANA COUNTY   OCCUPATION: TAILOR
     HEIGHT: 5' 11"   COMPLEXION: DARK   EYES: BLUE   HAIR: BROWN
     FARMER, SCHOOL DIRECTOR, POSTMASTER, STONEMASON
     ORIGIN: WEST MAHONING TWP., INDIANA COUNTY
     SWORN: OCT 12, 1861/3 YRS   MUSTER: NOV 4, 1864
     ENLISTED AS 2ND SGT   PROMOTED FROM SGT, SEP 1, 1863
     HOME 1890-1914: SMICKSBURG, INDIANA COUNTY, PA
     SERVED AS A CAPTAIN IN THE PA NATIONAL GUARD FOR 6 YEARS AFTER THE WAR
     SERVED AS COMMANDER OF THE GAR IN PLUMVILLE
     BURIED @ MAHONING BAPTIST CEMETERY IN HOME, PA, DIED: OCT 28, 1917
     REUNION AT CHICKAMAUGA 1897, KITTANNING 1900, INDIANA 1908.
     SERVED AS VP OF REUNION ASSOCIATION
     BURIED OLD MAHONING BAPTIST CEMETERY, HOME, PA
     FIRST WIFE: CATHERINE KEEL [1851], SECOND WIFE: SARAH R., THIRD WIFE: LYDIA W.

LEWIS, JOHN ** *   PVT   CO. A   AGE:21
     SWORN: AUG 5, 1862/3 YRS   DISCHARGED: JUN 19, 1865
     BORN: INDIANA COUNTY   OCCUPATION: FARMER
     HEIGHT: 5' 8"   COMPLEXION: FAIR   EYES: BROWN   HAIR: BROWN
     HOME 1890-1914: SMICKSBURG, INDIANA COUNTY, PA
     LIFETIME REPUBLICAN   WIFE: SARAH ELLEN DAVIS; 1844-1913
     ATTENDED THE REGIMENTAL REUNION AT INDIANA, PA, IN 1908.
     BURIED OLD MAHONING BAPTIST CEMETERY, HOME, PA, NOV 20, 1840-JUN 10, 1922
     BROTHER JOSHUA LEWIS

LEWIS, JOHN C.   PVT   CO. A   AGE:18
    PARENTS GEORGE LEWIS-DIED 1846; SUSAN C. SPEAR 1815-1904
    BORN: SMICKSBURG, INDIANA COUNTY, PA, 1842
    SWORN: OCT 12, 1861/3 YRS   DIED: AT LOUISVILLE, DEC 15, 1863
    BORN: INDIANA COUNTY   OCCUPATION: LABORER
    HEIGHT: 5' 7½"   COMPLEXION: DARK   EYES: BLUE   HAIR: BROWN
    CAPTURED AT STONES RIVER; SENT TO LIBBY PRISON AND EXCHANGED
    BURIED: NATIONAL CEMETERY LOUISVILLE; SECTION.B, RANGE.16, GRAVE.29
    SAMUEL LEWIS' BROTHER

LEWIS, JOSHUA   PVT   CO. A   AGE:18
LEWIS, JOSIAH
    SWORN: OCT 12, 1861/3 YRS   MUSTER: NOV 4, 1864
    BORN: INDIANA COUNTY   OCCUPATION: LABORER
    HEIGHT: 5' 5"   COMPLEXION: DARK   EYES: BLUE   HAIR: BLACK
    HOME 1890-1914: CHAMBERSVILLE, INDIANA COUNTY, PA
    REUNION CHICKAMAUGA 1897, INDIANA 1908.
    BURIED OLD MAHONING BAPTIST CEMETERY, HOME, PA: DIED: JUN 1921
    BROTHER JOHN LEWIS

LEWIS, JOSHUA P.   PVT   CO. A   AGE: 18
LEWIS, JOSIAH P.
    SWORN: OCT 12, 1861/3 YRS   MUSTER: NOV 4, 1864
    BORN: INDIANA COUNTY   OCCUPATION: LABORER
    HEIGHT: 5' 6"   COMPLEXION: FAIR   EYES: BLUE   HAIR: BROWN
    HOME 1897: VENUS, VENANGO COUNTY, PA
    HOME 1914: RYBURG, CLARION COUNTY, PA
    REUNION CHICKAMAUGA 1897, INDIANA 1908.

LEWIS, LEWIS *   PVT   CO. F   AGE: 44
LEWIS, LOUIS
    SWORN: OCT 12, 1861/3 YRS   TRANS: AUG 1, 1863 TO VRC
    BORN: FREEPORT, PA   OCCUPATION: LABORER
    HEIGHT: 5' 5"   COMPLEXION: SALLOW   EYES: GREY   HAIR: BROWN
    SOME FAMILIES RECEIVED $100 BOUNTY UPON ENLISTMENT
    RESIDENT OF DAYTON [PA] SOLDIER'S HOME IN 1886
    DIED: SOLDIERS HOME DAYTON BEFORE 1905
    BURIED FREEPORT CEMETERY, FREEPORT, PA   WIFE: MARY

LEWIS, ROBERT *   PVT   CO. B   AGE:31
    SWORN: OCT 12, 1861/3 YRS   DIED: JAN 17, 1863 AT MURFREESBORO, TN
    BORN: ARMSTRONG COUNTY   OCCUPATION: FARMER
    HEIGHT: 5' 10"   COMPLEXION: DARK   EYES: BLACK   HAIR: BLACK
    MORTALLY WOUNDED/THIGH AT STONES RIVER
    BURIED AT NATIONAL CEMETERY STONES RIVER, GRAVE #307

LEWIS, SAMUEL **   PVT   CO. A   AGE: 18
    PARENTS GEORGE LEWIS-DIED 1846; SUSAN C. SPEAR 1815-1904
    BORN: SMICKSBURG, INDIANA COUNTY, PA
    SWORN: AUG 5, 1862/3 YRS   DISCHARGED: JUN 19, 1865
    BORN: INDIANA COUNTY   OCCUPATION: FARMER
    HEIGHT: 5' 8"   COMPLEXION: DARK   EYES: BROWN   HAIR: BROWN
    1890 CENSUS: CANOE TWP., INDIANA COUNTY, PA
    HOME IN 1897: ROCHESTER MILLS, INDIANA COUNTY, PA
    REUNION CHICKAMAUGA 1897, INDIANA 1908.
    BURIED: INDIANA COUNTY, PINE GROVE CEMETERY, CANOE TWP., 1844-1914
    JOHN C. LEWIS' BROTHER

LEWIS, WILLIAM T.   PVT   CO. A   AGE:20
LEWIS, WILLIAM TAYLOR
    SWORN: OCT 12, 1861/3 YRS   MUSTER: NOV 4, 1864
    BORN: INDIANA COUNTY   OCCUPATION: LABORER
    HEIGHT: 5' 2"   COMPLEXION: FAIR   EYES: BROWN   HAIR: BROWN
    REUNION IN FREEPORT 1886
    HOME 1886-1890 AMBROSE, INDIANA COUNTY, PA
    BURIED: INDIANA COUNTY, MARION CENTER CEMETERY, JUL 22, 1839-APR 16, 1908

LIAS, McKENDRIA M. *   MUC   CO. G   AGE:22
    SWORN: OCT 12, 1861/3 YRS   DIED: DEC 11, 1861 AT CAMP NEGLEY

BORN: RURAL VALLEY, PA   OCCUPATION: FARMER
HEIGHT: 5' 5"   COMPLEXION: FAIR   EYES: BROWN   HAIR: BROWN
LINDSEY, JAMES W.   PVT   CO. H   AGE:20
   SWORN: OCT 12, 1861/3YRS   MUSTER: NOV 4, 1864   BOUNTY: $100.
   BORN: BUTLER COUNTY   OCCUPATION: FARMER
   HEIGHT: 5' 7"   COMPLEXION: DARK EYES: GREY   HAIR: BROWN
LITTLE, JAMES   PVT   CO. A   AGE: 20
   SWORN: OCT 12, 1861/3 YRS   KILLED: MAY 27, 1864 @ PICKETT'S MILL
   BORN: INDIANA COUNTY   OCCUPATION: FARMER
   HEIGHT: 5' 5½"   COMPLEXION: LIGHT   EYES: GREY   HAIR: BLOND
   WOUNDED/NECK AT STONES RIVER
LLOYD, ABSALOM *   PVT   CO. K   AGE:19
   SWORN: OCT 12, 1861/3 YRS   MUSTER: NOV 4, 1864
   BORN: ARMSTRONG COUNTY   OCCUPATION: UNDERTAKER
   HEIGHT: 5' 8"   COMPLEXION: DARK   EYES: BLACK   HAIR: DARK
   WOUNDED AT STONES RIVER
   HOME 1890-1914: KITTANNING, PA
   BURIED: KITTANNING CEMETERY [1840-1922]   WIFE: HATTIE J.
LLOYD, JOHN   PVT   CO. D   AGE: 19
   SWORN: OCT 12, 1861/3 YRS   DIED: FEB 19, 1862 AT LOUISVILLE
   BORN: INDIANA COUNTY, CHERRY TREE   OCCUPATION: FARMER
   HEIGHT: 6' 1"   COMPLEXION: FAIR   EYES: BLUE   HAIR: DARK
   BURIED: NATIONAL CEMETERY LOUISVILLE: SECTION.A, RANGE.11, GRAVE.21
LOCKE, DAVID E.   PVT   CO. H   AGE:18
   SWORN: OCT 12, 1861/3YRS   DIED: NOV 28, 1862 AT NASHVILLE OF TYPHOID
   FEVER AND DIPTHERIA
   BORN: MERCER COUNTY   OCCUPATION: TEAMSTER
   HEIGHT: 5' 6"   COMPLEXION: DARK   EYES: DARK   HAIR: DARK
   BURIED AT NATIONAL CEMETERY NASHVILLE. GRAVE #B-187
LONG, JACOB S. *   PVT   CO. I   AGE:19
   SWORN: OCT 12, 1861/3 YRS   MUSTER: NOV 4, 1864
   BORN: SALTSBURG, PA   OCCUPATION: LABORER
   HEIGHT: 5' 6"   COMPLEXION: LIGHT   EYES: GRAY   HAIR: LIGHT
   ATTENDED THE REGIMENTAL REUNION AT INDIANA, PA, IN 1908.
   BURIED: BLAIRSVILLE CEMETERY, BLAIRSVILLE, PA 1842-1912
LONG, JAMES C.   PVT   CO. H   AGE:16
   BUTLER COUNTY ENLISTEE   BOUNTY: $100
   SWORN: OCT 12, 1861/3YRS   MUSTER: NOV 4, 1864
   BORN: BUTLER COUNTY   OCCUPATION: CABINET MAKER
   HEIGHT: 5' 10"   COMPLEXION: FAIR   EYES: GREY   HAIR: BROWN
   HOME IN 1897: PHILADELPHIA, PA   HOME 1914: CHICAGO, ILL
LONG, JOHN R. **   PVT   CO. H   AGE:19
   BORN: JAN 20, 1843 IN WESTMORELAND COUNTY.
   SWORN: MAR 30, 1864/3 YRS   MUSTER: SEP 11, 1865
   ENLISTED AT ALLEGHENY CITY, PA
   BORN: ARMSTRONG COUNTY   OCCUPATION: FARMER
   HEIGHT: 5' 5½"   COMPLEXION: FAIR   EYES: HAZEL   HAIR: DARK
   WORKED AS AN ENGINEER @ JONES & LAUGHLIN STEEL AFTER THE WAR
   BECAME THE VICE PRESIDENT OF THE FIRST NATIONAL BANK, LEECHBURG, PA
   1886 REUNION IN FREEPORT, INDIANA 1908
   HOME 1886-1925: LEECHBURG, ARMSTRONG COUNTY, PA
   BURIED AT EVERGREEN CEMETERY, LEECHBURG, PA   DIED: JUN 15, 1925
LONG, SOLOMON *   PVT   CO. B   AGE: 34
   BORN: FEB 17, 1837
   OCCUPATION: FARMER   TEACHER IN RED BANK
   SWORN: OCT 12, 1861/3 YRS   MUSTER: NOV 4, 1864
   BORN: ARMSTRONG COUNTY   OCCUPATION: FARMER
   HEIGHT: 5' 10"   COMPLEXION: LIGHT   EYES: BLUE   HAIR: DARK
   1890 CENSUS: RED BANK, ARMSTRONG COUNTY, PA
   HOME 1901-1914: EDDYVILLE, PA   REUNION IN KITTANNING 1901
   WIFE: MARY SNYDER   2nd WIFE: LEVINA CLEMENZA KELLS
LOVE, JOHN *   PVT   CO. I   AGE:26

SWORN: OCT 12, 1861/3 YRS   MUSTER: NOV 4, 1864
BORN: SMICKSBURG, PA   OCCUPATION: LABORER
HEIGHT: 5' 11½"   COMPLEXION: LIGHT   EYES: BLUE   HAIR: LIGHT
1890 CENSUS: SLIGO, CLARION COUNTY, PA

LOWRY, WILLIAM A. "WILL"   CPL   CO. H   AGE: 19
LOWREY, WILL
SWORN: OCT 12, 1861/3YRS   DISCHARGED: MAR 1863 AS A 2LT IN THE PA 103RD INF;
REGIMENT CAPTURED AND SENT TO ANDERSONVILLE BEFORE LOWERY REPORTED IN.
BORN: BLAIR COUNTY   OCCUPATION: STUDENT
HEIGHT: 6' ¼"   COMPLEXION: FAIR   EYES: BLUE   HAIR: LIGHT
PARENTS: ALEXANDER AND MARGARET LOWRY
ACTING 1ST SGT: DEC 1862.
DETAILED TO MILLER'S CAV ESCORT DEC 1862
PROMOTED TO CPL, FEB 1, 1862 WOUNDED AT STONES RIVER
SENT TO HOSPITAL IN NEW ALBANY, INDIANA, JANUARY 1863
ELECTED VICE PRESIDENT OF THE 78th REUNION COMMITTEE IN 1886
REUNION FREEPORT 1886, PUNXSUTAWNEY 1899, KITTANNING 1901, INDIANA 1908
DEMOCRATIC PROTHONOTARY OF BUTLER COUNTY, PA IN 1908
SECRETARY/TREASURER OF 78th REUNION COMMITTEE 1870-1908
COMMANDER OF ALFRED REED G.A.R. POST
WIFE: ANNIE T. ZEIGLER
HOME 1886-1914: 136 E. DIAMOND, BUTLER, PA
BURIED: NORTH CEMETERY, BUTLER, PA; 1842-1921

LOWRY, ALEXANDER   PVT   CO. G   AGE:60
SWORN: OCT 12, 1861/3 YRS   MEDICAL: OCT 1, 1862
DIED BEFORE THE REGIMENTAL HISTORY WAS PUBLISHED IN 1905

LOWRY, ADAM   1LT   REGIMENTAL STAFF   AGE: 32
ORIGIN: INDIANA COUNTY   REGIMENTAL QUARTER MASTER
ENLISTED AS 2nd SERGEANT, CO. A
SWORN: OCT 18, 1861/3 YRS   DIED: SEP 28, 1863 AT CHATTANOOGA, TN
HEIGHT: 5' 11"   HAIR: BROWN   EYES: BLUE   COMPLEXION: DARK

LOWRY, JOSEPH MARTIN   COM/SGT   STAFF   AGE:16
SWORN: OCT 12, 1861/3 YRS   MUSTER: NOV 4, 1864
BORN: INDIANA COUNTY   OCCUPATION: INNKEEPER
HEIGHT: 5' 7½"   COMPLEXION: FAIR   EYES: GREY   HAIR: DARK
PROMOTED FROM PVT CO. D, APR 25, 1864
HOME 1886: INDIANA, PA   HOME 1897-1901: ALLEGHENY, PA
REUNION FREEPORT 1886, KITTANNING 1901
BURIED: INDIANA COUNTY, OAKLAND CEMETERY, WHITE TWP.,
NOV 10, 1845-DEC 21, 1904

LOWRY, SAMUEL   PVT   CO. C   AGE: 53
BORN: MAY 9, 1809 IN COUNTY DOWN, IRELAND
SWORN: AUG 28, 1862/3 YRS   DISCHARGED: JUN 19, 1865
BORN: IRELAND   OCCUPATION: FARMER
HEIGHT: 5' 9"   COMPLEXION: DARK   EYES: BLUE   HAIR: BROWN
WOUNDED AT STONES RIVER/HIP   DIED: NEW BETHLEHEM, PENNSYLVANIA
DIED BEFORE THE REGIMENTAL HISTORY WAS PUBLISHED IN 1905
WIFE: ELIZABETH BARNHART,   REUNION IN FREEPORT 1886
HOME 1886-1890: NEW BETHLEHEM, CLARION COUNTY, PA

LUCKHART, JOHN   CPL   CO. A   AGE:19
LUKECART, JOHN   LUKEHART, JOHN   VETERAN
SWORN: OCT 12, 1861/4 YRS   MUSTER: SEP 11, 1865
BORN: INDIANA COUNTY   OCCUPATION: FARMER
HEIGHT: 5' 10"   COMPLEXION: LIGHT   EYES: BLUE   HAIR: BROWN
HOME 1886: PLUMVILLE, PA; HOME 1890-1897: DENTON, INDIANA COUNTY, PA
BURIED @ MAHONING BAPTIST CEMETERY IN HOME, PA
ATTENDED THE DEDICATION OF THE CHICKAMAUGA BATTLEFIELD, NOV 1897

LUSHER, JOHN   CPL   CO. E   AGE: 19
SWORN: OCT 12, 1861/3 YRS   MUSTER: NOV 4, 1864
BORN: VENANGO COUNTY   OCCUPATION: FARMER
HEIGHT: 5' 9"   COMPLEXION: DARK   EYES: BROWN   HAIR: BLACK
PROMOTED TO CPL, APR 27, 1863

HOME IN 1897: NEW CASTLE, LAWRENCE COUNTY, PA
BECAME A LUTHERAN MINISTER
HOME 1914: PARKER'S LANDING, PA
REUNION CHICKAMAUGA 1897, INDIANA 1908.

LUTE, CHRISTOPHER H.   PVT   CO. D   AGE: 29
LUTZ, CHRISTOPHER H.
    SWORN: OCT 12, 1861/3 YRS   MUSTER: NOV 4, 1864
    BORN: INDIANA COUNTY, UTAH   OCCUPATION: FARMER
    HEIGHT: 5' 6"   COMPLEXION: SANDY   EYES: GREY   HAIR: SANDY
    HOME IN 1897: NEW FLORENCE, WESTMORELAND COUNTY, PA
    HOME 1914: VINTONDALE, CAMBRIA COUNTY, PA
    BURIED: INDIANA COUNTY, McDOWELL CEMETERY, GREEN TWP.,
    APR 14, 1832-JUN 16, 1914

LYDICK, ALEXANDER   PVT   CO. D   AGE: 42
    SWORN: OCT 12, 1861/3 YRS   MUSTER: OCT 26, 1864
    BORN: INDIANA COUNTY, UTAH   OCCUPATION: CARPENTER
    HEIGHT: 5' 8½"   COMPLEXION: FAIR   EYES: BLUE   HAIR: DARK
    TRANS: NOV 25,1863 TO VRC
    ATTENDED 1886 REUNION IN FREEPORT
    HOME 1886-1899: UTAH, INDIANA COUNTY, PA; WIDOW MARGARET
    BORN 1819, DIED: JUL 1899 AT UTAH, PA
    BURIED: INDIANA COUNTY, TAYLORSVILLE CEMETERY, GREEN TWP.,

LYTLE, CONSTANTINE W.E.   *   PVT   CO. K   AGE:18
    SWORN: FEB 27, 1864/3 YRS   MUSTER: SEP 11, 1865 - NOT AT FINAL MUSTER
    BORN: VENANGO COUNTY   OCCUPATION: BOATMAN
    HEIGHT: 5' 5"   COMPLEXION: LIGHT   EYES: BLUE   HAIR: LIGHT
    BORN: MAR 20, 1846   DIED: MAR 9, 1898
    1890 CENSUS: APOLLO, PA
    ENUMERATOR OF 1890 CENSUS IN APOLLO, PA
    BURIED: APOLLO CEMETERY, APOLLO, PA   WIFE: CHRISTINIA

LYTLE, DAVID S.   PVT   CO. E   AGE: 23
LITTLE, DAVID S.
    SWORN: OCT 12, 1861/3 YRS   MUSTER: NOV 4, 1864
    BORN: HUNTINGTON COUNTY   OCCUPATION: LABORER
    HEIGHT: 5' 4"   COMPLEXION: DARK   EYES: GREY   HAIR: DARK
    HOME IN 1897: SENECA, VENANGO COUNTY, PA

McAFOOS, JACOB R. *   1LT   CO. G   AGE:31
McAFFOSE, JACOB R.
    BORN: SEPT 9, 1829, IN ARMSTRONG COUNTY TO DANIEL AND CATHERINE
    SWORN: OCT 12, 1861/3 YRS   MUSTER: NOV 4, 1864
    BORN: DAYTON, PA   OCCUPATION: CARPENTER
    HEIGHT: 5' 10"   COMPLEXION: FAIR   EYES: BLUE   HAIR: SANDY
    PROMOTED FROM 2ND LT AUG 26, 1863
    WIFE: SARAH RUPP
    1890 CENSUS: WEST MILLVILLE, CLARION COUNTY, PA
    DIED: MILLVILLE, CLARION COUNTY, PA
    BROTHER, ABSOLOM OF THE 14th PA CAVALRY DIED AT ANDERSONVILLE

McBRIDE, EDWARD H.C. **   PVT   CO. C   AGE: 19
    SWORN: SEP 22, 1863/3 YRS   MUSTER: SEP 11, 1865, SICK AT MUSTER
    BORN: WASHINGTON COUNTY   OCCUPATION: LABORER
    HEIGHT: 5' 7"   COMPLEXION: DARK   EYES: BLACK HAIR: BLACK

McBRIDE, ENOS   PVT   CO. G
    SWORN: MAR 12, 1862/3 YRS   DIED: DEC 30, 1862 AT NASHVILLE
    BURIED @ NASHVILLE, BATES

McBRIDE, GEORGE D.   PVT   CO. H   AGE:24
    SWORN: OCT 12, 1861/3YRS   TRANS: MAY 15, 1864 TO VRC
    BORN: BUTLER COUNTY   OCCUPATION: TEACHER
    HEIGHT: 5' 11"   COMPLEXION: FAIR   EYES: GREY   HAIR: BROWN
    HOME 1914: GALLIPOLIS, OH

McBRIDE, JAMES C.   CPL   CO. C
    SWORN: AUG 28, 1862/3 YRS   DISCHARGED: JUN 19, 1865
    BORN: CLARION COUNTY   OCCUPATION: BLACKSMITH

HEIGHT: 5' 11"   COMPLEXION: FAIR   EYES: BLUE   HAIR: SANDY
PROMOTED TO CORPORAL IN CO. B Π
ATTENDED 1886 REUNION IN FREEPORT
HOME 1886-1899: SLIGO, CLARION COUNTY, PA   DIED: 1899

McBRIDE, SAMUEL J.   1LT   CO. H   AGE:21
SWORN: OCT 12, 1861/3YRS   MUSTER: NOV 4, 1864
BORN: BUTLER COUNTY   OCCUPATION: PAINTER
HEIGHT: 6' $^{1}/_{3}$"   COMPLEXION: SANDY   EYES: BLUE   HAIR: SANDY
WOUNDED AT STONES RIVER;   LED CO. AT STONES RIVER AS SGT
PROMOTED FROM SGT TO 2ND LT FOR BRAVERY AND LEADERSHIP AT STONES
RIVER FEB 20, 1863   PROMOTED TO 1LT APR 16, 1863.
HOME 1897: EAST BROOK, LAWRENCE COUNTY, PA
ATTENDED THE DEDICATION OF THE CHICKAMAUGA BATTLEFIELD, NOV 1897
DIED: JUL 16, 1907 IN LAWRENCE COUNTY; BURIED AT RICH HILL CHURCH YARD

McBRIER, ARCHIBALD M.   CPL   CO. A   AGE:21
McBRIDE, ARCHIBALD
SWORN: OCT 12, 1861/3 YRS   MUSTER: NOV 4, 1864
BORN: INDIANA COUNTY   OCCUPATION: FARMER
HEIGHT: 5' 7½"   COMPLEXION: FAIR   EYES: BLUE   HAIR: SANDY
HOME: 1886-1897: ROUSEVILLE, VENANGO COUNTY, PA
ATTENDED THE DEDICATION OF THE CHICKAMAUGA BATTLEFIELD, NOV 1897

McCAIN, ALEXANDER   PVT   CO. E   AGE: 21
SWORN: OCT 12, 1861/3 YRS   DIED: APR 24, 1864 IN FREEPORT, PA
BORN: CLARION COUNTY   OCCUPATION: LABORER
HEIGHT: 6'   COMPLEXION: LIGHT   EYES: BLUE   HAIR: LIGHT

McCAIN, JAMES *   1ST MUC   CO. F   AGE:36
SWORN: OCT 12, 1861/3 YRS   MEDICAL: JUN 23, 1863
BORN: FREEPORT, PA   OCCUPATION: LABORER
HEIGHT: 5' 10"   COMPLEXION: LIGHT   EYES: BLUE   HAIR: LIGHT

McCALL, ELI   PVT   CO. E   AGE: 27
SWORN: JAN 3, 1862/3 YRS   MUSTER: SEP 11, 1865
BORN: CLARION COUNTY   OCCUPATION: FARMER
HEIGHT: 5' 10"   COMPLEXION: SANDY   EYES: GREY   HAIR: LIGHT
PRISONER AT STONES RIVER/PAROLED
1890 CENSUS: TOBY, CLARION COUNTY, PA; WIDOW SARAH

McCANDLESS, GEORGE WASHINGTON *
McCANDLASS, GEORGE W.   PVT   CO. H   AGE:18
SWORN: APR 22, 1861/3 MONTHS, CO B, NINTH PENNSYLVANIA   BOUNTY: $100.
COLONEL SIRWELL'S NEPHEW   SERVED WITH SIRWELL'S BRADY ALPINES
SWORN: OCT 12, 1861/3YRS   MUSTER: NOV 4, 1864   VETERAN
BORN: BUTLER COUNTY   OCCUPATION: TEAMSTER
HEIGHT: 5' 9½"   COMPLEXION: DARK   EYES: BLUE   HAIR: DARK
ARRESTED FOR FRACTURING A CO. F SOLDIER'S SKULL WITH A CLUB; ON APR 2,   1862,
WAS DRUNK AT THE TIME.   BROKE OUT OF GUARD HOUSE APR 4.
SERVED WITH PIONEER BRIGADE DURING BATTLE AT STONES RIVER
HOME IN 1897-1914: 621 MONROE AVE, BELLVUE [BELLEVUE], ALLEGHENY COUNTY, PA
ATTENDED THE DEDICATION OF THE CHICKAMAUGA BATTLEFIELD, NOV 1897

McCANNA, BARNABAS ***   PVT   CO. A
SWORN: JAN 19, 1864/3 YRS   MEDICAL: MAY 26, 1865.
1890 CENSUS: BROOKVILLE, JEFFERSON COUNTY, PA

McCANNA, MARTIN M.   CPT   CO. B   AGE: 27
SWORN: APR 22, 1861/3 MONTHS, CO B, NINTH PENNSYLVANIA
SWORN: JUL 24, 1861/3 YRS   MUSTER: NOT ON ROLLS
SWORN: OCT 12, 1861/3 YRS   MUSTER: NOV 4, 1864
BORN: ARMSTRONG COUNTY   VETERAN
HEIGHT: 6' 1"   COMPLEXION: DARK   EYES: GREY
SHELL WOUND LEFT FOOT, DATE & BATTLE UNKNOWN
SERVED WITH SIRWELL'S ORIGINAL CO. B.   APPTD CO. COMMANDER: DEC 26, 1862
COMMENDED BY SIRWELL FOR BRAVERY AT STONES RIVER
AFTER MUSTER WITH THE 78th, RAISED A CO. THAT JOINED THE PA 104TH INF
FINAL MUSTER: AUG 25, 1865
HOME 1890-1897: KNOX, CLARION COUNTY, PA

HOME 1901: EDENSBURG, CLARION COUNTY, PA
REUNION IN CHICKAMAUGA 1897, KITTANNING 1901

McCANNA, WILLIAM *   CPL   CO. B   AGE:29
    SWORN: OCT 12, 1861/3 YRS   MEDICAL: JAN 28, 1862
    BORN: ARMSTRONG COUNTY   OCCUPATION: FARMER
    HEIGHT: 6'   COMPLEXION: DARK   EYES: BLACK   HAIR: DARK

McCLEARY, JAMES   PVT   CO. H   AGE:24
    SWORN: OCT 12, 1861/3YRS   MUSTER: NOV 4, 1864   BOUNTY: $100.
    BORN: BUTLER COUNTY   OCCUPATION: FARMER
    HEIGHT: 5' 11½"   COMPLEXION: LIGHT   EYES: BROWN   HAIR: BLACK
    DEMOTED FROM SEVENTH CPL AUG 4, 1863
    WOUNDED/FACE AT PICKETT'S MILL, MAY 27, 1864

McCLEARY, THOMAS *   CPL   CO. G
    SWORN: FEB 2, 1864/3 YRS   MUSTER: SEP 11, 1865
    HOME IN 1897: TEMPLETON, ARMSTRONG COUNTY, PA
    1890 CENSUS: EAST FRANKLIN TWP., ARMSTRONG COUNTY, PA
    ATTENDED THE DEDICATION OF THE CHICKAMAUGA BATTLEFIELD, NOV 1897

McCLELLAND, JEREMIAH C.   PVT   CO. C   AGE: 20
McCLELLAN, JERIMIAH C.   McLELLAND, JEREMIAH   VETERAN
    SWORN: OCT 12, 1861/4 YRS   DISCHARGED: MAY 19, 1865
    BORN: PENNSYLVANIA
    HEIGHT: 5' 10"   COMPLEXION: SANDY   EYES: GREY   HAIR: SANDY
    BURIED: UNION BAPTIST CEMETERY, SLATE LICK, PA [1843-1903]
    WIFE: MARY
    1890 CENSUS: PORTER TWP., CLARION COUNTY, PA

McCLELLAND, SAMUEL A. ***   CPL   CO. K   AGE:19
    SWORN: OCT 12, 1861/4 YRS   MUSTER: SEP 11, 1865   NOT AT FINAL MUSTER
    BORN: ALLEGHENY COUNTY   OCCUPATION: FARMER
    HEIGHT: 5' 7½"   COMPLEXION: DARK   EYES: GREY   HAIR: DARK
    PROMOTED TO CORPORAL CO. B II   VETERAN
    WOUNDED AT STONES RIVER DIED: JUN 7, 1903 AT ALLEGHENY CITY, PA
    1886 REUNION IN FREEPORT: HOME, SLATE LICK, PA

McCLOSKEY, JAMES P.   SGT   CO. D   AGE: 18
    SWORN: OCT 12, 1861/3 YRS   MUSTER: NOV 4, 1864
    BORN: INDIANA COUNTY, TYLERSBURG   OCCUPATION: LUMBERMAN
    HEIGHT: 5' 7"   COMPLEXION: DARK   EYES: DARK   HAIR: DARK
    PROMOTED APR 16, 1863   HOME IN 1897: LEEPER, CLARION COUNTY, PA
    PUT UNDER ARREST, MAR 18, 1863
    1890 CENSUS: SCOTCH HILL, CLARION COUNTY, PA
    HOME 1914: KUSKEQUA, McKEAN COUNTY, PA

McCOLL, JASPER   PVT   CO. E   AGE: 18
McCOOL, JASPER
    SWORN: OCT 12, 1861/3 YRS   MUSTER: NOV 4, 1864
    BORN: BUTLER COUNTY   OCCUPATION: LABORER
    HEIGHT: 5' 8"   COMPLEXION: DARK   EYES: BLACK   HAIR: BROWN

McCOLLUM, HENRY *   PVT   CO. B   AGE:23
    SWORN: OCT 12, 1861/3 YRS   KILLED: MAY 27, 1864 AT PICKETT'S MILL
    BORN: ARMSTRONG COUNTY   OCCUPATION: FARMER
    HEIGHT: 5' 10"   COMPLEXION: LIGHT   EYES: BLUE   HAIR: LIGHT

McCOLLUMS, JAMES *   7TH CPL   CO. G   AGE:28
COLLUMS, JAMES M.   McCULLONS, JAMES
    SWORN: OCT 12, 1861/3 YRS   DIED: FEB 17, 1862 AT CAMP WOOD
    BORN: KITTANNING, PA   OCCUPATION: FARMER
    HEIGHT: 5' 8"   COMPLEXION: DARK   EYES: GREY   HAIR: BROWN

McCOMBS, WILLIAM   PVT   CO. D   AGE: 19
    SWORN: OCT 12, 1861/3 YRS   DIED: JAN 2, 1862 AT CAMP WOOD
    BORN: INDIANA COUNTY, DIAMOND   OCCUPATION: FARMER
    HEIGHT: 5' 6½"   COMPLEXION: FAIR   EYES: BLUE   HAIR: DARK

McCORMICK, ROBERT *   PVT   CO. B   AGE:52
    SWORN: OCT 12, 1861/4 YRS   DIED: DEC 14, 1865 AT NASHVILLE
    BORN: IRELAND   OCCUPATION: FARMER   VETERAN
    HEIGHT: 5' 7"   COMPLEXION: DARK   EYES: GREY   HAIR: GREY

BURIED AT NATIONAL CEMETERY NASHVILLE, GRAVE #C-84

McCORMICK, ROBERT H.   CPT   CO. D   AGE:36
   ORIGIN: HOLIDAYSBURG, PA
   SWORN: OCT 12, 1861/3 YRS   MUSTER: NOV 4, 1864
   BORN: INDIANA COUNTY, CHERRY TREE TWP.
   OCCUPATION: TURNER [LATHE OPERATOR]
   HEIGHT: 5' 10" COMPLEXION: SANDY   EYES: BROWN   HAIR: SANDY
   SERVED IN PIONEER BRIGADE DURING STONES RIVER
   PROMOTED APR 16, 1863 FROM 1LT
   1886 REUNION IN FREEPORT: HOME, CHERRY TREE, PA
   HOME 1890-1897: GRANT, INDIANA COUNTY, PA   DIED: JUN 22, 1898
   BURIED: INDIANA COUNTY, IOOF CEMETERY, CHERRY TREE, MONTGOMERY TWP.,
   AUG 26, 1825-JUN 22, 1898

McCOY, ANDREW   PVT   CO. E   AGE: 38
   SWORN: OCT 12, 1861/3 YRS   MUSTER: NOV 4, 1864
   BORN: WESTMORELAND COUNTY   OCCUPATION: LABORER
   HEIGHT: 5' 7"   COMPLEXION: DARK   EYES: BROWN   HAIR: BLACK

McCOY, JOSEPH P.   PVT   CO. H   AGE:30
   SWORN: OCT 12, 1861/3YRS   MUSTER: NOV 4, 1864
   BORN: MERCER COUNTY   OCCUPATION: MILLER
   HEIGHT: 5' 11" COMPLEXION: DARK   EYES: BLUE   HAIR: BLACK
   BOUNTY: $100.   HOME IN 1897: GROVE CITY, PA
   ATTENDED THE DEDICATION OF THE CHICKAMAUGA BATTLEFIELD, NOV 1897

McCRACKEN, GEORGE ***   PVT   CO. F   AGE: 20
McCRACKAN, GEORGE
   SWORN: OCT 31, 1863/3 YRS   MUSTER: SEP 11, 1865
   BORN: WESTMORELAND COUNTY   OCCUPATION: FARMER
   HEIGHT: 5' 9"   COMPLEXION: DARK   EYES: GREY   HAIR: BROWN
   BROTHER NATHAN IN SAME COMPANY
   BURIED: SLATE LICK CEMETERY, SLATE LICK, PA [1842-1930]
   HOME 1886-1930 SLATE LICK, ARMSTRONG COUNTY, PA
   REUNION IN FREEPORT 1886, CHICKAMAUGA 1897, KITTANNING 1901, INDIANA 1908
   HELD ONE OF THE LATER REGIMENTAL REUNIONS ON HIS FARM
   ATTENDED GAR DINNER IN TARENTUM IN MAY, 1927

McCRACKEN, JAMES*   PVT   CO. G
   SWORN: OCT 12, 1861/3 YRS   MUSTER: NOV 4, 1864
   WOUNDED AT STONES RIVER/ARM
   DIED BEFORE THE REGIMENTAL HISTORY WAS PUBLISHED IN 1905
   1886 REUNION IN FREEPORT: HOME, ADRIAN, PA
   1890 CENSUS: ADRAIN, EAST FRANKLIN TWP., ARMSTRONG COUNTY, PA

McCRACKEN, NATHAN *   PVT   CO. F   AGE: 20
   SWORN: OCT 12, 1861/3 YRS   MUSTER: NOV 4, 1864
   BORN: FREEPORT, PA   OCCUPATION: FARMER
   HEIGHT: 5' 7"   COMPLEXION: DARK   EYES: BLUE   HAIR: BROWN
   BROTHER GEORGE IN SAME COMPANY   HOME: DENVER COLORADO

McCRADY, GEORGE *   PVT   CO. G
McCREADY, GEORGE
   SWORN: OCT 12, 1861/3 YRS   DIED: OCT 12, 1862 AT NASHVILLE
   BURIED AT NATIONAL CEMETERY NASHVILLE, GRAVE #A-708

McCUE, MARTIN **   PVT   CO. C
   SWORN: OCT 22, 1863/3 YRS   MUSTER: SEP 11, 1865
   BATTLES: BUZZARD'S ROOST, RESACA,   PICKETT'S MILL, BUZZARD'S ROOST II

McCUE, WILLIAM B. *   1LT   CO. F   AGE:22
McCOE, WILLIAM B.
   SWORN: OCT 12, 1861/3 YRS   RESIGNED: NOV 29, 1862
   BORN: FREEPORT, PA   OCCUPATION: MERCHANT/CHEMIST
   HEIGHT: 5' 9"   COMPLEXION: DARK   EYES: GREY   HAIR: BLACK
   MARRIED CAPTAIN GILLESPIE'S WIDOWED SISTER-IN-LAW.
   RESWORN: FEB 29, 1864/3 YRS   MUSTER: SEP 11, 1865
   PROMOTED FROM SGT TO 1LT, DEC 2, 1864
   PROMOTED TO REGIMENTAL QUARTERMASTER DEC 4, 1864
   DIED: MAR 31, 1867 [WPGS]

McCULLOUCH, AZEL S.   2LT   CO. C   AGE:25
   ORIGIN: CLARION COUNTY
   BORN: CLARION COUNTY   OCCUPATION: CARPENTER
   HEIGHT: 5' 7½"   COMPLEXION: FAIR   EYES: BLUE   HAIR: SANDY
   SWORN: OCT 12, 1861/3 YRS   MUSTER: NOV 4, 1864
   PROMOTED: JUL 22, 1863, FROM 1ST SGT
   HOME 1890-1897: KNOX, CLARION COUNTY, PA
   HOME 1914: SOLDIER'S HOME, DAYTON, OHIO
McCULLOUGH, DR. WILLIAM P.*   ASST SUR/78th   REGIMENTAL STAFF
   FRIEND OF SIRWELL'S
   ORIGIN: KITTANNING, ARMSTRONG COUNTY
   SWORN: MAR 19, 1863/3 YRS   MUSTER: NOV 4, 1864
   SERVED IN GENERAL HOSPITAL, MURFREESBORO: APRIL 11, 1863-OCT 14, 1863
   DIED: SEP 17, 1867 [WPGS]
McCURDY, JAMES W.   PVT   CO. B   AGE:18
   SWORN: OCT 12, 1861/3 YRS   DIED: JUN 4, 1864 AT KINGSTON, GA
   BORN: ARMSTRONG COUNTY   OCCUPATION: FARMER
   HEIGHT: 5' 10"   COMPLEXION: DARK   EYES: BLACK   HAIR: BLACK
   MORTALLY WOUNDED AT PICKETT'S MILL
McDONALD, THEODORE ***   PVT   CO. F   AGE: 35
McDONALD, STRODER   McDONALD, STROTHER
   ORIGIN: BUTLER COUNTY
   SWORN: FEB, 28, 1864/3 YRS   DISCHARGED: JUN 7, 1865
   BORN: BUTLER, PA   OCCUPATION: FARMER
   HEIGHT: 5' 11"   COMPLEXION: BLACK   EYES: BLACK   HAIR: BLACK
McDONALD, WESLEY *   PVT   CO. B   AGE:18
   SWORN: OCT 12, 1861/3 YRS   MUSTER: NOV 4, 1864
   BORN: ARMSTRONG COUNTY   OCCUPATION: FARMER
   HEIGHT: 5' 11"   COMPLEXION: DARK   EYES: BLACK   HAIR: DARK
McELHINEY, WILLIAM G. *   CPL   CO. G   AGE: 31
McELHANEY, WILLIAM GEMMILL
   SWORN: OCT 12, 1861/3 YRS   MUSTER: NOV 4, 1864
   BURIED: INDIANA COUNTY, OAKLAND CEMETERY, WHITE TWP.,
   MAY 17, 1830-MAY 5, 1925
McELROY, DAVID W. *   PVT   CO. A   AGE:19
   BOYHOOD HOME IN 1897: RURAL VALLEY, PA
   SWORN: OCT 12, 1861/3 YRS   MUSTER: NOV 4, 1864
   BORN: ARMSTRONG COUNTY   OCCUPATION: MERCHANT
   HEIGHT: 5' 7½"   COMPLEXION: FAIR   EYES: DARK   HAIR: BROWN
   WOUNDED/LEG AT STONES RIVER
   HOME 1886-1908: KEOKUK, IOWA   OWNER: McELROY IRON WORKS CO.
McELROY, JAMES   PVT   CO. E
   SWORN: FEB 29, 1864/3 YRS   MUSTER: SEP 11, 1865
   BATTLES: BUZZARD'S ROOST, RESACA,   PICKETT'S MILL, BUZZARD'S ROOST II
McELROY, JOHNSTON *   PVT   CO. I   AGE:30
   SWORN: OCT 12, 1861/3 YRS   MUSTER: NOV 4, 1864
   BORN: N. WASHINGTON   OCCUPATION: FARMER
   HEIGHT: 5' 7½"   COMPLEXION: LIGHT   EYES: GRAY   HAIR: DARK
   TAKEN PRISONER AT STONES RIVER/PAROLED   SERVED IN AMBULANCE CORP
   HOME 1914: OAKLAND CROSS ROADS, PA
McELWEE, JOSEPH *   CPL   CO. G
   SWORN: OCT 12, 1861/3 YRS   MUSTER: NOV 4, 1864
   HOME 1890-1901: DAYTON, ARMSTRONG COUNTY, PA
   REUNION CHICKAMAUGA 1897, KITTANNING 1901, INDIANA 1908.
McFADDEN, HUGH F. *   PVT   CO. F   AGE:24
   SWORN: OCT 12, 1861/3 YRS   MUSTER: NOV 4, 1864
   BORN: SUGAR CREEK TWP   OCCUPATION: FARMER
   HEIGHT: 5' 10½"   COMPLEXION: LIGHT   EYES: BLUE   HAIR: LIGHT
   BORN: SUGAR CREEK, ARMSTRONG COUNTY, FEB 10, 1837
   DEMOTED FROM 3RD CPL
   HOME 1886: GREER, PA; 1897-1901: RATTIGAN, BUTLER COUNTY, PA
   REUNION FREEPORT 1886, CHICKAMAUGA 1897, KITTANNING 1901

BROTHER. MANASSA J. McFADDEN, 32nd INDIANA, WAS SEVERLY WOUNDED AT
NEW HOPE CHURCH, GA.
BROTHER, MICHAEL McFADDEN WAS KILLED IN 1863 SERVING IN THE PA 14th CAVALRY
WIFE: NANCY RODGERS

McFARLAND, J.F. #   LT   CO. A
WOUNDED/SHOULDER AT STONES RIVER; NO INFORMATION ON THIS SOLDIER OTHER
THAN SIRWELL'S REPORT TO THE KITTANNING NEWSPAPER

McFARLAND, WILLIAM T.*   PVT   CO. A/H   AGE:17
SWORN: OCT 12, 1861/3 YRS   MUSTER: NOV 4, 1864
ENLISTED AT KITTANNING; AUG 27, 1861
BORN: ARMSTRONG COUNTY   OCCUPATION: FARMER
HEIGHT: 5' 6"   COMPLEXION: DARK   EYES: BROWN   HAIR: BROWN
WOUNDED/SHOULDER AT STONES RIVER
1890 CENSUS: DAYTON BOROUGH, ARMSTRONG COUNTY, PA
COULD BE WIDOW THAT FILED INFORMATION ON CENSUS
BURIED: METHODIST CEMETERY, RURAL VALLEY, PA   DIED: 26 OCT, 1866

McGARVEY, EDWARD *   PVT   CO. B   AGE:22
SWORN: OCT 12, 1861/3 YRS   MUSTER: NOV 4, 1864
BORN: IRELAND   OCCUPATION: FARMER
HEIGHT: 5' 4"   COMPLEXION: DARK   EYES: BLACK   HAIR: BLACK

McGAUGHEY, GEORGE W.   PVT   CO. A   AGE:18
SWORN: OCT 12, 1861/3 YRS   MUSTER: NOV 4, 1864
BORN: ARMSTRONG COUNTY   OCCUPATION: FARMER
HEIGHT: 5' 9"   COMPLEXION: DARK   EYES: GREY   HAIR: BROWN
TAKEN PRISONER AT STONES RIVER/PAROLED
BURIED: INDIANA COUNTY, WASHINGTON CEMETERY, RAYNE TWP.,
1842-OCT 21, 1887

McGEE, PATRICK H. *   PVT   CO. F   AGE: 18
SWORN: FEB 28, 1864/3 YRS   DESERTED: JUN 15, 1864 @ BIG SHANTY, GA
BORN: BUTLER, PA   OCCUPATION: FARMER
HEIGHT: 5' 7"   COMPLEXION: FAIR   EYES: BLUE   HAIR: FAIR
RETURNED AND WAS JAILED; STILL CONFINED AT FINAL MUSTER

McGLAUGHLIN, JOHN N. *   PVT   CO. F   AGE: 30
McLAUGHLIN, JOHN
SWORN: OCT 12, 1861/3 YRS   MUSTER: NOV 4, 1864
BORN: CLEARFIELD, PA   OCCUPATION: TEACHER
HEIGHT: 6' ½"   COMPLEXION: BROWN   EYES: BROWN   HAIR: DARK
WOUNDED AT DALLAS, GA, MAY 31, 1864
HOME IN 1897: ROUGH RUN, BUTLER COUNTY, PA   DIED: OCT 9, 1905
1886 REUNION IN FREEPORT: HOME, COYLESVILLE, PA

McGRATH, DR. JOHN   SURGEON/78th   REGIMENTAL STAFF
ORIGIN: PHILADELPHIA
SWORN: APR 14, 1862/3 YRS   RESIGNED: JUN 23, 1863.

McGRAW, GEORGE W. ***   1ST SGT   CO. F   AGE:25
SWORN: OCT 12, 1861/3 YRS   MUSTER: NOV 4, 1864
BORN: FREEPORT, PA   OCCUPATION: GLASS BLOWER
HEIGHT: 5' 7½"   COMPLEXION: DARK   EYES: GREY   HAIR: BROWN
PROMOTED FROM 5TH SGT MAY 1, 1864
HOME 1897: TYRONE, BLAIR COUNTY, PA; HOME 1914: CHESWICK, PA
REUNION CHICKAMAUGA 1897, INDIANA 1908.
BURIED: PROSPECT CEMETERY, TARENTUM, PA; DIED APR 25, 1921

McHENRY, R. HARVEY   PVT   CO. A   AGE:19
SWORN: OCT 12, 1861/3 YRS   TRANS: SIG CORPS, OCT 22, 1863.
BORN: INDIANA COUNTY   OCCUPATION: FARMER
HEIGHT: 5' 11"   COMPLEXION: LIGHT   EYES: BLUE   HAIR: BROWN

McHUGHES WILLIAM M. *   CPL   CO. F   AGE:21
SWORN: OCT 12, 1861/3 YRS   DIED: JAN 20, 1862 @ CAMP WOOD, KY
BORN: FREEPORT, PA   OCCUPATION: BLACKSMITH
HEIGHT: 5' 7½"   COMPLEXION: LIGHT   EYES: BLUE   HAIR: LIGHT

McILRAVY, JOHN *   PVT   CO. I   AGE: 25
McILRANY. JOHN
SWORN: OCT 12, 1861/3 YRS   MUSTER: NOV 4, 1864

BORN: KITTANNING, PA   OCCUPATION: LABORER
HEIGHT: 5' 7½"   COMPLEXION: SANDY   EYES: BLUE   HAIR: SANDY
BURIED: KITTANNING CEMETERY
DIED BEFORE THE REGIMENTAL HISTORY WAS PUBLISHED IN 1905
1886 REUNION IN FREEPORT: HOME, KITTANNING, PA

McILWAINE, JAMES A.   PVT   CO. E   AGE: 18
SWORN: OCT 12, 1861/3 YRS   MUSTER: NOV 4, 1864
BORN: CLARION COUNTY   OCCUPATION: FARMER
HEIGHT: 5' 10"   COMPLEXION: LIGHT   EYES: BLUE   HAIR: BROWN
WOUNDED AT STONES RIVER/HEAD
1890 CENSUS: POLLOCK, CLARION COUNTY, PA

McILWAIN, JOHN S. *   2ND LT   CO. I   AGE:20
McLLWAIN, JOHN S.
SWORN: OCT 12, 1861/3 YRS   MUSTER: NOV 4, 1864
BORN: KITTANNING, PA   OCCUPATION: MARBLE CUTTER
HEIGHT: 5' 9"   COMPLEXION: SANDY   EYES: GREY   HAIR: LIGHT
PROMOTED FROM 1ST SGT TO 2LT, FEB 18, 1863
BURIED: APOLLO CEMETERY, APOLLO, PA, DIED BEFORE 1905

McILWAINE, JOSIAH   PVT   CO. E   AGE: 28
SWORN: OCT 12, 1861/3 YRS   MEDICAL: MAR 5, 1862
BORN: ARMSTRONG COUNTY   OCCUPATION: FARMER
HEIGHT: 5' 8"   COMPLEXION: SANDY   EYES: BLUE   HAIR: BROWN

McKELVEY, JAMES   PVT   CO. A
SWORN: FEB 29, 1864/3 YRS   KILLED: FEB 16, 1865 IN ACTION
AT SPRING HILL, TN, WHILE FIGHTING GUERRILLAS THAT HAD ATTACKED A TRAIN
HE WAS GUARDING.
ORIGINAL ENLISTMENT IN CO. E
BURIED AT NATIONAL CEMETERY NASHVILLE, GRAVE #G-556

McKELVEY, WILLIAM *   PVT   CO. B   AGE:36
McCELVY, WILLIAM
SWORN: OCT 12, 1861/3 YRS   DIED: MAR 30, 1864
BORN: ARMSTRONG COUNTY   OCCUPATION: FARMER
HEIGHT: 5' 8"   COMPLEXION: LIGHT   EYES: GREY   HAIR: BLACK
DIED AT LOOKOUT MOUNTAIN/CAMP STARKWEATHER

McLAUGHLIN, ARCHIBALD   PVT   CO. D   AGE: 20
SWORN: OCT 12, 1861/3 YRS   DIED: DEC 1861 AT LOUISVILLE
BORN: INDIANA COUNTY, DIAMOND   OCCUPATION: FARMER
HEIGHT: 5' 11½"   COMPLEXION: SANDY   EYES: DARK   HAIR: DARK

McLAUGHLIN, HARRISON   PVT   CO. D   AGE: 22
ORIGIN: UTAH, PA
SWORN: OCT 12, 1861/3 YRS   DIED: MAR 4, 1862 AT MUNFORDSVILLE, KY

McLAUGHLIN, HARRISON   PVT   CO. D   AGE:22
SWORN: OCT 12, 1861/3 YRS   DIED: FEB 4, 1863 AT NASHVILLE
BURIED AT NATIONAL CEMETERY NASHVILLE, GRAVE #B-1158
BORN: INDIANA COUNTY, DIAMOND   OCCUPATION: FARMER
HEIGHT: 6' 1"   COMPLEXION: SANDY   EYES: DARK   HAIR: DARK
FROM UTAH, PA

McLAUGHLIN, JOSEPH C. *   PVT   CO. I   AGE:18
SWORN: OCT 12, 1861/3 YRS   MUSTER: NOV 4, 1864
BORN: APOLLO, PA   OCCUPATION: SHOEMAKER
HEIGHT: 5' 8"   COMPLEXION: DARK   EYES: GREY   HAIR: LIGHT
BURIED: APOLLO CEMETERY, APOLLO, PA

McLAUGHLIN, THOMAS   PVT   CO. D   AGE: 18
SWORN: OCT 12, 1861/3 YRS   DIED: JAN 24, 1862 AT CAMP WOOD
BOWEL INFLAMMATION
BORN: INDIANA COUNTY, DIAMOND   OCCUPATION: FARMER
HEIGHT: 5' 8½"   COMPLEXION: DARK   EYES: DARK   HAIR: DARK

McLEAN, JAMES D. *   PVT   CO. A   AGE:23
McLAIN, JAMES D.
SWORN: OCT 12, 1861/3 YRS   MUSTER: NOV 4, 1864
BORN: ARMSTRONG COUNTY   OCCUPATION: FARMER
HEIGHT: 5' 11"   COMPLEXION: DARK   EYES: GREY   HAIR: BROWN

BRIEFLY MISSING IN ACTION AT STONES RIVER
HOME 1890-1915: ATWOOD BORO, ARMSTRONG COUNTY, PA
REUNION CHICKAMAUGA 1897, INDIANA 1908.
BURIED: ATWOOD CEMETERY, COWANSHANNOCK, ARMSTRONG COUNTY, 1837-1919

McLEOD, JAMES N. *   PVT   CO. G
    SWORN: OCT 12, 1861/3 YRS   MUSTER: NOV 4, 1864
    WOUNDED AT STONES RIVER DEC 31, 1862/FOOT   DIED: AT KITTANNING, PA
    BURIED: KITTANNING CEMETERY, DIED BEFORE 1905

McLEOD, JOHN N.   PVT   CO. G
    SWORN: OCT 18, 1861/3 YRS   MUSTER: NOV 4, 1864
    REDUCED IN RANK FROM REGT QM SGT, TRANSFERRED TO CO. G AS A PVT MAR 1, 1862.

McMEANS, JAMES *   PVT   CO. I   AGE:25
    SWORN: OCT 12, 1861/3 YRS   DIED: JUL 8, 1863 AT NASHVILLE
    BORN: FREEPORT, PA   OCCUPATION: LABORER
    HEIGHT: 5' 7½"   COMPLEXION: DARK   EYES: BLACK   HAIR: DARK
    MORTALLY WOUNDED AT STONES RIVER/ARM
    BURIED @ NASHVILLE, BATES

McMILLAN, HARVEY M.   PVT   CO. C   AGE: 22
McMULLEN, HARVEY
    SWORN: OCT 12, 1861/3 YRS   DIED: NOV 12, 1861 AT LOUISVILLE
    BORN: CLARION COUNTY
    HEIGHT: 5' 7½"   COMPLEXION: DARK   EYES: GREY   HAIR: BROWN
    BURIED: NATIONAL CEMETERY LOUISVILLE; SECTION.A, RANGE.1, GRAVE.5

McMILLAN, WILLIAM   PVT   CO. C   AGE: 29
McMULLEN, WILLIAM   McMILLEN, WILLIAM
    SWORN: AUG 28, 1862/3 YRS   DIED: JAN 15, 1863 AT MURFREESBORO
    BORN: CLARION COUNTY   OCCUPATION: CARPENTER
    HEIGHT: 5' 9"   COMPLEXION: DARK   EYES: BROWN   HAIR: DARK
    MORTALLY WOUNDED AT STONES RIVER/HIP
    BURIED AT NATIONAL CEMETERY NASHVILLE, GRAVE #B-139

McMILLEN, DANIEL *   PVT   CO. G   AGE: 23
    SWORN: SEP 10, 1862/3 YRS   MUSTER: SEP 11, 1865
    BORN: ARMSTRONG COUNTY   OCCUPATION: LABORER
    HEIGHT: 5' 5½"   COMPLEXION: FAIR   EYES: GREY   HAIR: DARK
    BRIEFLY MISSING IN ACTION AT STONES RIVER   DESERTED AND RETURNED
    1890 CENSUS: DAYTON BOROUGH, ARMSTRONG COUNTY, PA

McMILLEN, GEORGE W. *   PVT   CO. I   AGE:32
    SWORN: APR 22, 1861/3 MONTHS, CO B, NINTH PENNSYLVANIA
    SERVED WITH SIRWELL IN ORIGINAL THREE MONTH CO.
    SIRWELL'S BRADY ALPINES
    SWORN: OCT 12, 1861/3 YRS   MEDICAL: JAN 1, 1864   VETERAN
    BORN: APOLLO, PA   OCCUPATION: FARMER
    HEIGHT: 6' ½"   COMPLEXION: SANDY   EYES: BLUE   HAIR: AUBURN
    DEMOTED FROM CORPORAL
    ABSENT/SICK AT FINAL MUSTER   DIED: AT SALTSBURG, PA
    1886 REUNION IN FREEPORT: HOME, SALTSBURG, PA
    BURIED: INDIANA COUNTY, EDGEWOOD CEMETERY, SALTSBURG, FEB 1829-MAY 1898

McMILLER, JAMES M.   PVT   CO. C   AGE: 24
McMILLEN, JAMES M.
    SWORN: OCT 12, 1861/3 YRS   MUSTER: NOV 4, 1864
    BORN: CLARION COUNTY
    HEIGHT: 5' 7"   COMPLEXION: FAIR   EYES: GREY   HAIR: LIGHT
    1890 CENSUS: FULLER, JEFFERSON COUNTY, PA

McNABB, JOSEPH B. *   1ST SGT   CO. B   AGE:40
McNOBB, JAMES B.   ORDERLY   McNABB, JOHN B.
    SWORN: OCT 12, 1861/3 YRS   DISCHARGED: AUG 26, 1862
    BORN: COLUMBANA, OHIO   OCCUPATION: CARPENTER
    HEIGHT: 5' 10"   COMPLEXION: DARK   EYES: BLACK   HAIR: LIGHT
    RESIDENT OF DAYTON [PA] SOLDIER'S HOME IN 1886
    1890 CENSUS: WALK CHALK, EAST FRANKLIN TWP., ARMSTRONG COUNTY, PA

McNEES, DAVID L.   PVT   CO. H   AGE:22
    SWORN: OCT 12, 1861/3YRS   MEDICAL: JUL 11, 1864

BORN: BUTLER COUNTY   OCCUPATION: FARMER
HEIGHT: 5' 8½"   COMPLEXION: SANDY   EYES: BLUE   HAIR: SANDY
PROMOTED FROM 4th CPL TO SGT, MAY 1, 1863
DEMOTED TO PVT, NOV 16, 1863; DIED: BUTLER, PA BEFORE 1905

McNUTT, JAMES   CPL   CO. E   AGE: 22
   SWORN: OCT 12, 1861/3 YRS   MUSTER: NOV 4, 1864
   BORN: DONEAGLE, IRELAND   OCCUPATION: FARMER
   HEIGHT: 5' 10"   COMPLEXION: SANDY   EYES: BLUE   HAIR: FAIR
   WOUNDED AT STONES RIVER/SIDE   PROMOTED TO CPL, SEP 17, 1863
   HOME 1897: CHICORA, BUTLER COUNTY, PA
   HOME 1901: SHERRETT, PA
   REUNION CHICKAMAUGA 1897, KITTANNING 1901

McPHERSON, ELI *   PVT   CO. G   AGE: 17
   BORN: CLARION COUNTY, AUG 28, 1845   VETERAN
   SWORN: MAR 4, 1862/3 YRS   MUSTER: SEP 11, 1865
   1890 CENSUS: EWING, PA
   HOME IN 1897: BUTLER, PA; 1914: 128 SECOND ST, BUTLER, PA
   ATTENDED THE DEDICATION OF THE CHICKAMAUGA BATTLEFIELD, NOV 1897
   BROTHER DAVID SERVED IN 155th PA   WIFE: JOANNA WILLIAMS
   BURIED: NORTH CEMETERY, BUTLER, PA; 1846-1917

McPHERSON, JAMES A.   PVT   CO. E   AGE: 18
   SWORN: OCT 12, 1861/3 YRS   MUSTER: NOV 4, 1864
   BORN: VENANGO COUNTY   OCCUPATION: LABORER
   HEIGHT: 5' 10"   COMPLEXION: LIGHT   EYES: BLUE   HAIR: LIGHT
   HOME IN 1897: PITTSBURGH, PA   DIED: PITTSBURGH, PA
   ATTENDED THE DEDICATION OF THE CHICKAMAUGA BATTLEFIELD, NOV 1897

McQUISTON, DAVID SR.   PVT   CO. H   AGE:46
McQUISTION, DAVID SR.   ENLISTED AT BEAVER, PA
   SWORN: SEP 22, 1862 /3 YRS   DIED: FEB 8, 1864 AT NASHVILLE OF CHRONIC DIARHREA
   BORN: BEAVER COUNTY   OCCUPATION: MASON
   HEIGHT: 5' 8½"   COMPLEXION: DARK EYES: GREY HAIR: BROWN
   BURIED AT NATIONAL CEMETERY NASHVILLE, GRAVE #D-58

McQUISTON, DAVID JR.   PVT   CO. H   AGE:18
McQUISTION, DAVID JR.   BUTLER COUNTY ENLISTEE
   BORN: BEAVER COUNTY   OCCUPATION: SHOEMAKER
   HEIGHT: 5' 6"   COMPLEXION: DARK EYES: GREY HAIR: BROWN
   SWORN: OCT 12, 1861/3YRS   MUSTER: NOV 4, 1864   BOUNTY: $100.

McQUISTON, JOHN K.   PVT   CO. H   AGE:28
McQUISTION, JOHN K.
   SWORN: OCT 12, 1861/3YRS   MUSTER: NOV 4, 1864   BOUNTY: $100.
   BORN: BUTLER COUNTY   OCCUPATION: FARMER
   HEIGHT: 5' 4"   COMPLEXION: LIGHT EYES: GREY HAIR: BROWN

McSWINEY, PETER   PVT   CO. A   AGE:19
McSWEENY, PETER
   SWORN: AUG 28, 1862/3 YRS   DISCHARGED: MAY 27, 1865   BOUNTY: $29
   BORN: INDIANA COUNTY   OCCUPATION: FARMER
   HEIGHT: 5' 9"   COMPLEXION: FAIR   EYES: GREY   HAIR: BROWN
   BROTHER DENNIS SERVED IN THE PA 103rd; 1st LIGHT ARTILLERY, 14th RESERVES AND THE
   46th PA INF. DENNIS WAS WOUNDED AT DERCHARD STATION, TN, JUL 13, 1863
   BURIED: INDIANA COUNTY, CATHOLIC CEMETERY, WHITE TWP., DIED: MAR 27, 1864
   DISCHARGE AND DEATH DIFFER

McVEY, DAVID L. *   PVT   CO. G   AGE:40
McVAY, DAVID L.   BORN: MAY 22, 1817   VETERAN
   SWORN: APR 22, 1861/3 MONTHS, CO B, NINTH PENNSYLVANIA
   SERVED WITH SIRWELL IN ORIGINAL THREE MONTH CO.
   SIRWELL'S BRADY ALPINES
   SWORN: OCT 12, 1861/3 YRS   MUSTER: NOV 4, 1864
   BORN: KITTANNING, PA   OCCUPATION: STONE MASON
   HEIGHT: 5' 9"   COMPLEXION: FAIR   EYES: BLUE   HAIR: BROWN
   DEMOTED FROM 1ST SGT   DIED: AT KITTANNING, PA, NOV 12, 1878
   BURIED: KITTANNING CEMETERY

MACKEY, DAVID H.   PVT   CO. B

SWORN: FEB 9, 1864   MUSTER: SEP 11, 1865
MACKAY, DAVID H.   SGT   CO. H   AGE:36
MACKEY, DAVID H.   VETERAN   BUTLER COUNTY ENLISTEE
SWORN: OCT 12, 1861/4 YRS   MUSTER: SEP 11, 1865
WOUNDED AT CHICKAMAUGA   PROMOTED FROM PVT SEP 23, 1864
MAHAN, EBENEZER   PVT   CO. A   AGE:21
MAHON, EBENEZER
SWORN: OCT 12, 1861/3 YRS   KILLED: MAY 27, 1864 AT PICKETT'S MILL
BORN: INDIANA COUNTY   OCCUPATION: FARMER
HEIGHT: 5' 9"   COMPLEXION: DARK   EYES: GREY   HAIR: BLACK
BURIED @ MARIETTA, ROW G, GRAVE #1119, BATES
MAINS, DANIEL ***   PVT   CO. A/G   AGE: 35/42
MEANS, DANIEL
SWORN: MAR 4, 1862/3 YRS   MUSTER: SEP 11, 1865
BORN: ARMSTRONG COUNTY   OCCUPATION: LABORER
HEIGHT: 5' 9½"   COMPLEXION: FAIR   EYES: BLUE   HAIR: DARK
DIED: AT KITTANNING, PA BURIED: KITTANNING CEMETERY [1827-1888]
1890 CENSUS: KITTANNING, ARMSTRONG COUNTY, PA; WIDOW MARTHA J.
MAITLAND, ALFRED *   CPL   CO. C   AGE: 18
SWORN: OCT 12, 1861/4 YRS   MUSTER: SEP 11, 1865
BORN: VENANGO COUNTY   VETERAN
HEIGHT: 5' 8"   COMPLEXION: FAIR   EYES: GREY   HAIR: LIGHT
BRIEFLY MISSING IN ACTION AT STONES RIVER
PROMOTED TO CPL CO. B IN 2ND REGIMENT
1890 CENSUS: NEW BETHLEHEM, CLARION COUNTY, PA
MAIZE, WILLIAM R.   1LT   CO. A   AGE:20
ORIGIN: INDIANA COUNTY   OCCUPATION: CLERK
HEIGHT: 5' 7"   COMPLECTION: FAIR   HAIR: LIGHT   EYES: BLUE
SWORN: OCT 12, 1861/3 YRS   MUSTER: NOV 4, 1864
COMMANDED CO. G AT STONES RIVER, WOUNDED/LEG, DEC 31, 1862.
COMMENDED BY COLONEL SIRWELL FOR BRAVERY AT STONES RIVER
SERVED AS SIRWELL'S BRIGADE ADJ, ORDANANCE OFFICER AND TOP. ENGIN. 1863
HOME 1914: US GRANT HOTEL, SAN DIEGO, CA
JOINED THE REGULAR ARMY AS A SECOND LIEUTENANT AT THE WAR'S END;
PROMOTED TO MAJOR
MALONE, RODNEY O.*   PVT   CO. K   AGE:18
SWORN: OCT 12, 1861/3 YRS   MUSTER: NOV 4, 1864
BORN: HANCOCK, VA   OCCUPATION: LABORER
HEIGHT: 5' 6½"   COMPLEXION: FAIR   EYES: GREY   HAIR: LIGHT
TAKEN PRISONER AT STONES RIVER/PAROLED AT VICKSBURG
MARKET, VALENTINE *   PVT   CO. F   AGE: 20
SWORN: OCT 12, 1861/3 YRS   TRANS: DEC 1, 1862 TO 4TH CAV
BORN: JOHNSTOWN, PA   OCCUPATION: COLLIER
HEIGHT: 5' 6"   COMPLEXION: FRESH   EYES: BROWN   HAIR: SANDY
MARKLE, FRANCIS   PVT   CO. C   AGE: 19
SWORN: OCT 12, 1861/3 YRS   DIED: DEC 14, 1861 AT LOUISVILLE
BORN: CLARION COUNTY
HEIGHT: 5' 7½"   COMPLEXION: DARK   EYES: BROWN   HAIR: BROWN
BURIED: NATIONAL CEMETERY LOUISVILLE: SECTION.A, RANGE.2, GRAVE.19
MARKLE, WILLIAM H.   PVT   CO. E   AGE: 19
SWORN: OCT 12, 1861/3 YRS   MEDICAL: DEC 14, 1862
BORN: HUNTINGTON COUNTY   OCCUPATION: LABORER
HEIGHT: 5' 10"   COMPLEXION: SANDY   EYES: BLUE   HAIR: BROWN
1890 CENSUS: BRADYS BEND TWP., ARMSTRONG COUNTY, PA
MARKS, DR. JOHN I.   SUR/78th   REGIMENTAL STAFF
ORIGIN: MIFFLIN COUNTY
SWORN: OCT 18, 1861/3 YRS   RESIGNED: AUG 30, 1862.
MARLIN, FRANKLIN   PVT   CO. A   AGE:20
MARLIN, BENJAMIN FRANKLIN
BORN: JUN 17, 1841 TO JESSE AND ANN McLAUGHLIN MARLIN IN WASHINGTON TWP.,
INDIANA COUNTY, PA
SWORN: OCT 12, 1861/3 YRS   MEDICAL: FEB 20, 1864

BORN: INDIANA COUNTY   OCCUPATION: FARMER
HEIGHT: 6' 1½"   COMPLEXION: LIGHT   EYES: GREY   HAIR: BROWN
BROTHER, THOMAS JEFFERSON MARLIN, COLOR BEARER 155th PA
BROTHER, SIDNEY MARLIN, SIGNAL CORP.
WIFE: MARY COCHRAN   DIED: JUL 30, 1895
DIED IN GREELEY TWP., SALINA COUNTY, KANSAS

MARLIN, JOHN M.   CPT   CO. A   AGE:25
MARLIN, JOHN MILTON
BORN: JAN 29, 1836 TO JESSE AND ANN McLAUGHLIN MARLIN IN WASHINGTON TWP.,
INDIANA COUNTY, PA   OCCUPATION: MILLER
HEIGHT: 6' 1"   HAIR: SANDY   EYES: GREY   COMPLEXION: FAIR
SWORN: OCT 12, 1861/3 YRS   MUSTER: NOV 4, 1864
WOUNDED AT STONES RIVER, DEC 31, 1862
COMMENDED BY SIRWELL FOR BRAVERY AT STONES RIVER
PROMOTED FROM 1LT, SEP 1, 1863
BROTHER, THOMAS JEFFERSON MARLIN, COLOR BEARER 155th PA
BROTHER, SIDNEY MARLIN, SIGNAL CORP.
1886 REUNION IN FREEPORT
HOME 1886-1897: WILLET, INDIANA COUNTY, PA
DIARY USED IN WRITING ORIGINAL REGIMENTAL HISTORY IN 1905
ATTENDED THE DEDICATION OF THE CHICKAMAUGA BATTLEFIELD, NOV 1897
WIFE: MARY A. WALLACE   DIED: OCT 29, 1904
BURIED: OAKLAND CEMETERY, INDIANA, PA

MARSH, ABSOLOM K. *   PVT   CO. I   AGE:36
SWORN: OCT 12, 1861/3 YRS   MEDICAL: FEB 24, 1864
BORN: APOLLO, PA   OCCUPATION: LABORER
HEIGHT: 5' 10"   COMPLEXION: DARK   EYES: GRAY   HAIR: DARK
REUNION FREEPORT 1886, KITTANNING 1901
HOME 1886-1905: SALTSBURG, INDIANA COUNTY, PA
BURIED: EDGEWOOD CEMETERY, SALTSBURG, 1835-MAY 26, 1905

MARSH, GEORGE P.   PVT   CO. E   AGE: 24
SWORN: OCT 12, 1861/3 YRS   DIED: MAR 1, 1863 AT MURFREESBORO
BORN: CLARION COUNTY   OCCUPATION: FARMER
HEIGHT: 5' 9"   COMPLEXION: DARK   EYES: BLUE   HAIR: BROWN
MORTALLY WOUNDED AT STONES RIVER
BURIED: NATIONAL CEMETERY STONES RIVER, GRAVE #O-5815

MARSHAL, HENRY M.   PVT   CO. E   AGE: 21
SWORN: OCT 12, 1861/3 YRS   CAPTURED: SEP 8, 1863 NEAR CHATTANOOGA
BORN: ARMSTRONG COUNTY   OCCUPATION: LABORER
HEIGHT: 5' 8"   COMPLEXION: LIGHT   EYES: BROWN   HAIR: LIGHT
DIED AT ANDERSONVILLE   BURIED @ ANDERSONVILLE GRAVE #1722.
IMPRISONED @ ANDERSONVILLE

MARSHALL, JAMES W. *   PVT   CO. G   AGE: 17
SWORN: OCT 12, 1861/3 YRS   MUSTER: NOV 4, 1864
WOUNDED AT PICKETT'S MILL/"FINGERS SHOT OFF" MAY 27, 1864
HOME 1890-1901: SMICKSBURG, INDIANA COUNTY, PA
HOME 1914: PLUMVILLE, PA
REUNION CHICKAMAUGA 1897, KITTANNING 1901, INDIANA 1908.
BURIED: INDIANA COUNTY, UNION CEMETERY, SMICKSBURG, JAN 16, 1844-JUL 7, 1924

MARSHALL, ROBERT L.*   CPL   CO. G
SWORN: OCT 12, 1861/3 YRS   MUSTER: NOV 4, 1864

MARSHALL, WILLIAM A. *   PVT   CO. G   AGE: 18
BORN: JAN 12, 1843   PARENTS: ARCHIBALD & ELIZABETH
SWORN: OCT 12, 1861/3 YRS   MUSTER: NOV 4, 1864
BROTHER DAVID L. IN PA 5th HEAVY ARTILLERY
MARRIED: SUSAN E. SOXMAN, AUG 25, 1868.

MARTIN, GEORGE *   PVT   CO. B   AGE:18
SWORN: OCT 12, 1861/3 YRS   KILLED: MAY 27, 1864 @ PICKETT'S MILL
BORN: ARMSTRONG COUNTY   OCCUPATION: NONE
HEIGHT: 5' 4"   COMPLEXION: DARK   EYES: BLUE   HAIR: DARK

MARTIN, HUGH D.   1ST CPL   CO. H   AGE:37
SWORN: OCT 12, 1861/3YRS   MEDICAL: JUN 27, 1862

BORN: MERCER COUNTY   OCCUPATION: TAILOR
HEIGHT: 6' 1½"   COMPLEXION: FAIR   EYES: BLUE   HAIR: LIGHT
DIED AT OIL CITY, PA BEFORE THE REGIMENTAL HISTORY WAS PUBLISHED IN 1905

MARTIN, JOHN W. *   PVT   CO. I   AGE:21
SWORN: OCT 12, 1861/3 YRS   MEDICAL: JUN 25, 1862
BORN: APOLLO, PA   OCCUPATION: LABORER
HEIGHT: 5' 10"   COMPLEXION: DARK   EYES: GRAY   HAIR: DARK

MARTIN, LEWIS   QUARTER MASTER SGT   REG STAFF   AGE: 30
SWORN: OCT 12, 1861/3 YRS   MUSTER: NOV 4, 1864
BORN: JUNIATA COUNTY   OCCUPATION: CARPENTER
HEIGHT: 5' 10"   COMPLEXION: SANDY   EYES: BROWN   HAIR: DARK
PROMOTED FROM PVT CO. E, MAR 1, 1862.
HOME 1886-1897: WEST FREEDOM, CLARION COUNTY, PA
ATTENDED THE DEDICATION OF THE CHICKAMAUGA BATTLEFIELD, NOV 1897

MARTIN, WILLIAM *   SGT   CO. K   AGE: 38
SWORN: OCT 12, 1861/3 YRS   MUSTER: NOV 4, 1864   VETERAN
BORN: ARMSTRONG COUNTY   OCCUPATION: LABORER
HEIGHT: 6' 1"   COMPLEXION: DARK   EYES: GREY   HAIR: DARK
WOUNDED AT STONES RIVER/ARM
SENT NORTH TO CINCINNATI HOSPITAL ON STEAMER LENORA
PROMOTED TO SGT, MAR 1, 1863, SERVED WITH PA 104TH, CO. K: MAR 18-AUG 25, 1865
BURIED: APPLEBY MANOR PRESBYTERIAN CEMETERY, FORD CITY, PA
BATTLES/DUTY: PETERSBURG, FORTRESS MONROE, PORTSMOUTH

MATHIAS, DAVID *   PVT   CO. B   AGE:35
MATTHAIS, DAVID   VETERAN
SWORN: DEC 25, 1861/4 YRS   MUSTER: SEP 11, 1865
BORN: ARMSTRONG COUNTY   OCCUPATION: COLLIER
HEIGHT: 5' 9"   COMPLEXION: DARK   EYES: LIGHT   HAIR: DARK
BURIED: KITTANNING CEMETERY

MATTHEWS, JOHN W.   PVT   CO. A   AGE: 37
SWORN: AUG 25, 1862/3 YRS   MUSTER: SEP 11, 1865.

MATTHEWS, JOHN W. *   PVT   CO. B   VETERAN
SWORN: OCT 12, 1861/4 YRS   MUSTER: SEP 11, 1865
BORN: HUNTINGTON COUNTY   OCCUPATION: CARPENTER
HEIGHT: 6' ½"   COMPLEXION: LIGHT   EYES: BLUE   HAIR: LIGHT
BURIED: DAYTON CEMETERY, DAYTON, PA

MATTHEWS, WILLIAM *   CPL   CO. B   AGE:40
SWORN: OCT 12, 1861/3 YRS   DIED: JAN 16, 1863
BORN: ARMSTRONG COUNTY   OCCUPATION: FARMER
HEIGHT: 6' 1"   COMPLEXION: DARK   EYES: BLACK   HAIR: LIGHT
MORTALLY WOUNDED/LEG AT STONES RIVER

MAXWELL, WILLIAM W. *   CPL   CO. K   AGE:26
SWORN: OCT 12, 1861/3 YRS   MUSTER: NOV 4, 1864
BORN: BUTLER COUNTY   OCCUPATION: JOINER
HEIGHT: 5' 10"   COMPLEXION: DARK   EYES: BROWN   HAIR: BLACK
PROMOTED TO CPL MAY 27, 1862; TO SGT, 2ND ORGANIZATION
1886 REUNION IN FREEPORT: HOME, BUTLER, PA
BURIED: NORTH CEMETERY, BUTLER, PA

MECHLING, FRANKLIN *   2LT   REGIMENTAL STAFF
ORIGIN: ARMSTRONG COUNTY   OCCUPATION: LAWYER
SWORN: OCT 12, 1861/3 YRS   MUSTER: NOV 4, 1864
WOUNDED AT STONES RIVER
COMMENDED BY SIRWELL FOR BRAVERY AT LAVERGNE AND NEELY'S BEND.
COMMENDED BY COLONEL SIRWELL, COLONEL MILLER AND GENERAL ROSECRANS
FOR BRAVERY AT STONES RIVER
PROMOTED FROM SGT MAJOR TO 2ND LT CO. B, DEC 26, 1862.
HOME 1886-1897: NORTH JEFFERSON ST., KITTANNING, ARMSTRONG COUNTY, PA
"LOVED FLOWERS AND BASEBALL"
ATTENDED 1886 REUNION IN FREEPORT; BURIED: KITTANNING CEMETERY; DIED 1900

MECHLING, JACOB   PVT   CO. H   AGE:19
SWORN: OCT 12, 1861/3YRS   DIED: MAY 26, 1863 AT MURFREESBORO, TN
OF ERYSIPELAS: A CONTAGIOUS SUBCUTANEOUS SKIN INFECTION

BORN: BUTLER COUNTY   OCCUPATION: FARMER
HEIGHT: 5' 11¼"   COMPLEXION: DARK   EYES: GREY   HAIR: BROWN
BURIED AT NATIONAL CEMETERY STONES RIVER
MECHLING, JOSEPH B.   1LT   CO. H   AGE:23
   SWORN: OCT 12, 1861/3YRS   RESIGNED: NOV 30, 1862
   BORN: ARMSTRONG COUNTY   OCCUPATION: STUDENT
   HEIGHT: 5' 6¾"   COMPLEXION: FAIR   EYES: DARK   HAIR: LIGHT
   COMMANDED CO. K AFTER DeWITT HERVEY'S RESIGNATION JUN 22, 1862 UNTIL HIS   OWN
RESIGNATION BY ORDER OF ROSECRANS
   ARRESTED NOV 13, 1862 FOR BEING DRUNK AND AWAY FROM HIS POST.
   ATTENDED 1886 REUNION IN FREEPORT: HOME, BUTLER, PA
MECKLING, LAIRD O. *   PVT   CO. K   AGE:18
MECHLING, LAIRD
   SWORN: SEP 12, 1862/3 YRS   MEDICAL: MAR 7, 1863
   BORN: ARMSTRONG COUNTY   OCCUPATION: FARMER
   HEIGHT: 6' ½"   COMPLEXION: FAIR   EYES: GREY   HAIR: DARK
MEEKER, HEEBER M.   PVT   CO. E   AGE: 25
MEEKER, HEBER B.   MEKER, HEBER B.
   SWORN: OCT 12, 1861/3 YRS   MUSTER: NOV 4, 1864
   BORN: CLARION COUNTY   OCCUPATION: FARMER
   HEIGHT: 5' 9"   COMPLEXION: DARK   EYES: BROWN   HAIR: BLACK
   MEEKER BROTHERS IN SERVICE WERE: ADOLPHUS [PA14thCAV-KILLED @ ROCKY GAP],
   EDWIN [CO. G, PA155th], ALBERT [CO. A, PA103rd-IMPRISONED @ ANDERSONVILLE] AND
   E. HAMMETT [CO. H, PA155th-IMPRISONED @ ANDERSONVILLE; DIED THERE]
MEREDITH, JOHN *   PVT   CO. F   AGE: 18
   SWORN: OCT 12, 1861/3 YRS   MUSTER: NOV 4, 1864
   BORN: ALADIN, PA   OCCUPATION: COLLIER
   HEIGHT: 5' 8"   COMPLEXION: SALLOW   EYES: GREY   HAIR: BROWN
   VOLUNTEERED FOR PIONEER BRIGADE AT STONES RIVER
   SERVED ENLISTMENT IN BATTALION COMMISSARY
   HOME IN 1897/1914: 804 MAIN ST., TOWANDA, BRADFORD COUNTY, PA
   ATTENDED THE DEDICATION OF THE CHICKAMAUGA BATTLEFIELD, NOV 1897
MESSICK, HIRAM*   PVT   CO. F   AGE: 20
MESSIRK, HIRAM
   BORN: SARVERVILLE, PA   OCCUPATION: BLACKSMITH
   HEIGHT: 5' 7½"   COMPLEXION: SALLOW   EYES: LIGHT BROWN   HAIR: DARK BROWN
   SWORN: OCT 12, 1861/3 YRS   KILLED: DEC 31, 1862 AT STONES RIVER
   ACCIDENTLY STRUCK BY A TRAIN: AUG 9, 1862 AT PULASKI, TN
   DAVID KENNISTON KILLED IN THE SAME ACCIDENT.
MEYER, JACOB   PVT   CO. F
   SWORN: MAR 10, 1863/3 YRS   NOT AT FINAL MUSTER
MEYER, JOSEPH   PVT   CO. F
   SWORN: AUG 5, 1863/3 YRS   NOT AT FINAL MUSTER
MEYERS, FRANCIS *   PVT   CO. F   AGE: 40
MEYER, FRANK H.
   SWORN: OCT 12, 1861/3 YRS   MUSTER: NOV 4, 1864
   BORN: FREEPORT, PA   OCCUPATION: COLLIER
   HEIGHT: 5' 5"   COMPLEXION: DARK   EYES: BLACK   HAIR: DARK BROWN
   1890 CENSUS: FRYBURG, CLARION COUNTY, PA
   DIED: AT FRYBURG, PA BEFORE 1905
MICHAEL, JOHN *   PVT   CO. B   AGE:22
   SWORN: AUG 25, 1862/3 YRS   DIED: MAR 21, 1863 AT MURFREESBORO, TN
   HEIGHT: 5' 11"   COMPLEXION: DARK
   BURIED AT NATIONAL CEMETERY STONES RIVER, GRAVE #70
MILLER, HARVEY J.   3RD CPL   CO. H   AGE:26
MILLER, HANEY J.   MILLER, J.H.
   SWORN: OCT 12, 1861/3YRS   TRANS: APR 28, 1864 TO VRC
   BORN: BUTLER COUNTY, APR 18, 1835   OCCUPATION: CHAIR MAKER
   HEIGHT: 5' 6½"   COMPLEXION: LIGHT   EYES: GREY   HAIR: BROWN
   WOUNDED @ STONES RIVER DEC 31, 1862 WHILE SERVING WITH A BATTERY
   HIS BROTHERS: JOHN, NEWTON, HENRY AND PRESLEY SERVED IN THE WAR
MILLER, HENRY *   PVT   CO. B

SWORN: AUG 25, 1862/3 YRS   DISCHARGED: JUN 19, 1865
HOME 1914: KINGSVILLE, PA
MILLER, HENRY   PVT   CO. C   AGE: 25
SWORN: AUG 28, 1862/3 YRS   MEDICAL: JUN 26, 1863
BORN: GERMANY   OCCUPATION: FARMER
HEIGHT: 5' 6" COMPLEXION: DARK EYES: BLUE   HAIR: LIGHT
1890 CENSUS: KINGSVILLE, CLARION COUNTY, PA
MILLER, HENRY A. *   SGT MAJOR   REGIMENTAL STAFF   AGE:29
SWORN: OCT 12, 1861/3 YRS   MUSTER: NOV 4, 1864
WOUNDED IN THE ARM AT STONES RIVER, DEC 31, 1862
BORN: BUTLER COUNTY   OCCUPATION: STUDENT
HEIGHT: 5' 5½"   COMPLEXION: LIGHT EYES: BLACK   HAIR: BROWN
COMMENDED BY COLONEL SIRWELL, COLONEL MILLER AND GENERAL ROSECRANS
FOR BRAVERY AT STONES RIVER
PROMOTED FROM SGT CO. H, FEB 18, 1863.
DETAILED TO FORWARD CONSCRIPTS: AUG 7, 1863-NOV 8, 1863
ATTENDED THE REGIMENTAL REUNION AT INDIANA, PA, IN 1908.
HOME 1886: PITTSBURGH; ATTORNEY AT LAW
BURIED: NORTH CEMETERY, BUTLER, PA; 1841-1908; WIFE: FRANCES S.; 1843-1919
MILLER, JACOB **   PVT   CO. A
SWORN: SEP 14, 1864/1 YEAR   DISCHARGED: JUN 19, 1865.
1890 CENSUS: RED BANK, ARMSTRONG COUNTY, PA
MILLER, JACOB   PVT   CO. C   AGE: 38
SWORN: OCT 12, 1861/3 YRS   MEDICAL: JUN 26, 1862
BORN: CLARION COUNTY
HEIGHT: 5' 11"   COMPLEXION: DARK   EYES: GREY   HAIR: BROWN
MILLER, JAMES #   PVT   CO. I
SWORN: UNKNOWN   DIED: JUN 28, 1865
BURIED @ NASHVILLE, ROW J, GRAVE #1396, BATES
MILLER, JAMES M.   1ST SGT   CO. A   AGE:33
BORN: INDIANA COUNTY   OCCUPATION: TAILOR
HEIGHT: 5' 8"   HAIR: BROWN EYES: BLACK   COMPLEXION: DARK
SWORN: OCT 12, 1861/3 YRS   MUSTER: NOV 4, 1864
WOUNDED/SHOULDER AT STONES RIVER
HOME 1886-1897: WILLET, INDIANA COUNTY, PA
ATTENDED THE DEDICATION OF THE CHICKAMAUGA BATTLEFIELD, NOV 1897
BURIED: INDIANA CTY, PRESBYTERIAN CEM, WASHINGTON TWP.,   1828-1898
MILLER, JOHN   PVT   CO. A
ORIGIN: INDIANA COUNTY
SWORN: OCT 12, 1861/3 YRS   TRANS: JUN, 1864 TO VRC
MILLER, JOHN ***   PVT   CO. F   AGE: 19
SWORN: SEP 20, 1862/3 YRS   MUSTER: SEP 11, 1865
BORN: PITTSTON, PA   OCCUPATION: CARPENTER
HEIGHT: 5' 7"   COMPLEXION: DARK   EYES: HAZEL HAIR: DARK BROWN
PROMOTED TO CPL IN 2ND REGIMENT, DEC 1, 1864; TO COMMISSARY SGT MAY 1, 1865
1886 REUNION IN FREEPORT: HOME, PITTSTON, PA
MILLER, VICTOR D.   ASSISTANT SURGEON/78th   REGIMENTAL STAFF
SWORN: AUG 1, 1862/3 YRS   RESIGNED: MAR 9, 1863. ORIGIN: FRANKLIN COUNTY
CONDEMNED FOR COWARDICE AT THE BATTLE OF STONES RIVER BY CHIEF
SURGEON ARMY OF THE CUMBERLAND, DOCTOR EBENEZER SWIFT
MILLEN, WILLIAM A.   SGT   CO. A   AGE:20
MILLER, WILLIAM A.   VETERAN
SWORN: OCT 12, 1861/4 YRS   MUSTER: SEP 11, 1865
BORN: INDIANA COUNTY   OCCUPATION: FARMER
HEIGHT: 5' 9½"   COMPLEXION: FAIR   EYES: BLUE   HAIR: BROWN
PROMOTED FROM CPL, JUN 20, 1865.
HOME: 1886-1897: PARKWOOD, INDIANA COUNTY, PA
ATTENDED THE DEDICATION OF THE CHICKAMAUGA BATTLEFIELD, NOV 1897
BURIED: INDIANA COUNTY, WEST UNION CEMETERY, ARMSTRONG TWP.,
MAR 31, 1841-JUN 25, 1909
MILLER, WILLIAM H.H.   CPL   CO. C   AGE: 20
MILLEN, WILLIAM

SWORN: OCT 12, 1861/3 YRS   MEDICAL: MAY 14, 1863
BORN: CLARION COUNTY
HEIGHT: 5' 9½"   COMPLEXION: FAIR   EYES: GREY   HAIR: LIGHT
WOUNDED AT STONES RIVER/KNEE
DIARY USED IN WRITING REGIMENTAL HISTORY
BURIED: GAR PLOT IN LEECHBURG CEMETERY, LEECHBURG, PA

MILLIGAN, JOHN P.   PVT   CO. B
MILLIKEN, JOHN P.
    SWORN: DEC 25, 1861   MUSTER: NOV 4, 1864

MILLISON, ELI   PVT   CO. C   AGE: 34
MILLIRON, ELI
    SWORN: OCT 12, 1861/3 YRS   DIED: JAN 11, 1862 AT CAMP WOOD OF PNEUMONIA
    BORN: ARMSTRONG COUNTY
    HEIGHT: 5' 9"   COMPLEXION: FAIR   EYES: BROWN   HAIR: LIGHT

MINTEER, SAMUEL A. *   PVT   CO. K   AGE:23
MINTON, SAMUEL A.
    SWORN: SEP 10, 1862/3 YRS   DIED JUN 28, 1863 AT NASHVILLE
    BORN: ARMSTRONG COUNTY   OCCUPATION: FARMER
    HEIGHT: 5' 9"   COMPLEXION: FAIR   EYES: GREY   HAIR: DARK
    BORN: ARMSTRONG COUNTY   BOUNTY: $29
    BURIED AT NATIONAL CEMETERY NASHVILLE, GRAVE #E-568

MITCHELL, FRANCIS ***   PVT   CO. F   AGE: 19
    SWORN: OCT 12, 1861/3 YRS   MUSTER: NOV 4, 1864
    BORN: E. TARENTUM, PA   OCCUPATION: FARMER
    HEIGHT: 5' 9½"   COMPLEXION: DARK   EYES: BLUE   HAIR: LIGHT
    BORN: DEC 1, 1841   DIED: MAY 6, 1907
    HOSPITALIZED IN LOUISVILLE, JAN 1862
    SERVED AS A MOUNTED SCOUT IN EARLY 1863
    ATTENDED REUNION IN FREEPORT 1886
    HOME 1886-1897: NATRONA, ALLEGHENY COUNTY, PA   WIFE: ALMIRA
    BURIED: PLEASANT HILLS CEMETERY, LEECHBURG, PA

MITCHELL, ROBERT M. **   PVT   CO. F   AGE: 19
    SWORN: OCT 12, 1861/3 YRS   MUSTER: NOV 4, 1864
    BORN: TARENTUM, PA   OCCUPATION: LABORER
    HEIGHT: 5' 7"   COMPLEXION: LIGHT   EYES: DARK BROWN   HAIR: BROWN
    BRIEFLY MISSING IN ACTION AT STONES RIVER

MOHNEY, ADAM   PVT   CO. C   AGE: 19
MOONEY, ADAM
    SWORN: OCT 12, 1861/3 YRS   MUSTER: NOV 4, 1864
    BORN: CLARION COUNTY
    HEIGHT: 5' 7½"   COMPLEXION: FAIR   EYES: BROWN   HAIR: BROWN
    HOME 1890-1914: EMERICKSVILLE, PA

MOHNEY, DAVID   1LT   CO. C   AGE:37
    BORN: CLARION COUNTY
    HEIGHT: 5' 8"   COMPLEXION: LIGHT   EYES: GREY
    SWORN: OCT 12, 1861/3 YRS   RESIGNED: JAN 30, 1863
    HOME 1886-1890: NEW BETHLEHEM, CLARION COUNTY, PA
    ATTENDED REUNION IN FREEPORT 1886
    DIED: NEW BETHLEHEM, PA BEFORE 1905

MOHNEY, JACOB G.   PVT   CO. C   AGE: 22
MOONEY, JACOB G.
    SWORN: OCT 12, 1861/3 YRS   MUSTER: NOV 4, 1864
    BORN: CLARION COUNTY
    HEIGHT: 5' 7½"   COMPLEXION: DARK   EYES: GREY HAIR: BLACK

MOHNEY, JOSEPH   PVT   CO. C   AGE:30
    SWORN: OCT 12, 1861/3 YRS   MUSTER: NOV 4, 1864
    DEMOTED FROM FOURTH CPL
    BORN: CLARION COUNTY
    HEIGHT: 5' 8"   COMPLEXION: FAIR   EYES: BLUE

MOHNEY, LEWIS   PVT   CO. C   VETERAN
    SWORN: FEB 29, 1864/3 YRS   MUSTER: SEP 11, 1865

MOHNEY, REUBEN   CPL   CO. C   AGE: 18

MOONEY, REUBEN
    SWORN: OCT 12, 1861/3 YRS   MUSTER: NOV 4, 1864
    BORN: CLARION COUNTY
    HEIGHT: 5' 7½"   COMPLEXION: DARK   EYES: GREY HAIR: BROWN
MOHNEY, SAMUEL   PVT   CO. C   AGE: 23
MOONEY, SAMUEL
    SWORN: OCT 12, 1861/3 YRS   MUSTER: NOV 4, 1864
    BORN: CLARION COUNTY
    HEIGHT: 5' 9"   COMPLEXION: FAIR   EYES: BLUE   HAIR: BROWN
    WOUNDED AT STONES RIVER/LEG   HOME IN 1897: VERONA, PA
    REUNION IN FREEPORT 1886, CHICKAMAUGA 1897
    HOME 1886-1914: 722 FRONT ST., VERONA, PA
MOHNEY, SAMUEL G.   PVT   CO. C   AGE: 22
MOONEY, SAMUEL G.
    SWORN: OCT 12, 1861/3 YRS   MUSTER: NOV 4, 1864
    BORN: CLARION COUNTY
    HEIGHT: 5' 7"   COMPLEXION: DARK   EYES: BLACK   HAIR: BLACK
    1890 CENSUS: OAKRIDGE, ARMSTRONG COUNTY, PA
MONROE, JAMES M. *   PVT   CO. K   AGE: 23
    SWORN: OCT 12, 1861/3 YRS   MEDICAL: NOV 27, 1862
    BORN: ARMSTRONG COUNTY   OCCUPATION: FARMER
    HEIGHT: 5' 10"   COMPLEXION: FAIR   EYES: GREY HAIR: FAIR
MONTGOMERY, GILBERT S.   PVT   CO. C   AGE: 18
MONTGOMERY, GILMORE S.
    SWORN: MAR 21, 1864/3 YRS   DIED: JUL 21, 1864 AT NASHVILLE
    BORN: JEFFERSON COUNTY   OCCUPATION: LABORER
    HEIGHT: 5' 7"   COMPLEXION: DARK   EYES: BROWN HAIR: DARK
    MORTALLY WOUNDED: MAY 27, 1864 AT PICKETT'S MILL
    BURIED AT NATIONAL CEMETERY NASHVILLE, GRAVE #H-714
MOORE, DAVID   PVT   CO. H   AGE:25
    SWORN: AUG 28, 1862/3 YRS   DISCHARGED: JUN 19, 1865
    ENLISTED AT NEW BETHLEHEM, PA
    BORN: BUTLER COUNTY   OCCUPATION: LABORER
    HEIGHT: 5' 8½"   COMPLEXION: FAIR EYES: GREY HAIR: AUBURN
    REUNION FREEPORT 1886, CHICKAMAUGA 1897, KITTANNING 1901
    HOME IN 1886-1914: OAKLAND, ARMSTRONG COUNTY, PA
    DIED: 1919   WIFE: MATILDA
    BURIED: OAKLAND CEMETERY, DISTANT, PA
MOORE, GIBSON G.   PVT   CO. E   AGE: 18
    SWORN: OCT 12, 1861/3 YRS   TRANS: FEB 14,1863 TO VRC
    BORN: CLARION COUNTY   OCCUPATION: LABORER
    HEIGHT: 5' 8"   COMPLEXION: SANDY   EYES: GREY   HAIR: LIGHT
    WOUNDED AT STONES RIVER/LEG
    REUNION IN FREEPORT 1886, INDIANA 1908
    HOME 1886: SAXONBURG, PA;   HOME 1914: FOLSOM, WVA
MOORE, MARTIN *   PVT   CO. A   AGE:21
    SWORN: OCT 12, 1861/3 YRS   MUSTER: NOV 4, 1864
    BORN: ARMSTRONG COUNTY   OCCUPATION: FARMER
    HEIGHT: 5' 4"   COMPLEXION: DARK   EYES: BROWN   HAIR: BROWN
    1890 CENSUS:COWANSHANNOCK TWP., ARMSTRONG COUNTY, PA
    HOME IN 1897/1915: BERNARDS, ARMSTRONG COUNTY, PA
    BURIED: METHODIST CEMETERY, RURAL VALLEY, PA; DIED: 1925
MOORE, ROBERT C.   PVT   CO. H   AGE:20
    SWORN: AUG 31, 1862/3 YRS   DISCHARGED: JUN 19, 1865
    BORN: BUTLER COUNTY   OCCUPATION: LABORER
    HEIGHT: 5' 9½"   COMPLEXION: FAIR EYES: GREY HAIR: AUBURN
    ENLISTED AT NEW BETHLEHEM, PA BY CAPT. BRINKER
MOORE, WILLIAM C. *   PVT   CO. K   AGE:20
    SWORN: OCT 12, 1861/3 YRS DIED: JAN 28, 1862 AT CAMP WOOD OF PNEUMONIA
    BORN: ARMSTRONG COUNTY   OCCUPATION: FARMER
    HEIGHT: 5' 7"   COMPLEXION: FAIR   EYES: BLACK HAIR: DARK
MOORE, WILLIAM JOHN   CPL   CO. H   AGE: 21

SWORN: OCT 12, 1861/3YRS   DIED: FEB 24, 1863 AT MURFREESBORO
BORN: BUTLER COUNTY   OCCUPATION: FARMER
HEIGHT: 5' 6¼"   COMPLEXION: SANDY   EYES: BLUE   HAIR: SANDY
PROMOTED TO CPL OCT 10, 1862
MORTALLY WOUNDED/FOOT AT STONES RIVER
BURIED AT NATIONAL CEMETERY STONES RIVER, GRAVE #O-5867
MOORHEAD, JAMES *   CPL   CO. B   AGE:19
MOREHEAD, JAMES
    SWORN: OCT 12, 1861/3 YRS   MUSTER: NOV 4, 1864
    BORN: ARMSTRONG COUNTY   OCCUPATION: FARMER
    HEIGHT: 5' 11"   COMPLEXION: DARK   EYES: BLACK   HAIR: LIGHT
    REPORTEDLY GIVEN A MEDICAL: JAN 28, 1862
    PROMOTED TO CPL, DEC 11, 1863
    REPRIMANDED BY LT. COLONEL BLAKELEY JAN 17, 1864
    1890 CENSUS: BLANKET HILL, ARMSTRONG COUNTY, PA
    HOME 1897: SALTSBURG, INDIANA COUNTY, PA
    HOME 1911-1915: LEECHBURG, PA
    ATTENDED THE DEDICATION OF THE CHICKAMAUGA BATTLEFIELD, NOV 1897
    MOORHEAD, JAMES & FRANKLIN BROTHERS
    BROTHER WALKER SERVED IN THE PA 14th CAV
MOOREHEAD, FRANKLIN *   PVT   CO. B   AGE:22
MOOREHEAD, FRANKLIN
    SWORN: OCT 12, 1861/3 YRS   MUSTER: NOV 4, 1864
    BORN: MAY 8, 1842 IN CLARION COUNTY OCCUPATION: FARMER
    HEIGHT: 6' 1"   COMPLEXION: DARK   EYES: BLACK   HAIR: LIGHT
    HOME 1890-1901: GREENDALE, ARMSTRONG COUNTY, PA
    HOME 1914: KITTANNING, PA [RD 7]; REUNION IN KITTANNING 1901
    MOORHEAD, JAMES & FRANKLIN BROTHERS;   BROTHER WALKER IN THE PA 14th CAV
MOOREHEAD, WILLIAM L.   PVT   CO. A   AGE:18
    SWORN: OCT 12, 1861/3 YRS   DIED: AT NASHVILLE, JAN 3, 1863
    BORN: ARMSTRONG COUNTY   OCCUPATION: FARMER
    HEIGHT: 5' 10"   COMPLEXION: FAIR   EYES: GREY   HAIR: BROWN
    MORTALLY WOUNDED AT STONES RIVER
    BURIED @ NASHVILLE, ROW B, GRAVE # 482, BATES
MORGAN, HUGH   PVT   CO. H   AGE:21
    SWORN: OCT 12, 1861/3YRS   MUSTER: NOV 4, 1864   BOUNTY $100
    BORN: IRELAND   OCCUPATION: "FULLER"
    HEIGHT: 5' 7½"   COMPLEXION: LIGHT EYES: GREY   HAIR: BROWN
    IN MAR OF 1863, MILTON WELSH OF CO. H WAS DRUNK AND STABBED HUGH MORGAN
    HOME IN 1897: BUTLER, PA
    HOME 1914: EAU CLAIRE, BUTLER COUNTY, PA
    ATTENDED THE DEDICATION OF THE CHICKAMAUGA BATTLEFIELD, NOV 1897
MORRISON, GEORGE D. #   PVT
    INFORMATION FROM PRESIDENTS, SOLDIERS AND STATESMEN
    BRIGADE WAGON-MASTER FOR GENERAL JAMES NEGLEY
    ORIGIN: ALLEGHENY COUNTY
    FATHER, JAMES IN SAME POSITION
    BROTHER, JAMES A. IN PA 4th CAVALRY
MORRISON, JAMES #   PVT
    INFORMATION FROM PRESIDENTS, SOLDIERS AND STATESMEN
    BRIGADE WAGON-MASTER FOR GENERAL JAMES NEGLEY
    ORIGIN: ALLEGHENY COUNTY   WIFE: ANNIE GIRT
    SON, GEORGE D. IN SAME POSITION
    SON, JAMES A. IN PA 4th CAVALRY
MORROW, JOHN *   PVT   CO. F   AGE: 18
    SWORN: OCT 12, 1861/3 YRS   DISCHARGED: FEB 5, 1865
    BORN: SUNBURY, PA   OCCUPATION: SHOEMAKER
    HEIGHT: 5' 8"   COMPLEXION: DARK   EYES: BROWN   HAIR: BROWN
    CAPTURED AT CHICKAMAUGA; IMPRISONED @ ANDERSONVILLE
    PRISONER FROM SEP 20, 1863 TO NOV 20, 1864 @ ANDERSONVILLE
    1886-1908: KITTANNING, ARMSTRONG COUNTY, PA
    BURIED: KITTANNING CEMETERY [1842-1908]

ATTENDED 1886 REUNION IN FREEPORT
ATTENDED THE DEDICATION OF THE PA MONUMENT AT ANDERSONVILLE, DEC 7, 1905
HOME 1905: 245 CHESTNUT ST, KITTANNING, PA

MORTIMER, WILLIAM S.   PVT   CO. E   AGE: 18
SWORN: OCT 12, 1861/3 YRS   DIED: MAR 5, 1863
BORN: CLARION COUNTY   OCCUPATION: FARMER
HEIGHT: 5' 10"   COMPLEXION: LIGHT   EYES: BLUE   HAIR: LIGHT
MORTALLY WOUNDED AT STONES RIVER/SIDE
BURIED AT NATIONAL CEMETERY NASHVILLE, GRAVE #E-667

MOTT, HENRY *   PVT   CO. I   AGE:20
SWORN: OCT 12, 1861/3 YRS   DIED: JAN 15, 1862 AT LOUISVILLE
BORN: KITTANNING, PA   OCCUPATION: LABORER
HEIGHT: 5' 8½"   COMPLEXION: SANDY   EYES: GRAY   HAIR: LIGHT
BURIED: NATIONAL CEMETERY LOUISVILLE; SECTION.A, RANGE.8, GRAVE.2

MURPH, DANIEL *   PVT   CO. G

MURPHY, DANIEL
SWORN: OCT 12, 1861/3 YRS   DIED: JAN 5, 1863
MORTALLY WOUNDED AT STONES RIVER DEC 31, 1862/THIGH
BURIED AT NATIONAL CEMETERY NASHVILLE, GRAVE #B-654
1890 CENSUS: KITTANNING, ARMSTRONG COUNTY, PA; WIDOW SARAH

MURPHY, ANDREW N.   PVT   CO. H   AGE:23
SWORN: OCT 12, 1861/3YRS   TRANS: 4TH U.S.CAV, DEC 1, 1862,
KILLED IN ACTION
BORN: CHESTER COUNTY   OCCUPATION: CLERK
HEIGHT: 5' 7¼"   COMPLEXION: DARK   EYES: DARK   HAIR: BLACK

MURPHY, JONATHAN D.*   2ND LT   CO. F   AGE:21
BORN IN OHIO: FEB 2, 1840   PARENTS: WILLIAM & MARY DUGAN MURPHY
SWORN: OCT 12, 1861/3 YRS   MUSTER: NOV 4, 1864
BORN: FREEPORT, PA   OCCUPATION: MUSICIAN
HEIGHT: 5' 6"   COMPLEXION: LIGHT   EYES: BROWN   HAIR: DARK BROWN
ON "DETACHED SERVICE" NOV 30, 1862-MAR 1, 1863
PROMOTED FROM 1ST SGT TO 2LT, NOV 30, 1862 or MAR 1, 1863
LED COMPANY AT CHICKAMAUGA
HOME 1886-1914: ST. PETERSBURG, CLARION COUNTY, PA
ATTENDED 1886 REUNION IN FREEPORT   MUSIC TEACHER
WIFE: MARY W. BOWMAN OF PITTSBURGH [m. 1866]
ATTENDED THE DEDICATION OF THE CHICKAMAUGA BATTLEFIELD, NOV 1897

MURPHY, WILLIAM C.*   SGT   CO. I   AGE:32
SWORN: OCT 12, 1861/3 YRS   TRANS: AUG 1, 1863 VRC
BORN: PETERSBURG, IL   OCCUPATION: NAILOR
HEIGHT: 5' 6"   COMPLEXION: SANDY   EYES: GREY   HAIR: RED
WOUNDED AT STONES RIVER/FOOT
COMMENDED BY SIRWELL FOR BRAVERY AT STONES RIVER
ADMITTED TO HOSPITAL #12, LOUISVILLE MAR 1, 1863
ATTENDED THE REGIMENTAL REUNION AT INDIANA, PA, IN 1908.

MYERS, CHARLES   PVT   CO. E   AGE: 38
SWORN: OCT 12, 1861/3 YRS   MUSTER: NOV 4, 1864
BORN: CENTER COUNTY   OCCUPATION: LABORER
HEIGHT: 5' 11"   COMPLEXION: SANDY   EYES: BLUE   HAIR: SANDY
WOUNDED AT STONES RIVER/WRIST

MYERS, DAVID R.P.   PVT   CO. C   AGE: 22
SWORN: OCT 12, 1861/4 YRS   MUSTER: SEP 11, 1865   VETERAN
BORN: CLARION COUNTY
HEIGHT: 5' 5½"   COMPLEXION: FAIR   EYES: GREY   HAIR: LIGHT
WOUNDED AT STONES RIVER/BREAST

MYERS, JAMES   PVT   CO. H   AGE:20
SWORN: OCT 12, 1861/3YRS   KILLED: DEC 30, 1862 AT STONES RIVER
BORN: ARMSTRONG COUNTY   OCCUPATION: TEACHER
HEIGHT: 5' 7½"   COMPLEXION: DARK   EYES: GREY   HAIR: DARK
REGIMENTS 1ST CASUALTY AT STONES RIVER

MYERS, JOSEPH L.*   PVT   CO. G   AGE: 22
OCCUPATION: TAILOR   HEIGHT: 5' 7"

SWORN: OCT 12, 1861/3 YRS   MUSTER: NOV 4, 1864
BORN: INDIANA, PA   OCCUPATION: TAILOR
HEIGHT: 5' 8"   COMPLEXION: FAIR   EYES: GREY   HAIR: LIGHT
HAD BEEN AWOL OCT 18, 1861/NEVER REPORTED
DEMOTED FROM 2ND MUC   REPORTED IN AUGUST 18, 1862
1890 CENSUS: PURCHASE LINE, INDIANA COUNTY, PA
DIED: AT UTAH, PA BEFORE 1905
1886 REUNION IN FREEPORT: HOME, UTAH, PA
BURIED: INDIANA CTY, MAHONING BAPTIST CEMETERY, GRANT TWP., 1839-AUG 13, 1888

MYRTLE, ARTHUR L/S. *   8TH CPL   CO. G   AGE:20
SWORN: OCT 12, 1861/3 YRS   KILLED: DEC 31, 1862 AT STONES RIVER
BORN: KITTANNING, PA   OCCUPATION: FARMER
HEIGHT: 5' 7"   COMPLEXION: FAIR   EYES: GREY   HAIR: LIGHT
1890 CENSUS: FAIRMOUNT, CLARION COUNTY, PA; WIDOW MARY ROBERTSON

MYRTLE, HENRY A. *   PVT   CO. G   AGE:52
SWORN: OCT 12, 1861/3 YRS   MUSTER: NOV 4, 1864   ABSENT/SICK AT FINAL MUSTER
DIED BEFORE THE REGIMENTAL HISTORY WAS PUBLISHED IN 1905
1890 CENSUS: KITTANNING, ARMSTRONG COUNTY, PA

MYRTLE, JACOB B. *   PVT   CO. G
SWORN: FEB 2, 1864/3 YRS   MUSTER: SEP 11, 1865

NEAL, ALBERT J. *   PVT   CO. A   AGE:18
NEEL, ALBERT
SWORN: OCT 12, 1861/3 YRS   DIED: APR 13, 1863 AT NASHVILLE OF "CRAMP"
BORN: ALLEGHENY COUNTY   OCCUPATION: FARMER
HEIGHT: 6'   COMPLEXION: FAIR   EYES: BLUE   HAIR: BROWN
BURIED @ NASHVILLE, BATES

NEEDHAM, JONATHAN *   PVT   CO. F   AGE: 33
SWORN: OCT 12, 1861/3 YRS   MUSTER: NOV 4, 1864
BORN: PITTSBURGH, PA   OCCUPATION: BLACKSMITH
HEIGHT: 5' 8"   COMPLEXION: FLORID   EYES: BLUE   HAIR: LIGHT
WOUNDED AT STONES RIVER/LEG

NEELY, WILLIAM   PVT   CO. H   AGE:20
NEELEY, WILLIAM
SWORN: OCT 12, 1861/3YRS   MEDICAL: JUN 23, 1863
BORN: BUTLER COUNTY   OCCUPATION: MINER
HEIGHT: 5' 11½"   COMPLEXION: DARK   EYES: DARK   HAIR: BROWN
DIED BEFORE THE REGIMENTAL HISTORY WAS PUBLISHED IN 1905

NEFF, JACOB C.   PVT   CO. D   AGE: 18
NAVE, JACOB
SWORN: OCT 12, 1861/3 YRS   MUSTER: NOV 4, 1864
BORN: INDIANA COUNTY   OCCUPATION: FARMER
HEIGHT: 5' 8"   COMPLEXION: DARK   EYES: GREY   HAIR: DARK
WOUNDED AT STONES RIVER/KNEE
HOME 1890-1914: PUNXSUTAWNEY, JEFFERSON COUNTY, PA
ATTENDED THE DEDICATION OF THE CHICKAMAUGA BATTLEFIELD, NOV 1897

NELSON, ELIAS   PVT   CO. H   AGE:22
SWORN: OCT 12, 1861/4 YRS   MUSTER: SEP 11, 1865   VETERAN
BORN: LAWRENCE COUNTY   OCCUPATION: MINER
HEIGHT: 5' 7¼"   COMPLEXION: LIGHT   EYES: HAZEL   HAIR: LIGHT
WOUNDED/HEAD AT STONES RIVER
GENERAL COURT MARTIAL DURING SERVICE RE-ENLISTED FEB 2, 1864
HOME IN 1897: JOHNSTOWN, PA
ATTENDED THE DEDICATION OF THE CHICKAMAUGA BATTLEFIELD, NOV 1897

NEVILLE, JOHN B.*   PVT   CO. B   AGE:18
SWORN: OCT 12, 1861/3 YRS   TRANS: VRC AUG 1, 1863
BORN: ARMSTRONG COUNTY   OCCUPATION: FARMER
HEIGHT: 5' 8"   COMPLEXION: LIGHT   EYES: BLUE   HAIR: LIGHT
WOUNDED/LEG AT STONES RIVER

NEYMAN, WILLIAM J.   PVT   CO. H   AGE:18
SWORN: OCT 12, 1861/3YRS   MUSTER: NOV 4, 1864   BOUNTY: $100.
BORN: BUTLER COUNTY   OCCUPATION: FARMER
HEIGHT: 5' 10½"   COMPLEXION: LIGHT   EYES: GREY   HAIR: SANDY

NICHOLS, ALBERT G.   PVT   CO. C   AGE: 19
    SWORN: OCT 12, 1861/3 YRS   MUSTER: NOV 4, 1864
    BORN: WESTMORELAND COUNTY
    HEIGHT: 5' 10"   COMPLEXION: FAIR   EYES: HAZEL   HAIR: BROWN
    DIED: OAKLAND, ARMSTRONG COUNTY, PENNSYLVANIA
    BORN: MAY 5, 1842   DIED: JAN 17, 1894 WIFE: MARY L.
    1890 CENSUS: OAKLAND, ARMSTRONG COUNTY, PA
    BURIED: OAKLAND CEMETERY, DISTANT, PA

NICHOLS, ANDREW J.   PVT   CO. C   AGE: 20
    SWORN: MAR 10, 1863/3 YRS   MUSTER: SEP 11, 1865
    BORN: COLUMBIA COUNTY   OCCUPATION: LABORER
    HEIGHT: 5' 8" COMPLEXION: FAIR EYES: BLUE   HAIR: BROWN

NICHOLS, GEORGE W.   PVT   CO. E   AGE: 28
    SWORN: AUG 28, 1862/3 YRS   DISCHARGED: AUG 9, 1865
    BORN: CLARION COUNTY   OCCUPATION: FARMER
    HEIGHT: 5' 7"   COMPLEXION: FAIR   EYES: BROWN   HAIR: DARK
    WOUNDED AT STONES RIVER/HEAD; HOME 1890-1914: WEST FREEDOM, PA

NICHOLS, JAMES #   PVT/78th   CO. F
    SWORN: UNKNOWN   DIED: SEP 12, 1865
    BURIED @ NASHVILLE, ROW E, GRAVE #244, BATES

NICHOLS, JAMES G.   PVT   CO. E   AGE: 19
    SWORN: OCT 12, 1861/3 YRS   MUSTER: NOV 4, 1864
    BORN: CLARION COUNTY   OCCUPATION: LABORER
    HEIGHT: 5' 9"   COMPLEXION: FAIR   EYES: GREY   HAIR: LIGHT
    1890 CENSUS: WEST FREEDOM, CLARION COUNTY, PA

NICHOLS, WILLIAM A.   CPL   CO. C   AGE: 19
    SWORN: JAN 12, 1864/3 YRS   MUSTER: SEP 11, 1865
    BORN: CAMBRIA COUNTY   OCCUPATION: LABORER
    HEIGHT: 5' 10" COMPLEXION: FAIR EYES: GREY HAIR: DARK
    PROMOTED FROM PVT TO CORPORAL CO. B Π

NOLDER, MARTIN *   PVT   CO. I   AGE:18
    SWORN: OCT 12, 1861/3 YRS   MUSTER: NOV 4, 1864
    BORN: APOLLO, PA   OCCUPATION: SHOEMAKER
    HEIGHT: 5' 8½"   COMPLEXION: FAIR   EYES: GREY   HAIR: LIGHT
    1890 CENSUS: KITTANNING, ARMSTRONG COUNTY, PA
    HOME 1914: WHITESBURG, PA
    DIED: FEB 8, 1924 @ WHITESBURG, ARMSTRONG COUNTY, PA @ 82
    BURIED @ ST. JOHN'S LUTHERAN, KITTANNING, PA

NOLF, DAVID H.   PVT   CO. C   AGE: 18
NOLPH, DAVID   BORN: PENNSYLVANIA
    SWORN: OCT 12, 1861/3 YRS   MUSTER: NOV 4, 1864
    HEIGHT: 5' 11"   COMPLEXION: FAIR   EYES: GREY   HAIR: BROWN
    HOME 1897-1901: ELEANOR, JEFFERSON COUNTY, PA
    REUNION IN FREEPORT 1886, CHICKAMAUGA 1897, KITTANNING 1901

NOLF, ISAAC   PVT   CO. C   AGE: 44
NOLPH, ISAAC   BORN: PENNSYLVANIA
    SWORN: OCT 12, 1861/3 YRS   MEDICAL: DEC 17, 1863
    HEIGHT: 6' 2"   COMPLEXION: SANDY   EYES: BLUE   HAIR: BROWN
    DIED: SENECA, PENNSYLVANIA
    1886 REUNION IN FREEPORT: HOME, NEW BETHLEHEM, PA

NOLF, JAMES O. *   PVT   CO. B
    SWORN: AUG 28, 1863/3 YRS   MUSTER: JUN 19, 1865
    PROBABLY THE SAME MAN AS JAMES O. NULPH

NOLF, SIMON *   PVT   CO. B   AGE:36
    SWORN: AUG 25, 1862/3 YRS   MUSTER: SEP 11, 1865
    BORN: ARMSTRONG COUNTY   OCCUPATION: FARMER
    HEIGHT: 6' 1"   COMPLEXION: LIGHT   EYES: DARK   HAIR: SANDY
    1890 CENSUS: PUTNEYVILLE, ARMSTRONG COUNTY, PA

NUGENT, WILLIAM J.   1LT   CO. D   AGE:25
NUGENT, WILLIS OR WILLES   NUGENT, WILLIS J. [TOMBSTONE]
    HOME, BEFORE THE WAR: MORRISON'S COVE, BLAIR COUNTY
    SWORN: OCT 12, 1861/3 YRS   MUSTER: NOV 4, 1864

BORN: INDIANA COUNTY, PLUMSVILLE   OCCUPATION: TEACHER
HEIGHT: 5' 8"   COMPLEXION: FAIR   HAIR: RED
PROMOTED APR 16, 1863 FROM 2ND LT
PRESENTED A $100 SWORD AND SASH MAR 1863 BY MEN OF COMPANY
COMMANDED COMPANY DURING EARLY 1863
COMMANDED COMPANY F DURING LATER PART OF 1863
ELECTED VICE PRESIDENT OF THE 78th REUNION COMMITTEE IN 1886
1886 REUNION IN FREEPORT: HOME, GRANT, PA
HOME IN 1897: GRANT, INDIANA COUNTY, PA
JUSTICE OF THE PEACE, TEN TERMS IN WEST BRANCH VALLEY
ATTENDED THE DEDICATION OF THE CHICKAMAUGA BATTLEFIELD, NOV 1897
BURIED: INDIANA CTY, IOOF CEMETERY, CHERRY TREE, MONTGOMERY TWP., 1836-1905

NULPH, JAMES O.   PVT   CO. H   AGE:25
NOLPH, J.C.
ENLISTED AT NEW BETHLEHEM, PA BY CAPT. BRINKER
SWORN: AUG 28, 1862/3 YRS   DISCHARGED: JUN 19, 1865
BORN: ARMSTRONG COUNTY   OCCUPATION: FARMER
HEIGHT: 5' 6½"   COMPLEXION: LIGHT EYES: GREY   HAIR: LIGHT
HOME 1886-1890: NEW BETHLEHEM, CLARION COUNTY, PA
ATTENDED 1886 REUNION IN FREEPORT

NUPP, CYRUS   PVT   CO. D   AGE: 25
BORN: SOMERSET COUNTY, JAN 3, 1836 TO DANIEL AND LEAH
SWORN: OCT 12, 1861/3 YRS   MUSTER: NOV 4, 1864
BORN: INDIANA COUNTY, HILLSDALE   OCCUPATION: FARMER
HEIGHT: 5' 7½"   COMPLEXION: SANDY   EYES: GREY   HAIR: FAIR
BROTHER, JOHN HENRY NUPP KILLED AT THE WILDERNESS, CO. C, 67th PA
HOME 1890-1897: PURCHASE LINE, INDIANA COUNTY, PA
BURIED EAST MAHONING CHURCH, INDIANA COUNTY
CYRUS AND FRANKLIN NUPP WERE COUSINS
ATTENDED THE REGIMENTAL REUNION AT INDIANA, PA, IN 1908.
HOME 1914: PURCHASE LINE, PA
BURIED: INDNA CTY, E. MAHONING BAPTIST CEM., GRANT TWP., JAN 3, 1836-FEB 4, 1921

NUPP, FRANKLIN   PVT   CO. D   AGE: 23
SWORN: OCT 12, 1861/3 YRS   MUSTER: NOV 4, 1864
BORN: INDIANA COUNTY, HILLSDALE   OCCUPATION: FARMER
HEIGHT: 5' 4½"   COMPLEXION: DARK   EYES: GREY   HAIR: FAIR
1890 CENSUS: PURCHASE LINE, INDIANA COUNTY, PA
HOME IN 1897: SPRUCE, INDIANA COUNTY, PA
CYRUS AND FRANKLIN NUPP WERE COUSINS
REUNION CHICKAMAUGA 1897, INDIANA 1908.
HOME 1914: WINDBER, CAMBRIA COUNTY, PA

O'CONNOR, FESTUS J.*   PVT   CO. F   AGE: 18
SWORN: OCT 12, 1861/3 YRS   TRANS: DEC 1, 1862 TO 4TH CAV
BORN: WORTHINGTON, PA   OCCUPATION: COLLIER
HEIGHT: 5' 6"   COMPLEXION: FAIR   EYES: GREY   HAIR: BROWN

O' DONNELL, CHARLES   PVT   UNASSIGNED
SWORN: FEB 26, 1864   NOT ON MUSTER-OUT ROLL

O'HARRA, WILLIAM   PVT   CO. B   AGE:18
O'HARA, WILLIAM   O'HARROW, WILLIAM
SWORN: OCT 12, 1861/3 YRS   MUSTER: NOV 4, 1864
BORN: CLEARFIELD COUNTY   OCCUPATION: FARMER
HEIGHT: 5' 7"   COMPLEXION: DARK   EYES: GREY   HAIR: DARK
BURIED: INDIANA COUNTY, NORTH POINT CEMETERY, W. MAHONING TWP.,
1843-JUL 20, 1925

ORR, JOHN G. #   PVT   CO. A
SWORN: AUG 27, 1861/3 YRS   MEDICAL:OCT 1, 1861
1890 CENSUS: ATWOOD BORO, ARMSTRONG COUNTY, PA
MUSTERED OUT BEFORE LEAVING CAMP ORR IN KITTANNING, PA

ORR, WILLIAM   PVT   CO. C   AGE: 19
SWORN: SEP 13, 1862/3 YRS   MEDICAL: APR 14, 1863
BORN: CLARION COUNTY   OCCUPATION: FARMER
HEIGHT: 5' 8"   COMPLEXION: FAIR   EYES: GREY   HAIR: BROWN

1890 CENSUS: CRATES, CLARION COUNTY, PA

OSWALD, BENJAMIN * SGT CO. K AGE:19
 SWORN: OCT 12, 1861/3 YRS MUSTER: NOV 4, 1864
 BORN: KITTANNING OCCUPATION: PRINTER
 HEIGHT: 5' 8" COMPLEXION: DARK EYES: BROWN HAIR: DARK
 PROMOTED TO CPL, MAY 26, 1862; TO SGT, MAR 1, 1863
 HOME 1886: KITTANNING, PA HOME 1901: KITTANNING, PA
 HOME 1897: FORD CITY, ARMSTRONG COUNTY, PA
 BURIED: KITTANNING CEMETERY; DIED: AUG 29, 1928
 REUNION FREEPORT 1886, CHICKAMAUGA 1897, KITTANNING 1901

OTTERMAN, CHARLES * PVT CO. F AGE: 18
 SWORN: OCT 12, 1861/3 YRS DIED: MAR 17, 1862 AT BOWLING GREEN
 BORN: FREEPORT, PA OCCUPATION: FARMER
 HEIGHT: 5' 3" COMPLEXION: SALLOW EYES: BROWN HAIR: DARK BROWN

OVER, CHRISTIAN PVT CO. E AGE: 28
 SWORN: OCT 12, 1861/3 YRS MIA: JAN 1, 1863 AT STONES RIVER
 BORN: CLARION COUNTY OCCUPATION: FARMER
 HEIGHT: 5' 9" COMPLEXION: DARK EYES: BLUE HAIR: BLACK

PAINTER, JOHN *** PVT CO. K AGE: 29
 SWORN: OCT 12, 1861/3 YRS MUSTER: NOV 4, 1864
 SERVED AS A CPL AT CAMP ORR
 BORN: ALLEGHENY COUNTY OCCUPATION: BLACKSMITH
 HEIGHT: 5' 6" COMPLEXION: FAIR EYES: GREY HAIR: FAIR
 WOUNDED AT STONES RIVER/LOST THREE FINGERS FROM LEFT HAND
 TAKEN PRISONER AT STONES RIVER/PAROLED
 SERVED AS DIVISION BLACKSMITH DURING 1864

PAINTER, JOSEPH R. PVT CO. E AGE: 20
 SWORN: MAR 31, 1864/3 YRS MUSTER: SEP 11, 1865
 BORN: CLARION COUNTY OCCUPATION: FARMER
 HEIGHT: 6' 1" COMPLEXION: FAIR EYES: GREY HAIR: BROWN
 1886 REUNION IN FREEPORT: HOME, CALENSBURG, PA
 1890 CENSUS: POLLOCK, CLARION COUNTY, PA

PAINTER, PETER A. * PVT CO. K AGE: 18
 SWORN: OCT 12, 1861/3 YRS MEDICAL: MAR 29, 1863
 SERVED AS A CPL AT CAMP ORR
 BORN: BUTLER COUNTY OCCUPATION: FARMER
 HEIGHT: 5' 7¼" COMPLEXION: FAIR EYES: BROWN HAIR: LIGHT
 TRANSFERRED FROM NASHVILLE TO LOUISVILLE HOSPITAL MAR 9, 1863

PAINTER, SAMUEL *** CPL CO. K AGE:18
 SWORN: OCT 12, 1861/4 YRS MUSTER: SEP 11, 1865 VETERAN
 BORN: ALLEGHENY COUNTY OCCUPATION: LABORER
 HEIGHT: 5' 7" COMPLEXION: FAIR EYES: GREY HAIR: LIGHT
 BRIEFLY MISSING IN ACTION AT STONES RIVER
 PROMOTED PVT TO CPL CO. B, SECOND REGIMENT

PALMER, GEORGE C. PVT CO. A AGE:19
POLMER, GEORGE C.
 SWORN: OCT 12, 1861/3 YRS TRANS: 4TH CAV, DEC 1, 1862.
 BORN: INDIANA COUNTY OCCUPATION: FARMER
 HEIGHT: 5' 6" COMPLEXION: DARK EYES: GREY HAIR: BROWN
 STEPSON OF JOHN LUCAS, ARMSTRONG TWP., INDIANA COUNTY, PA

PALMER, JEFFERSON J. PVT CO. A AGE:21
 SWORN: OCT 12, 1861/3 YRS MUSTER: NOV 4, 1864
 BORN: INDIANA COUNTY OCCUPATION: FARMER
 HEIGHT: 5' 7" COMPLEXION: DARK EYES: BLUE HAIR: BROWN
 BRIEFLY MISSING IN ACTION AT STONES RIVER
 STEPSON OF JOHN LUCAS, ARMSTRONG TWP., INDIANA COUNTY, PA
 BURIED: OAKLAND CEMETERY, INDIANA, PA, 1841-JUN 9, 1885

PALMETER, LUMAN B. ** PVT CO. C AGE: 18
 SWORN: SEP 15, 1863/3 YRS DESERTED: FEB 19, 1865
 BORN: BROOKVILLE, PA OCCUPATION: FARMER
 HEIGHT: 5' 7" COMPLEXION: FAIR EYES: GREY HAIR: LIGHT
 HOME 1897: COCHRANTON, CRAWFORD COUNTY, PA

PVT PALMETER'S RECORD INDICATES THAT HE DESERTED; IT IS UNUSUAL THAT HE
ATTENDED THE DEDICATION OF THE CHICKAMAUGA BATTLEFIELD, NOV 1897
PARKER, JOHN   PVT   CO. H   AGE:22
   SWORN: OCT 12, 1861/3YRS   MUSTER: NOV 4, 1864   BOUNTY: $100.
   BORN: BUTLER COUNTY   OCCUPATION: FARMER
   HEIGHT: 6' 3¾"   COMPLEXION: DARK   EYES: GREY   HAIR: BLACK
   HOME 1897-1902: PARKER'S LANDING, ARMSTRONG COUNTY, PA
   DIED: APR 1902 AT PARKER'S LANDING
   REUNION CHICKAMAUGA 1897, KITTANNING 1901
PATRICK, WASHINGTON C. *   SGT   CO. B   AGE:19
   SWORN: OCT 12, 1861/3 YRS   MUSTER: NOV 4, 1864
   BORN: ARMSTRONG COUNTY   OCCUPATION: FARMER
   HEIGHT: 5' 11"   COMPLEXION: DARK   EYES: BLACK   HAIR: DARK
   WOUNDED/HAND AT STONES RIVER
   1890 CENSUS: KITTANNING, ARMSTRONG COUNTY, PA
   HOME IN 1897/1914: BLANKET HILL, ARMSTRONG COUNTY, PA
   U.S. PENSION, 1894: $6.00
PATTERSON, DANIEL   PVT   CO. H   AGE:23
   SWORN: OCT 12, 1861/3YRS   DIED: FEB 9, 1862 AT WOODSONVILLE, KY OF MEASLES
   BORN: BUTLER COUNTY   OCCUPATION: FARMER
   HEIGHT: 5' 11"   COMPLEXION: DARK   EYES: GREY   HAIR: BROWN
PATTERSON, JOHN F.   PVT   CO. H   AGE:23
   SWORN: OCT 12, 1861/3YRS   TRANS: FEB 6, 1864 TO VRC
   BORN: IRELAND   OCCUPATION: FARMER
   HEIGHT: 5' 9"   COMPLEXION: SANDY   EYES: BLUE   HAIR: SANDY
   DIED: GARNETT, KS, APR 1896
PATTON, SAMUEL J. **   PVT   CO. H   AGE:25
PATTEN, SAMUEL J.   PADDEN, SAMUEL J.
   SWORN: SEP 1, 1864/3 YRS   DISCHARGED: JUN 19, 1865
   ENLISTED AT ALLEGHENY CITY, PA
PENCE, BENJAMIN J.   PVT   CO. C   AGE: 19
   SWORN: OCT 12, 1861/3 YRS   DIED: FEB 6, 1862 CAMP WOOD OF PNEUMONIA
   BORN: CLARION COUNTY
   HEIGHT: 6'   COMPLEXION: DARK   EYES: BROWN   HAIR: BLACK
PENNINGTON, JAMES *   PVT   CO. A   AGE: 20
   SWORN: OCT 12, 1861/4 YRS   DISCHARGED: AUG 2, 1865   VETERAN
   BORN: SUCCESS, PA   OCCUPATION: FARMER
   HEIGHT: 5' 4"   COMPLEXION: FRESH   EYES: DARK BROWN   HAIR: BROWN
PENNMAN, JAMES *   PVT   CO. F   AGE: 19
PENMAN, JAMES
   SWORN: OCT 12, 1861/3 YRS   DIED: JAN 8, 1863 AT MURFREESBORO
   BORN: ALADAN, PA   OCCUPATION: COLLIER
   HEIGHT: 5' 7"   COMPLEXION: SALLOW   EYES: BLUE   HAIR: DARK BROWN
   MORTALLY WOUNDED AT STONES RIVER/HEAD
   BURIED AT NATIONAL CEMETERY STONES RIVER, GRAVE #N-5523
PEOPLES, JAMES   PVT   CO. C   AGE: 44
   SWORN: OCT 12, 1861/3 YRS   MEDICAL: JUN 1, 1862
   BORN: CLARION COUNTY
   HEIGHT: 6' 2"   COMPLEXION: SANDY   EYES: BLUE   HAIR: SANDY
PHENICIE, SAMUEL   PVT   CO. E   AGE: 22
PHINICI, SAMUEL
   SWORN: OCT 12, 1861/3 YRS   MUSTER: NOV 4, 1864
   BORN: MERCER COUNTY   OCCUPATION: LABORER
   HEIGHT: 5' 9"   COMPLEXION: DARK   EYES: BROWN   HAIR: BLACK
   TAKEN PRISONER AT STONES RIVER/PAROLED
   HOME 1890-1897: PARKER'S LANDING, ARMSTRONG COUNTY, PA
PIERCE, ERASTUS *   CPL   CO. K   AGE: 21
   SWORN: OCT 12, 1861/3 YRS   MEDICAL: DEC 8, 1862
   BORN: WESTMORELAND COUNTY   OCCUPATION: FARMER
   HEIGHT: 5' 6"   COMPLEXION: FAIR   EYES: BLACK HAIR: LIGHT
PIFER, CONRAD *   PVT   CO. I   AGE:18
PIPHER, CONRAD

SWORN: OCT 12, 1861/3 YRS   MUSTER: NOV 4, 1864
BORN: ARMSTRONG COUNTY   OCCUPATION: LABORER
COMPLEXION: DARK   EYES: BLACK   HAIR: DARK

PIGLEY, JOSEPH H. *   PVT   CO. B   AGE:19
SWORN: OCT 12, 1861/3 YRS   MUSTER: NOV 4, 1864
BORN: CLARION COUNTY   OCCUPATION: FARMER
HEIGHT: 5' 8"   COMPLEXION: DARK   EYES: BLACK   HAIR: BLACK

POLLIARD, DANIEL   PVT   CO. C   AGE: 42
SWORN: OCT 12, 1861/3 YRS   TRANS: OCT 1, 1863 TO VRC
BORN: CLARION COUNTY
HEIGHT: 5' 8"   COMPLEXION: DARK   EYES: GREY   HAIR: BROWN

POOL, WILLIAM V. *   PVT   CO. G
PAUL, WILLIAM V.
SWORN: OCT 12, 1861/3 YRS   MEDICAL: JUL 20, 1863
HAD BEEN AWOL OCT 18, 1861   DIED: MAR 16, 1903
HOME 1890-1901: APOLLO, PA   REUNION KITTANNING 1901
BURIED: APOLLO CEMETERY, APOLLO, PA

PORTER, WILLIAM M. *   PVT   CO. G
SWORN: OCT 12, 1861/3 YRS   DIED: DEC 1, 1861 AT LOUISVILLE
BURIED: NATIONAL CEMETERY LOUISVILLE; SECTION.A, RANGE.3, GRAVE.9

POWELL, JOSEPH W. *   1LT   REGIMENTAL STAFF
ORIGIN: CLARION COUNTY
SWORN: OCT 18, 1861/3 YRS   MUSTER: NOV 4, 1864
REGIMENTAL ADJUTANT 1861, 1862, 1864
RECRUITING DUTY 1863
COMMENDED BY BLAKELEY FOR PERFORMANCE OF DUTIES

PRICE, JOHN   PVT   CO. C   AGE: 42
SWORN: OCT 12, 1861/3 YRS   DIED: OCT 19, 1864 OF WOUNDS
RECEIVED IN THE ATLANTA CAMPAIGN
BORN: PENNSYLVANIA
HEIGHT: 5' 10"   COMPLEXION: DARK   EYES: BROWN   HAIR: SANDY
BURIED @ NASHVILLE, ROW G, GRAVE #217, BATES

PRICIOUS, ADAM *   PVT   CO. I
PROCIUS, ADAM
SWORN: MAR 4, 1864/3 YRS   MUSTER: SEP 11, 1865

PRITCHARD, WILLIAM H.   SGT   CO. E   AGE: 31
BORN IN MONMOUTH, ENGLAND
SWORN: OCT 12, 1861/3 YRS   DIED: OCT 31, 1862 AT NASHVILLE
BORN: MONMOUTH, ENGLAND OCCUPATION: SHOEMAKER
HEIGHT: 5'5"   COMPLEXION: SANDY   EYES: DARK   HAIR: BROWN
PROMOTED FROM PVT TO SGT, DEC 16, 1861
BURIED @ NASHVILLE, ROW A, LOT #789

PROSSER, ABRAHAM B.   PVT   CO. H   AGE:19
SWORN: OCT 12, 1861/3YRS   MUSTER: NOV 4, 1864   BOUNTY: $100.
BORN: BUTLER COUNTY   OCCUPATION: SHOEMAKER
HEIGHT: 5' 3¼"   COMPLEXION: DARK   EYES: BROWN   HAIR: DARK
DIED: APR 18, 1905 AT PLEASANT HILL, MO

PRUNKARD, DAVID *   PVT   CO. K   AGE:19
SWORN: OCT 12, 1861/3 YRS   MUSTER: NOV 4, 1864
BORN: FRANKLIN COUNTY   OCCUPATION: LABORER
HEIGHT: 5' 9½"   COMPLEXION: DARK   EYES: GREY   HAIR: DARK
WOUNDED AT STONES RIVER

PRUNKARD, JOHN *   PVT   CO. K   AGE:24
SWORN: OCT 12, 1861/3 YRS   MUSTER: NOV 4, 1864
BORN: FRANKLIN COUNTY   OCCUPATION: LABORER
HEIGHT: 5' 8½"   COMPLEXION: DARK   EYES: GREY   HAIR: DARK

PUGH, JACKSON *   PVT   CO. K   AGE:26
SWORN: OCT 12, 1861/3 YRS   MUSTER: NOV 4, 1864
BORN: BUTLER COUNTY   OCCUPATION: LABORER
HEIGHT: 5' 9"   COMPLEXION: FAIR   EYES: GREY   HAIR: FAIR

PUGH, JOSEPH K. *   PVT   CO. K   AGE:18
SWORN: OCT 12, 1861/3 YRS   DESERTED: DEC 22, 1863

BORN: BUTLER COUNTY   OCCUPATION: FARMER
HEIGHT: 5' 9½"   COMPLEXION: DARK   EYES: GREY   HAIR: DARK
QUINN, MICHAEL   PVT   CO. C   AGE: 18
   SWORN: OCT 12, 1861/3 YRS   MEDICAL: DEC 4, 1862
   BORN: PENNSYLVANIA
   HEIGHT: 5' 5½"   COMPLEXION: SANDY   EYES: GREY   HAIR: LIGHT
RADER, ISAAC   PVT   CO. C   AGE: 21
   ORIGIN: CLARION COUNTY
   SWORN: OCT 12, 1861/3 YRS   MEDICAL: DEC 4, 1862
   BORN: PENNSYLVANIA
   HEIGHT: 5' 9"   COMPLEXION: DARK   EYES: BLACK   HAIR: BROWN
   COUSIN TO SHINDLEDECKERS
RADER, WILLIAM H.A.   PVT   CO. C   AGE: 18
READER, WILLIAM H.A.
   SWORN: JUL 2, 1863/3 YRS   DIED: NASHVILLE OCT 15, 1863
   BORN: CLARION COUNTY   OCCUPATION: SHOEMAKER
   HEIGHT: 5' 6"   COMPLEXION: DARK   EYES: GREY   HAIR: AUBURN
   BURIED AT NATIONAL CEMETERY NASHVILLE, GRAVE #E-1026
RAFENACHT, EMMUEL ***   PVT   CO. F
ROFENACHT, EMMEL   PAID SUBSTITUTE
   SWORN: AUG 5, 1864/3 YRS   NOT AT MUSTER
RAMSEY, JOHN W.   PVT   CO. E   AGE: 20
   SWORN: OCT 12, 1861/3 YRS   MUSTER: NOV 4, 1864
   BORN: CLARION COUNTY   OCCUPATION: FARMER
   HEIGHT: 5' 10"   COMPLEXION: SANDY   EYES: DARK   HAIR: DARK
   DIED: IN CLARION COUNTY, PA
RAMSEY, WILLIAM J.   CPL   CO. E   AGE: 18
   SWORN: OCT 12, 1861/3 YRS   MUSTER: NOV 4, 1864
   BORN: CLARION COUNTY   OCCUPATION: FARMER
   HEIGHT: 5' 6"   COMPLEXION: DARK   EYES: GREY   HAIR: BLACK
   PROMOTED TO CPL, MAY 21, 1863
   1890 CENSUS: CHURCH, CLARION COUNTY, PA
   HOME 1914: MONROE, PA
RANKIN, AUSTIN   TEAMSTER   CO. D   AGE: 17
RANKIN, AUSTIN C.   RENKIN, AUSTIN
   SWORN: OCT 12, 1861/3 YRS   MUSTER: NOV 4, 1864
   BORN: INDIANA COUNTY, HILLSDALE   OCCUPATION: FARMER
   HEIGHT: 5' 8½"   COMPLEXION: DARK   EYES: GREY   HAIR: DARK
   COMPANY TEAMSTER
   HOME 1890-1914: HILLSDALE, INDIANA COUNTY, PA
   REUNION CHICKAMAUGA 1897, INDIANA 1908.
   BURIED: IND CTY, THOMPSON'S CEM, HILLSDALE, MONTG TWP., FEB 12, 1844-DEC 1, 1924
RANKIN, DAVID A.   SGT   CO. A   AGE:21
   ORIGIN: INDIANA COUNTY   ENLISTED AS FIFTH CPL   VETERAN
   SWORN: OCT 12, 1861/4 YRS   MUSTER: SEP 11, 1865
   BORN: INDIANA COUNTY   OCCUPATION: FARMER
   HEIGHT: 5' 9"   HAIR: BROWN   EYES: GREY   COMPLEXION: DARK
   PROMOTED TO 2ND LT, DEC 3, 1864; TO CPT MAR 26, 1865.
RANKIN, DAVID K.   PVT   CO. A   AGE:21
   SWORN: OCT 12, 1861/3 YRS   MUSTER: NOV 4, 1864
   BORN: INDIANA COUNTY   OCCUPATION: FARMER
   HEIGHT: 5' 10"   COMPLEXION: DARK   EYES: GREY   HAIR: BLACK
   BRIEFLY MISSING IN ACTION AT STONES RIVER
RANKIN, JOHN F.   MUS   CO. A   AGE:16
   SWORN: OCT 12, 1861/3 YRS   MUSTER: NOV 4, 1864
   BORN: INDIANA COUNTY   OCCUPATION: FARMER
   HEIGHT: 5' 4"   COMPLEXION: DARK   EYES: BLUE   HAIR: BROWN
   ENLISTED AS 1ST MUSICIAN
   HOME 1886-1897: WILLET, INDIANA COUNTY, PA
   REUNION CHICKAMAUGA 1897, INDIANA 1908.
   BURIED: INDIANA COUNTY, PRESBYTERIAN CEMETERY, WASHINGTON TWP.,
   DEC 22, 1846-APR 10, 1917

RARAH, JAMES B.   PVT   CO. A   AGE:20
REARICK, JAMES
    SWORN: OCT 12, 1861/3 YRS   MUSTER: NOV 4, 1864
    HEIGHT: 5' 8½"   COMPLEXION: LIGHT
    1890 CENSUS: OAKLAND, ARMSTRONG COUNTY, PA
RARAH, JAMES W. #   PVT   CO. A   AGE: 20
RARAIGH, JAMES W.   REARICK, JAMES W.
    SWORN: OCT 12, 1861/3 YRS   MUSTER: NOV 4, 1864
    BORN: ARMSTRONG COUNTY   OCCUPATION: FARMER
    HEIGHT: 5' 8½"   COMPLEXION: LIGHT   EYES: GREY   HAIR: LIGHT
    1890 CENSUS: GRANT, INDIANA COUNTY, PA
    BURIED: UNIONTOWN CEMETERY, UNIONTOWN, INDIANA COUNTY, PA 1841-1896
RARAH, DANIEL B. *   PVT   CO. A   AGE:20
    SWORN: OCT 12, 1861/3 YRS   MUSTER: NOV 4, 1864
    BORN: ARMSTRONG COUNTY   OCCUPATION: FARMER
    HEIGHT: 5' 11"   COMPLEXION: DARK   EYES: GREY   HAIR: BLACK
    U.S. PENSION, 1894: $8.00   HOME: OAKLAND
REA, LEMUEL S. *   PVT   CO. K   AGE:19
    SWORN: SEP 10, 1862/3 YRS   DISCHARGED: JUN 19, 1865
    BOUNTY: $29   HOME IN 1897: ALLEGHENY CITY, PA
    BORN: ARMSTRONG COUNTY   OCCUPATION: FARMER
    HEIGHT: 5' 8½"   COMPLEXION: FAIR   EYES: GREY   HAIR: LIGHT
    1890 CENSUS: SLATE LICK, ARMSTRONG COUNTY, PA
    HOME 1901: KINO, PA
    BURIED: PRESBYTERIAN CEMETERY, SLATE LICK, PA   [1843-1908]
    REUNION CHICKAMAUGA 1897, KITTANNING 1901
REAGAN, JAMES *   PVT   CO. F   AGE: 20
REGAN, JAMES   ORIGIN: BUTLER COUNTY
    SWORN: OCT 12, 1861/3 YRS   MEDICAL: MAY 31, 1862
    BORN: SARVERSVILLE, PA   OCCUPATION: FARMER
    HEIGHT: 5' 8"   COMPLEXION: DARK   EYES: BLACK   HAIR: DARK
REARDON, ANDREW J.   CPL   CO. E   AGE: 19
    SWORN: AUG 19, 1861/3 YRS   MUSTER: SEP 11, 1865   VETERAN
    BORN: CLARION COUNTY   OCCUPATION: FARMER
    HEIGHT: 5' 10"   COMPLEXION: LIGHT   EYES: BLUE   HAIR: LIGHT
    PROMOTED TO CPL IN 2ND REGIMENT
    1890 CENSUS: CLARINGTON, FOREST COUNTY, PA
REARICK, DANIEL B. #   PVT   CO. A
    DIED: JAN 3, 1882 @ AGE 60
    COULD BE DANIEL B. RARAH
    TOMBSTONE SAYS A MEMBER OF THE 78th
    BURIED: OAKLAND CEMETERY, DISTANT, PA
REED, ALFRED G.   2ND SGT   CO. H   AGE: 22
    PVT CO. H, 13th PA/THREE MONTH SERVICE   VETERAN
    SWORN: OCT 12, 1861/3YRS   TRANS: AUG 15, 1862 TO PA 134TH
    BORN: BUTLER COUNTY, JUL 2, 1839   OCCUPATION: STUDENT
    HEIGHT: 5' 6¾"   COMPLEXION: LIGHT   EYES: DARK   HAIR: BROWN
    WOUNDED AT STONES RIVER;   LED CO. AT STONES RIVER AS SGT
    PROMOTED TO 1LT/134th; TO ADJ/134th, OCT 1, 1862
    DIED: DEC 28, 1862 IN WASHINGTON, D.C. FROM WOUNDS RECEIVED AT THE
    BATTLE OF FREDERICKSBURG, VA WHILE ASSALTING MARYE HEIGHTS ON DEC 13, 1862
    AGE:22 IN DESCRIPTIVE REGIMENTAL ROSTER   AGE:32 ON MUSTER OUT PAPERS
    BUTLER G.A.R. POST #45/105 NAMED IN HIS HONOR
REED, GEORGE   PVT   CO. C   AGE: 21
    SWORN: FEB 4, 1862/3 YRS   DIED: JAN 16, 1864 AT NASHVILLE
    BORN: CLARION COUNTY   OCCUPATION: BLACKSMITH
    HEIGHT: 5' 6"   COMPLEXION: FAIR   EYES: BLUE   HAIR: SANDY
    BURIED AT NATIONAL CEMETERY NASHVILLE, GRAVE #E-193
REED, GEORGE S. *   PVT   CO. G
    SWORN: OCT 12, 1861/3 YRS   MUSTER: NOV 4, 1864
REED, JOHNSTON *   PVT   CO. F   AGE: 20
    SWORN: OCT 12, 1861/3 YRS   MUSTER: NOV 4, 1864

BORN: SUCCESS, PA   OCCUPATION: LABORER
HEIGHT: 5' 7"   COMPLEXION: LIGHT   EYES: BLUE   HAIR: BROWN
HOME 1897-1901: INGLESIDE, WESTMORELAND COUNTY
REUNION CHICKAMAUGA 1897, KITTANNING 1901

REED, JOSEPH L. *   PVT   CO. I   AGE:24
   SWORN: MAR 31, 1864/3 YRS   MUSTER: SEP 11, 1865
   BORN: JEFFERSON COUNTY   OCCUPATION: FARMER
   HEIGHT: 5' 8"   COMPLEXION: FAIR   EYES: BLUE   HAIR: SANDY

REED, SAMUEL   PVT   CO. H   AGE:24
   SWORN: AUG 5, 1863/3 YRS   DIED: NOV 16, 1863 NASHVILLE, CHRONIC DIARHREA
   ENLISTED AT JOHNSTOWN, PA   BOUNTY $27
   BORN: MAINE   OCCUPATION: COOPER
   HEIGHT: 5' 7"   COMPLEXION: FAIR   EYES: BLUE   HAIR: LIGHT
   BURIED AT NATIONAL CEMETERY NASHVILLE, GRAVE #E-101

REESE, EDWARD M. *   PVT   CO. C   AGE: 18
   SWORN: AUG 21, 1862/3 YRS   DISCHARGED: JUN 19, 1865
   BORN: CLARION COUNTY   OCCUPATION: LABORER
   HEIGHT: 5' 6"   COMPLEXION: FAIR   EYES: BLUE   HAIR: BROWN
   1890 CENSUS: FAIRMOUNT, CLARION COUNTY, PA

REESE, GEORGE J.   SGT MAJ   CO. B   AGE: 19
   SWORN: FEB 1, 1864/3 YRS   MUSTER: SEP 11, 1865
   BORN: CLARION COUNTY   ORIGINAL ENLISTMENT IN CO. C
   HEIGHT: 5' 9"   COMPLEXION: FAIR   EYES: BROWN   HAIR: BROWN
   PROMOTED TO QUARTERMASTER SGT, APR 1, 1865; STAFF II
   HOME 1890-1897: HORTON, INDIANA COUNTY, PA
   PHYSICIAN AND DENTIST AFTER THE WAR; HOME 1914: KITTANNING, PA
   ATTENDED THE DEDICATION OF THE CHICKAMAUGA BATTLEFIELD, NOV 1897
   BURIED: INDIANA COUNTY, MARION CENTER CEMETERY, 1842-JUN 5, 1914

REESE, LEVI   PVT   CO. B
   SWORN: AUG 29, 1861   MUSTER: SEP 11, 1865
   1890 CENSUS: NEW BETHLEHEM, CLARION COUNTY, PA

REESE, LEWIS   PVT   CO. C
   SWORN: OCT 12, 1861/3 YRS   MUSTER: NOV 4, 1864

REESE, THOMAS   PVT   CO. E
   SWORN: OCT 12, 1861/3 YRS   MUSTER: NOV 4, 1864
   BORN: UNION COUNTY   OCCUPATION: BLACKSMITH
   HEIGHT: 5' 10"   COMPLEXION: SANDY   EYES: BLUE   HAIR: BROWN
   REDUCED FROM SIXTH CPL
   APPOINTED TEAMSTER NOV 1, 1862

REIBER, JOHN J.   PVT   CO. H   AGE:20
   SWORN: OCT 12, 1861/3YRS   MUSTER: NOV 4, 1864   BOUNTY: $100.
   BORN: NEW YORK, NY   OCCUPATION: CLERK
   HEIGHT: 5' 3"   COMPLEXION: DARK   EYES: BROWN   HAIR: BROWN
   PROMOTED TO CPL MAY 1, 1863   DEMOTED AUG 4, 1863
   HOME IN 1897: BUTLER, PA   DIED: JAN 2, 1901 AT BUTLER, PA
   REUNION CHICKAMAUGA 1897, KITTANNING 1900
   SERVED AS VP OF REUNION ASSOCIATION

REICHERT, THOMAS L.   PVT   CO. E   AGE: 18
   SWORN: OCT 12, 1861/3 YRS   MUSTER: NOV 4, 1864
   BORN: CLARION COUNTY   OCCUPATION: FARMER
   HEIGHT: 5' 10"   COMPLEXION: LIGHT   EYES: BLUE   HAIR: LIGHT

REISINGER, GEORGE W. *   PVT   CO. I   AGE:19
WEISSINGER, GEORGE W.
   SWORN: OCT 12, 1861/3 YRS   MUSTER: NOV 4, 1864
   BORN: WHITESBURG, PA   OCCUPATION: LABORER
   HEIGHT: 5' 10½   COMPLEXION: DARK   EYES: DARK   HAIR: LIGHT
   HOME IN 1897: DUQUESNE, ALLEGHENY COUNTY, PA

REPINE, ISRAEL   PVT   CO. A   AGE:47
   SWORN: OCT 12, 1861/3 YRS   MUSTER: NOV 4, 1864
   BORN: ARMSTRONG COUNTY   OCCUPATION: PLASTERER
   HEIGHT: 5' 10"   COMPLEXION: FAIR   EYES: BLUE   HAIR: LIGHT
   BURIED: INDIANA COUNTY, OAKLAND CEMETERY, WHITE TWP., 1813-FEB 22, 1872

REPROGLE, JOHN   PVT   CO. A   AGE:21
   ORIGIN: UTAH, INDIANA COUNTY   VETERAN
   SWORN: OCT 12, 1861/4 YRS   MUSTER: SEP 11, 1865
   BORN: CAMBRIA COUNTY   OCCUPATION: LABORER
   HEIGHT: 5' 7"   COMPLEXION: DARK   EYES: GREY   HAIR: BROWN
RETTINGER, ELIAS W. *   PVT   CO. B   AGE:18
   SWORN: OCT 12, 1861/3 YRS   MUSTER: NOV 4, 1864
   BORN: ARMSTRONG COUNTY   OCCUPATION: FARMER
   HEIGHT: 5' 7"   COMPLEXION: DARK   EYES: BLACK   HAIR: DARK
   SENT TO LOUISVILLE HOSPITAL #1 [NINTH & BRODWAY] ON 12/23/1862.
   ..BEFORE THE BATTLE OF STONES RIVER.
   HOME 1914: 1375 COOK AVE, LAKEWOOD, OHIO
REYNOLDS, THOMAS HAMILTON   REGIMENTAL SUTLER/78th   AGE: 44
   HOME: KITTANNING, PA
   CONTRACTED: OCT 18. 1861   KILLED: CIRCA JULY 9, 1862
   KILLED DURING THE WAR AT AGE 45, BETWEEN FRANKLIN AND COLUMBIA, TN
   REPORTEDLY REBEL SYMPATHIZERS ATTACKED AND KILLED REYNOLDS. HIS BODY
   HAD 12 BULLETS IN IT. HIS BROTHER SENT HIS BODY HOME.
RHOADS, DAVID C. *   PVT   CO. B   AGE:30
RHODES, DAVID C.   RHODES, B.
   SWORN: OCT 12, 1861/3 YRS   DIED: MAR 16, 1862 AT LOUISVILLE, KY
   BORN: ARMSTRONG COUNTY   OCCUPATION: PAINTER
   HEIGHT: 5' 8"   COMPLEXION: DARK   EYES: BLACK   HAIR: DARK
   BURIED @ LOUISVILLE, ROW A, GRAVE #19, BATES
RHODES, JOHN *   PVT   CO. K   AGE:35,
   SWORN: OCT 12, 1861/3 YRS   DIED: DEC 15, 1863 AT NASHVILLE
   BORN: GORZEIN, GERMANY   OCCUPATION: LABORER
   HEIGHT: 5' 6¾" COMPLEXION: DARK   EYES: BROWN HAIR: DARK
   BURIED AT NATIONAL CEMETERY NASHVILLE, GRAVE #C-324
RICHARDS, EDWARD *   PVT   CO. D   AGE: 41
   SWORN: SEP 20, 1862/3 YRS   MEDICAL: DATE UNKNOWN
   BORN: INDIANA COUNTY, NEW SALEM   OCCUPATION: STILLER
   HEIGHT: 5' 9½" COMPLEXION: BROWN EYES: GREY   HAIR: BROWN
   DIED BEFORE THE REGIMENTAL HISTORY WAS PUBLISHED IN 1905
RICHARDS, GEORGE *   PVT   CO. C
   SWORN: SEP 21, 1864/1 YR   DISCHARGED: MAY 30, 1865
RICHEY, ABRAHAM B.   PVT   CO. H   AGE:19
RICHEY, ABRAM   RITCHEY, A.B.
   SWORN: OCT 12, 1861/3YRS   MUSTER: NOV 4, 1864   BOUNTY: $100.
   BORN: BUTLER COUNTY, JAN 1842   OCCUPATION: SHOEMAKER
   HEIGHT: 5' 6¼" COMPLEXION: LIGHT EYES: GREY   HAIR: LIGHT
   SERVED AS PROVOST GUARD AT NEGLEY'S HQ IN FALL OF 1863
   HOME 1886-1901: BUTLER, PA   WIFE: AMANDA CHRISTY
   REUNION FREEPORT 1886, CHICKAMAUGA 1897, KITTANNING 1901
RICHEY, WILLIAM A. *   PVT   CO. K   AGE:18
RITCHIE, W.A.
   SWORN: SEP 10, 1862/3 YRS   DISCHARGED: JUN 19, 1865
   BORN: ARMSTRONG COUNTY   OCCUPATION: LABORER   BOUNTY: $29
   HEIGHT: 5' 6½" COMPLEXION: FAIR   EYES: BLACK   HAIR: LIGHT
   REUNION IN FREEPORT 1886   HOME 1886: WITCHITA, KS
RICHIE, EPHRAIM N.   PVT   CO. A   AGE:24
RITCHIE, EPHRAIM   RICHEY, EPHRAIM N.
   SWORN: OCT 12, 1861/3 YRS   MEDICAL: AUG 26, 1863
   BORN: INDIANA COUNTY   OCCUPATION: FARMER
   HEIGHT: 6' 1"   COMPLEXION: DARK   EYES: GREY   HAIR: BROWN
   HOME 1886-1890: SMICKSBURG, INDIANA COUNTY, PA
   HOME 1914: FALLS CREEK, PA   REUNION INDIANA, 1908.
RIGBY, REUBEN M.***   PVT   CO. K   AGE:18
RIGLEY, REUBEN M.
   SWORN: OCT 12, 1861/3 YRS   TRANS: DEC 1, 1862 TO 4TH U.S. CAV
   BORN: ALLEGHENY COUNTY   OCCUPATION: LABORER
   HEIGHT: 5' 5"   COMPLEXION: FAIR   EYES: HAZEL   HAIR: DARK

RILEY, MICHAEL   PVT   CO. C   AGE: 24
    SWORN: OCT 12, 1861/3 YRS   MIA: DEC 31, 1862 @ STONES RIVER
    BORN: IRELAND
    HEIGHT: 5' 5"   COMPLEXION: DARK   EYES: BROWN   HAIR: BROWN
    SIRWELL'S REPORT STATED RILEY WAS MISSING IN ACTION AT STONES RIVER
    INFORMATION FROM ORIGINAL DESCRIPTIVE LIST
RIPPEY, THOMAS B. *   PVT   CO. F   AGE: 24
RAPPEY, THOMAS B.
    SWORN: OCT 12, 1861/3 YRS   MEDICAL: JAN 20, 1864
    BORN: KITTANNING, PA   OCCUPATION: FARMER
    HEIGHT: 6'   COMPLEXION: SANDY   EYES: BROWN   HAIR: BROWN
    HOME 1890-1901: WORTHINGTON, ARMSTRONG COUNTY, PA
    REUNION KITTANNING 1901
RIVERS, JOHN ***   PVT   CO. F   AGE: 20
    BORN: BUTLER COUNTY, MAR 2, 1844
    SWORN: FEB 29, 1864/3 YRS   MUSTER: SEP 11, 1865
    BORN: BUTLER, PA   OCCUPATION: FARMER
    HEIGHT: 5' 5"   COMPLEXION: FAIR   EYES: GREY   HAIR: LIGHT
    FATHER-IN-LAW, PETER KENNEDY IN CO. E, 2ND 78th REGIMENT
    HOSPITALIZED @ LOOKOUT MOUNTAIN, MAY 2-JUL 15, 1864
    HOSPITALIZED @ CHATTANOOGA, SEP 18-NOV 20, 1864
    1886 REUNION IN FREEPORT: HOME, CARBON, PA
    PENSION: $12.00   WIFE: ELLEN KENNEDY
    JR DIED: JAN 26, 1912 IN BUTLER TWP., BUTLER COUNTY, PA
ROBINSON, JAMES H.   PVT   CO. A   AGE:23
    SWORN: OCT 12, 1861/4 YRS   MUSTER: SEP 11, 1865
    BORN: INDIANA COUNTY   OCCUPATION: TEACHER
    HEIGHT: 5' 9"   COMPLEXION: DARK   EYES: GREY   HAIR: BLACK
    BRIEFLY MISSING IN ACTION AT STONES RIVER
    VETERAN, DIED IN KANSAS BEFORE 1905
ROBINSON, SAMUEL B. *   PVT   CO. B   AGE:28
    SWORN: OCT 12, 1861/3 YRS   MUSTER: NOV 4, 1864
    BORN: ARMSTRONG COUNTY   OCCUPATION: MINER
    HEIGHT: 5' 6"   COMPLEXION: LIGHT   EYES: BROWN   HAIR: LIGHT
    HOME IN 1897: MONONGAHELA, PA
    HOME 1914: NEW EAGLE, WASHINGTON COUNTY, PA
ROESSLER, CHRISTIAN *   PVT   CO. A/B   AGE: 18
RESSLER, CHRISTIAN
    SWORN: FEB 2, 1864/3 YRS   MUSTER: SEP 11, 1865
    BORN: ARMSTRONG COUNTY   OCCUPATION: SADDLER
    HEIGHT: 5' 4"   COMPLEXION: DARK   EYES: BLACK   HAIR: DARK
    HOME 1914: SALEM, OHIO
ROGERS, HUGH H. *   PVT   CO. I   AGE:19
RODGERS, HUGH F.
    SWORN: OCT 12, 1861/3 YRS   MUSTER: NOV 4, 1864
    BORN: KITTANNING, PA   OCCUPATION: LABORER
    HEIGHT: 5' 8½"   COMPLEXION: LIGHT   EYES: BLUE   HAIR: LIGHT
    HOME 1897-1914: 533 MARWOOD AVE., McKEES ROCKS, PA
    OCCUPATION: ENGINEER ON THE PITTSBURGH AND LAKE ERIE RR.
    DROVE THE YOUNGSTOWN FLYER
    REUNION CHICKAMAUGA 1897, KITTANNING 1901
RONEY, JAMES M. *   PVT   CO. F
    ORIGIN: BUTLER COUNTY
    JAMES M. RONEY AND MARTIN RONEY COULD BE THE SAME MAN
    SWORN: OCT 12, 1861/3 YRS   MUSTER: NOV 4, 1864
RONEY, JOHN W. *   PVT   CO. K   AGE: 21
ROWEN, JOHN W.
    SERVED AS A SGT AT CAMP ORR
    SWORN: OCT 12, 1861/3 YRS   MUSTER: NOV 4, 1864
    BORN: BUTLER COUNTY   OCCUPATION: FARMER
    HEIGHT: 5' 11½"   COMPLEXION: FAIR   EYES: GREY   HAIR: LIGHT
    TRANS: OCT 21, 1863 TO SIGNAL CORP TO DEC 1863

HOME 1900: CHICAGO, IL   OCCUPATION: NEWSPAPERMAN
REUNION IN KITTANNING 1900
RONEY, MARTIN   PVT   CO. F   AGE: 22
JAMES M. RONEY AND MARTIN RONEY COULD BE THE SAME MAN
SWORN: OCT 12, 1861/3 YRS   MUSTER: NOV 4, 1864
BORN: SARVERSVILLE, PA   OCCUPATION: FARMER
HEIGHT: 5' 10"   COMPLEXION: DARK   EYES: GREY   HAIR: DARK BROWN
ROOF, JOHN C. *   CPL   CO. G
SWORN: OCT 12, 1861/3 YRS   TRANS: NOV 30, 1862 TO 4TH CAV
ROPER, WILLIAM B.   PVT   CO. C
SWORN: OCT 12, 1861/3 YRS   DIED: MAR 11, 1864
BORN: PENNSYLVANIA
COMPLEXION: DARK   EYES: BLUE   HAIR: BROWN
ASSISTANT HOSPITAL STEWARD, 1862.
FELL FROM POINT LOOKOUT OFF LOOKOUT MOUNTAIN DURING PHOTO SESSION;
INSTANTLY KILLED
ROSE, GEORGE   PVT   CO. H   AGE:24
SWORN: OCT 12, 1861/3YRS   MUSTER: NOV 4, 1864   BOUNTY: $100.
BORN: WESTMORELAND COUNTY   OCCUPATION: PAINTER
HEIGHT: 5' 5^{1}/8"   COMPLEXION: LIGHT   EYES: BROWN   HAIR: BLACK
WOUNDED/LEG AT STONES RIVER
HOME 1897: PITTSBURGH, PA
HOME 1914: 212 W 38th ST, MARION, INDIANA
ROSS, ELIJAH W.   ASSISTANT SUR/78th   REGIMENTAL STAFF
ORIGIN: CHESTER COUNTY
SWORN: MAY 16, 1862/3 YRS   RESIGNED: JAN 13, 1863.
ROSS, JOHN K.***   PVT   CO. F   AGE: 27
ROSS, JOHN E.
SWORN: OCT 12, 1861/3 YRS   MUSTER: NOV 4, 1864
BORN: TARENTUM, PA   OCCUPATION: LABORER
HEIGHT: 5' 7½"   COMPLEXION: FRESH   EYES: BLUE   HAIR: BROWN
REUNION IN FREEPORT 1886
HOME 1886-1897: TARENTUM, PA
BORN: DEC 25, 1834   DIED: JUN 15, 1910
BURIED: PROSPECT CEMETERY, TARENTUM, PA   WIFE: R. JANE
ROSS, JOHN W.   1ST SGT   CO. D   AGE: 21
SWORN: OCT 12, 1861/3 YRS   MUSTER: NOV 4, 1864
BORN: INDIANA COUNTY, CHERRY TREE   OCCUPATION: FARMER
HEIGHT: 5' 10½"   COMPLEXION: LIGHT   EYES: BLUE   HAIR: BROWN
PROMOTED APR 16, 1863 FROM SGT
HOME IN 1897: BRUSH VALLEY, INDIANA COUNTY, PA
HOME 1901: PITTSBURGH, PA
HOME 1914: APOLLO, PA
BURIED: APOLLO CEMETERY, APOLLO, PA [1840-1935]
REUNION KITTANNING 1901, INDIANA 1908.
ROTH, GEORGE WASHINGTON   PVT   CO. H   AGE:20
ROTH, DAVID   ROTH, GEORGE W.
NATIVE OF PROSPECT, PA   BORN: 1842
SWORN: OCT 12, 1861/3YRS   DIED: DEC 12, 1861 AT CAMP NEGLEY, TYPHOID FEVER
BORN: BUTLER COUNTY   OCCUPATION: STUDENT
HEIGHT: 6'   COMPLEXION: LIGHT   EYES: GREY   HAIR: BROWN
SISTER: MARIETTA "MET" ROTH; FRIEND: FRED WIEHL, ALSO OF CO. H
GEORGE'S BROTHER, HENRY WARREN ROTH, BECAME THE FIRST PRESIDENT OF
THEIL COLLEGE, HIS YOUNGER BROTHER BECAME PRESIDENT OF THE COLLEGE, TOO.
ROTHROCK, R.K.   PVT   CO. C   AGE: 30
ROTHROCK, ROSWELL
SWORN: OCT 12, 1861/3 YRS   DISCHARGED: JAN 18, 1865
BORN: PENNSYLVANIA
HEIGHT: 5' 7"   COMPLEXION: DARK   EYES: GREY   HAIR: BROWN
TAKEN PRISONER AT McLEMORE'S COVE, SEP 18, 1863; PAROLED: NOV 25, 1864
DIED: 1900 AT McCLURE, PENNSYLVANIA
ROW, CHRISTOPHER *   PVT   CO. I   AGE:18

SWORN: OCT 12, 1861/3 YRS   TRANS: DEC 1, 1862, 4TH CAV
BORN: LEECHBURG, PA   OCCUPATION: LABORER
HEIGHT: 5' 5"   COMPLEXION: DARK   EYES: BROWN   HAIR: DARK
DIED: BENTON HARBOR, MI, BEFORE 1905

ROW, JOSEPH *   PVT   CO. K   AGE:36
SWORN: OCT 12, 1861/3 YRS   MEDICAL: FEB 10, 1862
BORN: WESTMORELAND COUNTY   OCCUPATION: FARMER
HEIGHT: 5' 5"   COMPLEXION: DARK   EYES: HAZEL   HAIR: DARK

ROWDYBUSH, MICHAEL *   PVT   CO. G   AGE: 18
ROWDERBUSH, MICHAEL   ROUDYBUST, MICHAEL
SWORN: MAR 24, 1862/3 YRS   MUSTER: SEP 11, 1865
BORN: BLAIR COUNTY   OCCUPATION: LABORER
HEIGHT: 5' 4½"   COMPLEXION: FAIR   EYES: GREY   HAIR: SANDY
DESERTED: JUN 2, 1864/RETURNED
RE-ENLISTED AND DESERTED WHILE AT HOME IN KITTANNING WHILE ON VETERAN
FURLOUGH
HOME IN 1897: McKEES GAP, BLAIR COUNTY, PA
ATTENDED THE DEDICATION OF THE CHICKAMAUGA BATTLEFIELD, NOV 1897
DIED BEFORE THE REGIMENTAL HISTORY WAS PUBLISHED IN 1905

ROWLAND, ISAAC   PVT   CO. A   AGE:24
SWORN: OCT 12, 1861/3 YRS   MEDICAL: JUN 28, 1863
BORN: INDIANA COUNTY   OCCUPATION: LABORER
HEIGHT: 5' 8"   COMPLEXION: DARK   EYES: GREY   HAIR: BROWN

ROWLAND, JAMES   PVT   CO. D
SWORN: OCT 12, 1861/3 YRS   TRANS: OCT 7, 1863   MEDICAL: FEB 24, 1865

ROWLEY, GEORGE W.   PVT   CO. D   AGE: 19
SWORN: OCT 12, 1861/3 YRS   DIED: FEB 22, 1862 AT CAMP HAMBRIGHT
BORN: INDIANA COUNTY, HILLSDALE   OCCUPATION: FARMER
HEIGHT: 6' 1"   COMPLEXION: DARK   EYES: BLUE   HAIR: DARK

ROWLEY, WESLEY *   PVT   CO. F   AGE: 26
SWORN: OCT 12, 1861/3 YRS   MUSTER: NOV 4, 1864
BORN: FREEPORT, PA   OCCUPATION: CARPENTER
HEIGHT: 5' 3"   COMPLEXION: FRESH   EYES: BLACK   HAIR: DARK BROWN
1886 REUNION IN FREEPORT: HOME, FREEPORT, PA
DIED: 1891; BURIED: FREEPORT CEMETERY

RUFFNER, DANIEL *   PVT   CO. G
SWORN: OCT 12, 1861/3 YRS   MUSTER: NOV 4, 1864
1890 CENSUS:COWANSHANNOCK TWP., ARMSTRONG COUNTY, PA

RUFFNER, SIMON *   PVT   CO. G
SWORN: OCT 12, 1861/3 YRS   MUSTER: NOV 4, 1864
1890 CENSUS: BLANKET HILL, ARMSTRONG COUNTY, PA

RUFFNER, WILLIAM H. ***   PVT   CO. G   AGE: 15
SWORN: MAR 3, 1862/3 YRS   MUSTER: SEP 11, 1865
1890 CENSUS: SHELOCTA, INDIANA COUNTY, PA
BURIED: INDIANA COUNTY, OAKLAND CEMETERY, WHITE TEP., 1847–APR 21, 1916

RUMBAUGH, PETER K.   PVT   CO. H   AGE:19
SWORN: OCT 12, 1861/3YRS   DIED: MAR 19, 1862 AT LOUISVILLE, CONSUMPTION
BORN: BUTLER COUNTY   OCCUPATION: SHOEMAKER
HEIGHT: 5' 10"   COMPLEXION: LIGHT   EYES: BLUE   HAIR: BROWN
BURIED: NATIONAL CEMETERY LOUISVILLE; SECTION.A, RANGE.16, GRAVE.4

RUMBERGER, PETER J.*   PVT   CO. B   AGE:25
SWORN: OCT 12, 1861/3 YRS   MUSTER: NOV 4, 1864
BORN: ARMSTRONG COUNTY   OCCUPATION: CARPENTER
HEIGHT: 5' 8"   COMPLEXION: DARK   EYES: BLACK   HAIR: DARK
HOME IN 1897: HARRISBURG, PA
ATTENDED THE DEDICATION OF THE CHICKAMAUGA BATTLEFIELD, NOV 1897

RUNYAN, JAMES W.   PVT   CO. H   AGE:20
RUYAN, JAMES W.
SWORN: OCT 12, 1861/3YRS   KILLED: DEC 31, 1862 AT STONES RIVER
BORN: CLARION COUNTY   OCCUPATION: FARMER
HEIGHT: 5' 4"   COMPLEXION: LIGHT   EYES: BLUE   HAIR: LIGHT

RUNYAN, PHINEAS D. *   PVT   CO. G   AGE: 29

SWORN: OCT 12, 1861/3 YRS   MUSTER: NOV 4, 1864
1890 CENSUS:COWANSHANNOCK TWP., ARMSTRONG COUNTY, PA
BURIED: INDIANA COUNTY, ST. JOHN'S LUTHERAN CEMETERY, SOUTH MAHONING,
APR 17, 1832-AUG 8, 1927 [95]

RUPERT, SALATHIEL M.   PVT   CO. E   AGE: 18
SWORN: OCT 12, 1861/3 YRS   DIED: FEB 17, 1862
BORN: CLARION COUNTY   OCCUPATION: FARMER
HEIGHT: 5' 10"   COMPLEXION: FAIR   EYES: BLUE   HAIR: LIGHT

RUPP, ADAM   PVT   CO. A   AGE: 18
BORN: ARMSTRONG COUNTY, PA TO GEORGE RUPP & ELIZABETH REEDY
GEORGE DIED IN 1850; ELIZABETH REMARRIED TO JOHN EDWARDS IN 1853
SWORN: OCT 12, 1861/3 YRS   DIED: OCT 18, 1864 AT NASHVILLE, RHEUMATIC HEART
BORN: ARMSTRONG COUNTY   OCCUPATION: FARMER
HEIGHT: 5' 8¾"   COMPLEXION: FAIR   EYES: BLUE   HAIR: BROWN

RUPP, CHRISTOPHER   PVT   CO. A
SWORN: SEP 17, 1861/3 YRS   DISCHARGED: OCT 1, 1861
NEVER LEFT CAMP ORR
1890 CENSUS: WIDNOON, MADISON TWP., ARMSTRONG COUNTY, PA

RUPP, NATHANIEL *   PVT   CO. A   AGE:22
RAPP, NATHANIEL
SWORN: OCT 12, 1861/3 YRS   MUSTER: NOV 4, 1864
BORN: ARMSTRONG COUNTY   OCCUPATION: FARMER
HEIGHT: 5' 6"   COMPLEXION: DARK   EYES: BLUE   HAIR: BROWN
WOUNDED AT STONES RIVER JAN 2, 1863

RUTTER, JOHN *   PVT   CO. B   AGE:21
RITTER, JOHN
SWORN: OCT 12, 1861/3 YRS   MUSTER: NOV 4, 1864
BORN: ARMSTRONG COUNTY   OCCUPATION: NONE
HEIGHT: 5' 7"   COMPLEXION: DARK   EYES: BLACK   HAIR: LIGHT

RYERS, VALENTINE #   PVT   CO. C
REYERS, VALENTINE
SWORN: UNKNOWN   DIED: JAN 31, 1863
BURIED AT NATIONAL CEMETERY NASHVILLE, GRAVE #B-1030, BATES

SAEGERS, LEWIS   PVT   CO. C   AGE: 18
SWORN: OCT 12, 1861/3 YRS   DIED: JAN 5, 1863
BORN: CLARION COUNTY
HEIGHT: 5' 5"   COMPLEXION: FAIR   EYES: GREY   HAIR: BROWN
MORTALLY WOUNDED/LUNG AT STONES RIVER WHILE SERVING ON BATTERY

SAGASER, HENRY H.   PVT   CO. H   AGE:24
SAGASER, HENRY S.   SAGASSER, HENRY H.
SWORN: FEB 22, 1864/3 YRS   MUSTER: SEP 11, 1865

SALTSGIVER, ISAAC *   PVT   CO. K   AGE: 26
SWORN: OCT 12, 1861/3 YRS   LEFT REGIMENT AUG 15, 1863/ILLNESS
ABSENT/SICK AT FINAL MUSTER
BORN: ARMSTRONG COUNTY   OCCUPATION: SHOEMAKER
HEIGHT: 5' 6¼"   COMPLEXION: DARK   EYES: GREY   HAIR: DARK
1890 CENSUS: WEST LEBANON, PA; WIDOW MARY

SARVER, BENJAMIN *   PVT   CO. F   AGE: 26
BORN: BUTLER COUNTY, JUN 15, 1835
SWORN: OCT 12, 1861/3 YRS   TRANS: APR 10,1864 TO VRC
BORN: SARVERSVILLE, PA   OCCUPATION: FARMER
HEIGHT: 5' 8½"   COMPLEXION: FRESH   EYES: GREY   HAIR: DARK BROWN
CAPTURED AT STONES RIVER; FREED BY FELLOW 78th MEMBERS
WIFE: ISABELLE La FEVER   HOME: EKASTOWN, PA

SARVER, LYNUS T. *   PVT   CO. I   AGE: 21
SWORN: OCT 12, 1861/3 YRS   DIED: JAN 15, 1862 AT LOUISVILLE
BORN: CLARKSBURG, PA   OCCUPATION: LABORER
HEIGHT: 5' 8"   COMPLEXION: SANDY   EYES: GREY   HAIR: LIGHT
BURIED: NATIONAL CEMETERY LOUISVILLE; SECTION.A, RANGE.2, GRAVE.24

SAY, THOMAS   PVT   CO. E   AGE: 21
SWORN: OCT 12, 1861/3 YRS   MUSTER: NOV 4, 1864
BORN: VENANGO COUNTY   OCCUPATION: FARMER

HEIGHT: 6'   COMPLEXION: FAIR   EYES: BLUE   HAIR: BLACK
1890 CENSUS: ASHLAND TWP., CLARION COUNTY, PA
HOME IN 1897: NICKELVILLE, VENANGO COUNTY, PA
ATTENDED THE DEDICATION OF THE CHICKAMAUGA BATTLEFIELD, NOV 1897

SCHAFFNER, GEORGE   CPL   CO. H   AGE: 19
    SWORN: OCT 12, 1861/3YRS   DISCHARGED: OCT 12, 1864
    BORN: BUTLER COUNTY   OCCUPATION: FARMER
    HEIGHT: 5' 8^{1}/3" COMPLEXION: DARK EYES: BROWN HAIR: BROWN
    PROMOTED TO CPL, DEC 17, 1863.   BORN: SLIPPERY ROCK, PA, DEC 17, 1841
    WOUNDED/RT SHOULDER & LEFT HAND AT PICKETT'S MILL MAY 27, 1864
    HOME 1897-1914: 330 LOOKOUT AVE., BUTLER, PA
    DIED: NOV 1923 IN BUTLER, PA   CONTRACTOR BY TRADE
    BROTHER, SAMUEL IN PA 6th HVY ARTILLERY, SAM'S WIFE: JOSEPHINE HINCHBERGER

SCHECKLER, GEORGE #   PVT   CO. A
    SWORN: OCT 12, 1861/3 YRS
    BORN: INDIANA COUNTY   OCCUPATION: FARMER
    LISTED ONLY IN ROSTER AND DESCRIPTIVE BOOK NO ADDITIONAL INFORMATION

SCHELLENBERGER, GEORGE W.   PVT   CO. C   AGE: 28
SHALLENBERGER, G.W.
    SWORN: OCT 12, 1861/3 YRS   MUSTER: NOV 4, 1864
    BORN: PENNSYLVANIA
    HEIGHT: 5' 8" COMPLEXION: DARK EYES: BLUE HAIR: BLACK
    HOME 1890-1914: NEW BETHLEHEM, CLARION COUNTY, PA

SCHICK, ADAM *   PVT   CO. C   AGE: 19
    SWORN: OCT 12, 1861/4 YRS   MUSTER: SEP 11, 1865
    BORN: CLARION COUNTY   VETERAN
    HEIGHT: 5' 10" COMPLEXION: DARK EYES: GREY HAIR: BROWN

SCHICK, ADAM M.   PVT   CO. C   AGE: 18
    SWORN: OCT 12, 1861/3 YRS   MUSTER: NOV 4, 1864
    BORN: CLARION COUNTY
    HEIGHT: 5' 9" COMPLEXION: DARK EYES: BLACK HAIR: BROWN
    1890 CENSUS: RED BANK, ARMSTRONG COUNTY, PA

SCHICK, CHRISTIAN *   PVT   CO. I
SHICK, CHRISTIAN
    SWORN: FEB 29, 1864/3 YRS   MUSTER: SEP 11, 1865
    1890 CENSUS: RED BANK, ARMSTRONG COUNTY, PA
    HOME 1901: MILLVILLE, PA   REUNION KITTANNING 1901

SCHICK, JOHN *   PVT   CO. C   AGE: 21
    SWORN: OCT 12, 1861/3 YRS   MEDICAL: MAY 1, 1862
    BORN: CLARION COUNTY
    HEIGHT: 5' 9" COMPLEXION: DARK EYES: BLUE HAIR: BLACK
    DIED: WEST MILLVILLE, PA BEFORE 1905

SCHICK, JOHN H. *   CPL   CO. C   AGE: 24
    SWORN: AUG 28, 1862/3 YRS   MUSTER: SEP 11, 1865
    BORN: CLARION COUNTY   OCCUPATION: LUMBERMAN
    HEIGHT: 5' 8" COMPLEXION: FAIR EYES: BLUE   HAIR: LIGHT
    1890 CENSUS: BROOKVILLE, JEFFERSON COUNTY, PA
    DIED: BROOKVILLE, PA BEFORE THE REGIMENTAL HISTORY WAS PUBLISHED IN 1905

SCHICK, JOHN R. *   PVT   CO. C   AGE: 44
SHICK, JOHN R.   SHICK, JONAS R.   SHICK, JONATHAN
    SWORN: AUG 21, 1862/3 YRS   DIED: JUN 23, 1865 AT RINGGOLD, PENNSYLVANIA
    BORN: BERKS COUNTY   OCCUPATION: FARMER
    HEIGHT: 5' 9" COMPLEXION: DARK EYES: GREY   HAIR: BROWN
    MEDICAL: AFTER SERVING 2 YEARS, 9 MONTHS
    1890 CENSUS: HEATHVILLE, JEFFERSON COUNTY, PA; WIDOW SUSANNAH RICHARDS

SCHICK, JOSEPH *   PVT   CO. B   AGE:23
SHICK, JOSEPH
    SWORN: OCT 12, 1861/3 YRS   MUSTER: NOV 4, 1864
    BORN: JEFFERSON COUNTY   OCCUPATION: FARMER
    HEIGHT: 5' 8" COMPLEXION: LIGHT EYES: LIGHT   HAIR: BLACK
    1890 CENSUS: RED BANK, ARMSTRONG COUNTY, PA

SCHICK, REUBEN M. *   PVT   CO. C   AGE: 20

SHICK, REUBEN M.
    SWORN: OCT 12, 1861/3 YRS   MEDICAL: JUN 1, 1862
    BORN: CLARION COUNTY   OCCUPATION: LUMBERMAN
    HEIGHT: 5' 6½"   COMPLEXION: DARK   EYES: BLUE   HAIR: LIGHT
    SENT HOME WITH TYPHOID FEVER
    RE-ENLISTED: MAR 29, 1864   MUSTER: SEP 11, 1865
    1890 CENSUS: BROOKVILLE, JEFFERSON COUNTY, PA, DIED IN BROOKVILE BEFORE 1905
SCHICK, WILLIAM F. *   PVT   CO. C
    SWORN: MAR 9, 1864/3 YRS   MUSTER: SEP 11, 1865
    1890 CENSUS: FAIRMOUNT, CLARION COUNTY, PA
SCHMIDT, KARL   PVT   CO. H   AGE:29
SCHMIDT, CARL   VETERAN
    SWORN: OCT 12, 1861/4 YRS   MUSTER: SEP 11, 1865
    BORN: GERMANY   OCCUPATION: MINER
    HEIGHT: 5' 7½"   COMPLEXION: LIGHT EYES: GREY   HAIR: BROWN
    LEFT SICK IN TULLAHOMA, JULY 1863;   RE-JOINED REGIMENT FEB 2, 1864
SCHRECENGHOST, CHRISTOPHER   PVT   CO. A   VETERAN
SCHECENGHOST, C.   SCHRECENGOST, CHRISTOPHER
    SWORN: AUG 27, 1861/3 YRS   MUSTER: SEP 11, 1865
    1890 CENSUS: CLARKSBURG, INDIANA COUNTY, PA
    BURIED: INDIANA COUNTY, PRESBYTERIAN CEMETERY, CLARKSBURG,
    AUG 7, 1842-OCT 5, 1905
SCHRECENGOST, ALFRED   PVT   CO. G   AGE:32
    SWORN: OCT 12, 1861/3 YRS   DESERTED: OCT 18, 1861
    U.S. PENSION, 1894: $8.00   HOME: KITTANNING
    SERVED IN THE SECOND BATTALION PENNSYLVANIA MILITIA 1862
SCHRECENGOST, W. *   PVT   CO. G   AGE:23
SCHRECHENGHOST, WILSON   SCHRECENGHOST, WILSON
SCHRECENGOST, D.W.
    SWORN: OCT 12, 1861/3 YRS   MUSTER: NOV 4, 1864
    1890 CENSUS:COWANSHANNOCK TWP., ARMSTRONG COUNTY, PA
    HOME IN 1897: RURAL VALLEY, ARMSTRONG COUNTY
    ATTENDED THE DEDICATION OF THE CHICKAMAUGA BATTLEFIELD, NOV 1897
    BURIED: METHODIST CEMETERY, RURAL VALLEY, PA   DIED: 1926
SCHRECHENGOST, ISAAC *   CPL   CO. G
SCHRECENGOST, ISAAC   SCHRECONGOST, ISAAC
    DIED: KITTANNING PA
    SWORN: OCT 12, 1861/3 YRS   MUSTER: NOV 4, 1864
    U.S. PENSION, 1894: $6.00   HOME: KITTANNING
    1890 CENSUS: KITTANNING, ARMSTRONG COUNTY, PA
    BURIED: KITTANNING CEMETERY, RAYBURN TWP., DIED BEFORE 1905
SCHRECKONGASTER, CHRISTOPHER,
SCHRECENGHOST   PVT   CO. A   AGE:19
    SWORN: OCT 12, 1861/4 YRS   MUSTER: SEP 11, 1865   VETERANS
    BORN: ARMSTRONG COUNTY   OCCUPATION: FARMER
    HEIGHT: 5' 7½"   COMPLEXION: DARK   EYES: BLUE   HAIR: BROWN
    HOME 1897: CLARKSBURG, INDIANA COUNTY, PA
    ATTENDED THE DEDICATION OF THE CHICKAMAUGA BATTLEFIELD, NOV 1897
SCHREFFER, JACOB   PVT   CO. D   AGE: 38
SHREFFER, JACOB
    SWORN: AUG 25, 1862/3 YRS   DIED: MAR 9, 1863 AT NASHVILLE
    BORN: ARMSTRONG COUNTY   OCCUPATION: FARMER
    HEIGHT: 5' 8½"   COMPLEXION: FAIR   EYES: GREY   HAIR: BROWN
    BURIED AT NATIONAL CEMETERY NASHVILLE, GRAVE #E-921
SCOTT, ROBERT P. "PRES"   PVT   CO. H   AGE:19
    SWORN: OCT 12, 1861/3YRS   MUSTER: NOV 4, 1864   BOUNTY: $100.
    BORN: BUTLER COUNTY   OCCUPATION: DEPUTY SHERIFF
    HEIGHT: 5' 7$^1/_3$"   COMPLEXION: FAIR EYES: GREY   HAIR: LIGHT
    SUFFERED WITH PNUEMONIA IN EARLY 1862
    HIS BOYHOOD FRIEND, WILLIAM J. MOORE, CO. H, WAS KILLED AT STONES RIVER.
    HOME IN 1897-1914: 411 N. MAIN ST., BUTLER, PA
    REUNION CHICKAMAUGA 1897, PUNXSUTAWNEY 1899,

KITTANNING 1900, 1901, INDIANA 1908.
SERVED AS PRESIDENT OF THE REUNION ASSOCIATION

SCOTT, WILLIAM *   PVT   CO. B   AGE:22
    SWORN: OCT 12, 1861/3 YRS   MUSTER: NOV 4, 1864
    BORN: IRELAND   OCCUPATION: MINER
    HEIGHT: 5' 9"   COMPLEXION: LIGHT   EYES: DARK   HAIR: BLACK

SEIP, JAMES H.   PVT   CO. E   AGE: 19
    SWORN: OCT 12, 1861/3 YRS   MUSTER: NOV 4, 1864
    BORN: CLARION COUNTY   OCCUPATION: TEAMSTER
    HEIGHT: 5' 6"   COMPLEXION: FAIR   EYES: BLUE   HAIR: DARK
    WOUNDED AT STONES RIVER/SHOULDER

SEMPKINS. ALBERT P. "BUCK" *   SGT   CO. K   AGE: 22
SIMKINS, ALBERT P. "BUCK"   LIMKINS, ALBERT
    SWORN: OCT 12, 1861/3 YRS   MUSTER: NOV 4, 1864
    BORN: FAYETTE COUNTY   OCCUPATION: JOINER
    HEIGHT: 5' 6¼"   COMPLEXION: FAIR   EYES: BLUE   HAIR: AUBURN
    PROMOTED TO CPL, OCT 18, 1862; TO SGT, MAR 1, 1863
    ATTENDED 1886 REUNION IN FREEPORT
    HOME 1886–1897: CORSICA, JEFFERSON COUNTY, PA

SERENE, SAMUEL L.   CPL   CO. A   AGE:26
SERINES, SAMUEL L.
    SWORN: OCT 12, 1861/3 YRS   MUSTER: NOV 4, 1864
    BORN: ARMSTRONG COUNTY   OCCUPATION: FARMER
    HEIGHT: 5' 8"   COMPLEXION: FAIR   EYES: GREY   HAIR: BROWN
    PROMOTED TO CPL   WOUNDED/LEG AT STONES RIVER
    HOME 1914: PEPIN, WISCONSIN

SHAFER, HENRY S.   PVT   CO. E   AGE: 22
SHEFFER, HENRY
    SWORN: OCT 12, 1861/3 YRS   TRANS: SEP 1, 1863 TO VRC
    BORN: LEHIGH COUNTY   OCCUPATION: CARPENTER
    HEIGHT: 5' 10"   COMPLEXION: SANDY   EYES: BLUE   HAIR: DARK

SHAFER, LEWIS C.   PVT   CO. G
    SWORN: SEP 13, 1864   DISCHARGED: JUN 19, 1865
    SERVED UNDER SIRWELL

SHAFER, ISRAEL   PVT   CO. G
    SWORN: SEP 13, 1864   DISCHARGED: JUN 19, 1865
    SERVED UNDER SIRWELL

SHAFFER, ADAM *   PVT   CO. B   AGE:38
SHOFER, ADAM
    SWORN: AUG 25, 1862/3 YRS   DIED: JAN 9, 1863 AT FIELD HOSPITAL
    BORN: ARMSTRONG COUNTY
    HEIGHT: 5' 11"   COMPLEXION: DARK   EYES: GREY   HAIR: DARK
    MORTALLY WOUNDED AT STONES RIVER
    BURIED AT NATIONAL CEMETERY STONES RIVER, GRAVE #K-4461
    1890 CENSUS: RED BANK, ARMSTRONG COUNTY, PA; WIDOW POLLY

SHAFFER, GEORGE H. *   PVT   CO. B   AGE:20
SHIFFER, GEORGE H.
    SWORN: OCT 12, 1861/3 YRS   DIED: MAR 13, 1862 AT LOUISVILLE, KY
    BORN: JEFFERSON COUNTY   OCCUPATION: FARMER
    HEIGHT: 5' 10"   COMPLEXION: DARK   EYES: BLACK   HAIR: BLACK
    BURIED: NATIONAL CEMETERY LOUISVILLE; SECTION.A, RANGE.14, GRAVE.23

SHAFFER, ISRAEL   PVT   CO. G   AGE: 16
SHAFER, ISRAEL
    OCCUPATION: FARMER IN RED BANK, ARMSTRONG COUNTY
    SWORN: SEP 13, 1863/3 YRS   DISCHARGED: JUN 19, 1865
    BROTHER: LEWIS C.; CO. G, 78th, JOHN C. CO. A 78th
    PARENTS: CHRISTIAN & MAGDALENA FUERINGER
    1890 CENSUS: RED BANK, ARMSTRONG COUNTY, PA
    ENTERED THE WHOLESALE PRODUCE BUSINESS IN PITTSBURGH
    ALLEGHENY COUNTY TREASURER 1899
    ALLEGHENY COUNTY COMMISSIONER SEPT 30, 1911

SHAFFER, JACOB   2 MUS   CO. C   AGE:21

SHEFFER, JACOB
    SWORN: OCT 12, 1861/3 YRS   MUSTER: NOV 4, 1864
    HEIGHT: 5' 8½"   COMPLEXION: DARK   EYES: GREY
SHAFFER, JOHN   PVT   CO. A
    SWORN: SEP 14, 1864/1 YEAR   DISCHARGED: JUN 19, 1865
    ONE OF "THE LAST DOZEN" LIVING IN ARMSTRONG COUNTY IN 1936
    1890 CENSUS: RED BANK, ARMSTRONG COUNTY, PA
    PO BOX: RED BANK TWP, OAK RIDGE, PA
SHAFFER, JOHN C. *   PVT   CO. A
SHAFER, JOHN C.   SCHAFFER, J.C.
    SWORN: SEP 14, 1864/1 YEAR   DISCHARGED: JUN 19, 1865
    1890 CENSUS: RED BANK, ARMSTRONG COUNTY, PA
    HOME: 1914: OAK RIDGE, PA   STILL ALIVE IN 1936.
    BROTHER: LEWIS C.; CO. G/78th, ISRAEL CO. G/78th
    PARENTS: CHRISTIAN & MAGDALENA FUERINGER
SHAFFER, LEWIS C. *   PVT   CO. G   AGE: 24
SHAFER, LEWIS C.   SCHAEFFER, LEWIS C.
    SWORN: JUL 6, 1863/90 DAYS   DISCHARGED: AUG 17, 1863
    FIRST ENLISTMENT: PA 57th REGIMENT, CO. K
    SWORN: SEP 13, 1864/1 YEAR   DISCHARGED: JUN 19, 1865
    BORN: APR 27, 1840 IN RED BANK TWP.,   DIED: FEB 22, 1925
    OCCUPATION: FARMER
    1890 CENSUS: RED BANK, ARMSTRONG COUNTY, PA
    HOME 1901: PIERCE, PA
    BURIED: MOUNT TABOR [DRY RIDGE] ARMSTRONG COUNTY, PA
    WIFE: CAROLINE MILLER [8/6/1842-6/29/1913]   VETERAN
    BROTHER: JOHN C.; CO. A, JOHN C. CO. A
    PARENTS: CHRISTIAN & MAGDALENA FUERINGER
    REUNION KITTANNING 1901
SHAFFER, SAMUEL, SR. *   PVT   CO. F   AGE: 55
SHOFFER, SAMUEL, SR.   SHEFFER, SAMUEL, SR.
    SWORN: OCT 12, 1861/3 YRS   MEDICAL: SEP 8, 1862 @ PITTSBURGH
    BORN: FREEPORT, PA   OCCUPATION: LABORER
    HEIGHT: 5' 5"   COMPLEXION: SHALLOW EYES: BROWN   HAIR: GREY
    LAY ILL FOR EIGHT WEEKS OR MORE BEFORE DISCHARGE   WIFE: JANE
    1886 REUNION IN FREEPORT: HOME, BUTLER, PA
SHAFFER, SAMUEL, JR. *   PVT   CO. F   AGE: 20
SHAFER, SAMUEL   SHEFFER, SAMUEL, JR
    SWORN: OCT 12, 1861/3 YRS   MUSTER: NOV 4, 1864
    BORN: FREEPORT, PA   OCCUPATION: LABORER
    HEIGHT: 5' 9"   COMPLEXION: SHALLOW EYES: BLACK   HAIR: DARK BROWN
    HOME 1886: BELLEFONTE, PA   HOME 1897: ALLEGHENY CITY, PA
    REUNION IN FREEPORT 1886, INDIANA 1908
SHANAHAN, EDWARD #   PVT   CO. D
    SWORN: UNKNOWN   DIED: MAY 3, 1865
    BURIED @ NASHVILLE, ROW J, GRAVE #1567, BATES
SHANER, JOSEPH E.   PVT   CO. B   AGE:23
    SWORN: OCT 12, 1861/3 YRS   MUSTER: NOV 4, 1864
    BORN: ARMSTRONG COUNTY   OCCUPATION: BLACKSMITH
    HEIGHT: 5' 11"   COMPLEXION: DARK   EYES: BLACK   HAIR: BLACK
SHANER, PATRICK *   SGT   CO. B   AGE:27
SHARRER, PATRICK
    SWORN: OCT 12, 1861/3 YRS   DIED: JUL 1, 1864
    BORN: ARMSTRONG COUNTY   OCCUPATION: FARMER
    HEIGHT: 6' 1"   COMPLEXION: DARK   EYES: BLACK   HAIR: DARK
    DIED AT HOME AT PUTNEYVILLE, PA   BURIED PUTNEYVILLE CEMETERY
    DIED OF CONSUMPTION WHILE ON RECRUITING DUTY
SHANER, SAMUEL R.   PVT   CO. E   AGE: 20
    SWORN: OCT 12, 1861/3 YRS   MUSTER: NOV 4, 1864
    BORN: CLARION COUNTY   OCCUPATION: BLACKSMITH
    HEIGHT: 5' 9"   COMPLEXION: LIGHT   EYES: BLUE   HAIR: BROWN
    REUNION IN FREEPORT 1886, CHICKAMAUGA 1897

HOME 1886-1897: SALEM, CLARION COUNTY, PA
HOME 1914: LARMARTINE, PA

SHANNON, GEORGE B. *   PVT   CO. C
   OCCUPATION: TEACHER
   SWORN: MAR 29, 1864/3 YRS   MUSTER: SEP 11, 1865
   1890 CENSUS: WORTHVILLE, JEFFERSON COUNTY, PA

SHANNON, GEORGE W. *   PVT   CO. G   AGE: 22
   SWORN: AUG 30, 1862/3 YRS   DISCHARGED: JUN 19, 1865
   BORN: CLARION COUNTY   OCCUPATION: TEACHER
   HEIGHT: 5' 10"   COMPLEXION: FAIR   EYES: HAZEL   HAIR: BLACK
   REUNION KITTANNING 1901
   HOME 1901: WHITESBURG, ARMSTRONG COUNTY, PA

SHANNON, JAMES *   PVT   CO. G   AGE: 19
   SWORN: AUG 30, 1862 /3 YRS   DISCHARGED: JUN 19, 1865
   BORN: ARMSTRONG COUNTY   OCCUPATION: FARMER
   HEIGHT: 6' "   COMPLEXION: FAIR   EYES: BROWN   HAIR: DARK
   WOUNDED AT STONES RIVER/LEG TAKEN PRISONER AT STONES RIVER/PAROLED

SHANNON, JAMES E.   PVT   CO. C   AGE: 20
   SWORN: OCT 12, 1861/3 YRS   MEDICAL: APR 11, 1862
   BORN: CLARION COUNTY
   HEIGHT: 5' 9"   COMPLEXION: FAIR   EYES: BROWN   HAIR: BROWN

SHANNON, JOHN S.   PVT   CO. C   AGE: 18
   SWORN: OCT 12, 1861/3 YRS   MUSTER: NOV 4, 1864
   BORN: PENNSYLVANIA
   HEIGHT: 5' 8"   COMPLEXION: DARK   EYES: BLUE   HAIR: LIGHT

SHANNON, OLIVER *   PVT   CO. I   AGE:21
   SWORN: JAN 4, 1864/3 YRS   MUSTER: SEP 11, 1865
   BORN: WESTMORELAND COUNTY   OCCUPATION: BLACKSMITH
   HEIGHT: 5' 6"   COMPLEXION: FAIR   EYES: BLUE   HAIR: SANDY
   BURIED: SARDIS CEM, SALTSBURG RD [RT #286] SARDIS, WESTMORELAND CTY, PA.

SHARP, JOSEPH H. #   PVT   CO. A   AGE: 27
   SWORN: UNKNOWN   MUSTER: UNKNOWN
   HEIGHT: 6'   COMPLEXION: FAIR   EYES: BLUE   HAIR: BROWN
   LISTED IN ORIGINAL DISCRIPTIVE LIST; NOT IN ORIGINAL HISTORY

SHAW, CHARLES E. *   CPL   CO. F   AGE: 18
   SWORN: OCT 12, 1861/3 YRS   MUSTER: NOV 4, 1864
   BORN: FREEPORT, PA   OCCUPATION: COOPER
   HEIGHT: 5' 11"   COMPLEXION: SHALLOW   EYES: GREY   HAIR: LIGHT
   PROMOTED TO CPL, AUG 7, 1863

SHAW, LEWIS Z.   SGT   CO. D   AGE:32
SHAW, LEWIS D.
   SWORN: OCT 12, 1861/3 YRS   DIED: MAY 29, 1863 AT MURFREESBORO
   BORN: COOKPORT, PA   OCCUPATION: BLACKSMITH
   HEIGHT: 5' 9"   COMPLEXION: FAIR   EYES: BROWN
   PROMOTED FROM THIRD CPL, APR 11, 1863
   WOUNDED AT STONES RIVER
   BURIED AT NATIONAL CEMETERY STONES RIVER, GRAVE #O-5722

SHAY, JOHN *   PVT   CO. B
   SWORN: UNKNOWN   DIED: DEC 29,1864 AT NASHVILLE OF TYPHOID
   BURIED AT NATIONAL CEMETERY NASHVILLE, GRAVE #F-82

SHEA, THOMAS *   4TH CPL   CO. G   AGE:41
   SWORN: OCT 12, 1861/3 YRS   MUSTER: NOV 4, 1864
   BORN: ARMSTRONG COUNTY   OCCUPATION: TAILOR
   HEIGHT: 5' 11"   COMPLEXION: FAIR   EYES: BLUE   HAIR: GREY
   1890 CENSUS: RIMERSBURG, CLARION COUNTY, PA DIED: JAN 2, 1905

SHEARER, DANIEL *   PVT   CO. F   AGE: 20
SHARER, DANIEL
   SWORN: OCT 12, 1861/3 YRS   MUSTER: NOV 4, 1864
   BORN: SHEARER'S CROSS ROADS   OCCUPATION: LABORER
   HEIGHT: 5' 5½"   COMPLEXION: SHALLOW   EYES: GREY   HAIR: DARK BROWN
   DETAILED TO REGIMENTAL HOSPITAL AS A NURSE IN 1863
   1890 CENSUS: RIMERSBURG, CLARION COUNTY, PA; WIDOW ELIZABETH

SHEEN, PATRICK   PVT   CO. H   AGE:32
SHEAN, PATRICK   SHEEHAN, PATRICK   BOUNTY $27
    SWORN: JUL 25, 1863   MUSTER: SEP 11, 1865
    ENLISTED AT JOHNSTOWN, PA BY CAPT. BRINKER
    BORN: KERRY, IRELAND   OCCUPATION: LABORER
    HEIGHT: 5' 7" COMPLEXION: FAIR   EYES: GREY   HAIR: DARK
    GENERAL COURT MARTIAL DURING SERVICE CAUSED ABSENSE DURING FINAL MUSTER
SHEESLEY, AMONS   PVT   CO. A   AGE:20
SHEESLEY, AMOS
    SWORN: APR 8, 1863/1 YEAR   MUSTER: SEP 11, 1865
    BORN: HARRISBURG, PA   OCCUPATION: LABORER
    HEIGHT: 5' 5"   COMPLEXION: DARK   EYES: BLACK   HAIR: BLACK
SHEFFER, WILLIAM H. *   8TH CPL   CO. F   AGE:22
    SWORN: OCT 12, 1861/3 YRS   MUSTER: NOV 4, 1864
    HEIGHT: 5' 5½" COMPLEXION: DARK   EYES: BROWN   HAIR: BLACK
    BORN: FREEPORT   OCCUPATION: CARPENTER
    REUNION FREEPORT 1886, CHICKAMAUGA 1897, KITTANNING 1901, INDIANA 1908
    HOME 1886-1901: ALLEGHENY, PA
SHELDON, SAMUEL *   PVT   CO. F   AGE: 23
    SWORN: OCT 12, 1861/3 YRS   MUSTER: NOV 4, 1864
    BORN: FREEPORT, PA   OCCUPATION: ENGINEER
    HEIGHT: 5' 5"   COMPLEXION: DARK   EYES: BROWN   HAIR: DARK
    1886 REUNION IN FREEPORT: HOME, PETROLIA, PA
SHETLER, JOHN *   PVT   CO. A   AGE:18
SHETLE, JOHN
    SWORN: OCT 12, 1861/3 YRS   MUSTER: NOV 4, 1864
    HEIGHT: 5' 7½"
SHERMAN, JOHN *   PVT   CO. C   AGE: 21
    SWORN: AUG 21, 1862/3 YRS   DISCHARGED: JUN 19, 1865
    BORN: CLARION COUNTY   OCCUPATION: FARMER
    HEIGHT: 5' 8" COMPLEXION: DARK EYES: DARK   HAIR: DARK
    HOME 1890-1897: STRATTONVILLE, CLARION COUNTY
    ATTENDED THE DEDICATION OF THE CHICKAMAUGA BATTLEFIELD, NOV 1897
SHETLER, JOHN   PVT   CO. A   AGE:18
    SWORN: OCT 12, 1861/3 YRS   MUSTER: NOV 4, 1864
    BORN: ARMSTRONG COUNTY   OCCUPATION: FARMER
    HEIGHT: 5' 7½" COMPLEXION: DARK   EYES: GREY   HAIR: BROWN
SHETTLER, JOHN   PVT   CO. D   AGE:30
SHETTERS, JOHN   SHELTER, JOHN   VETERAN
    BORN IN GERMANY SEP 20, 1831
    SWORN: OCT 12, 1861/3 YRS   MEDICAL: JUN 23, 1862
    INDIANA COUNTY, HILLSDALE   OCCUPATION: FARMER
    HEIGHT: 5' 8" COMPLEXION: DARK   EYES: GREY
    REDUCED IN RANK FROM 8TH CPL
    RE-ENLISTED IN CO. E, PA 206TH INFANTRY 1863
    SWORN: AUG 25, 1864   MEDICAL: JUN 26, 1865
    DIED AND BURIED 1904, FRANKLIN COUNTY, ILLINOIS
SHICK, FREDERICK   PVT   CO. I
    SWORN: SEP 21, 1864/1 YRS   NOT AT FINAL MUSTER
SHIELDS, CORNELIUS JOHN *   PVT   CO. I
    BORN IN GERMANY
    SWORN: OCT 12, 1861/3 YRS   MUSTER: NOV 4, 1864
    HOME: 1890-1914: WORTHINGTON, ARMSTRONG COUNTY
    REUNION FREEPORT 1886, CHICKAMAUGA 1897, KITTANNING 1901
SHIELDS, JOSEPH D.   PVT   CO. A   AGE:19
    SWORN: OCT 12, 1861/3 YRS   MEDICAL: AUG 6, 1863
    BORN: INDIANA COUNTY   OCCUPATION: FARMER
    HEIGHT: 5' 6" COMPLEXION: DARK   EYES: BLACK HAIR: BLACK
SHIELDS, JOHN D. #   PVT   CO. A
    SWORN: UNKNOWN   DIED: AUG 9, 1863.
    THIS COULD POSSIBLY BE JOSEPH SHIELDS.
    BURIED AT NATIONAL CEMETERY NASHVILLE, GRAVE #C-340

SHIELDS, ROBERT *   PVT   CO. K   AGE: 18
    SWORN: OCT 12, 1861/3 YRS   MUSTER: NOV 4, 1864
    BORN: ARMSTRONG COUNTY   OCCUPATION: FARMER
    HEIGHT: 5' 10¼" COMPLEXION: FAIR   EYES: BLUE   HAIR: FAIR
    HOME 1886-1890: SLATE LICK, ARMSTRONG COUNTY, PA
    HOME 1897: BOGGSVILLE, ARMSTRONG COUNTY, PA
    REUNION FREEPORT 1886, CHICKAMAUGA 1897
SHINDLEDECKER, ADAM, JR   PVT   CO. C   AGE: 23
    SWORN: AUG 21, 1862/3 YEAR   DISCHARGED: JUN 19, 1865
    BORN: CLARION COUNTY   OCCUPATION: FARMER
    HEIGHT: 5' 6"   COMPLEXION: DARK EYES: BROWN   HAIR: BLACK
    BORN: OCT 9, 1838 IN RED BANK TO ADAM & UTILLA FIKE SHINDLEDECKER
    1890 CENSUS: WEST MILLVILLE, CLARION COUNTY, PA
    HOME 1897-1901: HAWTHORN, CLARION COUNTY, PA
    REUNION KITTANNING 1901
    BROTHER, JOHN IN SAME COMPANY; BROTHER VALENTINE ALSO SERVED
SHINDLEDECKER, F.   PVT   CO. C
SHINDLEDECKER, FULTON
    SWORN: SEP 21, 1864/1 YR   DISCHARGED: AUG 5, 1865
    1890 CENSUS: REYNOLDSVILLE, JEFFERSON COUNTY, PA
SHINDLEDECKER, JOHN   PVT   CO. C
    BORN: IN RED BANK TO ADAM & UTILLA FIKE SHINDLEDECKER
    SWORN: SEP 21, 1864/1 YR   DISCHARGED: JUN 19, 1865
    BROTHER, ADAM IN SAME COMPANY; BROTHER VALENTINE ALSO SERVED
    1890 CENSUS: CLARION, CLARION COUNTY, PA
SHINDLER, ADAM *   TEAMSTER   REGIMENTAL STAFF   AGE: 27
    SWORN: OCT 12, 1861/3YRS   MUSTER: NOV 4, 1864   BOUNTY: $100
    BORN: GERMANY   OCCUPATION: FARMER
    HEIGHT: 5' 10"   COMPLEXION: SANDY   EYES: BROWN   HAIR: BROWN
    ORIGINAL ENLISTMENT IN CO. H AS A TEAMSTER, DIED BEFORE 1905
SHIRLEY, JOHN F.   1ST MUS   CO. H   AGE:18
SHIRLEY, JOHN T.
    SWORN: OCT 12, 1861/3YRS   MUSTER: NOV 4, 1864   BOUNTY: $100.
    BORN: ARMSTRONG COUNTY   OCCUPATION: CLERK
    HEIGHT: 5' 8½"   COMPLEXION: LIGHT EYES: BROWN   HAIR: BROWN
    HOME IN 1897-1914: FREEPORT, PA
SHIRLEY, JOHN R.   PVT   CO. H   AGE:43
    SWORN: FEB 28, 1864/3 YRS   DISCHARGED: MAY 27, 1865
    ENLISTED AT OIL CITY, PA
    BURIED: SOUTH CEMETERY, BUTLER, PA
SHOMO, JOSEPH E. *   PVT   CO. B
SHOMER, JOSEPH E.
    SWORN: OCT 12, 1861/3 YRS   MUSTER: NOV 4, 1864
    HOME IN 1897: MANORVILLE, ARMSTRONG COUNTY, PA
    1890 CENSUS: KITTANNING, ARMSTRONG COUNTY, PA
SHULL, JOHN W.   PVT   CO. H   AGE:21
    SWORN: OCT 12, 1861/3YRS   MUSTER: NOV 4, 1864   BOUNTY: $100. .
    BORN: BUTLER COUNTY   OCCUPATION: COOPER
    HEIGHT: 5' 8½"   COMPLEXION: LIGHT EYES: GREY   HAIR: SANDY
    HOME IN 1897-1914: HARRISVILLE, BUTLER COUNTY, PA
    ATTENDED THE DEDICATION OF THE CHICKAMAUGA BATTLEFIELD, NOV 1897
SHULTZ, HENRY J.   PVT   CO. C   AGE: 24
    SWORN: OCT 12, 1861/3 YRS   MUSTER: NOV 4, 1864
    BORN: CLARION COUNTY
    HEIGHT: 5' 10"   COMPLEXION: FAIR   EYES: GREY   HAIR: BROWN
    HOME IN 1897: GROVE CITY, MERCER COUNTY, PA
SILL, CONRAD ***   PVT   CO. F   AGE: 23
SELL, CONRAD
    ORIGIN: BUTLER COUNTY
    SWORN: MAR 31, 1864/3 YRS   MUSTER: SEP 11, 1865
    HOSPITALIZED ON LOOKOUT MOUNTAIN
SILVIS, AMOS   PVT   CO. C   AGE: 30

BORN: IN RED BANK TO CONRAD AND ANNA NOLL SILVIS
SWORN: AUG 28, 1862/3 YRS   MEDICAL: FEB 18, 1864
BORN: CLARION COUNTY   OCCUPATION: SHOEMAKER
HEIGHT: 5' 8" COMPLEXION: FAIR EYES: BLUE HAIR: LIGHT
HOME 1890-1897: FAIRMOUNT CITY, CLARION COUNTY
HOME 1901: NEW BETHLEHEM, PA   REUNION KITTANNING 1901
BROTHERS: AMOS, JEREMIAH AND WILLIAM ALL IN CO. C

SILVIS, JEREMIAH *   PVT   CO. C   AGE: 19
BORN: IN RED BANK TO CONRAD AND ANNA NOLL SILVIS
SWORN: OCT 12, 1861/4 YRS   MUSTER: SEP 11, 1865   VETERAN
BORN: CLARION COUNTY
HEIGHT: 5' 10" COMPLEXION: FAIR EYES: GREY HAIR: BROWN
BROTHERS: AMOS, JEREMIAH AND WILLIAM ALL IN CO. C
1890 CENSUS: NEW BETHLEHEM, CLARION COUNTY, PA

SILVIS, JONATHAN *   PVT   CO. I   AGE: 18
SILVUS, JONATHAN   SYLVIS, JOHNATHAN
SWORN: SEP 13, 1862/3 YRS   MEDICAL: SEP 25, 1863
BORN: CLARION, PA   OCCUPATION: LABORER
HEIGHT: 6' COMPLEXION: FAIR EYES: GREY HAIR: LIGHT

SILVIS, WILLIAM   PVT   CO. C   AGE: 23
BORN: JUL 27, 1838 IN RED BANK TO CONRAD AND ANNA NOLL SILVIS
SWORN: OCT 12, 1861/3 YRS   MUSTER: NOV 4, 1864
BORN: CLARION COUNTY
HEIGHT: 5' 11" COMPLEXION: DARK EYES: BROWN HAIR: BROWN
HOME 1890-1897: NEW BETHLEHEM, CLARION COUNTY, PA
ATTENDED THE DEDICATION OF THE CHICKAMAUGA BATTLEFIELD, NOV 1897
BROTHERS: AMOS, JEREMIAH AND WILLIAM ALL IN CO. C

SIMPSON, CHARLES C.   PVT   CO. A   AGE:23
SWORN: OCT 12, 1861/3 YRS   MUSTER: NOV 4, 1864
BORN: ARMSTRONG COUNTY   OCCUPATION: FARMER
HEIGHT: 5' 7¼" COMPLEXION: DARK EYES: BLUE HAIR: BROWN
HOME 1890-1897: HORTON, INDIANA COUNTY, PA

SIMPSON, HENRY M. *   PVT   CO. A   AGE:20
SIMPSON, HENRY W.
SWORN: OCT 12, 1861/3 YRS   MUSTER: NOV 4, 1864
BORN: RURAL VALLEY, ARMSTRONG COUNTY   OCCUPATION: FARMER
HEIGHT: 5' 9" COMPLEXION: FAIR EYES: GREY HAIR: BROWN
DIED @ EVANSTON, WYOMING ON FEB 4, 1914 @ 73

SINDORF, JOHN *   PVT   CO. F   AGE: 22
BORN: SLATE LICK, PA   OCCUPATION: BLACKSMITH
HEIGHT: 5' 8" COMPLEXION: FRESH EYES: BLACK HAIR: DARK
SUFFERED FROM MUMPS DEC 1861
SWORN: OCT 12, 1861/3 YRS   MUSTER: NOV 4, 1864

SIPE, SOLOMON *   PVT   CO. K   AGE: 21
SIFE, SOLOMON
SWORN: OCT 12, 1861/3 YRS   MUSTER: NOV 4, 1864
BORN: BUTLER COUNTY   OCCUPATION: BLACKSMITH
HEIGHT: 5' 9" COMPLEXION: FAIR EYES: GREY HAIR: FAIR
WOUNDED AT STONES RIVER/THIGH
ADMITTED TO HOSPITAL #12, LOUISVILLE MAR 1, 1863
HOME 1914: FARRELL, WYOMING

SIRWELL, WILLIAM GRAHAM *   COL   REGIMENTAL COMMANDER   AGE:40
BORN: AUG 10, 1820 IN PITTSBURGH [LAWRENCEVILLE] PA   VETERAN
PENNSYLVANIA MILITIA 1840-1861
BORN: ALLEGHENY COUNTY   OCCUPATION: JEWELER
HEIGHT: 6' 2" COMPLEXION: DARK EYES: HAZEL HAIR: BLACK
SWORN: APR 22, 1861/3 MONTHS   CAPTAIN OF CO. B, NINTH PENNSYLVANIA
SIRWELL'S COMPANY WAS THE FIRST TO WAR IN ARMSTRONG COUNTY, 18 APR 1861
BROTHER-IN-LAW, SAM McCANDLESS IN PA EIGHTH RESERVES
NEPHEW, GEORGE McCANDLESS IN PA 78th
SWORN: OCT 12, 1861/3 YRS   MUSTER: NOV 4, 1864
OCCUPATION: JEWELER, WATCH MAKER.

COMMENDED BY GENERAL WILLIAM ROSECRANS AND COL JOHN MILLER FOR
BRAVERY AT STONES RIVER.
COMMENDED BY GENERAL GEORGE THOMAS AND GENERAL JAMES NEGLEY FOR
BRAVERY CHICKAMAUGA.
COMMENDED BY GENERAL GEORGE THOMAS AND COL BENJAMIN SCRIBNER FOR
BRAVERY AT PICKETT'S MILL.
ARRESTED NOV 30, 1862 BY ORDER OF GENERAL NEGLEY.
SIRWELL HAD PERMITTED MEN UNDER HIS COMMAND [MEN FROM THE 19TH ILLINOIS]
TO "STEAL" AND KILL SEVERAL HOGS AND TURKEYS.
PROMOTED TO BRIGADE COMMANDER JUN 19, 1863
RESIGNED: NOV 17, 1863   RE-COMMISSIONED: JAN 9, 1864
RAN, UNSUCCESSFULLY, FOR STATE SENATE IN SEPTEMBER 1865
FIRST PRESIDENT REGIMENTAL ASSOCIATION IN 1882
DIED: SEP 9, 1885 AT KITTANNING

SLABRY, WILLIAM H.R.   PVT   CO. B
   SWORN: OCT 12, 1861/3 YRS   MEDICAL: SEP 6, 1862
SLAGLE, DANIEL   PVT   CO. B   AGE:19
   SWORN: OCT 12, 1861/3 YRS   MUSTER: NOV 4, 1864
   BORN: ARMSTRONG COUNTY   OCCUPATION: FARMER
   HEIGHT: 5' 5"   COMPLEXION: LIGHT   EYES: BROWN   HAIR: DARK
   WOUNDED RIGHT EYE; ELKTON, ALABAMA JUL 1862;
   ULTIMATELY LOST SIGHT IN THAT EYE.
   WOUNDED/RIGHT FOREARM AT STONES RIVER: JAN 2, 1863, HOSPITALIZED NASHVILLE
   U.S. PENSION, 1894: $17.00
   1890 CENSUS: TEMPLETON, ARMSTRONG COUNTY, PA
   HOME 1894-1901: APOLLO, ARMSTRONG COUNTY, PA
   HOME 1908-1915: TEMPLETON, PA
   ATTENDED THE DEDICATION OF THE CHICKAMAUGA BATTLEFIELD, NOV 1897
   REUNION IN KITTANNING 1901
SLAGLE, JACOB   PVT   CO. B   AGE:18
   SWORN: OCT 12, 1861/3 YRS   MUSTER: NOV 4, 1864
   HEIGHT: 5' 4"   COMPLEXION: DARK   EYES: BROWN
   PROMOTED TO CPL, DATE UNKNOWN
   U.S. PENSION, 1894: $10.00   HOME: LEECHBURG
   MOST LIKELY JACOB AND JACOB A. SLAGLE ARE THE SAME MAN
SLAGLE, JACOB A. *   SGT   CO. B   AGE: 18
SLAGLE, JACOB   VETERAN
   SWORN: OCT 12, 1861/3 YRS   MUSTER: SEP 11, 1865
   BORN: ARMSTRONG COUNTY   OCCUPATION: FARMER
   HEIGHT: 5' 4"   COMPLEXION: DARK   EYES: BROWN   HAIR: DARK
   PROMOTED TO CPL, DATE UNKNOWN
   PROMOTED FROM CPL, TO SGT, FEB 2, 1864; CO. A Π
SLATER, EVAN W.   PVT   CO. E   AGE: 21
SLAYLOR, EVAN W.
   SWORN: OCT 12, 1861/3 YRS   DESERTED: 1863
   BORN: CLARION COUNTY   OCCUPATION: FARMER
   HEIGHT: 5' 9"   COMPLEXION: SANDY   EYES: GREY   HAIR: LIGHT
SLANGENHAUPT, B.   6TH CPL   CO. C   AGE:23
SLAUGHENHAUPT, B.F.   SLAUGENHAUPT, B.F.   SLANGENHAUPT, BENJAMIN FRANKLIN
   PARENTS: WILLIAM AND MARY SLAUGENHAUPT OF NEW BETHLEHEM, PA
   SWORN: OCT 12, 1861/3 YRS DIED: JAN 21, 1862 AT CAMP WOOD OF PNEUMONIA
   HEIGHT: 5' 8½"   COMPLEXION: DARK   EYES: BLUE
SLANGENHAUPT, G.   PVT   CO. C   AGE: 28
SLAUGENHAUPT, GIDEON   SCHLANGENHAUPT, G.
SCHLANGENHAUPT, GIDEON   VETERAN
   PARENTS: WILLIAM AND MARY SLAUGENHAUPT OF NEW BETHLEHEM, PA
   SWORN: OCT 12, 1861/3 YRS   MUSTER: SEP 11, 1865
   BORN: CLARION COUNTY
   HEIGHT: 5' 9½"   COMPLEXION: DARK   EYES: BROWN   HAIR: BLACK
   DIVISION TEAMSTER: NOV 6, 1863 - NOV 4, 1864
   DIED: OCT 7, 1879
   1890 CENSUS: FOXBURG, CLARION COUNTY, PA; WIDOW JEMIMA

WIFE: JEMIMA JENNIE DUNKLE   DIED: AUG 3, 1903
SLAUGENHAUPT, J. DANIEL   PVT   CO. E   AGE: 24
SLAUGENHAUPT, JOHN D.
    SWORN: OCT 12, 1861/3 YRS   KILLED: MAY 27, 1864 AT PICKETT'S MILL
    BORN: CLARION COUNTY   OCCUPATION: FARMER
    HEIGHT: 5' 8"   COMPLEXION: DARK   EYES: BROWN   HAIR: BLACK
SLAUGENHAUPT, J.A.   PVT   CO. E   AGE: 21
SLAGENHAUPT, JAMES A.   ORIGIN: MATILDAVILLE, CLARION COUNTY
    SWORN: OCT 12, 1861/3 YRS   MUSTER: NOV 4, 1864
    BORN: CLARION COUNTY   OCCUPATION: FARMER
    HEIGHT: 6' 2" WEIGHT: 132 lbs EYES: BLUE   HAIR: BLACK   COMPLEXION: FAIR
    HOME 1887: FRANKLIN, PA   PENSION: $6-12/MO   DIED: DEC 1900
    WIFE: NANCY JANE YINGLING
SLEASE, SAMUEL *   PVT   CO. G
    SWORN: FEB 2, 1864/3 YRS   MUSTER: SEP 11, 1865 ABSENT/SICK AT FINAL MUSTER
SLOCUM, ALBERT G.C.   PVT   CO. C   AGE: 28
    SWORN: AUG 28, 1862/3 YRS   TRANS: APR 13, 1865
    BORN: KENT, RI   OCCUPATION: GARDENER
    HEIGHT: 5' 7" COMPLEXION: FAIR EYES: BLUE   HAIR: LIGHT
    WOUNDED AT STONES RIVER/HAND
SLUSSER, JAMES M. *   6TH CPL   CO. F   AGE:21
    SWORN: OCT 12, 1861/3 YRS   DISCHARGED: OCT 15, 1864
    HEIGHT: 5' 9"   COMPLEXION: DARK   EYES: BROWN   HAIR: BLACK
    BORN: FREEPORT   OCCUPATION: PLASTERER
    SOME FAMILIES RECEIVED $100 BOUNTY UPON ENLISTMENT
    WOUNDED AT PICKETT'S MILL   HOME IN 1897: FREEPORT, PA
    1886 REUNION IN FREEPORT: HOME, FREEPORT, PA
    ATTENDED THE DEDICATION OF THE CHICKAMAUGA BATTLEFIELD, NOV 1897
SLUSSER, SAMUEL *   PVT   CO. F   AGE: 18
    SWORN: AUG 28, 1862/3 YRS   DIED: JAN 9, 1863
    SOME FAMILIES RECEIVED $100 BOUNTY UPON ENLISTMENT
    MORTALLY WOUNDED AT STONES RIVER/THIGH
    BURIED: ST. MARY'S, FREEPORT, PA
SMAIL, DANIEL *   PVT   CO. I   AGE: 36
SNAIL, DANIEL
    SWORN: OCT 12, 1861/3 YRS   MEDICAL: OCT 15, 1862
    BORN: LEECHBURG, PA   OCCUPATION: FARMER
    HEIGHT: 5' 9" COMPLEXION: SANDY EYES: GREY HAIR: DARK
    BURIED: ZION LUTHERAN CEMETERY, LEECHBURG; DIED BEFORE IN 1905
SMALL, PETER   PVT   CO. A   AGE:30
SMAIL, PETER
    SWORN: SEP 10, 1862/3 YRS   DISCHARGED: JUN 19, 1865   BOUNTY: $29
    BORN: WESTMORELAND COUNTY   OCCUPATION: FARMER
    HEIGHT: 5' 10"   COMPLEXION: DARK   EYES: BLUE   HAIR: BROWN
    BURIED: INDIANA COUNTY, ST. JOHN'S LUTHERAN, SOUTH MAHONING
SMETZER, JOHN *   PVT   CO. B   AGE:27
SMELTZER, JOHN   SMELTZEN, JOHN SMULTZER, JOHN
    SWORN: OCT 12, 1861/3 YRS   MEDICAL: SEP 6, 1862
    BORN: ARMSTRONG COUNTY   OCCUPATION: FARMER
    HEIGHT: 5' 10"   COMPLEXION: DARK   EYES: BLACK   HAIR: DARK
SMITH, ANDREW J. *   PVT   CO. B
    DRAFTED: SEP 21, 1864   DISCHARGED: JUN 19, 1865
    BURIED: APPLEBY MANOR PRESBYTERIAN CEMETERY, FORD CITY, PA
SMITH, CHARLES F.   SGT   CO. H   AGE:29
SMITH, CHARLES S.
    SWORN: OCT 12, 1861/3YRS   DISCHARGED: OCT 12, 1864
    BORN: BUTLER COUNTY   OCCUPATION: MINER
    HEIGHT: 5' 8¾"   COMPLEXION: LIGHT   EYES: GREY   HAIR: BROWN
    WOUNDED/HEAD AT STONES RIVER
    HOME 1897-1901: SARVERSVILLE, BUTLER COUNTY, PA
    HOME 1914: TARENTUM, ALLEGHENY COUNTY, PA
    REUNION KITTANNING 1901, INDIANA 1908.

SMITH, GEORGE D. *   PVT   CO. B   AGE:20
    SWORN: AUG 25, 1862/3 YRS   MUSTER: SEP 11, 1865
    HEIGHT: 5' 6½"   COMPLEXION: LIGHT
    BORN: MAR 8, 1841   DIED: JUN 20,1921 AT NEW BETHLEHEM, PA
    WOUNDED AT STONES RIVER, BAYONET WOUND RIGHT WRIST/12/31/62
    WOUNDED AT PICKETT'S MILL, HEAD WOUND
    PROMOTED TO CPL, NOV 4, 1864
    1890 CENSUS: RED BANK, ARMSTRONG COUNTY, PA
    HOME 1897: EDDYVILLE, ARMSTRONG COUNTY, PA
    HOME 1914: NEW BETHLEHEM, PA
    REUNION CHICKAMAUGA 1897, INDIANA 1908.
SMITH, GEORGE H.   PVT   CO. H   AGE:17
    SWORN: OCT 12, 1861/3YRS   DIED: FEB 26, 1862 AT "BELL'S FARM"
    CAMP FRY, KY OF TYPHOID FEVER
    BORN: OHIO   OCCUPATION: FARMER
    HEIGHT: 5' 9¼"   COMPLEXION: LIGHT EYES: BLUE   HAIR: LIGHT
SMITH, GEORGE M. *   PVT   CO. C   AGE: 19
    SWORN: JAN 23, 1864   MUSTER: SEP 11, 1865
    BORN: ARMSTRONG COUNTY   OCCUPATION: FARMER
    HEIGHT: 5' 8"   COMPLEXION: FAIR EYES: BLUE   HAIR: BROWN
SMITH, GEORGE W.   PVT   CO. H   AGE:21
    SWORN: FEB, 26, 1862/3 YRS   DISCHARGED: FEB 25, 1865
    BORN: BUTLER COUNTY   OCCUPATION: LABORER
    HEIGHT: 5' 7½"   COMPLEXION: FAIR EYES: GREY   HAIR: LIGHT
    HOME IN 1897: PUNXSUTAWNEY, JEFFERSON COUNTY, PA
    ATTENDED THE DEDICATION OF THE CHICKAMAUGA BATTLEFIELD, NOV 1897
SMITH, HENRY C.   PVT   CO. E   AGE: 24
    SWORN: OCT 12, 1861/3 YRS   MUSTER: NOV 4, 1864
    BORN: VENANGO COUNTY   OCCUPATION: TEACHER
    HEIGHT: 5' 8"   COMPLEXION: LIGHT   EYES: BLUE   HAIR: LIGHT
SMITH, JACOB C. *   PVT   CO. K   AGE: 27
    SWORN: OCT 12, 1861/3 YRS   DESERTED: APR 10, 1864 WHILE ON FURLOUGH
    BORN: GERMANY   OCCUPATION: FARMER
    HEIGHT: 5' 11½"   COMPLEXION: DARK   EYES: BROWN   HAIR: BLACK
    RE-ENLISTED AND DESERTED WHILE AT HOME ON VETERAN FURLOUGH
SMITH, JOSEPH B. *   CPT   CO. K   AGE: 41
    ORIGIN: ARMSTRONG COUNTY   JUL9, 1820-OCT 4, 1901
    SWORN: OCT 12, 1861/3 YRS   MUSTER: NOV 4, 1864
    ACTING REGIMENTAL QUARTERMASTER JUN 30, 1862 UNTIL PROMOTION
    PROMOTED TO CAPTAIN FEB 17, 1863   BRIGADE COMMISSARY 1863
    1890 CENSUS: NORTH BUFFALO, ARMSTRONG COUNTY, PA
SMITH, LEVI "HAM" *   PVT   CO. K   AGE:18
SMITH, LEVI HAMILTON
    SWORN: SEP 10, 1862/3 YRS   DISCHARGED: MAY 25, 1865
    BORN: ARMSTRONG COUNTY   OCCUPATION: FARMER
    HEIGHT: 5' 9½"   COMPLEXION: FAIR   EYES: GREY   HAIR: DARK
    BORN: ARMSTRONG COUNTY   BOUNTY: $29
    WOUNDED AT STONES RIVER
    SERVED AS GENERAL JOHN MILLER'S ORDERLY NOV 1864
    HOME 1914: RD #4; KITTANNING, PA   OCT 14, 1844-MAR 2, 1917
    REUNION KITTANNING 1901   HOME 1901: McHADDON, PA
SMITH, PHILIP *   CPL   CO. B   AGE:20
SMITH, PHILLIP
    SWORN: OCT 12, 1861/3 YRS   MUSTER: NOV 4, 1864
    BORN: ARMSTRONG COUNTY   OCCUPATION: FARMER
    HEIGHT: 5' 9"   COMPLEXION: LIGHT   EYES: GREY   HAIR: DARK
SMITH, RICHARD H. *   PVT   CO. K   AGE: 24
SMITH, RICHARD NORMAN   JAN 12, 1837-OCT 12, 1900
    SWORN: OCT 12, 1861/3 YRS   MUSTER: NOV 4, 1864
    BORN: ARMSTRONG COUNTY   OCCUPATION: FARMER
    HEIGHT: 5' 8½"   COMPLEXION: DARK   EYES: BROWN   HAIR: DARK
SMITH, RICHARD W. *   PVT   CO. K

SWORN: OCT 12, 1861/3 YRS   MUSTER: NOV 4, 1864
SMITH, ROBERT H. #   PVT   CO. K   AGE: 31
    SWORN: OCT 12, 1861/3 YRS   MUSTER: NOV 4, 1864
    BORN: JEFFERSON COUNTY   OCCUPATION: FARMER
    HEIGHT: 6' 2½"   COMPLEXION: FAIR   EYES: GREY   HAIR: AUBURN
    LISTED IN ORIGINAL ROSTER
SMITH, ROBERT M. *   MAJ   CO. K   AGE: 41
    ORIGIN: ARMSTRONG COUNTY   BORN: JUL 9, 1820
    SWORN: OCT 12, 1861/4 YRS   MUSTER: SEP 11, 1865   VETERAN
    BORN: ARMSTRONG COUNTY   OCCUPATION: CARPENTER
    HEIGHT: 5' 6"   COMPLEXION: FAIR   EYES: BLACK HAIR: BLACK
    AGE ON TOMBSTONE AND ENLISTMENT DIFFER; 26 ON ENLISTMENT vs. 41 ON STONE
    BATTLEFIELD PROMOTION FROM SGT JAN 2, 1863 TO 2ND LT
    COMMENDED BY SIRWELL FOR BRAVERY AT STONES RIVER
    PROMOTED TO CAPTAIN IN CO. B; SECOND ORGANIZATION, DEC 3, 1864
    PROMOTED TO MAJOR MAR 5, 1865; REGIMENTAL STAFF
    RESIDENT OF CHEROKEE, IOWA IN 1886
    DIED: OCT 4, 1901   BURIED: PRESBYTERIAN CEMETERY, SLATELICK, PA
SMITH, SAMUEL   PVT   CO. B   AGE:21
    SWORN: AUG 25, 1862/3 YRS   DISCHARGED: JUN 19, 1865
    BORN: ARMSTRONG COUNTY
    HEIGHT: 5' 10"   COMPLEXION: FAIR   EYES: BLUE   HAIR: LIGHT
    PO BOX 1914: NEW BETHLEHEM, PA [RD 4]
SMITH, SAMUEL S. *   PVT   CO. A   AGE: 23
    SWORN: OCT 12, 1861/4 YRS   MUSTER: SEP 11, 1865
    BORN: INDIANA COUNTY   OCCUPATION: FARMER
    HEIGHT: 5' 9"   COMPLEXION: DARK   EYES: GREY   HAIR: BROWN
    REUNION RECORDS STATE RANK OF 1SGT.
    HOME 1886: CLAY CENTER, KANSAS
    1890 CENSUS: RED BANK, ARMSTRONG COUNTY, PA
    HOME 1897-1901: EDDYVILLE, ARMSTRONG COUNTY, PA
    REUNION CHICKAMAUGA 1897, KITTANNING 1901
    BURIED: INDIANA COUNTY, MARION CENTER CEMETERY, 1845-1915
SMITH, WILLIAM *   PVT   CO. F   AGE: 18
    SWORN: OCT 12, 1861/3 YRS   MEDICAL: MAY 13, 1862
    BORN: SLATE LICK, PA   OCCUPATION: LABORER
    HEIGHT: 5' 4"   COMPLEXION: FRESH   EYES: GREY   HAIR: DARK BROWN
SMITH, WILLIAM A.   PVT   CO. H   AGE:23
    SWORN: OCT 12, 1861/3YRS   MUSTER: NOV 4, 1864   BOUNTY: $100.
    BORN: MERCER COUNTY   OCCUPATION: FARMER
    HEIGHT: 6'   COMPLEXION: LIGHT EYES: BLUE   HAIR: DARK
    HOME IN 1897: GROVE CITY, PA
    ATTENDED THE DEDICATION OF THE CHICKAMAUGA BATTLEFIELD, NOV 1897
SMITH, WILLIAM A.   PVT   CO. G
    SWORN: SEP 13, 1864   DISCHARGED: JUN 19, 1865
    SERVED UNDER SIRWELL
SMITH, WILLIAM W. ***   SGT   CO. K   AGE: 36
    SWORN: OCT 12, 1861/3 YRS   DIED: JAN 18, 1863
    BORN: ALLEGHENY COUNTY   OCCUPATION: TEACHER
    HEIGHT: 5' 10½"   COMPLEXION: DARK   EYES: BLACK HAIR: BLACK
    MORTALLY WOUNDED AT STONES RIVER/HEAD & THIGH DEC 31, 1862
    COMMENDED BY SIRWELL FOR BRAVERY AT STONES RIVER
    BURIED: SLATE LICK CEMETERY, SLATE LICK, PA
SMULLIN, HENRY *   PVT   CO. I   AGE:18
SMULLEN, HENRY
    SWORN: OCT 12, 1861/3 YRS   MUSTER: NOV 4, 1864
    BORN: CLARION, PA   OCCUPATION: LABORER
    HEIGHT: 5' 9½"   COMPLEXION: LIGHT   EYES: BLUE   HAIR: LIGHT
SNYDER, ALBERT *   PVT   CO. I   AGE: 22
    SWORN: SEP 5, 1862/3 YRS   DISCHARGED: JUN 19, 1865
    BORN: PITTSBURGH, PA   OCCUPATION: LABORER
    HEIGHT: 5' 5"   COMPLEXION: FAIR   EYES: GREY   HAIR: DARK

BROTHER WILLIAM SERVED IN THE PA 14th CAVALRY

SNYDER, CHRISTIAN   PVT   CO. E   AGE: 20
    SWORN: OCT 12, 1861/3 YRS   MIA: JAN 1, 1863 AT STONES RIVER
    BORN: WELSHIMO, GERMANY   OCCUPATION: SHOEMAKER
    HEIGHT: 5' 8"   COMPLEXION: LIGHT   EYES: BLUE   HAIR: BROWN

SNYDER, FREDERICK *   PVT   CO. I   AGE:21
    SWORN: OCT 12, 1861/3 YRS   MUSTER: NOV 4, 1864
    BORN: KITTANNING, PA   OCCUPATION: LABORER
    HEIGHT: 5' 10"   COMPLEXION: LIGHT   EYES: GREY   HAIR: DARK

SNYDER, JOHN   PVT   CO. E   AGE: 18
SNIDER, JOHN
    SWORN: OCT 12, 1861/3 YRS   MUSTER: NOV 4, 1864
    BORN: MERCER COUNTY   OCCUPATION: LABORER
    HEIGHT: 5' 7"   COMPLEXION: FAIR   EYES: BLUE   HAIR: LIGHT

SNYDER, JOHN S. *   PVT   CO. G
    SWORN: OCT 12, 1861/3 YRS   MUSTER: NOV 4, 1864
    1890 CENSUS: DAYTON BOROUGH, ARMSTRONG COUNTY, PA
    BURIED: DAYTON CEMETERY, DAYTON, PA

SNYDER, KIMBALL M.   PVT   CO. B   AGE:18
SNYDER, KIMBER M.
    SWORN: MAR 31, 1864   MUSTER: SEP 11, 1865
    BORN: ARMSTRONG COUNTY   OCCUPATION: FARMER
    HEIGHT: 5' 9"   COMPLEXION: LIGHT   EYES: BLUE   HAIR: LIGHT
    PROMOTED TO CPL, SECOND REGIMENT

SNYDER, THEODORE *   PVT   CO. I   AGE:18
    SWORN: OCT 12, 1861/3 YRS   MUSTER: NOV 4, 1864
    BORN: KITTANNING, PA   OCCUPATION: LABORER
    HEIGHT: 5' 8½"   COMPLEXION: DARK   EYES: BROWN   HAIR: DARK

SOLINGER, PERIS G. *   PVT   CO. K   AGE:19
SALINGER, PARIS G.
    SWORN: MAR 3, 1864/3 YRS   MUSTER: SEP 11, 1865
    BORN: BUTLER COUNTY   OCCUPATION: LABORER
    HEIGHT: 5' 8½"   COMPLEXION: DARK   EYES: DARK   HAIR: DARK

SONG, ADAM #   PVT   CO. A   AGE:20
    SWORN: MAR 31, 1864/ YRS   MUSTER: UNKNOWN
    BORN: LANCASTER COUNTY   OCCUPATION: FARMER
    HEIGHT: 5' 8¼"   COMPLEXION: LIGHT   EYES: HAZEL   HAIR: DARK
    LISTED IN ORIGINAL DISCRIPTIVE LIST; NOT IN ORIGINAL HISTORY

SONG, JACOB #   PVT   CO. I
    SWORN: SEP 16, 1861/3 YRS   MUSTER: NOV 4, 1864
    1890 CENSUS: MILLWOOD DISTRICT, WESTMORELAND COUNTY, PA

SOSSA, LEWIS *   PVT   CO. F   AGE: 26
SARSE, LEWIS   ORIGIN: BUTLER COUNTY
    SWORN: OCT 12, 1861/3 YRS   KILLED: DEC 31, 1862 AT STONES RIVER
    BORN: FREEPORT, PA   OCCUPATION: LABORER
    HEIGHT: 5' 7"   COMPLEXION: DARK   EYES: BLACK   HAIR: DARK BROWN
    BURIED AT NATIONAL CEMETERY STONES RIVER, GRAVE #L-4647

SOUTHWORTH, JERRY *   PVT   CO. K   AGE:21
    SWORN: OCT 12, 1861/3 YRS   MUSTER: NOV 4, 1864
    BORN: BUTLER COUNTY   OCCUPATION: LABORER
    HEIGHT: 5' 6¼" COMPLEXION: FAIR   EYES: BROWN HAIR: DARK
    PRISONER AT STONES RIVER/PAROLED; HOSPITALIZED, SEP 16, 1863
    BURIED: OLD PRESBYTERIAN CEMETERY [ELGIN CEMETERY], COWANSHANNOCK TWP.,
    ARMSTRONG COUNTY

SOWERS, HENRY *   PVT   CO. G   AGE: 18
    SWORN: SEP 13, 1862/3 YRS   DIED: MAY 11, 1863 AT MURFREESBORO
    BORN: ARMSTRONG COUNTY   OCCUPATION: FARMER
    HEIGHT: 6'   COMPLEXION: FAIR   EYES: GREY   HAIR: FAIR
    BURIED AT NATIONAL CEMETERY STONES RIVER, GRAVE #O-5904
    MEMORIAL: OLD PRESBYTERIAN CEMETERY, COWANSHANNOCK TWP., ARMSTRNG CTY
    WIFE: SUSANAH; MAR 15, 1825 - NOV 15, 1851

SOWERS, JOHN N. *   PVT   CO. G   AGE: 19

SOWERS, JOSEPH N.   BORN: 9 APR 1843
    SWORN: AUG 30, 1862 /3 YRS   DISCHARGED: JUN 19, 1865
    BORN: ARMSTRONG COUNTY   OCCUPATION: FARMER
    HEIGHT: 6' 2"   COMPLEXION: FAIR   EYES: BROWN   HAIR: DARK
    WOUNDED AT STONES RIVER   HOME IN 1897: BLANCO, ARMSTRONG COUNTY, PA
    1890 CENSUS:COWANSHANNOCK TWP., ARMSTRONG COUNTY, PA
    REUNION CHICKAMAUGA 1897, KITTANNING 1901, INDIANA 1908.
    HOME 1901-1914: YATESBORO, PA
    BURIED: MARGARET, PA   DIED: 26 JUN 1918
SOWERS, SAMUEL H. *   PVT   CO. G
    SWORN: OCT 12, 1861/3 YRS   MUSTER: NOV 4, 1864
    HOME IN 1897: GREENDALE, ARMSTRONG COUNTY, PA
    1890 CENSUS: GREENDALE, ARMSTRONG COUNTY, PA
    HOME 1914: RD #2, KITTANNING, PA
    ATTENDED THE DEDICATION OF THE CHICKAMAUGA BATTLEFIELD, NOV 1897
SOWERS, WILLIAM *   PVT   CO. G   AGE: 23
    SWORN: OCT 12, 1861/3 YRS   MUSTER: NOV 4, 1864
    1890 CENSUS: MANORVILLE, ARMSTRONG COUNTY, PA
    HOME IN 1897: ATWOOD, ARMSTRONG COUNTY, PA
    ATTENDED THE REGIMENTAL REUNION AT INDIANA, PA, IN 1908.
    BURIED: ATWOOD CEMETERY, COWANSHANNOCK, ARMSTRONG COUNTY, 1838-1913
SOXMAN, HENRY F. *   PVT   CO. G
    SWORN: OCT 12, 1861/3 YRS   MUSTER: NOV 4, 1864
    WOUNDED AT STONES RIVER DEC 31, 1862/THIGH
SPANGLER, ABRAHAM *   PVT   CO. K   AGE: 20
    SWORN: OCT 12, 1861/3 YRS   DIED: JAN 4, 1862
    BORN: ARMSTRONG COUNTY   OCCUPATION: FARMER
    HEIGHT: 5' 9¾"   COMPLEXION: FAIR   EYES: BLUE   HAIR: FAIR
    BURIED: NATIONAL CEMETERY LOUISVILLE; SECTION.A, RANGE.3, GRAVE.1
SPENCER, HIRAM L. *   PVT   CO. A
    SWORN: FEB 17,1864/3 YRS   MEDICAL: FEB 26, 1865
    1890 CENSUS: DAYTON BOROUGH, ARMSTRONG COUNTY, PA
SPENCER, JOHN J. *   PVT   CO. B   AGE:18
SPENCES, JOHN J.
    SWORN: OCT 12, 1861/3 YRS   MUSTER: NOV 4, 1864
    BORN: ARMSTRONG COUNTY   OCCUPATION: FARMER
    HEIGHT: 5' 4"   COMPLEXION: LIGHT   EYES: BLUE   HAIR: LIGHT
    WOUNDED/HIPS AT STONES RIVER
SPENCER, PETER **   PVT   CO. A
    SWORN: SEP 15, 1864/3 YRS   DISCHARGE: JUN 19, 1865
    1890 CENSUS: KITTANNING, ARMSTRONG COUNTY, PA; WIDOW MARY
SPICE, JOHN *   PVT   CO. B   AGE:19
SPECIE, JOHN   SPACE, JOHN
    SWORN: OCT 12, 1861/3 YRS   TRANS: 4TH CAV, DEC 1, 1862.
    BORN: ARMSTRONG COUNTY   OCCUPATION: FARMER
    HEIGHT: 5' 11"   COMPLEXION: LIGHT   EYES: GREY   HAIR: LIGHT
SPIKER, CHRISTIAN   PVT   CO. C   AGE: 33
SPIKER, CHRISTOPHER
    SWORN: OCT 12, 1861/3 YRS   DIED: AUG 31, 1862 AT NASHVILLE
    BORN: CLARION COUNTY
    HEIGHT: 5' 9"   COMPLEXION: DARK   EYES: GREY   HAIR: BLACK
    BURIED @ NASHVILLE, ROW A, GRAVE #655, BATES
SPROUL, WILLIAM J.*   PVT   CO. F   AGE: 23
SPROULL, WILLIAM J.
    SWORN: OCT 12, 1861/3 YRS   MEDICAL: DEC 19, 1863
    BORN: FREEPORT, PA   OCCUPATION: LABORER
    HEIGHT: 5' 9"   COMPLEXION: FRESH   EYES: GREY   HAIR: DARK BROWN
    HOSPITALIZED DEC 1862   DIED: AT PARNASSUS, BEFORE 1905
    ATTENDED 1886 REUNION IN FREEPORT
    HOME 1886-1890: PARNASSUS, WESTMORELAND COUNTY, PA
STACKPOLE, JAMES B. #   PVT   CO. H
    SWORN: UNKNOWN   DIED: MAR 23, 1865

BURIED @ NASHVILLE, ROW R, GRAVE #248, BATES
STAHL, SAMUEL, I   PVT   CO. D   AGE: 21
    SWORN: OCT 12, 1861/3 YRS   MUSTER: NOV 4, 1864
    BORN: INDIANA COUNTY, CHERRY TREE   OCCUPATION: LUMBERMAN
    HEIGHT: 5' 10"   COMPLEXION: DARK   EYES: GREY   HAIR: BROWN
    SERVED IN CAVALRY SQUAD, 1863
STAHL, SAMUEL, II   PVT   CO. D   AGE: 19
    SWORN: OCT 12, 1861/3 YRS   TRANS: DEC 1, 1862 TO 4TH CAV
    BORN: INDIANA COUNTY, CHERRY TREE   OCCUPATION: LUMBERMAN
    HEIGHT: 6' 1"   COMPLEXION: FAIR   EYES: GREY   HAIR: BROWN
    CAPTURED NEAR SELMA, ALABAMA; DIED AT ANDERSONVILLE
    IMPRISONED @ ANDERSONVILLE
STAHLMAN, HARRISON   SGT   CO. C   AGE: 19
STUHLMAN, HARRISON
    SWORN: OCT 12, 1861/3 YRS   KILLED: MAY 27, 1864 AT PICKETT'S MILL
    BORN: CLARION COUNTY
    HEIGHT: 5' 11"   COMPLEXION: FAIR   EYES: BLUE   HAIR: BROWN
STAHLLMAN, GEORGE W.   PVT   CO. B
    SWORN: SEP 21, 1864/3 YRS   DISCHARGED: JUN 19, 1865
    SERVICE: GUARD DUTY, NASHVILLE 1865
STALEY, WILLIAM H.R. *   PVT   CO. B   AGE:35
STALEY, WILLIAM W.
    SWORN: OCT 12, 1861/3 YRS   DISCHARGED: SEP 6, 1862
    HEIGHT: 6' 1"   COMPLEXION: LIGHT   EYES: BLUE   HAIR: LIGHT
STARK, JOSEPH M.P. *   PVT   CO. I   AGE:26
    SWORN: OCT 12, 1861/3 YRS   DIED: MAR 14, 1862 AT NASHVILLE
    BORN: WHITESBURG, PA   OCCUPATION: CARPENTER
    HEIGHT: 6' 1¼"   COMPLEXION: SANDY   EYES: GREY   HAIR: DARK
    BURIED AT NATIONAL CEMETERY NASHVILLE, GRAVE #L-602
STARK, ROBERT B. *   PVT   CO. I   AGE:19
    SWORN: OCT 12, 1861/3 YRS   DIED: DEC 6, 1862 AT CAMP NEGLEY
    BORN: WHITESBURG, PA   OCCUPATION: CARPENTER
    HEIGHT: 6'   COMPLEXION: DARK   EYES: GREY   HAIR: DARK
    BURIED @ CAVE HILL CEMETERY, LOUISVILLE, DIV 4, ROW D, GRAVE # 54
STAUFFER, JOHN   CPL   CO. A   AGE:21
STAUFFER, JOHN W.
    SWORN: OCT 12, 1861/3 YRS   MUSTER: NOV 4, 1864
    BORN: HUNTINGTON COUNTY   OCCUPATION: FARMER
    HEIGHT: 6'   COMPLEXION: DARK   EYES: GREY   HAIR: BROWN
    PROMOTED TO CPL
    REUNION CHICKAMAUGA 1897, INDIANA 1908.
    HOME 1886: PUNXSUTAWNEY, PA
    HOME 1897: LINDSEY, JEFFERSON COUNTY, PA
    HOME 1914: BOX 254, JEANETTE, PA
STUTTS, ALEXANDER #   PVT   CO. K
    SWORN: UNKNOWN   DIED: AUG 16, 1865
    BURIED @ NASHVILLE, BATES
STEAR, JOHN K.   PVT   CO. A   AGE:19
STEER, JOHN K.
    SWORN: OCT 12, 1861/3 YRS   MUSTER: NOV 4, 1864
    BORN: INDIANA COUNTY   OCCUPATION: FARMER
    HEIGHT: 5' 10"   COMPLEXION: DARK   EYES: GREY   HAIR: BROWN
    HOME 1914: COZAD, NEBRASKA
STEELE, SAMUEL R.**   PVT   CO. K   AGE:14
    LIED ABOUT AGE UPON ENLISTMENT
    SWORN: OCT 17, 1861/4 YRS   MUSTER: SEP 11, 1865
    BORN: ARMSTRONG COUNTY   OCCUPATION: FARMER
    HEIGHT: 5' 8"   COMPLEXION: FAIR   EYES: BLACK   HAIR: BROWN
    BORN: ARMSTRONG COUNTY, APR 1, 1847   VETERAN
    FARMER AFTER THE WAR [W.R. WILSON, GRANDSON; 3/10/95]
    REUNION FREEPORT 1886, CHICKAMAUGA 1897, INDIANA 1908.
    ATTENDED GAR DINNER MAY 30, 1927 IN TARENTUM, PA

        HOME 1886-1936: SLATE LICK, ARMSTRONG COUNTY, PA
        ONE OF "THE LAST DOZEN" LIVING IN ARMSTRONG COUNTY IN 1936
        HOME/1927: FREEPORT, PA   DIED DEC 27, 1936
        BURIED: SLATELICK CEMETERY, SLATELICK, PA
STEPP, LEVI *   SGT   CO. K   AGE:20
STEP, LEVI   STET, LEVI   VETERAN
        BORN: JAN 9, 1842, BUTLER COUNTY TO MICHAEL & CATHERINE HECKERT
        MOVED TO ARMSTRONG COUNTY IN 1859
        SWORN: OCT 12, 1861/4 YRS   MUSTER: SEP 11, 1865
        BORN: BUTLER COUNTY   OCCUPATION: LABORER
        HEIGHT: 5' 8"   COMPLEXION: DARK   EYES: GREY   HAIR: DARK
        WOUNDED AT STONES RIVER
        PROMOTED FROM PRIVATE TO SERGEANT; CO. B Π
        U.S. PENSION, 1894: $4.00   HOME: WORTHINGTON
        ATTENDED 1886 REUNION IN FREEPORT
        PO BOX 1886-1914: WORTHINGTON, PA
        BROTHERS: LEVI AND WILLIAM H.H. BOTH IN PA 78th
        COUSIN WILLIAM IN PA 14th CAVALRY
        BLACKSMITH IN SLATE LICK AFTER THE WAR.
        INNKEEPER IN WORTHINGTON "STEPP HOUSE"
        WIFE: MARY FERRY; FATHER-IN-LAW, FERRY, JOHN C. PVT/139th, CO. C
        REUNION KITTANNING 1901, INDIANA 1908
STEPP, WILLIAM H.H. *   1LT   CO. K   AGE: 21
STEP, WILLIAM H.H.
        PARENTS MICHAEL & CATHERINE HECKERT
        MOVED TO ARMSTRONG COUNTY IN 1859
        SWORN: OCT 12, 1861/4 YRS   MUSTER: SEP 11, 1865
        BORN: BUTLER COUNTY   OCCUPATION: CARPENTER
        HEIGHT: 5' 11½"   COMPLEXION: DARK   EYES: BLUE   HAIR: AUBURN
        PROMOTED TO 2LT CO. B Π, MAR 15, 1865; TO 1LT AUG 7, 1865
        U.S. PENSION, 1894: $4.00   HOME: SLATE LICK
        DIED: AT SLATELICK, PA, 1900
        BROTHERS: LEVI AND WILLIAM H.H. BOTH IN PA 78th
        COUSIN WILLIAM IN PA 14th CAVALRY   VETERAN
STEPHENS, JOHN C.   PVT   CO. D   AGE: 18
        SWORN: OCT 12, 1861/3 YRS   MUSTER: NOV 4, 1864
        BORN: INDIANA COUNTY   OCCUPATION: LABORER
        HEIGHT: 5' 6"   COMPLEXION: DARK   EYES: GREY   HAIR: DARK
        1886 REUNION IN FREEPORT: HOME, NEW FLORENCE, PA
        HOME 1890-1897: NEW FLORENCE, WESTMORELAND COUNTY, PA
        ATTENDED THE DEDICATION OF THE CHICKAMAUGA BATTLEFIELD, NOV 1897
        DIED BEFORE THE REGIMENTAL HISTORY WAS PUBLISHED IN 1905
        BURIED: INDIANA COUNTY, LURAL HILLS FURNACE, FLORENCE
STERNTS, PETER   PVT   CO. E   AGE: 44
        SWORN: MAR 21, 1864/3 YRS   DIED: JUL 9, 1864 AT NASHVILLE
        BORN: WESTMORELAND COUNTY   OCCUPATION: FARMER
        HEIGHT: 5' 8"   COMPLEXION: DARK   EYES: HAZEL   HAIR: DARK
STEWART, ALEXANDER K.   PVT   CO. A   AGE: 45
        SWORN: MAR 31, 1864/3 YRS   MUSTER: SEP 11, 1865
        NEPHEW JOHN R. STEWART OF CO. A IN REGIMENT
        1890 CENSUS: DAVIS, INDIANA COUNTY, PA
        BURIED: INDIANA COUNTY, WASHINGTON CEMETERY, RAYEN TWP., 1819-JAN 11, 1898
STEWART, ALLEN   PVT   CO. E
        SWORN: JAN 3, 1862/3 YRS   MUSTER: SEP 11, 1865   VETERAN
        HOME 1890-1897: TOBY, CLARION COUNTY, PA   DIED: INDIANA COUNTY, PA
        DIED BEFORE THE REGIMENTAL HISTORY WAS PUBLISHED IN 1905
        ATTENDED THE DEDICATION OF THE CHICKAMAUGA BATTLEFIELD, NOV 1897
STEWART, CHRISTOPHER ***   PVT   CO. F   AGE: 35
        SWORN: AUG 6, 1864/3 YRS   DISCHARGED: JUN 19, 1865
        BORN: BUTLER, PA   OCCUPATION: FARMER
        HEIGHT: 5' 9"   COMPLEXION: FLORID   EYES: GREY   HAIR: DARK
STEWART, JOHN R.   PVT   CO. A   AGE:23

SWORN: OCT 12, 1861/4 YRS   MUSTER: SEP 11, 1865   VETERAN
BORN: INDIANA COUNTY   OCCUPATION: FARMER
HEIGHT: 5' 9½"   COMPLEXION: LIGHT   EYES: GREY   HAIR: LIGHT
UNCLE ALEXANDER K. STEWART OF CO. A IN REGIMENT
ATTENDED REUNION IN FREEPORT 1886; INDIANA 1908
HOME 1886-1914: PLUMVILLE, INDIANA COUNTY, PA
BURIED: INDIANA COUNTY, BARACHA CEMETERY, SOUTH MAHONING, 1838-APR 8, 1917
STEWART, JOHN ROBERT #   SGT   CO. A
BORN IN IRELAND
SWORN: OCT 12, 1861/4 YRS   MUSTER: SEP 11, 1865
HEIGHT: 5' 9½"   COMPLEXION: LIGHT
PROMOTED FROM CPL JUN 29, 1865   VETERAN
HOME 1886-1897: PLUMVILLE, INDIANA COUNTY, PA
ATTENDED THE DEDICATION OF THE CHICKAMAUGA BATTLEFIELD, NOV 1897
STIFFLER, WILLIAM   PVT   CO. D   AGE: 18
STIFFLER, WILLIAM T.
SWORN: OCT 12, 1861/3 YRS   MUSTER: NOV 4, 1864
BORN: INDIANA COUNTY, CHERRY TREE   OCCUPATION: LUMBERMAN
HEIGHT: 5' 8" COMPLEXION: DARK   EYES: BROWN   HAIR: DARK
1890 CENSUS: PURCHASE LINE, INDIANA COUNTY, PA
HOME IN 1897: GRANT, INDIANA COUNTY, PA
DIED: 1907 AT GLEN CAMPBELL, PA
ATTENDED THE DEDICATION OF THE CHICKAMAUGA BATTLEFIELD, NOV 1897
CAVALRY SERVICE DURING 1863
BURIED: INDIANA CTY, IOOF CEMETERY, CHERRY TREE, MONTGOMERY TWP., 1845-1908
STITT, JAMES H. *   CPL   CO. I   AGE:19
SWORN: OCT 12, 1861/3 YRS   MUSTER: NOV 4, 1864
BORN: LEECHBURG, PA   OCCUPATION: STUDENT
HEIGHT: 5' 11"   COMPLEXION: LIGHT   EYES: BLUE   HAIR: DARK
PROMOTED TO CPL, APR 30, 1863; DIED BEFORE 1905
STIVENSON, GEORGE   PVT   CO. I   AGE:18
STIVENSON, GEORGE W.   STEVENSON, GEORGE
SWORN: OCT 12, 1861/3 YRS   MUSTER: NOV 4, 1864
BORN: LEECHBURG, PA   OCCUPATION: FARMER
HEIGHT: 5' 6½"   COMPLEXION: DARK   EYES: GREY   HAIR: DARK
DIED BEFORE THE REGIMENTAL HISTORY WAS PUBLISHED IN 1905
BURIED: APOLLO CEMETERY, APOLLO, PA
STIVERS, ABRAM *   PVT   CO. F   AGE: 19
SWORN: AUG 28, 1862/3 YRS   DIED: NOV 25, 1863 AT NASHVILLE
BORN: LUZERNE COUNTY, PA   OCCUPATION: LABORER
HEIGHT: 5' 7"   COMPLEXION: FAIR   EYES: GREY   HAIR: DARK BROWN
BURIED AT NATIONAL CEMETERY NASHVILLE, GRAVE #B-1213
STOKES, SIMON *   PVT   CO. C   AGE:29
SWORN: OCT 12, 1861/3 YRS   MEDICAL: MAY 13, 1863
HEIGHT: 5' 11"   COMPLEXION: FAIR   EYES: GREY
DEMOTED FROM FIRST CPL
TRANSFERRED FROM NASHVILLE TO LOUISVILLE HOSPITAL MAR 9, 1863
REUNION IN FREEPORT 1886, KITTANNING 1901
HOME 1886: HULTON, PA
HOME 1890-1914: PUNXSUTAWNEY, JEFFERSON COUNTY, PA
STONE, SYLVESTER C.   PVT   CO. C   AGE: 19
SWORN: MAR 21, 1864/3 YRS   MUSTER: SEP 11, 1865
BORN: ALLEGHENY, NY   OCCUPATION: LABORER
HEIGHT: 5' 9"   COMPLEXION: DARK   EYES: GREY   HAIR: BLACK
BATTLES: RESACA, PICKETT'S MILL, BUZZARD'S ROOST II
SERVICE: GUARD DUTY, NASHVILLE 1865
STORVERS, SIMEON   PVT   CO. C   AGE: 23
STOWERS, SIMEON
SWORN: OCT 12, 1861/3 YRS   MUSTER: NOV 4, 1864
BORN: CLARION COUNTY
HEIGHT: 5' 9"   COMPLEXION: DARK   EYES: BLUE   HAIR: LIGHT
HOME IN 1897: OAKMONT, PA

ATTENDED THE DEDICATION OF THE CHICKAMAUGA BATTLEFIELD, NOV 1897
STOUGHTON, THOMAS J.   PVT   CO. H   AGE:20
SLOUGHTON, THOMAS J.   DIED BEFORE 1905
    SWORN: OCT 12, 1861/3YRS   MEDICAL: MAY 20, 1863
    BORN: BUTLER COUNTY   OCCUPATION: FARMER
    HEIGHT: 5' 6½"   COMPLEXION: LIGHT EYES: BLUE   HAIR: LIGHT
STREET, WILLIAM *   PVT   CO. F   AGE: 18
    SWORN: OCT 12, 1861/3 YRS   MUSTER: NOV 4, 1864
    BORN: SUCCESS, PA   OCCUPATION: COLLIER
    HEIGHT: 5' 7½"   COMPLEXION: FRESH EYES: BLUE   HAIR: BROWN
    BRIEFLY MISSING IN ACTION AT STONES RIVER
STROKLEY, JAMES L.   PVT   CO. H   AGE:18
STOKELEY, JAMES L.
    BORN: ALLEGHENY COUNTY   OCCUPATION: FARMER
    HEIGHT: 5' 5"   COMPLEXION: DARK EYES: BLACK HAIR: DARK
    SWORN: OCT 12, 1861/3YRS   MUSTER: NOV 4, 1864   BOUNTY: $100.
    DIED: AT PITTSBURGH, JUL 1877
STROYICK, JOHN G.***   PVT   CO. K   AGE: 25
STRAYICK, JOHN G.   STRAYEIK, JOHN K.
    SWORN: OCT 12, 1861/3 YRS   MEDICAL: AUG 29, 1863
    BORN: PITTSBURGH   OCCUPATION: MILLER
    HEIGHT: 5' 5¾"   COMPLEXION: FAIR   EYES: GREY   HAIR: FAIR
    TAKEN PRISONER AT STONES RIVER/PAROLED AT VICKSBURG
    HOME 1914: HOT SPRINGS, SD
STUART, ARCHIBALD M. *   PVT   CO. B   AGE:20
STEWART, ARCHIBALD M.
    SWORN: OCT 12, 1861/3 YRS   MUSTER: NOV 4, 1864
    BORN: ARMSTRONG COUNTY   OCCUPATION: FARMER
    HEIGHT: 5' 6"   COMPLEXION: LIGHT   EYES: GREY   HAIR: LIGHT
    1890 CENSUS: SCHENLEY, ARMSTRONG COUNTY, PA
STUART, GEORGE W.***   PVT   CO. K   AGE:20
STEWART, GEORGE W.
    SWORN: OCT 12, 1861/3 YRS   MUSTER: NOV 4, 1864
    BORN: ALLEGHENY COUNTY   OCCUPATION: LABORER
    HEIGHT: 5' 9"   COMPLEXION: FAIR   EYES: BLUE   HAIR: FAIR
    1890 CENSUS: KELLERSBURG, MADISON TWP., ARMSTRONG COUNTY, PA
    HOME 1914: CLIMAX, CLARION COUNTY, PA
STUCHAL SAMUEL   PVT   CO. D   AGE: 22
    SWORN: OCT 12, 1861/3 YRS   DIED: DEC 16, 1861 AT LOUISVILLE
    BORN: INDIANA COUNTY   OCCUPATION: FARMER
    HEIGHT: 5' 4½"   COMPLEXION: DARK   EYES: GREY   HAIR: BROWN
    BURIED: NATIONAL CEMETERY LOUISVILLE; SECTION.A, RANGE.2, GRAVE.15
SUGOSS, ADAM   PVT   CO. B
    SWORN: FEB 24, 1864/3YRS   MUSTER: SEP 11, 1865
    1890 CENSUS: NEW MAYSVILLE, CLARION COUNTY, PA
SULLIVAN, MARK *   CPL   CO. B   AGE:23
    SWORN: OCT 12, 1861/3 YRS   MUSTER: NOV 4, 1864
    BORN: IRELAND   OCCUPATION: MOULDER
    HEIGHT: 6'   COMPLEXION: LIGHT   EYES: BLUE   HAIR: LIGHT
    WOUNDED/LEG AT STONES RIVER
    REPRIMANDED BY LT. COL BLAKELEY JAN 17, 1864
    1890 CENSUS: BLANKET HILL, ARMSTRONG COUNTY, PA
SULLIVAN, MICHAEL *   PVT   CO. F   AGE:32
    SWORN: OCT 12, 1861/3 YRS   DIED: JAN 13, 1863
    BORN: FREEPORT, PA   OCCUPATION: LABORER
    HEIGHT: 5' 8½"   COMPLEXION: DARK   EYES: BLUE   HAIR: DARK BROWN
    BORN: FREEPORT   DEMOTED FROM 4TH CPL
    MORTALLY WOUNDED AT STONES RIVER/LEG
    BURIED AT NATIONAL CEMETERY NASHVILLE, GRAVE #B-45
SUMMERVILLE, SAMUEL M. *   PVT   CO. K   AGE: 21
    SWORN: OCT 12, 1861/3 YRS   MUSTER: NOV 4, 1864
    BORN: ARMSTRONG COUNTY   OCCUPATION: FARMER

HEIGHT: 5' 7½"   COMPLEXION: FAIR   EYES: BLUE   HAIR: FAIR
HOME IN 1897: MERWIN, WESTMORELAND COUNTY, PA
HOME 1914: KELLY & HALE STS, PITTSBURGH, PA
SUPPLEE, PETER *   PVT   CO. F   AGE: 27
SUPLEE, PETER
    SWORN: OCT 12, 1861/3 YRS   MUSTER: NOV 4, 1864
    BORN: WAYNESBURG, PA   OCCUPATION: FARMER
    HEIGHT: 5' 6"   COMPLEXION: FRESH   EYES: BROWN   HAIR: BROWN
    WOUNDED AT STONES RIVER DEC 31, 1862/BACK
    1886 REUNION IN FREEPORT: HOME, SUPLEE, PA
SUXFORD, JOHN   PVT   CO. A
    SWORN: AUG 25, 1862/3 YRS   DISCHARGED: JUN 19, 1865
SWAGER, SAMUEL   PVT   CO. A
    SWORN: SEP 17, 1864/1 YRS   NOT AT FINAL MUSTER
SWARTZLANDER, WILLIAM *   PVT   CO. K   AGE: 20
    SWORN: OCT 12, 1861/3 YRS   MUSTER: NOV 4, 1864
    BORN: ARMSTRONG COUNTY   OCCUPATION: FARMER
    HEIGHT: 5' 7"   COMPLEXION: DARK   EYES: DARK   HAIR: DARK
    1886 REUNION IN FREEPORT: HOME, ROBELIA, PA
    HOME IN 1897: PITTSBURGH, PA
SYKES, THOMAS M.C.   PVT   CO. H   AGE:21
    BORN: BEAVER COUNTY   OCCUPATION: SHOEMAKER
    HEIGHT: 5' 5$^{1}/_{3}$ "   COMPLEXION: SANDY EYES: BROWN   HAIR: LIGHT
    SWORN: OCT 12, 1861/3YRS   MUSTER: NOV 4, 1864   BOUNTY: $100.
    WOUNDED/HEAD AT STONES RIVER
SYKES, WILLIAM C. **   PVT   CO. H   AGE:20
    SWORN: OCT 12, 1861/3YRS   MUSTER: NOV 4, 1864   BOUNTY: $100.
    BORN: BEAVER COUNTY   OCCUPATION: SADDLER
    HEIGHT: 5' 6¼"   COMPLEXION: FAIR   EYES: BROWN   HAIR: LIGHT
TANNER, JOHN L.   PVT   CO. I
TARMER, JOHN L.
    FROM NEAR MURFREESBORO, POSSIBLE REBEL SPY
    SWORN: DEC 17, 1862/3 YRS   DIED: JAN 2/4, 1863 AT NASHVILLE OF PNEUMONIA
    BURIED AT NATIONAL CEMETERY NASHVILLE, GRAVE #A-1161
TAYLOR, GEORGE W. *   PVT   CO. F   AGE: 22
    SWORN: OCT 12, 1861/3 YRS   MUSTER: NOV 4, 1864
    BORN: SHEARSBURG, PA   OCCUPATION: LABORER
    HEIGHT: 6'   COMPLEXION: DARK   EYES: BLACK   HAIR: BLACK
    WOUNDED AT STONES RIVER DEC 31, 1862/THIGH, HOSPITALIZED IN NASHVILLE
    1886 REUNION IN FREEPORT: HOME, FREEPORT, PA
TEITSWORTH, JAMES R.   PVT   CO. E   AGE: 21
TUTSWORTH, J.R.
    SWORN: OCT 12, 1861/3 YRS   MUSTER: NOV 4, 1864
    BORN: BUTLER COUNTY   OCCUPATION: FARMER
    HEIGHT: 5' 9"   COMPLEXION: SANDY   EYES: BROWN   HAIR: BLACK
    WOUNDED AT STONES RIVER/HEAD   DIED: AT EMLENTON, PA
    ATTENDED 1886 REUNION IN FREEPORT
    DIED BEFORE THE REGIMENTAL HISTORY WAS PUBLISHED IN 1905
    [OBVIOUSLY INCORRECT]
    HOME: 1886-1914: EMLENTON, PA
    SERVICE: GUARD DUTY, KY, TN, GA 1861-1862; BATTLES: ALL
TEMPLETON, SILAS F.   PVT   CO. D   AGE: 22
    SWORN: OCT 12, 1861/3 YRS   MUSTER: NOV 4, 1864
    BORN: INDIANA COUNTY, COOKPORT   OCCUPATION: FARMER
    HEIGHT: 5' 10"   COMPLEXION: FAIR   EYES: GREY   HAIR: FAIR
    HOME 1890-1901: DECKER'S POINT, INDIANA COUNTY, PA
    BURIED: INDIANA COUNTY, SHILOH CEMETERY, DECKER'S POINT, 1839-AUG 28, 1901
THOMAS, JACOB *   PVT   CO. C   AGE: 21
    SWORN: OCT 12, 1861/3 YRS   MUSTER: SEP 11, 1865   VETERAN
    BORN: ARMSTRONG COUNTY
    HEIGHT: 5' 8"   COMPLEXION: FAIR   EYES: BLUE   HAIR: LIGHT
    PROMOTED TO CPL IN 2ND REGIMENT

THOMAS, JACOB * CPL CO. I AGE:18
 SWORN: MAR 9, 1864/3 YRS MUSTER: SEP 11, 1865
 BORN: CLARION COUNTY OCCUPATION: LABORER
 HEIGHT: 5' 4½" COMPLEXION: DARK EYES: HAZEL HAIR: BROWN
 PROMOTED TO CORPORAL CO. B Π
 HOME IN 1897: MEADVILLE, PA
THOMAS, JAMES M. PVT CO. D AGE: 21
 SWORN: OCT 12, 1861/3 YRS MUSTER: NOV 4, 1864
 BORN: INDIANA COUNTY, HILLSDALE OCCUPATION: LABORER
 HEIGHT: 5' 6½" COMPLEXION: FAIR EYES: GREY HAIR: DARK
 DIED: 1897 IN SOUTH DAKOTA
THOMAS, JOHN B. * PVT CO. F AGE: 20
 SWORN: OCT 12, 1861/3 YRS MUSTER: NOV 4, 1864
 BORN: SUCCESS, PA OCCUPATION: COLLIER
 HEIGHT: 5' 7" COMPLEXION: FRESH EYES: BROWN HAIR: BROWN
 1890 CENSUS: HILLSDALE, INDIANA COUNTY, PA
THOMAS, WILLIAM CPL CO. A AGE:27
 SWORN: OCT 12, 1861/3 YRS MUSTER: NOV 4, 1864
 BORN: INDIANA COUNTY OCCUPATION: FARMER
 HEIGHT: 5' 9" HAIR: BROWN EYES: BLACK COMPLEXION: DARK
 ENLISTED AS 3RD CPL HOME 1886: KANSAS
THOMAS, WILLIAM H. 4TH SGT CO. C AGE:23
 SWORN: OCT 12, 1861/3 YRS MUSTER: NOV 4, 1864
 HEIGHT: 5' 6½" COMPLEXION: DARK
 WOUNDED AT STONES RIVER/LEG, DEC 30, 1862
 HOME 1890-1897: BLAIRS CORNERS, PA
 ATTENDED THE DEDICATION OF THE CHICKAMAUGA BATTLEFIELD, NOV 1897
THOMPSON, ANDREW JACKSON * SGT CO. G AGE:33
 SWORN: OCT 12, 1861/3 YRS MUSTER: NOV 4, 1864
 BORN: DAYTON, PA OCCUPATION: CARPENTER
 HEIGHT: 6' 2" COMPLEXION: DARK EYES: GREY HAIR: BROWN
 PROMOTED FROM 1ST CPL
 HOME IN 1897-1914: PHOENIX, ARMSTRONG COUNTY, PA
 REUNION CHICKAMAUGA 1897, KITTANNING 1901
THOMPSON, BENJAMIN PVT CO. A
 SWORN: AUG 23, 1864/1 YRS NOT AT FINAL MUSTER
THOMPSON, DALLAS J. PVT CO. H AGE:18
 SWORN: OCT 12, 1861/3YRS MUSTER: NOV 4, 1864 BOUNTY: $100
 BORN: KITTANNING, PA OCCUPATION: STUDENT
 HEIGHT: 5' 8¼" COMPLEXION: LIGHT EYES: BLUE HAIR: LIGHT
 WOUNDED/HIP AT STONES RIVER JAN 2, 1863
 SENT TO HOSPITAL IN NEW ALBANY, INDIANA
 HOME 1914: 52 SILVER ST., YOUNGSTOWN, PA
THOMPSON, DAVID PVT CO. C AGE: 22
 SWORN: OCT 12, 1861/3 YRS MUSTER: NOV 4, 1864
 BORN: CLARION COUNTY
 HEIGHT: 5' 8" COMPLEXION: DARK EYES: BROWN HAIR: BLACK
 1890 CENSUS: CLARION, CLARION COUNTY, PA
THOMPSON, DAVID K. * SGT CO. B AGE:33
THOMPSON, DAVIS K.
 SWORN: OCT 12, 1861/3 YRS MUSTER: NOV 4, 1864
 BORN: ARMSTRONG COUNTY OCCUPATION: FARMER
 HEIGHT: 6' COMPLEXION: LIGHT EYES: BLACK HAIR: DARK
 PROMOTED TO SGT: APR 30, 1862 WOUNDED/ARM AT STONES RIVER
 HOME 1890-1897: BIG RUN, JEFFERSON COUNTY, PA
THOMPSON, JOHN H. * PVT CO. G
 SWORN: OCT 12, 1861/3 YRS KILLED: AT STONES RIVER JAN 2, 1863
THOMPSON, JOHN W. * PVT CO. I AGE: 18
 SWORN: JAN 4, 1864/3 YRS MUSTER: SEP 11, 1865
 BORN: ARMSTRONG COUNTY OCCUPATION: CABINET MAKER
 HEIGHT: 5' 3½" COMPLEXION: LIGHT EYES: BROWN HAIR: FAIR
 OFFICE 1914: 631 LIBERTY AVE, PITTSBURGH, PA [OFFICE]

HOME 1914: 1257 FRANKLIN AVE., WILKENSBURG, PA
THOMPSON, McCLAIN   PVT   CO. C   AGE:17
    SWORN: MAR 31, 1864/3 YRS   MUSTER: SEP 11, 1865, NOT AT FINAL MUSTER
    BORN: CLARION COUNTY   OCCUPATION: LABORER
    HEIGHT: 5' 5"   COMPLEXION: FAIR   EYES: BLUE   HAIR: BROWN
THOMPSON, ROBERT R. **   PVT   CO. H   AGE:18
    ENLISTED AT ALLEGHENY CITY, PA
    SWORN: FEB 22, 1864/3 YRS   MUSTER: SEP 11, 1865
    HOME 1914: 315 FIRST ST., BUTLER, PA
THORN, ROBERT B. *   PVT   CO. I   AGE:18
    SWORN: OCT 12, 1861/3 YRS   MUSTER: NOV 4, 1864
    BORN: SLATE LICK, PA   OCCUPATION: STUDENT
    HEIGHT: 5' 4"   COMPLEXION: LIGHT   EYES: GREY   HAIR: LIGHT
THORN, SAMUEL   PVT   CO. E   AGE: 34
    HOME IN 1897: NORTH WASHINGTON, PA
    SWORN: OCT 12, 1861/3 YRS   DIED: NOV 13, 1861 AFTER SURGERY
    BORN: VENANGO COUNTY   OCCUPATION: BLACKSMITH
    HEIGHT: 5' 8"   COMPLEXION: SANDY   EYES: BLUE   HAIR: SANDY
    1ST MEMBER OF REGIMENT TO BE KILLED
    ACCIDENTLY SHOT WHILE ON PICKET DUTY AT CAMP NEVIN
    BURIED: IN THE LOCAL BAPTIST CEMETERY , MOVED TO LOUISVILLE
    NATIONAL CEMETERY LOUISVILLE; SECTION.D, RANGE.4, GRAVE.93
THORNBURG, JESSE S.   CPL   CO. H   AGE:22
THOMBURGH, JESSE
    SWORN: FEB 20, 1864   MUSTER: SEP 11, 1865
    PROMOTED FROM PVT TO CORPORAL CO. B II
    BATTLES: BUZZARD'S ROOST, RESACA,   PICKETT'S MILL, BUZZARD'S ROOST II
THORNBURG, JOHN R.   PVT   CO. H   AGE:25
THOMBURGH, JOHN
    SWORN: FEB 16, 1864   MUSTER: SEP 11, 1865
THORNE, JAMES   PVT   CO. A   AGE:16
THORN, JAMES
    SWORN: DEC 19, 1862/3 YRS   MUSTER: JUN 19, 1865
    BORN: TENNESSEE   OCCUPATION: FARMER
    HEIGHT: 5' 2"   COMPLEXION: FAIR   EYES: GREY   HAIR: BROWN
    ENLISTED BY COLONEL SIRWELL IN NASHVILLE
    AGE: 12 AS LISTED IN INDIANA HISTORY
    U.S. GOVERNMENT GAVE HIM AN "APPOINTMENT" FOR HIS BRAVERY AT STONES
    RIVER; REPORTEDLY HUNG BY EX REBEL SYMPATHIZERS [BEFORE 1880]
    AFTER THE WAR.
TINGLING, W.M.   CPL   CO. E
    SWORN: OCT 12, 1861/3 YRS   MUSTER: NOV 4, 1864
    PROMOTED TO CPL FEB 1, 1864
TITTLE, RICHARD J.*   PVT   CO. I   AGE:18
    BORN NEW ALEXANDRIA, WESTMORELAND COUNTY, PA, MAR 23, 1843
    FATHER: JAMES K. TITTLE   MOTHER: ELIZABETH JANE JACKSON [DIED 1848]
    SWORN: OCT 12, 1861/3 YRS   DIED: FEB 9, 1862 AT CAMP WOOD
    BORN: KITTANNING, PA   OCCUPATION: FARMER
    COMPLEXION: LIGHT   EYES: GREY   HAIR: LIGHT
    BURIED: KITTANNING CEMETERY
TORBETT, HENRY W.*   LT COL   CO. F   AGE:22
    ORIGIN: ARMSTRONG COUNTY   VETERAN
    SWORN: SEP 10, 1861/3 YRS   MUSTER: SEP 11, 1865
    BORN: FREEPORT, PA   OCCUPATION: POST MASTER
    HEIGHT: 5' 6"   COMPLEXION: LIGHT   EYES: GREY   HAIR: DARK BROWN
    SOME FAMILIES RECEIVED $100 BOUNTY UPON ENLISTMENT
    PROMOTED FROM 2LT CO. F, NOV 30, 1862
    COMMENDED BY COLONEL SIRWELL FOR BRAVERY AT STONES RIVER
    ACTING REGIMENTAL ADJUTANT 1863
    COMMENDED BY BLAKELEY FOR BRAVERY AT CHICKAMAUGA
    PROMOTED FROM 1LT CO. F, DEC 3, 1864 TO CPT IN 2ND REGIMENT
    PROMOTED TO LT COLONEL FROM CPT CO. A, MAR 26, 1865

ON DETACHED SERVICE WHEN REGIMENT MUSTERED OUT
JOINED 11 U.S. REGULAR ARMY AS 1LT   DIED: JUN 8, 1871 IN FREEPORT;
BURIED IN FREEPORT CEMETERY, FREEPORT, PA

TRAVAIS, GEORGE W.   PVT   CO. H   AGE:21
TRAVIS, GEORGE W.
    SWORN: OCT 12, 1861/3YRS   DIED: DEC 20, 1863 AT CAMP STARKWEATHER ON
    BORN: CLARION COUNTY   OCCUPATION: FARMER
    HEIGHT: 5' 8½"   COMPLEXION: FAIR   EYES: GREY   HAIR: BROWN
    LOOKOUT MOUNTAIN, TN OF CHRONIC DIARHREA

TRIMBLE, THOMAS   PVT   CO. H   AGE:18
    SWORN: OCT 12, 1861/3YRS   DIED: DEC 24, 1861 AT LOUISVILLE OF TYPHOID
    BORN: BUTLER COUNTY   OCCUPATION: CARPENTER
    HEIGHT: 5' 10½"   COMPLEXION: DARK   EYES: GREY   HAIR: BLACK

TROUTMAN, HENRY   PVT   CO. A
    SWORN: SEP 14, 1864/1 YEAR   DISCHARGED: JUN 19, 1865
    1890 CENSUS: SPRANKILLS MILLS, JEFFERSON COUNTY, PA

TROUTMAN, JACOB **   PVT   CO. A
    SWORN: SEP 14, 1864/1 YEAR   DISCHARGED: JUN 19, 1865
    U.S. PENSION, 1894: $4.00   HOME: PIERCE

TROUTNER, GEORGE W. *   PVT   CO. G   AGE: 23
    SWORN: MAR 4, 1864/3 YRS   MUSTER: SEP 11, 1865
    BORN: CLARION COUNTY   OCCUPATION: LABORER
    HEIGHT: 5' 10¼"   COMPLEXION: FAIR   EYES: BLUE   HAIR: SANDY
    HOME 1897: EAST BRADY, CLARION COUNTY, PA   DIED: JUN 15, 1902
    ATTENDED THE DEDICATION OF THE CHICKAMAUGA BATTLEFIELD, NOV 1897

TROUTNER, THOMAS *   PVT   CO. G   AGE: 22
    SWORN: OCT 12, 1861/3 YRS   TRANS: NOV 30, 1862 TO 4TH CAV
    VETERAN   MUSTER: DEC 1, 1865
    HOME 1890-1914: WORTHINGTON, PA
    REUNION KITTANNING 1901
    BURIED: WORTHINGTON LUTHERAN CEMETERY, WORTHINGTON, PA 1839-1923

TRUNICK, CHARLES W.   PVT   CO. D   AGE: 21
    SWORN: OCT 12, 1861/3 YRS   MUSTER: NOV 4, 1864
    BORN: PITTSBURGH, PA   OCCUPATION: LABORER
    HEIGHT: 6'   COMPLEXION: FAIR   EYES: GREY   HAIR: AUBURN
    VOLUNTEERED FOR PIONEER BRIGADE AT STONES RIVER

TRUXALL, BENJAMIN W.   8TH CPL   CO. H   AGE:21
    SWORN: OCT 12, 1861/3YRS   DIED: DEC 9, 1861 AT CAMP NEGLEY OF TYPHOID FEVER
    BORN: BUTLER COUNTY   OCCUPATION: STUDENT
    HEIGHT: 6'   COMPLEXION: LIGHT   EYES: GREY   HAIR: LIGHT

TURNER, GEORGE W.*   PVT   CO. C
    SWORN: OCT 23, 1862/1 YR   DISCHARGED: OCT 13, 1864
    OCCUPATION: TAILOR

TURNER, JOHN H.   PVT   CO. E   AGE: 21
    SWORN: OCT 12, 1861/3 YRS   MUSTER: NOV 4, 1864
    BORN: VENANGO COUNTY   OCCUPATION: TEACHER
    HEIGHT: 5' 10"   COMPLEXION: LIGHT   EYES: BLUE   HAIR: BROWN
    HOME 1897: FOXBURG, CLARION COUNTY, PA
    REUNION CHICKAMAUGA 1897, INDIANA 1908.

TURNER, JOHN M.   PVT   CO. E   AGE: 20
TURNER, JOHN H.
    BORN: BUTLER COUNTY, JAN 11, 1841
    BORN: BUTLER COUNTY   OCCUPATION: FARMER
    HEIGHT: 5' 8"   COMPLEXION: LIGHT   EYES: BLUE   HAIR: LIGHT
    SWORN: OCT 12, 1861/3 YRS   MUSTER: NOV 4, 1864
    HOME 1897: BUTLER, PA
    ATTENDED THE DEDICATION OF THE CHICKAMAUGA BATTLEFIELD, NOV 1897

TURNEY, HENRY *   PVT   CO. I   AGE:29
TWINEY, HENRY
    SWORN: OCT 12, 1861/3 YRS   MEDICAL: JUN 22, 1863
    BORN: APOLLO, PA   OCCUPATION: LABORER
    HEIGHT: 5' 6"   COMPLEXION: LIGHT   EYES: BLUE   HAIR: DARK

DIED BEFORE THE REGIMENTAL HISTORY WAS PUBLISHED IN 1905
    BURIED: APOLLO CEMETERY, APOLLO, PA

TURNEY, PETER JOHN*   PVT   CO. A   AGE:14
    BORN: MAR 5, 1847   DIED: MAR 30, 1899
    SWORN: OCT 12, 1861/4 YRS   MUSTER: SEP 11, 1865   VETERAN
    BORN: ARMSTRONG COUNTY   OCCUPATION: FARMER
    HEIGHT: 5' 4"   COMPLEXION: LIGHT   EYES: GREY   HAIR: LIGHT
    LIED ABOUT AGE AT ENLISTMENT, CLAIMED 18
    TRADE: CARPENTER   WIFE: REBECCA McELWAIN
    WOUNDED AT CHICKAMAUGA [BEERS]
    1890 CENSUS:COWANSHANNOCK TWP., ARMSTRONG COUNTY, PA
    HOME 1897: RURAL VALLEY, ARMSTRONG COUNTY
    ATTENDED THE DEDICATION OF THE CHICKAMAUGA BATTLEFIELD, NOV 1897

TUXFORD, JOHN *   PVT   CO. F   AGE: 24
TREXFORD, JOHN
    SWORN: AUG 28, 1862/3 YRS   MUSTER: SEP 11, 1865
    BORN: LINCOLNSHIRE, ENGLAND   OCCUPATION: LABORER
    HEIGHT: 5' 8"   COMPLEXION: LIGHT   EYES: GREY   HAIR: LIGHT BROWN
    HOME 1886: FREEPORT, PA
    ATTENDED 1886 REUNION IN FREEPORT
    1890 CENSUS: McVILLE, ARMSTRONG COUNTY, PA

UHL, JOSEPH A. *   PVT   CO. F   AGE: 18
    BORN: SUGAR CREEK, PA   OCCUPATION: FARMER
    HEIGHT: 5' 9½"   COMPLEXION: FAIR   EYES: BLUE   HAIR: LIGHT
    SWORN: OCT 12, 1861/3 YRS   MUSTER: NOV 4, 1864

UMBAUGH, JOHN *   PVT   CO. A   AGE:20
UNSBAUGH, JOHN
    SWORN: OCT 12, 1861/3 YRS   MUSTER: NOV 4, 1864
    BORN: ARMSTRONG COUNTY   OCCUPATION: FARMER
    HEIGHT: 5' 11"   COMPLEXION: DARK   EYES: BLUE   HAIR: BROWN
    HOME 1890-1901: RURAL VALLEY, COWANSHANNOCK TWP., ARMSTRONG COUNTY, PA
    HOME 1914: ECHO, PA [RD 2]   REUNION KITTANNING 1901

UNCAPHER, JOSEPH   PVT   CO. A   AGE:23
UNCAPHER, JOSEPH W.   UNCAPHER, JOSEPH WILSON
    BORN: NOV 17, 1837 WASHINGTON, INDIANA COUNTY
    SWORN: OCT 12, 1861/3 YRS   MUSTER: NOV 4, 1864
    BORN: INDIANA COUNTY   OCCUPATION: CARPENTER
    HEIGHT: 6'   COMPLEXION: DARK   EYES: BROWN   HAIR: BROWN
    HOME 1890-1915: INDIANA, INDIANA COUNTY, PA
    REUNION CHICKAMAUGA 1897, KITTANNING 1901, INDIANA 1908.
    BURIED: INDIANA COUNTY, OAKLAND CEMETERY, WHITE TWP., 1837-NOV 26, 1926

UNGER, JOHN W. *   PVT   CO. K   AGE:34
    SWORN: OCT 12, 1861/3 YRS   MEDICAL: JAN 29, 1863   VETERAN
    BORN: FRANKLIN COUNTY   OCCUPATION: MINER
    HEIGHT: 5' 10"   COMPLEXION: DARK   EYES: GREY   HAIR: DARK
    SERVED WITH PA 104TH, CO. K: MAR 18-AUG 25, 1865/CPL
    BATTLES/DUTY: PETERSBURG, FORTRESS MONROE, PORTSMOUTH

UNSBAUGH, JOHN   PVT   CO. A
    SWORN: OCT 12, 1861/3 YRS   MUSTER: NOV 4, 1864

UPTIGRAFF, JAMES *   PVT   CO. I   AGE:30
UPTEGRAFF, JAMES   UPDEGRAFF, JAMES
    SWORN: OCT 12, 1861/3 YRS   MUSTER: NOV 4, 1864
    BORN: APOLLO, PA   OCCUPATION: LABORER
    HEIGHT: 5' 5½"   COMPLEXION: DARK   EYES: GREY   HAIR: DARK
    WOUNDED AT STONES RIVER/HEAD
    HOME 1890-1897: IRWIN, WESTMORELAND COUNTY, PA
    HOME 1914: 308 MAGEE AVE., JEANETTE, PA
    ATTENDED THE DEDICATION OF THE CHICKAMAUGA BATTLEFIELD, NOV 1897

VAUGHAN, WILLIAM P.   PVT   CO. H   AGE:26
VOGAN, WILLIAM P.
    SWORN: OCT 12, 1861/3YRS   TRANS: JUL 27, 1863 TO VRC
    BORN: BUTLER COUNTY   OCCUPATION: FARMER

HEIGHT: 5' 9"   COMPLEXION: LIGHT   EYES: BLUE   HAIR: BROWN
DIED BEFORE THE REGIMENTAL HISTORY WAS PUBLISHED IN 1905

WADE, JACOB *   PVT   CO. K   AGE:39
   SWORN: OCT 12, 1861/3 YRS   MEDICAL: JUL 12, 1863
   BORN: BUTLER COUNTY   OCCUPATION: LABORER
   HEIGHT: 5' 6¼"   COMPLEXION: FAIR   EYES: GREY   HAIR: LIGHT

WADE, JOHN A.*   PVT   CO. K   AGE:20
   SWORN: OCT 12, 1861/3 YRS   MUSTER: NOV 4, 1864
   BORN: BUTLER COUNTY   OCCUPATION: LABORER
   HEIGHT: 5' 6"   COMPLEXION: FAIR   EYES: GREY   HAIR: LIGHT
   ATTENDED 1886 REUNION IN FREEPORT
   HOME 1886-1897: HITES [PITTSBURGH], ALLEGHENY COUNTY, PA
   ATTENDED THE DEDICATION OF THE CHICKAMAUGA BATTLEFIELD, NOV 1897

WADDING, JOHN H.   PVT   CO. A   AGE:21
   SWORN: OCT 12, 1861/3 YRS   MUSTER: NOV 4, 1864
   BORN: ARMSTRONG COUNTY   OCCUPATION: FARMER
   HEIGHT: 5' 9½"   COMPLEXION: FAIR   EYES: BLUE   HAIR: FAIR
   HOME 1890-1914: DAYTON BOROUGH, ARMSTRONG COUNTY, PA
   BURIED: DAYTON CEMETERY, DAYTON, PA
   REUNION IN KITTANNING 1901

WAGONER, JEREMIAH   PVT   CO. A   AGE:21
WAGGONER, JEREMIAH   WAGNER, JEREMIAH
   SWORN: OCT 12, 1861/3 YRS   DIED: AT NASHVILLE, DEC 27, 1862
   BORN: INDIANA COUNTY   OCCUPATION: FARMER
   HEIGHT: 5' 10"   COMPLEXION: DARK   EYES: BLACK   HAIR: BROWN
   BURIED AT NATIONAL CEMETERY NASHVILLE, GRAVE #A-1215

WALKER, ENOCH *   PVT   CO. B   AGE:23
   SWORN: OCT 12, 1861/3 YRS   MUSTER: NOV 4, 1864
   HEIGHT: 5' 6"   COMPLEXION: LIGHT   EYES: GREY

WALKER, HUGH B. "BARNEY"   PVT   CO. H   AGE:20
   SWORN: OCT 12, 1861/3YRS   MEDICAL: APR 10, 1864
   BORN: BUTLER COUNTY   OCCUPATION: MOULDER
   HEIGHT: 5' 7¼"   COMPLEXION: SANDY EYES: BLUE HAIR: BROWN
   HOSPITALIZED NOV 15, 1862
   DESERTED DEC 5, 1862 FROM HOSPITAL #13 AT NASHVILLE AND RETURNED
   DIED: OLD SOLDIERS HOME, DAYTON, OH, 1900

WALKER, JOHN R.*   PVT   CO. F   AGE: 33
   SWORN: FEB 26, 1864/3 YRS   NOT AT FINAL MUSTER
   BURIED: BROOKLAND CEMETERY, ALLEGHENY TWP. [1818-1889]

WALKER, ROBERT M.   PVT   CO. D   AGE:15
   SWORN: OCT 12, 1861/3 YRS   MUSTER: NOV 4, 1864
   BORN: APR 28, 1846 NEAR TARENTUM, PA
   DIED IN TARENTUM OCT 2, 1930
   BURIED: EVERGREEN CEMETERY, LEECHBURG, PA

WALKER, ROBERT M.   PVT   CO. D   AGE: 49
   SWORN: OCT 12, 1861/3 YRS   MUSTER: NOV 4, 1864
   BORN: INDIANA COUNTY, HILLSDALE   OCCUPATION: FARMER
   HEIGHT: 5' 9½"   COMPLEXION: LIGHT   EYES: BLUE   HAIR: DARK
   DESERTED AND RETURNED, JAN 3, 1864
   1890 CENSUS: HILLSDALE, INDIANA COUNTY, PA
   BURIED: INDIANA COUNTY, THOMPSON'S CEMETERY, HILLSDALE, MONTGOMERY TWP.

WALKER, "SQUIRE"   VOLUNTEER COMMISSARY   REGIMENTAL STAFF/78th
   SWORN: NO RECORD   DIED: FEB 18, 1862 AT CAMP WOOD
   "BARNEY" WALKER'S FATHER
   SQUIRE WALKER IS NOT LISTED IN ANY RECORDS;
   HOWEVER, THOMAS BLAKELEY AND WILL   LOWERY MENTION HIM IN LETTERS.

WALLACE, ABRAHAM   PVT   CO. A   AGE:28
   SWORN: MAR 28, 1864/3 YRS   MEDICAL: SEP 19, 1864
   BORN: INDIANA COUNTY   OCCUPATION: LABORER
   HEIGHT: 5' 6"   COMPLEXION: DARK   EYES: BLUE   HAIR: LIGHT
   HOME 1890-1897: HOMER CITY, INDIANA COUNTY, PA
   REUNION CHICKAMAUGA 1897, INDIANA 1908.

BURIED: INDIANA COUNTY, GREENWOOD CEMETERY, 1831-NOV 1, 1911

WALLACE, DAVID #   PVT   CO. H
    LISTED ONLY IN BUTLER COUNTY HISTORY; NO INFORMATION

WALLACE, SAMUEL SR.   PVT   CO. H   AGE: 26
    SWORN: OCT 12, 1861/3YRS   DIED: NOV 21, 1863 AT CHATTANOOGA OF
    CHRONIC DIARHREA
    BORN: BUTLER COUNTY   OCCUPATION: FARMER
    HEIGHT: 5' 10"   COMPLEXION: DARK   EYES: BLUE   HAIR: BROWN
    AGE 26 LISTED ON ORIGINAL ROSTER

WALLACE, SAMUEL JR.   PVT   CO. H   AGE: 24
    SWORN: OCT 12, 1861/3YRS   DESERTED:JUL 17,1863 FROM CULLEOKA, TN
    BORN: CLARION COUNTY   OCCUPATION: COLLIER
    HEIGHT: 5' 10½"   COMPLEXION: FAIR   EYES: GREY   HAIR: DARK

WALLACE, WILLIAM   PVT   CO. H   AGE:44
    MAPLE FURNACE, BUTLER COUNTY, PA
    SWORN: OCT 12, 1861/3YRS   MEDICAL: JUN 23, 1862
    BORN: BUTLER COUNTY   OCCUPATION: FARMER
    HEIGHT: 5' 9½"   COMPLEXION: LIGHT   EYES: HAZEL   HAIR: BROWN
    DIED BEFORE THE REGIMENTAL HISTORY WAS PUBLISHED IN 1905

WALTERS, COSTON *   PVT   CO. F   AGE: 23
    SWORN: OCT 12, 1861/3 YRS   DIED: MAR 28, 1862 AT NASHVILLE
    BORN: SARVERSVILLE, PA   OCCUPATION: FARMER
    HEIGHT: 5' 8"   COMPLEXION: SALLOW   EYES: GREY   HAIR: BROWN

WANDERLING, W.H. *   PVT   CO. I
    SWORN: MAR 28, 1864/3 YRS   DIED: JUL 21, 1864 AT CHATTANOOGA
    BURIED AT NATIONAL CEMETERY, GRAVE #44

WATSON, GEORGE A./D. *   SGT   CO. B   AGE:25
    SWORN: OCT 12, 1861/3 YRS   DIED: JUN 27, 1862 AT CAMP WOOD, KY
    BORN: ARMSTRONG COUNTY   OCCUPATION: FARMER
    HEIGHT: 5' 7"   COMPLEXION: LIGHT   EYES: BLUE   HAIR: DARK
    DIED OF TYPHOID

WEAVER, ABSOLOM R. *   ACTING LT   CO. F   AGE: 18 or 48
    SWORN: OCT 12, 1861/3 YRS   MEDICAL: APR 7, 1864
    BORN: FREEPORT, PA   OCCUPATION: OIL BORER
    HEIGHT: 5' 11½"   COMPLEXION: DARK   EYES: DARK   HAIR: DARK
    SOME FAMILIES RECEIVED $100 BOUNTY UPON ENLISTMENT
    BREVETED 2LT, DEC 15, 1862 BY COLONEL SIRWELL
    LED COMPANY AT STONES RIVER, WOUNDED AT STONES RIVER/SIDE
    COMMENDED BY SIRWELL AND ROSECRANS FOR BRAVERY AT STONES RIVER
    PROMOTED FROM 4TH SGT
    DIED: MARCH 13, 1864 BURIED: FREEPORT CEMETERY, FREEPORT, PA.
    BIRTH DATE ON TOMBSTONE: JUL 20, 1813; ENLISTMENT SHOWS 18 YEARS-OLD

WEAVER, HENRY S. *   PVT   CO. F   AGE: 14
    SWORN: OCT 12, 1861/3 YRS   KILLED: DEC 31, 1862 AT STONES RIVER
    BORN: FREEPORT, PA   OCCUPATION: LABORER
    HEIGHT: 5' 8"   COMPLEXION: SALLOW   EYES: BROWN   HAIR: DARK BROWN
    SOME FAMILIES RECEIVED $100 BOUNTY UPON ENLISTMENT
    THE YOUNGEST MAN OF THE REGIMENT EVER KILLED IN BATTLE
    BURIED: FREEPORT CEMETERY, FREEPORT, PA.
    FREEPORT G.A.R. #32 WAS NAMED FOR HIM

WEBB, JOHN G. *   MUS/78th   CO. A/G
    SWORN: MAR 4, 1862/3 YRS   MUSTER: SEP 11, 1865

WENNER, WILLIAM   PVT   CO. E   AGE: 18
    SWORN: OCT 12, 1861/3 YRS   DIED: DEC 7, 1861 AT LOUISVILLE
    BORN: BERKS COUNTY   OCCUPATION: FARMER
    HEIGHT: 5' 8"   COMPLEXION: DARK   EYES: DARK   HAIR: BLACK
    BURIED: NATIONAL CEMETERY LOUISVILLE: SECTION.D. RANGE.4. GRAVE.98

WEIR, ALFRED L.*   PVT   REGIMENTAL STAFF   AGE: 23
    SWORN: OCT 12, 1861/3 YRS   MUSTER: NOV 4, 1864
    BORN: FREEPORT, PA   OCCUPATION: ATTORNEY
    HEIGHT: 5' 5"   COMPLEXION: FRESH   EYES: BROWN   HAIR: BROWN
    SOME FAMILIES RECEIVED $100 BOUNTY UPON ENLISTMENT

ORIGINAL ENLISTMENT IN CO. F; COLONEL SIRWELL'S SECRETARY
COMMENDED BY COLONEL SIRWELL FOR BRAVERY AT STONES RIVER
1890 CENSUS: PARKER'S LANDING, ARMSTRONG COUNTY, PA
BURIED: VANDERGRIFT CEMETERY, VANDERGRIFT, PA [1839-1912]

WEIR, BENJAMIN F. *   PVT   CO. F   AGE: 19
  SWORN: OCT 12, 1861/3 YRS   MUSTER: NOV 4, 1864
  BORN: FREEPORT, PA   OCCUPATION: LABORER
  HEIGHT: 5' 3½"   COMPLEXION: LIGHT   EYES: GREY   HAIR: BROWN
  SOME FAMILIES RECEIVED $100 BOUNTY UPON ENLISTMENT
  ALFRED WEIR'S BROTHER
  BURIED: FREEPORT CEMETERY, SOUTH BUFFALO TWP.

WELSH, MILTON   PVT   CO. H   AGE:22
  SWORN: OCT 12, 1861/3YRS   MUSTER: NOV 4, 1864   BOUNTY: $100.
  BORN: ZELINOPLE, PA   OCCUPATION: PRINTER
  HEIGHT: 5' 6¼"   COMPLEXION: DARK   EYES: BLACK   HAIR: BLACK
  IN MAR OF 1863, MILTON WELSH WAS DRUNK AND STABBED HUGH MORGAN
  ALSO OF CO. H; DIED BEFORE 1905

WENNER, PETER   SGT   CO. E   AGE:20
WERNER, PETER   WENDER, PETER
  SWORN: OCT 12, 1861/3 YRS   MUSTER: NOV 4, 1864
  BORN: BERKS COUNTY   OCCUPATION: LUMBERMAN
  HEIGHT: 5' 10"   COMPLEXION: FAIR   EYES: BLUE   HAIR: DARK
  PROMOTED FROM 3RD CPL MAY 20, 1863
  1890 CENSUS: KNOX, CLARION COUNTY, PA

WENTZEL, ROBERT E.   PVT   CO. A   AGE:39
WENTZELL, ROBERT E.
  SWORN: SEP 10, 1862/3 YRS   DIED: JAN 28, 1865 OF TYPHOID
  BOUNTY: $29
  BORN: CENTER COUNTY   OCCUPATION: CARPENTER
  HEIGHT: 5' 7½"   COMPLEXION: LIGHT   EYES: BLUE   HAIR: LIGHT

WHEATCRAFT, GEORGE S. *   PVT   CO. B   AGE:29
WHEATCRAFT, GEORGE T.   WHEATCROFT, GEORGE
  SWORN: AUG 19, 1863   MEDICAL: NOV 3, 1864   BOUNTY $27
  BORN: ALLEGHENY COUNTY   OCCUPATION: FARMER
  HEIGHT: 5' 7"   COMPLEXION: SANDY   EYES: BLUE   HAIR: SANDY
  SERIOUSLY WOUNDED AT PICKETT'S MILL
  1890 CENSUS: PHOENIX, ARMSTRONG COUNTY, PA
  U.S. PENSION, 1894: $10.00   HOME: PHOENIX
  HOME IN 1897: BUTLER, PA
  ATTENDED THE DEDICATION OF THE CHICKAMAUGA BATTLEFIELD, NOV 1897

WHEELER, WILLIAM   PVT   CO. G
  SWORN: OCT 12, 1861/3 YRS   DESERTED: OCT 18, 1861
  NEVER REPORTED IN/AWOL

WHITE, GEORGE W.   PVT   CO. H   AGE:23
  SWORN: OCT 12, 1861/3YRS   MEDICAL: FEB 5, 1864
  BORN: MERCER COUNTY   OCCUPATION: FARMER
  HEIGHT: 6' ½"   COMPLEXION: LIGHT   EYES: BLUE   HAIR: BROWN

WHITE, JOHN C. *   SGT   CO. G   AGE:21
  SWORN: OCT 12, 1861/3 YRS   MEDICAL: JUL 20, 1863
  BORN: ARMSTRONG COUNTY   OCCUPATION: FARMER
  HEIGHT: 6'   COMPLEXION: FAIR   EYES: GREY   HAIR: BROWN
  PROMOTED FROM SIXTH CPL; WOUNDED AT STONES RIVER/ARM
  DIED BEFORE THE REGIMENTAL HISTORY WAS PUBLISHED IN 1905

WHITEHILL, HENRY H. "HARRISON"PVT   CO. E   AGE: 18
WHITDUL, HENRY H.   WHITEHALL, H.H.
  SWORN: OCT 12, 1861/3 YRS   DIED: JAN 9, 1863 AT MURFREESBORO
  BORN: CLARION COUNTY   OCCUPATION: FARMER
  HEIGHT: 5' 8"   COMPLEXION: LIGHT   EYES: BLUE   HAIR: BROWN
  MORTALLY WOUNDED AT STONES RIVER/SHOULDER
  TAKEN FROM THE FIELD AND TREATED BY CONFEDERATES
  DIED WITH A PICTURE OF "MISS MARY THOMSON"
  INITIALLY BURIED @ PRESBYTERIAN CEMETERY, MURFREESBORO

BURIED: NATIONAL CEMETERY STONES RIVER, GRAVE #K-4384

WHITLING, EDWARD   PVT   CO. E   AGE: 21
   BORN: JUL 15, 1839, TO FREDERICK AND CATHERINE RITTS WHITLING
   SWORN: OCT 12, 1861/3 YRS   MUSTER: NOV 4, 1864
   BORN: CLARION COUNTY   OCCUPATION: SHOEMAKER
   HEIGHT: 5' 7"   COMPLEXION: LIGHT   EYES: DARK   HAIR: BROWN
   1886 REUNION IN FREEPORT
   HOME 1886: SALEM, CLARION COUNTY, PA
   1890 CENSUS: LARMARTINE, CLARION COUNTY, PA
   AFTER THE WAR WAS A DRUGGIST AND POSTMASTER IN SALEM TWP., CLARION CTY
   WIFE: ELIZABETH BUSHY

WIANT, JOHN G.   SGT   CO. C   AGE: 22
WYANT, JOHN G.
   HOME/1908: VANDERGRIFT, PA
   SWORN: OCT 12, 1861/3 YRS   MUSTER: NOV 4, 1864
   BORN: PENNSYLVANIA
   HEIGHT: 5' 7"   COMPLEXION: DARK   EYES: BLACK   HAIR: BLACK
   BORN: 1839   DIED: 1925   WIFE: MARGARET R. 1847-1931
   1890 CENSUS: PORTER TWP., CLARION COUNTY, PA
   BURIED: VANDERGRIFT CEMETERY, VANDERGRIFT, PA

WICKENHAGEN, GUSTAVE *   PRINCIPAL MUS/78th   REGIMENTAL STAFF
WICKENHACKER, GUSTAVUS   WICKENHACKEN, GUSTAVUS   AGE: 18
   BORN: BUTLER COUNTY: JUN 24, 1844
   SWORN: OCT 12, 1861/3 YRS   MUSTER: NOV 4, 1864
   HOSPITALIZED ON LOOKOUT MOUNTAIN
   PROMOTED FROM PVT CO. K, MAR 17, 1864
   BORN: BUTLER COUNTY   OCCUPATION: FARMER
   HEIGHT: 5' 6¼"   COMPLEXION: FAIR   EYES: GREY   HAIR: FAIR
   HOME IN 1897-1915: BUTLER, PA
   ATTENDED THE DEDICATION OF THE CHICKAMAUGA BATTLEFIELD, NOV 1897
   WIFE: CAROLINE TRUMBLE

WIDMAN, DANIEL #   PVT   CO. A   AGE: 35
   SWORN: MAR 28, 1864/3 YRS   MUSTER: UNKNOWN
   BORN: LANCASTER COUNTY   OCCUPATION: LABORER
   HEIGHT: 5' 4½"   COMPLEXION: RUDDY   EYES: BROWN   HAIR: DARK
   LISTED IN ORIGINAL DISCRIPTIVE LIST; NOT IN ORIGINAL HISTORY

WIEHL, FREDERICK F.   2LT   CO. H   AGE:21
WIEHL, FRANK F.   ORIGIN: BUTLER COUNTY
   SWORN: OCT 12, 1861/3YRS   MUSTER: NOV 4, 1864
   BORN: ZELINOPLE, PA   OCCUPATION: STUDENT
   HEIGHT: 5' 9"   COMPLEXION: DARK   EYES: DARK   HAIR: BLACK
   WOUNDED AT STONES RIVER;   LED CO. AT STONES RIVER AS SGT
   PROMOTED FROM 3RD SGT APR 23, 1863; REGIMENTAL QM 1863
   ATTENDED 1886 REUNION IN FREEPORT
   HOME 1886-1900: CHATTANOOGA, TN;   DIED: SEP 1, 1900 AT CHATTANOOGA

WIGGINS, THOMAS S. #   PVT   CO. A
   SWORN: OCT 12, 1861/3 YRS   DIED: SEP 11, 1861 OF DIPTHERIA @ INDIANA
   LISTED ONLY IN ROSTER AND DESCRIPTIVE BOOK, NO ADDITIONAL INFORMATION
   INDIANA HISTORY REPORTS WIGGINS DIED IN SEP 1961, AND IS BURIED: INDIANA
   COUNTY, OLD PRESBYTERIAN CHURCH ON 7TH ST., INDIANA, PA. HIS GRAVE WAS
   SUBSEQUENTLY MOVED EITHER TO OAKLAND OR GREENWOOD.

WIKE, ABRAM B. "ABE"   PVT   CO. D   AGE:39
   SWORN: OCT 12, 1861/3 YRS   TRANS: DEC 12,1863 TO VRC
   BORN: INDIANA COUNTY   OCCUPATION: LUMBERMAN
   HEIGHT: 5' 8½"   COMPLEXION: FAIR   EYES: BLUE
   DEMOTED FROM FIFTH CPL, 1864   WOUNDED AT STONES RIVER/FOOT
   DIED BEFORE THE REGIMENTAL HISTORY WAS PUBLISHED IN 1905
   BURIED: INDIANA COUNTY, LUTHERAN CEMETERY, BRUSH VALLEY

WILLIAMS, JOHN B.   PVT   CO. H   AGE:30
   BORN: HUNTINGTON COUNTY   OCCUPATION: COLLIER
   HEIGHT: 5' 9"   COMPLEXION: FAIR   EYES: BLUE   HAIR: BROWN
   SWORN: OCT 12, 1861/3YRS   MUSTER: NOV 4, 1864   BOUNTY: $100.

WILLIAMS, JONATHAN N.   PVT   CO. E   AGE: 33
WILLIAMS, JONATHAN W.
    SWORN: OCT 12, 1861/3 YRS   MUSTER: NOV 4, 1864
    BORN: BUTLER COUNTY   OCCUPATION: FARMER
    HEIGHT: 6' 2"   COMPLEXION: SANDY   EYES: BLUE   HAIR: DARK
    PRISONER AT STONES RIVER/PAROLED
    HOME 1890–1897: BLAIRS CORNERS, CLARION COUNTY
    DIED: IN CLARION COUNTY, PA BEFORE 1905
WILLIAMS, WILLIAM J.   CPT   CO. G   AGE: 38
    ORIGIN: WESTMORELAND COUNTY; BORN: WESTMORELAND COUNTY
    SWORN: OCT 18, 1861/3 YRS   MUSTER: NOV 4, 1864
    HEIGHT: 5' 11"   COMPLEXION: FAIR   EYES: BLUE   HAIR: GREY
    PROMOTED FROM QUARTER MASTER SGT TO COMMISSARY SGT MAY 1, 1862.
    PROMOTED FROM COMMISSARY SGT TO 2LT CO. G, APR 24 1864
    PROMOTED TO CPT APR 13, 1864; DIED BEFORE 1905
WILLIAMSON, BENJAMIN FRANKLIN * PVT   CO. I   AGE:20
    SWORN: OCT 12, 1861/3 YRS   DIED: JUN 6, 1864 AT CHATTANOOGA
    BORN: LEECHBURG, PA   OCCUPATION: FARMER
    HEIGHT: 5' 8"   COMPLEXION: FAIR   EYES: BROWN HAIR: DARK
    MORTALLY WOUNDED AT PICKETT'S MILL MAY 27, 1864
    BURIED AT NATIONAL CEMETERY, GRAVE #917
WILSON, JAMES *   PVT   CO. F   AGE: 22
    SWORN: OCT 12, 1861/3 YRS   MEDICAL: DEC 27, 1862
    BORN: SHEARER'S CROSS ROADS   OCCUPATION: LABORER
    HEIGHT: 5' 11½"   COMPLEXION: SALLOOW   EYES: GREY HAIR: DARK BROWN
    1886 REUNION IN FREEPORT: HOME, SHEARERS CROSS ROADS, PA
WILSON, JAMES #   PVT   CO. K   AGE: 18
JAMES WILSON REED [ENLISTMENT NAME]
    SWORN: OCT 1862/3 YRS   MUSTER: NOV 4, 1864
    BORN A SLAVE IN TENNESSEE OCCUPATION: "COLORED" COOK
    1880 CENSUS: VENANGO COUNTY, FRANKLIN, PA; "HOTEL COOK"
    DIED: DEC 11, 1917 BURIED: FRANKLIN CEMETERY WIFE: CATHERINE DERRY
WILSON, JAMES F. *   PVT   CO. I   AGE: 21
    SWORN: OCT 12, 1861/3 YRS   MEDICAL: AUG 12, 1862
    BORN: APOLLO, PA   OCCUPATION: LABORER
    HEIGHT: 5' 9½"   COMPLEXION: FAIR   EYES: BLUE   HAIR: LIGHT
    HOME 1911: PARKS TOWNSHIP, ARMSTRONG COUNTY, PA
WILSON, JAMES S.   PVT   CO. H   AGE:20
    SWORN: OCT 12, 1861/3YRS   DISCHARGED: OCT 12, 1864
    BORN: BUTLER COUNTY   OCCUPATION: CLERK
    HEIGHT: 5' 5¼"   COMPLEXION: LIGHT EYES: BROWN HAIR: BROWN
    ATTENDED 1886 REUNION IN FREEPORT, CHICKAMAUGA 1897
    HOME 1886–1897: SLIPPERY ROCK, BUTLER COUNTY, PA
WILSON, THOMAS *   TEAMSTER   CO. G   AGE:58
    SWORN: OCT 12, 1861/3 YRS   DIED: MAR 15, 1862 AT NASHVILLE
    BORN: DAYTON, PA   OCCUPATION: TEAMSTER
    HEIGHT: 5' 7"   COMPLEXION: FAIR   EYES: GREY   HAIR: GREY
    DIED OF "OLD AGE - UNFIT"
    1890 CENSUS: DAYTON BOROUGH, ARMSTRONG COUNTY, PA; WIDOW MARY
WISE, JACOB   PVT   CO. D   AGE: 42
    SWORN: OCT 12, 1861/3 YRS   MUSTER: NOV 4, 1864
    BORN: KITTANNING   OCCUPATION: COLLIER
    HEIGHT: 5' 7"   COMPLEXION: FAIR   EYES: BLUE   HAIR: DARK
    1890 CENSUS: NEW BETHLEHEM, CLARION COUNTY, PA, DIED BEFORE 1905
WISE, WILLIAM H. H. *   PVT   CO. B   AGE: 18
    SWORN: FEB 2, 1864/3 YRS   MUSTER: SEP 11, 1865
    BORN: ARMSTRONG COUNTY   OCCUPATION: FARMER
    HEIGHT: 5'6"   COMPLEXION: LIGHT   EYES: GREY   HAIR: DARK
    PROMOTED TO CPL, NOV 4, 1864   HOME IN 1897: PITTSBURGH, PA
    1890 CENSUS: FORD CITY, ARMSTRONG COUNTY, PA
    HOME 1914: SOLDIER'S HOME, DAYTON, OHIO
    ATTENDED THE DEDICATION OF THE CHICKAMAUGA BATTLEFIELD, NOV 1897

WODFORD, BANKS   PVT   CO. D   AGE: 27
WOODFORD, BANKS
  SWORN: OCT 12, 1861/3 YRS   MUSTER: NOV 4, 1864
  DESERTED AND RETURNED, JAN 3, 1864
  BORN: BEAVER COUNTY   OCCUPATION: LABORER
  HEIGHT: 6' ¼" COMPLEXION: FAIR EYES: BLUE   HAIR: FAIR
WOLF, JOHN G. *   PVT   CO. K   AGE:18
WOLFF, JOHN G.
  SWORN: SEP 13, 1862/3 YRS   DISCHARGED: JUN 19, 1865
  BORN: ARMSTRONG COUNTY   OCCUPATION: FARMER
  HEIGHT: 5' 6" COMPLEXION: FAIR   EYES: GREY   HAIR: DARK
  BORN: ARMSTRONG COUNTY
  BROTHERS JOHN G. AND WILLIAM B. WOLFF
WOLF, JACOB *   PVT   CO. K   AGE:27
WOLFF, JACOB W.
  SWORN: OCT 12, 1861/3 YRS   DIED: JAN 2, 1862
  BORN: ARMSTRONG COUNTY   OCCUPATION: FARMER
  HEIGHT: 5' 6½"   COMPLEXION: FAIR   EYES: GREY   HAIR: LIGHT
WOLF, WILLIAM B. "BILLIE"   PVT   CO. K   AGE:18
WOLFF, WILLIAM S. ***
  SWORN: OCT 12, 1861/3 YRS   MUSTER: NOV 4, 1864
  BORN: ALLEGHENY COUNTY   OCCUPATION: FARMER
  HEIGHT: 5' 4"   COMPLEXION: DARK   EYES: GREY   HAIR: DARK
  BROTHERS JOHN G. AND WILLIAM B. WOLFF
  MARRIED TO "BIDDY" ON LOOKOUT MT. BY FATHER CHRISTY
WOODS, JOEL *   PVT   CO. I   AGE:28
  SWORN: OCT 12, 1861/3 YRS   MUSTER: NOV 4, 1864
  BORN: COWANSVILLE, PA   OCCUPATION: FARMER
  HEIGHT: 5' 8" COMPLEXION: FAIR EYES: BLUE HAIR: LIGHT
  HOME 1901: HENDERSON, IOWA HOME 1914: GARMONS MILLS, PA
  REUNION KITTANNING 1901
WOODSIDES, WILLIAM   PVT   CO. D   AGE: 18
  SWORN: OCT 12, 1861/3 YRS   MEDICAL: MAR 31, 1863
  BORN: INDIANA COUNTY, STRONGTOWN   OCCUPATION: FARMER
  HEIGHT: 5' 10" COMPLEXION: DARK EYES: BROWN   HAIR: DARK
  1890 CENSUS: GARMAN MILL, CAMBRIA COUNTY, PA
WOODWARD, WEST   PVT   CO. C   AGE: 19
  SWORN: OCT 12, 1861/3 YRS   MEDICAL: DEC 17, 1862
  BORN: PENNSYLVANIA
  HEIGHT: 6'   COMPLEXION: DARK EYES: BROWN   HAIR: BROWN
WOOLWEAVER, J.A.   PVT   CO. D   AGE: 19
WOOLWEAVER, JOHN A.
  BORN: INDIANA COUNTY, WHITE TWP., FEB 3, 1842
  PARENTS: CONRAD AND HARRIET   OCCUPATION: FARMER, COAL MINER
  SWORN: OCT 12, 1861/3 YRS   MUSTER: NOV 4, 1864
  HEIGHT: 5' 5½"   HAIR: LIGHT   EYES: GREY   COMPLEXION: FAIR
  CAVALRY SERVICE DURING 1863
  HOME IN 1890-1914: INDIANA, INDIANA COUNTY, PA
  WIFE: MATILDA HENRY
  ATTENDED THE DEDICATION OF THE CHICKAMAUGA BATTLEFIELD, NOV 1897
  BURIED: OAKLAND CEMETERY, INDIANA, PA, SEC I-160; DIED: NOV 21, 1920
WORKMAN, A.G.   CPL   CO. C   AGE: 44
WORKMAN, ALBERT G.
  SWORN: OCT 12, 1861/3 YRS   DIED: DEC 16, 1863 AT NASHVILLE
  BORN: PENNSYLVANIA
  HEIGHT: 5' 9" COMPLEXION: DARK EYES: HAZEL   HAIR: BROWN
  BURIED @ NASHVILLE, ROW D, GRAVE #341, BATES
WORNER, JACOB   PVT   CO. E   AGE: 19
WOMER, JACOB
  SWORN: OCT 12, 1861/3 YRS   MUSTER: NOV 4, 1864
  BORN: BUTLER COUNTY   OCCUPATION: FARMER
  HEIGHT: 5' 7"   COMPLEXION: DARK   EYES: BROWN   HAIR: DARK

WRIGHT, WILLIAM J.*　　　　SGT　　　　CO. I　　　　AGE: 30
　　SWORN: SEP 18, 1862/3 YRS　　DISCHARGED: JUN 19, 1865
　　BORN: FRANKLIN, PA　　OCCUPATION: CONSTABLE
　　HEIGHT: 6'　COMPLEXION: DARK　EYES: GREY　HAIR: DARK
　　PROMOTED FROM PVT OCT 1, 1864
　　1886 REUNION IN FREEPORT: HOME, KITTANNING, PA
　　1890 CENSUS: RIMER, MADISON TWP., ARMSTRONG COUNTY, PA
WYANT, FREDERICK *　　　　PVT　　　　CO. C　　　　AGE: 23
WIANT, FREDERICK
　　SWORN: OCT 12, 1861/3 YRS　　TRANS: OCT 1, 1863 TO VRC
　　BORN: CLARION COUNTY
　　HEIGHT: 5' 10"　COMPLEXION: DARK　EYES: BROWN　HAIR: BROWN
　　BORN: 1824
　　PARENTS: MARTIN & CHRISTEENA BOOHER
　　BROTHER JACOB KILLED AT McLEMORE COVE WITH THE 78th
　　BROTHER HENRY WAS IN THE PA 103rd; DIED AT ANDERSONVILLE
WYANT, JACOB *　　　　PVT　　　　CO. C　　　　AGE: 25
WIANT, JACOB
　　SWORN: OCT 12, 1861/3 YRS　　KILLED: SEP 11, 1863 @ DUG GAP, GA
　　BORN: CLARION COUNTY
　　HEIGHT: 6'　COMPLEXION: DARK　EYES: BROWN　HAIR: BLACK
　　PARENTS: MARTIN & CHRISTEENA BOOHER WYANT
　　BROTHER HENRY WAS IN THE PA 103rd; DIED AT ANDERSONVILLE
　　BROTHER FREDERICK WAS IN THE 78th, CO. C
YARGER, JOHN *　　　　PVT　　　　CO. B　　　　AGE:27
　　SWORN: AUG 25, 1863/3 YRS　　MUSTER: SEP 11, 1865
　　BORN: WESTMORELAND COUNTY
　　HEIGHT: 5' 10½"　COMPLEXION: DARK　EYES: BLUE　HAIR: DARK
YEAGER, JOHN　　　　PVT　　　　CO. D
　　SWORN: SEP 12, 1862/3 YRS　　DIED: FEB 1, 1863 AT NASHVILLE
　　BURIED AT NATIONAL CEMETERY NASHVILLE, GRAVE #B-382
YINGLING, CHAMBERS　　　　PVT　　　　CO. E　　　　AGE: 20
YINGLEY, CHAMBERS
　　SWORN: OCT 12, 1861/3 YRS　　MUSTER: NOV 4, 1864
　　BORN: CLARION COUNTY　　OCCUPATION: FARMER
　　HEIGHT: 5' 4"　COMPLEXION: SANDY　EYES: BROWN　HAIR: DARK
　　WOUNDED AT STONES RIVER/LEFT THIGH
　　ADMITTED TO HOSPITAL #12, LOUISVILLE MAR 1, 1863
　　1890 CENSUS: POLLOCK, CLARION COUNTY, PA
YINGLING, DAVID M.　　　　PVT　　　　CO. E
　　SWORN: OCT 12, 1861/3 YRS　　DIED: JUL 21, 1864 AT CHATTANOOGA
YINGLING, EMORY　　　　PVT　　　　CO. E
　　SWORN: MAR 31, 1864/3 YRS　　DIED: AUG 18, 1864 AT ANDERSONVILLE
　　CAPTURED & IMPRISONED @ ANDERSONVILLE
　　BURIED: ANDERSONVILLE, GA; GRAVE 6103
YINGLING, JOHN　　　　PVT　　　　CO. E　　　　AGE: 24
　　SWORN: OCT 12, 1861/3 YRS　　MUSTER: NOV 4, 1864
　　BORN: CLARION COUNTY　　OCCUPATION: CARPENTER
　　HEIGHT: 5' 10"　COMPLEXION: SANDY　EYES: BROWN　HAIR: SANDY
　　DIED: AT LARMARTINE, PA BEFORE 1905
YINGLING, JOSEPH　　　　PVT　　　　CO. E　　　　AGE: 19
　　SWORN: MAR 31, 1864/3 YRS　　MUSTER: SEP 11, 1865
　　BORN: CLARION COUNTY　　OCCUPATION: FARMER
　　HEIGHT: 5' 2"　COMPLEXION: FAIR　EYES: BLUE　HAIR: BROWN
YINGLING, WALKER M. #　　　　PVT　　　　CO. E　　　　AGE: 20
　　SWORN: OCT 12, 1861/3YRS　MUSTER: UNKNOWN
　　BORN: CLARION COUNTY　　OCCUPATION: FARMER
　　HEIGHT: 5' 4"　COMPLEXION: SANDY　EYES: BROWN　HAIR: LIGHT
YINGST, HENRY E. *　　　　PVT　　　　CO. G　　　　AGE: 18
　　BORN: ARMSTRONG COUNTY　　OCCUPATION: SHOEMAKER
　　HEIGHT: 5' 6"　COMPLEXION: FAIR　EYES: GREY　HAIR: FAIR
　　SWORN: OCT 12, 1861/3 YRS　　TRANS: JUL 1, 1862 TO VRC

HOME 1914: TORONTO, OH
YOCK, WILLIAM *   PVT   CO. B   AGE: 20
YOCKEY, WILLIAM
    SWORN: OCT 12, 1861/3 YRS   DIED: JAN 12, 1862 AT LOUISVILLE
    BORN: ARMSTRONG COUNTY   OCCUPATION: FARMER
    HEIGHT: 5' 10"   COMPLEXION: LIGHT   EYES: DARK   HAIR: LIGHT
    BURIED: NATIONAL CEMETERY LOUISVILLE; SECTION.A, RANGE.6, GRAVE.10
YOHE, JOHN   PVT   CO. E   AGE: 48
    SWORN: OCT 12, 1861/3 YRS   KILLED: APR 16, 1862 AT CAMP RUTHERFORD, TN,
    BORN: PERRY COUNTY   OCCUPATION: LABORER
    HEIGHT: 5' 10"   COMPLEXION: DARK   EYES: BROWN   HAIR: DARK
    WHILE ON PICKET DUTY "KILLED BY FRIENDLY FIRE"
YORK, JOSEPH McC #   PVT   CO. A   AGE:18
    SWORN: ≅ SEP 10, 1862/3 YRS
    HEIGHT: 5' 10"   COMPLEXION: FAIR   EYES: GREY   HAIR: SANDY
    LISTED IN ORIGINAL DISCRIPTIVE LIST; NOT IN ORIGINAL HISTORY
YOUNG, JOHN *   PVT   CO. K   AGE:36
    SWORN: OCT 12, 1861/3 YRS   MUSTER: NOV 4, 1864   VETERAN
    BORN: NEW CASTLE, DE   OCCUPATION: FARMER
    HEIGHT: 5' 11"   COMPLEXION: FAIR   EYES: BLUE   HAIR: LIGHT
    SERVED WITH PA 104TH, CO. K: MAR 18-AUG 25, 1865/PVT
    BURIED: WORTHINGTON LUTHERAN CEMETERY, WORTHINGTON, PA
    WIFE: HANNAH   JOHN: 1826-1913
YOUNG, JOHN P. *   PVT   CO. C   AGE: 19
    SWORN: AUG 28, 1862/3 YRS   DISCHARGED: JUN 19, 1865
    BORN: JEFFERSON COUNTY   OCCUPATION: FARMER
    HEIGHT: 5' 6"   COMPLEXION: FAIR   EYES: BROWN   HAIR: DARK
YOUNG, PHILIP   PVT   CO. A
    SWORN: AUG 5, 1864/1 YRS   NOT AT FINAL MUSTER
YOUNG, THEODORE *   PVT   CO. I   AGE:18
    SWORN: OCT 12, 1861/3 YRS   DIED: MAR 27, 1862 AT BOWLING GREEN
    BORN: FREEPORT, PA   OCCUPATION: FARMER
    HEIGHT: 5' 6"   COMPLEXION: DARK   EYES: GREY   HAIR: DARK
    BURIED @ NASHVILLE, BATES
YOUNG, WILLIAM *   CPL   CO. I   AGE:24
    SWORN: OCT 12, 1861/3 YRS   MUSTER: NOV 4, 1864
    BORN: COWANSVILLE, PA   OCCUPATION: BRICK MAKER
    HEIGHT: 5' 11½"   COMPLEXION: DARK   EYES: GREY   HAIR: DARK
    BRIEFLY MISSING IN ACTION AT STONES RIVER
    PROMOTED TO CPL JUN 1, 1863
    1890 CENSUS: BURRELL TWP., ARMSTRONG COUNTY, PA
YOUNKINS, JOHN F. *   PVT   CO. K   AGE:18
    SWORN: OCT 12, 1861/3 YRS   MUSTER: NOV 4, 1864
    BORN: WESTMORELAND COUNTY   OCCUPATION: FARMER
    HEIGHT: 5' 11"   COMPLEXION: FAIR   EYES: BLUE   HAIR: LIGHT
    MICHAEL YOUNKINS BROTHER
    BRIEFLY MISSING IN ACTION AT STONES RIVER
YOUNKINS, MICHAEL *   PVT   CO. K   AGE:28
    SWORN: OCT 12, 1861/3 YRS   MUSTER: NOV 4, 1864
    BORN: WESTMORELAND COUNTY   OCCUPATION: FARMER
    HEIGHT: 5' 8"   COMPLEXION: DARK   EYES: GREY   HAIR: DARK
    JOHN F. YOUNKINS BROTHER
    U.S. PENSION, 1894: $30.00   HOME: McHADDON
YOUNT, DANIEL *   PVT   CO. G
    SWORN: OCT 12, 1861/3 YRS   TRANS: AUG 1, 1862 TO VRC
    IT IS POSSIBLE THAT DANIEL YOUNT, 78th & 14th COULD BE THE SAME MAN
    BURIED: OLD PRESBYTERIAN CEMETERY, COWANSHANNOCK TWP., ARMSTRONG CTY
YOUNT, DAVID *   PVT   CO. B   AGE: 19
    SWORN: OCT 12, 1861/3 YRS   TRANS: 4TH CAV, DEC 1, 1862
    BORN: ARMSTRONG COUNTY   OCCUPATION: FARMER
    HEIGHT: 5' 9"   COMPLEXION: DARK   EYES: BROWN   HAIR: BLACK
YOUNT, JACOB *   PVT   CO. G   AGE: 19

SWORN: SEP 13, 1862/3 YRS   DIED: NOV 24, 1863 AT LOUISVILLE
BORN: ARMSTRONG COUNTY   OCCUPATION: STONE MASON
HEIGHT: 5' 9½"   COMPLEXION: FAIR   EYES: GREY   HAIR: LIGHT
BURIED: NATIONAL CEMETERY LOUISVILLE; SECTION.A, RANGE.28, GRAVE.10

YOUNT, WILLIAM *   PVT   CO. B   AGE: 23
SWORN: OCT 12, 1861/3 YRS   MEDICAL: APR 27, 1863
BORN: ARMSTRONG COUNTY   OCCUPATION: FARMER
HEIGHT: 6' 1"   COMPLEXION: DARK   EYES: BLACK   HAIR: BLACK
BORN: 1838   DIED: 1917
1890 CENSUS: KITTANNING, ARMSTRONG COUNTY, PA
BURIED: CEMETERY NEAR WHITESBURG
U.S. PENSION, 1894: $24.00   HOME: BLANKET HILL

ZERBY, DANIEL *   PVT   CO. F   AGE: 31
ZIRBY, DANIEL
SWORN: OCT 12, 1861/3 YRS   KILLED: OCT 20, 1862 AT HERMITAGE FORD
BORN: KITTANNING, PA   OCCUPATION: MILLER
HEIGHT: 5' 9"   COMPLEXION: DARK   EYES: GREY   HAIR: BROWN
FIRST MEMBER OF THE REGIMENT KILLED IN ACTION
BURIED AT NATIONAL CEMETERY NASHVILLE, GRAVE #B-341
ZERBY'S WIDOW, MARY, EVENTUALLY MARRIED ALEXANDER BURKET THE SON OF JOHN
BURKET OF COMPANY B/G, PA 78th. REPORTEDLY, THE MARRIAGE ENDED WHEN IT WAS
FOUND THAT ALEX FAILED TO DIVORCE HIS FIRST WIFE.

Roster of the Pennsylvania Seventy-Eighth Volunteer Infantry
Second Regiment

SERVICE: GUARD DUTY, NASHVILLE 1865

ACKELSON, JOHN   PVT   CO. F
    SWORN: FEB 23, 1865   MUSTER: SEP 11, 1865
ADAMS, JOHN   PVT   CO. C
    SWORN: FEB 14, 1865   DISCHARGED: AUG 21, 1865
    1890 CENSUS: GREENDALE, ARMSTRONG COUNTY, PA
ALCORN, HENRY H.   PVT   CO. G
    SWORN: FEB 27, 1865   MUSTERED: SEP 11, 1865
ALEXANDER, JACOB S.   PVT   CO. E
    SWORN: FEB 17, 1865   MUSTER: SEP 11, 1865
ALEXANDER, JOSEPH H.   PVT   CO. E
    SWORN: FEB 17, 1865   MUSTER: MAR 31, 1865
ALEXANDER, JACOB S.   PVT   CO. E
    SWORN: FEB 17, 1865   MUSTER: SEP 11, 1865
ALEXANDER, JOSEPH H.   PVT   CO. E
    SWORN: FEB 17, 1865   MUSTER: MAR 31, 1865
ALEY, ISAIAH   PVT   CO. G
    SWORN: FEB 27, 1865   DISCHARGED: SEP 18, 1865
ALLEBACH, KNOX P.   PVT   CO. C
    SWORN: FEB 24/16, 1865   MUSTER: NOT ON MUSTER OUT ROLLS
ALMS, SAMUEL A.   PVT   CO. I
ALMES, SAMUEL
    SWORN: FEB 20, 1865   MUSTERED: SEP 11, 1865
    1890 CENSUS: LONG RUN, ARMSTRONG COUNTY, PA
    BURIED: APOLLO CEMETERY, APOLLO, PA
ALTER, JACOB   PVT   CO. H
    SWORN: FEB 21, 1865   DISCHARGED: JUN 3, 1865
ALTER, JOSEPH H.   PVT   CO. C
    SWORN: FEB 18, 1865   MUSTER: SEP 11, 1865
ANDERSON, ALEXANDER S.   SGT   CO. G
    SWORN: FEB 27, 1865   MUSTERED: SEP 11, 1865
    PROMOTED TO CPL; MAR 2, 1865; TO SGT; MAR 3, 1865
ANDERSON, DAVID M.   PVT   CO. G
    SWORN: FEB 27, 1865   DISCHARGED: SEP 9, 1865
ANDERSON, JOHN   PVT   CO. G
    SWORN: FEB 27, 1865   MUSTERED: SEP 11, 1865
ANDERSON, WILLIAM   PVT   CO. G
    SWORN: FEB 14, 1865   MUSTERED: SEP 11, 1865
ANDREWS, ABIJAH   PVT   CO. I
    SWORN: FEB 17, 1865   MUSTERED: SEP 11, 1865
ANDREWS, GALEN   CPL   CO. I
    SWORN: FEB 17, 1865   MUSTERED: SEP 11, 1865
    PROMOTED FROM PVT TO CPL AUG 8, 1865
ARBUCKLE, ROBERT   PVT   CO. I
    SWORN: FEB 20, 1865   MUSTERED: SEP 11, 1865
ARCHIBALD, JAMES A.   PVT   CO. I
    SWORN: FEB 24, 1865   MUSTERED: SEP 11, 1865
ARFORD, JOHN H.   PVT   CO. K
    SWORN: MAR 6, 1865   DESERTED: AUG 15, 1865
    1890 CENSUS: PORTAGE, CAMBRIA COUNTY, PA
ARMSTRONG, B.H.   PVT   CO. G
    SWORN: FEB 27, 1865   DISCHARGED: JUN 8, 1865

ARMSTRONG, JOSEPH   PVT   CO. E
   SWORN: FEB 24, 1865   MUSTER: SEP 11, 1865
ARMSTRONG, WILLIAM   PVT   CO. E
   SWORN: FEB 24, 1865   MUSTER: SEP 11, 1865
ARNOLD, CYRUS   PVT   CO. G
   SWORN: FEB 27, 1865   DISCHARGED: JUN 12, 1865
ARNOLD, SIMON   PVT   CO. C
   SWORN: FEB 18, 1865   DISCHARGED: MAY 16, 1865
ASHBAUGH, ALEXANDER   PVT   CO. D
   SWORN: FEB 16, 1865   DESERTED: JUL 27, 1865
      1890 CENSUS, ASHBAUGH WESTMORELAND COUNTY/LEECHBURG, ARMSTRONG COUNTY, PA
ASHTON, JOHN C.   CPL   CO. G
   SWORN: FEB 27, 1865   MUSTERED: SEP 11, 1865
   PROMOTED TO CPL; AUG 12, 1865
ASHTON, STEPHEN M.   PVT   CO. G
   SWORN: FEB 27, 1865   MUSTERED: SEP 11, 1865
ATKINSON, JOHN   CPL   CO. D
   SWORN: FEB 17, 1865   MUSTERED: SEP 11, 1865
   PROMOTED TO CORPORAL SEP 1, 1865
ATKINSON, WILLIAM T.   PVT   CO. I
   SWORN: FEB 16, 1865   MUSTERED: SEP 11, 1865
ATTICKS, OLIVER   SGT   CO. D
   SWORN: FEB 20, 1865   MUSTERED: SEP 11, 1865
AUCHENBACH, J.N.   PVT   CO. D
   SWORN: FEB 17, 1865   MUSTERED: SEP 11, 1865
AUGUSTINE, JACOB   PVT   CO. E
   SWORN: FEB 20, 1865   DESERTED: AUG 8, 1865
AUMAN, JACOB   CPL   CO. K П
   SWORN: FEB 28, 1865   MUSTERED: SEP 11, 1865
AYERS, EDWIN   MUC   CO. G
   SWORN: FEB 27, 1865   MUSTERED: SEP 11, 1865
BAKER, ABRAHAM   PVT   CO. K
   SWORN: FEB 28, 1865   MUSTERED: SEP 11, 1865
BAKER, WILLIAM   PVT   CO. H П
   SWORN: FEB 21, 1865   MUSTERED: SEP 11, 1865
BAKER, WINFIELD S.   PVT   CO. K
   SWORN: FEB 28, 1865   MUSTERED: SEP 11, 1865
BALDWIN, THOMAS   PVT   CO. F
   SWORN: FEB 10, 1865   MUSTER: SEP 11, 1865
BANFORD, THOMAS   PVT   CO. G
   SWORN: FEB 27, 1865   MUSTERED: SEP 11, 1865
BARKER, GEORGE   1LT   CO. H
   SWORN: FEB 28, 1865   MUSTERED: SEP 11, 1865
BARNETT, DAVID   PVT   CO. K
   SWORN: FEB 28, 1865   MUSTERED: SEP 11, 1865
BARNHART, JACOB J.   CPL   CO. I   AGE: 21
   BORN: AUG 30, 1843, BUTLER COUNTY   VETERAN
   SWORN: AUG 7, 1862   MUSTERED: MAY 27, 1863; PVT PA 134th, CO. K
   SWORN: FEB 25, 1865   MUSTERED: SEP 11, 1865
   PROMOTED FROM PVT TO CPL AUG 8, 1865
   WIFE: ELIZABETH BARNHART, DAUGHTER OF FREDERICK BARNHART
   BATTLES: FREDERICKSBURG, CHANCELORSVILLE
BARR, HENRY   PVT   CO. G
   SWORN: FEB 27, 1865   MUSTERED: SEP 11, 1865
BARTLEY, NAAMAN F.   PVT   CO. E
   SWORN: FEB 17, 1865   MUSTER: SEP 11, 1865
BARTLEY, WASHINGTON   PVT   CO. E

SWORN: FEB 17, 1865   MUSTER: MAY 20, 1865
BARTLEY, WILLIAMSON   PVT   CO. E
BARTLEY, WILLIAM
    SWORN: FEB 17, 1865   MUSTER: SEP 11, 1865
    1890 CENSUS: POLLOCK, CLARION COUNTY, PA
BARTON, JAMES   CPL   CO. E
    SWORN: FEB 18, 1865   MUSTER: SEP, 9 1865
    PROMOTED TO CORPORAL; FEB 27, 1865
BATHELL, JOHN   PVT   CO. A
    SWORN: MAR 2, 1865/3 YRS   MUSTER: SEP 11, 1865
BAUMAN, FREDERICK   PVT   CO. E   AGE: 28
    BORN: SAXON VOIGLAND, GERMANY   ENLISTED AT ALLEGHENY CITY
    SWORN: FEB 15, 1865   MUSTER: SICK: ABSENT
    HOME 1886: SAXONBURG, BUTLER COUNTY, PA
    1886 REUNION IN FREEPORT   WIFE: LOUISA ADERHOLD
BEARCROFT, WILLIAM   PVT   CO. D
    SWORN: FEB 11, 1865   DIED: MAR 23, 1865 @ ALEXANDRIA, VA
BEARD, WILLIAM   PVT   CO. D
    SWORN: FEB 17, 1865   DISCHARGED: JUN 3, 1865
BEARLY, JACOB   PVT   CO. C
    SWORN: FEB 18, 1865   MUSTERED: SEP 11, 1865
BEAVER, HENRY   PVT   CO. K
    SWORN: MAR 7, 1865   MUSTERED: SEP 11, 1865
BEAVER, MICHAEL   CPL   CO. K
    SWORN: FEB 28, 1865   MUSTERED: SEP 11, 1865
BECK, JOSEPH   PVT   CO. B
    SWORN: JAN 14, 1865   DESERTED: AUG 11, 1865
BECKER, WILLIAM   PVT   CO. H
    SWORN: MAR 1, 1865   MUSTERED: SEP 11, 1865
BECKMAN, IRWIN   PVT   CO. E
    SWORN: FEB 15, 1865   MUSTER: SICK; ABSENT
BEDILLION, ROBERT   PVT   CO. E
    SWORN: FEB 15, 1865   MUSTER: SEP 11, 1865
BEERS, SAMUEL   1ST SGT   CO. E
    SWORN: FEB 15, 1865   MUSTER: SEP 11, 1865
BEHM, WILLIAM F.   PVT   CO. E
    SWORN: FEB 18, 1865   MUSTER: SEP 11, 1865
BELL, GEORGE   PVT   CO. H
    SWORN: FEB 21, 1865   MUSTERED: SEP 11, 1865
BENDER, CLOYD C.   PVT   CO. D
    SWORN: FEB 22, 1865   DESERTED: AUG 23, 1865
BENNER, GEORGE   PVT   CO. F
    SWORN: FEB 22, 1865   DISCHARGED: MAY 20, 1865
BENNETT, JOHN A.   CPL   CO. F
    SWORN: FEB 20, 1865   MUSTER: SEP 11, 1865
    PROMOTED FROM PRIVATE FEB 27, 1865
BENNETT, JOHN H.   PVT   CO. H
    SWORN: JAN 25, 1865   MUSTERED: ABSENT
    SERVING SENTENCE FROM GENERAL COURT MARTIAL
BENNETT, LEMUEL   PVT   CO. G
    SWORN: FEB 27, 1865   DIED: JUL 31, 1865 @ NASHVILLE
    BURIED @ NASHVILLE
BENINGER, WILLIAM #   PVT   CO. H
    NO INFORMATION
    1886 REUNION IN FREEPORT: HOME, BURRELL, PA
BENTZ, JOSEPH   PVT   CO. I
    SWORN: FEB 16, 1865   MUSTERED: SEP 11, 1865

BETZ, CONRAD   PVT   CO. I
    SWORN: FEB 18, 1865   MUSTERED: SEP 11, 1865
BIGLOW, ELIPHAS   PVT   CO. K
    SWORN: MAR 2, 1865   DISCHARGED: MAY 21, 1865
BILBEY, CHRISTOPHER   PVT   CO. F
    SWORN: MAR 17, 1865   MUSTER: SEP 11, 1865
BISHOP, GEORGE W.   PVT   CO. D
    SWORN: FEB 17, 1865   MUSTERED: SEP 11, 1865
BLACK, ADAM   PVT   CO. D
    SWORN: FEB 8, 1865   DISCHARGED: MAY 16, 1865
BLACK, JOHN   PVT   CO. H
    SWORN: FEB 20, 1865   MUSTERED: SEP 11, 1865
BLACK, LEWIS   PVT   CO. E
    SWORN: FEB 24, 1865   MUSTER: SICK, ABSENT
BLACK, SOLOMON   PVT   CO. F   AGE: 31
    BLACKSMITH   ORGIN: INDIANA COUNTY
    SWORN: FEB 14, 1865   MUSTER: SICK/ABSENT
    REMAINED IN NASHVILLE WITH TYPHOID
    BURIED: INDIANA COUNTY, OAKLAND CEMETERY, WHITE TWP., 1830-JUL 20, 1912
BLAIN, JAMES   PVT   CO. F
    SWORN: FEB 23, 1865   MUSTER: SEP 11, 1865
BLISS, HENRY   PVT   CO. I
    SWORN: FEB 21, 1865   MUSTERED: SEP 11, 1865
    BURIED: PROSPECT CEMETERY, TARENTUM, PA; DIED: DEC 25, 1902
BLOMAN, JOSEPH   PVT   CO. H
    SWORN: FEB 21, 1865   DISCHARGED: SEP 9, 1865
BLUME, CHRISTOPHER   PVT   CO. G
    SWORN: FEB 27, 1865   DISCHARGED: SEP 9, 1865
BLUNDIN, JAMES   PVT   CO. F
    SWORN: FEB 20, 1865   MUSTER: SEP 11, 1865
BODEN, WILLIAM H.   PVT   CO. D   AGE: 25
BODEN, W.W.
    SWORN: MAR 7, 1865   DISCHARGED: MAY 27, 1865
    1890 CENSUS: LONG RUN, ARMSTRONG COUNTY, PA
    BURIED: EDGEWOOD CEMETERY, SALTSBURG, INDIANA COUNTY, PA 1840-1916
BOGGS, DETMOR P.   MUS   CO. E Π
    SWORN: FEB 21, 1865   MUSTER: SEP 11, 1865
BOGGS, HENRY C.   PVT   CO. I
    SWORN: FEB 16, 1865   MUSTERED: SEP 11, 1865
BOGGS, PALMER   PVT   CO. I
    SWORN: FEB 16, 1865   DISCHARGED: JUN 3, 1865
BOGGS, ROBERT L./J.   CPT   CO. E
    SWORN: FEB 27, 1865   MUSTER: SEP 11, 1865
    1886 REUNION IN FREEPORT: HOME, ZELIENOPLE, PA
BOHN, CHARLES   PVT   CO. E
    SWORN: FEB 15, 1865   MUSTER: SEP 11, 1865
BOLLINGER, OLIVER P.   ASST SUR   STAFF   AGE:37
    SWORN: APR 3, 1865   RESIGNED: JUN 22, 1865
    BORN: JUL 8, 1827   DIED: JUL 4, 1895
    BURIED: APOLLO CEMETERY, APOLLO, PA
BOLLNER, H.P.   PVT   CO. G
    SWORN: FEB 27, 1865   MUSTERED: SICK, ABSENT
BONHAYRO, LEWIS   PVT   CO. D
    SWORN: FEB 16, 1865   MUSTERED: SEP 11, 1865   SUBSTITUTE
BOOKWALTERS, BENJAMIN F.#   PVT   CO. K
    SWORN: FEB 28, 1865   MUSTERED: SEP 11, 1865
    1890 CENSUS: CAVODE, INDIANA COUNTY, PA

BORDEL, ISRAEL   PVT   CO. K
    SWORN: MAR 2, 1865   MUSTERED: SEP 11, 1865
BOTT, WILLIAM C.   PVT   CO. D
    SWORN: FEB 20, 1865   DISCHARGED: JUN 2, 1865
BOWMAN, JOHN   PVT   CO. F
NOWMAN, JOHN
    SWORN: FEB 8, 1865   MUSTER: SEP 11, 1865
BOWN, GEORGE H.   PVT   CO. G
    SWORN: FEB 27, 1865   DISCHARGED: JUN 2, 1865
BOYDEN, THOMAS   PVT   CO. C
    SWORN: FEB 18, 1865   MUSTERED: SEP 11, 1865
BOYER, ELIAS R.   PVT   CO. F   AGE: 23
    BORN: BUTLER COUNTY, MAR 5, 1842
    SWORN: MAR 6, 1865   MUSTER: SEP 11, 1865
    FATHER, ISAAC SERVED IN PA 77th: 1861-1865 and WOUNDED JUN 25, 1863 @ TULLAHOMA
BRADY, JOHN C.   PVT   CO. K
    SWORN: MAR 27, 1865   MUSTERED: SEP 11, 1865
BRADY, SAMUEL R.P.   PVT   CO. D
    SWORN: FEB 17, 1865   MUSTERED: SEP 11, 1865
BRANNAN, WILLIAM F.   CPL   CO. G
    SWORN: FEB 27, 1865   MUSTERED: SEP 11, 1865
    PROMOTED TO CPL; MAR 2, 1865
BRANT, HENRY   PVT   CO. I
    SWORN: FEB 20, 1865   MUSTERED: SEP 11, 1865
BRANYAN, JOHN G.   CPL   CO. G
    SWORN: FEB 27, 1865   MUSTERED: SEP 11, 1865
    PROMOTED TO CPL; MAR 2, 1865
BRATTON, SAMUEL C.   PVT   CO. F
    SWORN: FEB 13, 1865   MUSTER: SICK/ABSENT
BRENNER, JACOB   PVT   CO. D
    SWORN: FEB 17, 1865   MUSTERED: SICK, ABSENT
BREWSTER, JOHN   CPT   CO. K
    SWORN: MAR 8, 1865   MUSTERED: SEP 11, 1865
BRICKER, JOSEPH   PVT   CO. D
    SWORN: FEB 11, 1865   MUSTERED: SEP 11, 1865
BRINDLE, LONATHAN   PVT   CO. K
    SWORN: FEB 28, 1865   DESERTED: AUG 15, 1865
BRINEY, JOHN   PVT   CO. I
    SWORN: FEB 17, 1865   MUSTERED: SEP 11, 1865
BRINKER, HENRY P.   PVT   CO. A
    SWORN: FEB 14, 1865/3 YRS   MUSTER: SEP 11, 1865
BRODE, SAMUEL E.   PVT   CO. K
    SWORN: MAR 6, 1865   MUSTERED: SEP 11, 1865
BROOM, DICKINSON   PVT   CO. C
    SWORN: FEB 18, 1865   MUSTERED: SEP 11, 1865
BROUGHT, JOHN A.   PVT   CO. C
    SWORN: FEB 18, 1865   MUSTERED: SEP 11, 1865
BROWN, DAVID   PVT   CO. F
    SWORN: FEB 20, 1865   DISCHARGED: MAY 12, 1865
BROWN, JOSEPH B.   1LT   CO. H
    SWORN: MAR 4, 1865   MUSTERED: SEP 11, 1865
BROWN, ROBERT   PVT   CO. H
    SWORN: FEB 20, 1865   MUSTER: SEP 11, 1865
BROWN, THOMAS   PVT   CO. H   AGE: 28
    SWORN: FEB 15, 1865   MUSTER: SEP 11, 1865
    1886 REUNION IN FREEPORT: HOME, FREEPORT, PA
    BURIED:ST. PAUL'S LUTHERAN CEMETERY, SARVER, PA [1837-1898]

BRUNSON, JOSIAH   PVT   CO. H
   SWORN: FEB 23, 1865   MUSTERED: SEP 11, 1865
BUCHANAN, JAMES W.   SGT   CO. K
   SWORN: FEB 28, 1865   MUSTERED: SEP 11, 1865
BUCHANAN, JOHN   SGT   CO. H
   SWORN: FEB 23, 1865   MUSTERED: SEP 11, 1865
BUCKWALTER, B.F.   PVT   CO. K
   SWORN: FEB 28, 1865   MUSTERED: SEP 11, 1865
BUNDU, EUGENE H.   PVT   CO. F
   SWORN: FEB 25, 1865   DISCHARGED: JUN 2, 1865
BURFORD, ANDREW J.   PVT   CO. G
   SWORN: FEB 14, 1865   DISCHARGED: MAY 20, 1865
BURKHOLDER, JOHN W.   PVT   UNASSIGNED
   SWORN: FEB 17, 1865   DISCHARGED: AUG 29, 1865   SUBSTITUTE
BURRY, FREDERICK   1ST SGT   CO. E
   SWORN: FEB 20, 1865   MUSTER: SEP 11, 1865
BURTT, CHARLES N.   PVT   CO. F
   SWORN: FEB 23, 1865   MUSTER: SEP 11, 1865
BURTT, WILLIAM S.   PVT   CO. F
   SWORN: FEB 23, 1865   MUSTER: SEP 11, 1865
BUSH, JACOB   PVT   CO. I
   SWORN: JAN 14, 1865   MUSTERED: SEP 11, 1865
BUSSOM, JAMES C.   PVT   CO. D
   SWORN: FEB 17, 1865   MUSTERED: SEP 11, 1865
BUZZARD, ANDREW   PVT   CO. K
   SWORN: MAR 7, 1865   DESERTED: JUL 18, 1865
BYERS, JONAS   CPL   CO. F
   SWORN: FEB 21, 1865   MUSTER: SICK/ABSENT
BYERS, WILLIAM #   PVT   CO. A
   SWORN: UNKNOWN   DIED: MAR 18, 1865
   BURIED @ CYPRESS HILL CEMETERY, LONG ISLAND
BYERS, WILLIAM   PVT   CO. G
   SWORN: FEB 25, 1865   DIED: AUG 25, 1865 @ NASHVILLE
   BURIED @ NASHVILLE, BATES
CALDWALDER, J.W.   PVT   CO. D
   SWORN: FEB 22, 1865   DISCHARGED: AUG 28, 1865
CAMERON, HUGH   PVT   CO. I
   SWORN: FEB 16, 1865   MUSTER: SEP 11, 1865
CAMPBELL, ALEXANDER   PVT   CO. I
   SWORN: FEB 18, 1865   MUSTER: SEP 11, 1865
CAMPBELL, JOHN   PVT   CO. H
COMPBELL, JOHN
   SWORN: FEB 23, 1865   DISCHARGED: SEP 9, 1865
CAMPBELL, JOHN A.   PVT   CO. I
   SWORN: FEB 20, 1865   MUSTER: SEP 11, 1865
CAMPBELL, THOMAS   PVT   CO. I
CAMPBELL, THOMAS WADE
   SWORN: FEB 16, 1865   MUSTER: SEP 11, 1865
   1890 CENSUS: NEW FLORENCE, WESTMORELAND COUNTY, PA
   BURIED: BETHEL CEMETERY, W. WHEATFIELD TWP., INDIANA COUNTY; 1847-1936
CANBY, WILLIAM   SGT   CO. F
   SWORN: FEB 16, 1865   MUSTER: SEP 11, 1865
CARUS, WILLIAM   PVT   CO. G
   SWORN: APR 3, 1865   MUSTERED: SEP 11, 1865
CAUGHEY SAMUEL W.   PVT   CO. F
   SWORN: FEB·23, 1865   MUSTER: SEP 11, 1865
CAVITT, LEWIS   PVT   CO. H

SWORN: FEB 20, 1865   MUSTERED: SEP 11, 1865
CHAMBERS, CHRISTOPHER   PVT   CO. H
    SWORN: FEB 21, 1865   MUSTERED: SEP 11, 1865
CHESTNUT, SAMUEL   SGT   CO. C
    SWORN: FEB 18, 1865   MUSTER: SEP 11, 1865
CHISHOLM, JAMES   PVT   CO. F
    SWORN: FEB 15, 1865   MUSTER: SEP 11, 1865
CHRISTIAN, RICHARD A.   PVT   CO. I
    SWORN: FEB 20, 1865   MUSTER: SEP 11, 1865
CHRISTMAS, FREDERICK   PVT   CO. G
CRISMAN, FREDERICK
    SWORN: MAR 17, 1865   DISCHARGED: MAY 31, 1865
    1890 CENSUS: SHIPPENVILLE, CLARION COUNTY, PA
CISSNIA, JAMES A.   PVT   CO. G
    SWORN: MAR 4, 1865   DIED: APR 22, 1865 @ NASHVILLE
    BURIED @ NASHVILLE, ROW J, GRAVE #743, BATES
CLAPPER, OLIVE W.   PVT   CO. K
    SWORN: FEB 28, 1865   MUSTERED: SEP 11, 1865
CLARK, ANDREW   PVT   CO. K
    SWORN: MAR 6, 1865   DIED: JUN 4, 1865 @ NASHVILLE
    BURIED @ NASHVILLE, BATES
CLARK, DAVID M.   MUC   CO. G
    SWORN: FEB 27, 1865   MUSTERED: SEP 11, 1865
CLAWSON, WILLIAM   PVT   CO. I
    SWORN: FEB 14, 1865   DISCHARGED: MAY 20, 1865
    1890 CENSUS: LONG RUN, ARMSTRONG COUNTY, PA
CLAYPOOLE, SAMUEL N.   PVT   CO. I   AGE: 33
CLAYPOLE, SAMUEL
    SWORN: FEB 15, 1865   MUSTER: SEP 11, 1865
    1890 CENSUS: GIRTY, ARMSTRONG COUNTY, PA
    BURIED: UNION BAPTIST CEMETERY, SLATE LICK, PA [1842-1900]
CLOUSE, JACOB   PVT   CO. F
    SWORN: FEB 14, 1865   MUSTER: SEP 11, 1865
CLOWES, JACOB #   PVT   CO. F
    SWORN: FEB 14, 1865   MUSTER: SEP 11, 1865
    1890 CENSUS: WILLET, INDIANA COUNTY, PA
COLPITZER, GEORGE   PVT   CO. K
    SWORN: MAR 2, 1865   DIED: JUL 6, 1865 @ NASHVILLE
    BURIED @ NASHVILLE, ROW B, GRAVE #1216, BATES
COMFORT, JOSEPH A.   PVT   CO. C
    SWORN: FEB 18, 1865   MUSTERED: SEP 11, 1865
COMFORT, SAMUEL M.   PVT   CO. C
    SWORN: FEB 18, 1865   DISCHARGED: JUN 7, 1865
CONNER, GEORGE E.   PVT   CO. C
    SWORN: FEB 18, 1865   DISCHARGED: JUN 7, 1865
COOK, DAVID S.   CPT   CO. G
    SWORN: MAR 2, 1865   MUSTERED: SEP 11, 1865
COOK, JOSIAH W.   PVT   CO. C
    SWORN: FEB 18, 1865   MUSTERED: SEP 11, 1865
COOPER, DAVID   PVT   CO. H
    SWORN: FEB 21, 1865   MUSTER: SEP 11, 1865
COOVER, GEORGE H.   SGT   CO. D
    SWORN: FEB 20, 1865   DIED: JUL 6, 1865 @ NASHVILLE
CORBIN, JOHN   PVT   CO. K
    SWORN: FEB 28, 1865   MUSTERED: SEP 11, 1865
CORNELIUS, GEORGE J.   PVT   CO. D
    SWORN: FEB 20, 1865   MUSTERED: SICK, ABSENT

CORNMAN, L.C.   SGT   CO. D
    SWORN: FEB 8, 1865   MUSTERED: SEP 11, 1865
    PROMOTED FROM CORPORAL, JUN 3, 1865
COUCH, GEORGE W.   PVT   CO. D
    SWORN: MAR 7, 1865   MUSTERED: SEP 11, 1865
COULTER, THOMAS J.   PVT   CO. K
    SWORN: MAR 7, 1865   DISCHARGED: MAY 23, 1865
COULTER, WILLIAM A.   HOSP STEWARD   STAFF
    SWORN: MAR 9, 1865   MUSTER: ABSENT, ON FURLOUGH
    PROMOTED FROM PVT, CO. B, MAY 1, 1865
COVERT, BENJAMIN F.   PVT   CO. E
    SWORN: FEB 18, 1865   MUSTER: SEP 11, 1865
COWAN, THOMAS   PVT   CO. H
    SWORN: MAR 27, 1865   DISCHARGED: AUG 28, 1865
COWDEN, JAMES R.   1LT   CO. G
    SWORN: FEB 27, 1865   MUSTERED: SEP 11, 1865
    PROMOTED FROM 2LT; JUL 1, 1865
CRABB, MARK M.   PVT   CO. H
    SWORN: FEB 23, 1865   DISCHARGED: JUN 8, 1865
CRADLE, PHILIP   MUS   CO. E
    SWORN: FEB 20, 1865   MUSTER: SEP 11, 1865
    BROTHER-IN-LAW, HENRY E. MILLER SERVED CO. G, PA 4th CAVALRY
CRAVEN, BENJAMIN   2LT   CO. G
    SWORN: FEB 27, 1865   MUSTERED: SEP 11, 1865
    PROMOTED FROM 1ST SGT; JUL 1, 1865
CRAVEN, JAMES   PVT   CO. G
    SWORN: FEB 27, 1865   DISCHARGED: JUN 12, 1865
CRAWFORD, PAUL   CPT   CO. H
    SWORN: MAR 4, 1865   MUSTERED: SEP 11, 1865
CRAWFORD, WILLIAM N.   PVT   CO. G
    SWORN: FEB 27, 1865   DIED: APR 15, 1865 @ NASHVILLE
    BURIED @ NASHVILLE, ROW J, GRAVE #1218, BATES
CRITCHLOW, JOHN C.   PVT   CO. E
    SWORN: FEB 20, 1865   MUSTER: MAY 23, 1865
CROSS, JOSEPH L.   PVT   CO. H
    SWORN: MAR 23, 1865   MUSTER: SEP 11, 1865
CULBERT, THOMAS.   PVT   CO. D
    SWORN: FEB 22, 1865   MUSTERED: SEP 11, 1865
CULLENBERGER, JAMES   PVT   CO. H
    SWORN: MAR 3, 1865   DISCHARGED: MAY 13, 1865
CUNNINGHAM, W.   PVT   CO. K
    SWORN: FEB 28, 1865   MUSTERED: SEP 11, 1865
DANIELS, OLIVER   PVT   CO. K
McDANIELS, OLIVER
    SWORN: MAR 7, 1865   MUSTER: SEP 11, 1865
    SHOWN AS UNASSIGNED [DANIELS]
DAUM, ADAM   CPL   CO. I
    SWORN: FEB 18, 1865   MUSTER: SEP 11, 1865
    PROMOTED FROM PVT TO CPL; MAY 23, 1865
DRAKE, JOHN T.   PVT   CO. G
    SWORN: MAR 2, 1865   MUSTERED: SEP 11, 1865
    U.S. PENSION, 1894: $12.00   HOME: FREEPORT
    1886 REUNION IN FREEPORT; HOME 1886-1890, SLATE LICK, ARMSTRONG COUNTY, PA
DRESHER, HENRY   PL MUS   STAFF
DRESCHER, HENRY
    SWORN: FEB 15, 1865   MUSTER: SEP 11, 1865
    PROMOTED FROM PVT, CO. E, APR 1, 1865; TO PRINCIPAL MUSICIAN SEP 1, 1865.

1886 REUNION IN FREEPORT: HOME, NEW CASTLE, PA
DRESHER, WILLIAM   PVT   CO. E
    SWORN: FEB 15, 1865   MUSTER: SEP 11, 1865
    1886 REUNION IN FREEPORT: HOME, SAXONBURG, PA
DUNCAN, WILLIAM   CPL   CO. E
    SWORN: FEB 22, 1865   MUSTER: MAY 15, 1865
EBERSOLE, MICHAEL   PVT   CO. D
    SWORN: FEB 18, 1865   DISCHARGED: JUN 8, 1865
EBERSOLE, WILLIAM   CPL   CO. D
    SWORN: FEB 20, 1865   DISCHARGED: JUL 18, 1865
EDWARDS, SAMUEL   ASST SUR   STAFF
    SWORN: FEB 16, 1865   MUSTER: SEP 11, 1865
    PROMOTED FROM SERGEANT CO. I, JUL 1, 1865.
    COMPANY RECORDS SHOW EDWARDS PROMOTED TO SGT MAJOR; JUL 1, 1865
EISENBEIS, SAMUEL   2LT   CO. C
    SWORN: FEB 20, 1865   MUSTER: SEP 11, 1865
ELDER, WILLIAM W.   PVT.   CO. F
    SWORN: FEB 14, 1865   MUSTER: SEP 11, 1865
ELDERINGHAM, H.   PVT   CO. H
    SWORN: FEB 21, 1865   MUSTER: SEP 11, 1865
ELLIOTT, DANIEL   PVT   CO. D
    SWORN: FEB 17, 1865   DISCHARGED: MAY 16, 1865
ENNEY, THOMAS J.   CPL   CO. C
    SWORN: FEB 18, 1865   MUSTER: SEP 11, 1865
ENYEART, DAVID G.   1LT   CO. K
    SWORN: MAR 8, 1865   MUSTERED: SEP 11, 1865
FAUSNAUGHT, BERN. #   PVT   CO. I
    SWORN: UNKNOWN   DIED: APR 16, 1865 AT NASHVILLE
    BURIED @ NASHVILLE, ROW J, GRAVE #874, BATES
FENNELL, DANIEL   PVT   CO. I
    SWORN: FEB 23, 1865   DISCHARGED: SEP 9, 1865
FENNELL, ISAAC   PVT   CO. I   AGE: 21
    OCCUPATION: FARMER   BORN: AUG 21, 1840
    WIFE: MARY McELFRESH; MARRIED MAY 31, 1865; SHE DIED IN 1867.
    2nd WIFE:NANCY KEIBLER [BEERS HISTORY]
    SWORN: FEB 23, 1865   DISCHARGED: SEP 9, 1865
    U.S. PENSION, 1894: $6.00   HOME: LOGANSPORT
    1890 CENSUS: BETHEL TWP., ARMSTRONG COUNTY, PA
FINLEY, JOHN BORLAND   COL
FINLAY, JOHN BORLAND
    COMMANDER OF CAMP ORR, KITTANNING, PA
    CASHIER AT THE KITTANNING BANK
    NEVER TRULY RECEIVED A COMMISSION, TITLE HONORARY
FLEMING, JOSEPH J.   PVT   CO. G
    SWORN: MAR 23, 1865   MUSTERED: SEP 11, 1865
FORBES, J.W.   PVT   CO. G
    SWORN: MAR 15, 1865   MUSTERED: NOT ON ROLLS
FORCE, GEORGE   PVT   CO. H
    SWORN: FEB 21, 1865   MUSTER: SEP 11, 1865
FORD, SAMUEL W.   PVT   CO. C
    SWORN: FEB 18, 1865   DIED: MAY 14, 1865 @ NASHVILLE
    BURIED @ NASHVILLE, BATES
FOREMAN, JAMES   PVT   CO. A/E
    SWORN: FEB 14, 1865   MUSTER: SEP 11, 1865
    1890 CENSUS: DAYTON BOROUGH., ARMSTRONG COUNTY, PA
    BURIED: DAYTON CEMETERY, DAYTON, PA
FRAZIER, JOHN   PVT   CO. G

SWORN: FEB 27, 1865   DISCHARGED: JUN 8, 1865
FRAZIER, JOHN T.   PVT   CO. G
  SWORN: FEB 27, 1865   MUSTERED: SEP 11, 1865
FRAZIER, JOSEPH C.   CPL   CO. G
  SWORN: FEB 27, 1865   MUSTERED: SEP 11, 1865
  PROMOTED TO CPL, JUL 1, 1865
FRAZIER, T.W. #   PVT   CO. K
  NO INFORMATION
  1886 REUNION IN FREEPORT: HOME, SAXONBURG, PA
  COULD BE THOMAS FRAZIER FROM THE 63rd
FRIEND, JEREMIAH   PVT   CO. C
  SWORN: FEB 18, 1865   DESERTED: AUG 17, 1865
FRY, BENJAMIN   PVT   CO. D
  SWORN: FEB 17, 1865   MUSTER: SEP 11, 1865
FRY, DAVID   CPL   CO. I
  SWORN: FEB 16, 1865   MUSTER: SEP 11, 1865
  PROMOTED FROM PVT TO CPL; JUL 1, 1865
FRY, GEORGE W.   PVT   CO. E
  SWORN: FEB 20, 1865   DIED: JUL 19, 1865 AT NASHVILLE
  BURIED @ NASHVILLE, ROW J, GRAVE #1342, BATES
FRY, JOHN P.   PVT   CO. F
  SWORN: FEB 23, 1865   DISCHARGED: JUN 12, 1865
FULLERTON, JOHN #   PVT   CO. F
  SWORN: FEB 22, 1865/3 YRS   MUSTER: SEP 11, 1865
  PREVIOUS SERVICE
  1890 CENSUS: CRAIGSVILLE, ARMSTRONG COUNTY, PA
GALLOWAY, GEORGE #   PVT   CO. D
  SWORN: UNKNOWN   DIED: AUG 29, 1865
  BURIED @ NASHVILLE, ROW E, GRAVE #2355, BATES
GARVIN, JAMES R.   PVT   CO. E
  SWORN: FEB 22, 1865   MUSTER: SEP 11, 1865
GASTON, ALEXANDER L.   PVT   CO. F   AGE: 35
  SWORN: FEB 14, 1865   MUSTER: SICK/ABSENT - SEP 22, 1865
  1890 CENSUS: INDIANA, INDIANA COUNTY, PA
  BURIED: INDIANA COUNTY, GREENWOOD CEMETERY, JAN 14, 1830-FEB 19, 1907
GIBSON, SAMUEL S.   PVT   CO. E   AGE: 21
  SWORN: APR 4, 1865   MUSTER: SEP 11, 1865
  BURIED: BLAIRSVILLE CEMETERY, BLAIRSVILLE, PA 1844-1917
GILLILAND, JOHN W.   PVT   CO. E
  SWORN: FEB 20, 1865   MUSTER: SICK AT MUSTER, ABSENT
GLENN, JOHN   CPL   CO. I
  SWORN: FEB 14, 1865   MUSTER: SEP 11, 1865
  PROMOTED FROM PVT TO CPL; MAY 18, 1865
GOEHRING, LEWIS   PVT   CO. E
  SWORN: FEB 14, 1865   MUSTER: SICK AT MUSTER, ABSENT
GOLD, WILLIAM J.   PVT   CO. E
  SWORN: FEB 25, 1865   DESERTED: AUG 8, 1865
GORDON, JOHN   PVT   CO. I   AGE: 40
  SWORN: MAR 23, 1865   MUSTERED: SEP 11, 1865
  BURIED: EDGEWOOD CEMETERY, SALTSBURG, INDIANA COUNTY, PA 1825-1907
GRAFT, SAMUEL #   PVT   CO. F
  SWORN: FEB 7, 1865   MUSTERED: SEP 11, 1865
  1890 CENSUS: CHAMBERSVILLE, INDIANA COUNTY, PA; WIDOW HARRIETT
GRAHAM, THEOPHILIS #   PVT   CO. E
  SWORN: AUG 28, 1862/3 YRS   MUSTER: JUN 1, 1863 [CO. D, 137th PA]
  SWORN: FEB 24, 1865/1 YRS   MUSTER: SEP 11, 1865
  BURIED: BLAIRSVILLE CEMETERY, BLAIRSVILLE, PA 1841-1917

GRAHAM, WILLIAM   PVT   CO. E
   SWORN: FEB 24, 1865   DISCHARGED: AUG 24, 1865
GRIFFITH, WILLIAM #   PVT   CO. F
   SWORN: UNKNOWN   DIED: AUG 29, 1865
   BURIED @ NASHVILLE, ROW E, GRAVE #2355, BATES
GROFF, SAMUEL   PVT   CO. F
GROFT, SAMUEL
   SWORN: FEB 7, 1865   DISCHARGED: JUN 2, 1865
   BURIED: INDIANA COUNTY, WASHINGTON CEMETERY, RAYNE TWP., 1826-JUN 19, 1877
GROSSMAN, JACOB G.   PVT   CO. I
   SWORN: MAR 9, 1865   MUSTER: SEP 11, 1865
GRUBBS, GEORGE W.   SGT   CO. I
   SWORN: FEB 16, 1865   MUSTER: SEP 11, 1865
   PROMOTED FROM PVT TO SGT: MAR 3, 1865
GRUBBS, PATTERSON   PVT   CO. E
   SWORN: FEB 14, 1865   DISCHARGED: AUG 28, 1865
HAGAR, DAVID   PVT   CO. H
   SWORN: MAR 14, 1865   DESERTED: JUL 30, 1865
HAHN, JOSEPH   PVT   CO. H
   SWORN: FEB 21, 1865   MUSTER: SEP 11, 1865
HALDEMAN, SAMUEL   PVT   CO. D
   SWORN: FEB 20, 1865   MUSTER: SEP 11, 1865
HALL, EPHRIAM   PVT   CO. H
   SWORN: FEB 15, 1865   MUSTER: ABSENT, ON FURLOUGH
HALL, THOMAS S.   PVT   CO. I
   SWORN: FEB 20, 1865   MUSTERED: SEP 11, 1865
HAMAKER, JAMES P.   PVT   CO. C
   SWORN: FEB 18, 1865   MUSTER: SEP 11, 1865
HAMAKER, WILLIAM W.   CPL   CO. C
   SWORN: FEB 18, 1865   MUSTER: SEP 11, 1865
HAMILTON, DAVID   PVT   CO. K
   SWORN: FEB 28, 1865   MUSTERED: SICK, ABSENT
HAMILTON, JOHN   PVT   CO. G
   SWORN: FEB 28, 1865   MUSTERED: SEP 11, 1865
HAMILTON, STEWART   PVT   CO. H
   SWORN: FEB 23, 1865   MUSTER: SEP 11, 1865
HAMOR, ADRIAN C.   PVT   CO. E
HAMER, ADRIAN C.
   SWORN: FEB 20, 1865   DIED: AUG 12, 1865 AT NASHVILLE
   BURIED @ NASHVILLE, BATES
HAMMEL, THOMAS   PVT   CO. B
   SWORN: JAN 28, 1865   MUSTER: SEP 11, 1865
HARDMAN, DAVID   PVT   CO. G
   SWORN: FEB 25, 1865   MUSTERED: SEP 11, 1865
HART, GEORGE W.   PVT   CO. C
   SWORN: FEB 18, 1865   MUSTER: SEP 11, 1865
HASTINGS, FRANK   PVT   CO. I
   SWORN: FEB 18, 1865   MUSTERED: SEP 11, 1865
HASWELL, JOHN   PVT   CO. F
   SWORN: FEB 15, 1865   MUSTER: SEP 11, 1865
HAWKINS, THOMAS   PVT   CO. H
   SWORN: FEB 25, 1865   DIED: SEP 2, 1865 IN CINCINNATI
   BURIED @ CINCINNATI, ROW C, GRAVE #44, BATES
HAYS, GEORGE   PVT   CO. E
   SWORN: FEB 18, 1865   MUSTER: SEP 11, 1865
HAYS, JAMES   PVT   CO. E
   SWORN: FEB 17, 1865   MUSTER: SEP 11, 1865

HAZLETT, WASHINGTON   PVT   CO. I   AGE: 22
    ORIGIN: TARENTUM, PA
    SWORN: JAN 10, 1862/3 YRS   DISCHARGED: NOV 28, 1862 [PA 103rd]
    SWORN: FEB 18, 1865   DESERTED: AUG 8, 1865
    1890 CENSUS: GREENSBURG, WESTMORELAND COUNTY, PA
    BATTLES: PENINSULAR, FAIR OAKS, SEVEN DAYS
HECKERT, AMOS   PVT   CO. E
    SWORN: FEB 15, 1865   MUSTER: SEP 11, 1865
    1886 REUNION IN FREEPORT: HOME, SAXONBURG, PA
HEIFFNER, ALLISON   PVT   CO. K
    SWORN: MAR 6, 1865   MUSTERED: SEP 11, 1865
HEIFFNER, JOSEPHUS   PVT   CO. K
    SWORN: MAR 6, 1865   MUSTERED: SEP 11, 1865
HEIFFNER, ORLADY   CPL   CO. K
    SWORN: FEB 28, 1865   DISCHARGED: JUN 21, 1865
HEIFFNER, PETER   PVT   CO. K
    SWORN: FEB 28, 1865   MUSTERED: SEP 11, 1865
HELLER, ERDMAN   PVT   CO. E
    SWORN: FEB 15, 1865   DISCHARGED, MAY 23, 1865
    1886 REUNION IN FREEPORT: HOME, SAXONBURG, PA
HENDERSON, CHARLES H.   1SGT   CO. C
    SWORN: FEB 18, 1865   MUSTER: SEP 11, 1865
HERMAN, FREDERICK   1SGT   CO. I
    SWORN: FEB 25, 1865   MUSTERED: SEP 11, 1865
    PROMOTED FROM PVT; MAR 2, 1865
HERWICK, JOHN D.   PVT   CO. I
    SWORN: FEB 16, 1865   MUSTERED: SEP 11, 1865
HESS, CHRISTIAN #   PVT   CO. A   VETERAN
    SWORN: SEP 21, 1861/3 YRS   MUSTER: OCT 22, 1864 [SGT/74th PA]
    SWORN: FEB 18, 1865   MUSTER: SEP 11, 1865
    1890 CENSUS: INDIANA, INDIANA COUNTY, PA
HESS, SAMUEL   PVT   CO. C
    SWORN: FEB 18, 1865   MUSTER: SEP 11, 1865
HESS, WASHINGTON   PVT   CO. D
    SWORN: FEB 18, 1865   MUSTERED: SEP 11, 1865
HICK, FRANK   PVT   CO. F
    SWORN: FEB 14, 1865   DESERTED: SEP 6, 1865
HICKS, JAMES   PVT   CO. K
    SWORN: FEB 28, 1865   DISCHARGED: AUG 28, 1865
HICKS, JONATHAN   PVT   CO. K
    SWORN: FEB 28, 1865   MUSTERED: SEP 11, 1865
HICKS, THOMAS H.   PVT   CO. K
    SWORN: MAR 6, 1865   DESERTED: AUG 12, 1865
HIGGINS, THOMAS   PVT   CO. D
    SWORN: FEB 22, 1865   DISCHARGED: JUN 3, 1865
HILTZ, MICHAEL   PVT   CO. I
    SWORN: FEB 18, 1865   DISCHARGED: MAY 20, 1865
HIMES, JOHN L.   PVT   CO. C
    SWORN: FEB 18, 1865   DISCHARGED BY SPECIAL ORDER; DATE UNKNOWN
HINCHBERGER, JOSEPH #   PVT   CO. H
    HOME IN 1897: BUTLER, PA
    RECORD FROM PRESIDENTS, SOLDIERS AND STATESMEN
HINEMAN, SEBASTIAN   PVT   CO. C
    SWORN: FEB 18, 1865   MUSTER: SEP 11, 1865
HINKLE WILLIAM   PVT   CO. D
    SWORN: FEB 7, 1865   DISCHARGED: MAY 23, 1865
HOFFMAN, CHARLES   2LT   CO. E

SWORN: FEB 27, 1865   MUSTER: SEP 11, 1865
PROMOTED FROM 1ST SERGEANT: JUN 1, 1865
1886 REUNION IN FREEPORT: HOME, SAXONBURG, PA
HOFFMAN, HENRY A.   PVT   CO. D
SWORN: FEB 8, 1865   MUSTERED: SICK, ABSENT
HOFFMAN, JOHN   PVT   UNASSIGNED
SWORN: APR 4, 1865   NOT ON MUSTER OUT ROLLS   SUBSTITUTE
HOFFMAN, JOHN D.   PVT   CO. G
SWORN: MAR 18, 1865   MUSTERED: SEP 11, 1865
HOGLE, GILBERT   PVT   CO. C
SWORN: FEB 18, 1865   MUSTER: SEP 11, 1865
HOLLAND, WILLIAM   PVT   CO. H
SWORN: FEB 23, 1865   DISCHARGED: JUL 15, 1865
HOLTON, JAMES   CPL   CO. G
SWORN: FEB 27, 1865   MUSTERED: SEP 11, 1865
PROMOTED TO CPL; MAY 17, 1865
HOOD, JOHN   PVT   CO. K
SWORN: FEB 28, 1865   MUSTERED: SEP 11, 1865
HOOPES, HARLAND A.   PVT   CO. D
SWORN: FEB 17, 1865   MUSTERED: SEP 11, 1865
HOOVER, ALBERT MATTHEW   PVT   CO. H   AGE: 21
SWORN: FEB 14, 1865   DISCHARGED: SEP 9, 1865
PROFESSION: PHYSICIAN & PHARMACIST
BORN: OCT 31, 1844, BUFFALO TWP., BUTLER COUNTY
SERVED AS COMPANY CLERK AND AS CLERK TO COLONEL BONNAFFON
SENT TO MOWER HOSPITAL IN PHILADELPHIA IN LATE JUL 1865; ILLNESS
PRESIDENT OF FIRST NATIONAL BANK, PARKER'S LANDING, PA
BROTHER N.M. HOOVER SERVED IN THE 61st OHIO, 10th VERMONT AND THE 87th PA AS A
PHYSICIAN AND ASST. SURGEON
HORN, JAMES   PVT   CO. E
SWORN: FEB 23, 1865   MUSTER: SEP 11, 1865
HORN, SIMON   PVT   CO. G
SWORN: FEB 8, 1865   DISCHARGED: MAY 19, 1865
HOSEY, JAMES   PVT   CO. G
SWORN: FEB 26, 1865   MUSTERED: SEP 11, 1865
HOULETTE, CHARLES W.   PVT   UNASSIGNED
SWORN: MAR 18, 1865   NOT ON MUSTER OUT ROLLS
HOWARD, GEORGE   PVT   CO. I   AGE: 54
SWORN: FEB 17, 1865   MUSTERED: SEP 11, 1865
BURIED: BLAIRSVILLE CEMETERY, BLAIRSVILLE, PA 1811-1883
HULLET, CHARLES W. #   PVT   CO. G
SWORN: UNKNOWN   DIED: APR 11, 1865
BURIED @ NASHVILLE, ROW C, GRAVE #126, BATES
HUMPHREYS, BENJAMIN   PVT   CO. H
SWORN: MAR 1, 1865   MUSTER: SEP 11, 1865
HUTCHINSON, GEORGE   PVT   CO. I
SWORN: FEB 17, 1865   MUSTERED: SEP 11, 1865
INGRAM, ROBERT   MUC   CO. I
SWORN: FEB 21, 1865   MUSTERED: SEP 11, 1865
IRWIN, THOMAS   PVT   CO. F
SWORN: FEB 23, 1865   MUSTER: SEP 11, 1865
IRWIN, WILLIAM   PVT   CO. G
SWORN: FEB 28, 1865   MUSTERED: SEP 11, 1865
ISENBERG, ALFRED P.   PVT   CO. K
SWORN: MAR 7, 1865   MUSTERED: SEP 11, 1865
ISENBERG, WILLIAM H.   PVT   CO. D
SWORN: MAR 7, 1865   DISCHARGED: JUN 3, 1865

BURIED: INDIANA COUNTY, UNIONTOWN CEMETERY, GREEN TWP.,

JACKSON, JAMES A.   PVT   CO. I
    SWORN: FEB 18, 1865   MUSTERED: SEP 11, 1865
JACKSON, MICHAEL   PVT   CO. C
    SWORN: FEB 18, 1865   DISCHARGED: MAY 20, 1865
JACOBS, JAMES H.   MUS   CO. C
    SWORN: FEB 18, 1865   MUSTER: SEP 11, 1865
JAMES, WILLIAM   PVT   CO. G
    SWORN: FEB 27, 1865   MUSTERED: SEP 11, 1865
JENKINS, JOHN   PVT   CO. K
    SWORN: MAR 2, 1865   MUSTERED: SEP 11, 1865
JOHNSTON, DANIEL   PVT   CO. B
    SWORN: FEB 23, 1865   MUSTER: MAY 16, 1865
JOHNSTON, JOHN B.   PVT   CO. I   AGE: 23
JOHNSON, JOHN B.
    SWORN: MAR 9, 1865   MUSTERED: SEP 11, 1865
    BURIED @ EDGEWOOD CEMETERY, SALTSBURG, PA; 1842-1920
    WIFE: CATHARINE 1848-1935
JOHNSTON, JOHN S.   MUC   CO. K
    SWORN: FEB 28, 1865   MUSTERED: SEP 11, 1865
JOHNSTON, THOMAS A.   PVT   CO. I   AGE: 35
JOHNSTON, THOMAS D.
    SWORN: MAR 23, 1865   MUSTERED: SEP 11, 1865
    1890 CENSUS: CREEKSIDE, INDIANA COUNTY, PA
    BURIED: INDIANA COUNTY, CHAMBERSVILLE BAPTIST CEMETERY, DEC 24, 1830-NOV 19, 1893
JOHNSTON, WILLIAM   1SGT   CO. H
    SWORN: FEB 23, 1865   MUSTERED: SEP 11, 1865
JOHNSTON, WILLIAM   PVT   CO. H
    SWORN: FEB 9, 1865   MUSTERED: SEP 11, 1865
JONES, DANIEL   PVT   CO. F
    SWORN: FEB 20, 1865   DIED: JUL 4, 1865 @ NASHVILLE
    BURIED @ NASHVILLE, ROW J, GRAVE #978, BATES
JONES, DAVID J.   PVT   CO. I
    SWORN: FEB 16, 1865   MUSTERED: SEP 11, 1865
JONES, JOHN J.   PVT   CO. H
    SWORN: FEB 20, 1865   MUSTERED: SEP 11, 1865
JONES, SAMUEL   PVT   CO. K
    SWORN: FEB 28, 1865   DISCHARGED: JUN 2, 1865
JONES, THOMAS   PVT   CO. F
    SWORN: FEB 20, 1865   MUSTER: ABSENT ON FURLOUGH
    COULD BE THE SAME AS THOMAS JONES IN CO. C
JONES, THOMAS   PVT   CO. C
    SWORN: FEB 18, 1865   DESERTED: AUG 24, 1865
KALTENBAUGH, J.   PVT   CO. E
    SWORN: FEB 20, 1865   MUSTER: SEP 11, 1865
KAY, JOHN   1ST SGT   CO. E
    SWORN: FEB 15, 1865   MUSTER: SEP 11, 1865
KEARNS, JEROME   PVT   CO. F
    SWORN: FEB 23, 1865   MUSTER: SEP 11, 1865
KEEFER, NELSON   PVT   CO. I
    SWORN: MAR 6, 1865   MUSTERED: SEP 11, 1865
KEIGHLY, WILLIAM H.   PVT   CO. F
    SWORN: FEB 16, 1865   MUSTER: SEP 11, 1865
KEITH, LEWIS   PVT   CO. K
    SWORN: MAR 7, 1865   MUSTERED: SICK, ABSENT
KELLER, JOHN J.   CPL   CO. D
    SWORN: FEB 20, 1865   MUSTERED: SEP 11, 1865

PROMOTED FROM PRIVATE; JUN 18, 1865
KELLEY, JOSEPH   CPL   CO. I
   SWORN: FEB 21, 1865   MUSTERED: SEP 11, 1865
   PROMOTED TO CPL; APR 25, 1865
KELLY, FRANCIS A.   PVT   CO. F
   SWORN: FEB 16, 1865   MUSTER: SICK/ABSENT
KELLY, HIRAM   PVT   CO. I
   SWORN: FEB 17, 1865   MUSTERED: SEP 11, 1865
KELLY, JAMES   PVT   CO. F
   SWORN: FEB 14, 1865   MUSTER: SEP 11, 1865
   1890 CENSUS: ORBERG, INDIANA COUNTY, PA
KENNEDY, JOHN   PVT   CO. D
   SWORN: MAR 25, 1865   DESERTED: APR 9, 1865
KENNEDY, PETER   PVT   CO. E
   SWORN: FEB 15, 1865   MUSTER: SEP 11, 1865
   SON-IN-LAW, JOHN RIVERS IN REGIMENT
   1886 REUNION IN FREEPORT: HOME, CARBON, PA
KEPFORD, JOHN   CPL   CO. D
   SWORN: FEB 17, 1865   DISCHARGED: AUG 28, 1865
   PROMOTED FROM PRIVATE; JUN 3, 1865
KERR, FREDERICK R.   PVT   CO. C
   SWORN: FEB 14, 1865   MUSTER: SEP 11, 1865
   1890 CENSUS: NEW BETHLEHEM, CLARION COUNTY, PA
KERR, REASON J.   PVT   CO. E
   SWORN: APR 4, 1865   MUSTER: SEP 11, 1865
KIER, THOMAS   PVT   CO. D
   SWORN: MAR 7, 1865   MUSTERED: SEP 11, 1865
KINNEY, WILSON   PVT   CO. D
   SWORN: FEB 22, 1865   MUSTERED: SEP 11, 1865
KIRK, DAVID D.   PVT   CO. G
   SWORN: FEB 27, 1865   MUSTERED: SEP 11, 1865
KIRK, GEORGE   PVT   CO. G
   SWORN: FEB 27, 1865   MUSTERED: SEP 11, 1865
KIRKER, MARTIN L.   PVT   CO. E
   SWORN: FEB 18, 1865   MUSTER: SEP 11, 1865
KIRKHAM, JAMES   PVT   CO. I
   SWORN: FEB 17, 1865   MUSTERED: SICK, ABSENT
KIRKLAND, JOHN   PVT   CO. A
   SWORN: FEB 14, 1865/3 YRS MUSTER: SEP 11, 1865
KITTING, WILLIAM H.   SGT   CO. C
   SWORN: FEB 18, 1865   MUSTER: SEP 11, 1865
KLINE, JACOB   PVT   CO. H
   SWORN: MAR 1, 1865   MUSTER: SEP 11, 1865
KLINGENSMITH, L.E.   PVT   CO. H
   SWORN: FEB 23, 1865   DESERTED: AUG 19, 1865
KLINGENSMITH, WILLIAM G.   PVT   CO. H   AGE: 35
   SWORN: MAR 3, 1865   MUSTER: SEP 11, 1865
   1890 CENSUS: INDIANA, INDIANA COUNTY, PA
   BURIED: INDIANA COUNTY, GREENWOOD CEMETERY, 1830-APR 9, 1899
KLUTZ, GEORGE   PVT   CO. C
   BORN IN GERMANY
   SWORN: OCT 12, 1861/3 YRS DESERTED: DEC 9, 1861
KNIPSCHIELD, MICHAEL   PVT   CO. I
   SWORN: FEB 18, 1865   DISCHARGED: MAY 20, 1865
   1890 CENSUS: LONG RUN, ARMSTRONG COUNTY, PA
KNOX, ALEXANDER   PVT   CO. G
   SWORN: FEB 27, 1865   MUSTERED: SEP 11, 1865

KOLLER, LUTHER   PVT   CO. D
    SWORN: FEB 17, 1865   MUSTERED: SEP 11, 1865
KRAFT, DANIEL J.   PVT   CO. C
    SWORN: FEB 18, 1865   MUSTER: SEP 11, 1865
KRAMER, CHARLES   PVT   CO. F
    SWORN: FEB 15, 1865   DESERTED: MAR 3, 1865
KRAMER, NICHOLAS   CPL   CO. E
    SWORN: FEB 15, 1865   MUSTER: SEP 11, 1865
KRENZLIEN, WILLIAM   PVT   CO. F
    SWORN: FEB 20, 1865   MUSTER: SEP 11, 1865
KRUMPE, CHARLES   PVT   CO. H
    SWORN: FEB 15, 1865   MUSTER: SEP 11, 1865
    BURIED: ST. PAUL'S LUTHERAN CEMETERY, SARVER, PA
KUHN, JAMES T.   PVT   CO. E
    SWORN: FEB 15, 1865   MUSTER: SEP 11, 1865
    BURIED: PROSPECT CEMETERY, TARENTUM, PA
    DIED: FEB 24, 1892   WIFE: SARAH J. 1844-1921
KUHNS, WILLIAM   MUC   CO. I
    SWORN: MAR 9, 1865   MUSTERED: SEP 11, 1865
KUPPENHOEFFER, J. #   PVT   CO. B
    SWORN: UNKNOWN   DIED: FEB 8, 1865
    BURIED @ NASHVILLE, BATES
LAMBING, DAVID M.   PVT   CO. I   AGE:25
LAMBING, DAVID B.
    SWORN: MAR 17, 1865   MUSTER: SEP 11, 1865
    BORN: NOV 22, 1840   DIED: MAY 6, 1906
    1890 CENSUS: OLIVET, ARMSTRONG COUNTY, PA
    BURIED: SPRING CHURCH, PA
LARRIMER, JOSEPH D.   PVT   CO. F
    SWORN: FEB 23, 1865   DISCHARGED: JUN 3, 1865
LAWALL, JOHN   PVT   CO. E
    SWORN: FEB 15, 1865   MUSTER: SEP 11, 1865
    BURIED: SOUTH CEMETERY, BUTLER, PA
    BORN: JAN 20, 1838   DIED; JAN 22, 1894 WIFE: KATHARINA
    1886 REUNION IN FREEPORT: HOME, SARVERSVILLE, PA
LAYTON, HENRY   PVT   CO. K
    SWORN: FEB 28, 1865   DIED: JUN 21, 1865 @ NASHVILLE
LEE, WILLIAM   PVT   UNASSIGNED
    SWORN: JAN 25, 1865   NOT ON MUSTER OUT ROLLS
LEEDY, DANIEL   PVT   CO. D
    SWORN: FEB 22, 1865   MUSTERED: SEP 11, 1865
LEES, JOHN   CPL.78th   CO. F
    SWORN: FEB 23, 1865   MUSTER: SEP 11, 1865
LEIGHTON, HENRY #   PVT   CO. K
    SWORN: UNKNOWN   DIED: JUN 21, 1865
    BURIED @ NASHVILLE, BATES
LEFEVER, JAMES M.   PVT   CO. H
    SWORN: FEB 15, 1865   MUSTERED: SEP 11, 1865
LEHMAN, CHRISTOPHER J.   PVT   CO. F
    SWORN: MAR 6, 1865   MUSTER: SEP 11, 1865
LEHR, LEWIS   PVT   CO. I
    SWORN: FEB 18, 1865   MUSTERED: SEP 11, 1865
LENSNER, JOHN G.   PVT   CO. E
    SWORN: FEB 15, 1865   MUSTER: SEP 11, 1865
    1886 REUNION IN FREEPORT: HOME, SAXONBURG, PA
LEREW, JESSE   PVT   CO. D
    SWORN: FEB 22, 1865   MUSTERED: SEP 11, 1865

LERNER, LEWIS *   PVT   CO. E   VETERAN
LERNER, LOUIS   AGE: 40
   ORIGIN: BUTLER COUNTY; BORN IN GERMANY   BOUNTY $100
   SERVED IN THREE MONTH SERVICE, CO. A, PA 1st BATTALION
   HEIGHT: 5' 5"   COMPLEXION: DARK   EYES: GREY   HAIR: DARK
   LIVED WITH WIFE CHRISTINE DEUTCH LERNER @ BLANKET HILL
   SWORN: FEB 15, 1865   MUSTER: SEP 11, 1865
LETZKUS, GEORGE   PVT   CO. F
   SWORN: FEB 16, 1865   MUSTER: SEP 11, 1865
LEWIS, SAMUEL   PVT   CO. F
   SWORN: FEB 13, 1865   DISCHARGED: JUL 12, 1865
LEWIS, WILLIAM G.   PVT   CO. F
   SWORN: FEB 23, 1865   MUSTER: SEP 11, 1865
LIBENGOOD, HENRY   PVT   CO. G
   SWORN: MAR 4, 1865   DISCHARGED: JUN 3, 1865
LIEB, SOBIESKI   PVT   CO. D
   SWORN: FEB 18, 1865   MUSTERED: SEP 11, 1865
LIGHTHILL, GEORGE W.   PVT   CO. H
   SWORN: FEB 21, 1865   MUSTERED: SEP 11, 1865
LINCOLN, GEORGE H.   SGT   CO. K
   SWORN: FEB 28, 1865   MUSTERED: SEP 11, 1865
LINDER, EDGAR T.   PVT   CO. G
   SWORN: FEB 25, 1865   MUSTERED: SEP 11, 1865
LITTIMER, WILLIAM   PVT   CO. D
   SWORN: APR 5, 1865   DISCHARGED: SEP 9, 1865
LITTLE, CHARLES F.   PVT   CO. C
   SWORN: FEB 18, 1865   DISCHARGED: MAY 20, 1865
LITTLE, JOHN   PVT   CO. I
   SWORN: FEB 17, 1865   MUSTERED: SEP 11, 1865
LLOYD, JOSEPH J.   PVT   CO. G
   SWORN: FEB 27, 1865   MUSTERED: SEP 11, 1865
LLOYD, TAYLOR   PVT   CO. K
   SWORN: FEB 28, 1865   DESERTED: JUL 27, 1865
LOGAN, CALVIN   PVT   CO. F
   SWORN: MAR 17, 1865   DISCHARGED: JUN 2, 1865
LONGWELL, SAMUEL M.   MUS   CO. D
   SWORN: FEB 17, 1865   MUSTERED: SEP 11, 1865
LOTZ, ADAM   PVT   CO. C
   SWORN: FEB 18, 1865   DISCHARGED: MAY 15, 1865
LOWMILLER, THOMAS   PVT   CO. C
   SWORN: FEB 18, 1865   MUSTERED: SEP 11, 1865
LOWRIE, SAMUEL   PVT   CO. K
   SWORN: FEB 28, 1865   MEDICAL: MAY 1, 1865
LOWRY, WILLIAM   PVT   CO. I
   SWORN: FEB 20, 1865   MUSTERED: SEP 11, 1865
LOYER, JACOB   PVT   CO. D
   SWORN: FEB 22, 1865   DIED: MAY 11, 1865 @ NASHVILLE
   BURIED @ NASHVILLE, ROW J, GRAVE # 858, BATES
LUCAS, SAMUEL H.   PVT   CO. I   AGE: 41
   SWORN: MAR 17, 1865   MUSTER: SEP 11, 1865
   DIED: JUN 28, 1899   BURIED: PLEASANT HILLS CEMETERY, LEECHBURG, PA
   75 YEARS OLD @ DEATH   TOMBSTONE SAYS CO. H
   1890 CENSUS, ASHBAUGH WESTMORELAND COUNTY/LEECHBURG, ARMSTRONG COUNTY, PA
LUCE, JOHN   PVT   CO. G
   SWORN: FEB 27, 1865   MUSTERED: SEP 11, 1865
LUKER, JAMES   CPL   CO. C
   SWORN: FEB 18, 1865   MUSTER: SEP 11, 1865

PROMOTED FROM PVT; JUN 3, 1865

LUTZ, JACOB   PVT   CO. E
SWORN: MAR 6, 1865   MUSTER: SEP 11, 1865

LYDICK, JOSEPH M.   PVT   CO. H   AGE: 36
INDIANA COUNTY ENLISTEE
BORN: INDIANA COUNTY, OCT 13, 1829
SWORN: FEB 14, 1865   MUSTERED: SEP 11, 1865
WIFE: HELEN SILVIS   DIED: FEB 9, 1913
BURIED: INDIANA COUNTY, GILGAL CEMETERY, EAST MAHONING TWP.,
1825-FEB 9, 1913

LYNCH, GEORGE   PVT   CO. G
SWORN: FEB 27, 1865   MUSTERED: SEP 11, 1865

LYNCH, JAMES   PVT   CO. G
SWORN: FEB 27, 1865   MUSTERED: SEP 11, 1865

McADOO, JOHN #   PVT   CO. D
SWORN: MAR 7, 1865   MUSTER: SEP 11, 1865
1890 CENSUS: LONG RUN, ARMSTRONG COUNTY, PA

McALICE, JOHN   PVT   CO. F
SWORN: FEB 15, 1865   DESERTED: MAR 4, 1865
RETURNED: MAY 10, 1865   MUSTERED: MAY 11, 1865

McCANDLESS, ALEXANDER M.   PVT   CO. I
SWORN: FEB 24, 1865   MUSTERED: SEP 11, 1865
BURIED: SOUTH CEMETERY, BUTLER, PA; 1822-1919
WIFE: MATILDA JANE; 1827-1877

McCOLLUM, ROBERT   PVT   CO. B
SWORN: FEB 22, 1865   MUSTER: JUN 13, 1865
BROTHER ALEX IN THE PA EIGHTH RESERVE
BORN: JUL 27, 1827   DIED: JUL 31, 1903
1890 CENSUS: KITTANNING, ARMSTRONG COUNTY, PA
BURIED: SLATE LICK, PA

McDANIELS, OLIVER   PVT   CO. K
DANIELS, OLIVER
SWORN: MAR 7, 1865   MUSTER: SEP 11, 1865
SHOWN AS UNASSIGNED [DANIELS]

McGARVEY, JAMES #   PVT   CO. F
ORIGIN: ARMSTRONG COUNTY
SIRWELL'S BRADY ALPINES
SWORN: APR 22, 1861   MUSTER: JUL 22, 1861 [PA 9th]
SWORN: FEB 16, 1865   MUSTER: SEP 11, 1865
1890 CENSUS: GALLITZIN, CAMBRIA COUNTY, PA
SERVICE: GUARD DUTY, DELEWARE AND NORTHERN VIRGINIA

McGINLEY, JOHN   PVT   CO. E
SWORN: FEB 22, 1865   MUSTER: SEP 11, 1865

McGRATH, DR. JOHN   SUR   STAFF
ORIGIN: PHILADELPHIA
SWORN: APR 14, 1862/3 YRS   RESIGNED: JUN 23, 1863.

McGREGOR, DANIEL C. #   PVT   CO. C
SWORN: FEB 18, 1865   MUSTER: SEP 11, 1865
1890 CENSUS: NORTH POINT, INDIANA COUNTY, PA

McINTYRE, GEORGE   PVT   CO. E
SWORN: FEB 23, 1865   MUSTER: SEP 11, 1865

McKALAP, WILLIAM #   PVT   CO. G
BURIED: MT. UNION LUTHERAN CEMETERY, SHELOCTA, PA
NO INFORMATION; GOVERNMENT STONE

MARBURGER, GEORGE   PVT   CO. E
SWORN: FEB 18, 1865   MUSTER: SICK/ABSENT
1886 REUNION IN FREEPORT: HOME, SAXONBURG, PA

MARS, BENJAMIN   PVT   CO. G
    SWORN: FEB 27, 1865/3 YRS   MUSTER: SEP 11, 1865
    1890 CENSUS: LUCINDA, CLARION COUNTY, PA
MARS, GEORGE   PVT   CO. G
    SWORN: FEB 27, 1865/3 YRS   MUSTER: SEP 11, 1865
MARTIN, AUGUSTUS, N.   PVT   CO. E
    SWORN: FEB 23, 1865   DISCHARGED: AUG 30, 1865
MARTIN, WILLIAM H.   PVT   CO. E
    SWORN: FEB 18, 1865   DESERTED AUG 5, 1865
MAXLER, FRANCIS   PVT   CO. E
    SWORN: FEB 14, 1865   MUSTER: SEP 11, 1865
    1886 REUNION IN FREEPORT: HOME, FREEPORT, PA
MAXWELL, JAMES A.   PVT   CO. F
    SWORN: FEB 26, 1865   DESERTED: SEP 6, 1865
MICHAEL, CHRIS   PVT   CO. E
    SWORN: FEB 15, 1865   MUSTER: SEP 11, 1865
MICHAEL, EDWARD   PVT   CO. E
    SWORN: FEB 15, 1865   MUSTER: SEP 11, 1865
MILLER, LEVI J.   PVT   CO. E
    SWORN: FEB 20, 1865   MUSTER: SEP 11, 1865
MILLER, SAMUEL C.   SGT   CO. D
    SWORN: FEB 20, 1865   MUSTERED: SEP 11, 1865
    PROMOTED FROM CORPORAL, JUN 3, 1865
MILLIGAN, JOHN   PVT   CO. G
    SWORN: MAR 15, 1865   DIED: JUN 2, 1865 @ NASHVILLE
    BURIED @ NASHVILLE, ROW J, GRAVE #1315, BATES
MOCHEL, MICHAEL   PVT   CO. E
MOCKEL, MICHAEL
    SWORN: FEB 15, 1865   MUSTER: SEP 11, 1865
    1886 REUNION IN FREEPORT: HOME, SARVERSVILLE, PA
MOORE, CHARLES   PVT   CO. H
    SWORN: FEB 21, 1865   MUSTERED: SEP 11, 1865
MORRISON, A.J.   PVT   CO. H
    SWORN: FEB 21, 1865   MUSTERED: SEP 11, 1865
    1886 REUNION IN FREEPORT: HOME, TARENTUM, PA
MORRISON, JAMES   PVT   CO. C
    SWORN: FEB 18, 1865   MUSTERED: SEP 11, 1865
MORRISON, HENRY H.   PVT   CO. H
MORRISON, HENRY HUEY
    SWORN: MAR 22, 1865   MUSTERED: SEP 11, 1865
    BURIED: INDIANA COUNTY, PRESBYTERIAN CEMETERY, WASHINGTON TWP.,
NEELY, THOMAS   PVT   CO. E
    SWORN: MAR 6, 1865   MUSTER: SEP 11, 1865
NICHOLAS, EDWARD   PVT   CO. F
    SWORN: FEB 15, 1865   MUSTERED: SEP 11, 1865
    1886 REUNION IN FREEPORT: HOME, CREIGHTON, PA
NICHOLS, JAMES #   PVT   CO. F
    SWORN: UNKNOWN   DIED: SEP 12, 1865
    BURIED @ NASHVILLE, ROW E, GRAVE #244, BATES
PAINTER, WILLIAM   PVT   CO. H
    SWORN: MAR 14, 1865   MUSTERED: SEP 11, 1865
PALMER, CHARLES   CPL   CO. I
    SWORN: FEB 17, 1865   MUSTERED: SEP 11, 1865
    PROMOTED TO CPL, MAY 30, 1865
PALMER, JACOB G.   PVT   CO. D
    SWORN: FEB 22, 1865   MUSTERED: SEP 11, 1865
PATTON, JOHN M. #   PVT

PA 78th: 1864   PA 109th: 1865

PEARCE, DAVID E.   PVT   CO. E
    SWORN: FEB 17, 1865   MUSTER: SICK/ABSENT
PHILLIPS, JOSEPH S.   PVT   CO. E
    SWORN: FEB 21, 1865   MUSTER: SEP 11, 1865
    BROTHER-IN-LAW, CHRISTY ROBB, IN THE REGIMENT
POTTS, JAMES   PVT   CO. E
    SWORN: FEB 17, 1865   DESERTED: AUG 8, 1865
POTTS, TAYLOR   PVT   CO. D
    SWORN: FEB 14, 1865   MUSTERED: SEP 11, 1865
POWELL, JOHN   PVT   CO. E
    SWORN: FEB 18, 1865   MUSTER: SEP 11, 1865
POWELL, WILLIAM   PVT   CO. F
    SWORN: FEB 13, 1865   MUSTERED: SEP 11, 1865
POWELL, WILSON   PVT   CO. E   AGE: 18
    SWORN: FEB 18, 1865   MUSTER: SEP 11, 1865
    BURIED: ALLEGHENY TWP. [CEMETERY ABOVE RIVER FOREST GOLF COURSE, FREEPORT]
    SEP 13, 1847-DEC 27, 1932
PRESCOTT, ISAAC   CPL   CO. H
    SWORN: FEB 20, 1865   MUSTERED: SEP 11, 1865
PRICE, ELIAS   PVT   CO. C
    SWORN: FEB 18, 1865   DISCHARGED: JUN 6, 1865
PRICE, JOHN   PVT   CO. C
    SWORN: FEB 18, 1865   MUSTERED: SEP 11, 1865
PRICE, WILLIAM   PVT   CO. D
    SWORN: FEB 9, 1865   MUSTERED: SEP 11, 1865
PRICE, WILLIAM   CPL   CO. I
    SWORN: FEB 27, 1865   MUSTERED: SEP 11, 1865
    PROMOTED TO CPL, MAR 3, 1865
PROCTOR, DAVID P.   PVT   CO. I   AGE: 38
    SWORN: MAR 6, 1865   MUSTERED: SEP 11, 1865
    BURIED: INDIANA COUNTY, PROCTOR CEMETERY, PURCHASE LINE, GREEN TWP.,
    1827-MAR 10, 1890
    FREE BLACK MAN; HAD "2 WHITE WIVES AND 8 DAUGHTERS"
RAABE, CHARLES   PVT   CO. E
    SWORN: FEB 15, 1865   MUSTER: SEP 11, 1865
RAABE, CHRISTIAN   PVT   CO. E
    SWORN: FEB 15, 1865   MUSTER: SEP 11, 1865
RABER, WILLIAM H. #   PVT   CO. D
    SWORN: UNKNOWN   DIED: APR 24, 1865
    BURIED @ NASHVILLE, ROW J, GRAVE #1211, BATES
RAMSEY, WILLIAM   PVT   CO. E   AGE: 21
    SWORN: FEB 18, 1865   DISCHARGED: SEP 8, 1865
    BURIED: NORTH CEMETERY, BUTLER, PA; 1844-1920
REARICK, DANIEL B. #   PVT   CO. A
    DIED: JAN 3, 1882 @ AGE 60   COULD BE DANIEL B. RARAH
    TOMBSTONE SAYS A MEMBER OF THE 78th
    BURIED: OAKLAND CEMETERY, DISTANT, PA
REDDICK, CHARLES   PVT   CO. E
REDICK, CHARLES
    SWORN: FEB 15, 1865   MUSTER: SEP 11, 1865
    1886 REUNION IN FREEPORT: HOME, SAXONBURG, PA
REED, JOHN   CPL   CO. H
    SWORN: FEB 23, 1865   MUSTERED: SICK/ABSENT
REED, THOMAS   PVT   CO. F
    SWORN: FEB 11, 1865   MUSTERED: SEP 11, 1865
REITEL, JOHN F. #   PVT   CO. UNKNOWN

SWORN: UNKNOWN   DIED: JUL 2, 1865
    BURIED @ NASHVILLE, BATES
REYNOLDS, JAMES   PVT   CO. F
    SWORN: FEB 14, 1865   DIED: MAY 12, 1865 @ NASHVILLE
    BURIED @ NASHVILLE, ROW J, GRAVE #1188, BATES
REYNOLDS, WALTER   2LT.   CO. F
    SWORN: FEB 27, 1865   MUSTER: SEP 11, 1865
  RHEA, JOSEPH   PVT   CO. D   AGE: 24
    SWORN: JUN 30, 1863   MUSTERED: AUG 17, 1863/ 54 PA REGIMENT
    SWORN: MAR 7, 1865   MUSTERED: SEP 11, 1865
    BURIED: INDIANA COUNTY, EDGEWOOD CEMETERY, SALTSBURG, 1841-1928
RICE, CORNELIUS   PVT   CO. K
    SWORN: FEB 28, 1865   MUSTERED: SICK, ABSENT
RICE, ISAAC B.   PVT   CO. F
    SWORN: MAR 6, 1865   MUSTERED: SEP 11, 1865
RICE JOHN B.   PVT   CO. E
    SWORN: MAR 6, 1865   MUSTER: SICK/ABSENT
RICE, MICHAEL   PVT   CO. I
    SWORN: FEB 17, 1865   MUSTERED: SEP 11, 1865
RICHARDS, GEORGE   PVT   CO. I
    SWORN: MAR 15, 1865   MUSTERED: SEP 11, 1865
RIDDLE, SAMUEL   PVT   CO. C
    SWORN: FEB 18, 1865   MUSTERED: SEP 11, 1865
RIDEN, GUSTIN P.   CPL   CO. C
    SWORN: FEB 18, 1865   MUSTER: JUN 2, 1865
RIDEN, LEWIS H.   PVT   CO. C
    SWORN: FEB 18, 1865   MUSTERED: SEP 11, 1865
RIDEN, SAMUEL N.   PVT   CO. K
    SWORN: FEB 28, 1865   DISCHARGED: JUN 7, 1865
RIDEN, WILLIAM C.   PVT   CO. C
    SWORN: FEB 18, 1865   DISCHARGED: JUN 8, 1865
RIEGER, HENRY   PVT   CO. I   AGE: 32
RIGGER, HENRY
    SWORN: FEB 25, 1865   MUSTERED: SEP 11, 1865
    BROTHERS: JACOB AND VALENTINE
    BURIED: SOUTH CEMETERY, BUTLER, PA
    BORN: MAY 20, 1833   DIED; MAR 2, 1897 WIFE: ANNA B.
RIEGER, JACOB   PVT   CO. I
RIGGER, JACOB
    SWORN: FEB 25, 1865   MUSTERED: SEP 11, 1865
    BROTHERS: HENRY AND VALENTINE
RIEGER, VALENTINE   PVT   CO. E   AGE: 38
RENGER, VALENTINE
    BORN: GERMANY, SEP 6, 1827
    SWORN: FEB 25, 1865   MUSTER: SEP 11, 1865
    BROTHERS: JACOB AND HENRY
RIGGLE, A.A. #   PVT   CO. K
    NO INFORMATION
    1886 REUNION IN FREEPORT: HOME, SCHENLEY, PA
    PROBABLY ABSALOM RIGGLE FROM THE 14th CAVALRY
RILEY, WILLIAM E.   PVT   CO. B ·
    SWORN: JAN 21, 1865   DESERTED: FEB 19, 1865
ROBB, CHRISTY   1ST SGT   CO. E   AGE: 30
    BORN: BUTLER COUNTY: SEP 5, 1835
    RETURNED FROM MISSIONARY WORK WITH NEBRASKA INDIANS TO JOIN THE REGIMENT.
    SWORN: FEB 21, 1865   MUSTER: SEP 11, 1865
    PROMOTED FROM CORPORAL; JUL 19, 1865   WIFE: LYDIA C. PHILLIPS

BROTHER-IN-LAW, JOSEPH S. PHILLIPS ALSO IN THE REGIMENT.
BROTHER, WILLIAM IN THE 134th PA
HOME: NEAR SONORA, BUTLER COUNTY

ROBB, GRANVILLE L.   SGT   CO. K
    SWORN: FEB 28, 1865   MUSTERED: SEP 11, 1865
    PROMOTED TO CPL, MAR 9, 1865; TO SGT, JUN 6, 1865

ROBB, WILLIAM C.   PVT   CO. K
    SWORN: FEB 28, 1865   MUSTERED: ABSENT, ON FURLOUGH

ROBINSON, GEORGE   CPL.   CO. F
    SWORN: FEB 23, 1865   DISCHARGED: JUL 12, 1865

ROBINSON, THOMAS   PVT   CO. I
    SWORN: FEB 21, 1865   MUSTERED: SEP 11, 1865

ROCKEY, MICHAEL   PVT   CO. D
    SWORN: FEB 17, 1865   MUSTERED: SEP 11, 1865   SUBSTITUTE

ROGERS, ARTHUR C.   PVT   CO. K
    SWORN: FEB 28, 1865   MUSTERED: SEP 11, 1865

ROGERS, CHARLES   PVT   CO. E
    SWORN: FEB 15, 1865   MUSTER: SEP 11, 1865

ROGERS, NEIL   PVT   CO. H
    SWORN: FEB 26, 1865   MUSTERED: SEP 11, 1865

ROOF, GEORGE W.   MUS   CO. F   AGE: 38
    SWORN: FEB 14, 1865   MUSTER: ABSENT/SICK - SEP 14, 1865
    1890 CENSUS: INDIANA, INDIANA COUNTY, PA
    BURIED: INDIANA COUNTY, OAKLAND CEMETERY, WHITE TWP., 1827-MAR 13, 1897

ROSS, ALEXANDER M.   PVT   CO. K
    SWORN: FEB 24, 1865   MUSTERED: SICK, ABSENT

ROTH, ALFRED   PVT   CO. E
    SWORN: FEB 23, 1865   MUSTER: SEP 11, 1865

ROTHROCK, JAMES   PVT   CO. C
    SWORN: FEB 18, 1865   DIED: MAR 27, 1865 @ NASHVILLE
    BURIED @ NASHVILLE, ROW R, GRAVE #337, BATES

ROWAN, GEORGE   SGT.   CO. F
    SWORN: FEB 16, 1865   MUSTER: SEP 11, 1865

ROWE, ROBERT S.   CPL   CO. C
    SWORN: FEB 18, 1865   MUSTER: SEP 11, 1865

RUBINCAM, JOSEPH H.   2LT   CO. H II
    SWORN: MAR 4, 1865   MUSTERED: SEP 11, 1865

RUBY, ANDREW   PVT   CO. E
    SWORN: FEB 21, 1865   MUSTER: SICK/ABSENT

RUDISILL, ABRAHAM W.   CPL   CO. D
    SWORN: FEB 17, 1865   MUSTERED: SEP 11, 1865

RUDISILL, WILLIAM   PVT   CO. G
    SWORN: FEB 25, 1865   MUSTERED: SEP 11, 1865

RUSH, JOHN H.   PVT   CO. F
    SWORN: FEB 16, 1865   DESERTED: MAY 15, 1865

RUSH, THOMAS   PVT   CO. F
    SWORN: MAR 17, 1865   MUSTERED: SEP 11, 1865

RUSSELL, GEORGE   PVT   CO. K
    SWORN: MAR 7, 1865   DISCHARGED: JUN 7, 1865

RUTTER, MARTIN   PVT   CO. K
    SWORN: FEB 28, 1865   MUSTERED: SEP 11, 1865

ST. CLAIR, JOHN W.   PVT   CO. E   AGE: 33
    BORN: BUTLER COUNTY, NOV 17, 1832   TRADE: CARPENTER
    SWORN: FEB 17, 1865   MUSTER: SEP 11, 1865
    DIED: BEAVER FALLS, PA, APR 4, 1889
    BURIED: ZION BAPTIST CHURCH   WIFE: MARY ANN SNYDER

SAEGER, JOSIAH   PVT   CO. C

SWORN: FEB 18, 1865 DESERTED: JUN 28, 1865
SAVAGE, ROBERT CPL CO. G
 SWORN: FEB 27, 1865 MUSTERED: SEP 11, 1865
 PROMOTED TO CPL; JUL 1, 1865
SCHAFFER, GEORGE W. PVT CO. E
 SWORN: FEB 20, 1865 MUSTER: SICK AT MUSTER
SCHELL, GEORGE W. PVT CO. K
 SWORN: MAR 7, 1865 MUSTERED: SICK, ABSENT
SCHROTH, CHRISTIAN PVT CO. E
 SWORN: FEB 15, 1865 MUSTER: SEP 11, 1865
SCOTT, WILLIAM PVT CO. F
 SWORN: FEB 28, 1865 DESERTED: MAR 2, 1865
SEAMAN, J.H. # PVT CO. G
 NO INFORMATION
 1886 REUNION IN FREEPORT: HOME, KITTANNING, PA
SEFTON, EDWARD PVT CO. E
 SWORN: FEB 15, 1865 MUSTER: SEP 11, 1865
 1886 REUNION IN FREEPORT: HOME, SAXONBURG, PA
SHAFFER, JOHN PVT CO. H
 SWORN: MAR 1, 1865 MUSTERED: SEP 11, 1865
SHANAHAN, EDWARD # PVT CO. D
 SWORN: UNKNOWN DIED: MAY 3, 1865
 BURIED @ NASHVILLE, ROW J, GRAVE #1567, BATES
SHANNON, JAMES E. PVT CO. C
 SWORN: OCT 12, 1861/3 YRS MEDICAL: APR 11, 1862
SHAW, WILLIAM PVT CO. I
 SWORN: FEB 16, 1865 MUSTERED: SEP 11, 1865
SHELL, GEORGE PVT CO. E
 SWORN: FEB 16, 1865 MUSTER: SEP 11, 1865
SHELLY, MARTIN PVT CO. E
 SWORN: FEB 21, 1865 MUSTER: SEP 11, 1865
SHICK, AMOS # PVT CO. G
 SWORN: UNKNOWN DIED: JUN 19, 1865
 BURIED @ NASHVILLE, ROW J, GRAVE #1136, BATES
SHIELDS, CHARLES G. PVT CO. C
 SWORN: FEB 16, 1865 MUSTERED: SEP 11, 1865
SHIELDS, SAMUEL PVT CO. G
 SWORN: FEB 27, 1865 MUSTERED: SEP 11, 1865
SHOWALTER, GEORGE W. PVT CO. D
 SWORN: FEB 17, 1865 DISCHARGED: JUN 14, 1865
SHOWALTER, SAMUEL PVT CO. D
 SWORN: FEB 17, 1865 DISCHARGED: JUN 24, 1865
SHULL, ABRAHAM D. PVT CO. C
 SWORN: FEB 18, 1865 DISCHARGED: AUG 28, 1865
SHULL, ALFRED L. PVT CO. G
 SWORN: MAR 22, 1865 MUSTERED: SEP 11, 1865
SHULTZ, ANTHONY PVT CO. K
 SWORN: MAR 3, 1865 MUSTERED: SEP 11, 1865
SHULTZ, AUGUST PVT CO. H
 SWORN: FEB 23, 1865 MUSTERED: SEP 11, 1865
SHULTZ, HENRY CPL CO. K
 SWORN: MAR 7, 1865 MUSTERED: SICK, ABSENT
SHULTZ, WILLIAM B. PVT CO. K
 SWORN: FEB 28, 1865 MUSTERED: SICK, ABSENT
SHUSTER, GOTTLIEB PVT CO. E
 SWORN: FEB 15, 1865 MUSTER: SICK/ABSENT
SLACKER, WILLIAM PVT CO. H

SWORN: FEB 20, 1865   MUSTERED: SEP 11, 1865
1890 CENSUS: GREENSBURG, WESTMORELAND COUNTY, PA

SLOAN, JOHN D.   PVT   CO. F
SWORN: MAR 17, 1865   MUSTERED: SEP 11, 1865

SLOAN, JOHN D.   PVT   CO. H
SWORN: FEB 23, 1865   MUSTERED: SEP 11, 1865

SLOAN, ROBERT   CPL   CO. H
SWORN: FEB 23, 1865   MUSTERED: SEP 11, 1865

SLUTTER, CHRISTIAN   PVT   CO. I
SWORN: FEB 24, 1865   MUSTERED: SEP 11, 1865

SLUTTER, WILLIAM   PVT   CO. I
SWORN: FEB 24, 1865   MUSTERED: SEP 11, 1865

SMITH, GEORGE W.   MUS   CO. F
SWORN: FEB 14, 1865   MUSTER: SEP 11, 1865

SMITH, JAMES H.   CPL   CO. G
SWORN: FEB 27, 1865   DISCHARGED: MAY 17, 1865

SMITH, JAMES W.   PVT   CO. C
SWORN: FEB 18, 1865   DISCHARGED: JUN 7, 1865

SMITH, JOHN E.   PVT   CO. A
SWORN: MAR 2, 1865   MUSTER: SEP 11, 1865
BURIED: INDIANA COUNTY, PRESBYTERIAN CEMETERY, SHELOCTA, WASHINGTON TWP.

SMITHERS, GEORGE W.   PVT   CO. C
SWORN: FEB 18, 1865   MUSTERED: SEP 11, 1865

SMITHERS, ROBERT   PVT   CO. C
SWORN: FEB 18, 1865   MUSTERED: SEP 11, 1865

SOWERS, WILLIAM   PVT   CO. F
SWORN: MAR 21, 1865   MUSTERED: SEP 11, 1865

SOWERS, WILLIM   PVT   CO. A II
SWORN: MAR 21, 1865   MUSTER: NOT ON MUSTER OUT ROLLS

SPANG, JOSIAH R.   PVT   CO. E
SWORN: FEB 14, 1865   DESERTED: FEB 28, 1865

STACKPOLE, JAMES B. #   PVT   CO. H
SWORN: UNKNOWN   DIED: MAR 23, 1865
BURIED @ NASHVILLE, ROW R, GRAVE #248, BATES

STAHLLMAN, GEORGE W.   PVT   CO. B
SWORN: SEP 21, 1864/3 YRS   DISCHARGED: JUN 19, 1865

STALEY, ADAM S.   PVT   CO. K
SWORN: MAR 2, 1865   DISCHARGED: MAY 12, 1865

STATES, ALEXANDER   PVT   CO. K
SWORN: FEB 28, 1865   DIED: AUG 16, 1865 @ NASHVILLE

STUTTS, ALEXANDER #   PVT   CO. K
SWORN: UNKNOWN   DIED: AUG 16, 1865
BURIED @ NASHVILLE, BATES

STEPP, MICHAEL *   PVT   CO. H
STEP, MICHAEL   STEPP, MICHAEL I.
SWORN: FEB 22, 1865   MUSTER: SEP 11, 1865 BOUNTY: $100
BORN: JAN 30, 1845 IN SLATE LICK, PA
PARENTS: JOHN & SARAH COOPER STEPP
CIVIL WAR PENSION: #957-907
DIED: JAN 16, 1931 IN ASHEVILLE, N.C.   WIFE: EMMA LOUISE NOBEL
BURIED: McVILLE CEMETERY, ROGERS CHAPEL CHURCH, CLINTON, PA

STONE, JACOB   PVT   CO. K
SWORN: FEB 28, 1865   MUSTERED: SICK, ABSENT

STONE, JACOB H.   PVT   CO. K
SWORN: MAR 7, 1865   DESERTED: AUG 13, 1865

STONE, JOHN L.   PVT   CO. K
SWORN: MAR 7, 1865   MUSTERED: SEP 11, 1865

STRAWBRIDGE, J.W.   SGT   CO. G
   SWORN: FEB 27, 1865   MUSTERED: SEP 11, 1865
   PROMOTED TO CPL. MAR 2, 1865; TO SGT, AUG 12, 1865
SUMMERS, DAVID   PVT   CO. K
   SWORN: FEB 28, 1865   MUSTERED: SEP 11, 1865
SUMMERS, HENRY H.   CPL   CO. K
   SWORN: FEB 28, 1865   MUSTERED: SEP 11, 1865
SWARTZLANDER, LEVI   PVT   CO. G
   SWORN: MAR 21, 1865   MUSTERED: SEP 11, 1865
   1890 CENSUS: CRAIGSVILLE, ARMSTRONG COUNTY, PA
SWEIZER, CHRISTIAN   PVT   CO. D   AGE: 30
SWITZER, CHRISTIAN
   SWORN: FEB 16, 1865   DESERTED: AUG 25, 1865
   1890 CENSUS: BERRINGER, INDIANA COUNTY, PA
   BURIED: INDIANA COUNTY, UNIONTOWN CEMETERY, GREEN TWP., 1835-1909
SWISHER, GEORGE   PVT   CO. I   AGE: 43-44
   ARMSTRONG COUNTY ENLISTEE; BORN SLATE LICK/FREEPORT AREA
   SWORN: FEB 27, 1865   DISCHARGED: JUN 22, 1865
   HEIGHT: 5' 7¼"   COMPLEXION: FAIR   HAIR: DARK   EYES: GREY
   BOUNTY: $470   PROFESSION: CARPENTER
   BURIED: BLUE SLATE, BOGGSVILLE
TAYLOR, GEORGE H.   PVT   CO. D
   SWORN: MAR 22, 1865   MUSTERED: SEP 11, 1865
TAYLOR, THOMAS   PVT   CO. G
   SWORN: FEB 27, 1865   MUSTERED: SEP 11, 1865
TAYLOR, SAMUEL   PVT   CO. H
   SWORN: FEB 28, 1865   DISCHARGED: MAY 20, 1865
THOMAS, McCONNELL   PVT   CO. C
   SWORN: FEB 18, 1865   DISCHARGED: JUN 6, 1865
THOMPSON, HENRY C.   PVT   CO. D
   SWORN: FEB 18, 1865   DIED: MAR 1, 1865 @ COLUMBUS, OHIO
THOMPSON, JAMES W.   PVT   CO. E
   SWORN: FEB 15, 1865   MUSTER: SICK/ABSENT
THONBURY, SAMUEL   PVT   CO. E
   SWORN: FEB 25, 1865   DISCHARGED: MAY 23, 1865
TOMAY, FRANCIS   PVT   CO. E
   SWORN: FEB 14, 1865   MUSTER: SEP 11, 1865
TOWNSEND, ISRAEL   PVT   CO. I   AGE: 22
   SWORN: MAR 17, 1865   MUSTERED: SEP 11, 1865
   1890 CENSUS: LONG RUN, ARMSTRONG COUNTY, PA
   BURIED: INDIANA COUNTY, EDGEWOOD CEMETERY, SALTSBURG, 1843-1892
TRIMBLE, SAMUEL   PVT   CO. E
   SWORN: FEB 15, 1865   DESERTED: AUG 5, 1865
VANDIVOORT, MILTON   PVT   CO. E
   SWORN: FEB 28, 1865   MUSTER: SEP 11, 1865
WALLACE, CALVIN   PVT   CO. K
   SWORN: FEB 28, 1865   MUSTERED: ABSENT, ON FURLOUGH
WALLACE, DAVID #   PVT
   LISTED ONLY IN BUTLER COUNTY HISTORY
WAREAM, EDMOND B.   PVT   CO. C
   SWORN: FEB 18, 1865   MUSTERED: SEP 11, 1865
WAREAM, JOHN A.   PVT   CO. C
   SWORN: FEB 18, 1865   MUSTERED: SEP 11, 1865
WAREAM, JOSEPH S.   SGT   CO. C
   SWORN: FEB 18, 1865   MUSTER: SEP 11, 1865
WATSON, SAMUEL   PVT   CO. F
   SWORN: FEB 8, 1865   DESERTED: MAR 2, 1865

RETURNED: JUN 10 1865 MUSTER: SEP 11, 1865
WEAVER, ADAM H. CPL CO. D
 SWORN: FEB 8, 1865 MUSTERED: SEP 11, 1865
WHITE, SAMUEL SGT CO. G
 SWORN: FEB 27, 1865 MUSTERED: SEP 11, 1865
 PROMOTED TO CPL; MAR 2, 1865
 PROMOTED TO SGT; JUL 1, 1865
WHITHOFF, HENRY PVT CO. C
 SWORN: FEB 18, 1865 MUSTERED: SEP 11, 1865
WHITNER, VALENTINE PVT CO. E
 SWORN: FEB 21, 1865 MUSTER: SEP 11, 1865
WISE, CHRISTOPHER C. PVT CO. G
 SWORN: FEB 28, 1865 MUSTERED: SEP 11, 1865
WISE, JOHN M. PVT CO. G
 SWORN: FEB 27, 1865 DISCHARGED: MAY 25, 1865
WISE, JOSHUA ** PVT CO. A
 SWORN: SEP 28, 1864/1 YEAR DISCHARGED: JUN 19, 1865
WISSA, F. # PVT
 NO INFORMATION ON THIS SOLDIER. HE IS LISTED IN THE BURIAL RECORDS
 AT STONES RIVER. COULD BE JACOB WYANT/WIANT.
 BURIED AT NATIONAL CEMETERY STONES RIVER, GRAVE #N-5522
WOLF, JAMES MUS CO. H
 SWORN: FEB 21, 1865 MUSTERED: SEP 11, 1865
WOLF, PHILIP D. PVT CO. D
 SWORN: FEB 16, 1865 MUSTERED: SEP 11, 1865
 1890 CENSUS: PUNXSUTAWNEY, JEFFERSON COUNTY, PA
WOLFF, JOHN H. PVT CO. I AGE: 32
WOLFE, JOHN H.
 SWORN: FEB 18, 1865 DESERTED: AUG 8, 1865
 BURIED: INDIANA COUNTY, SPRUCE CEMETERY, CHERRY HILL TWP., 1833–MAR 17, 1888
WONDERLY, JOSHUA PVT CO. I
 SWORN: FEB 14, 1865 MUSTERED: SEP 11, 1865
 BROTHER-IN-LAW, GEORGE WILSON, IN THE PA 6th HEAVY ARTILLERY
 BURIED: NORTH CEMETERY, BUTLER, PA
 BORN: JUN 7, 1832 DIED: NOVEMBER 2, 1911
YEAGER, JACOB PVT CO. F
 SWORN: FEB 25, 1865 MUSTERED: SEP 11, 1865
YINGLING, W.M. # PVT CO. E
 SWORN: UNKNOWN MUSTER: UNKNOWN
 PO BOX 1914: PARKER'S LANDING, PA
YINGST, FRED W. 1SGT CO. D
 SWORN: FEB 17, 1865 DISCHARGED: JUN 2, 1865
ZWANZIGER, JOHN PVT CO. E
 SWORN: FEB 20, 1865 MUSTER: NO RECORDS

"A Visit from a Civil War Soldier"

For a one-hour film on the history of the Seventy-Eighth
contact:
Preservation Enterprises
228 E. Pearl
Butler, PA 16001

"A Visit from a Civil War Soldier"
is the one man drama of the Civil War years.

Mr. Bill May presents a living story of
the Pennsylvania Seventy-Eighth through the eyes of his great grandfather
"Private Christian Hinchburger"
a member of the regiment.

This superb drama based on the diary and letters of
Christian Hinchburger
brings the story of the war to life.
Done in vivid color, period uniform and setting this work is more than a mere story

"A Visit from a Civil War Soldier"
contains the insightful years of research done by Bill May.
More importantly it is a story told with emotion.

A valued addition to any film library
"A Visit from a Civil War Soldier"
is available from
Preservation Enterprises
228 E. Pearl
Butler, PA 16001
for $19.95 + $3.00 Shipping & Handling

A portion of the proceeds from this tape are donated to the
preservation of the Civil War battlefields

Stones River
National Battlefield
& Cemetery

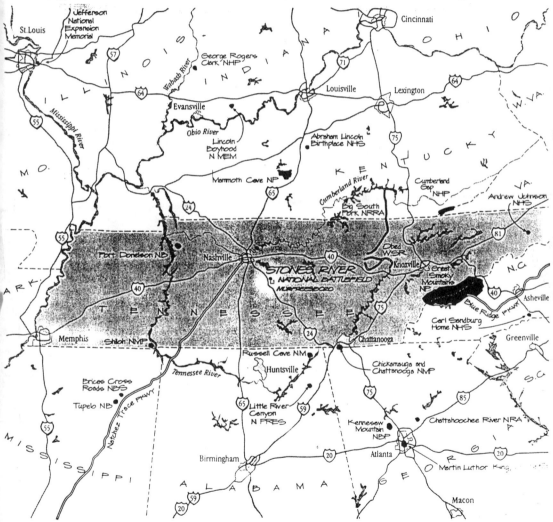

STONES RIVER
NATIONAL BATTLEFIELD
Murfreesboro, Tennessee

AREA
ENLARGED
ABOVE